GEORGE EASTMAN

GEORGE

EASTMAN

A BIOGRAPHY

Elizabeth Brayer

The Johns Hopkins University Press ☐ *Baltimore and London*

© 1996 The Johns Hopkins University Press
All rights reserved. Published 1996
Printed in the United States of America on acid-free paper
05 04 03 02 01 00 99 98 97 96   5 4 3 2 1

The Johns Hopkins University Press
2715 North Charles Street
Baltimore, Maryland 21218-4319
The Johns Hopkins Press Ltd., London

Library of Congress Cataloging-in-Publication Data
will be found at the end of this book.
A catalog record for this book is available from the British Library.

ISBN 0-8018-5263-3

Frontispiece: George Eastman, 1900. (EKC)

For Sheldon
and our children
Sarah, David, Anne, Jennifer, and Caroline
and grandchildren
Oliver, Harriett, Nicholas, and Olivia

CONTENTS

PREFACE AND
ACKNOWLEDGMENTS

■ ■ ▪ ───

George Eastman, who set the world to snapping pictures, was nervously ambivalent about being the subject of a biography. Although he aggressively sought publicity for his products, particularly after devising the "Kodak" trademark and "You press the button, we do the rest" slogan, he remained reticent about his community and personal life. He rarely granted interviews, shunned the limelight, and complained that serialized accounts of his career in the *New York Sun* (1913) and *Boston Post* (1920) were sensational or inaccurate. He refused to permit publication of even company-sponsored and expurgated biographies—such as one by Isaac F. Marcossen in 1923. The sole book-length biography of Eastman, written by Carl Ackerman and published in 1930, was financed and edited by Eastman. Contemporaries wrote that material about his life was removed before publication. Eastman's need for privacy that precipitated this dearth of published material is one of the major themes of his life.

The Eastman Kodak Company has jealously guarded its founder's privacy since his death in 1932. In 1934 company officials urged Ackerman to write a sequel in a more anecdotal and "human" vein, but this was not forthcoming. In 1940 biographer André Maurois conducted interviews and reached a tentative agreement with the company that also came to naught. In the 1950s Beaumont Newhall, curator and then director of the new George Eastman House of Photography, prepared a manuscript for a pictorial biography of Eastman, but the rights to this material were acquired by Kodak and turned over to the next potential biographer, Roger Butterfield. Following his acclaimed essay in *Life* magazine on the centenary of Eastman's birth in 1954, Butterfield conducted massive research on Eastman; after disagreements with Kodak officials, he never wrote his book. In the 1960s Wyatt Brummitt of Kodak's public relations department finished a 332-page typescript entitled "George Eastman of Kodak," which the company chose not to publish. In the 1970s Lawrence Bachmann completed the final draft of an unpublished biography, also commissioned by the company.

Thus Eastman biographical literature does not equal that of other American inventors and innovators such as Edison, Bell, the Wright brothers, Ford, or Land. Nor are there the inches of text about "America's most modest and least known millionaire," as the *Boston Post* grumbled, as there are about other financiers, business builders, or philanthropists such as Rockefeller, Carnegie, Gould, Duke, Watson, Morgan, Vanderbilt, Schwab, Frick, and the du Ponts.

Yet Eastman outflanked company timidity by insuring that future biographers would have access to an extensive record. Except for unexplained holes in personal account books of the 1870s, and in his business and personal correspondence of the 1880s, he apparently did not destroy or make inaccessible the bulk of his papers. More than two hundred thousand personal and business letters as well as a mountain of ephemera remain largely intact, "for possible future use," as he wrote in 1930.

Business smarts—another theme—were ingrained. A self-educated bank clerk began manufacturing dry plates in his mother's kitchen in 1879. Fifteen years later he headed the largest photographic materials company in the world, having wrested from Europe, where domination resided since 1839, leadership in products, enterprise, strategy, structure, and research. But no sooner had wealth begun to accumulate than he began dispersing it into the very technical, vocational, professional, and liberal education enterprises that he missed as a youth.

One can both like and dislike Eastman, a figure more complex and caring than the wooden character of legend. His feisty business skills included industrial spying, the cornering of all significant patents (except the primary one), and the squeezing out of competitors. But it is hard to fault his deep beliefs concerning the value of education, health care, racial and industrial relations, low-cost housing, and the importance to the human spirit of art, music, and designated park land.

His life was both easy and tough. A reticent, diminutive boy, he lost his father at age seven; yet that loss focused rather than diminished his life as he quickly assumed the role of head of family. Inventive, entrepreneurial, and managerial talents as well as dogged determination surfaced early. Yet the Eastman who emerges from his elaborate paper trail also regularly forsook the office for stimulating vacations, alternating hard work with hard play. His thirst for color and adventure led him to cycle into the wilds of czarist Russia in the 1890s and to undertake safaris when he was in his late seventies. Although he indulged in building the largest private home in town, acquired horses and carriages—and finally automobiles—by the dozen, he was never far from rural roots. Vegetable and flower gardens, greenhouses stuffed with flowers, palms, and bulbs for forcing augmented the prize cows in his home dairy.

Despite official retirement in 1925, Eastman showed little sign of slowing down. Late in life he designed a special camera for use in orthodontia and founded ground-breaking dental clinics for children in Europe and America. He established a medical school and campuses for two major universities, and oversaw a monumental music project with the goal that it be the best in the world. (In 1944 the Eastman School of Music tied for best graduate school for music in the nation.) Finally, he became the largest contributor to the education of African Americans during the 1920s.

My interest in George Eastman began as a sidebar about 1978. In researching a newspaper article about architecture in Rochester, New York, I learned that the identity of the architect of Eastman House was in question. During the ensuing search for the plans—they eventually surfaced in the engineering department of Kodak Park—I discovered much hitherto unpublished correspondence, source material, and interviews pertaining to Eastman. This material was then at the University of Rochester Library and the Eastman Kodak Company. In 1979 and 1980 I wrote almost fifty newspaper and magazine articles about Eastman, the majority pertaining to the construction of Eastman House. In the mid-1980s I became historical consultant for the restoration of Eastman House and its gardens. This provided access to more material, particularly Eastman's correspondence at the Eastman Kodak Company.

I am indebted to more individuals than I can recall or mention. In roughly chronological order they include: Andrew D. Wolfe, editor and publisher, Wolfe Publications, whose interest in the Eastman story led him to provide space in his newspapers for my continuing saga. Robert Doherty, director of the Eastman House in 1979, recalled that many glass negatives of the house and gardens were stored in the attic of the carriage house; some of these are used here. Kodak Engineering Department provided Photostats of 250 architectural plans, 1899–1950. Carl F. W. Kaelber Jr. of the successor architectural firm to Gordon & Kaelber provided information, photographs, and plans of the Eastman Theatre, the University of Rochester campus and medical school, and various dental clinics. Librarians at the New-York Historical Society alerted me to the McKim, Mead & White correspondence and plans there relating to Eastman House and the Eastman Theatre. At the University of Rochester Library, the late Alma Creek introduced me to a rich treasure trove of Eastman correspondence, photographs, ephemera, and interview files that were quietly collected, preserved, and indexed over many years. Some these files, notably the nitrate negatives, would never have survived but for the dedication of staff members to the principle that history takes precedence. Manuscripts librarian Karl Kabelac's assistance spans fifteen years and ranges from expertise regarding antique cars and the history of the University of Rochester to his important bibliographical publications about Eastman and Monroe County personalities and places.

At Eastman House, the House Restoration Committee under Elizabeth K. Harvey and then Georgia P. Gosnell, and the Garden Restoration Committee under Nancy R. Turner, gave me the opportunity to reopen the subject of Eastman in the mid-1980s. Interviews with Lucia Valentine, who as wife of University of Rochester president Alan Valentine lived in Eastman House from 1935 to 1947, provided unique insights.

In pursuit of Eastman I cycled through the same bulb fields near Hillegom, Holland, as he did a century earlier and interviewed the directors of Eastman dental clinics in Paris, Stockholm, and Rome. (The director of the Paris clinic spoke no English and I spoke no French, yet the interview proved productive.) I talked with persons who had met Eastman, albeit often as children or young adults. In Florida in 1989 Nancy Turner and I visited George Eastman Dryden, now in his nineties and the last surviving relative who knew George Eastman. I had many conversations with Gertrude Herdle Moore, director of the Memorial Art Gallery of the University of Rochester (1922–62) where Eastman was a board member (1912–32). Albert K. Chapman was hired by Eastman in 1918, became his assistant, and rose to become company president. General Edward Peck Curtis and William Vaughn (another president) worked at Kodak during the 1920s. Elizabeth Vaughn was Eastman's last organist. Alan McHose and Nicolas Slonimsky played the organ and piano respectively at Eastman House. Enid Knapp Botsford organized the Eastman Ballet. As cub reporter Henry Clune interviewed Eastman. Clayla Ward and Charlotte Whitney Allan knew Eastman socially. As Eastman Preparatory School student, Byron Johnson had personal tours of Eastman's trophies and was admonished not to pick the oranges from the trees in the Eastman House conservatory. Blanchard Bartlett Walker, daughter of the Rev. Murray Bartlett, stayed at Eastman House on several occasions. Katharine Whipple and Dorothy Burkhart Voorhis knew Eastman well. Dr. James Sibley Watson Jr., editor of *The Dial* in the 1920s, watched his father give Eastman tips on shooting clay pigeons in return for Kodak film and tips about photography. Charles Gleason, son of Harold Gleason, Eastman's organist (1919–30), and Marion Gleason, member of Eastman's Saturday luncheon club, the Lobster Quartet, shared recollections from childhood.

I spoke with Beaumont Newhall, second director of Eastman House, and Roger Butterfield. Both distinguished scholars urged me to complete this book. David Gibson, then director of the Kodak Patent Museum, made trial transcripts available and gently corrected my many misconceptions about Kodak cameras and company history. Nicholas Graver, Dr. James Zimmer, and Frank Brownell Mehlenbacher (grandson of Eastman's camera designer) shared extensive archival material and expertise concerning the history of photography. Without the conviction of Lois Gauch, head of Business Information Center at the Eastman Kodak Company, that I was the right person to pursue an Eastman biography, this book would not exist. She allowed me to read (for five years) all of the Eastman correspondence then in the company's private archives. Michael More, director of international news, communications, and public affairs, made available many of the photographs from the Eastman Kodak collection used here.

The staff of Eastman House under James Enyeart, director 1989–95, cooperated in many ways. In particular, Kathleen Connor, George Eastman House curator, ferreted out negatives with only the slightest clue as to their location among 13,000 inventoried images; Barbara Galasso printed them. The archives and archivists at the Massachusetts Institute of Technology proved helpful to Carl Ackerman in the 1920s and to me in the 1990s. Colin Rattee provided material pertaining to Kodak Limited.

Most of the suggestions of Thomas Fitzpatrick, first reader of my first draft, remain. Others who read the draft (or portions thereof) in its various states, offering corrections and comments without destroying old friend-ships, include Karl Kabelac, William Vaughn, Nina Anderson, David Gibson, Nicholas Graver, Mary Ann Hargrave, Margaret Bond, Michael More, and T. H. James. Ann Sayre and the late Ann Gibson encouraged me to complete the task.

Dr. Henry Y. K. Tom at Johns Hopkins University Press recognized the importance of a new biography of Eastman, then wielded a friendly scalpel in reducing my manuscript to manageable proportions.

Finally, I salute my husband, Sheldon Brayer, who cheerfully endured the single-minded focus and shared my fascination with George Eastman.

GEORGE EASTMAN

Prologue:
The Housewarming

The men arrive promptly at 6 P.M. Although many of the one hundred far-flung executives of the Eastman Kodak Company have just recently converged upon Rochester, New York, they hasten on to their final destination. The gala opening of George Eastman's baronial estate is a command performance.

On this balmy October evening in 1905, carriages and cabs (some of the horseless variety) traverse the circular gravel driveway to the Neo-Georgian mansion and discharge their passengers at its stately portico. The urban estate is ablaze with lights—gas, electric, Japanese lanterns, Roman candles. Inside bronze and glass doors, a slight yet commanding figure greets his "boys" before the light-splashed grand staircase of the marble and paneled main hallway. Strains of a string ensemble issue from the cavernous interior.

Intense blue eyes, steely cold during working hours, are twinkling with pride tonight. The mouth, typically set in a severe and firm line, breaks easily into a smile. The countenance may resemble Julius Caesar's[1] but the stance—feet apart, hands in back pockets with thumbs out, and chin protruding—accentuates the small paunch extending from the white waistcoat. The words are few but the striking language and rising inflections hint at coiled energy behind the quiet, dry exterior.

An air of loneliness in public, even amid colleagues he has known for decades, leads some to assume that he is incapable of close friendship. Bored and uncommunicative in large groups, he is animated with just a few companions, particularly women, and at his best as a correspondent. And in letters to him, an attorney can say, without fear of embarrassing his boss, "I have enjoyed your quintette and your orchids but I have missed you greatly; as much as I enjoy the music and flowers, I like you much better."[2]

How can this seemingly withdrawn personality be such a superb leader and organizer? Although known internationally as the man who made the photographic image a universal tool and at home as the city's largest employer and wealthiest citizen, his physiognomy is unknown to all but a few intimates. He is denied access to his own factory by a new watchman: "Glad to meet you; I'm John D. Rockefeller," scoffs the employee. Caught jaywalking, his explanation (that he had just returned from six months in Europe and had not noticed the new traffic sign) is rejected by the cop on the beat with a disdainful mutter: "Everybody in this town thinks he's George Eastman."[3]

The housewarming is Eastman's way of thanking the members of the large and talented organization he is still building. Twenty-five years before he performed all company functions himself; having institutionalized many roles, he now scours the universities and technical schools for the best talent to fill them. He needs good executives to keep pace with the research of chemists and engineers that almost daily opens new fields for expansion. Growth has been so rapid and all encompassing that the company may be in trouble with the government; at the very least, the Hearst papers and a small army of photographers and dealers are in full cry against the "Kodak Trust."

He is careful not to use the word "monopoly" in public. "He states emphatically" to a magazine reporter that the Eastman Kodak Company does "not desire to create a monopoly in photographic goods . . . [which] would be impossible to get. But any part of the photographic trade which they can get by giving the customer better and cheaper goods than any one else, or by giving the dealer a better profit so that it would be in his interest to push their goods—that part of the trade they are after . . . however much the anti-monopoly cry might be raised by their competitors. . . . "'That kind of monopoly is good for society at large'," Eastman tells the press, "'and just so far as it is good for it, will society encourage and permit it, and no further.' At any rate," the article concludes, "Mr. Eastman, as the moving spirit of this mammoth photographic company, seems assured of success, which he so well deserves."[4]

It is the trust-busting era. John D. Rockefeller's Standard Oil Company is mired in legal struggles as the government seeks to dismember that octopus. John D. is called "the greatest criminal of the age" by Senator Robert La Follette, and the Rockefeller family is referred to as "malefactors of great wealth" by President Theodore Roosevelt. Other capitalists see the richest man on earth differently: "Mr. Rockefeller is trying to do what he can for his fellow man in a most modest manner," says Frank Babbott—manufacturer, art collector, philanthropist, and Eastman's friend since childhood.[5] Rockefeller is worth $900 million in this age before billionaires and before income taxes, when a single dollar has the buying power that ten will have in the final decade of the century. Eastman, later listed as the sixth wealthiest man in the country (and the nation's wealthiest bachelor), could soon, with the right investments, be worth one-third of Rockefeller's assets, yet large chunks of his fortune are just sitting in bank accounts. He has lost interest in increasing his wealth: The driving force now is finding ways to put his money to work in the rest of society.

He still chooses his lieutenants carefully. In 1880 he used his father's handwriting test and intuition; now he seeks experts who understand the latest technology. Proving oneself "as always being ready to work and never anxious to drop the pick and shovel at the sound of the whistle" is another criterion. Dead wood never remains for long, and promotion is from within. The personality and values of the founder are reflected throughout the company: When in doubt, say nothing, is the credo of both.

Beyond the lieutenants is a rapidly growing labor force that does not push for unions. Eastman is staunchly opposed to unions and has easily won one skirmish with union organizers trying to gain a toehold. There is little discontent among the workers that could force a showdown: An occasional disgruntled employee is fired under suspicion of industrial espionage, but most perceive that Eastman provides higher wages and more benefits than other employers. Unionists go elsewhere.

The regal housewarming marks a stage in Eastman's metamorphoses from inventor and innovator to entrepreneur to manufacturer to financier to philanthropist. Just now he is deep into the financier stage. Having reorganized and refinanced the corporation in 1898 for $8 million in London, the world's financial capital, against the furious opposition of bankers and brokers there, he repeated the coup three years later with a capitalization of $35 million, again with no professional outside assistance. He enjoys putting together jigsaw puzzle mergers, those complex games that create order out of a jumble of companies and interests. Neither the planning of broad strategy nor the attention to minute detail escapes his eagle eye.

Wives are not included tonight because the host's eighty-four-year-old mother has recently broken her hip. Friends still hope that "GE," as he asks them to call him, a bachelor at fifty-one, will follow the lead of Andrew Carnegie who married at the same age shortly after the death of his beloved mother—but Eastman has always been the lone wolf among the tycoons of his time. His women friends—they are legion and mostly safely married— see a ray of hope in the time and attention he showers on Josephine Dickman, widow of his London manager, who now performs many wifely roles for him. Eastman just laughs them off with, "You women are always trying to take away my freedom." Household employees and Josephine's relatives say that except for her troubling heart condition the two would marry. The principals say nothing.[6]

Unlike the guests, the vodka fails to arrive in time for the beluga caviar, first of nine courses, but the Kirschwasser punch and Pommery sec champagne flow freely. The feast begins with bouillon and marrow balls, then the guests sample halibut timbales with truffles, sweetbreads with peas, tenderloin of beef with mushrooms, lima beans and Parisian potatoes, and partridges with bread sauce and salad. Dessert consists of pumpkin pie with cheese, Nesselrode pudding with apricot sauce, cakes, and coffee. The menu for the feast is handsomely recorded in a gilt-edged souvenir booklet illustrated with photographs of house and garden.

During dinner, which is served at tables for six and eight in the arcade running from dining room to palm house, a male vocal quartet is accompanied by the massive pipe organ in the flower-bedecked conservatory. Eight popular and patriotic renditions include "Marching through Georgia," "America," "Teasing," and Eastman's old nemesis, "Annie Laurie," the tune he spent two futile years as a youth trying to play on the flute.[7] The brick wall along one side of the arcade is illuminated by colored lights in the ivy, while a string orchestra on the porch provides pleasant music for dining. Vaudeville entertainment from New York City precedes group singing to the swells of the organ, all leading up to an *Illumination of the Gardens*. Eastman motions the Kodakers to the garden and asks for absolute quiet. Moments later a whistle sounds and twelve men stationed throughout the roses and shrubs touch off bombs, lights, and firecrackers as the whole garden bursts into pyrotechnics for the next twenty minutes. Policemen stationed in front of the house point curious onlookers to spots where they can best observe the illuminations. Upstairs in the mansion, Maria Kilbourn Eastman, the host's aged mother, watches as an artificial moon rises from behind the garden peristyle. Downstairs in garden and conservatory, host and guests climax this memorable housewarming with a rousing rendition of "Auld Lang Syne."[8]

"I want to gather around the table as many of the men as possible who have been instrumental in building up the great concern with which we are all connected," Eastman had written Thacher Clarke, when he learned that the "big bear," as he called Clarke, could not attend the housewarming of 7 October 1905. "Your part therein has been of more importance than you have ever seemed to realize."[9] It was a piece of the growing mystique of the Eastman Kodak Company that its new president (and still treasurer and general manager) would constantly remind his lieutenants how valuable each one was to the success of the company. When art dealers approach him he begs off, claiming that he is "not a collector"; he does collect people, however, and very selectively.

The turn of the century is the watershed of Eastman's life. It is then that he moves from the active and intensive work of the early years to a time of relative leisure and travel; from a period of amassing great wealth to having the fun of distributing it; from building a business, and the factories in support of it, to building institutions to serve humankind through music, medicine, dentistry, racial advancement, technical and liberal arts education, and so forth. But before he can effect this sea change, a photographic revolution is waiting to be completed.[10]

I

Beginnings

Eastmans and Kilbourns

■ ■ ▪ ————————————————————————————————

A quarter century before the Kodak chief's brilliant housewarming, observers glimpsed a very different kind of scene. As the liner pushed out of New York Harbor on 18 June 1879, fellow passengers on the Cunard steamship *Abyssinia* noted the young American's curiously blackened fingertips. Otherwise, he cut a respectable figure, with a voluminous greatcoat adding some bulk to his "thin as piecrust," five-foot-eight, 135 pound frame. The scruffy beginnings of a beard betrayed him as a twenty-four-year-old trying to appear just a little older. The seven-day voyage to London would help the beard along.

George Eastman's darkly stained fingers were the emblems of his enterprise. Two years of tinkering with photographic chemicals in the "lightless and dustless" laboratory he had set up in his mother's rooming house, during hours after his normal day as a bank clerk, had blackened his hands. He had also produced a photographic plate-coating machine, a model of which was crated below deck. He was writing that "my process reduces the cost of manufacture materially . . . wherever the plates are made in large quantity" and that "no one will coat plates by hand after he has seen this."[1] He was gambling that his invention would gain him entrée to the world capital of photography before him. The plan was to patent the machine in London, then sell it outright or at least the licensing rights to established firms; thus capitalized he could quit the bank job, go into business for himself back in Rochester, and get the boarders out of his mother's house. A heady design, but this young American about to test his acumen in the Island Empire was bankrolled for the attempt. After $144 for the steamship ticket and $25 for clothes out of his $3,600 savings, he still had on deposit with the ship's purser a total of $241. That, and a month's leave from the bank should do it.

George Eastman's ancestors had made the Atlantic voyage westward more than two centuries earlier. On the maternal side, Thomas Kilborne and family sailed from England in 1635 on the wooden ship *Increase* for a Dutch settlement in Connecticut. The Kilbornes (also recorded as Kilbourn, Kilbourne, Kilburnen, and Kilborn) were of yeoman stock and unlike many immigrants of the seventeenth century were not religious separatists but staunchly Church of England. The Eastmans were not far behind. Roger Eastman of Wales sailed from Southampton on the *Confidence* in 1638 to become an original settler of Salisbury (now Franklin, New Hampshire) in the Massachusetts Bay Colony. Roger's trade was carpentry (his eleventh-generation descendant would actively pursue many an elaborate construction project). From Roger, subsequent Eastmans in America would claim descendance. The branch of the family that produced George Eastman would move west, but those Eastmans who remained in New England had a distinguished heritage of their own. Abigail Eastman, one of Roger's granddaughters, became the mother of orator and statesman Daniel Webster. One grandson, Peter, built the first house in New Fairfield, Connecticut, while another, Deacon Joseph, survived capture by Indians. Captain Ebenezer Eastman was the first inhabitant of Concord, New Hampshire. General Francis Amasa Walker, an early president of the Massachusetts Institute of Technology to whom George Eastman wrote asking for chemists, was descended from Roger Eastman, and so were Sydney and Arthur Colgate of the soap and toothpaste empire (besides the blood relationship, George Eastman would count both the Colgates as friends). Still another Eastman married into the family that would produce the poet Emily Dickinson in Amherst, Massachusetts.[2]

   These facts were dug out by George Eastman himself. After a lifetime of affecting indifference to his lineage, the sixty-year-old Kodak leader would in 1916 begin to research and publish material about the genealogy of both Eastmans and Kilbourns. He learned of Eastman generals during the American Revolution, and of two forebears who had crossed the Delaware with Washington (one freezing to death). He found that his great-grandfather Hezekiah had fought with the militia when the British burned Danbury, Connecticut, and helped bond schooners and brigantines for the American naval forces that put out from Maryland. Peter Eastman was found among the ranks of the Minutemen of Boston. (In 1924, after donating $1 million to the Hampton Institute for the education of African Americans and Native

Americans, George Eastman was amazed to be informed by a distant cousin that "during the war with the Indians a whole branch of the Eastman family, except the father, was scalloped [sic] and burned."[3])

Both families separately pushed westward in the late eighteenth century. Joseph Eastman, after living in New Jersey, Connecticut, and Washington County, New York, left the coastal states for the New York frontier, which had not yet moved much beyond the rich agricultural and dairy township of Marshall, south of Utica in the center of the state. He purchased a farm there in 1797 that became the Eastman homestead, passing it to his eldest son Hezekiah, and then to Hezekiah's eldest son, Harvey, George Eastman's grandfather. Aside from the families of Harvey's sons Porter and Almon Russell, which settled in Ohio, and a few Eastmans who scattered to Missouri and California, neither family showed much desire to keep up the westward-ing. (Indeed, A. Russell later moved eastward from Ohio to Rochester.) Similarly, George Eastman, even with his propensity for world travel, was never inclined to permanently leave Upstate New York.

The homesteads the Eastmans and Kilbourns established in central New York were passed from generation to generation, usually to the eldest son, and so it was a stable and enduring agricultural life that greeted George Washington Eastman on 9 September 1815, and six years later, on 22 August 1821, Maria Kilbourn. George Eastman's parents were both the youngest children of large broods. Harvey and Anne Rundell Eastman reared ten children, six boys and four girls, nine of whom survived into adulthood, on their Marshall farm near Waterville; Thomas Kilbourn's wife Mary gave birth to seven, one boy and six girls, on their farm atop Paris Hill on the road from Waterville to Utica. The farms apparently provided an adequate living even for such large families (although there is one country lane off that main road that still bears the name "Hardscrabble Road"), but they were hardly large enough to partition among so many children.

While George W. and Maria were growing up in the fertile Mohawk Valley, James Fenimore Cooper was immortalizing the area to the southeast, the ancient territory of the Mohawk and Oneida nations of the Iroquois League. What DeWitt Clinton's Erie Canal had begun would be completed by wooden rails. The valley became the halfway point for commerce between Buffalo and New York City, the gateway to the lumbering industry, to the Adirondacks in the north, the Catskills in the south, and the Finger Lakes to the west. Waterways and rails of wood and iron brought new ideas into the region. The culture of central New York in the mid-nineteenth century was marked by evangelical piety in religion, devotion to progressive causes in politics, and faith in formal education as the key to self-improvement.

   The two families saw many an itinerant evangelist add sparks to the fiery
revivalism that so repeatedly swept over their area that it came to be known as
the "burned-over district." Calvinists from New England left their mark, but
so did such anti-Calvinists as Charles Grandison Finney, whose oratory engulfed Rome, Utica, and Rochester. In 1848 the Spiritualist movement began in Hydesville, New York, when two little sisters, Margaret and Katherine
Fox, heard "rappings" from a murdered man. The children were taken to
Rochester, where they lived in the house once occupied by the family of
Henry Strong, who would become president of the Eastman Kodak Company. Within months the rappings stirred worldwide interest and many people
declared themselves mediums.
   The utopian Oneida Community, whose members were derisively called
"Bible communists," was established in 1848 by John Humphrey Noyes.
Many of the ideas that George Eastman would develop have roots in Oneida:
the concept that all work was dignified, the imposition of eugenic principles
to produce healthy and intelligent children, and equal rights in the workplace for women. The intense spirituality of the period produced the
Church of Jesus Christ of Latter-day Saints, and Joseph Smith's visions while
living at Palmyra (twenty miles east of Rochester) made that community a
Mormon shrine.
   A New York farmer, William Miller, predicted the end of the world and
the Second Coming for 1843, gaining legions of converts. In October of
Miller's doomsday year a young Maria Kilbourn wrote to her missionary
sister, Emily Cope, in Ceylon of the ambivalence of many: "If this doctrine is
of men it will soon come to nought but if it is of God it will be a fearful thing to
be found fighting against." When 1843 passed without cosmic incident,
religious enthusiasm abated. Maria preferred the fiery evangelical mood; as
she wrote from Kingsville in 1842, "The churches in this place are beginning
to awake from the dreadful state of coldness and stupidity in which they have
been."[4] The Eastmans and Kilbourns embraced more conventional denomi-
nations. George W.'s grandfather, Elder Hezekiah Eastman, was a Baptist
clergyman, and the grandson flirted with becoming a Baptist preacher himself. Reared in the Anglican faith of her progenitors, Maria and her children
attended the Baptist church in Waterville but after G. W.'s death she and her
son, then age sixteen, became Episcopalians.[5]
   All this high-powered piety left in the district a residue of idealism and a
steady belief in the redeemability of humankind. Coupled with a fundamen-
talist work ethic, it made Upstate New York the point of origin of many of the
progressive social movements of the century. Later an ex-slave named Frederick Douglass would thunder forth his abolitionist creed in his Rochester
newspaper the *North Star*, while a Rochester schoolteacher named Susan B.
Anthony would begin her long march toward full women's suffrage. But in
the 1830s it was still unusual for the family of a young woman like Maria

Kilbourn to provide her with an education as thorough as that of her future husband. George Washington Eastman attended Hamilton Academy at Clinton (where he was taught by the father of Elihu Root) and Amenia Seminary in Dutchess County. The Kilbourns sent Maria to the Vernon Academy and to Kellogg's Seminary, both schools of abolitionist sympathies. She was educated in chemistry, mental philosophy, rhetoric, astronomy ("the geography of heaven"), and botany by young ministers from the radical Oberlin Theological Seminary. After classes, her sewing society worked on items to be donated to a colony of runaway slaves in Toronto, Canada. The Kilbourn home provided an antidote to rural provinciality—the house was crowded with art objects from Ceylon and Madura, India, sent to Marshall by Maria's missionary sister, Emily. Maria's mementos of this period were two copies of the *Book of Common Prayer*, three hymnals, and the poems of John Milton.[6]

The Eastmans were also involved in the antislavery movement. The homestead in Marshall would later be a stop on the Underground Railway—in the barn stood a special carriage, always ready to spirit away to Canada the next "bale of Southern goods" that arrived in "Quaker bonnets" in the dead of night. G. W.'s brother Porter had a similar arrangement in Kingsville, and his nephew Harvey Gridley Eastman "guilelessly imported some noted Eastern abolitionists" to lecture in a business college he started in St. Louis in 1858. Harvey was driven out of town.[7] As young people both George W. and Maria witnessed and approved of the pre–Civil War move to racial justice, and this concern was passed down to their son. George Eastman's friendship with Booker T. Washington, his strong support of educational institutions devoted to racial advancement, and his easy acceptance from people of various backgrounds are evidence of the two families' ethical legacy.

George Washington Eastman's aptitude for penmanship translated into an enthusiasm and then a vocation. At age seventeen he offered classes at Hamilton Academy and Amenia Seminary "the winter he was in attendance there," then private lessons in Waterville and vicinity.[8] Through his Kingsville brothers, G. W. learned of Platt Rogers Spencer, also of Ashtabula County, Ohio, who had developed a system of handwriting that was standardizing the craft. Everyone wanted to learn this ornate style of penmanship, marked by rounded letters slanted to the right. Children had to perfect "a fine Spencerian hand"; G. W. saw this as an opportunity to become a "writing master." A decade after he began teaching penmanship, he took leave of farming and opted for the commercial world of business education. For its boldness and creativity, G. W.'s move was remarkable. It is one thing for a younger son of a farming family to be forced off the land and make his way to the city, there to scratch around for a new occupation. It is quite another thing for a young man to create a new life and profession for himself out of thin air and a couple of instructional manuals. If George Washington

Eastman left his son nothing else, this life model would prove to be enough of a bequest.

G. W. made a start on the new life by moving to Rochester, the coming community of the Genesee Valley, in 1842. From a bachelor's room in a boarding house, surrounded by traveling drummers, he hung up a shingle over a rented space at Wamstet's Marble Block and had himself listed as a penmanship teacher in the city directory. Apparently, his prospects were encouraging, for it was not long before he was negotiating with the Kilbourns for Maria's hand.

It was a natural match. The two families had been close and, in fact, had already intermarried. G. W.'s older brother Almon Russell had married Sophia Wells Kilbourn in 1836, and the pair had moved to Kingsville, Ohio. Maria visited her older sister there in 1842, and saw an old playmate, also visiting his brother, in a new light. "George [Washington] Eastman . . . is trying to do something for the cause of Temperance in this place which with all the other good causes of the day has been sadly neglected," she wrote Emily in faraway Ceylon. Maria saw G. W. in his temperance phase when he had joined his older brothers as a Washingtonian Lecturer and was employing his considerable vigor in saving souls from demon rum. The pretty, usually serene Maria (whose daguerreotype suggests that early trouble with her teeth produced a stiff-lipped grimace that passed for a smile) chafed at spinsterhood. Her letters are full of complaints that her friends are all getting married, and that she has found no congenial company in Kingsville except Sophia's family—and George Washington Eastman. Kingsville saw the marriage of Maria Kilbourn and George Washington Eastman on 25 September 1844.[9]

When G. W. brought his bride back to Rochester in 1844, they found a city of almost 25,000 that ranked just behind Pittsburgh and Cincinnati as an industrial center in America's interior. Its economic base was flour milling along the Genesee River, whose two major waterfalls preceded its flow northward into Lake Ontario. The inchoate community of Rochesterville (population 332 in 1815) became the seat of Monroe County in 1821; the building of the Erie Canal in the 1820s transformed it into an incorporated city of 13,000 in 1834. Colonel Nathaniel Rochester's one hundred acres of swamp, purchased as a speculation in 1803 for $1,750, had been chosen over a dozen other communities as the point where the canal would be carried by aqueduct to cross the Genesee River. And so Rochester became what its twentieth-century historians would call "America's first boomtown."[10]

By 1855 clothing and footwear manufacture would be vying with the flour mills for industrial leadership, and the city had added cooper shops, lumber mills, boat yards, breweries, and optical plants (through the 1853 enterprise of German lens makers John Jacob Bausch and Henry Lomb) as well as cabinet and furniture factories. West of Rochester grazed half a million sheep; the city's two woolen mills made it a key market. In 1851 a group of Rochesterians led by Hiram Sibley put together the telegraph company combine that five years later would be called Western Union. Many of the Irish immigrants who built the canal settled in Rochester, joining the transplanted New Englanders and descendants of the city's founders—Nathaniel Rochester, William Fitzhugh, and Charles Carroll. The revolutions of 1848 in the German states instigated new immigration; Protestant, Catholic, and Jewish emigrants would be the city's largest foreign-born minority for the next half century. It was a burgeoning city with an economy on an upswing— just the place for an enterprising twenty-nine-year-old like G. W. to make his mark without handling hops and apples.

For Maria, it was a lonely place. She missed both her friends and the settled farms and tree-lined streets of the older Oneida communities. "I find residence in Rochester very pleasant, but I still love the country and if it were as favorable for my husband's business should prefer living there." The young couple spent the winter at the Blossom House, "a new and elegant Hotel," but sensing that "it would be pleasanter to live more retired," had found "an English cottage about three quarters of a mile from the centre of the city." The house was in the middle of a garden, surrounded by flowers and shrubbery on all sides, and in the back there were fruit trees and a vegetable garden. G. W. had not shaken his Oneida agricultural past, for he tended the trees and made the garden for his wife when he was not giving lessons in writing and bookkeeping.[11] He attracted enough business to enlist an Eastman brother, Almon Russell of Ohio, and their nephew Harvey Gridley, son of another brother (Horace Haveland of Waterville), in the growing enterprise and to add bookkeeping and accounting to the writing classes. In 1847 he wrote and published, with Levi S. Fulton, what would become a standard textbook—*Fulton and Eastman's Bookkeeping, Single and Double Entry*. The next year the same authors published *Chirographic Charts*, a handwriting book that employed maxims to be used as writing exercises.

The Eastmans needed the income. On 4 November 1845 their first child, Ellen Maria, was born, an event recorded in the family bible inscribed, "A New Year's Gift from George Washington Eastman to his Wife."[12] About four years later the Eastmans bought a ten-acre farm in Waterville for $3,000 and the family moved back in 1849. The house that has come down in legend as "George Eastman's birthplace"[13] was "a comfortable sort of old fashioned dwelling," a modest Greek Revival frame house with a barn.[14] The house stood on Stafford Avenue as it curved toward the plank road to Utica just outside Waterville. Maria may have been pleased to be back among familiar scenes and people, but she encountered loneliness of a different sort. G. W. now had to commute between Waterville and Rochester and saw his family infrequently. Maria would drive him in a wagon over the toll road to Utica, where he would board the New York Central train to Rochester. He would probably not return until the following weekend. While in Rochester he boarded at the Blossom House, the Waverly House, or the Osborn House. "I find it unpleasant to have him away," Maria wrote soon after she and baby Ella were settled in Waterville. But she filled her days: "I cleaned the chambers yesterday, baked a little, and churned, beside putting up the washing. Was not that right smart?" Her consolation was in religion: "We are both endeavoring to serve the Lord. Pray for us that we may 'continue faithful until death that we may receive a crown of life.'"[15]

G. W. and his brother A. Russell opened a business school in Waterville. Next he published his own *Complete System of Penmanship*, enlisting Fulton once again to co-write *A Practical System of Bookkeeping by Single and Double Entry Containing Forms of Books and Practical Exercises Adapted to the Use of the Farmer, Mechanic, Merchant and Professional Man*. He meant to make the farm pay as well. He stocked it with roses and fruit trees and advertised their availability in the *Waterville Times*.[16] In 1851 George W. contemplated opening another commercial college, this time in Ohio.

His son would later call this hedging of financial bets "covering the alternative," and G. W. was successful enough at it to plan for expansion. In January 1850 he had a seventeen-year-old apprentice architect, Andrew Jackson Warner of Rochester, draw up some "plans for the home of George Washington Eastman." We don't know if the house on Stafford Avenue was merely to be expanded—a second child, Emma Kate, was born on 6 August 1850—or if this was the genesis of it. Half a century later, Warner's son would be hard at work on much grander plans for the home and factories belonging to George Eastman.[17]

Emma Kate was a sickly child from age fourteen months when Tommy Cope, son of Maria's missionary sister, noted that "Little Katy has got a sick foot, arm, and wrist. This evening she lifted her sick foot very well in trying to walk to her father."[18] All the "very wells" of forced optimism couldn't disguise the nature of Emma Kate's disease: infantile paralysis, or polio. Deemed too delicate for schooling during the winter months and condemned to a sedentary existence, she would be dependent for the rest of her short life on the earning power of first her father and then her younger brother. But worse was to come. In 1852 a son, planned to carry the father's name and dreams, did not survive long after birth.[19]

By 1854 G. W. was apparently living on his own in Rochester from November through April. From spring through fall, however, he seems to have stayed in Waterville with the family, cultivating his orchard. Into this household, financially comfortable if precarious, with the father gone for half the year so that its atmosphere was set by the mother and sisters, on 12 July 1854, an infant son was born. Had the parents read the *Rochester Daily Union* that Wednesday they would have noticed the area's big news: the inauguration the previous day of the first president of the fledgling University of Rochester who, in his maiden address, "disposed of the popular objections against a liberal education in masterly fashion."[20] Seven decades later the Eastmans' son, having similarly disposed of his own objections against a liberal education, would make that university the principal recipient of his largess.

This son's name was entered into the family bible as just "George Eastman." Throughout his adult life, he would bristle if someone sought to insert "Washington" as his middle name.

For a boy whose ancestors had lived on American soil since the 1630s in family homesteads that were passed along from generation to generation, it must have seemed an unsettled childhood, what with the ambitious George Washington Eastman's divided existence. Most of the year he resided in Rochester as president of a fledgling commercial college that had year-round matriculation. Weekends and vacations the absentee husband and father, more special visitor than family member, traveled to Waterville, some 120 miles to the east, to oversee his nursery business.

Almost the first excursions the infant George had were, portentously, to a bank. His nine-year-old sister Ellen Maria would wheel him in a carriage and later pull him in Katy's little rattan wagon to Waterville's short Main Street to do her father's banking. In "one of his rare spells of loquaciousness," G. W. Eastman told his neighbor, R. Wilson Roberts, that he believed the only way to bring up children was by letting them learn by actual experience—the same philosophy he followed in his commercial school. Roberts recalled the father's theories on child rearing: "I wouldn't have a child of mine that couldn't do any sort of an errand after it was five years old." Other elderly Waterville residents remembered the Kodak tycoon as "far from a quiet baby. . . . But as he began to play about the big spacious yard, or was able to toddle after his father into the orchard with its young trees, George was a surprisingly well-behaved child," to quote one woman. "The baby boy was his father's especial favorite, and as he grew into boyhood he often accompanied his father as he drove his team to Paris, the shipping point in those days—13 miles each way over Paris Hill."[21]

When George was a little older, he visited Eastman and Kilbourn cousins on nearby farms as well as in Gilbertsville and Marcellus, New York, and Ashtabula County, Ohio. On the next street lived Frank Lusk Babbott, almost exactly George's age, who would be his boon companion for seventy-seven years. As the youngest child and only boy, George was the center of attention at home, even though Katy, four years older, was the invalid. It was a somewhat somber household, if George's memories of seventy years later are accurate: "I never smiled until I was forty. I may have grinned but I never smiled. Since then I've tried to win back something of the fun that other men had when they were boys."[22]

Its "chief beauty," a New York City newspaper of the 1850s enthused over Waterville, was "its cozy nestling among the lofty hills, its beautiful streams . . . for good fishing. . . . The streets were wide with plank side-walks on either side and thickly shaded by elms between expansive Italianate and Greek Revival residences. Beautiful villas, costly mansions and snugly nestled cottages peep out from their maple and ailanthus surroundings."[23] Waterville was originally a manufacturing and service center for its farming hinterland: Farmers brought grain, butter, eggs, fruit, and meat to village stores and took home shoes, calico, sugar, coffee, and flour bought with store credits. Tools and machinery were made in the village. After hops were introduced in the 1830s, the village became the national exchange center for this product. Diversified farming was eclipsed until the end of the century, when depletion of the soil and "the blue mold" revived it.[24]

The Eastmans did not grow hops but concentrated on pear, apple, cherry, peach, plum, chestnut, and quince trees, as well as roses and other ornamental shrubs. Flowers were "selected with great care . . . from the best greenhouses in Utica and Rochester."[25] In 1852 G. W. purchased an additional ten acres adjoining his farm, causing the *Waterville Times* to take note of "the nursery and grounds of Mr. George W. Eastman": "We never witnessed so large a collection of prize winners. . . . Mr. Eastman has something like 30 acres under cultivation and he will be able to throw into market this fall about 40,000 fruit trees."[26] Tommy Cope worked summers in the nurseries of his uncles, George W. and Horace. He reported to his parents, the itinerant missionaries, how intensely interested his uncle was, not just in the new writing school but in all aspects of horticulture, including a system called "terra culture." Tommy, seventeen years older than baby George, lived with the Eastmans from July until December, attending his uncle's writing school when he was not "budding," grafting, or becoming "lame from working too hard" in the fields.[27]

Waterville's population of two thousand residents was sufficient to draw traveling entertainers, reformers, and photographers. Although a Utica portrait studio advertised "beautiful Photographic likenesses" in the *Waterville Times,* and daguerreotype studios adjoined Eastman's Commercial College in Rochester, and itinerant photographers set up temporary shop on Waterville's Main Street, which had not one but two permanent galleries, it does not appear that the Eastman family was enthralled by the infant craft of photography. From the 1850s only one daguerreotype of Maria survives, along with three photographs of G. W. (one to advertise the college), none of the daughters, and but a single ambrotype of young George, age three— with the next photograph of him a tintype of a decade later.

As Eastman's Commercial College and its branches grew, G. W. added merchandising, banking, insurance, and jobbing—"to qualify the pupil to act as book-keeper in the most extensive and diversified establishments." It became, his son wrote in 1901, "the prototype of similar schools of the present day the first commercial school in which the scholars were actually carried through the regular business transactions . . . by means of dummy banks, warehouses and factories . . . [and by] using samples of stocks, real estate, insurance, banking, steamboat and railroad forms." G. W. acknowledged he was strict—"All accounts must be kept with absolute accuracy in every detail"—but that was necessary, he said, to fit his pupils for "lucrative positions." In 1854 the college moved to the top floor of the Reynolds Arcade, Rochester's commercial and cultural center. And so, at the very hub of a city on an antebellum economic rise, George's father seemed to have the American Dream at his fingertips. But his health began to deteriorate in 1857, when at the age of forty-two, he was housebound with inflammatory rheumatism. It may have been a factor in his giving up the Waterville business in May 1858. October saw him put the Waterville house up for sale, but the house did not sell immediately, perhaps because these were hard economic times. Finally, in 1860, the house and nursery had been sold and the Eastmans moved back to Rochester to a rented house at 10 South Washington Street, within walking distance of the business district and the Commercial College, but also close to the bustling, noisy, and ripely malodorous Erie Canal. The *Rochester Union & Advertiser* welcomed them back, noting that George W. had "superior qualifications as a teacher as well as manager of one of the finest institutions of the age." Business smarts, strictness, managerial and horticultural skills—all these would be the legacy of father to son.

Then, total calamity. On 2 May 1862, between columns reporting the Civil War news (New Orleans had been captured by Union troops), the *Rochester Union and Advertiser* announced George Washington's death of a "brain disorder."[28] He was buried in the family plot in Waterville. Two months shy of his eighth birthday, George Eastman had experienced a drastic reversal of fortunes that was to indelibly mark his youth and early manhood. Born into a rural, easy-going environment, he was thrust into a scrambling urban roughness. The heir of a well-off, if not affluent family, he had suddenly to make his way hampered by genteel poverty. His father's death forced him into dependence on his mother alone for parental guidance and, ultimately, into an early and remarkable self-reliance. Eastman's contemporaries remembered, too, that he harbored resentments toward his father, particularly for the debts he had incurred.[29]

For Maria Kilbourn Eastman, widowed at forty-one and with three young children (one an invalid), life looked grim. She had little money, receiving a percentage of the business school profits that grew less each year and royalties from her husband's books that trickled in. Although shortly before or after her husband's death the family moved to another modest frame house in Livingston Park, within the boundaries of Rochester's fashionable ("Ruffled Shirt") Third Ward, she had no recourse but to adopt that usual

nineteenth-century expedient of widows: taking in boarders. The extra
money allowed her to send George to "Mr Carpenter's . . . the best private
school for boys in the city," as the youngster wrote Uncle Horace.[30] Mr.
Carpenter's school with its "seventy scholars" was housed in the old United
States Hotel where the University of Rochester had made its debut in 1850,
then removed in 1861 to Azariah Boody's cow pasture on the undeveloped
east side of Rochester.

Up to his first job as an office boy in 1868 George's boyhood had been
fairly conventional. There was the usual brush with schoolboy cruelty. Once,
in order to join a secret club, the sweet-faced, small George underwent an
initiation ceremony: In the shadowy confines of Darwin Smith's barn the
boys dripped hot candle wax from the loft onto his outstretched arms, hoping to raise a whimper. They had invited him for the fun of initiating him,
not from any desire to have this shy boy as a member. But when George stood
firm and unflinching, his status went up and his self-control was admired. As
an adult, Eastman would boast of his stoicism and proudly show the scars of
this fraternity.[31]

There were still visits with Tompkins cousins in Marcellus and Eastman
cousins in Ashtabula during the summer, treats at Christmas, baseball
games, and matching pennies with a neighbor, Albert O. Fenn. The picture
that emerges from childhood letters is one of a balanced and busy life within
a close family of modest means. The family's financial condition was more
shabbily genteel than grindingly poverty-stricken, even though poverty is
the myth helped along by Eastman's own selective memory. The boy's decision to drop formal education for work may be seen as an act of rugged
independence rather than one born of absolute necessity. And it was not
Maria's idea, as Eastman always took pains to point out. From 8 A.M. to 6 P.M.
every day but Sunday, he would sweep Captain Waydell's office, stoke the
stove, run errands, clean off the desks, and empty the cuspidors. His pay was
$3 a week and he gloried in being a man of independent means. Employing
one of his father's favorite textbook axioms, "No one should trust transactions of a pecuniary nature to his memory alone," he began an account book
and became an assiduous figure keeper, of both income and expense. He
enjoyed plopping down $5 to pay the coal bill. He earned a little on the side
by creating puzzles "made up of rings pinned together on a tuning fork, the
object [of which] was to get them off and place them on again without
disturbing their order," then selling them to friends for ten cents apiece. For
adults he fashioned $5 book shelf brackets out of black walnut with a filigree
design in the workshop his mother outfitted for him one Christmas. He
budgeted largess: photographs for his Sunday school teacher, a book called
The Token, or Affection's Gift for sister Ella, the fee to send crippled Katie for a
ride in a carriage, and a quarter a week to the Sunday school of St. Luke's
Episcopal Church.[32]

He was a neat dresser, buying a suit or two each year while not neglecting hats, ties, shoes, slippers, collars, a key ring, and well-repaired boots. Every two weeks he had a fifteen-cent haircut, but it cost $1.25 to get a tooth pulled. (Like his mother, he had dental problems.) He bought a fishing pole, dumbbells, two flutes (one for $3, the second for $14), and subscriptions to *Harper's* and *Youth's Companion*. Lectures were not neglected; dancing lessons cost $10. A $5 membership in Shadders Gymnasium began a lifelong dedication to physical fitness; another $10 (more than three weeks' pay) went for a ticket to New York City. His taste for travel whetted, he went farther afield each year thereafter. A trip to Waterville, Utica, Oneida, and Sidney in 1869 cost $12.46 (he then earned $6 a week). The next year it was Buffalo and vicinity as seen from an omnibus and carriage and in 1872, at age eighteen, he splurged on a trip to New England, staying a while at Squirrel Island, sailing and fishing. In 1873 he bought berths and went "west"—as far as Chicago.[33]

He left Captain Waydell when the insurance man failed to give him a raise and took a job with the rival firm of Buell & Brewster. (That firm shortly became Buell & Hayden when Harris H. Hayden, a young man in his twenties whom George perceived to be a "comer," was made a partner.) He took charge of his own education by haunting the Steele & Avery Bookshop. He would ask clerk Tommy Brown to see a certain volume of an encyclopedia (which Tommy had to go to the basement to find), then stand around in the store reading it. In 1870 he bought a French reader, grammar book, and dictionary—and paid for some French lessons. His young imagination was fired by the reading of a series of "boy's books," written by the pseudonymous "Oliver Optic"—really William Taylor Adams (1822–97), a Boston schoolteacher. The heroes of these tales, armsful of which George would lug home from Scrantom's Lending Library, were entranced by travel, geography, and science, and their fascinations would propel them into action-packed adventures. The titles alone of Optic adventures (Adams wrote 126 books and over a thousand magazine articles) foreshadow Eastman's life: *Work and Win; A Millionaire at Sixteen; Poor and Proud; In School and Out; Watch and Wait; Seek and Find, or, The Adventures of a Smart Boy; Try Again;* and *Little by Little*.[34]

The late 1860s brought more changes. In 1866, perhaps as an economy move, the four Eastmans left the fashionable Third Ward for the more pedestrian address of 9 Elizabeth Street—on the "wrong" side of the canal, hard by a sooty railroad station. They also left the fashionable St. Luke's for the solid middle class parish of Trinity Episcopal Church. Maria still took in boarders, but she was selective: her sister Cornelia Tompkins and Cornelia's daughter Eliza; a second cousin named Morton Rundel, who came to Rochester from the hinterlands to study at the Eastman Commercial College; a young bank clerk named Tom Husband; and a seamstress, Mrs. Ranney.

Throughout his childhood George shared his Christmas and birthday presents with Katie (also spelled Katy), be they pictures, candy, or figs. He worried about the delicate state of her health because her bout with polio had left her not only in a wheelchair but susceptible to many illnesses: "Katy has been to school this fall but it is getting so cold that she can not go any more so she is going to recite to Mother," he wrote when he was ten and she was fourteen. Katie's health did not improve and six years later, on 3 December 1870, she died. George bought a new $30 suit for her funeral and paid for her last ride to Waterville, where she was buried next to her father. Maria gave her daughter's prize possession, a lovely china tea set, to Emma Kate's namesake and Tommy Cope's daughter, and immediately began to throw herself more fervently into religion. She was confirmed in Trinity Episcopal Church on 30 April 1871, and George, now sixteen, allowed himself to be baptized the same day with Maria and her friend Caroline Lee as his sponsors. Even though George never showed any impulse toward piety, he was willing to go through the motions to please his mother.[35] But in matters religious and ethical, as in almost all aspects of his life, George Eastman would go his own way.

During this period, two families—Andrus and Strong—entered George's life who would play major roles in the years ahead. Shortly after George left school for work in 1868, his sister Ella married George Worthington Andrus in the Eastman living room on Elizabeth Street, and soon after moved to Cleveland. George considered his Ohio brother-in-law somewhat vulgar, so his wedding present to Ella of a lady's parasol may have been a nudge in the ribs to the earthy Andrus. The first child of that union, christened George Eastman Andrus, died in infancy, but Ellen Amanda Andrus, born in 1871, and Royal Vilas Andrus, born in 1878, would become George's surrogate children—particularly after sister Ella died in 1884 and Andrus remarried. From the time of his mother's death in 1907 until his own in 1932, Ellen Andrus Dryden would be George Eastman's closest relative.

Katie's death in 1870 had coincided with a fire in the Elizabeth Street home of a neighbor. Loneliness may have had something to do with it, as well as the prospect of extra income, but Maria invited the lively Henry Alvah Strong family to board with her and her son. For more than a year the irrepressible Henry, his crankily devout wife Helen, and their three children, Gertrude, Helen, and Harry, lived with the Eastmans. In such an accidental way did the sixteen-year-old George begin to forge a bond with the thirty-two-year-old Henry Strong that would radically change both of their lives.

Henry seemed the most problematic of men—particularly to his newspaper publisher father, Alvah, and his intellectual, high-achieving older brother, Augustus, who headed the prestigious Rochester Theological Seminary. The gregarious Henry's "mind did not seem to run in the line for study," nor did he show any "fixed will or purpose" in his life, Alvah noted

sadly in his autobiography. His talents lay elsewhere—sales and human relations were his forte. Henry dropped out of school at sixteen, shunned efforts
to provide him with tutors, and tried a little banking in New York City, but
ended up running off to sea "as a common sailor before the mast." A risk-
taker, even danger-seeker, "he feared nothing but disgrace," Alvah noted
presciently. Henry would later regale family and friends with stories of "ignorant, profane, brutal," and drunken skippers as well as "many providen-
tial, hairbreath escapes from fractured head, limbs, and watery grave." He
jumped ship in France, "a stranger in a strange land, unable to speak the
language and out of money!" but as usual landed on his feet, eventually
returned to America, and in 1859 went into business with a cousin in St.
Louis. The business failed almost immediately—"a total loss." So off he went
to climb Pike's Peak in the dead of winter with a caravan of ox teams. During
the Civil War he served as a paymaster in the navy but before that, married a
conventional young woman who was bent on domesticating the roaming
Henry. "Having sown his wild oates," Alvah concluded with relief, Henry
finally settled down to "regular business" in Rochester as a principal in the
family's Strong-Woodbury Whip Company.[36]

After Ella's marriage and Katie's death, there were but two Eastmans left at 9
Elizabeth Street. Maria would continue to scold her son and complain of her
ailments, but delight in her flower garden, wait upon George's every need,
charm his colleagues, run his social life, become his sounding board in business matters, and remain the center of his emotional world. George always
remained comfortable with, and even glad of, the arrangement. It was as if
Maria provided the stability at the core of his existence, the conventional and
secure launching pad from which he could soar into the heady atmosphere
of risk taking and adventure.

2

An Amateur There

■ ■ ·—————————————————————————

The Caribbean island of Hispaniola in 1877 would seem an unlikely catalyst for a series of events that changed the development of photography and altered forever American popular culture, but history will have its fortuitous accidents. The Grant administration was considering purchasing land around Samana Bay for a U.S. naval base, in order to prevent Spain from establishing, for a third time, colonial control over the island. A naval base would make real estate there increase in value, so American land speculators began to cast hungry eyes in the direction of Santo Domingo.[1] One of them was George Eastman. Barely twenty-three, he had been out in the commercial world for nearly a decade. His career as first insurance agent, then bank clerk, was progressing, but like his father before him he was not content with a safe seat on the career carousel. He had a yen for the brass ring, for the individual enterprise that would transform his life.

The potential land boom in Santo Domingo struck Eastman's fancy, and, after carefully figuring out the expense, he discussed the trip with a fellow bank employee who had been assistant to a photographer with the famous Powell Survey of the Grand Canyon in 1871. The colleague suggested a camera would be the best way to record the island. The voyage to Hispaniola never came off, but, "In making ready, I became totally absorbed in photography."[2]

Earlier, at age seventeen, Eastman had been Buell & Hayden's prodigy: The Chicago fire of 1871 brought in so much new business that even lowly clerks like Eastman got to write "new policies to the amount of three-

quarters of a million or more," as he boasted to his Ohio cousin, Mary
Eastman. His private sums were adding up: The insurance firm was paying
him $41.66 a month, and moonlighting as a Rochester fireman added anoth-
er $8. He was drawing interest on a mortgage, with another $200 invested in
building lots. Then in 1874 Tom Husband, one of Maria's boarders and a
clerk at the Rochester Savings Bank, alerted George to a job opening. Eastman applied, was voted in by the directors over seven other candidates on the
third ballot, and named "clerk at a salary of $700." That was in April. By
January he had been promoted to second assistant bookkeeper. Not yet
twenty-one, his salary was now $1,000 a year, at a time when $300–$400 was
the average annual wage. He seemed headed for a conventional career as a
successful banker.[3]

He knew how to spend as well as save. By 1876 he and his mother had
moved from Elizabeth Street to a rented house at 49 Jones Avenue, near
Jones Park, a spectacularly verdant spot that would be redesigned in 1888 by
Frederick Law Olmsted, most famous for his design of Central Park in New
York City. He made his first art purchases to decorate the new place—
reproductions of three popular pictures, *Carthage*, *Beatrice*, and *Two More
Return*.[4] His fortunes were on the ascent and his social life broadening.
Befitting his young-man-about-town image, his account books itemize tickets
for masquerade balls, concerts, lectures, and the theater. He is squiring
young women, taking "Kitty" to The Powers Block with its art gallery, fun
house mirrors, museum of stuffed birds, and the first passenger elevator in
western New York. The next week he goes out with "Edith," the following
week with "Louise." He rents hacks to take his dates down Charlotte Boulevard (later rechristened Lake Avenue) to Lake Ontario, ten miles from
downtown, to the pavilions and elaborate resort hotels at the sandy juncture
of the lake and the Genesee River—the bustling playground of Ontario
Beach, known as "the Coney Island of the West." He attends a Valentine
masquerade for $1.50, buys a necktie and some "Mille Fleurs" perfume, and
has his gloves dyed. Goggles and a duster are purchased for trips to Elmira
and New York. He sends presents to sister Ella (a slate) and baby Ellen
Amanda Andrus. He buys a revolver for $12.50 and some life insurance on
himself to protect his mother. The account book records his first philanthropy (not counting his contributions to St. Luke's or Trinity Church): a
dollar for an injured boy in 1871.[5]

According to Elizabeth Street friends, including the Strong family, Eastman was preoccupied during this period with a young woman who had
visions of a musical career but gave up the liaison to go abroad and study. If
Rochester had had a music conservatory then, the singer might have stayed
nearby, these friends argued. Gertrude Strong Achilles always believed that
Eastman's contributions to music, especially a school dedicated to fostering
American music, were in part a reaction to this defeat.[6] There does appear a

curious gap in George's otherwise meticulously kept ledgers. He faithfully kept a record of his social activities, expenses, and so on, from 1 March 1868 to 18 March 1874. Suddenly, nothing. Although spaces are ruled off for the next several months, nothing is recorded until April 1876, when the Eastmans move into a new house. A frenzy of notation then picks up. The reentry into his life in 1927 of Susan Brown, whom Eastman as a youth saw off to Europe with a bunch of violets and who wrote him love letters, lends credence to the story.[7]

A year later, in 1877, he found photography a welcome way of using up surplus time and energy. On 13 November 1877 Eastman climbed the stairs at 12 State Street to the shop of Henry D. Marks, who advertised himself as a "dealer in walnut, gilt, and rosewood frames, and photographic materials of every description." For $49.58, he bought a five- by eight-inch camera box, a view tripod, a darkroom tent, and twenty-four other photographic items. The outfit, which he paid for in two installments, was impressive for its shortcomings and difficulties. Eastman's layout, "which included only the essentials," had in it a camera "about the size of a soap box," a tripod the heft and strength of which "could support a bungalow," a plate holder, the darkroom tent, a nitrate bath, and a container for water. The plates for that holder were called "wet," that is, panes of heavy glass that the photographer had to coat with collodion and nitrate of silver just before exposure. The whole procedure was "intricate and cumbersome and the expense was considerable." Only professionals could be expected to understand it, so "people took it for granted that every man who owned a camera made a living out of it. Amateurs were all but unknown. There were only two in Rochester." The bulk of the paraphernalia "worried" Eastman: "It seemed that one ought to be able to carry less than a pack-horse load." But tote it he did and "took my views." Lugging the wet-plate apparatus all the way to Michigan to photograph the natural bridge on Lake Huron's Mackinac Island, he found that wherever he set up "a crowd drew around as though I were going to open a patent-medicine show."[8]

Gone now were dates with young women, trips to Shadders Gym, visits to Ashtabula. Yet the seminary girls who were "exercised" daily outside the Rochester Savings Bank were more fascinated by the "serious blond young man who never left his work" than by the the "bank boys whose custom it was to be at the window" when the feminine parade passed by.[9] When George was not working (and sometimes while he was) he was reading, thinking, dreaming, or practicing photography. He hung around the studio and gallery of John H. Kent, portrait photographer. He looked out of the bank window and saw Professor Charles Forbes going into the Rochester Free Academy next door with a camera under his arm and rushed over to see the professor's photographs, then pointed his own camera at the fountain of

"Little Black Sambo" in the courtyard of the bank.[10] He bought photo-graphic manuals.

He sought out two photographers for lessons, and both would remain influential in his life for decades. For a $5 fee in his downtown Rochester office, the professional George Monroe taught Eastman the rudiments. And it may have been from the back window of Monroe's studio on the Main Street Bridge looking south toward the aqueduct carrying the Erie Canal that the amateur took what has come down to us as his first picture—a well-composed shot of mill buildings and bridges along the Genesee.[11] Eastman's second mentor was George B. Selden, patent attorney, automobile inventor, and—along with Forbes—one of the two amateur photographers in town. Selden never forgot his first sight of "a slight young man coming up the stairs, a bank clerk who painted as a hobby and was interested in photo-graphic wet plates." From Selden's attic workshop Eastman "looked out of the window and suggested that the beauty of the grove of trees which sur-rounded the house was a good subject for the camera."[12] After he had the basics down, it did not take long for Eastman to decide that photography could be his entrée into where he might spend the rest of his life. A way to do that was to somehow liberate photography from the wet-plate process, the laboriousness of which Eastman described well when he talked of his field trips with Monroe:

> We used the wet collodion process, taking a very clean glass plate and coating it with a thin solution of egg white. This was to make the subse-quent emulsion stick. Then we coated the plate with a solution of guncot-ton and alcohol mixed with bromide salts. When the emulsion was set, but still moist, the plate was dipped into a solution of nitrate of silver, the sensitizing agent. That had to be done in the dark. The plate, wet and shielded from the light, was put in the camera. Now you took your picture.[13]

In February 1878 he subscribed to the *British Journal of Photography*, and in that very first issue[14] read of Charles Bennett's breakthrough formula for a dry-plate emulsion that was ripened by prolonged heating to produce a considerable increase in speed. The possibility of making a dry plate that was even faster than the wet medium seemed at hand. "The English article started me in the right direction," and he immediately ("in my spare time—for I was still working at the bank") began to work up his own formula. "My first results did not amount to much, but finally I came upon a coating of gelatine and silver bromide that had all the necessary photographic qualities. . . . At first I wanted to make photography simpler merely for my own convenience, but soon I thought of the possibilities of commercial production."

On 5 July 1878 Eastman, in the persona of "G. E. (Rochester, N.Y.)," enters the literature of photography with a letter published in the same magazine that had inspired his own experiments four months earlier. Eastman, of course, had no formal training in chemistry. What he knew he got from voraciously consuming foreign photography journals and exchanging ideas with other amateurs. His method was empirical in the strictest sense: What seemed to work, he kept; what did not, he tossed. Upon leaving the bank each day he carried on experiments "from 3 P.M. until breakfast." Mornings, his mother found him asleep on the floor. Weekends he recharged.

When he found an expert who seemed to possess some useful information, he was relentless in his questioning. To M. Carey Lea, whose manual Eastman had purchased in 1877, he was initially decorously apologetic: "If I did not think I had faithfully tried your formula I should hesitate to trespass on your good nature . . . but . . . " Then, rapid fire: "1st. Can you suggest the cause of my failures? 2nd. Do you still use your formula in preference to others published since? 3rd. Would it be practical to add an organifier directly to the emulsion before pouring it out to set, and then drying the pellicle before washing to obtain greater density?"[15] His teachers were soon overtaken by the pupil. A correspondent from the *Philadelphia Photographer* interviewed Monroe and reported that the professional "works the modified Bennett Process, but modestly disclaims any credit of his own, giving all the honor, whatever there may be, to Mr. George Eastman, an amateur there, who worked it all out his own way and gave it to Mr. Monroe."[16] Eastman's formula of ripened gelatin and silver bromide worked, but applying it to plates had chancy results. He poured the hot emulsion from a tea kettle and smeared it around the glass with a rod—a process "necessarily slow and tedious, and therefore expensive." Clearly needed was a machine to uniformly coat the dry plates, to do it in quantity and, therefore, cheaply. The coater he devised was simple, even graceful, in concept and design. It looked like a large version of a stamp wetter, combining suction cups to hold the glass from above and a roller beneath to coat it evenly. The India rubber and brass roller was activated by a crank (eventually by a motor) and partly immersed in a trough of warmed, melted emulsion. The trough was designed to be placed in warm water to keep the gelatin liquid. Held by the vacuum cups, the glass plate was gently pushed across the roller as it moved in the opposite direction and a fairly even if sometimes bubbly coating of emulsion was applied to the underside of the glass. The plate was then dried and cut into smaller pieces. Eager to try out his new outfit, and as always seeking to simplify further, Eastman had the Scovill Manufacturing Company build a special "4 × 5 camera of much lighter construction" than what one could get ready-made. He set up his tripod and pointed it out the window of the house on Jones Avenue at the grand Italianate edifice of Charles P. Ham across the street. A Rochester landmark until the 1950s when it was demolished, all that remains of the Ham house is a gelatin negative coated and taken by George Eastman.[17]

On 10 January 1878 he shared his hopes for making and marketing dry plates in a letter, asking Uncle Horace Eastman to invest in this new business. The request shows a certain self-centeredness and lack of feeling in the nephew, for the seventy-two-year-old Horace had just been forced to put his elderly wife in an insane asylum. When the Waterville uncle rebuffed him in a kindly, albeit formal note, Eastman hatched another "scheme" (not a pejorative then). London in 1879 was both the financial center of the world and its photographic capital, and he had already had one bad experience at the U.S. Patent Office with a furnace grate—already patented by someone else. English companies—the Liverpool Dry Plate Company, Wratten & Wainwright, Ltd., Mawson and Swan, and B. J. Edwards—were making dry plates by the old handicraft methods and marketing them for a growing trade. The plan: Go to London to patent his coating machine, and then sell off the rights. Capitalized, he would return home to set up his own business. So Eastman raided his savings account of $400, and like an American version of Dick Whittington, though without so much as a cat to guide him, steamed for London.

No sooner had the *Abyssinia* landed in Liverpool at 6 P.M. on Saturday, 28 June 1879, than George Eastman, bewhiskered, greatcoat flapping, hustled down the gangplank with a sheaf of drawings and the prototype dry plate-coating machine. He found time on this, his first trip across the Atlantic, for a three-hour tour of Liverpool before boarding a train on a second-class ticket. Arriving in London at 6 A.M. Sunday morning, he spent the day "skirmishing around," trying to locate a room during the height of the season, and planning a side trip to Paris.[18] But early Monday morning he called on W. B. Bolton, editor of the prestigious *British Journal of Photography* and owner of the Liverpool Dry Plate and Photographic Printing Company, in business since 1864. Bolton's imprimatur would mean everything.[19]

"I have been to see the editor," he wrote in a hasty note to his mother with "CONFIDENTIAL" emblazoned across the cheap stationery. "He was rather incredulous when I told him what I could do and was a little cool but the next day I showed him the drawing confidentially. He was surprised and offered to do anything for me that he could." Eastman then journeyed to Kingston-on-Thames, twenty miles from London, to see Samuel Fry, a manufacturer who advertised "instantaneous" plates in the *British Journal Almanac*. Fry, Eastman reported, was "a live man [who] caught right on, . . . took my portrait three times, [and] was so impressed that he immediately telegraphed his partner to come up from the city." The partner was the renowned Charles

Bennett, whose formula Eastman had adapted for his own use. Looking around Fry and Bennett's firm was an eye-opener: Eighteen employees were unable to fill all the orders for what Eastman considered the best plates made. Fry estimated his secret process to be worth £2,500.[20]

Next, Eastman engaged London solicitors Hazeltine, Lake & Company to start patent proceedings for his machine; accordingly applied for on 22 July was patent no. 2967 UK, a device for coating glass plates in "large numbers . . . with great rapidity and of better quality than is practicable by hand-work." He appointed W. B. Bolton as his agent to sell the patent on the Continent, offering the solicitor a 25 percent commission. Then he began dickering with Fry. He wanted the Englishman to either pay him £500 ($2,500) outright for the patent or buy a license—"we call it a shop right," said Eastman—and pay a royalty of a penny per plate. Fry was interested, courted the American with hospitality ("took me down to his house to wine, showed me all over town"), and pointed him toward the local tourist attraction of Hampton Court across the Thames. But Fry began to dither over signing a contract, so Eastman determined upon adventure. "The hard work of sight seeing is good for me," he decided. From Kingston he cabled Roswell Hart at the Rochester Savings Bank for an additional week's leave, then boarded a train and steamer to slip off to Paris. There he was startled by the high prices (hotels at $6 a day compared with $4 in New York), but charmed by the City of Light. "I should like to live here a year," he wrote his mother. "It would take that long to experience it."[21]

For now he had to take a cautious "maybe" from his potential customers. His time was up and his English patent would not be final until January 1880.[22] Five weeks after embarking from America, Eastman returned on the Cunard liner *Gallia*. Back in Rochester he engaged his erstwhile photography tutor, George Selden, in his other role as patent attorney. Applied for in September 1879, American patent no. 226503 was granted the following April. In researching the patent, Selden discovered two possible infringements (one a gluing machine) but got his client's patent through.[23]

Selden, son of the man who had been New York's lieutenant governor and the defender of Susan B. Anthony at her 1873 trial on charges of voting illegally, shared many qualities with George Eastman. Like his client, Selden had a creative imagination that teemed with inventive ideas. Unlike Eastman, however, he was never able to follow through and reap the rewards of his notions. After being thrown from a horse, Selden sought to develop "a safe, simple, and cheap road locomobile." He succeeded in producing a gasoline engine that could run for three minutes, and applied for a patent in this same year, 1879—a full six years before the German inventors Gottlieb Daimler and Carl Benz, working independently, built operable motor cars. But instead of pursuing the idea with a prototype, he was content to keep his patent application alive for sixteen years by scribbling amendments to it.

Selden collected license fees on every automobile manufactured until 1911, when Henry Ford successfully brought suit against him. Selden's lethargy marked his courtroom manner as well. Eastman finally dismissed him in 1887 with the words, "Selden was there but would not open his mouth. . . . We want a *fighter*."[24]

Eastman continued to press his British counterparts to some action, finding the delaying tactics of Fry and Bolton maddening. By October, having received no communication from Bolton, he swiftly "revoked authority given you to collect the royalty and withdraw my offer to give you a commission to sell my patent, nor shall I recognize you as my agent." He told a correspondent that "The English patent is being used by Mawson & Swan and Samuel Fry & Co.," at the same time as he was sending dunning letters to them. "Englishmen as a rule are business hyenas," he decided, indicting a nation after a few bad experiences, "and it is not safe to turn around without a written opinion from your counsel." He found it difficult to tolerate the deliberate pace of negotiations with the British (theirs was the nation, after all, that Charles Dickens could imagine having invented The Circumlocution Office). He began dickering. How about only £400 pounds for the patent? he wired Fry and Hazeltine & Lake. To sweeten the pot he offered Fry the commission for "negotiating the sale of the French, German, and Belgian rights." His own business barely off the ground, Eastman was already looking to explore international markets.[25]

Each letter to Fry, Bolton, and others tended to give the impression that Eastman had a factory already in operation. Word was getting around photographic circles about the machine that could coat plates. Mawson & Swan, the London firm that owned the Liverpool Dry-Plate and Photographic Printing Company, contacted Hazeltine and then wrote to Eastman directly. "They want me to set a price and say they desire to come to terms," Eastman noted. Selden seized upon the Mawson & Swan inquiry as an acknowledgment of the validity of Eastman's patent claims,[26] so the young businessman instructed his British solicitors "to accept on my behalf except for one right which you will retain in your name subject to my disposal." Keeping a subtle pressure on his British customers, he wrote to Mawson & Swan directly that he had previously accepted Fry's verbal offer of royalty payments "more to get the machine working on a large scale . . . but . . . I prefer to sell out the balance in a lump." This, he assured his customers, was a great bargain for them. Fry further delayed paying Eastman by a quibble. He believed that a stamp gummer already on the market might invalidate Eastman's patent. (It did not.)[27]

From his standup desk at the bank he dashed off two chatty notes in October 1879 to his mother, then off visiting relatives in Kingsville, indicating that he was about to take the plunge and go into business for himself. He was concerned about capital, but he thought he had found an investor in

Emerson W. Peet, an insurance examiner by profession and cousin Amelia Kilbourn Eastman's husband, who had "said he would lend me the money to start the business if I did not sell the English patent. This was his offer. I did not ask him." Amelia, twenty years George's senior, was his cousin twice-over: her mother was Maria's sister, her father G. W.'s brother. Her husband, a widower she had married in 1874, was one of the few family members financially able to invest in the "biz," as Eastman was now calling his moonlighting operation. Eastman was grateful for the safety net Peet offered but would find a more suitable partner.[28] All of this shifting, haggling, and strategy that Eastman employed to get off the ground in Rochester shows he had already developed the business sense that would characterize his later, manifestly successful enterprise. He was holding his own in the treacherous terrain of patent law (although, as we shall see, he could stumble). The patented plate coater led him to try for another with only a minor variant in its workings—the addition of a hollow tube with a slot in it—for which he received "provisional protection only." In 1882 he was granted a patent for photographic paper pads made from sheets in the popular sizes and glued along the edges. Insignificant as these were, he was learning how he could manipulate patents to control the nascent industry. The plate coater that he was so eager for the British to take up was a contraption he was rendering obsolete while peddling it. An amazing deal it was. Here was Eastman selling, by transatlantic mail, a mechanism on which he hadn't received a final patent, at the same time that he was perfecting a better apparatus in his home workshop.

By 1880 Eastman's bank career was prospering; he was now first assistant bookkeeper at Rochester Savings, earning a salary of $1,400 a year. Controlling the alternative, he would keep the job until September 1881. In this, he was heeding the advice of Harris Hayden, his former insurance colleague. Eastman had approached him with the idea of becoming a partner in the photographic enterprise, but Hayden declined, recommending that Eastman try manufacturing dry plates on a small scale before establishing an incorporated business. In April 1880 Eastman rented a room above a music store in the Martin Building at 73 State Street, two blocks from the bank and at the heart of the business and financial district of Rochester. The coating machine was moved in, and the first dry plates turned out. They were sold to professional photographers, a few retail shops, and within the coterie of correspondents that Eastman had developed. Word spread that a superior, relatively streak-free product at a reasonable price was on the market. Once set up to coat plates, Eastman continued to improve the process with innovations, which he immediately tried to sell too. Having noted that in Fry's setup plates were dried by the use of fans blowing over blocks of ice, Eastman allowed that this contrivance "will set the plates no doubt, but it seems as if the air would be damp and the plates long in drying." By July he wished he could move the whole "factory" to Denver, where "we should not require any special drying apparatus, the air being dry the year around."[29]

Eastman's plates were produced at a factory as tidy and compartmentalized as the rest of his endeavors. He constructed cubbyholes for his supplies, identified as "clothes pins, printing labels, boxes, straw, glass, gelatin, silver, chloroform, chimney matches, towels, bottles, nails, lamps." Six ruby globes sketched and patented by him, then ordered from the Corning Glass Company, were fitted as darkroom lamps. He took pride in being handy. He did everything himself, from hiring to firing, from inventing, mixing, and building to selling, bookkeeping, and corresponding. He rode to the bank on an English bicycle, having strapped onto it in the morning a shoe box containing his lunch (and sometimes the pickle juice leaked). At 3 P.M. he moved over to his "factory," where he worked into the night, providing himself with a hammock, which he designed, made, and hung in one corner of a room to be used for catnaps between emulsion stirrings.[30]

Soon he needed help and more space. He expanded to the third-floor loft, a twenty- by fifty-foot space. He hired a young "supervisor," age twenty and appropriately named Glaser, to coat the glass plates while he was at the bank.[31] Florence (like Evelyn Waugh's, his first name would cause a lifetime of confusion) S. Glaser would make a career with Eastman, rising to become superintendent of the Eastman Kodak State Street Works. Celia Roberts, "the first girl employed by Mr. Eastman," stayed with him well into the next century. Edward Gilman and James T. Costello, "us two kids," did "general shop work," as Costello would later recall. In March 1881 Eastman had six employees on the job—a salesman, a bookkeeper, packers, two women to coat the plates by hand (including Hattie Brumen, writer Henry Clune's mother)—and, by the end of that year, sixteen. His cousin Eliza Thompkins, a thirty-eight-year-old spinster who worried as much over the "biz" as Eastman did, came "afternoons only." As "the head of our laboratory," she weighed the chemicals, washed the "noodled" emulsion with chilled water to eliminate excess salts, and packed the finished plates carefully in straw for shipment. For these duties, Eastman paid her $10 a week—a measure of his regard for her competence, for he paid other employees between $2.50 and $3.[32]

Three months after transforming the loft above the music store into a factory—on Independence Day, tellingly enough—he announced to solicitor W. R. Lake of Hazeltine & Lake in London the news of a second, improved coating machine, requesting Lake to apply for a patent. "As soon as you get the application in, please cable me 'Go Ahead' as I want to write Mawson & Swan."[33] No rival patents being unearthed, he got the "Go Ahead" from Hazeltine & Lake and immediately began firing off messages to other prospective customers: "It is not expensive, it is simple, easy to clean . . . not liable to get out of order . . . no parallel streaks and waves. . . . In short, it is an eminently practical apparatus."[34]

The irony here, after all the finagling and bargaining, is that this coating machine in any of its various versions never did work right—for either Eastman or his customers/competitors. It broke down, it was hard to clean after a run, it was wasteful of the expensive emulsion, and it was always likely to cause bubbles, waves, and streaks on the plates—all this despite Eastman's claims to the contrary. We have later court testimony from Glaser, who "had full charge of the plate-coating department at that time," and from Hattie Brumen that Eastman's own factory eschewed the machine in favor of hand coating: "We tried to use the machine," Glaser said, "off and on . . . for about a year along in 1881 [but] it did not prove satisfactory . . . or pay to use as compared with flowing plates by hand."[35] For Eastman the machine was a tool to exert maximum leverage in the photographic world, to get his "foot in the door." Constant innovation and perpetual tinkering could give him an advantage in marketing strategy. Sixteen years later he would describe what was by then habitual practice: "I have come to think that the maintenance of a lead in the apparatus trade will depend greatly upon a rapid succession of changes and improvements. . . . If we can get out improved goods every year nobody will be able to follow us and compete with us."[36] His probe of international markets was beginning to get some responses. An inquiry from Romain Talbot of Berlin about the machine brought a savvy reply from this twenty-six-year-old bank clerk, showing that he never needed tutoring in financial dealings. The German license was available for £400 sterling, he wrote Talbot. "I have not patented it in Russia or Austria, but if desired . . . will sell the rights for a nominal sum, say Russia $50 and Austria $100."[37]

While eventually Eastman would easily outstrip all other American competitors in diversification, innovation, advertising, and attention to foreign markets, at the beginning he had to labor diligently to get a foothold in the domestic photographic industry. Although still in its infancy, the photographic world already had an establishment, the leading firm of which was E. & H. T. Anthony of New York City. Conservative and suspicious of outsiders, the house had been founded by Edward Anthony, a civil engineer educated at Columbia University, who had purchased daguerreotype lessons from Samuel F. B. Morse. Anthony traveled as a photographer on a survey of the northeast boundary of the United States in 1840, and in 1842, twelve years before Eastman's birth, opened a daguerreotype gallery in Manhattan, and soon expanded into selling photographic supplies. Thirteen years later sales had reached a quarter of a million dollars, Edward had been joined in partnership by his banker brother Henry, and the Anthony company was one of the top two in the trade (the other being Scovill, a branch of Scovill

Brass of Waterbury). In 1870 Colonel Vincent Meigs Wilcox, at one time a clerk, became a partner. Manufacturing continued to be a sideline for Anthony, which functioned mainly as a national jobber or supply house. To forge a relationship with Anthony was a coup for any manufacturer, and particularly for an unknown one like Eastman.[38]

George Monroe knew Edward Anthony, and met with him at the latter's summer home in the Thousand Islands in August 1880. He brought along Eastman's plates and managed to deflect some of Anthony's skepticism. Studio photographers, Anthony's main customers, were rigid and slow to change ingrained habits. For the most part they continued to cling to the old technology of the wet collodion process. Dry plates began to make inroads through those intrepid amateurs who specialized in outdoor photography but expected Anthony to supply them with plates from the established companies abroad (Scovill got its plates from Holland). But Eastman had noted that the British firms like Mawson & Swan had not let competition reduce prices on this side of the Atlantic. "This leads me to think that perhaps a really good plate could hold its own here," he wrote to Anthony, who had tried to manufacture dry plates with indifferent results—the quality was not up to European standards.[39]

Eastman was quick to try to slip through this small crack in the establishment wall. On 18 August he wrote to Anthony: "I shall commence manufacture as soon as my laboratory is fitted up. . . . The capacity of the new works will be . . . capable of rapid expansion as the demand requires. My formula is excellent . . . thoroughly tested. . . . The apparatus will materially reduce the cost of manufacture upon a large scale. . . . I should be happy to furnish you with prints or negatives or to show you the great simplicity of manipulation of my plates."[40] Anthony and Eastman met face to face in New York in September 1880, and came to a verbal agreement; Eastman later sent a memorandum for the older man's signature, insisting on his terms rather than theirs. But he did offer two concessions: Anthony's orders would take precedence, and he would list Anthony as his trade agent in all advertisements. Of course this was only agreeing to what he had agreed to before. Clearly, Eastman wanted the relationship with Anthony, but not at the price of limiting himself in any way. The Anthonys and Wilcox (who was emerging as the administrator of the firm) "looked with more or less amusement on my attempts," Eastman recalled a half century later, "and their patronizing ways sometimes got on my nerves."[41] But they ordered $1,053.08 worth of plates in December 1880. Later, as Eastman proved that patronizing amusement would not stop him, their irritation turned to anger.

As the 1880s began so did recovery from the economic depression of the previous decade. Money was out there to be made, and competition in dry plates geared up. Local manufactories sprouted in many communities, but two, started at the same time as Eastman's and by professional photographers with strong backgrounds in chemistry, posed the strongest competitive threat. John Carbutt, who emigrated from England to Chicago in the 1850s, founded the Keystone Dry Plate Works in Philadelphia in 1879, and landed an exclusive contract with Scovill. Gustav "Papa" Cramer and Hermann Norden, schooled in chemistry in their native Germany, set up a professional studio in St. Louis in the 1860s and produced dry plates for their own use. By 1879 they were marketing them commercially, although Norden shortly withdrew from the business. For the next forty years Eastman would alternately combat, cooperate with, or absorb these formidable rivals.[42]

Competitive pressure lay in Eastman's future; for now, the beginnings of mechanized production and one of America's premier photographic houses as his exclusive agent had given him the jump. As 1880 closed, he could look back on the previous two years and marvel at how far he had come. His profits stood at more than $4,000. There were some irritants: He still was plagued by the reluctance of the British to pay him his due in any regular way, and he had run across a mundane but vexing problem—dust had necessitated designing and fabricating a whole new dryer, which delayed a shipment of plates to Anthony. Obstacles were soon overshadowed by at last succeeding in attracting a partner and a heathy infusion of capital in the person and purse of Henry Alvah Strong.

When Henry Strong returned to Rochester after his Civil War duty as a navy paymaster, he joined his Uncle Myron Strong in the whip business, later acquired the uncle's interest, and continued in business with Edmund F. Woodbury. Their factory grew until it was the second largest such concern in the country, employing one hundred people, producing almost a million whips a year, and giving the partners enough income for outside investment.[43] The conservative Edmund Frost Woodbury stuck to local rental properties, while Strong, who always liked a little cliff-hanging excitement in his portfolio, looked westward to first Michigan and then to the boomtown of Tacoma, Washington, for his risk taking. Strong loved a gamble and was always on the lookout for a "killing" to be made on the new and unfamiliar. He noticed the young George Eastman right away, according to his daughter Gertrude, and even in the depths of their worst troubles would say, "I have great faith in that young man. He is doing wonders." A personal bond developed early on between the two, and in 1921 Gertrude wrote to Eastman that "You were more of a son to father than was Harry or any of his sons-in-law. He was so reticent that I doubt if anyone, except myself, knew how much he loved you." Gertrude may well have been the only human on earth to ever call the gregarious Henry Alvah Strong "reticent."[44]

There was always something faintly bogus about Strong's personality, something about his grandiose verbalizing (not to mention his girth) that had a touch of Falstaff to it. The navy, of course, has no title of "Colonel," so where did Strong pick it up? George Eastman himself may have been the tagger, for he delighted in pinning the honorific on Strong. For the next forty-nine years Eastman plagued Strong with the constant use of it, even wiring ahead to hotels where the Strongs were about to stay, telling them to expect "Colonel Strong and company."[45] In Henry Strong, Eastman had found not just an investor, but a full partner with implicit faith in the young man's genius, who would share the ups and downs, the splendors and the miseries, over the formative years of the company. On 23 December 1880 Strong would plunk down $1,000 and sign a contract creating the Eastman Dry Plate Company, with himself as president and Eastman as treasurer—effective 1 January 1881. (This was the same day a newspaper[46] headlined a story "Jay Gould Predicts a Crash," going on to note that the financier believed "a great crash is coming before long, with a greater panic than has ever before been known.") Strong put in another $1,000 that January, $1,873 more in March, and by August had turned over a total of $5,000 to the venture. Eastman had found an older man who could display the paternal confidence in him that Maria contributed from the distaff side. This did not mean that Strong replaced the father Eastman had lost at a young age. It did mean that Eastman always regarded Strong with the deepest affection and gratitude: "What a bully old boy he is. I love him from the bottom of my heart."[47]

The Eastman Dry Plate Company was now a growing concern, but regardless of the young proprietor's ambitions for it, the company had to remain a sideline for Eastman throughout much of 1881. By March he had moved his apparatus, materials, and employees to larger quarters, taking over 101 and 103 State Street. But he was still putting in a full day six times a week at the bank—as well as Tuesday and Thursday evenings—so time and attention devoted to the company had to be squeezed into an already crammed schedule.

He was pleased with the contraption he had rigged in the loft so that cousin Eliza Tompkins could wash the "noodled" emulsion: "A big cask to hold 120 gals in the corner of the wash-room, cased in sawdust to hold water and ice, pipe through the floor down into the cellar where the ice water can be drawn directly into the jars. The emulsion is to be stirred by machinery so that $\frac{3}{4}$ of the work and all of the sloppiness will be done away with." He was also happy about hiring a new assistant for Eliza, "a big good natured Irish woman. . . . If she is not too old to learn she will be a capital person."[48] That adjective, "capital," along with "bully," favorites of that "regular fellow," Theodore Roosevelt, sum up the zeal and vitality Eastman possessed in these years. Nothing seemed beyond him; anything balky yielded to his energy.

True to his work/play axiom, the twenty-seven-year-old persisted in wedging in time and space for recreation away from both bookkeeping and photography. Enthused about cycling, he ordered new fifty-inch Challenge bicycles from England for himself and two friends. The cycle company's slow delivery of seven weeks and casual treatment of customers—"not such as we were warranted in expecting for orders accompanied by funds"—were filed away for contemplation: Treating customers with prompt courtesy encourages loyalty. When the English cycles arrived he noted: "American bikes are fast approaching English in finish and having interchangeable parts requiring less extensive repairs." Quality and standardized parts would become Eastman hallmarks.[49]

Though his social life was limited because of work, Eastman was beginning to put in orbit around him a number of close friends and relatives who served as a kind of extended family. The Strong household, now living on upscale Lake Avenue, was the first place he headed after the workday. When Maria tarried with relatives, "Auntie" Cornelia Kilbourn Tompkins kept house for Eastman, her daughter Eliza, and the rest of the boarders. In return Eastman handled Eliza's investments, arranging for her to take a $1,500 mortgage in Henry Strong's boomtown of Tacoma, putting another $1,500 of her earnings in the hands of Harris Hayden, now treasurer of a wallpaper company in New York but still handling some of Eastman's investments. Young Ellen Andrus was ten in 1881, old enough for her mother Ella to put her on a train alone from Cleveland to Rochester, where she arrived after a three-hour delay that sorely taxed her young uncle's patience.

Cousin Almon Eastman, thirteen years Eastman's senior, had left Ohio in 1861 for Poughkeepsie, New York, where he took a course at the Eastman Business College, founded by another cousin, Harvey Gridley Eastman, on G. W.'s principles. Almon stayed on as secretary and instructor until Harvey moved to Colorado; Almon then founded a business college of his own in Atlanta. Almon had married Cordelia Conger of Waterville in 1866 and in 1870 they returned there to join Delia's three brothers in operating the large Hanover dairy and hop farm. The hop industry was at its zenith, with Hanover Farms producing five hundred bales in a good year. A dapper, distinguished man of small stature, Almon was emphatically a lover of country life. He was active in Waterville affairs and trustee of the State College of Agriculture at Cornell. He conducted the Farmers Institute for years, was an officer of the state agriculture society, and was regarded as an authority on the raising of dairy cattle—as such he would advise his cousin George for years.[50] Almon and Delia's presence in Waterville gave Eastman the opportunity to revisit scenes he had left as a boy, and they became his closest cousins. Part of their appeal was that they never asked him for money; indeed they would invest their Hanover profits in Kodak stock. Delia was a

sweet, dreamy woman who loved to conjure up visions of far away places—
and go to them. The pair being extensive travelers, their home was filled with
treasures collected abroad. Delia had no children herself but loved to mother
Eastman, smothering him with fond notes of encouragement and scolding
him for not taking better care of his health. Eastman accepted the mothering
and cared deeply for Delia. Correspondence with Almon gave him holidays
from photographic matters, and the pair exchanged a voluminous correspondence about cattle breeding, the "unholy oleomargarine law," alfalfa
growing, and other interminable agricultural details.[51]

Though Eastman's personal myth would have it that he and his mother
were obliged to pinch pennies throughout his second and third decades, this
seems to be an exaggeration. He could afford a cook at 49 Jones Avenue and
a part-time handy man named Kelly to take care of such things as sink traps.
New stationery for the "Office of the Eastman Dry Plate Company, 101 and
103 State Street, Rochester, New York," was ordered, along with engraved
calling cards to nudge Maria into the genteel custom of "calling"—his idea,
not hers. She always seemed to be traveling during this period.[52] With just a
few months left in the exciting year of 1881, an objective observer would
have to see George Eastman comfortably ensconced in a catbird seat of his
own fashioning. His job at the bank was paying him $1,500 a year and he had
hopes of improving on that. He had found a partner for his new business
who not only supplied him with always needed funds, but also was an avuncular complement to his own personality. The dry-plate concern challenged
Eastman, gave him an outlet for his creativity and energy, and was correctly
situated to take financial advantage of a burgeoning industry. But all unaware, Eastman was about to enter the crucible. In the next six months he
would face the two most pressing crises of his young adulthood.

3

Scoop the World

■ ■ ▪ ●─────────────────────────────────

"The resignation of George Eastman as first assistant bookkeeper read and on motion accepted." This notation, from the minutes of a board of trustees meeting of the Rochester Savings Bank of 5 September 1881, was the end result of an act of nepotism so blatant that Eastman had immediately resigned on account of it. His superior left the bank, and Eastman, who was fully conversant with the work and well qualified to step into the position, was passed over in favor of a relative of one of the bank directors. The episode would have consequences for Kodak, since Eastman made a vow that favoritism would have no place in his company. "It wasn't fair; it wasn't right; it was against every principle of justice," he fumed even years later to the *New York Times*. For now, it represented a break with a cautionary past. His notion that one should always preserve an alternative, hedge one's bet in the rough and tumble world of entrepreneurship, was now abandoned. Eastman placed his entire stake on the dry-plate square. Many thought he was crazy for doing so. "George is a damn fool," scoffed one banker, "to give up a wonderful position for a will o'the wisp."[1]

As if in fulfillment of the bank official's ominous prediction, in February 1882 dealers began complaining that exposed Eastman plates either were registering no image at all or were badly fogged. Eastman immediately went to the Anthony establishment in New York to test samples from the stock, but the examination provided no answer. Baffled, he recalled the plates, and perceptive, he reimbursed the angry dealers. For two years the plates had been satisfactory; now they were failing. Why? Eastman at first suspected that because of the seasonal nature of photography, the emulsions on the plates on the back of the dealers' shelves had deteriorated with age. Yet too many plates had spoiled, both old and new. He had always insisted on the purest ingredients, and had mother-henned each batch. Returning to Rochester, Eastman took drastic steps. He shut down the factory completely, and embarked upon 'round-the-clock cookings and testings. He moved in for the duration, hanging up the hammock and divorcing himself from all diversions save a pile of pulp novels. His professional life was riding on breaking this chemical conundrum, but 454 attempts at remixing in various proportions got him only "Trials show slight red fog & slight veil." Eighteen more attempts and then the "bottle broke & lost all."[2]

Financially, he stood at the brink. He had just purchased a lot at State and Vought streets (the present address of the Eastman Kodak Company),[3] and had engaged Thomas Finucane to build a new four-story building, sixty-six by ninety feet. The plant was under construction with the most modern equipment available: Edison's new-fangled electric lights, a kind of air conditioning for the storage areas, a drying room with ventilators and blowers, and an adjacent power plant. He had bought a two-horsepower engine for the power plant when only one-horsepower was needed, reasoning that the business would grow up to it. When Eastman was unable to pay his creditors, Finucane pressed for foreclosure. Strong and attorney Walter Hubbell painted a rosy picture of the company's prospects; Finucane agreed to wait and both he and Hubbell found their wagons hitched to a rising Kodak star.

After 469 unsuccessful experiments to resolve the crisis, Eastman gathered up Strong and Walter Butler, his emulsion assistant, bought three tickets on the RPNS *Germanic*, and on 11 March 1882 steamed for England, source of both formula and materials. In London, Eastman and Butler rushed straight to Mawson & Swan while the colonel settled comfortably into the elegant and insular routine of Rochester expatriots at the Savoy. Mawson & Swan became the heroes. Forgiving Eastman his deception in selling them an obsolete machine, they allowed him to "stand in the works" and solve his puzzle in less than a week. It was the gelatin binding that killed the emulsion. Eastman's English supplier had changed his source of gelatin without notifying customers. (It is now surmised that it was not an impurity that fogged the emulsions but the lack of an ingredient. It would be forty years before the presumed missing element—sulphur—would be identified in Kodak's Research Laboratory by Samuel Sheppard as having the power to both speed up the emulsion or destroy all sensitivity. According to legend and Dr. C. E. Kenneth Mees's 1936 book, *Photography*, the calves scheduled to be reduced to gelatin had not grazed in pastures where sulphur-rich mustard grew. Enough for now to note that the difficulty could be overcome by simply switching back to the original source.[4])

Eastman took the London opportunity to cut a new deal with Mawson &

Swan. The British company offered him $2,000 for the details of manu-
facturing dry plates. Eastman countered: his manufacturing secrets for
Mawson & Swan emulsion know-how. The agreement reached, he stood
once again in the works from 20 March to 4 April until he had absorbed
every detail of the British operation.[5] Returning to Rochester via the 4 April
steamer *Republic*, his back still up against the financial wall, he signed an
onerous ten-day note for $600 to reopen the factory on 28 April. By May the
emulsion was all right. He cut the price of his plates by 25 percent to reattract
the customers he had lost, and was back in the market by June. Years later he
recalled that "when the plates fogged it was a terrible experience—like waking in the morning with a clear mind and paralysis in every muscle."[6]

Into Eastman's life in 1884 came the valuable but tempestuous relationship
with his second partner, William Hall Walker. Like Eastman, Walker, eight
years older, had left school while in his teens in Scio, Michigan, to help
support a widowed mother. Arriving in Rochester in 1880 as the photographic business called "Wm. H. Walker, Amateurs' Supplies," a short block
from the Martin Building, Walker soon teamed up with Charles Forbes, one
of Eastman's mentors and other partners. By 1883 Walker's firm was offering a new brand of dry plates and had opened a factory that the partners
described as "the best appointed and most complete of any in this country."[7]
Walker also designed and marketed a small camera for amateurs. Although
"Walker's Pocket Camera" was ingeniously put together and would anticipate Eastman's goal of interchangeable, standardized parts, it was not the
whopping commercial success that the Kodak camera would be, and this
would rankle Walker always. Yet in 1883, for reasons we can only hypothe-
size, Walker gave up making cameras, and the Rochester Optical Company
was formed by his former partners from the sale of the business. Perhaps
Walker's overambitious factory had bankrupted him or perhaps his (eventually) well-documented inability to get along with people led his partners to go
it alone. But Eastman took note of Walker's talents—to say nothing of the
emulsion knowledge he must have soaked up through his various partnerships—and made Walker an offer of a small salary and a stock option. The
new partner accepted as of the first day of 1884.[8]

   Eastman was now pursuing a complete replacement for dry plates—a
"rollable" substance, a lighter, more flexible, and unbreakable substitute for
glass. The idea was not new; as Eastman himself said in 1925, "an exposing
mechanism called a 'roll holder' for sensitized paper had been made as early
as 1854, the year that I was born." Eastman and Walker split the work.
Eastman, with his experience as emulsion maker and producer of bromide
paper, concentrated on coming up with a suitable film. Walker, who knew

cameras and accessories, focused his attention on designing a roll holder and the machinery to apply the emulsion to the film. They found it easier to divide the labor than to get along personally. Walker was as volatile as Eastman was calm and self-controlled, and his emotional explosions were memorable. As British chemist Walter Krohn, who would work under Walker in the late 1880s, remembered, Walker was always angled to "go off the deep end if things went wrong, stamp around the room, letting himself go completely." Because Walker also had a depressive side to his nature, Eastman could count on him for gloom-and-doom letters, expressing hopeless fatalism over inconsequential matters. The normally optimistic Eastman found Walker's dark growlings an irritant. Walker harbored deep resentments of Eastman, never forgetting for a moment that Eastman's company was succeeding while his parallel venture had failed; and in a well-known psychological quirk, Walker disliked being beholden to the man who had rescued him from unemployment.[9] For a time, however, Eastman got along with his two partners, the exuberant, ebullient Strong and the dyspeptic Walker—the Shem and Shaun of the photographic world—and moved toward his goal. He believed that the first photographic company to market a flexible but tough, transparent but inert substitute for glass would have an enormous advantage over the hundreds of small plate companies struggling to survive in the 1880s. John Wesley Hyatt's 1869 invention of celluloid, the first synthetic plastic, was seen as a breakthrough.

As early as 1881 Eastman had begun experiments with collodion, a mixture of cotton cellulose and nitric acid. He coated paper and glass with it and added a coat of the photographic emulsion. He would then strip off the resulting transparent film from the support and see what he had—usually a material of insufficient strength. In order to be first on the market, he turned to paper as a stopgap support. Paper was light, smooth, and strong, but not transparent; it also had a fiber grain. By rubbing it with hot castor oil and glycerine (and later a cold substance marketed as Translucine), he could achieve translucency and eliminate some grain. Next he figured out a way to strip the paper away. A soluble gelatin layer was added between paper and emulsion and after exposure the negative floated in a hot bath to dissolve the gelatin. The film could then be squeegeed to glass and the paper peeled away, much as a decalcomania is transferred. The remaining film was varnished with thick gelatin and glycerine, dried, and stripped from the glass—ready for printing. From 4 March 1884 when he applied for a patent on what he called "American Film," to 1895 when it was discontinued in America, Eastman made numerous improvements to the process.[10]

Eastman and Walker designed a roll holder that would enable existing cameras to use paper film. The film was wound on a wooden spool, and the spool placed in a handsome, brass-tipped mahogany case. The film was stretched over guide rollers to a second spool and the case attached to the back of the camera in place of the glass-plate holder. Early in December 1884 Eastman opened the doors of the newly incorporated (as of 1 October) Eastman Dry Plate and Film Company to a reporter from the *Rochester Union*. "The Gelatin Paper Dry Plate—A Wonderful Invention by Rochester Citizens," the headline read, and beneath those words, "the new process will save photographers about a quarter million dollars yearly." Eastman explained that the paper dry plate would replace glass, and the new roll holder would reduce the weight of the apparatus required for outdoor photography by about one-half. The reporter then fed Eastman a straight line that foretells the subsequent history of photography: "This will delight the amateurs, won't it?" Although the term "amateur" then meant those who loved the craft of photography rather than those who were complete novices, Eastman's reply represents the basis of his future marketing strategy of going beyond the needs of established photographers. "It can't be otherwise," he said. "Let me show you this little self-registering machine all ready to put into a camera. There you see two spools of paper film. As fast as one unwinds the other winds up. The thumbscrew enables the operator to turn the paper along . . . and thus take 50 distinct photographs on the one spool of paper film . . . in an hour. . . . [It] weighs two and three-quarters pounds. A corresponding amount of glass plates and holders would weigh 50 pounds. . . . [The amateur] can then quietly keep his selection in his pocket until he gets ready to transfer such as he wants to a glass plate and print."[11]

A patent for the Eastman–Walker Roll Holder was granted 5 May 1885, just in time for Walker to take what the partners billed as "At Last a Complete System of Film Photography" to London for the International Inventions Exhibitions. "We shall be able to popularize photography to an extent as yet scarcely dreamed of," Eastman wrote the organizers in April 1885. Because this would be his first exhibit, he desired "to have it creditable in every way."[12] What he didn't mention was that he had just started coating his paper negative in March, and that it would not be put on the market until June, along with the company's first catalog. Even so, the system garnered the highest award of a gold medal, and a number of others. Next came the gold medal of the Exposition Universelle in Paris, followed by similar awards in Florence, Melbourne, Moscow, and Geneva. With seventeen standardized roll-holder components, the partners were bringing interchangeable parts—and the potential for mass production—to the world of photography. It would be another twenty-eight years before that historically vaunted innovator, Henry Ford, would bring the same ideas to the automotive assembly line.[13] Eastman was determined to reach them all—amateurs, professionals, and camera manufacturers. By 1885 he had salesmen and demonstrators hitting the road in all directions, while he kept constant tabs on them with letters and telegrams—exhorting, encouraging, setting the tone, and, at age thirty-two, clucking over their health. He had no more need for Anthony's as jobbers. He severed the relationship in March 1885, one more step in personally controlling all aspects of his business.

Early in 1885, his old mentor George Selden had some uncomfortable news for Eastman. One part of the roll holder, a pointed metal stud that indicated exposure length by perforating the film, infringed a patent held by David Houston, a farmer in the Dakota Territory who had patented (but never manufactured) a hand-held camera in 1881. Finding the cost of the patent too high, Eastman purchased a shop right for Monroe County for $700. Houston was something of a brilliant crank, a prolific inventor—of paper patents only—but he proved to be Eastman's gadfly. Over the next two decades Eastman purchased several of Houston's patents and ran amuck of several others. Nor did it end with Houston's death in 1906. For another decade Eastman paid his widow and son royalties. And Houston continued to haunt the fringes of the Eastman story long after both antagonists were in their graves. In 1942 Houston's niece and hagiographer, Mina Fisher Hammer, published a book that insisted her uncle was the real inventor of the Kodak camera and, moreover, had contrived the word "Kodak" itself, naming the company after his beloved Dakota Territory. The Houston family's claim was reported to Eastman in February 1917 by B. C. Forbes, who would found *Forbes* magazine in September of that same year but who at the time was writing about Eastman's achievements for *Leslie's*. Eastman was astounded: "I never knew that the late David H. Houston . . . ever claimed to be the inventor of the Kodak, or that he claimed to have originated the name, and I can hardly believe that he ever did make any such claim. He certainly never had the nerve to mention it to me."[14]

In the spring of 1883 Eastman had turned his thoughts to increasing his working capital, again looking for advice from Emerson W. Peet, cousin Amelia's husband, insurance actuary, and someone whom Eastman regarded as a financial maven. Peet suggested that he "form a Stock co. with $200,000 capital. Strong & Eastman sell to the co. all the property and business and . . . issue stock."[15] The subsequent reincorporation of 1884 prompted the first public offering of stock at $100 a share, the three partners keeping $160,000 worth and selling $40,000 in stock to ten other stockholders. Strong received the most, 750 shares: $10,000 as repayment of notes, $40,000 for his stake in the patents, and $25,000 compensation for his past services and interest in the original company. Eastman was the recipient of 650 shares for $40,000 in patents, plus $25,000 for services and value of the original company. Walker, named secretary, received 200 shares for patents and his work on the roll holder. Twenty shares were distributed to those who had helped Eastman or Strong (including one for Eliza Tompkins).[16]

In the midst of all this financial dealing, Eastman's sister Ellen Maria ("Ella") died on 25 June 1884, leaving a daughter, Ellen Amanda, age thirteen; a son, Royal Vilas, age six; and her Cleveland husband George W. Andrus. Eastman's reaction is puzzling, because he seems to have had no emotional response at all. Preoccupied with the recapitalization, he spent most of that summer badgering Andrus to buy some Eastman stock himself. "Bro. Andrus," Eastman then scolded, "I cannot imagine why you should pay me so scurvy a trick as failure to answer would imply. . . . You placed me in an embarrassing position."[17] He expressed no sense whatsoever that the widower might be undergoing some strain (although he does at times bid hello "to Ella & the boy"). Maria, though, was devastated and never forgot her firstborn. Four years after the older Ellen's death she wrote to her sister, Emily Cope: "I sent for a bunch of pansies to put in a little vase under Ellen's picture (that was her favorite flower) some carnations, tulips, and jonquils. These we will place in the windows."[18]

In the spring of 1885 Eastman managed both to expand his operations to Europe and put some distance between himself and his difficult partner. Walker stayed on after the International Inventions Exhibition to manage the London agency that he and Eastman opened. But bachelor Eastman, ever mindful of the company coffers, did not allow Walker to send for his wife and invalid daughter (like Katie Eastman, Gertrude Walker was afflicted with polio) until the agency was off the ground. In 1912 Eastman was amazed to learn that Walker still harbored resentments on that score. Thousands of miles of separation could not mute the discord between such two clashing personalities. At the moment, however, all was harmony and gleeful anticipation of a glorious future as Eastman crowed to Walker in a transatlantic message: "Brace yourself for a grand boom. . . . Paper negatives are okay for portraits, landscapes, and anything and everything. We struck it yesterday in hot oil! Don't say a word to nobody whether we are going to make films or paper, but get your office arranged, hire your man and get ready for the goods. . . . We will be ready to scoop the world in a few weeks!"[19]

With yet another grand enterprise in mind and brimming with confidence, Eastman walked the two blocks from Jones Avenue to rent the ten-room frame "cottage" that E. F. Woodbury had built one lot removed from his own substantial brick house on Lake Avenue. "I have been trying to rent it ever since it was built two years ago," George told his brother-in-law. The Eastmans' new address was 59 Ambrose Street. Maria's boarding house was closed forever.[20]

Eastman was far from having the field of photographic materials to himself in the final two decades of the century. Many competitors surfaced, but few survived. Some were bent on quick exploitation, choosing, as Eastman put it, "to boom it and drop it like a new toy."[21] They would pay impressive dividends for a time, then sell out. Others, such as Thomas Blair, would plow all profits back into production, leaving the firm financially moribund and unattractive to investors. Although he characterized his approach as "conservative," Eastman's way took more of a middle course between the quick-profit schemes of those who wanted only dividends (his partners Strong and Walker) and his own impulse to constantly reinvest profits. "As long as we can pay for all our improvements and also some dividends I think we can keep on the upper road," he assured Strong. In the end his "conservative" policies would prove sufficient to provide both generous dividends and capital for expansion—"it is a slower matter with me than it might be with someone else. . . . But when we get there we 'get there to stay.'"[22] Stock ownership was cautiously placed; as late as 1910 over 80 percent of Eastman Kodak stock still remained in the hands of the original partnership. The financial plan was conservative, but its aim was radical: control of the market.

First, however, Eastman had to create the market. Professional studio photographers and those who were then called "amateurs"—people who indulged in the craft for the love of it rather than for the financial rewards—were slow to leave plates for film. They had the equipment for plates; glass was inert and so did not react with the hypersensitive emulsion; and glass could provide negatives up to twenty by twenty-four inches which, when contact printed, gave a marvelous sharpness to details. Eastman accommodated with plates of different sizes and emulsions and cameras such as the Interchangeable View, Genesee, and Eastman Enlarging cameras. But he soon realized that the number of photographers in both these categories that the economy could support was finite and his mind took a turn that changed the history of the craft. "When we started out with our scheme of film photography," he recalled, "we expected that everybody who used glass plates would take up films, but we found that the number which did so was relatively small, and in order to make a large business we would have to reach the general public."[23] The general public would demand simplicity of operation over fine photographic quality.

While presenting the roll holder and paper-backed film to the world as great advances, Eastman privately believed that they were makeshifts on the way to a simple, inexpensive, universal system. The roll holder was an accessory; the key would be a simple camera designed to exploit a roll of flexible transparent film. His eagerness to develop an improved film base that, with the right camera, could deliver the photographic market into his hands, did not deter him from seizing opportunities as they arose. The machinery on which Eastman made negative paper film, consisting of roller, trough, heating device, and a hang-up drying mechanism, had been developed to produce bromide paper, for which there was already a demand. Thirty-five years later Eastman testified that the paper-coating machine was still "so satisfactory that the machinery has never been changed, except in detail, since."[24]

Eastman's Permanent bromide paper, introduced in 1885, was something new—a developing-out paper (DOP) on which prints were quickly made by lamplight and the latent image chemically developed in a darkened room. Bromide paper was so "fast" that if accidentally exposed to light, it would fog. By contrast, printing-out paper (POP), such as albumen paper that photographers sensitized just before using, yielded prints by natural light. As sunlight gradually brought out the latent image, the photographer could remove the print at any stage and chemically fix it. The long exposures (forty minutes for a solar enlargement) made it a time-consuming process but the photographer had the visual control he thought he needed.[25] Eventually, almost all developing would be done in the dark rather than on the roof, but that was twenty years in the future. To help his demonstrators promote the new paper, Eastman started a printing and enlarging service in the spring of 1886, a service that thrives more than one hundred years later. By late 1886, despite the use of automatic printing equipment with Edison's new electric arc lamps and the capacity to process from five thousand to ten thousand prints in a ten-hour day, the printing and enlarging department was hard pressed to get out the orders.

All was not roses. Sales of the roll-holder system were dropping at the same time as price wars continued among the multitudinous dry-plate concerns. Eastman's situation was not helped by criticism from the media. *Walzl's Photographic Monthly* ("Devoted to Practical Photography") reported on the show that opened at the Buffalo Armory Hall in July 1885. Praising the Scovill and Anthony wares, it then took a swipe at "what is claimed to be the greatest improvement in the present era of photography, viz: The Eastman Film Negative. Their chief characteristic is an extreme want of brilliancy giving gray, sickly looking prints. . . . Below mediocrity," the critique continued, "the difference between them and a glass plate being as great as between an inferior tin type and a first-class Daguerreotype." The *Detroit Free Press* ridiculed roll holders, and when Scovill reprinted the article in its journal, Eastman moved to control the damage. He sent a free roll holder to the reporter and an objection to Scovill, the company he had already contacted to make the first roll-holder camera, an important advance for the entire industry: "We think everyone should be able to take a joke in good part, and the article . . . will do us no great harm. But . . . we do not think it . . . to your interest or ours to . . . throw cold water on an enterprise when it is likely to be of great value to us both." J. Traill Taylor, editor of the influential *British Journal of Photography*, dismissed the roll holder as a pale "imitation of [Leon] Warnerke," who had produced a roll-holder system in the 1870s. "There is about the same similarity between it and our holder as there is between an old flint lock blunderbuss and a Smith & Wesson self-acting six shooter," Eastman fumed. "We understand that this very scoffer at photography is going to take one of [our] roll holders with him on an extended foreign trip this summer. The camera," he aphorized, "is getting to be as necessary to newspaper correspondents as the pen."[26]

Damage control was a stopgap. Better film and a lightweight camera small enough to be used without a tripod were needed. The former was a chemical problem, the latter a mechanical one that would be solved first. Try as he would, Eastman could not produce a flexible, inert, transparent film support on his own. He enumerated the kitchen remedies he had tested since 1881: "I have tried purifying the gelatine with ether, soap, alcohol and ammonia but with no effect." With emulsion problems continuing to plague him as well, Eastman contacted Dr. Samuel A. Lattimore, head of the chemistry department of the University of Rochester. Since leaving the former United States Hotel for Azariah Boody's cow pasture on Prince Street, the university had expanded to include departments of chemistry and physics. Lattimore was an expert on chemical formulas but an amateur when it came to mechanics. Eastman sent Lattimore a roll holder in 1885 as "an experiment to find out how the instrument would work in the hands of an inexperienced person. . . . It was a good opportunity to determine whether any weak points . . . would be developed."[27]

Now the situation had shifted and Eastman needed an experienced chemist. On Lattimore's recommendation of his undergraduate assistant, Henry Reichenbach, Eastman hired the "ingenious, quick-witted fellow, to devote his time entirely to experiments" in August 1886. In September a separate budget for research was established. "He knows nothing about photography," Eastman told Walker. "I told him what was wanted and that it might take a day, a week, a month or a year to get it, or perhaps longer, but that it was a dead sure thing in the end."[28]

Eastman was figuring out ways to profit on Reichenbach's early findings in an area (glass negatives) that he was simultaneously trying to replace with film. His insistence on secrecy was growing (he sent Walker "a phial of the mixture" rather than directions for making up a sample). Despite his public position that Eastman emulsions were the best in the field, he was experiencing difficulties. Emulsion mixing was hit or miss. ("When we get the emulsion quick enough the plates won't keep.") Each batch was different and on hot summer days the plant had to shut down. Reichenbach spent part of his time trying to get the emulsion up to snuff, but more and more Eastman had him concentrate on finding a substitute for paper as film base. He tried each of the varnishes and solutions that Eastman suggested but for the next two years found nothing suitable. Either the film was too thin or it wrinkled or developed tears. There were spots, pits, and other imperfections, or the film cracked when rolled. Sometimes it was objectionable in color, sometimes too greasy to be coated with a sensitive photographic emulsion. But the chemist persevered. As Reichenbach gradually took over Eastman's role as experimenter, the boss turned his energies to advertising and promotion. He wrote all the copy himself, and every piece of art was subject to his aesthetic judgment. He decided where the ads were placed, and he personally chose and trained all demonstrators who were sent into the field. He worked with one eye on the laboratory, one on the Patent Office, and both on the salesmen, advertisers, ad agencies, and suppliers. "We would like you to get up a design that would be striking but not flashy," he told an agent. "The girl on the front piece don't disconcert anybody in this pious concern, but she is too devilishly homely to make anything of." Rather than take an expensive ad in the *Philadelphia Photographer*, Eastman tried to get the editor "to write a good vigorous article on the permanence of bromide paper . . . for $25 or even $50. I would not ask you to do this, but I gathered from your conversation that you were as firm a believer in bromide paper as I am myself."[29]

Prospective salesmen and demonstrators had to pass a handwriting test and come for a personal interview. "We should like to see you," Eastman wrote Gustav Milburn. "From what we hear of you we think that we can make you useful at $75 a month. We do not want to make an offer, however, until we see you. . . . If you cannot succeed for any reason, or if we cannot make your services pay, there shall be no dissatisfaction at our calling it quits." Customers were asked to express their opinions about a demonstrator: "Will you have the kindness to write us confidentially and tell us what you think of his skill and ability? We do not want to make permanent arrangements with a man who cannot give our customers first rate satisfaction." Once Eastman even hired a Pinkerton agent to "shadow" his star salesman "for a few days" and tempt him with a phony job. In exchange for a testimonial, a free camera was sent in 1886 to W. H. Pickering, professor of chemistry at the Massachusetts Institute of Technology, perhaps the first contact between Eastman and an institution he would support munificently. Another harbinger was his first substantial philanthropic gift—at a time when his own weekly salary was less than $60—to Rochester's trade and technical college, Mechanics Institute. "I am in receipt of the pamphlet left by you at our factory," he told Captain Henry Lomb of Bausch and Lomb, who founded the institute in 1885. In 1887 Eastman wrote Lomb: "I am thoroughly in sympathy with the object of this enterprise and enclose check for $50.00 to help it along."[30] The gift was probably the result of two influences: the public-spiritedness inherited from his mother and his perception that trained technicians were of use to his business.

Overriding matters philanthropic, on New Year's Day 1887, Eastman noticed that two of his most trusted employees were missing.[31] Franklin Millard Cossitt was a valued technician who had made several camera models for Eastman (indeed, he shared with Eastman the patent for the "Detective," the company's first box camera) and was foreman in charge of paper making. David Cooper was Eastman's top demonstrator-salesman, who often accompanied Eastman and Strong to conventions. He had been the recipient of many Eastman letters, one in August 1885 cautioning him about "the position Anthony has taken in regard to our goods" (it wouldn't handle roll holders) and exhorting him that "The chief end of our business is orders. We cannot live on faith. . . . Immediate results are what we are after, and I write plainly that there may be no mistake as to our expectations."[32] It soon was revealed that the pair had defected to the Anthony company, Eastman's first major customer and now a major enemy.

The difficulties between the two firms had begun as differences in ways of doing business and escalated into bitterness. Anthony disdained mechanized equipment (which was more costly for them to adopt than for Eastman, who had started from scratch). The old, autocratic house had been around since 1841, the very beginning of photography, and had most of the trade cornered. Eastman was never satisfied that Anthony pushed his products: "Anthony & Co. do their utmost to avoid selling any of our goods, and to prevent their customers using any of our goods."[33] In 1885 squabbles developed over Tropical Plates, which Eastman made exclusively for Anthony. To Eastman, the name of the game was success and he played hard to win. To Anthony, Eastman was an upstart, and a ruthless one to boot. Eastman terminated his exclusive contract with Anthony in 1885, and Eastman salesmen began pushing products in the field to Anthony's detriment and annoyance. Retaliating, Anthony began producing its own warm-weather plates. This led to a price war. Eastman drove down the price of paper until Anthony was obliged to undercut him. By 1886 Eastman was in the midst of large-scale production of bromide paper by coating webs of paper, on the run, with sensitized gelatin, using the Eastman–Walker machine he had also adapted for coating American film. Anthony was still hand coating paper and probably marketing it at a loss. Still one jump ahead of his rival, Eastman brought out a new and cheaper paper, called Eureka. Anthony had to follow suit. Anthony received a bromide paper patent and issued a circular threatening Eastman dealers with suit. Eastman countered: "If the Messrs. Anthony ever deem it wise to bring their suit to trial, we shall show that Mr. Roche did not invent Bromide Paper, and that no paper we ever sold infringes his patent."[34]

Pirating Eastman's employees was Anthony's latest move, and a serious one. Eastman's informers told him that Cooper was "working up a bromide paper company in the interest of Anthony" while Cossitt was busy duplicating the Eastman web coater for his new employer. Eastman resolved to heat up the cold war between the rival firms. "We propose to show the d___d scoundrels that when it comes to 'funny' work the country men from Monroe County are not to be sneezed at." Infuriated at Cossitt's "duplicity" and "lack of Principle," Eastman felt no compunction over planting one of his "operatives" as Cossitt's roommate in New York and having the spy pose as the technician's "most intimate friend." Eastman himself seems to have slipped into the Anthony plant in some sort of disguise, since he told Walker that "I have been in the shop where they are building their machinery, have seen the drawings and castings. A mechanical expert went with me as witness." He had enough evidence to prove in court, he thought, that Anthony had infringed on his patent. Seeing a golden opportunity to scotch the Anthony challenge with one blow, Eastman eagerly looked forward to his day in court: "If we beat Anthony we shall have a clear field hereafter. . . . A successful litigation will make our stock worth double what it is now. . . . If we can prevent competition such dividends will be regular." The hoped-for result of the "pretty a case against Anthony as anybody could hope for" would put Eastman in the position sought by most capitalists in the years before passage of the Sherman Antitrust Act— "monopolist of gelatin-argentic paper." Eastman's "detective operations" did him little good in the end. In March 1887 he brought suit against Anthony for infringement of patents, but was disappointed when the motion for a preliminary injunction was denied. "Judge Shipman dissolved the stay, but compelled A & Co. to sign a stipulation not to use or allow our machine to let it go out of their possession until after the final hearing. Our opponents made the point that they stopped using our machine as soon as they saw our patent and had no intention of infringing. There being no infringement," Anthony claimed, "there ought to be no injunction."[35]

Meanwhile, Walker was growing restive in his duties for the firm in England. Perhaps seeing an opportunity while Eastman was preoccupied with courtroom strategy, he pressed him with some new demands. Walker asked for a salary increase and to be relieved of his contract requiring him to give the company the benefit of his ideas and inventions. He requested that notice to cancel his contract be reduced to three months and that the company give him a bond of indemnity for any loss he might sustain in assuming obligations abroad.

Back in Rochester, Eastman had another distraction—of an incendiary sort. On 10 February 1888, past 2 A.M., an alarm was sent in from "the dreaded box 37, at the corner of Mill and Platt streets," the *Rochester Democrat & Chronicle* reported. "Every member of the department understands that [to be] a disastrous fire." A general alarm was sounded, with all available apparatus and fire brigades ordered to the scene, only to find the hydrants frozen. The fire, which originated in the chemical rooms, smoldered unobserved in the nearly windowless five-story building, eating its way through the floors. "At 3:25 o'clock the flames burst through the roof and ran down the elevator well. . . . The firemen were driven from the building and at that hour it was thought impossible to save any portion of the plant." By 4:30, however, "the fire was substantially under control. The front portion of the building was not extensively damaged. The rear is gutted."[36] Eastman's careful planning for a "fire-proof brick wall extending from cellar to roof" separated the rear of the building from the front, and thus saved the front offices, the accumulated records, and the stock of roll holders and cameras. In spite of this catastrophe, Eastman's overall safety record was good, even though he worked daily with volatile and dangerous substances. But the fire did destroy the paper and plate-coating machines in the rear, and water from the noble efforts of the brigades made worthless his stock of American film and bromide paper. Still, Eastman presented the fire brigade with a $100 check as a reward for saving what it could. He received a healthy insurance settlement ("HURRAH for you!" cabled Strong).[37] Within weeks the coating machines had been rebuilt, goods were rationed and sent out, and plans for a new building were on the boards.

Feeling that with all of his troubles at home he could not risk an open rift with the difficult Walker across the Atlantic, Eastman endeavored to "harmonize Walker's views with those of the Board." A new three-year contract was negotiated that included a directive to Walker to "rent a desirable location on Oxford Street" for the company's first retail store. Realizing that Walker would have to be replaced eventually, Eastman quietly hired Joseph Thacher Clarke in 1886 to be his "scientific expert for Europe." Urbane, cultured, and enigmatic, Clarke would become Eastman's artistic guide, cycling companion, and eyes and ears on the Continent.[38]

Thacher Clarke's (he went by his middle name) father, a Boston physician, had died when the boy was twelve. His mother took him to Germany, where schooling was less expensive. At the Dresden Gymnasium Clarke studied architecture, archeology, and the cello, became a facile linguist, and returned to Boston at age sixteen to study architecture. He teamed up with another student, Francis Bacon, brother of Henry Bacon, later the designer of the Lincoln Memorial, to join an archeological expedition excavating Assos, near the site of ancient Troy. (Francis Bacon would later design the furniture for Eastman House.) Clarke's interest in the lighting of Greek temples led him to take up photography. After two years on the dig he went to England to write up his findings for the British Museum and settled there. Having found available cameras unsatisfactory for his archeological work, Clarke constructed his own prototype, the Frena. The Frena used cut pieces of film in place of glass plates but never became a commercial success. Clarke tried to interest Eastman in improving and pushing the Frena, but Eastman saw it as merely an intermediate and unnecessary sidestep in his own search for a simple, infallible roll-film camera any child could operate. Instead, in what became a pattern when dealing with inventors or small businessmen looking for assistance, Eastman bought the rights, hired the man, and put him to work on some aspect of the business where such an expert was needed.

Fluent in German, Spanish, and Italian, and conversant in science, art, food, and wine, Clarke lived with his family in Harrow, England. Eastman called the corpulent (250 pounds) and bearded Clarke "Big Bear." He advised Eastman on foreign patents, technical information, and property. He participated in negotiations for acquisitions abroad and in recruiting personnel. Clarke was charged with linking the company—through George Eastman personally—with European photographic developments and with protecting Eastman innovations in Europe. On a personal level, he became Eastman's self-educated guide to European civilization. Clarke's two sons, Hans and Eric, knew Eastman from the time they were small boys. When Hans grew up, Eastman allowed him to play the clarinet with his quartet at Eastman House and hired him as a Kodak Park research chemist. Eric became the manager of the Eastman Theatre in 1924.[39]

The competition and litigation between Eastman and Anthony would continue for years, but similar scuffles with other manufacturers—Blair, Scovill, Cramer—erupted now as well. Eastman liked to combine provocation with conciliation, thus keeping his competitors off balance. The Blair Camera Company of Boston, with textile manufacturer Darius Goff as president and photographer Thomas Blair as treasurer and general manager, was trying to follow Eastman's lead in becoming a complete manufacturer by combining patented innovations, world markets, diversification, and simpler cameras for the amateur market.[40] Blair marketed what he called a Combination camera, then complained when Eastman used the word "combination" to describe one of his models—the Eastman View camera. Eastman, who was beginning to formulate his own views on the value of a simple, distinct, and strong trademark, rejected Blair's claim that "combination" could be construed as a trademark. "The word is purely descriptive, . . . used to describe tools and apparatus capable of multiple uses," he wrote. "If the word [was exclusively Blair's] you could prevent your fellow citizens from using the English language."[41] He felt compelled, moreover, to use the opportunity to cast aspersions on a rival product, "because if there is anything that we do not care to imitate . . . , it is the style and workmanship of the Blair Camera. This is a cold, naked fact, and we feel compelled to state it plainly without desiring to give offense." Offense he gave, of course.

The Cramer Dry Plate Company also got the back of Eastman's hand: "We are aware that Cramer claims to have a plate so rapid that he can catch the flight of a cannon ball! Perhaps in a little while he will get out a plate that can catch the 'flight of fancy.'"[42]

As the Eastman company began manufacturing roll holders for American film, it found itself in direct competition with the Scovill Manufacturing Company, soon to become the Scovill & Adams Company. Eastman thought Scovill made the best cameras—his own early cameras were custom built by that company—and after Eastman's break with Anthony, relations between Eastman and Scovill became fairly close. Eastman added roll holders to Scovill cameras at customers' requests. When Eastman turned to manufacturing cameras, it became a different story. Scovill's attitude was that it had created the market for cameras and related apparatus and now Eastman, who heretofore concentrated on film and paper, was horning in. As the howls from Scovill increased, Eastman blandly explained "that in order to make the films the greatest success they are capable of, we have to make apparatus especially adapted to it. I realize this puts us [in direct competition with] the Scovill Company, and I sincerely regret it. . . . Of course the number of cameras we make would not be a fly speck in their immense business, but sometimes a little thorn causes a big irritation."[43]

Earlier, Eastman had urged Scovill to build a light, portable film camera to meet the "numberless inquiries that we are getting" for a camera "fitted with the roll holder." Prophetically Eastman told Adams that "The concern first in the market . . . with a complete photographic outfit . . . will be sure to reap a great advantage." Scovill did not chose to develop that simple camera, however, nor were they reassured by Eastman's explanations. Feelings grew more heated and Eastman's subsequent letters were even less conciliatory, while purring that "we do not see how the Scovill Co can reasonably make any objection to our little efforts." Nervous about Eastman's "little efforts," Scovill's lawyers contacted Eastman. He was already in court with Anthony and so urged Irving Adams of Scovill to "postpone any preemptory action until we can have the conference which you suggested," adding sarcastically that Adams should "kindly advise us whether you have singled us out for an especial victim, or whether you propose to proceed against every other camera manufacturer."[44]

Eastman got the break he wanted in December 1887 when H. S. Lewis of Scovill wrote, independently of the camera squabble, to propose that Eastman and Scovill join forces in foreign trade. Eastman responded eagerly and the flurry of correspondence let him play for time. While this intense jockeying for position in the photographic world was going on, with Eastman holding the upper hand in most areas, a minor event went unnoticed that would have greater repercussions than all the Blairs, Scovills, Anthonys, and Cramers combined.

On 2 May 1887 the Reverend Hannibal Goodwin of Newark, New Jersey, filed an application for the patent of a transparent, flexible film for photographic purposes.[45] The film had a nitrocellulose base. Goodwin had been looking for a less cumbersome support than glass for his lantern slides of the Holy Land. He first tried the celluloid collars from men's shirts, but with the invention of the Eastman–Walker roll holder, Goodwin and other experimenters—including George Eastman—turned their attentions to rollable film and found that celluloid sheet film was too thick for roll holders. Goodwin and the others then began experimenting with flowing and evaporating nitrocellulose in various solvents in search of a thinner film.

Goodwin's film awaited Eastman down the road.

II

"You Press the Button . . ."

"...We Do the Rest"

Tapping the huge potential of the amateur market was now George Eastman's objective. Some manufacturers (such as William Walker before he joined forces with Eastman) made sporadic forays in that direction, centering around an inexpensive plate camera. But none pursued the goal with the determination and method of George Eastman. His idea was to build up his paper business and continue his search for a transparent celluloid film so that when the right camera came on the market (fitted with an Eastman–Walker roll holder) his business would grow to the point where "it will dazzle the eyes of the gentle beholder. . . . About four out of five amateurs have cheap cameras," he told W. J. Stillman of Scovill before the break with that company, "and when we fit them a holder it makes their old camera look so poverty stricken that they cannot rest until they have a new camera. This indication of the way the wind is going to blow is of significance to you as the manufacturer of the best apparatus in the country." Scovill, he felt in 1885, was "much inclined to boom things if we give them a show" and indeed Stillman told him what was needed was a camera that would act as a "photographic notebook."[1] When Scovill sued instead of boomed, Eastman was drawn into coming up with his own entry to capitalize on a fad of the late 1880s—the detective camera.

Detective cameras, disguised as books or boxes, were originally designed for police work. They were so named by Thomas Bolas in 1881. The public was fascinated and scooped them up as novelties. Soon manufacturers were producing cameras that were disguised as parcels, canes, guns, suitcases, picnic baskets, binoculars, opera glasses, and even hats. The Patent Detective camera, invented by William Schmid of Brooklyn in 1883 and sold through the Anthony company, was the first commercially produced, hand-held box camera. It took a plate holder and cost $55. Subsequent models could be fitted with a roll holder, but because of Eastman's tight control of roll-holder patents, it was difficult for his competitors to design film systems of their own. The earliest hint that Eastman was working on a detective camera of his own came in November 1885, when he alerted prospective customers that a new camera would be ready for the spring trade. On 1 March 1886 Eastman and his technician Frank Cossitt applied for a patent that was issued on 30 November, just a month before Cossitt defected to the Anthony company.

Eastman's Detective camera, six by six by ten inches, took negative paper film with forty-eight exposures. Smooth and simple design was promised. "Everything will be enclosed in a box of the smallest possible compass, with no inconvenient springs, catches and levers projecting outside to interfere with its convenient carrying and handling." Leather-covered, with carrying case and shoulder strap, it looked "much like a small traveling bag." Then Eastman, who would have a lifelong love affair with guns, lapsed into the language of ordnance (as did many camera manufacturers, with their "ready, aim, cock, shoot" talk): "At short distances a gunner can kill without bringing his rifle or pistol to the eye. The Detective camera will be perfectly adapted to taking groups unobserved." Eastman hoped his Detective camera might be "put on the market at such a low price that it would be a leading card with us and defy competition from other makers." The U.S. patent shows it with a roll holder; the British patent, with a plate holder.[2] It was fitted with a most unusual shutter: a hollow funnel of sheet metal in which "the jaws," as Eastman called them, traveled across the sensitive material. "The Detective camera is complete," he declared in May 1886, "works beautifully, and we have a large number in the shop." He confidently expected to place the camera on the market "in a few days." In June models were exhibited at the St. Louis Photographic Convention. In July came the first sign of trouble and each letter therafter pushes the date of delivery a little farther into the future.

In early November Eastman predicted his Detective camera would be on the market momentarily with "extra quick American film." Yet ten days later he admitted that "we have been the victims of annoying delays." These were variously described as failure to get brass rods for the plate holders, a rubber shortage, waiting for faster film, and the impossibility of producing the camera at a price that would allow a reasonable profit. After the first flush of enthusiasm, there was stalling, although orders were taken and customers assured that delivery was imminent. By June 1887, with the price fixed at $45, a total of fifty Detective cameras were finished and "awaiting careful trial. I shall use one tomorrow. We have not sent any out yet except three or four to be used for a special enterprise on time exposures." Soon, however, Eastman lost patience and resolved to remainder his stock of forty Detective cameras. "We shall not make any more of them," he told W. H. Walmsley, a Philadelphia dealer, in January 1888. "We . . . want to get rid of these without distributing them all over the country. . . . Can you not make a specialty of them?" His eagerness to have done with the Eastman Detective camera can be explained by what was going on at the Rochester factory—he was readying its permanent successor. The Kodak camera was in the wings.

What became of this stock of Detective cameras remains a mystery. Eastman sent Walmsley a model; then the fire ravaged the Eastman factory. Some Detective cameras must have survived, because individual inquirers were offered them on approval. There is no record of the cameras being shipped to Philadelphia. Maybe Eastman destroyed the lot because he had a better product on hand. In any case, there is only one known example of the Eastman Detective camera in existence—in the collection of the Smithsonian Institution.[3] Months before, on 22 October 1887, Eastman alluded to what would be the Kodak camera in a letter to Stillman of Scovill. "Speaking to you confidentially, I will say that I believe that I have got the little roll holder breast camera perfected, but there is always delay in making tools and getting stock of anything. Our experience with the Detective camera has been very annoying and I will never be caught advertising anything again until I have it in stock. . . . [The experience] will enable us to avoid most of the difficulties of manufacture. The trouble with the Detective is that no matter how successfully it works, it will always be hard to make."[4]

By 1888 Scovill had changed its mind about lawsuits and was pressing Eastman to buy the company out. Too late, "impractical," Eastman replied, and Waterbury was too far from Rochester for an "apparatus factory, it being absolutely necessary that the experiments conducted shall be under the personal supervision of the writer." Although many would later attack Eastman for indiscriminately gobbling up all photographic concerns, in reality he often turned down mergers when they did not involve valuable patents or had no immediate practical value, or when the firms involved were financially weak. Instead of Scovill, Eastman turned to Frank Brownell, a State Street neighbor whose cabinet and camera shop had produced the Eastman–Walker roll holder. About 10 October 1887, as he later testified, "I first conceived the invention," commencing the wood working on 12 October. Two days later he explained his drawing of the shutter to machinists Yawman & Erbe. By 6 November he was taking pictures and nine days later had five more twenty-two-ounce box cameras, $6\frac{3}{4}$ by $3\frac{3}{4}$ by $3\frac{3}{4}$ inches, with fixed focus lens by Bausch & Lomb; woodworking by Brownell; metal parts, shutters, and assembly by Yawman & Erbe. All were Rochester concerns that

Eastman supervised closely as he formulated plans to mass produce the new camera. The "little roll holder breast camera" was covered by seven patents, including Eastman's main patent of 4 September 1888 that completely described it. Others assigned to the Eastman Dry Plate and Film Company were roll-holder patents—from Houston, Stoddard, and Bannister—which Eastman had purchased to protect his system from infringement or duplication.[5]

In outward appearance the little breast camera resembled the Eastman Detective camera. But instead of a removable roll holder for American film, the spools were built in. The clumsy internal shutter had been replaced by a revolving shutter of equally ingenious design, becoming the camera's chief mechanical novelty. Eastman had placed the lens in a tube with two holes in it that revolved when a button on the side of the camera was pressed. As the holes passed across the lens, the exposure was made. The shutter was cocked by pulling a string that tensed a spring. Furthermore, the shutter was self-capping.[6] Eastman's revolving shutter operated on a continuous basis, thus simplifying the operation. The lens, a simple symmetrical doublet, produced a curvature of field and chromatic aberration that were remedied by masking the image into circular negatives $2\frac{1}{2}$ inches in diameter. Later models with different lenses would produce the familiar rectangular image. It was possible to make as many as twenty separate exposures in one minute—and so the speed of the motion picture camera was not far down the line.

The camera was to be hand-held securely against the chest rather than placed on a tripod or table—hence the description "little roll holder breast camera." Leather-covered and fitted with its own carrying case and shoulder strap and a roll of one hundred frames of American film, it sold for $25. That was half the price of the Eastman Detective camera. The *Philadelphia Photographer* found it "incredible that so many possibilities should rest within the confines of so tiny a structure, and such an unpretentious one. . . .[It] is a model of compactness, neatness, and ingenuity." Eastman's goal was a camera that "could be put into any ordinary man's hands with satisfactory results."[7] But simplicity had its drawbacks. With no view finder it was difficult to guess what might be framed in the finished picture. And although a revolving indicator showed when a fresh exposure was in place, it was difficult to remember how many of the one hundred exposures might be left. A small printed card was soon introduced to remedy both defects. Converging lines on one side formed a view finder; the picture was lined up by placing the card on the top of the box and pointing the "V" at the subject. Everything beyond six feet was in focus. (Later the "V" sight was embossed into the morocco covering of the camera.) The other side of the card had numbers from 1 to 100 for the photographer to check off as he wound the film.[8]

If the photographer was determined to process his own film, he would involve himself in such complexity that it was sure to immobilize the novice (or "Kodaker," as the directions called him). All one needed was a totally dark room, an Eastman Orange Candle Lamp, six sheets of clear glass, four trays (one for stripping), a camel's hair brush, two graduated measures, a velvet rubber squeegee, developing powders, bromide potassium (restrainer), hyposulphite soda (fix), Eastman's collodion (varnish), Eastman's rubber solution, intensifier, gelatin skins, a mackintosh blanket (to squeegee through), two pails (for water and waste), and a dipper. A sample negative came with the outfit that the Kodaker could compare by orange candle to his own emerging image. Then came developing, fixing, transferring to glass, stripping, applying the gelatin skin, and collodionising. By then one had four negatives; only ninety-six more to go. "The Finished Negative," said the directions, "consists of a very thin image-bearing film, supported on the gelatine skin, and enclosed between two films of collodion varnish." Few amateurs would want to take on such a task, but Eastman had the alternative—factory developing and printing. The camera with exposed film could be sent to Rochester where for $10 the film would be processed; the camera was then reloaded with fresh film and returned to the owner. All those months that Eastman talked about his "little roll holder breast camera," he knew exactly what he was going to call it. So did Church & Church, patent attorneys, after 28 January 1888: "We send you today two Kodak cameras," Eastman wrote, "to serve as the model for the patent drawing. Please use up the film and return to us for finishing. . . . Make a search. . . . Is it going to infringe?"

This is Eastman's first public use of the name "Kodak." According to tradition, Eastman hit upon the appellation while playing anagrams with his mother ("trying out a great number of combinations of letters that made words starting and ending with 'K'"). He liked the letter "K" because it was "strong and incisive . . . firm and unyielding." It was pronounced the same in every language, and was the first letter of his mother's family name. Registered as a trademark on 4 September 1888, Eastman later explained the word's merits to the British Patent Office: "*First*: It is short. *Second*: It is not capable of mispronunciation. *Third*: It does not resemble anything in the art and cannot be associated with anything in the art except the Kodak." He told one correspondent that "there is, you know, a commercial value in having a peculiar name; it cannot be imitated or counterfeited. . . . You are in error if you think Kodak is a foreign word. It is truly American. . . . It was born in this country. It is not pretty but it protects the advertising, and besides, it is not 'Detective,' a name I detest."[9] He told *Pathfinder* magazine that when he coined the word he was looking for a term that would be both "euphonious and snappy."[10] There are other versions of the origin of the name that vie with one another in degrees of the preposterous—for example, "kodak" resembled the sound the shutter made when it opened and closed. This version may be based on a 1938 press release the company put out on *The Origin of the Word Kodak*, which noted that "Philologically the word 'Kodak' is as meaningless as a child's first 'goo.' Terse, abrupt to the point of rudeness, literally bitten off by ice-cutting consonants at both ends, it snaps like a Kodak shutter." One woman swore that Eastman told her over luncheon that he had come up with the name while gazing into a bowl of alphabet soup, an incident that confirms his prankish nature and love of inventing conflicting stories. Best to take the founder at his word— whichever version one chooses.[11]

The first convert to the new camera was none other than the company's president, Henry Strong. In spite of his association with Eastman and photography, "he never realized that it was a possible thing to take pictures himself." Eastman gave Strong a Kodak to take along with him on a trip to Tacoma in May 1888, and the complete tyro's enthusiasm was instantaneous. "It was the first time he had ever carried a camera, and he was as tickled with it as a boy with a new top. I never saw anybody so pleased over a lot of pictures before," Eastman observed.[12]

> Oh Kodak, are you so void of sense
> That you so stoically take
> The pressure of her fingers fair,
> While all my nerves do shake?
>
> ("To My Sweetheart's Kodak," 1890s)

While there is no record of George Eastman quivering like this lovesick swain, the Kodak camera did involve him in a one-sided near-romance. Mrs. Cornelia J. Hagan, a young widow who worked for the federal government in Washington, D.C., had several dates with the thirty-three-year-old Eastman in 1887 and 1888 when he was visiting the Johnston family, friends of Strong who lived in the nation's capital. Cornelia was especially close to Frances Benjamin Johnston (1864–1952), a photographer who achieved some fame with pictures of egg-rolling contests on the White House lawn and candid portraits of President Benjamin Harrison's grandchildren.[13]

After some afternoon horseback rides in Rock Creek Park, Cornelia made a number of ladylike bids for Eastman's affections in letters to Rochester she wrote on delicate stationery (with a nest-building robin in the upper corner). Eastman chose to overlook her flirtatious manner, but because Cornelia was interested in photography, he continued the correspondence and sent her new photographic products to try out. He also promised to visit her soon. "I trust your visit to Washington may not be long postponed," Cornelia replied coyly, "for I am already exceedingly interested in the 'most fascinating amusement of the age,' as you choose to term it, and I am sure it must be. With such an able instructor, it could not be otherwise than fascinating."

Ignoring the personal overtures, Eastman continued to stick to business. He predicted a great photographic future for Cornelia and told her of "a new small camera" he was perfecting and sent her some pictures he had taken of Strong's wife and daughter. But Cornelia's overtures persisted in another note: "I sent you yesterday some trailing arbutus which grows in quantity all about Washington—I hope it will not lose all of its freshness—before reaching you—It is one of our sweetest spring flowers." In January 1888 Eastman visited Washington and promised to return. He brought Kodak cameras for Cornelia and Frances Johnston to try out. In May Cornelia wrote that "If only I can remember the instructions received from you I shall get some superior views," and then got down to the real purpose: "I hope, however, your trip to New York may *necessitate* your coming to Washington too—*then* you will give me the final instructions and 'diploma.'"

Eastman pointedly did not detour to Washington. He continued to correspond, criticizing the "lights and shadows" of Cornelia's work, but she was beginning to get the larger picture, that Eastman's interest in her was friendly but professional. Then a promised visit did not come off: "I put on my best holiday attire last Sunday and staid at home all the afternoon—thinking perhaps your 'visit deferred' might be accomplished—but my efforts on your behalf were wasted. . . . Another shock like that might prove fatal—and we are not willing to 'skuse George' again." Despite her jocular air, Cornelia seems to have given up any romantic hopes she may have entertained of Eastman, who during these early Kodak days was always very much otherwise engaged. "I am grateful for the interest manifested in my progress," she concluded, "and hope for the sake of my instructor that I shall become accomplished in the art."[14]

A romance with Cornelia seems never to have kindled any ardor in Eastman. He coolly wrote to Strong in 1892: "Mrs. Hagan and I are fully as good friends as ever. I have seen her twice since she got home, once in Rochester and once in Washington. She is as bright and charming as ever." Eastman kept his packet of letters from Cornelia Hagan all his life. In October 1889 Cornelia reopened the correspondence in a friendly manner, but stuck strictly to business talk. She purchased Kodak stock as it became available over the years and sometimes would write him about that. At least once, she, Eastman, and Fanny Johnston had a weekend rendezvous in England, where all three were traveling. Something might be assumed about Cornelia from her close association with Fanny—highly respected for her photography but an unconventional woman for her times. The best-known photograph of Johnston (taken in 1896) shows her with cigarette in one hand, beer stein in the other, petticoats hiked up to display her leg to the knee (in an era when a glimpse of ankle was shocking). Other than this association, not much is known about Mrs. Hagan. As for Eastman, his diffidence can at least partly be accounted for by his preoccupation at the time with the "baby" (as cousin

Almon called the Kodak) he was rearing. In the next century, as a much older man, he would seek out friendships with women.

Even Eastman may not have been prepared for what happened next.

By late April 1888 production machinery was under construction and the application for the patent had been filed. In May the first Kodak camera was sold but then suddenly Yawman & Erbe had to shut down their works for several weeks and the next few cameras were not put on the market until 10 June.[15] In July twenty-five Kodak cameras spent "a very hot week" at the convention of the Photographers' Association of America in Minneapolis, where one of the professional photographers remarked to the assembled fraternity, "George Eastman is here with the cutest little trick box of a camera he calls a Kodak."[16] Then, the little camera won a first medal. Eastman received other awards for various inventions, but it was the Kodak camera that swept the convention— "a great success among the professional photographers [who bought all twenty-five and placed orders for many more]. I hardly thought they would take hold of it so quickly."[17] On his way home he stopped in Cleveland and brought Ellen Andrus home with him, presenting his niece with a Kodak camera so that she could go on to become arguably the best photographer in the family. She was a "natural" when choosing subjects and composing shots— so good in fact that on the 150th anniversary of photography in 1989 the *National Geographic* magazine editors chose one of Ellen Andrus's first Kodak snapshots to lead off their article, completely unaware of her identity.[18]

It was clear that something spectacular was about to occur. By August Eastman was having trouble keeping up with orders. He corrected a dealer who wrote "If the Kodak is a success . . . " by responding "The Kodak is a very decided success" even though circulars had not yet been sent to the trade. During the next six months, five thousand cameras were sold, yielding a profit of $269,059, compared with $154,547 for the same six month-period in 1887.[19] Intimations of success spurred innovation. Soon Eastman and his lieutenants were working on three new camera models. In December 1888 he decided to replace the revolving shutter with an equally effective but less expensive arrangement. After the introduction of the No. 2 Kodak (which took larger but still round pictures) in October 1889, the second newly shuttered version of the original camera was named in retrospect the "No. 1 Kodak," a designation still used by collectors today but which would have been meaningless in 1888 and early 1889.[20]

Eastman's correspondence in these days shows him constantly probing for leverage. Late in 1888 Eastman in his role as marketing manager began pressing Walmsley to take some Kodak cameras. Walmsley replied that he already had four dozen Kodaks purchased from Scovill, which was *not* pushing Eastman's cameras, roll holders, or film. Besides, Walmsley was being squeezed out of his job and hoped that Eastman would open a retail store that Walmsley could manage. Diversification for Eastman did not extend to retailing but because Walmsley was the sole American agent for some English lenses Eastman badly wanted, he offered Walmsley a job in Rochester. "Everybody who has ever come into this concern has done well," he wrote Walmsley, citing his partner Walker's example. "When Walker came with us he came on a small salary but he has made a good thing of it as you doubtless know." Small salaries but large stock options would become the Eastman method for attracting and keeping outstanding people. But Walmsley did not think that he wanted to leave Philadelphia for Rochester and his refusal may have planted the seed in Eastman's mind that in order to attract the best people, he might have to make Rochester a more attractive place in which to live and work.[21]

Eastman knew that amateurs fell into two groups. The first, what he called "true amateurs," were willing and able to devote the time and expense "to acquire skills in developing, printing, toning, etc.," and valued photography as something between a challenging craft and an art form. The second group, exemplified by the snap-happy Strong, wanted to produce a kind of personal record "of their everyday life, objects, places or people that interest them in travel, etc." They loved to press the button, but were hardly interested in processing the result—indeed, they were mostly incapable of doing so. But these latter, Eastman sensed, were legion in number. He resolved to cater to both groups, and as the century neared its end he fully realized that the second group could eventually expand to include virtually everyone on the planet.

By separating the two main functions of photography—the picture taking and the processing—Eastman revolutionized the industry. The service department he started for professionals and to promote his bromide paper was now expanded to include developing and stripping the American film that was returned to the factory in Kodak cameras. "We do the rest" was literally true. At Eastman's factory, "we" removed the film from the camera, cut it into strips of twelve exposures, developed and stripped it, pressed it in contact with a clear gelatin skin, and dried it. Then "we" made prints from each negative and pasted them on gilt-edged, chocolate-colored mounts and returned them with the negatives and the Kodak camera loaded with a fresh roll of film. "We" had done more than invent a camera; "we" had a vision and were developing a whole system that included the machinery and standardized parts to deliver it. The last major gap between everyman and photography was filled in.

Eastman needed an instruction manual and a primer to accompany what by March 1888 he was casually referring to as "the K camera," so he hired Kilbourne Tompkins, a New York advertising writer, to compose one. He sent "Kib" Tompkins a camera so he might better understand how the Kodak functioned. Eastman's twenty-one-letter correspondence with Tompkins shows the young inventor-businessman at his most creative and dynamic, as well as at his most willful and impatient. It soon became apparent that in Kib he had on his hands a "camera-ignoramus" of the most invincible type. At first he patiently explained the workings of the Kodak to the writer, thus learning the shortcomings himself. In instructing Kib, Eastman inadvertently made some basic points—"Hold the camera steady. Hold it level. Do not point it at the sun. You cannot get nearer than five or six feet"—to include in the manual. He also decided that "There are fifty thousand amateur photographers in this country today and they are our first and tenderest meat." Eventually Kib "got some daisys. Your interiors are a success. The group of children is one of the best things I have ever seen." So Eastman inquired, "How did you hold the camera in these attempts?"

Kib's writing was no more acceptable to Eastman than his photography: "You are far off . . . in writing directions [because] *you are ignorant of the reason why.* That is all right for an idiot or a dog who is expected to do just exactly as you tell him, but . . . I never yet knew any man to follow the simplest written directions exactly. I never did it myself and never succeeded in making anybody else do it." In sending Tompkins $200 as partial payment of the $500, Eastman grouched: "It makes me tired to think of the time that has been wasted on this pesky manual. . . . It requires experience to write instructions. . . . I shall have to finish this job up here."

Eastman found Kib's $4,800 bill for personal services "excessive," declining to pay it, but was willing to submit the matter to an arbitrator. Now Tompkins declined. "We have just finished up a vexatious lawsuit in New York," Eastman eventually told Walker. "It has bothered me a great deal. A fellow sued us . . . and got a snap judgement against us for $5,065. We opened it up and had it tried last week. He got a verdict of $420 and had to pay costs. We licked him and made a good thorough job of it, but . . . it bothered me."[22] What Eastman didn't mention was that Kilbourne Tompkins was his cousin and childhood playmate at Marcellus, brother of the faithful Eliza. The hazards of hiring a kinsman (and one six years older) was what really bothered him. Then Eastman sat down and in five hours wrote the text for the first *Kodak Primer,* which said in part, "*For Twenty Years* the art of photography stood still. . . . *Four Years Ago* the amateur photographer was confined to heavy glass plates for making his negatives, *Today* photography has been reduced to a cycle of three operations: 1. Pull the String. 2. Turn the Key. 3. Press the Button." Five months later, he had the essence of the Kodak system further reduced to eight words: "You press the button, we do the rest."[23]

Eastman realized from the beginning that it would be the sale of film, not cameras, that was the key to the sucess of the system. Although the Kodak camera was marketed with American film, Henry Reichenbach continued his experiments to produce a transparent, flexible film. Just as collodion, a nitrocellulose material, was instrumental in the shift from daguerreotype to glass plate/paper print photography at midcentury, so a solution of nitrocellulose flowed and evaporated into a thin, flexible film would complete the shift to a roll-film system in the 1890s. Other companies were marketing cut celluloid sheets as a substitute for glass. The Celluloid Manufacturing Company had introduced and patented a method of producing thick, clear blocks and a shaving mechanism. John Carbutt sold this sheet film coated with dry-plate emulsion beginning in 1888 as did the Anthonys and others. But allegations that the camphor in the celluloid reacted adversely with the emulsion were heard, and the shaved celluloid was too thick and inflexible to be used for roll holders.

By December 1888 Reichenbach had produced a nitrocellulose solution in wood alcohol. On being flowed over a glass plate, the solution dried to a smooth, clear finish. It had little strength, however, tore easily, and had a tendency to peel while drying, thus forming a wavy, irregular surface. Next the chemist added a high solution of camphor—60 percent—to strengthen and soften the film. Eastman knew the chemist was getting close to a formula that would do away with the intermediate step of stripping the film, and so he began to design a new production apparatus. Late in January he requested Philipp and Church to obtain copies of all celluloid patents and to meet with him to prepare applications for the production of thin celluloid films. On 28 February 1889 he presented to his board of directors a methodical plan for initiating production of transparent film by flowing and evaporating the right combination of chemicals. The plan included cost estimates of raw materials from suppliers, drawings and cost data of machinery needed, and samples of Reichenbach's film. He then spent $15,000 to equip the new film-manufacturing plant ("double what I first figured," he told Strong, "but Court Street is going to be a Daisy"). Twelve new coating tables were assembled by joining four twenty-foot sheets of glass to form a three- by eighty-foot slab. All stood in readiness for Reichenbach's perfection of the process. By adding fusel oil and amyl acetate, the chemist found that the camphor was retained in solution during the drying of the film.[24] This solution, known in the trade as "dope," was poured over the glass to dry into thick but flexible "skins" of film. Under a safelight, the sensitive emulsion was poured over the film. When dried, the film could be peeled, cut into strips, spooled, and put into light-tight containers.

In a soft mood brought on by his gratitude for the young chemist's part in the process, Eastman returned the first draft of the patent application submitted by Church & Church on 3 March 1889: "I find that the fusel oil claims . . . must come out as I can lay no claim to the chemical part of the process. The mechanical part only is mine and the chemical part Henry M.

Reichenbach. . . . As the claims are at present drawn, neither Reichenbach nor myself could father them, as they combine the chemical and mechanical features, which are separate inventions. . . . I should like very much to have Reichenbach's name connected with these applications and think it would please him." It did not please the chemist enough. Three years later, a second New Year's drama would lead to an irreconcilable Eastman–Reichenbach split.[25]

On 27 August 1889 the first roll of nitrocellulose film went on sale. Within months, it was difficult to meet the demand. While defects would not be eliminated for many years, Eastman was proved right that it was film that amateurs would constantly need to replenish once they became infatuated with photography. Fully controlling the market for film meant controlling the market through patents. So anxious was he to achieve this that in playing all the angles, Eastman's patent, filed for in April 1889, was found to interfere with Reichenbach's as well as with Hannibal Goodwin's application. The difference in reactions is noteworthy: Goodwin, upon being advised by the examiner that part of his claim might be patentable if amended, did nothing. Eastman immediately dropped some of his own claims and removed some of Reichenbach's that might be subsumed under Goodwin's. The result was that Goodwin's application was denied as too general while Reichenbach's, which contained specific proportions of nitrocellulose, camphor, and solvents, was issued on 10 December 1889. Two additional film patents were granted to Eastman and Reichenbach in 1892.

Nine years after George Eastman introduced his box camera and the hullabaloo that followed, photographer Alfred Stieglitz made a statement that on the face of it is remarkable for its obtuseness. "Photography as a fad is well nigh on its last legs, thanks principally to the bicycle craze," said Stieglitz, the father of modern photography as an art form, while casting his eye on the inventions of Eastman, the father of modern photography as a cultural and consumer phenomenon. Amateur photography may have passed through its fad phase, but was not to fade away into the oblivion of passing fancies. Thanks to the Kodak camera, by 1897 photography was firmly fixed in popular culture, an event foreseen by the *Chicago Tribune* in 1891: "The craze is spreading fearfully. Chicago has had many fads whose careers have been brilliant but brief. But when amateur photography came, it came to stay."[26] Calling the spread of photography a craze is not an overstatement. Overnight, the complex, expensive task had been simplified, made convenient and enjoyable, and put into the hands of anyone who could spare $25. Eastman had changed his corner of the world. The art of photography was democratized and the camera became a tool—a recording tool, a voyeuristic tool, a tool of power—now that "the mirror with a memory" was accessible to everyone. The recorders of social phenomena spread the fad. "Beware the Kodak," cautioned the *Hartford Courant*. "The sedate citizen can't indulge in any hilariousness without incurring the risk of being caught in the act and having his photograph passed around among his Sunday School children." One resort posted the notice, "PEOPLE ARE FORBIDDEN TO USE THEIR KODAKS ON THE BEACH."

Amateurs seemed to have "an inexhaustible fund of original ideas in posing," the *Tribune* observed, citing "Mrs. Dr. Shears" who took "interior views of an unusual nature: In order to assist her husband in surgical work she photographs tumors, cancers, and other cheerful things of like character. She has 'taken' a man before, during, and after an epileptic fit."[27] That such uses of the Kodak might lead to medical photography was not apparent to journalists in 1891, who saw them only as grotesque and comic tales. The San Francisco story that "amateurs are running through Chinatown photographing opium dens" may today be seen as archetypal photojournalism. The word from Buffalo that "a dentist hides his Kodak under a cloth and takes pictures of patients at their worst" foreshadows one of the primary uses of x-ray film.

Eastman's product knew no national boundaries. President Grover Cleveland owned one, although in his case the Kodak was not quite simple enough. The president took one along on a hunting trip and although he dutifully pressed the button one hundred times, he never turned the key to advance the film. And when the Dalai Lama came down from his isolated Tibetan capital for the first time, he brought with him his Kodak camera.[28]

The Kodak and Eastman's slogan became catchphrases and supplied the punch lines of many a lame joke. A popular song of 1891, "You Press the Button, We Do the Rest," used the Kodak as the emblem of rapid invention and progress. Jokey doggerel filled the popular press and versifying comedians must have looked on the Kodak as manna from humor heaven. Eastman in London hastened to see his Kodak stand on the very pinnacle of popular culture thanks to Gilbert and Sullivan, who gave the camera a firmer grasp on immortality by including it and Eastman's slogan in their operetta, *Utopia*:

> Then all the crowd take down our looks
> In pocket memorandum books.
> To diagnose
> Our modest pose
> The Kodaks do their best:
> If evidence you would possess
> Of what is maiden bashfulness
> You only need a button press—
> And *we* do the rest!

Eastman capitalized on the craze by introducing the Kodak Girl, a wholesome outdoor type who would advertise his products for the next century.

Friends sent him their souvenirs of daily life, providing thumbnail sketches of the impact of the Kodak system on American and even world culture. He gave a Kodak camera to Ed Hickey, a friend who had moved to Pennsylvania, and in thanking Eastman, Hickey included some circular cyanotypes of his toddlers. His postscript illustrates how important Eastman's "exceedingly ingenious" system would become to ordinary families as they found a way to commemorate the passage of their lives: "I look at those pictures of my family every day and they will be more and more valuable to me as the children grow older and I can see them again as babies. Do you imagine that anybody could take them away from me at any price? Of course they can only be of passing interest to others. Show the enclosed to Mrs. Eastman and ask if she does not wish there had been Kodaks when her children were babies."[29]

There was a downside to the wide use of the term "Kodak." The public was so smitten with Eastman's little camera that manufacturers saw their chance for a free publicity ride. Candy makers turned out "Kodak Bon-Bons" until they were stopped by injunction. The letter "K" turned up everywhere—in King Kodak, Kodak Komics, the Kodak Kid (Eastman), new Kodaks for Kristmas, or even Kolumbus Day. Some of these were Eastman advertising gimmicks, but they were so emulated that Eastman's attorneys were kept busy. Book titles and characters exploited the craze. *Captain Kodak: A Camera Story* by Alexander Black was a popular novel for young adults published in 1898. By 1912 banks were distributing "Kodisks" or "snapshots in sound," and stores and photo finishers were displaying the Kodak name in such a way that it appeared they were branches of the company. By 1915 there was a phony Kodak Company in Florida. At first Eastman was pleased that he had "made a new word to express the whole thing" and that he could "eliminate the word camera." But he had seen the Celluloid Company lose its trademark as the word "celluloid" passed into generic use and came to mean at first any thermoplastic, then to stand for the film used in shooting motion pictures, and finally to evolve into a sobriquet for motion pictures themselves. Even within Eastman's lifetime, efforts were made to protect that valuable asset, the word "Kodak" as a trademark. The Eastman Kodak Company of the late twentieth century carefully insists upon the usage "Kodak camera" or "Kodak film" and never "the Kodak" or "kodak as you go." However "kodak" as a verb—as Strong and other early aficionados used it— is still listed in *Webster's Third New International Dictionary*.

Ten years of continuous innovation, sometimes radical, sometimes gradual, was drawing to a close. Order and simplification were coming to the world of photography. The stage was set to bring it to the masses. What once had been the province of artists and scientists would become a gigantic business based on the heady proposition that everyman could become a photographer.

England and America

The foreign trade will "distribute our eggs and pad the basket at the same time," Eastman had told William Hall Walker upon sending him to London in 1885. With the introduction of the Kodak system, advertising, sales, and profits increased as dramatically abroad as they had in the United States but the latter two leveled off when overloaded Rochester facilities could not keep up with the demand. Walker complained that the European business was suffering because shipments from Rochester were late. Emulsions spoiled during transatlantic trips. New factories and more capital were clearly needed. In early 1889 the board of directors considered whether to sell the foreign branch or develop it as a manufacturing and marketing center. Eastman favored the establishment of an independent company and directed Walker to set it up. For manufacturing "we ought to have 10 acres of meadow land where there is no dust, no smoke, good water, good drainage and easy access to Oxford Street. . . . We will have to hump ourselves to get a factory started in nine or ten months." He instructed Walker to "interest only first class people" as directors, employees, and stockholders. "No shysters."[1]

From the start Walker and Eastman were on divergent paths. First, Walker claimed that his contract did not include making financial deals and would need to be rewritten so that he was paid more for this additional service. No, the boss decreed. Strong and I will raise the money and you will just buy the property and organize the plant, both of which are covered in your present contract. Second, Eastman's philosophy was always to plow profits back into the business. Walker wanted the "stock listed on the exchange and then we

can easily boom it and sell out our shares at a premium when it is hot."
Eastman took strong exception to such a plan. Third, Walker's British contacts were with photographers rather than businessmen and the board he
eventually lined up included men Eastman would consider either incompe-
tent or "shysters." Indeed, Eastman had prejudices about Englishmen in
general. "You, in England, are too cautious and afraid of making mistakes.
We in the States make our mistakes and straighten them out before you even
begin to make them," he told an English chemist, but admitted that "the
English do sometimes get there with both their big feet."[2]

In July 1889 Eastman, Strong, and Fred Church steamed for England to
apply for film patents and to investigate expanding and incorporating the
English subsidiary. Also on the passenger list of the liner *Paris* were the
names of Mrs. Strong, Mrs. Eastman, and a Mrs. Dickman. It was Maria
Eastman's first and only trip to Europe. This may have been when Eastman
met George and Josephine Dickman, the beginning of a long business association and a deep friendship for Eastman. They were present at a dinner
given by the Walkers, and after this visit, Eastman's letters to Walker often
end, "Give my love to Mrs. Walker and Mrs. Dickman."

Quiet and self-effacing, George Dickman was a member of the Society of
Friends (Quakers); but he was also fun-loving and sophisticated—a kind of
transatlantic citizen who felt equally at home in England or in his native
America. The son of a sea captain, Dickman had learned the intricacies of
machinery during hours spent in engine rooms of wave-tossed ships. He had
started a business in Japan, but later returned to London and in 1889 was
manager of the Mabey Todd Company, an American firm that sold gold
pens and other devices. "Dickman and wife have just come in smiling and
hearty as ever," Walker commented once, realizing that Dickman's personality eclipsed his own. "I wish I had his *smile*."[3]

Josephine Haskins Dickman, also an American, had a trained voice and
sang for the assembled company that evening at the Walkers' home. Mrs.
Dickman and Maria got along splendidly from the start. Spirited, intelligent,
gracious, and talkative, Josephine Dickman would accompany George Eastman on later shopping trips to select gloves and hats, china and silver, or
pieces of jewelry for him to take home to his mother. ("Mrs. D. thinks you are
too loved to live," he told Maria.[4]) From 10 July to 12 September 1889
Eastman conducted his business in London and Paris, then spent his weekends escorting his mother to galleries, museums, and theaters. During the
week, Josephine Dickman or her "duenna" (hired companion) stepped in to
accompany the sixty-eight-year-old Maria. How Maria felt about it all is not
recorded except by her son, for whom it was the culmination of a dream.
"The trip did Mother a world of good," he told Walker with satisfaction. "She
has not been so well in fifteen years."[5]

In September 1889 Eastman and his mother returned to Rochester, leaving Strong to complete the deal with Mr. Ogle, the promoter Walker had hired. But Ogle was apparently a "shyster" and Strong had a lapse. On 21 October Eastman wrote with fervor to "Dear Old Crazy Loon," who had offered to guarantee the new stock in such a way as to potentially bankrupt Eastman and Strong. "If you are such a g____d d____d fool as to mortgage this Co in the above manner you ought to have a commission in lunacy appointed," Eastman wrote at the height of his agitation. "For gods sake come home before you give your business and my business and the business of the Eastman Dry Plate & Film Co. away." As a postscript, he instructed Strong to "Drop Ogle—he is too sharp."[6]

By November Strong had switched promoters (to H. W. Bellsmith) and closed the deal. The question of a name for the new company was still to be settled; Eastman suggested "The Anglo Eastman Company" or "The East-man Company in Europe," cautioning Strong not to use "The Eastman Company" as that was reserved for the American company Eastman was in the process of reincorporating. Late one night in a more mellow mood, Eastman wrote that "All hands have been made happy by your telegram that Bellsmith's Scheme No. 1 has been virtually closed. . . . You will be backed up in anything you have done short of a guarantee on the Dividends. . . . It has just occurred to me that it would be a good thing to call the English Co 'The Eastman–Walker Company.' That would probably be a name that would not damage the advertising—and it would be a deserved compliment to Walk-er."[7] "The Eastman–Walker Company" was never used, and, as subsequent events would prove, this was a good thing for Eastman. Instead the Eastman Photographic Materials Company, Ltd. was capitalized in November 1889 for £150,000 ($750,000), incorporated to take over the business and good-will of the Rochester company in London, Paris, Berlin, Milan, St. Pe-tersburg, Melbourne, Sydney, Shanghai, Canton, Constantinople, Japan, "and all other countries outside the Western Hemisphere." Five English directors—Colonel James T. Griffin, chairman; Colonel J. Noel Allix, George Davison, Andrew Pringle, and H. W. Bellsmith—joined Eastman and Walker to comprise the board.

On the other side of the Atlantic, Eastman drew up several plans for reorganizing the parent company. One that increased both working capital for buildings and machinery and the shareholders' dividends was adopted. In November 1889 Eastman and Strong, with directors John H. Kent, Edwin O. Sage, Brackett H. Clark, and William R. Seward (representing Walker), applied for incorporation of The Eastman Company ("Dry Plate and Film" being dropped from the corporate name). Strong was elected president; Kent, vice president; Clark, secretary; and Eastman, treasurer. The compa-ny owned the State Street office and factory and leased the Court Street factory from Strong. Authorized capital was $1 million. Ten thousand shares were issued at $100 par and distributed on the basis of $3\frac{1}{3}$ shares for each share held. Fifty shares were given to Reichenbach for agreeing to give the company all of his photographic inventions while employed by Eastman. Eastman's salary for 1890 was set at $7,500. The Rochester company retained 78 percent of the stock of its foreign subsidiary.[8] By handling much of the paper work connected with both capitalizations, Eastman was learning empirically about corporate financing as a decade earlier he had learned about the chemistry of photography through reading and cooking. On 22 February 1890 Eastman and Church embarked to England again to find that Walker, now threatening to retire, had done nothing about setting up a London plant. Eastman urged Walker to take a vacation but not to quit until a replacement was found. Against a background of escalating tension, Eastman looked at available sites himself and purchased one just outside London in the borough of Harrow. He spent the next month with architects, engineers, and contractors before leaving for Paris with Church and Thacher Clarke.

The relationship between Eastman and his London manager continued to be a complex and often vexing one. Eastman thought enough of Walker to put him in charge of the entire company outside of the Western Hemisphere. But it gradually became clear that Walker's talents were primarily in the laboratory; he was inept at day-to-day business details. For a time Walker's removal to England smoothed the relationship. The Walkers bought a home in Maresfield Garden, Hampstead, and lived in a style to which they rapidly became accustomed. Eastman and Walker exchanged cabinet portraits of each other. Eastman was forever sending Carrie Walker a flour sifter, or maple syrup, or her silver, or other American trifles she bemoaned doing without.

At first Eastman handled his dyspeptic partner with kid gloves, writing of the "liability of misunderstanding when conducting transactions at long range." He deferred on occasion to Walker's judgment. The squabbles developed in the areas of management skills, collections on outstanding stock, Walker's overreliance on his board of directors for decisions Eastman thought the manager should make himself, Walker's general pessimism, and Walker's lack of confidence in the company's future. Eastman expected the London branch to provide a continuing source of capital for the whole company: "Money is as scarce as hens' teeth here. Send the proceeds of your sales to help pay the December dividend." In spite of these urgings, Walker neglected billings. Relentlessly, Eastman kept it upbeat, trying to boost his gloom-beset partner. Noting problems developing with the English board, Eastman gingerly urged Walker to replace Colonel J. Noel Allix with "somebody who has more business experience such as George Dickman. I believe it will be a good thing for Dickman and an agreeable change for you. If not, you are not obliged to follow this suggestion."[9]

"I can truly say I should prefer Mr. Dickman," Walker replied. But Walk-

er, while complaining that "the entire board are deadheads," lacked Eastman's gumption in effecting the swift hiring and firing of board members
and subordinates. "Allix . . . if ousted would naturally feel affronted and
attempt to retaliate," he vacillated, and "Dr. Pritchard has the largest individual interest in this company & he has twice asked me to get him on the Board
if a vacancy should occur and this I have promised to do. . . . Above all we
must be *politic* and not excite hostile criticism and breed suspicions." So
nothing was done to change the composition of the board.[10]

The delay in getting the Harrow factory running, Eastman lamented,
meant that "tourists are in despair and supplying themselves with dry plate
cameras." From his personal account and at 6 percent interest, Eastman
loaned the English company $20,000 to get itself on its feet. Finally, two
buildings and a power house for the seven-acre site were begun in 1890 and
completed early in 1891. Yet halfway through the project, Walker developed
cold feet again and in December 1890 an annoyed Eastman wrote sarcastically, "If you have any doubt about the practicality of an English factory
it is rather late to find out now." The Harrow factory went on to completion,
with J. B. B Wellington named manager and F. W. T. Krohn hired as chemist.
By October 1891 no more shipments of film to England were needed.

But the internecine squabbles continued to volley back and forth across
the Atlantic. In his letters, Walker was forever carping about how Rochester
got all the best new equipment and Harrow only a second-hand sausage
machine for breaking up the emulsion. Employees were a perennial problem
and getting them to follow Walker's direction was "like pushing a wet rope."
With each complaint came the threat to retire. "You ought to have somebody
in training if you want to get out," Eastman warned, then suggested Dickman
as available and qualified.[11]

George Dickman, having joined the company in March 1892 and risen
quickly to senior staff member, was also well on his way to becoming Eastman's favorite subordinate. The period was a difficult one on both sides of
the Atlantic; the English company was barely running on a bank overdraft.
Although the Oxford Street headquarters had expanded to include No. 117,
the Harrow factory was mired in production difficulties. Complaints of
desensitized film led to the recall of thousands of spools and financial losses.
In France, Paul Nadar, Eastman's agent in Paris since 1886, sued the company for breach of contract. Eastman appointed George W. de Bedts to take
over the Paris branch. The financial situation was worsened by some shareholders' nonpayment for 1891 shares and compounded by Walker's inertia
in calling in those payments.

Walker led Eastman to believe the German company was underway; when
Eastman discovered to the contrary, sparks flew. Once again Walker ten-
dered his resignation and this time Eastman called his bluff and accepted it.
Dickman was sent from Harrow to London to take over for Walker begin-

ning January 1893. Walker, however, remained the third largest stockholder of the Eastman Kodak Company and a member of the English board. Eastman asked him to remain as consultant to start companies in France and Germany, beginning with a stop in Berlin for negotiations on his way back from his Italian holiday. "I infer from what you say," Walker sniffed, "that you propose to thrust the burden of this whole German matter on me." A party was held for Mr. and Mrs. Walker. Special trains carrying employees from Harrow, representatives from Paris and Nice, the successor Dickman and his wife, and the Oxford Street staff all converged upon Bloomsbury Hall to present Walker with a solid silver salver. Scanning the account of the festivities in the London company's *Social Notes*, Eastman underlined the last words of "It was stated that Mr. Walker would remain on the Eastman board, and would continue to devote himself *to certain departments of film construction.*" and queried Dickman: "What does *that* mean?"[12] It meant, of course, that Walker had no intention of ever retiring from his laboratory.

To shoulder the burden of dumping Walker and passing the dividend in England while still paying for a new Solio paper building and retaining enough money in case the Nadar suit went against the company, Eastman dispatched company president Henry Strong to London. "I shall not kick as long as you get rid of Walker," was Eastman's parting message. In these days when he was being stripped of power, Walker was behaving erratically both in his letters to Eastman and at the directors' session in London. Strong's heart was no more in this London business than it was in running the emulsion department or fending off creditors and employees in Rochester—tasks Eastman assigned him when he was out of town. Personal relations *was* Strong's forte, however. Soon he even had Walker and Dickman dining together.[13]

In spite of his perhaps misplaced sympathy for Walker, Strong agreed that business reasons did dictate his replacement by Dickman. Mission accomplished, Strong went off to play in Europe. With Strong gallivanting, Eastman turned his attention to grooming his new joint managing director, peppering Dickman with a crash course in the Eastman way of doing business. "The failure to market ABC Kodaks in Europe is a gross mistake," he admonished. "Walker takes the advice of men who have no commercial instinct. He has allowed his men to lie down upon the goods. . . . You have been living in the Walker, Pringle, and Davison atmosphere all the time that you have been in photography and I want you to be put on guard against their impractical ideas. . . . You have got to sell the goods!" As more advice flowed from his pen, the Eastman college of business knowledge expanded in curriculum: "I am a believer in one man management and that a Board of Directors is valuable only as an advisory instrument to a good manager. I would strongly advise you to adopt the same course. . . . Call on your Board for advice only as to general policy and never as to details. . . . I have confidence in you and will back you, mistakes or no mistakes, until you have had a fair chance to show what you can do." Eastman reposed a great deal of trust in Dickman, and he would prove worthy of it. But he also allowed Dickman a peek behind the arras, a glance at his own perception of Strong: "I hope you will be able to keep [Strong] out of an insane asylum. I do not want to break him down like [competitor] Richard Anthony."[14]

Eastman was able to take in stride passing difficulties arising from expansion and the seemingly endless train of lawsuits that followed in the wake of his company's progress. Strong could not. He worried about handling disappointed investors who failed to receive dividends, he was driven practically to distraction when Paul Nadar's suit against the company netted the Frenchman £2000,[15] and even though Walker was on his way out the door, he caused Strong some grief. Walker was continuing to experiment with film, and Strong worried that he might "succeed and makes a new film! Where are we at? . . . It will be well to be on the safe side for there is no knowing where lightning will strike next. Why not personally invite Walker to come over? Consider carefully and show your diplomacy." By this time Eastman was fed up with Walker and could see no need for diplomacy: "I cherish the hope that I may never see him again," he fumed at Strong. To Walker himself, Eastman sent a cold, impersonal letter of rejection from the treasurer of the Eastman Kodak Company. When Walker howled at this treatment, Eastman sent a more personal note, which included both a complaint that Walker had been making company life miserable for many years by his erratic business methods and a small gesture of reconciliation that since they were now disassociated as business partners, "I shall be only too happy to meet you on the most friendly terms." Eventually Eastman and Walker were able to correspond in a friendly, if wary, manner once they no longer had anything of a business nature to bring them to loggerheads.[16]

The problems did not evaporate when Dickman picked up the reins; indeed, in July 1894 Dickman tendered his resignation, which Eastman refused to accept. The Paris store was losing money. George W. de Bedts wanted to start a separate French company making paper, plates, and film supported by a "few great rich capitalists," yet had no contacts in mind. Then Dickman discovered that de Bedts had his hand in the till and had to fire him. Everyone agonized because de Bedts was "personally, a capital fellow," not to mention a handy one—he was Eastman's contact for exquisite French wine and had been combing Brussels for a good cook for the Eastman household.[17] In August Eastman crossed the Pond to straighten things out by obtaining a raise for Dickman and Walker's resignation from the board.

Dickman inherited problems with Wellington and Krohn, both of whom Walker had once labeled "traitors." Walker later admitted that "the comments I once made concerning Wellington are not strictly true. . . . They were made during the building of the factory and I was vexed and angered beyond endurance." Although Dickman was able to persuade Krohn to stay, Wellington went on to found his own company. Immediately after Wellington's departure, Dickman took over the management of the Harrow works himself in addition to his London duties as managing director. Eastman then worried that Dickman was spreading himself too thin. Finally, Harold Senier took over Harrow; though American-born, he had worked in London as a pharmaceutical chemist for some twenty years and eventually became an excellent emulsion maker. Together Dickman and Senier founded the Kodak Recreation Society that provided entertainments, dances, and "smoking concerts" for employees in local halls and hotels. The bills Eastman was glad to foot. Dickman's morale-building innovations for British employees began the extensive recreational and social programs for which the American company would become famous. Dickman brought a knowledge of English law, customs, and business that the English company lacked previously. Along with Thacher Clarke, Dickman added a certain flair and sophistication to the English company. Because he was so capable, conscientious, and uncomplaining, Eastman worked him to the bone.

The Dickmans functioned as personal purchasing agents for Eastman, sending knickknacks for his house and gloves for his mother through George Mabie, "my old employer in gold pens," and international stamps for Royal Andrus's collection.[18] Dickman was free enough with his employer to affect the British public school manner of referring to him as "Eastman" in direct address. Dickman's brand of easy-going charm and self-mocking, expansive humor was replacing Walker's pessimism, as he welcomed Eastman and some companions to "the Mother country . . . from which land thy Ancestors strayed, and their children returneth. Our modern Prodigal [Eastman] returneth not as in days of yore, with empty wallet . . . rather cometh . . . with jeans replete with plunks. . . . Strain thy eyes as thou approacheth the shore of Liverpuddledum and thou shalt behold the beaming face of thy well wisher and friend."[19]

Perhaps the greatest of Dickman's accomplishments was that suddenly the English company began to pay its own way, including installments on a long-standing loan from the American company: "If I were subject to heart disease your cable . . . might have been attended with fatal results," Eastman wrote. "To have two thousand pounds dumped in upon us while we thought you were still suffering for money was a great surprise. . . . The money will come in very handy. I am anxious to know how you got it."[20]

The British factory at Harrow was under way, but Eastman's Rochester facilities were proving more and more inadequate. There was room for but one creaky and overworked coating machine at State Street, and it produced all the stripping film and bromide paper for sale in America. Glass plates and the new transparent film came out of the leased Court Street building down-town. It was difficult to keep up the standards of cleanliness needed for film production in this ancient edifice—it seemed to leak dust itself besides doing little to keep out the dirt from the crowded streets. Fire was always a threat—Eastman put one out himself in the "skin room" with the help of a "daisy" of a Babcock extinguisher that he had acquired by swapping a Kodak. And there was no room for expansion downtown.

Eastman once again turned his thoughts to the farmland along Charlotte Boulevard in the town of Greece, a rural community between the city and Lake Ontario located three miles north of the Eastman offices in downtown. There was no grit in the air, drilling wells could produce an independent water supply, and there was room for a reservoir. The Genesee River was nearby for dumping waste and carrying it, out of sight, out of mind, north to the lake. In June 1890 Eastman dispatched Brackett Clark, director and major stockholder, to investigate three parcels of land in the area. The largest, a little over ten acres with a 500-foot frontage on Charlotte Boulevard and a depth of 1,000 feet, was selling for $15,000. The second, an adjoining 2.5 acres with a 150-foot frontage on the boulevard, would cost $6,000; the third, 2 acres for $1,800, "gives us an outlet toward the railroad and has an elegant sand bank for mortar."[21]

The photographic materials industry was still suspect in many quarters, especially in conservative Rochester. But Clark was a barrel manufacturer, and had no trouble obtaining a sixty-day option on the three parcels with the implication that he would build a barrel stave factory. When a source of water was found at a depth of 118 feet, the deal was clinched. Thus was thwarted the city fathers' plan for a grand boulevard leading to the lake, lined with high-tone residences. Once Eastman's factory was built, Charlotte Boulevard (soon to be called Lake Avenue) would become a wide thoroughfare with churches, automobile dealerships, apartment buildings, movie houses, and only a scattering of the palatial homes originally envisioned. Rochester's mansions, and its version of a silk-stocking district, would be built along East Avenue, surrounding the home of Kodak's founder, in the southeast quad-rant of the city.

On 1 October 1890 ground was broken for the first three buildings: a power plant, a film factory, and a testing laboratory. The film factory had electric lights and motors, and the emulsion room was air-conditioned by means of a fifty-ton ice machine. The plant was insured for $250,000 (with the value of the stone foundations estimated at $20,000). Six months after completion, in June 1891, plans to double the capacity of the plant were in the offing. The new factory was carefully landscaped, with "brick pavements around the emulsion house and boiler house," lined, within a few years, with gardens. William ("Billy") Waltjen, a Netherlands-born gardener, tended them and sent fresh flowers to the boss's office each morning. Plantings were supervised by Darragh de Lancey, mechanical engineer, and the versatile Eliza Tompkins, whose weighing and measuring functions were transferred to the boulevard plant. Not surprisingly, Eastman took an interest in things horticultural. "Here is some seed," he wrote Tompkins. "Please get your florist assistant to plant it this fall in a box so that we can transplant it in the spring."[22] Surveying the finished factory and environs, the boss saw that it was good: "It looks very neat and clean. The buildings sit in the center of a field of grass of about 14 acres."[23] By 1895 there were flower beds and shrub borders too, designed by Samuel Parsons, the supervisor of Central Park, New York City. Even earlier, the boulevard plant was being called Kodak Park—one of the first such industrial "parks." To staff the new plant, Eastman recruited young men who seemed in most ways to be mirror images of his younger self when he started out in Maria's kitchen. Chemist Henry Reichenbach, of course, was the most crucially important employee. Like Eastman, he had an "infinite capacity for taking pains," but at the same time he also possessed a boldness that made him unafraid of making mistakes. This latter trait would eventually develop into a maverick streak, but for now Eastman rewarded his services by naming him the manager of the new plant in addition to being chief emulsion maker. Reichenbach's brother Homer was brought on board as well, and employees of the time remember the high spirits the brothers brought to their daily tasks. Eastman hired an analytical chemist, S. Carl Passavant ("an excitable little chap"), to assist Reichenbach, take charge of the manufacture of transparent film, and oversee the operation at Court Street until that was transferred to the new plant.[24]

"My experience with Tech men began in 1890," Eastman would recall in a rare radio speech he gave in the 1920s to assembled alumni of the Massachusetts Institute of Technology. It marked "the beginning of the transition from empirical to scientific methods in the photographic business," and the young man who made the difference was Darragh de Lancey, whom MIT made an engineer and Eastman an instant expert in ivy and manure. His "veins were full of red blood and by the way he had red hair. He made good and soon rose to be manager of the plant." A native of East Orange, New Jersey, de Lancey was not yet twenty when he graduated from MIT in June; he went to work for Eastman a month later. (As he had done with the University of Rochester earlier, and thereby discovered Reichenbach, Eastman had contacted MIT, hoping the institution could find him a specialist.) Reichenbach and de Lancey after him represented the new wave of academically and theoretically trained scientists entering Eastman's employ. Historically, the period of individualist inventors was passing and the era of scientifically trained researchers working in large institutions was beginning. Eastman must have assumed that he had his heirs apparent in place. It was not to be. A second generation of heirs—Stuber and Lovejoy—would come on board before Eastman could realize the institutionalization of his initial functions, a goal that was formulated in part as response to his growing need to take long vacations from the business. ("When I am away the business always seems to increase and the boys usually manage to bust the record," he rationalized.[25])

Now that Eastman had decided to produce sensitive materials in England as well as America, the first project he assigned de Lancey was to design and build the machinery for making and coating film for the new Harrow plant. Such secrecy was called for that for eight months the area where the machines were under construction was identified only by a sign that read "Darragh de Lancey, Mechanical Engineer."

Reichenbach and de Lancey were the bright young men, well educated and with a theoretical bent, but for cameras, Eastman relied on a genius-tinkerer and perfectionist like himself, a man from his own generation, Frank Brownell. From roll-holder days he had engaged Brownell for wood-working and assembly of apparatus. In 1876 Brownell emigrated from Canada, his millwright father believing that the "Flour City" of Rochester afforded greater opportunities for his trade. Five years Eastman's junior, Brownell had the same inventive turn of mind. Experimenting at home and apprenticing with Yawman & Erbe, Brownell made a plate camera that was accepted by the Union View Camera company. This gave him the confidence to open a shop on State Street in 1883, thereby coming to the notice of George Eastman. Before signing his exclusive contract with Eastman, Brownell manufactured a large variety of studio and professional cameras. By the 1890s the Brownell Manufacturing Company was well on its way to becoming the largest volume producer of cameras in the world. Eastman had designed the original Kodak camera and left it to Brownell to manufacture the wooden parts and trundle them in a pushcart to Yawman & Erbe for shutters and assembly; but beginning with the first Folding Kodak camera of 1889, Brownell did much of the designing. (Eastman called his folding camera the "Collapsing Kodak" until persuaded that the name was ill-chosen.)[26]

Convinced that constant improvement of product was the way to stay on top of the heap, in 1890 Eastman introduced four new models of the Kodak camera—now taking rectangular pictures instead of round ones and selling for between $40 and $50 dollars—and three models of the Folding Kodak camera with bellows, taking four- by five-inch or five- by seven-inch pictures. Limitations on film production dictated the number of cameras made as Eastman wanted no dissatisfied customers growling for film. Late the next year the company marketed a daylight-loading cartridge and cartridge camera developed by Brownell.[27] By 1891 Eastman was pushing "CHEAP KODAKS FOR THE CHRISTMAS TRADE: Our tocsin for Christmas will be, 'Kodaks at any price, $5 to $50.'" This was his first dip into a really affordable camera.

Yet the A Ordinary Kodak camera (priced at $6) didn't sell, perhaps because of its naked wood box. Later low-priced models would be the Pocket Kodak of 1895 for $5 and the Bullet camera for $8, leading to the ultimate in inexpensive cameras, the Brownie of 1900. From 1885 to October 1902 all cameras, in excess of sixty models and related apparatus marketed under the Eastman or Kodak label, were manufactured by the Brownell Company. During that seventeen-year period, Brownell himself designed and patented many of the models. These included such cameras as the Genesee View, Eastman Detective, Folding Kodak, Ordinary Kodak, Daylight Kodak, Pocket Kodak, Bullet, Falcon, Eureka, Panoram, Flexo, Stereo Kodak, Cartridge Kodak, Folding Pocket Kodak, and the Brownie.

Eastman was beginning to put trained personnel in place to take over the technical tasks that had once been his sole responsibility. But he continued to keep a hand in the business. Although Eastman liked to call himself a "pessimist," and indeed his customary greeting to associates was, "Tell me the worst you know," he seemed really to welcome technical problems and to relish opportunities for problem solving. The new transparent film, for example, had a tendency to curl. This could be alleviated, Eastman found in 1890, by double coating the film with gelatin, a thin coat on the emulsion side, thicker on the back. Although he encountered many manufacturing difficulties, he kept at it, and in 1904 a noncurling film was finally marketed.

He liked to have a colleague such as Strong or Walker far from Rochester so he could organize his technical thoughts in weekly letters. (Later this role would be assumed by George Dickman, then Charles Abbott, George Davison, William S. Gifford, Frank C. Mattison, and Charles Case—successively the English managers—as well as Thomas Baker and then J. J. Rouse in Australia.) These long, interpolated memos essentially to himself provide a fascinating glimpse of Eastman talking aloud, letting his mind have free play. Here he is on a tangent in a letter to Walker, mulling over the problem of static discharges from film in cold weather. Walker had asked him how he "struck the Nitrate of Ammonium" as a solution. "Purely a matter of deduction," writes Eastman, affecting a Holmesian manner, and then he is off:

> One day, reflecting upon the theory that the discharge was caused by two surfaces, one of which was positive and the other negative, it occurred to me that if one of the surfaces was metallic there could be no generation. The idea of making one of the surfaces metallic naturally followed. A little further reflection, however, staggered me, because it seemed that the emulsion must be metallic, but I knew that it would spark as badly almost as any dope. I finally decided that every metallic particle in the emulsion must be insulated by the surrounding gelatine.[28]

His theorizing led to directions for Reichenbach, which in turn led to "a perfect cure." The final result was triumphantly pragmatic: "It will be worth big money to us because we can get a good patent on it and prevent other manufacturers from using it in any kind of celluloid film."[29]

"You will not recognize our new office," Eastman told Strong. "The President will have to wear a plug hat and fop coat after this if he is going to hang around the State Street building."[30] Eastman's office was on the second floor, allowing him to bound up the stairs two at a time to take on his myriad tasks (among them being his first outside directorship, in 1890, of the Flour City National Bank). He had by this time gathered about him an office staff that regardless of various upsets over the years served him faithfully and well. From these staffers we have virtually the only available personal glimpses of Eastman as he entered his late thirties. He was by this time firmly wedded to the company, and few outsiders had impressions of him that could be called intimate.

Eastman once said: "Tom Craig occupies a unique position in the Eastman Company." Craig's latter-day title as head of ciné processing and repair was something of a blind. His real function could be defined as George Eastman's man: trouble shooter, ambassador, persuader, liaison officer, and, in his older years, zealous guardian of the Eastman cult. Not that the latter prevented Craig from recognizing his employer's faults. Craig knew that Eastman was not always liked by the employees, particularly in later years when he was, to most of them, merely "Mr. Eastman," and their personal contacts with him were limited to chance meetings. Eastman's lack of warmth in responding to their respectful "Good Mornings" was accepted as the prerogative of the man in charge. Eastman's power of concentration was so overwhelming that nothing penetrated the fog. Often he would not realize anyone was in his vicinity; upon being greeted, he would start out of a brown study, gaping in amazement to find that there were people there. Yet he was sensitive enough to be hurt if anyone else adopted the cold treatment he himself dispensed. Eastman's most glaring fault stemmed entirely, Craig thought, from the man's painful shyness. In the early days, Eastman tried to socialize with his employees. He would attempt a jaunty and friendly air at the annual company picnic to little success. Finally, he gave up attending such affairs, thinking that in spite of his efforts, his frosty and awkward exterior just spoiled everyone else's fun.

Craig was a young man when he joined Kodak in 1895. As errand boy extraordinaire, he trudged through the plant and about Rochester with the good grace only a fledgling can muster. Eastman was in Europe when Craig was hired, and his youthful imagination pictured a venerable ogre. Besides, he had all he could do to cope with that hot-tempered, jovial, "handsome old goat," Henry Strong. When Eastman returned, the day Craig had been dreading arrived. A telegram came for "GE" and Craig was told to deliver it.

The young man he saw sitting in the boss's office could not be Eastman, he decided. "Are you Mr. Eastman?" Craig asked. "Yes," came the terse reply. Pop-eyed, Craig dropped the telegram on the desk and fled. After that Craig saw a lot of Eastman, who more or less appropriated him as general dogsbody. Henceforth Craig's activities were governed by the omnipresent whistle from Eastman on the speaking tube, the only means of interoffice communication. (The one telephone was for outside calls.) When the whistle tooted, it was often a summons for Craig. "Tommie come up here!" the command sounded, a token of Eastman's oblique humor, as he knew Tom hated the nickname. Yet it was also a sign of affection and esteem. "Why Tommie's one of my best friends," he fairly crowed when introduced to Craig's mother. In spite of his odd manners, Eastman inspired a surprising depth of loyalty in his staff. Working for the man in those days was like a crusade, with Eastman carrying the banner—or so it seemed to Craig. None of his employees could hope to match Eastman's own energy and capacity for work, but his example stirred emulation. They gladly worked overtime, faithful to the employer who often stayed at State Street until 3 A.M.[31]

The venerable Edwin O. Sage, who now ran the company in Strong's and Eastman's absence, was by his own description Eastman's "*demoralizing* Kicking Director." Sage went off to Martha's Vineyard for the summer of 1890 with the exit line, "While you are pressing the button, I am taking a rest." Semiretired from his shoe-manufacturing business, Sage, like Brackett Clark, hung around the office a great deal, looking over Eastman's shoulder, making comments, giving advice, and generally being the company's back seat driver. Sage lamented that "younger men are now coming to the front & we old fellows have to go way back and sit down" but that did not keep him from admonishing or suggesting. Mrs. Sage thought she could take advantage of what she considered her husband's special relationship by secretly asking Eastman to employ their son George, noting that the elder Sage often spoke of the great help he had been in the early days. Eastman demurred, both to hire George and to accept her account of the founding of the company.[32] On the other hand, the venerable George Ellwanger, who became a director in 1890, never seems to have darkened the Kodak Office door although Eastman deferred to him with elaborate respect and relied heavily on his advice about everything from fruit trees to business. During Ellwanger's lingering illness (he died in 1906 in his ninetieth year) the board met often in the patrician's rambling domicile at the center of his world-famous nursery. Sometimes it was the only way to achieve a quorum.

Very few people knew George Eastman in the days when he rode to the office on a high-wheeled bicycle, with his lunch in his hip pocket, the pickle juice leaking through the brown bag. Minnie Hoefler did; she had come to work for his company in 1888. At age fifteen she decided that she wanted a job in industry—a revolutionary thought for a young female of the day. With the grudging consent of her parents, she applied to her cousin, Florence S. Glaser, Eastman's first employee and now a superintendent, who put her to work in the pasting room. For $3 a week (a munificent sum for her sex and era) she glued labels on film boxes from 7 A.M. to 6 P.M., six days a week, with an hour out for lunch. If there was a rush, she worked overtime until 10 P.M. for twenty-five cents extra to pay for her supper. Parental disapproval might have been avoided had Minnie elected to work for one of the old, established firms of the city. But the Eastman company was held in poor repute, not just because of its youth but also because of its nature. Despite the Kodak craze, the average citizen had no confidence in the future of the photographic materials business. Rochesterians who invested in the Eastman company were thought to be giddy speculators who would soon get their comeuppance.

The eight women employed by the company when Minnie began were a congenial, close-knit group who took their work to heart and looked upon the business as their own. "The inspiration for this attitude," a Kodak interviewer wrote in 1950 after talking with an aged Minnie Hoefler Cline, "seems to have been GE himself. There is indication of a personal magnetism and drive that was buried later but which, in the early years, was intense enough to make working for him approximate loyalty to a cause." Partly this was because of Eastman's own unflagging application. Minnie chuckled over the times Eastman would come to the pasting room late at night and awkwardly try to help her glue labels. He was more hindrance than help, Minnie said, and "when it struck him that this was so, he would wander off and visit some other department." Working day and night on the new transparent film, a "nervous, ragged wreck" of a man, Eastman kept everything "very hush-hush—we only knew that no film was being shipped."[33]

Minnie's sister Millie also worked for Eastman and in his absent-minded way, he usually called Minnie Millie. The real Minnie felt that because he knew all of his employees as individuals and was interested in their welfare, the confusion may have been a means of teasing. A kind and thoughtful man, was Minnie's impression of the boss: "He always said goodbye to the employees personally before leaving on a trip, and brought them gifts upon his return." There was no hesitation in approaching him with a question or a grievance. "He heard each employee out—but his answer was final. He directed the business with an iron hand and an eagle eye." Grueling and boring as the work might be, judged by today's standards, conditions were accepted as normal then. Nobody had a vacation or thought of asking for one. When Eastman said "no" to a petition, no one thought of rebelling. The women depended on this one man's authority and abided by his decisions.

He was particularly concerned for Minnie because of her youth, and counseled her not to go to the developing room in the skylighted attic above the fifth floor of the office building where two "hard-bitten" women were employed. She also recalled getting up at 5:30 each morning, trudging over miles of 1888 terrain, her long skirts trailing through mud and snow, so that by the time she reached the office, the bottom of her dress was sopping. She and the other girls would change into calico working dresses and hang their dripping finery in the boiler room to dry. Eastman looked askance at this, telling them how he wished they would not wear cotton dresses "to the office." Almost in one breath, the girls chorused, "If you'd pay us more wages, Mr. Eastman, we could afford better dresses." Without a word, he turned on his heels and left.[34]

In April 1890 Eastman and Fred ("Chappie") Church, patent attorney, returned from England after getting the Harrow plant under way. The business had grown to the point that Eastman was falling behind in his correspondence. No longer was there time enough at night after all the hands had gone home to answer all the letters that came that day. His flowing, barely legible Spencerian script was not up to speed. The very next month a tall, attractive brunette from Kalamazoo visited friends in Rochester. Alice K. Whitney, graduate of the Buffalo Business School, was looking for a job. An Eastman company employee mentioned that the boss needed someone to answer the speaking tube and the correspondence but added the cautionary note that the employer was "a difficult man to work for." She called at the State Street office anyway, noted that Eastman's private speaking tube had a motto posted next to it ("A soft answer turneth away wrath"), and applied for the job. For the next forty-two years she worked for the "difficult man." The job and Eastman absorbed most of her waking hours. She typed his letters, business and personal, surreptitiously corrected his grammar and syntax without destroying his colorful language, and added quaint postscripts of her own.

The hiring provoked some distress among the green-eyed feminine contingent. Anonymous letters to Eastman would complain that he remembered Alice Whitney more generously at Christmas than her counterparts at Kodak Park. She shielded Eastman from unwanted interruptions, advised visitors and employees as to the best times for an audience, and, not surprisingly, gave rise to the speculation that she was in love with her boss. But in the background was a quiet, thirty-year courtship between her and her cousin Charlie Hutchison, who came to work with Kodak in 1894. Many days during those thirty years, Charlie would arrive at the sixteenth floor of Kodak Office to escort Eastman's secretary to lunch. Finally, in 1927, they married. Much gossip focused on this vegetable love. Was she secretly enamored of Eastman? Or did she bow to her employer's prejudice against married women working? Or were the two cousins worried about genetic repercussions in any offspring? Most likely, the timing of their marriage was related to the fact that both lived with and were the sole support of widowed mothers. When the mothers died, the children married.

Eastman and his secretary were very much alike: austere, reserved, almost rigid at times, and so devoted to the work ethic that while each commanded respect neither evoked warm affection in the workplace. They successfully preserved an inner sanctum impervious to speculation. Even after her marriage, Alice Whitney Hutchison never revealed any of Eastman's confidences to her husband. One day, Eastman was heard to exclaim of his secretary: "Next to my mother, she's the angel of my life."[35]

On New Year's Day 1892 George Eastman, standing at his desk in an empty office, wrote identical, brief letters to Henry Reichenbach, his brother Homer, Carl Passavant, and Gus Milburn: "Your services are no longer required by this company." "I recently discovered what might be called a conspiracy on the part of Reichenbach, Passavant, and Milburn to leave the concern and start another company outside," he explained the next day to his New York attorney, Moritz Phillip. "They claimed to my informants that they had the backing of some capitalists here and also of the Celluloid Co. . . . I discharged them all instantly. . . . They were greatly surprised and excited by my sudden action. The question is whether they are in a position to do harm . . . to our patent suits."[36] Reichenbach's defection was a bitter pill. Not only was Eastman genuinely fond of the young man, but he considered the chemist's job as nothing less than "the future of photography." At the time of his dismissal Reichenbach was second in command and heir apparent. Both Milburn, a camera maker and traveling salesman, and Passavant, a chemist, humbly asked that they be allowed to remove personal belongings; Eastman made the necessary arrangements through Darragh de Lancey, the new manager. There were rumors of other defections to come: James B. B. Wellington, the manager of Harrow, had been approached by Reichenbach, Walker reported, so Eastman, looking forward to litigation, asked Wellington for an affidavit of this contact. For a time even chemist Walter Krohn was suspect.[37]

Before leaving, Reichenbach approved forty thousand feet of imperfect film to be sent to dealers, and "the Reichenbach gang" spoiled 1,417 gallons of emulsion. In all, $50,000 worth of materials were ruined and the manufacture of film ground to a halt. Krohn was cleared of suspicion. As reports of sabotage circulated, frightened stockholders began to unload shares in anticipation of the company's collapse. The "conspirators" continued to weave tangled webs even after they had left Eastman's employ. Milburn soon regretted casting his lot with Reichenbach, and tried many times to get back in Eastman's good graces. Yet Eastman never would trust him again, although he did respond to Milburn's requests for loans (and even more pathetic pleas for Eastman's cast-off wardrobe).[38]

Eastman needed a manager to replace Reichenbach, and out of loyalty to his old friend, and also because he plainly liked him, he offered the job to Harris Hayden. Besides acting as Eastman's wholesale wallpaper source and stockbroker, Hayden always had five or six "wildcat enterprises," as Eastman called them, going at once in Manhattan. He turned down Eastman again, and perhaps because Hayden disappointed him at a time when he needed loyal friends, things were never quite the same between the two old friends again. As a result, Eastman made the twenty-one-year-old Darragh de Lancey plant manager. "It was a large order," a reporter would write in 1934, "but the youth's ambition knew no limits to venture or endurance." De Lancey himself would recall that the "work [was] so delicate, so specialized, so new" that he immediately installed a new-fangled gadget, the telephone, by his bed in the boarding house. When frantic calls came from the coating area in the middle of the night, he would stumble to a nearby livery stable, hire a horse and buggy, and drive the three miles to Kodak Park.[39]

De Lancey impressed some co-workers such as Krohn as "very boyish and full of fun"—but a hard worker for all that. Women employees found him to be "a mean son-of-a-gun and high-handed." Others thought he was "hot-tempered but fair." The seeds of de Lancey's eventual breakdown in 1898 were probably sown, said Charlie Hutchison, de Lancey's one-time assistant, when he came to Kodak straight out of MIT and found himself, with insufficient time to grow in the job, as the manager of an establishment that was mushrooming at a frantic rate. De Lancey probably exaggerated but little in claiming to have "laid the foundation of every department" at the park. "Selecting managers and presidents in embryo was a difficult task," he would recall, referring to the pipeline he kept open to MIT over which came Harriet Gallup, chemist, in 1897, Frank Lovejoy as de Lancey's assistant in 1897, and James Haste as manager of the chemical plant in 1897. De Lancey reorganized the laboratory and put Harriet Gallup in charge. "Her successful career was cut short," De Lancey would recall, "by her wise or unwise acceptance of a proposal of marriage from me in 1897."[40]

Meanwhile, the three defectors raised sufficient capital to start the Photo Materials Company and to build a modern factory in Rochester. Reichenbach sold $10,000 in Eastman stock, had $10,000 in cash, and was worth at least that much additionally, Eastman figured. Milburn sold his stock for $12,000 "and probably is worth $15,000 to $20,000 besides. We are informed by a close friend of Passavant that he is the only one who has no money." Most disturbing to Eastman were the formulas in the former employees' heads, particularly the one for Solio, the popular new printing-out paper. Eastman was able to get a perpetual restraining order preventing the use of any Eastman-owned patents or techniques. He learned that the defectors expected support not only from local capitalists but also from the Celluloid Corporation, with whom his company was involved in litigation. The settlement of the Celluloid suit may be one reason that support did not materialize—and one reason that Eastman chafed under the agreement, as part of that settlement, to buy all his dope from the Celluloid Zapon Company. That dope turned out to be dirty and yellow, sticking to the glass: "We *never* had any trouble with the Cooper dope," Eastman growled. "Don't come up here to see, you'll just find the same problems we did. Change the dope instead."[41]

The Photo Materials Company survived a short time before its founders abandoned it. Eastman Kodak would buy the liquidated company in July 1898, mostly to get the building and production machinery at a bargain.[42]

For Eastman, 1892 was the best of times and the worst of times: The year had opened with trouble, and would see more with film and emulsion failures on both sides of the Atlantic as well as a fire in Brownell's factory. As harbingers of problems to come, on 18 January 1892 a second interference between the Reichenbach and Goodwin patents was declared. On the national industrial scene, 1892 was the year the Standard Oil trust was dissolved under terms of the Sherman Antitrust Act. Kodak's turn would come early in the next century. Because the success and permanence of his company was now Eastman's raison d'être—the specter of poverty, if it ever existed, was gone—reincorporation as the Eastman Kodak Company in 1892 was both a watershed and a reward for hard work and difficulties overcome. The rapid expansion of the Eastman company since 1889 required substantial new capital; in 1892 the capitalization was increased fivefold and the corporate name changed for the last time.

"The new company," Eastman wrote Cornelia Hagan, "is to have five million dollars capital and each stockholder of the Eastman Co. will receive four shares of the Eastman Kodak Co. in exchange for each one share of the former company which they [sic] hold. The balance of the stock, one million dollars, will go into the treasury to be used in extending the business."[43] Eastman's knowledge in interpreting the various and changing laws governing incorporation was obviously growing. In May 1892 the interim New Process Film Company, created to take advantage of a quirk in corporation law, gave way to the Eastman Kodak Company. The stock split dropped the premium price on each share back down to its par value of $100 but the climb would soon resume. At the same time, George Eastman's salary was raised to $10,000 per annum and the *New York Tribune* included his name in a list of "tariff-made American millionaires," much to his objection. The distinction was significant: Most of the burgeoning U.S. industries of the period relied heavily on tariff protection.

The Kodak craze appeared to continue unabated. In 1892 the Secretary of War rescinded his order that no Kodak cameras could be taken up the Washington Monument. Yet actual sales peaked after three years and by

1892 were on the slide. In November Grover Cleveland was elected president again. (Republican Benjamin Harrison had sandwiched a term in between Cleveland's two and campaigned for reelection at Kodak Park in the company of Frederick Douglass.) With business off, defections up, court costs increasing, and what he considered an unfriendly administration in Washington, at year's end Eastman cut everyone's salary, including his own, by 25 percent. As it turned out, the whole country was on the edge of a severe financial panic.

As 1893 began farm mortgages were foreclosed, railroads went into bankruptcy, and strikes occurred in major industries. The public was suspicious of silver and customers overran the banks demanding gold. Many banks closed. "We are still on deck, but the deck is a little slippery," Strong reported from his Tacoma bank. All Rochester banks stayed afloat, yet by the fall of 1893 Rochester payrolls were cut in half and those without work survived on charity alone. "Times are getting worse all the while," Eastman wrote. "Self-preservation is the first law of nature and the Company must be protected for the sake of its stockholders. . . . In my judgment this winter is going to be the hardest time this country has seen for many years." The Eastman Kodak Company, in the midst of expansion at Kodak Park and Brownell's Camera Works and troubled by film and emulsion problems, passed a dividend for the first time. Yet Kodak ended one of the worst economic years in American history with a net profit of $87,717—down only $28,000 from 1892. The surprise showing was attributable to the expanding sales of its new Solio paper. "The good ship Kodak will weather every storm," said Harrow chemist Walter Krohn with satisfaction.[44]

The Panic of '93 did not keep the company from throwing a "grand ball" to celebrate the opening of the "Brownell Building" on Valentine's Day. "It is not a usual thing for a business building to be opened with a ball," the Rochester papers marveled. The reporter was impressed not just with Eastman's hospitality but with his building. Known as "The Crystal Palace" because of the immense amount of glass, iron supports, brick and Portland cement (an early use) piers, and fourteen-inch posts of Georgia pine, the Brownell Building was "the lightest manufacturing building in this part of the country." After the party, the basement would be used for cutting up lumber for camera cases, the first floor for offices and assembling leather cases, the second floor for the machine shop and metal working, the third for woodworking, the fourth for assembling, and the fifth for varnishing and polishing. The sixth was unoccupied. A one-story boiler house adjoined. For plans and construction, architect Charlie Crandall and contractor Tom Finucane were paid in Kodak stock. Eastman's "scheme" was to purchase all of Brownell's machinery and tools, paying him in stock, renting the plant to him at 6 percent of cost. Brownell was to furnish materials and labor and manufacture Eastman goods exclusively.[45]

"You will remember that when we opened Kodak Park, you promised to fill the emulsion tank with champagne," Eastman ruminated in a letter to Strong in London. "I am just now debating in my mind whether the authority you gave me then would warrant my filling one of the [Camera Works] boilers with the fluid. If I do, the six bottles that you owe me on the foreign exchange bet will be applied on the bill and the balance will be deducted out of your next dividend."[46]

6

Prayers and Paper Wars

■ ■ ▪ ──

Emulsions were the single most important component Eastman manu-factured—and the most chancy. Emulsion making in the 1890s was not a science but an art somewhat akin to alchemy. One day the emulsion was fine, the next spoiled—and no one knew why. Eastman pondered this with an anecdote about a St. Louis rival, the M. A. Seed Company: "Seed emulsifies for seven days and when the emulsion goes wrong takes ten days to straight-en it up," he wrote Walker. "In the meantime, all hands are called to prayer meeting to pray for the emulsion. I am considering," Eastman joked rue-fully, "whether we shall start a Praying Department." To which Walker shot back: "I was not aware that the Seed Company was religiously inclined as a company."[1]

After the departure of Reichenbach, Eastman needed a good emulsion maker to get the plant in operation again. In February 1892 he learned that his former mentor, George Monroe, to whom he had once paid $5 for lessons in wet-plate technology and under whose tutelage he had taken his first photograph, was available. What probably interested Eastman most was that Monroe had spent time in various photographic factories in St. Louis that had better plate emulsions than Eastman was able to produce. Monroe came aboard, and immediately a rivalry with de Lancey was created. Then suddenly, late in June as Eastman was leaving for Europe, reports came that film was deteriorating on dealers' shelves. Monroe was summarily fired. He simply wasn't qualified for the job, Eastman decided, and besides he talked too much.[2] With the Reichenbach experience fresh in his mind, Eastman's

guard was up. Walter O. Butler, who had accompanied Eastman and Strong
to London during the fogged plate crisis a decade before, begged for a
chance to prove his mastery of emulsion making. He got it, but had no more
luck than Monroe did. As he had done in 1882 when the dry plates went bad,
Eastman took the film off the market and made good. Monroe's and Butler's
failures brought Eastman back to the experiment table. Film making at
Kodak Park ceased from 20 September to 20 November 1892. Experiments
yielded no clues to the perplexed Eastman: "100 emulsions made in September kept perfectly well. Six made with nitrate to prevent electricity mottled
[yet all] emulsions made the day before and after with nitrate did not mottle
but retained their quality perfectly. . . . So there you are. It is impossible to
locate the trouble."

Next, Professor Charles Forbes, one of Eastman's early mentors and an
early photographic pioneer in Rochester, was hired at Strong's suggestion.
But he failed as well to "make an emulsion like we need." Eastman was stuck
with widespread customer dissatisfaction and a big drop in camera and film
sales during 1893 and 1894. He knew in his bones how inexact a science
emulsion making was and that he desperately needed an expert on board.
For the first time he ran up against his own limitations. He simply could not
continue to run the entire company and at the same time muck about with
test tubes and stirrings. Then came a classic confrontation between an American businessman and the press. In November 1892 the *Chicago Tribune*
published a long tale about "the kodak fiend abroad in the land" and worthless Kodak film ("long transparent celluloid ribbons on spools . . . that
turned out to be no better than no film at all"). "Amateurs are not in a happy
frame of mind," the *Tribune* warned. In the tradition of the best defense
being a good offense, Eastman replied (but "not for publication") that when
certain films that had passed the test suddenly deteriorated and lost sensi-
tiveness, they were removed from stock and manufacturing changes made—
that is, Monroe was fired. When that remedy was "only partially effective,"
another change was made (Butler was fired) and the replacing of defective
film commenced again. He continued to describe, in equally euphemistic
terms, the hiring and firing of Forbes, how the manufacture and shipping of
films had ground to a halt, and how the use of new dope, as required by the
settlement of the Celluloid suit, was the probable root cause of all troubles.
"Every sensitive photographic material is known to deteriorate," he concluded, "but this is the first time in the Company's history that considerable
loss has been caused to its customers. . . . Film photography, while it has
been brought to a practical stage, will require several years of experiment
and improvement to perfect it." The company also regretted the bad press
and the field day headline writers were having with Eastman's slogan during
these difficult times. This, from the *Denver Republican*: "Doesn't do the
Rest/Kodakers Press the Button and the Picture Won't Materialize."[3]

When he unveiled his mechanical plate coater in 1879, Eastman had boasted that his invention would ensure that "no one will coat plates by hand." In this case Eastman rhetoric was not father to the deed. The plate-coating machine never worked satisfactorily—not even for Eastman's own company, which continued to coat plates by hand until film made the whole process obsolete. His impatience with what he saw as soon-to-be-outmoded technology perhaps kept his company's product from competing successfully with the plate emulsions produced by the Standard Dry Plate Company of Lewiston, Maine, and the St. Louis companies of Seed, Hammer, and Cramer. Eastman firmly believed that roll-film systems would make glass plates obsolete for all but special high-precision work,[4] but for now, the professionals and serious amateur photographers wanted the plate technology and regarded Eastman's product as inferior. The satisfaction of being right in the long run would be cold comfort for loss of business in the short term, so Eastman resolved to capture a share of the plate market. He decided to build and staff a dry-plate building at Kodak Park, but he needed someone to come up with an improved emulsion and to direct operations. In solving his dry-plate problem, he would also solve the film emulsion problem of the past two years.

At age thirty, William G. Stuber of Louisville, Kentucky, had a national reputation as a portrait photographer as well as a half-interest in a new plate-coating machine made by the renowned Dr. John Henry Smith of Zurich. Indeed, Stuber had just spent six months in Switzerland studying Smith's emulsion techniques. Eastman met Stuber at a photographic convention, most probably in 1893, and his interest in the young man's techniques was stirred. In December 1893 Eastman invited Stuber to "come here for an interview. . . . There is some prospect of the position of foreman of our transparency plate department being open." (Indeed, there is some evidence that the transparency plate department itself was nonexistent in 1893.) Eastman also wondered aloud about getting a "clear title . . . to the Smith coating machine . . . free from the payment of royalty." Stuber came, bringing along his wife and infant son, and on 4 January 1894 was offered the job at $30 a week plus "1% on the net receipts for glass dry plates, the arrangement to be continued as long as your services are satisfactory; either party to have the privilege of terminating this contract at any time." Stuber's services would prove more than satisfactory.[5]

When Eastman asked Stuber why Kodak film would not keep longer than six months, Stuber replied that it was because of the way the emulsion was made. Eastman was startled: "You've never been in our Emulsion Department!" "It's the way your emulsions act in handling," Stuber replied, and his further theories and explanations led Eastman into the laboratory to test them. Within days, Stuber recalled, "he asked me if I would make an emulsion for the film."[6]

Straightaway thirty-year-old Stuber collided with his immediate boss, twenty-four-year-old Darragh de Lancey. "After making a few experiments I was ready to coat an emulsion on the film base," Stuber would recall, "but the manager of Kodak Park refused to allow me to make this coating." But de Lancey was hardly the final court of appeal. "Mr. Stuber will furnish the emulsion, under your directions, for coating film," Eastman notified de Lancey, when he heard of the dispute. "It is my desire to substitute his emulsion for Butler's as soon as it is safe to do so. Mr. Stuber's opinion as to the quality . . . is considered final." Stuber's film was then compared with the current Kodak film: "The result showed plainly that the experimental emulsion would keep for years. I was then put in charge of the Emulsion Department."[7] Eastman was greatly relieved. Stuber's fast start and "the fact that the emulsion [was] running so well" had put reliance on the supernatural to the side: "It is deemed unnecessary at present to start a Praying Department. Such a department is so much out of my line anyway," he admitted to Walker, "that I hesitate to get involved."[8]

Film making had so many variables it was hard to determine which one had caused the defective film. "It's like the combination of a lock," Eastman said. "Change one component . . . and everything changes."[9] Because of the Celluloid suit, the dope source had changed. Because of electrical discharges, nitrate salts had been added. After Reichenbach's defection, there had been several emulsion makers. The upshot was that the problems with emulsion gave Eastman serious concern, which is belied by his light-hearted comments about the need for prayer. With film unavailable except from Blair, who made the most of the situation in his ads, sales in film cameras dropped. It began to look as if film photography was a flash-in-the-pan. In the end it would be Eastman's unyielding persistence that led to the replacement of glass plates by the roll film system.

In the meantime, Stuber as emulsion maker was a gamble Eastman had to take, in spite of the young man's lack of technical training. (Years later when Stuber filled out the section in his personnel file dealing with education, degrees, advanced degrees, etc., the then chairman of the Eastman Kodak Company wrote simply "grammar school.") Eastman had begun to hire university-trained technicians—Reichenbach, de Lancey, Jones—but he continued to have an essential faith in empirical, self-trained craftsmen like himself and Stuber. The secrets of emulsion making seemed to resist scientific principles. He placed his hopes in another sleeves-rolled-up empiricist.

As Stuber began to break in, with "what we call Stuber's emulsion replacing Butler's emulsion" because of its "remarkable clarity and keeping quality," Eastman watched the results like a hawk: "Mr. Wm. Hoyt, a prominent amateur here in the city, in talking about your film emulsion, said he had considerable difficulty at first in getting good results owing to the tendency of the negative to flatten out unless held back in the developer," Eastman reported to Stuber. "If the negative begins to flatten it is impossible to get density. . . . The film is hard to work but gives beautiful results if properly handled," he concluded. These qualities were all right for professionals, but Eastman was after the larger market. "In mixing your emulsion to get the proper quality," Eastman instructed Stuber, "do not forget . . . that it is manifestly better from a commercial point of view to put out a sensitive product that can be easily worked to good average results than to put one out that requires such skillful manipulation as would give superlative results."[10] Eastman further mapped out mass production methods and detailed instructions on all phases of the business for his top employees. No detail was too small for his attention. And because of the rapid turnover in emulsion makers, only Eastman provided continuity.

Stuber did not have entirely smooth sailing. After his formula was sent to Harrow, the British chemists were unable to get the same results and wired back to Rochester for help. "The emulsion maker must use his own judgment in small matters," Stuber pointed out. "Your chemicals and water might be different from ours . . . so no rule can be given. Making a few lots will show you."[11] In 1892 Eastman solved one sticking problem by switching from chalk to grease, then, in 1893, he solved the same problem by switching back from grease to chalk.[12] Stuber's phrase "no rule can be given" aptly summarized the fact that no one could figure out why a substance would work one time but not another. Reduce the quantity of camphor, one expert wrote in a suggestion that would have far-reaching ramifications. Apparently the amount of camphor was reduced in 1892—even though Reichenbach had no trouble making film with a substantial percentage of camphor from 1889 to 1891—and this action would eventually put Eastman in conflict with the Rev. Hannibal Goodwin's not-yet-patented formula for film.

"Everytime we try to prove Blair is dead," George Dickman remarked, "he pops up serenely." Thomas Blair had moved his business to England during the final confusing months of the Walker tenancy at the Eastman Photographic Materials Company and now was calling at Oxford Street to meet the new joint managing director. (Eastman was the other joint managing director; for the time being he would look over Dickman's shoulder, no matter how much he liked and trusted him, just as he had monitored Walker.) While Blair was sizing up Dickman, the latter gave Blair the once-over: "He was overdressed in a long frock coat, silk facings, white necktie, new gloves, patent leather boots, swinging a silver headed cane. I thought it meant a failing man of business trying to keep up appearances."[13] In Eastman's opinion, Walker had been coddling Blair either out of friendship or fear: So Eastman was pleased, he told Strong, that Dickman had seen "Mr. Blair as, notwithstanding his claims to the contrary, a bluffer pure and simple."[14]

The Blair Camera Company in Boston was experiencing a shift in personnel: Darius L. Goff was still president and the Anthonys remained large
stockholders, but both Blair and Samuel Turner had left. The Blair company's board of directors had voted "no-confidence" in its treasurer and general manager and on 9 August 1894 Blair resigned. With the two prime inventive minds gone, the Blair company sunk into stagnation. With the Blair
company's permission, Turner had resumed his own business under the
name of Boston Camera Manufacturing Company. Blair's English company
became essentially a retail outlet for Turner's cameras. Goff, meanwhile,
continued to press Eastman to buy out the American Blair company; the pair
met regularly but without coming to terms. Back in September 1892 Thomas
Blair himself had "elaborated a plan of consolidation" of the two companies. "The scheme proposed," Eastman had told his board of directors, "involves the closing of the Boston camera works or reducing it to a mere repair
shop and removing the common work to the Brooklyn factory and the fine
work to our new works in Rochester; . . . and the running of the Blair Co.
generally as a vigorous competitor to our competitors and a feeder of the
Eastman Kodak Co. The Blair Camera Co. has not made any money for two
years and the people who are running it, although wealthy, are somewhat
discouraged," Eastman continued. Goff did not want to close operations
completely, preferring to sell out to Eastman to "putting more money into it
and setting it on its feet." Thomas Blair had, Eastman asserted, spent inordi-
nate sums on advertising and created an enormous amount of unsalable
stock, particularly Kamaret cameras. And there were "considerable discrep-
ancies" between the financial statement Blair filed in June and the one he
gave Eastman in August. With such a negative assessment by their astute
treasurer, the Kodak directors voted to reject the merger. Blair was bitter—
Eastman had been just toying with him, he said, in order to have a peek at his
finances. Yet Eastman had also outlined four advantages of the deal to the
Eastman Kodak Company, provided the price was right: "controlling our
principal competitor, cessation of all patent suits, strengthening of the bromide coating patents, and acquisition of our only competitor in bromide
paper." The catch was the price. Eastman's own figures reached a startling
conclusion: "We are giving them Kodak stock for about 33 cts." The merger
was off.[15]

Blair then went to England, acquired a new wife, and, as Dickman observed, refused to stay buried. He started the European Blair Camera Company in 1893 as an independent concern, although for a time he remained
vice president and general manager of the Blair Camera Company of Boston. Blair's lack of business acumen was underscored by the fact that even
though he was the sole supplier of roll film during Eastman's film crisis of
1892 through 1894, the company still lost money in 1893. Further complications ensued from the four lawsuits pending between the Eastman and Blair

companies. Even so, Eastman was anxious to get control of Blair's patents. As the first to patent and commercially produce a roll-film system, Eastman had created what he hoped was an impenetrable patent barrier. Blair and Turner, with the help of other inventors, notably David Houston, circumvented the barrier with innovations that made Eastman increasingly nervous. Then, in June 1894, Judge Colt decided for Eastman in "the roll holder suit involving the marking and indicating device." Eastman immediately began enforcing the decision. The Blair company, despite dwindling business and resources, appealed. All this constituted a drain on both Blair's and Eastman's time, money, and energy but a determined Eastman sent his attorneys back into the fray and the decision was upheld. A jubilant Eastman went to Boston to settle with Goff. The roll-holder decision of June 1894 was perhaps the high point in Eastman's use of patents. Once the court decisions began to go against him or the cost of enforcing them became prohibitive, he would shift his emphasis from patent protection to product innovation in the ongoing scramble to stay on top of the heap.

Eastman next turned his attention to Samuel Turner's Bulls-Eye camera. Initially Eastman had been sure he could remove from the market Turner's Bulls-Eye, a camera he sincerely admired as "the best thing Blair has going for him." So confident was he that he had Brownell start production of Pocket Kodak cameras and a blatant copy of the Bulls-Eye. He first called the latter the Cows-Eye in deference to his fondness for those bovine creatures, but then changed his mind. How best to hit the Bulls-Eye? With a Bullet, of course. Eastman's Bullet camera, so similar to the Bulls-Eye that customers would forever order the wrong camera or case, was patented by Brownell and introduced in March 1895.[16]

And then, in May 1895, George Eastman was sitting in his office, perusing, as was his habit, the weekly list received from the Patent Office. Something caught his eye, and so he rang up Chappie Church. Turner had just patented a light-tight cartridge or daylight-loading film spool that "covered the Bullet and Pocket Kodak" and caught Eastman with inadequate patent coverage. Each new camera piling up in Brownell's Camera Works represented a possible infringement. Turner's application had been lying around the patent office since 1892; Eastman had assumed it was going nowhere and confidently designed his two cameras based on Turner's system. Eastman and Church saw seven possible anticipations to Turner's patent "and the state of the art developed by these references." The earliest was an 1855 device: "Barr used a strip of black calico longer than his films and indicated numbers on a second strip. . . . Warnerke used a red window to look at numbers and cutting marks marked on the back of the film; and Marcy used a flanged spool wound with sensitized film protected by black paper at the ends. . . . Turner uses a flanged spool with a sensitized film, protected by opaque paper at each end to form a light-tight film roll." Eastman did some investigating on his own, including a visit to a drygoods store, where he "found an old man . . . who sold ribbon . . . which was spooled with paper, having marks upon it indicating the number of yards remaining." In early June, Turner's attorney notified Eastman that he was infringing both Turner's daylight-loading system and David Houston's front roll design of 1886, a patented device that placed the film in front of the focal plane for which Turner had the exclusive license. Eastman's attorneys reluctantly agreed.[17]

Eastman negotiated and on 25 July 1895 signed an agreement with Turner giving the Eastman Kodak Company an exclusive license and the right to set a minimum price on the film for the system. Turner continued to press Eastman to buy his whole business. In August, Eastman capitulated, buying the patent, the trademark Bulls-Eye, the finished and unfinished camera stock, three Boston properties including a plant, and a Waterbury plant. As it worked out, a decade later the Patent Office and courts would agree with Eastman's 1892 assessment that Turner had shown no invention. In 1903 Anthony & Scovill would manufacture a box camera based on Turner's patent, now owned by Eastman. Eastman would sue and in 1906 the United States Court of Appeals would declare Turner's patent null and void on the basis of the anticipations. That ironic twist was in the future, however. In November 1895 Thomas Blair came roaring back into this confusing scene with a claim circulated through the Anthony publications that the Bulls-Eye camera had been originally designed and manufactured by Blair (Turner was only the selling agent). Eastman was therefore infringing, this line of reasoning went, while he, Blair, would continue to market cameras as Birds-Eyes or Buck-Eyes and apply for the trademark Bulls-Eye in England.

"We are out for the blood of the pirates," Eastman growled to Strong, "and propose to get their scalps."[18]

Budding entrepreneurs of the 1890s, hoping to break into the expanding photographic business, found that George Eastman effectively controlled film photography through his film and camera patents. One recourse was to manufacture commodities impervious to patent control such as dry plates or photographic paper. Dozens of small manufactories in both of these specialties sprung up, and the price wars that ensued threatened the profits of established paper and dry plate companies. New antitrust laws prohibited formal agreements among competing companies, but informal pools for "price fixing" were popular, albeit ineffective. Eastman had not joined the dry-plate pool, possibly because his own plate output was so meager. With the coming of Stuber, Eastman revitalized the dry-plate department, passing a dividend or two to pay for new buildings where dry plates and "Solio" paper were produced. After Reichenbach's Photo Material's Company marketed Kloro to undercut Solio, Eastman decided it was time to get the paper sector better organized and tackle some of those fly-by-night companies. It was paper that saved the day when emulsions, films, banks, and economies failed.[19]

Although both plate and paper emulsions contained silver salts suspended in gelatin, the two emulsions were quite different in character and method of coating. Thus while the gelatin-silver revolution began with dry plates, plate manufacturers did not generally enter the paper field. The principal exception was Eastman, who perceived and capitalized on the revolutionary potential of the gelatin emulsion for paper. He became the first, and from 1885 to 1887, the only American manufacturer of gelatin bromide developing-out paper (DOP), a product involving a whole new technology that required a darkroom and special enlarging equipment. But photographers were loathe to invest the time and money necessary to master a radical new technology involving a paper so fast that visual control was lost and fogging likely. If professionals wanted a larger image, they could use glass plates up to eighteen by twenty-four inches or a solar enlarger. Eastman's market had to await the growth of the amateur segment. Competitors were content to stay with albumen paper. Eastman, with his boundless energy and willingness to take capital risks, tried the new; when it failed, he moved on to something else.

When photographers finally changed to factory-sensitized paper, most chose a printing-out paper (POP) they could work in sunlight as they had the albumen paper. Responding to this need a new American competitor, the American Aristotype Company in Jamestown, New York, dramatically entered the paper market in 1889 with a collodion chloride POP.[20] Charles S. Abbott, a New York advertising man, surfaced as the leader of the group. Like Eastman, Abbott had a natural flair for combining technical innovation with mechanized production and the latest marketing techniques. Abbott soon negotiated an exclusive contract with Anthony, emerging almost overnight as the dominant producer of collodion paper and a major force in the general paper market. Several smaller companies, among them the Western Collodion Paper of Cedar Rapids, Iowa, also began producing a collodion POP.

Then a gelatin chloride POP was introduced from Europe in the early 1890s. Again, small firms with no background in manufacturing photographic materials, among them New York Aristotype and Bradfisch & Hopkins, entered the field with this single product, marketing their paper through New York jobbers—Anthony, Scovill, Gennert, or Murphy. Eastman knew that paper was Kodak's bread-and-butter seller and that these new producers represented a challenge to his hegemony. He had been experimenting with a gelatin chloride POP since before 1888, but it took a young chemist, Jack Hawley, to hit upon the formula that was marketed in February 1892 as Solio—so named by Eastman after Hawley wrote down "Solio" as a possibility, and Eastman, seeing a dot on the paper above the "h," misread it.[21] It was a capital name for a paper printed by sunlight, but British courts denied him a trademark for that reason, and Eastman realized once more why "Kodak" was the perfect trademark.

In England, Krohn hit upon an improved matte paper formula and Eastman was so pleased that the chemist's salary was raised. But then the company was sued by Jahr, a German firm, which proved to the satisfaction of the courts that an identical formula had appeared earlier in a Spanish publication. The episode indicates the degree of proliferation of "secret" trade information during the 1890s as companies merged, or employees such as Monroe, Cossitt, Forbes, and Reichenbach changed employment. Eastman's employee contracts began including a clause about departing employees not reentering the photographic industry for five, ten, or twenty years, depending on the access a particular employee had to trade secrets. As a mark of William Stuber's value to Eastman, his contract stipulated that he could *never* work for another company.[22]

Eastman called Krohn's new paper "Platino Bromide" because it "enables us to get a picture exactly like platinum" even though it had no platinum in it. "Is this illegal?" he asked Philipp. If so, he would have to settle for "Platinoeffect-Bromide." One glossy bromide paper developed in England was named "Nikko," the Japanese word for bright and beautiful—this from Dickman, who had spent many years in Japan. The "fighting brands," cheap papers produced to compete in the paper wars of the 1890s, were Dekko and Karsak, also featuring the "double-k" sound Eastman favored. Although not as long-lasting as the difficulties with film, paper developed its own problems, primarily in the form of black spots caused by iron. The orders from 343 State Street to Kodak Park and Harrow came fast and furiously: "Get aluminum coating pans. Try maple rollers for the hang-up machine. Use rubber tubing and distilled water. . . . Burn the defective Eureka paper."[23]

From across the Atlantic, Eastman masterminded the design of Harrow's Solio building. The first British plans were "too cut up," so Eastman and a Rochester draughtsman prepared an improved design. He then tackled the logistics of production: "For cutting, sorting and packing 12,000 feet of paper a day, one foreman, one cutter, two choppers, and fifteen girls will be needed. The paper cutter should be run by small electric motors and a long treadle," he advised.[24] In the mid-1890s Eastman remained enmeshed in every detail and on top of every mechanical and chemical process related to his business. But a process was underway, beginning with a court decision in Great Britain requiring that the Eastman Photographic Materials Company pay cumulative dividends to preferred shareholders, which would gradually switch Eastman's personal interests from production and technology to finance and world marketing, forcing him to delegate some of his original responsibilities.

To market his papers Eastman sent an army of thirty salesmen into the field and advised Dickman to do the same: "The permanent and rapid introduction of Solio and Aristotype paper must depend on men who can give their entire time to it." Salesmen were installed in Chicago, St. Louis, Boston, New York, and Philadelphia and worked adjacent territories: "Their business is to sell Solio and start photographers using it. Go to all galleries in a town, leave paper. . . . Seeing prints made from their own negatives is generally conclusive and they place an order."[25] To keep an eye on the salesman, Eastman had J. B. B. Millington, his private detective, hire ambitious young men in various cities to watch and report.

"The Old Nick is to pay with the paper trade," Eastman grumbled to Strong.[26] The paper wars that heated up in 1893 would consume much of his energy for the next two years. He soon mounted a five-pronged attack on his rivals: dictating terms to his dealers, marketing cut-rate papers, price fixing through the Merchant Board of Trade, acquisition of paper companies, and, predictably, another patent suit. "Small makers will demoralize the business if allowed to," Eastman decided. "Terms of sale" to dealers began about 1894. Eastman prescribed that no discounts will be allowed to dealers "who sell our paper at less than list from now on. . . . We feel strong enough to do this." By 1899 retailers were signing contracts preventing them from stocking competitors' goods. Eastman rationalized that this policy protected the public from inferior and imitation goods. He could show, too, that Kodak's onward march toward monopoly was bringing lower prices and better quality. Believing that customers were willing to pay for value received, he insisted that Solio's quality remain high and its price unchanged—too hard to raise when the war is over, he maintained. But after Reichenbach's Kloro began to cut into his sales, Eastman decided to undercut it with Karsak paper. But while Eastman's sales remained high, profits steadily dropped as a higher percentage of sales went to low-priced Karsak. Reichenbach's threat continued, tempting Eastman to "cut him down to size through a lawsuit." Reichenbach's challenge proved ephemeral, however: 1895 was the only year the Photo Materials Company showed a profit, due entirely to the short-term success of Kloro paper.[27]

Eastman initially assumed that he could use patents to keep competitors out of the paper business, as he had done with roll holders, roll film, and roll-film cameras. In 1891 he devised a scheme, presented to Richard Anthony, Thomas Blair, and others, whereby the principal paper and film manufacturers would recognize the validity of Kodak's coating and machinery patents. In return he would license certain companies to use the patents, provided they agreed to maintain prices. Eastman's plan would have put teeth into the informal pooling arrangements by enforcing fair-trade prices through patents; the royalties, he confidently told Walker, would pay for litigation and leave a little for profit. The paper wars would last for five years, and the principal siege engine would be the Photographic Merchant Board of Trade. Eastman was the prime mover behind its formation, rationalizing that

> Dealers give [*fair-traded paper*] preference because they can make more money. . . . If the manufacturer cuts, dealers won't handle. If the dealer cuts, manufacturers won't furnish. . . . Other manufacturers, seeing our success, fall into line and . . . finally it comes to pass that a dealer cannot cut prices, cannot get any good goods. . . . It is not an illegal combination because there is nothing further than a tacit understanding among manufacturers and dealers and there is no penalty for falling out except to incur the displeasure of the rest . . . and a serious loss in trade.[28]

Eastman admitted that the arrangement "undoubtedly . . . favors the big manufacturer with greater facilities for introducing goods and keeping them before the public." He was skirting at the edge of the law as he pushed "this organization which is derisively called the 'combine' by the hoi polloi" and alerted his dealers with a "WARNING: Do not use the word 'combine' in any correspondence."[29] All like-minded dealers and manufacturers were welcome to join, for, he claimed to John Carbutt, "I am not and never have been in favor of freezing out anybody, and I consider that any endeavor to restrict the number of dealers . . . closer than their natural limits will do the association more harm than good."[30]

The stumbling block in Eastman's elaborate plans turned out to be not the Photo Materials Company, nor Anthony, nor Blair, who might have accepted such terms to keep their struggling companies afloat, but the new star on the paper horizon, American Aristotype. Charles Abbott, head of the Jamestown, New York company, declined categorically to recognize the validity of the Eastman patents and was rumored to be purchasing a bromide paper manufacturer. A new theater of war was about to heat up, although Eastman at first joked about it: "We have made such rapid strides . . . that they are evidently beginning to weaken in their confidence in the collodion paper which they heretofore manufactured exclusively." Then he soberly reconsidered: "They intend to wage vigorous warfare against us in the sale of bromide paper. . . . They will be the most formidable competitors that we could meet because they are thoroughly well liked by the trade and keep more traveling men on the road than we do."[31]

The major thrust of the war was between gelatin and collodion chloride paper; dealers, Eastman decreed, had better pick one or the other. While pooling may have been deemed illegal by courts in the 1870s, mergers and acquisitions were not. It was time, Eastman decided, to cover the collodion alternative. Rather than spend the time and money developing his own collodion department, he made his first acquisition with the purchase of the Western Collodion Paper Company of Cedar Rapids, Iowa, in December 1894. The company was small but ranked second to American Aristotype in quality and sales. He arranged for the deal quietly, sending an employee out to investigate, then boarding the train himself in early December. He closed the plant and brought the proprietors to Rochester to head the new collodion department he was building. The collodion acquisition was a risk involving a second new building and skipped dividends, but it also controlled the alternative, no matter which way popular favor went. But Eastman was never able to overcome American Aristotype's lead—"a failure," he admitted in 1896. So he paid off the former owners of Western Collodion, cut his losses, and waited for the next happening on the paper horizon.[32]

In 1894 Charles Abbott marketed two new collodion papers of superior formula and technology. In advertising them Abbott cast aspersions on Solio, claiming that it lacked permanence. The smoldering war exploded. Rising to the height of indignation, Eastman challenged Aristo to prove its claims. At the same time, though, not wishing to totally alienate Abbott, Eastman sent a somewhat conciliatory letter to his rival to remind him that "money spent in the detraction of our rival products will simply discredit them both and can better by used in making converts from our common rival albumen."[33] Following the vigorous price war of 1894–96 American Aristotype and Eastman Kodak dominated the market in their respective fields—Eastman in gelatin chloride POP (Solio) and bromide DOP and Charles Abbott in collodion chloride POP. The great majority of smaller concerns were battle casualties—few survived the cross fire between the two major powers.

Eastman opened a barrage on another flank with a coating machine suit against the Buffalo Dry Plate and Argentic Paper Company, subsidiary of Anthony and Blair. M. B. Phelps, Moritz Philipp's law partner, gained entrance to the Buffalo plant through an employee, Mollie Stephenson, and persuaded her to testify as to the similarity of Getz and Hoover's coating machine to Eastman's. Eastman urged Dickman to use the same tactics in England: "I have never found any difficulty whatever in getting into any works where I thought they were infringing our patents. It is merely a matter of expense."[34] Buffalo Argentic retained George B. Selden, Eastman's erstwhile lawyer who was making a career out of working for Eastman's competitors. Selden argued, among other things, that many coating machines existed before Eastman and Walker patented theirs in 1884, including machines that coated wallpaper. The case had bizarre ramifications. "Phelps is not a brilliant man," Eastman told Strong, "but he is a corker when it comes to getting evidence and as a running mate for Philipp he is a daisy, . . . oscillating between Rochester and Buffalo and having a red hot time. He got one of Hoover's girls down here to testify and Hoover got her father to come down and try to take her away by force. . . . Detectives and policemen and police court warrants have figured extensively in the case; also a revolver in the name of the irate father, who threatened to kill our detective. There have been several sensational articles in the Rochester and Buffalo newspapers but they did not succeed in getting the girl away from us."[35]

Mollie Stephenson was secretly ensconced in one of the houses bordering Kodak Park that the company owned to rent to employees or to temporarily house colleagues from abroad. Harry Strong, the son of Eastman's partner, was charged with bringing the young woman her meals under cover of darkness. Hardly had Eastman told Walker that he regretted "to hear the bad news about Richard Anthony. . . . I hope his insanity will be but temporary," than the scion of his old rival appeared in Rochester and learned of Mollie's whereabouts. Phelps had Anthony arrested for threatening a witness (he was later convicted), the countersuits began, the newspapers had an orgie, and George Eastman mused about "Mad Dick" Anthony.

> He has seen us slip out of the grasp of his father's old established concern and grow to be a much larger concern than they ever thought of being. . . . In the meantime his house has maintained less and less prominence and bids fair to sink into a mere retail business. We have hitherto been able to frustrate all of their evil designs upon us so there is therefore no reason we should not look with compassion upon his present unfortunate condition.[36]

Two years would pass before a decision was rendered, and it was not favorable to the Eastman Kodak Company. Perhaps because the American way is to favor the underdog, as the company grew to dominate the industry, the court decisions went against Kodak. The failure of Eastman's coating machine suit strategy would lead to new paper tactics during the second half of the decade.[37]

Because coating machine patents had proved inadequate to control the paper market, Eastman decided to try other ploys. Any company that became the exclusive North American agent for the two European mills that manufactured the world's finest paper could place the competition in a bind. In order not to contaminate the emulsion, photographic paper must be made with mineral-free water, be of a high-rag content, and be manufactured in clean plants. For forty years, beginning about 1860, the photographic world depended on two paper mills—Steinbach of Malmedy near the Belgian-Prussian border and Blanchet Freres and Kleber of Rives,

France—for all of its raw paper. "The gloss is simply magnificent," Eastman purred about the Steinbach paper he used for his "elegant Solio." He was already a friend of Gaston and Maurice Kleber and August Blanchet: In 1893 he and his mother and Henry Strong had accompanied Blanchet to the pier in New York, dining and feting him and wishing him a safe return to France. To lay the groundwork for a raw-paper deal, Eastman instructed Dickman to contact Thacher Clarke. "Clarke is such a good talker," he explained. Clarke talked for five years, finally softening up the paper cartel for Eastman to clinch the deal with a flying trip to Europe in 1898.[38]

As old adversaries squared off following Eastman's second acquisition, the paper wars sputtered to an end—or at least to a ceasefire. By 1896 prices had stabilized once more and a year later Eastman and Charles Abbott took a transatlantic voyage together where a strange thing happened: The two adversaries found that they liked each other—and a business marriage (merger) was in the offing. "The paper sky is a little less frowning," Eastman reported to Strong. Best of all, the whole roll-film system was coming back into popularity. "Hello Papa," he boasted to his partner. "We have another spell on. This time it's the Pocket Kodaks."[39]

Photos by the Mile

"That's it, now work like hell!" Thomas Edison shouted when he examined Eastman's transparent film in 1889.[1] His exclamation signaled a quantum leap in the nascent motion picture industry. Edison had first tried film from Carbutt, then Eastman, then Blair, and finally Eastman again and was impressed by Eastman's efforts to produce a film that did not tear in his machines. Edison called his brainchild "motioned pictures," and a variant of that ungrammatical phrase stuck. The development of motion pictures, from curiosity to commercial potential, was infinitely more complex and far-reaching than that of the x-ray, another innovation that presented new possibilities to Eastman in the 1890s.

Simultaneously, George Dickman and Henry Strong sensed the vast potential of "cinématographic" film; Eastman was slower to perceive that there might be outlets for film outside of amateur still photography. (His motto in this regard was, "I think baby deserves to have his picture taken often."[2]) Three separate technical areas—persistence of vision, photography, and projection—had to be understood, developed, and come together at the right moment.

The Eastman–Walker roll holder and paper film gave a tremendous boost to the development of the technology of film. Commercial cinematography, like mass amateur photography, had to await the development of fast gelatin emulsions and continuous roll film before significant strides were taken.[3] Among the experimenters was Edison, already famous for his work with the incandescent light and phonograph, but not versed in photography. In the

1880s he sought to extend his phonograph, a cylinder apparatus, with a visual counterpart or second cylinder of motion pictures on the same axle; immediately problems of coordination arose. Edison's staff of some sixty laboratory assistants included William Kennedy Laurie Dickson, who was knowledgeable about photography. However, Dickson's ideas about projection did not appeal to Edison, who still did not envision motion pictures as a separate invention. Instead, the inventor believed that success lay in "individual exhibition" and in 1891 he proudly presented the first Kinetoscope. Instead of projection for a large audience, Edison and Dickson devised a magnifying eyepiece for one observer to watch images going through one machine. Edison secured the patent for his new "marvel"; he now held the rights to a reel-to-reel system using magnification, perforated film, an intermittent shutter, and a continuous light source. For about $150 more, he could have internationally patented the system as well, but Edison, who never let business concerns occupy his thoughts for long, failed to protect it in Europe. And he remained committed to individual machines, even though he failed to find financial backing for what appeared to earlier supporters (such as Henry Villard) or observers (such as Eastman) as just an elaborate toy. Next Edison and Dickson collaborated in actual filmmaking. In 1892 the first motion picture studio was constructed on the Edison compound in West Orange, New Jersey, and called the "Black Maria."

At the end of May 1889 Edison ordered a loaded Kodak camera from the Eastman company. Then on 30 July Gus Milburn, Eastman's "traveling man" (and three years later one of the Reichenbach "conspirators"), led a group of demonstrators from the Eastman company to the New York Society of Amateur Photographers. In the audience was Edison's man Dickson, who pocketed a sample strip of Reichenbach's new negative film and took it back to the Edison compound. Edison's excited response linked the inventor and Eastman for years to come.[4] Edison had been using sheet film that had to be cut into strips and pasted together and so was easily torn and frayed. While Eastman's film represented an improvement—"I never succeeded in getting this substance in such straight and long pieces," Dickson marveled—it was still too thin for the wear and tear caused by the sprockets and multiple rollers of the Edison machines. Thin film was fine for Kodak cameras but not for the Kinetoscope. On 23 July 1891 Eastman sent Reichenbach "a small fragment of film furnished by Edison for his phonograph arrangement. He perforates it on both edges and delivers it by means of cog wheels. The film has to move forty times a second." Six months later Edison was ordering strips, one and one half inches wide, fifty feet long, one order in the highest speed (for negatives) and one in low speed (for positives).[5]

Then static electricity was found to be pitting the double-coated film. Eastman instructed Reichenbach on 8 December 1891 to "persist in your experiments" because it was "quite necessary that we perfect our method of making double coated film." Unfazed by the then preoccupied chemist's slowness, Eastman reentered the laboratory and divorced electricity from motion pictures himself. The search for a way to make film base as long continuous strips rather than on fifty-, one hundred-, or two hundred-foot tables begs the conclusion that the demand for ciné film spurred these experiments. But Eastman had dismissed the Kinetescope and its mutants as short-lived wonders. The continuous-flow method of film making and coating on gigantic wheels, developed by Darragh de Lancey and introduced in 1900, was primarily to reduce costs and speed up production of regular film. The endless strips needed for motion pictures were a lucky by-product.[6]

Edison dismissed Dickson in 1895, having suspected him of wanting to join a rival group. (Edison as well as Eastman had his "conspirators." The fear that trade secrets would be lost was widespread.) Dickson and his new colleagues eventually did come out with a successful projector. In France, Louis and Auguste Lumière patented a projector they called the Cinématographe in 1895. The fact that the Lumières did not have to worry about Edison's patents gave them free rein to incorporate the many cinematographic ideas then in the air.

People flocked to view films as an audience, and soon the popularity of the Kinetoscope was waning. Finally aware of the trend, Edison obtained the right to market Thomas Armat's projector, calling it the Edison Vitascope, thus giving it the commercial advantage of his famous name. On 23 April 1896 Edison presented the first theatrical showing of motion pictures in New York. A year later, Edison was granted a broad motion picture patent covering everything except film. This wide-reaching patent, sustained in 1907, would have ramifications for the future of motion pictures during the first two decades of the twentieth century.

X-rays were discovered almost by accident by German physicist Wilhelm Conrad Röntgen in 1895. The February 1896 issue of *The New Light*, a British photographic journal, published a translation of Röntgen's paper that announced that "photographic dry plates show themselves susceptible to x-rays." Walker conveyed the news that this German professor had discovered "a new kind of rays" with which one could take "shadowgrams." He sent Eastman x-ray plates of both "a living hand" and a "living frog . . . exposure twenty minutes."[7] X-ray machines began appearing on both sides of the Atlantic, albeit slowly; at first they were constructed as novelty items by hobbyists. Although a market for x-ray printing paper developed almost immediately in Europe—from England Dickman cabled for one thousand sheets of bromide paper in separate envelopes—it was months before the first machine was brought to the United States, and then only as a sideshow draw. Eastman dispatched William Stuber to walk the four blocks down State

Street to the Dime Museum in the Powers Building to see the strange new contraption. Stuber experimented with plates, films, and paper emulsions that had to be faster than Röntgen's plates for medical use. Eastman and Stuber advocated bromide paper from which many prints could be made—glass, being relatively opaque to the rays, had to be exposed one plate at a time—but the quality was lacking since images on paper were not as sharp, subtle, accurate, or legible as on plates.

Then Eastman heard that Edison maintained that his new fluoroscope, by means of which the x-ray image could be viewed directly, made photographs unnecessary. Always up for a challenge, Eastman gave Stuber the "go ahead" to try his hand with dental x-ray packets, defying Edison to place a Crookes tube inside a patient's mouth. The first packets were made of either glass or film wrapped in black paper. Clumsy by present standards—no patient enjoyed having glass placed inside his or her mouth—film finally won out in 1914 when the supply of Belgian glass was cut off by the war.[8] The term "plate" persisted, however. The speed of the emulsion was a factor too: It had taken an hour to get an image of Frau Röntgen's hand. Stuber did not achieve instant success—the time needed for producing an x-ray image only gradually lessened—but he would eventually solidify Kodak's reputation as the firm with the finest x-ray products.[9]

Fundamental differences existed between Edison and Eastman. Seven years older than Eastman, Edison invented the electric incandescent light in 1879, the year Eastman obtained his first patent. By then, Edison had already patented the phonograph, an electric vote-recording machine, and made improvements to the stock ticker, the mimeograph machine, and the telephone transmitter. Edison was a genius, and probably the greatest inventor in history—he towered above Eastman in the field of invention. He was rich in ideas, vision, and ability; over his lifetime he owned nearly 1,100 basic patents and therefore saw no need to control any alternative. Whereas Eastman immediately set his sights on capturing the world for his Kodak system, Edison was interested in everything he experienced and spun out dazzling bursts of invention in unrelated spectrums. His vision may have been ubiquitous, but in a sense he was less focused. He lacked the understanding of or the interest in the worldwide commercial opportunities engendered by his inventions. It would be Edison's secretary, Samuel Insull, who would see the full monetary potential of Edison's inventions to become the leading public utility financier prior to the 1929 crash of Wall Street. In manufacturing, their positions were reversed. If Edison was the great inventor of the era, Eastman was the great industrialist. Despite his failure to purchase the Goodwin patent and his caveat that he was wrong 35 percent of the time, Eastman made no major blunders in the exploitation of his inventions.

Although Edison began experimenting with motion pictures in 1887, he devoted his attention to ore mill experiments in 1890 and 1891. He had only a desultory interest in motion pictures until it was obvious they were the wave of the future. In later years he would claim to have invented the motion picture apparatus. The courts would agree with Edison in 1907, but not so with Eastman when he tried to prove that Kodak held the basic patent for film.

Eastman and Edison corresponded as early as 1882, but would not meet until 1907. They became close acquaintances only in the 1920s while earlier assuming the posture of cordial business associates—at least in public. (Surviving correspondence indicates they never achieved a first-name friendship.) Eastman had the highest regard for the inventive genius of his counterpart: "In him were combined a phenomenal mind, a tremendous energy, and—even up to his declining years—an almost boyish enthusiasm for the successful solving of the problem of the moment."[10] But privately Eastman was contemptuous of Edison's business practices. "Edison is probably the greatest inventor that ever lived," he wrote in 1922, "but when it comes to economics he is about as half baked as Henry Ford, who holds the record as far as I know up to date. I have not any sympathy for Ford but it is a pity that Edison is so intent on showing his weakness."[11] That opinion did not stop Eastman from showing the Wizard of Menlo Park all proper deference, noting that "along with his wizardry in matters electrical went a human kindliness that endeared him to the whole world."[12]

Eastman was in Europe in 1896 when the orders for ciné film began to pour in from Edison, the Mutoscope people (Dickson's group), and motion picture makers. Henry Strong was at the helm in Rochester and he waxed rhapsodic in the company correspondence as he saw business increase under his guardianship. His only problem was keeping up with the new demand. "If the disease breaks out seriously," he warned, "we will have no surplus film."[13]

In London, George Dickman was so swamped by requests from French filmmakers that Eastman joked about his English manager's sanity: "We cannot imagine what you are doing with these goods."[14] Soon Strong and the "crazy" Dickman would prove right about the "disease," and Rochester was inundated with orders as well. Credit for foresight here must be given to Dickman and Strong, who were earlier and more firmly convinced than Eastman that ciné film was an important new market and not just a mirror of a passing public enthusiasm. Eastman was wary of arcades and faddish entertainment schemes. However, his reluctance was soon overcome by ciné film's gargantuan leaps in economic potential: By 1910 ciné film would equal Kodak's traditional film output.

The birth of motion pictures had coincided with a resurgence of interest in film photography and Eastman was forced to choose between focusing on the service of old customers or gambling on this new market. Even with two extra film factories (one in Rochester and one at Harrow) built to cover the alternative in case of fire, there was suddenly not enough film for both cartridge and ciné film users. Eastman chose the former even after George Dickman came to Rochester to plead his case. "You must do the business as if Rochester would not make any ciné film for us,"[15] a chastened Dickman reported to Hedley Smith, Kodak's Paris manager. For once in his career, Eastman was reluctant to accept new technology. This retrograde attitude would be echoed in the 1920s, when he confronted the introduction of the "talkies."

The sudden demand for ciné film created problems beyond simply having enough for both the still camera and motion picture markets. The omnipresent puzzle of stabilizing the emulsion was now compounded by the need for a thicker base and two types of emulsion—fast for the negative film used to actually shoot the movies, and slow for the positive film used to project them—in addition to the thinner cartridge film for cameras. "Film is not like flour that can be turned out under any and all circumstances at a moment's warning and without limit,"[16] Strong told the clamoring customers. The need for producing more film led to discussions of doubling, even tripling the two hundred-foot tables and the buildings that contained them. Eastman vetoed that but when Dickman pondered whether Lumière was producing ciné film, Eastman jokingly suggested he send "a competent party down to Lyon to find out whether Lumière has built a long building. . . . If not, you can rest easy."[17] As cinema theaters began springing up around the world, distributors wanted more than one print from each reel that was shot. For every negative film, twenty to forty positive copies would be needed for distribution. The Eastman Kodak Company had the only factory capable of coming close to the demand, and it could not even meet the domestic need. Eventually European filmmakers resorted to regenerating used Kodak positive film and recoating it with emulsion. Thus did many early film classics bite the dust.

By the turn of the century motion pictures seemed to many—Eastman included—to be a fad that had run its course. Screen entertainment was too closely attached to vaudeville theaters, and thus perceived as lower-class entertainment. The short, plotless films were repetitive. However, audiences were soon entranced by the introduction of foreign films of two hours' length and more. New projectors and specialized theaters stimulated an enormous wave of popularity. In 1902 the Electric Theater, the first movie house in the country, opened in Los Angeles. In 1903 Edwin S. Porter directed *The Great Train Robbery*, the first American motion picture to tell a story with a convincing and exciting plot. In 1904 the Bijou, designed by

J. Foster Warner as Rochester's first movie theater, opened its Main Street doors. Fierce competition for new films among movie houses, distributors, and producers created an enormous demand on raw-film makers. Kodak, because of its superior product, became virtually the only film supplier, with sales in the United States alone increasing sevenfold in three years. Several other companies (most of them European), anxious about the limited supply of raw film and seeking frantically to create alternate sources, did attempt to enter the ciné film market. However, Kodak film proved to be the toughest and most uniformly sensitive; no one else was able to approach Eastman's standards.

Pathé built a film plant in a Paris suburb to become Eastman's toughest competitor. Yet Pathé remained a good Kodak customer, selling retread Kodak film to customers—sometimes in Kodak boxes—and buying some one hundred thousand meters of Kodak film per day for their own use because it was better film. Eastman observed that ciné film as the largest and most profitable item of Kodak's output was "not on account of the existence of patents, or other restraints on competition, but is owing to the difficulties of manufacture which have been surmounted by us in a larger degree than by anyone else."[18]

To avoid antagonizing his customers, Eastman made the policy decision not to enter into the making of "screen plays"—a departure from the usual practice. It was tacitly assumed that one man or company would see to the production from the manufacture of the raw film stock, to the shooting of the action, to the marketing of the finished product. Screen plays were clearly beyond Eastman's area of interest or expertise. Also, the first decade of the new century was a fiercely competitive one for filmmakers as rival producers went to enormous lengths of chicanery and dirty tricks to outdo one another. Edison and others had the jump on apparatus—although later, after a safe, noninflammable film had been perfected, Eastman would enter the field of cameras and projectors for "home movies." For the orderly Eastman, the current situation was too chaotic. Edison controlled the basic patents for everything but film and was suing everybody at home and abroad all the way down to the nickelodeon operators while simultaneously being forced to compete with them to maintain his patents. Eastman was the largest manufacturer of film in the world. He could argue from strength whereas Edison could not. Accordingly, Eastman suggested the first meeting that took place in Orange in 1907.[19]

Edison's monopolizing the motion picture industry was not a good idea, Eastman argued at that first meeting, because several minds could originate a greater variety of subjects for narrative film. Edison seemed to agree. Then in October 1907 Edison sustained a substantial court victory upholding his patents and strengthening his position. Shortly before Christmas of that year, Eastman met with two Edison representatives. Under Edison's and

Eastman's guidance the moguls of the film industry in the United States and France would merge as the Motion Picture Patents Company (MPPC), pooling all their patents (about twelve) and agreeing to pay Edison royalties. In turn, Eastman shrewdly made sure of his own financial success. Because the monopoly was solely dependent upon Eastman for its film, he would supply film only to members of the trust, charging one-half cent per foot extra as a royalty for the holders of the patents. The attraction from Eastman's vantage was that the market for film would be unified, assured, protected. Attractive to the MPPC was its ability to refuse to sell or lease either films or projectors to exhibitors who did business with nonmember companies. In addition, a tax of $2 per week was levied upon the MPPC's own licensed exhibitors.[20]

"The scheme looks like a good one," Eastman wrote, although he was still concerned about getting a working agreement with French filmmakers, "providing Edison . . . gets all the legitimate picture makers into it to start with."[21] Eastman sailed for Paris with Edison's carte blanche to negotiate a similar arrangement with the French. Subsequently, Pathé was willing to sign with provisos about their own film. Raymond Poincaré, attorney and later president of the French Republic, advised Eastman that he could run afoul of French law if he entered into a European cartel.[22] However, Eastman had already worked out the alternative: If Pathé would agree to pay Edison royalties, Eastman would "ignore" the retread film in Kodak boxes: "The reason I was anxious to reestablish relations with [Pathé] is that I was afraid that, being driven into a corner, he would make some foolish contract which would prevent our dealing with him again."[23] In his dealings with Pathé, as in his earlier arrangements with Edison and the Motion Picture Producers, Eastman's cleverness was remarkable.[24]

Thacher Clarke, Eastman's European advisor, then alerted Eastman that Lumière was coating celluloid obtained from England and that a German chemical company, Aktien Gesellschaft für Anilin Fabrikation (AGFA), was about to manufacture film on a giant scale. Clarke scouted it from outside the seven-foot fence surrounding the plant—"bigger than Kodak Park," he reported—and sent pictures of the construction. Eastman remained cool, realizing that "surmounting difficulties of manufacture," rather than elephantine building plans, was what kept Kodak "a long distance in advance of our competitors." Clarke urged a price war to keep the competition in check, but Eastman countered that "the best thing for us to do . . . [is to] bring our product up to the very highest state of perfection and reduce our price when we have to. . . . The money we would lose by cutting prices between now and the time the concern gets going would keep us from starvation during a good long fight."[25]

In response to a series of theater fires caused by the highly flammable nitrate film, Eastman began his experiments to find a more fireproof film. In 1906 a chemist was put on the project and, two years later, acetate film was introduced. Immediate complaints from exhibitors claiming, among other things, that the new film was too expensive, not as tough, and sometimes separated from the emulsion, coupled with Eastman's failure to influence the passage of legislation that would require fireproof film, indicated that "non-flam" acetate film was an idea whose time had not yet come. Eastman would initially feel the sting of failure with this expensive gamble but live to see the concept vindicated when he marketed acetate for the amateur home moviemaker.

The patents company cartel included all the established filmmakers in the world at the time the agreement was struck: Biograph, Kleine, Vitagraph, Lubin, Selig, Essanay, Pathé, Kalem, and Melies. But the concept of a monopoly contained the seeds of its own downfall, putting too tight a rein on a still new and very risky industry. Despite Eastman's warning to Edison, creativity was inhibited. One tenet of the agreement, for example, standardized movies as single-reel units. The inherent large profits for the in-group made it an easy target. Amateur filmmakers began to spring up all over the landscape and were finding it difficult to obtain film. The best and most aggressive of these were a talented group of first-generation Americans who banded together, calling themselves the Independents.

Eastman had inserted a proviso in the agreement that left him free to sell up to 2 percent of the total footage to smaller companies of his choice. "I finally convinced [the original licensees] that it was a foolish thing to do—to try to bar out their competitors in any way; that the result of it would be that they would bunch themselves together and make an opposition that would break up the whole scheme." However, Eastman's "safety" measure proved to be too small as well: Two percent could hardly satisfy the Independents. Lumière's New York agent, Jules Brulatour, became involved with the Independents, loading their cameras with whatever scraps of film he could come up with. The exuberant Brulatour, thirty-five years old in 1910, spoke fluent French and Spanish; he was a bon vivant who would entertain Eastman in New York, loan him his posh limousines and a chauffeur, and of course, be wined and dined in Rochester in return. Brulatour's second wife was the silent film star Hope Hampton.

Eastman's long friendship with Brulatour confounded his Kodak colleagues, who saw them as diametrical opposites. The colorful Creole from Louisiana—intense, urbane, and enterprising—was long on charm but short on profundity and quite a gambler. Eastman was a gambler, too, General Edward Peck Curtis who knew both of them said in 1980, but "*not* in the way Jules was." Brulatour was a playboy and a first-nighter who backed Broadway plays and musicals and often lost his shirt. He was a poor record keeper and he let the Independents buy all the film they wanted on credit and take all the time they wanted to pay, which meant nothing but more debt to Brulatour. He was a photographic dealer when he became the New York agent for Lumière ciné film early in the century. He took Eastman to Europe in 1910 with the hope that Kodak would buy out the family firm, but when Eastman saw the state of the Lumière plant and the nonexistence of account books the deal was off. Although Brulatour imported a half-million feet of film per week from France for the Independents, the Lumière film was so full of defects and its supply so undependable that the high-powered Independents—bright, aggressive men whose names (William Fox, Carl Laemmle, Adolf Zucker, Marcus Loew, Jesse Lasky, P. A. Powers, and Samuel Goldwyn) would make film history—demanded Kodak film. Because of Kodak's contractual agreement of 1908 to sell only to Edison's MPPC members, they could not get it. Brulatour saw before anyone else that the future of movies lay with the Independents, not with the moribund patents company, and convinced Eastman of this. By 1911 Eastman had a modification in his contract with the Edison group that allowed him to make Brulatour a Kodak representative selling to the Independents on a strict commission basis.

"The new deal permits us to sell to the 'Independents,'" he would tell Strong, "and it also results in our getting individual contracts with the Motion Picture licensees, under which they will use our film exclusively until July 1, 1912." This was practically, as Curtis noted, a license for Brulatour to print money because within a few years the Independents would grow from 5 percent of the raw film market to almost 100 percent while the original members of the patents company would fold or sell out.[26] Even in that age when motion pictures were engulfing the world as, in the words of Herbert Hoover, "the most penetrating and persuasive of all methods of world communication," shortsightedness and overwhelming greed could make some drop the horn of plenty. Eastman rarely made that sort of foolish mistake.

1. George Washington Eastman (1815–62) had two careers: as nurseryman in Waterville(1849–60) and as founder of a groundbreaking business college in Rochester (1842–62). This oil portrait (1927) is by Philip de Laszlo from an 1850 daguerreotype. (EKC)

2. Maria Kilbourn Eastman (1821–1907), an educated, well-poised woman, greatly influenced her son. In 1927 Eastman had de Laszlo paint an oil portrait from this 1850 daguerreotype. (EKC)

3. From 1849 to 1860 the Eastmans lived in this modest Greek Revival house, sited on a thirty-acre nursery of roses and fruit trees in Waterville. The portico resembles the much grander one on the George Eastman House, although Eastman did not consciously order the imitation. (EKC)

4. The earliest photograph of George Eastman is this ambrotype—a collodium positive on glass backed by dark paper—the instant photography of 1857. It could have been made by an itinerant photographer in Waterville, New York, or in a studio in nearby Utica, or in one of the studios adjoining Eastman's Commercial College in the Reynolds Arcade, Rochester. (GEH)

5. As a youth, George Eastman adopted various hirsute remedies to make himself appear older. Yet well into his sixties, his unlined face caused strangers to assume that he was the son of the founder of the Eastman Kodak Company. (GEH)

6. By age thirteen, Eastman no longer attended school. Starting work in 1868, he kept careful records of every cent earned and spent. His father, who had taught bookkeeping and penmanship, would have been proud of young George's meticulous entries and Spencerian script. (EKC)

7. Eastman's first photograph, a well-composed ambrotype made in October 1877, features the historic aqueduct that carried the Erie Canal over the Genesee River. Eastman pointed the stereo camera in George Monroe's studio on the Main Street Bridge south, and incidentally caught the future site (upper left) of the University of Rochester. A few blocks north of the bridge, the present Kodak Office would begin to rise in 1882. (EKC)

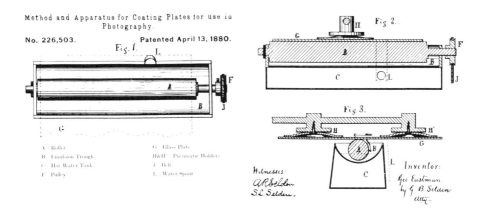

Method and Apparatus for Coating Plates for use in Photography.

No. 226,503.   Patented April 13, 1880.

Fig. 1.

Fig 2.

Fig. 3.

A – Roller
B – Emulsion Trough
C – Hot Water Tank
F – Pulley
G – Glass Plate
H&H' – Pneumatic Holders
J – Belt
L – Water Spout

Witnesses
Q R Selden
S L Selden.

Inventor:
Geo Eastman
by G B Selden
atty

8. In July 1879 Eastman steamed to England to patent a dry plate–coating mechanism; by September he had an improved version for his patent attorney, automobile inventor George B. Selden, to file. The American patent was issued in April 1880. (EKC)

9. Two years after taking up photography as a hobby, Eastman was producing gelatin dry plates for his own use. By 1880 he was selling them through the country's premier photographic house, E. & H. T. Anthony & Company. (EKC)

10. Investments during 1880 by whip manufacturer Henry Alvah Strong totaling $5,000 were a great boost to the struggling Eastman Dry Plate Company. Eastman made Strong company president as of 1 January 1881, a position he held in subsequent companies until his death in 1919. (EKC)

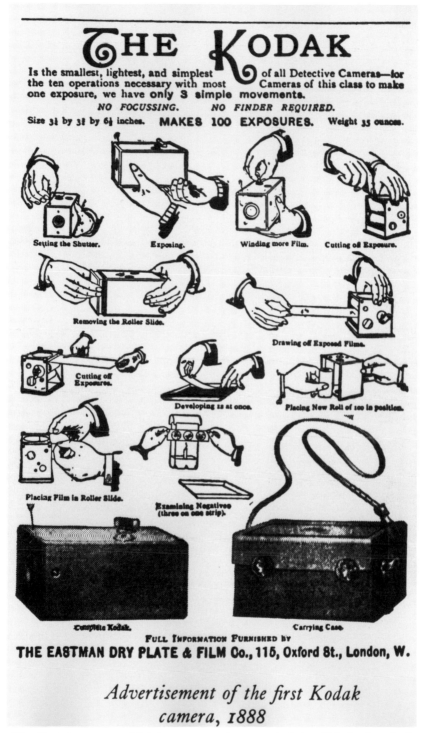

Advertisement of the first Kodak camera, 1888

11. The Kodak camera, which burst upon the scene in July 1888, "reduced photography," as Eastman's ads noted, "to three motions." (EKC)

12. One of Eastman's first Kodak shots was of his nephew and niece, Royal Vilas Andrus, age ten, and Ellen Amanda Andrus, age seventeen, in the backyard of his Ambrose Street, Rochester home. The children donned Uncle George's coats and hats for this mock duel before the camera in 1888. (GEH)

13. In February 1890 Eastman and patent attorney, Frederick "Chappie" Church, embarked for Europe aboard the mail steamer *Gallia*. Church photographed Eastman aiming his own Kodak camera at Church. These early-model cameras took round pictures. (EKC)

14. Nadar, famous Parisian photographer, made several studio portraits of Eastman in 1890. Nadar's son, Paul, was Eastman's dealer for France. (GEH)

15. In 1895 Kodak management consisted of partners Eastman and Strong (both wearing top hats), here visiting the Rives Paper factory in France. The best photographic paper in the world, made from essentially mineral-free water, came from this area near the French-German-Belgian borders. The partners' goal, resoundingly achieved in 1898, was to form exclusive contracts with paper makers of the region. (GEH)

16. Kodak employees garbed in their best finery pose by the factory door in 1890. For work, the women changed into calico dresses; office workers and salesmen such as Martin Freidel (*left*) wore suits; those in the laboratories or assembly rooms donned aprons or vests over shirtsleeves. (EKC)

17. Employees at work in the Kodak laboratories of the early 1890s. (EKC)

18. Eastman introduced Solio, a printing-out paper that capitalized on sunlight, as its name suggests. Printing sheds were built atop offices and factories. In 1894 employees loaded about seven thousand negatives a day into frames, exposed the frames in racks to daylight, and eyeballed each print until the correct exposure was slowly reached. (EKC)

19. Because of the volatile materials of nitrate photography, fire drills and buildings of slow-burning construction became the norm at Kodak Park. This scene is from 1899. (EKC).

20. The Kodak Girl, a significant advertising icon (1888–1960s), evolved contemporaneously with and outlived the Gibson Girl. She is usually pictured in a blue-and-white striped dress or swimsuit of whatever period she represents. (EKC)

21. One of the first Kodak Girls was Kitty Kramer, an employee who posed in the company studio with a No. 2 Kodak camera in 1889. (EKC)

22. Beginning in 1885, Eastman exhibited his wares prominently at international trade fairs. Here, the joint exhibit of Eastman Kodak and General Aristo, a Kodak subsidiary, at the Pan-American Exposition in Buffalo, 1901. (EKC)

23. The Kodak Office force of 1901 included Alice K. Whitney (*second from left*), who came in 1890 and remained as Eastman's personal secretary until after his death forty-two years later. (EKC)

24. The shipping room of the Chicago branch of the Eastman Kodak Company, 1902 or 1903. (EKC)

25. Workers ca. 1904 assembling the No. 4A Folding Kodak camera, considered to be the ancestor of all modern folding roll cameras. (EKC)

26. From 1860 until 1894 the Eastmans lived in a succession of six rented houses in various parts of Rochester. Then this Richardsonian Romanesque pile on East Avenue became available for purchase. The Soule House, as it is still called in memory of its first owner, a patent medicine king, was photographed by Eastman from every angle and remained his home until Eastman House was completed in 1905. (GEH)

27. Maria Kilbourn Eastman, 1890s. (EKC)

28. Eastman's first automobile was a Locomobile steamer, delivered April 1900. By 1902 he owned five cars. He tested this early model in Rochester's Seneca Park with Pauline and Charlie Abbott—Kodak's number two man and an avid automobiler. The rest of this series of pictures shows that there was as much tinkering with the car that day by the chauffeur (who took this picture) as there was driving it. (GEH)

29. From 16 January to 22 February 1901 Eastman rented the private car *Grass-mere* from the Wagner Palace Car Company for a trip from Rochester to New Orleans and Mexico City and return via a dozen or more railroads. Pictured here (*from left*) are Maria Eastman and her nurse, Louisa Knorr; Eastman's niece, Ellen Andrus; Eastman; Josephine Dickman; and the Rev. Murray Bartlett. (GEH)

30. A fishing trip to Nova Scotia in 1901 included Albert H. Overman (*second from left*), automobile manufacturer and co-owner with Eastman of Oak Lodge in North Carolina; Eastman; and Frank Seaman (*right*), Eastman's advertising agent in New York City. (GEH)

31. In 1891 the Kodak Office at 343 State Street, built 1882, was still fronted by a grassy plot with tree. The company name and motto changed over the years. The photofinishing department as fifth story was added about 1886. (EKC)

32. In 1898 Eastman commissioned J. Foster Warner, architect of the Soule House and later Eastman House, to design a new office in front of the 1882 building. He considered the result flimsy and overwrought but nonetheless appealing, and decorated it exuberantly for its Fourth of July opening. (EKC)

33. By 1906 the Kodak complex engulfed two blocks of State Street: (*left*) is the Camera Works (Brownell Building), Rochester's "Crystal Palace" of 1892, so-called for the generous amount of glass that brought daylight to camera assemblers; (*middle*) the 1898 Warner office building; (*right*) the 1904 addition, designed by Charles Crandall; (*far right*) the last remnant of an earlier era, now used for Kodak storage. (EKC)

III

The Goose
Hangs High

The Gay Nineties

Domestic duties could now be pleasures because money was coming in at a steady clip. Maria Eastman was cited by the city during the hot, dry summer of 1887 for a water use violation, but Eastman cheerfully paid up. "As the lessee I am doubtless responsible, for I am a big user of water at the factory and know the regulation." It was the family servant, he explained pointedly, who "did not know the regulation, but wanted to go home early" and therefore had sprinkled down the dusty street in front of the house before sundown.[1] Another financial arrangement that same year was more important since it symbolized for Maria a new affluence and for George a break with part of his past. Finding that keeping track of the small royalty payments that had come to Maria from G. W.'s textbook *Fulton & Eastman's Bookkeeping* was more trouble than it was now worth, Eastman cancelled the royalty by accepting a check for $25 from A. S. Barnes to "close up the copyright matter."[2] In 1886 he began to look at lots along Lake Avenue for a permanent residence and farther out, beyond the city limits toward Lake Ontario, for land for a factory. Neither search yielded exactly what he wanted. He "was offered 12 acres [of farmland] on the west side of the Charlotte road extending from the railroad north at $300 per acre, but I prefer a larger piece of land" and none of those adjoining were available at the right price. As a stopgap, he rented a building on Court Street from Strong and fitted it up as a film factory. The Court Street factory was conveniently near the falls for water power but, unfortunately for the sensitive photographic materials, too close to the dusty industrial area.[3]

City boosters had tagged Lake Avenue (formerly Charlotte Boulevard) the "*Champs Elysees* of Rochester," and it was fast becoming the city's fashionable residential street. The city fathers hoped Rochester would develop as Cleveland and Chicago had, with its Great Lake as focus, and planned Lake Avenue to be the gateway. The Strongs as well as the Woodburys lived there now. So did the Motleys, a prominent milling family whose fortunes rose back when Rochester was the "Flour City" of the country. The Motleys, with their six daughters, were providing wives for many of Eastman's neighbors and cronies: Bertie Fenn, Bert Eastwood, John Woodbury, and Charlie Angle. More out of friendship for the serious little dry-plate and film manufacturer than out of any hope of making a killing, these friends and neighbors would buy a little Eastman stock from time to time. Eastman thought of joining the gentry and even hired Charles F. Crandall ("Friend Charlie") of Otis and Crandall, architects of the State and Vought Street plant, to draw up plans. But he could not find a satisfactory lot.[4] He had not written off land near the lake for the factory. The location was good—the trolley to Ontario Beach could bring workers to a factory—but he had more ambitious ideas than twelve acres could accommodate. And perhaps it was best not to build a fancy residence on the thoroughfare that employees would use twice a day.

Ellen Andrus, age fourteen, came to live with the Eastmans for much of the year after her mother died in 1884. Besides Ellen's growing bond to her grandmother, she began thinking of Uncle George, albeit preoccupied with business and often absent on trips, as more of a father than her own father. Ellen's brother Royal, age eight, remained in Cleveland with his father, visiting his grandmother only during school vacations. During the 1880s and 1890s Royal and his usually distracted uncle had a pleasant enough relationship; Eastman saved the stamps that came off letters and testimonials from the United Kingdom, Europe, Kashmir, Bombay, South America, Canada, and the forty-some states and territories for Royal[5]; bought the boy bicycles and air guns (the better to shoot sparrows); and photographed Royal and Ellen clowning in the backyard of 59 Ambrose Street.

"Royal arrived safely," Eastman would report to Andrus, "and we were glad indeed to have his bright cheery face with us again." Once, when Royal, who was thirteen, arrived with an unnamed disease of the scalp, described by Uncle George as "repulsive," "a shocking condition," and "a frightful sight with his hat off," the Eastmans had a long-distance disagreement with Andrus as to treatment, fearing that "the local treatment [Andrus favored instead of the 'constitutional treatment' the Eastmans favored] will kill the hair follicles remaining in the scalp."[6] Unfortunately it did, and Royal in later years would wear a wig, which evoked acute embarrassment and perhaps contributed to his mostly unhappy adult life. All went reasonably well with this avuncular relationship until about 1900 when Royal, at age twenty-two, secretly sold the Kodak stock he had been given for Christmases and birthdays to pay off some debts; after that he and Uncle George never did hit it off.

Eastman's relationship with George Andrus rallied after the fallouts over the stock issue, because Andrus, who worked for a railroad, could obtain free or cut-rate passes for his brother-in-law's many business and pleasure trips. Then came an invitation to George and "Mother Eastman" to attend Andrus's marriage to Merie D. Reddy on 13 September 1886.[7] There is no recorded reaction to the marriage ("GE could keep silent in several languages," a friend once observed.[8]) Eastman's social life was now spartan and perfunctory. He attended debutante balls at the Powers Hotel and occasionally brought home young ladies such as Lizzie Coleman of Canandaigua to meet Mother (and indeed to accompany the Eastmans and the Strongs on a trip to Washington, D.C.). Lizzie wrote in a burst of rhapsody to thank Eastman for the photographs he sent as "souvenirs of another enjoyable trip. The last are better than any yet. . . . Those of the fishing excursion will recall one of the most pleasant days I ever spent. . . . We could not have had a more delightful time." Harris Hayden, his old insurance colleague and mentor, married, and in thanking Eastman for the "bowl and creamer," described his "pleasant little flat" on West 43rd Street, New York, urging his old colleague to follow his example: "I trust your business is prospering and that you are likely at a not very distant day to follow my illustrious example and look up a partner for life." Eastman visited the honeymooners in New York. "Mr. Hayden's wife is much more of a girl than I thought," he told his mother. "She makes him sit up and purr."[9] No one was making George sit up and purr. A little wistfully he told Ed Hickey, another boyhood friend, now living in Athens, Pennsylvania, "You are getting a long start on me in raising a family." He never would catch up to Hickey.[10]

Not yet forty years of age, Eastman was already referred to, in tycoon style, by his initials alone. "GE would like this done by the end of the week," his employees at the State Street office would say. "GE will be at the factory site today," his workers down at the rural end of Charlotte Boulevard would be memoed. "GE will send Clarke to Berlin to learn about the German laws regarding the formation of Companys and survey the entire photographic field incognito," the London staff would be informed. "No one can ever settle this matter to your satisfaction but GE," Walker would huffily write to Eastman, "so don't hop up swear bloody murder and say you cant & wont come." And so he formed his public persona, aloof and distant, but omnipresent in the organization. Employees could never slouch comfortably behind their desks come a new morning, lest there be memos written in a soft green pencil to be faced (and woe to the underling who wrote in green within company walls—that was GE's color, and his alone).

"GE" he would be and remain to employees (always "Mr. Eastman" to his face) and eventually by his own request to younger friends; but to Maria Eastman he was forever "Your loving son, George," and she to him, "My dear mother." The relationship continued to be close over the years, and no matter how much success came Eastman's way, he continued to pay Maria what to a modern sensibility seems excessive deference. Ironically, it was the son's success that in 1890 provoked a difference between them, and the curious and humorous working out of their dispute gives the best picture of George and Maria's relationship. For years Eastman had been after her to slough off her Waterville-born frugality and start enjoying the fruits of his labors. He practically had to drag her to the dressmakers for new clothes, and after one shopping expedition he emerged with a new fur coat while she could only be talked into a muff, a collar, and a fur-*trimmed* cloth coat. In a letter of 1890 he writes: "I think we had better begin to enjoy our money just as fast as we can, or we will not get the full benefit of it."[11]

What is bred in the bone or put there by hard experience is not easily relinquished. Maria had learned caution early in life—the ambitious plans of her husband ruined by his untimely death, her scraping—by widowhood, the holding on to genteel position in the community by dint of will—and even her son's rising fortunes did not make her eager to throw it to the winds. She had been here before: early success in a fledgling profession (her husband's penmanship and business school) brought low by unforeseen misfortune. She had enough of moving. Her roots were now planted on the west side of Rochester in the modest neighborhoods of Elizabeth Street, Jones Avenue, and Ambrose Street. The ten-room Victorian frame house in E. F. Woodbury's backyard was her home; in this year, 1890, she was still keeping up with her hometown news by subscribing to the *Waterville Times*.

But her son was eager to leave the west side of town. He eyed a house at 13 Arnold Park, owned by absentee landlord H. S. Finch of Richford, Tioga County, and decided to sublet it from George A. Curran at a reduced rate ($1,200 a year). It was a three-story clapboard structure with elaborately turned and jigsawn gingerbread above the wide veranda, under the eaves, and throughout the vergeboards of the gables. Since leaving the Greek Revival house in Waterville, the Eastmans had lived in a succession of modest if modish Victorian houses. With its fifteen rooms, the house on Arnold Park was the largest and most elaborate of these carpenter gothic efforts. To the rear of the small lot was a small carriage barn. Arnold Park was not unlike Livingston Park—a fashionable enclave surrounding a tree-lined mall that was enclosed at either end by iron gates between stone posts. The narrow streets on both sides of the mall were paved with creosoted tree rounds, an elegant alternative to the oiled dirt of most city streets (but a slippery one for horse hooves and carriage wheels, especially when the streets were covered with wet leaves). Livingston Park and the rest of the old "Ruffled Shirt Ward" was beginning to slide into shabbiness, but Arnold

Park, by virtue of its proximity to East Avenue, was on the rise.

But how to convince Maria that the move was advisable? Resistance could be predicted. She was used to the solid middle-class neighborhoods that had formed along the west bank of the Genesee—well-kept if modest houses and park greenery. Not only was George proposing to move his mother far from familiar landmarks and friends such as the Strongs but also to deny her the daily companionship of the Tompkins women. Over matters much more petty than this uprooting she had set her small feet and large will in concrete. Eastman took the least valorous but perhaps most expedient way out. He presented her with a fait accompli, and went off to Europe while the move was effected. With the Atlantic yawning between them, Maria could do nothing to change the situation, but she did not go gentle to Arnold Park. Complaints about the wallpapering in the new house, objections to the plumbing and heating, and other domestic grievances poured from Maria's pen and dogged Eastman's travels from London to Paris. She added a stream of objections to and worries about the terrible financial burdens they were assuming in following her son's quest for the outward trappings of upward mobility. Eastman may have succeeded in avoiding some face-to-face confrontations with his determined mother, but Maria made him pay the piper in her own way. From England and France Eastman wrote her, sometimes twice in twenty-four hours, trying to distract her from carrying on about the new house—to little avail. She ignored all of his tidbits of travel lore.

He told her of ducking into Westminster Abbey, picking up a *Schedule of Hymns and Anthems* for her (despite being clearly labeled "Not to be taken away at Morning Service"), and including it in his letter of 18 March 1890: "This will reach you," he wrote, "about the time [27 March] you are moving." Pocketed paeans to her Lord did not soothe Maria, for two days later he complained, "Your letter was pretty short, but I was glad to get it. I hope this will find you comfortably moved and not worn out." This time he included a description of a dinner he had given the night before and even a sketch of the seating arrangements, along with the program from a Royal Lyceum Theater production starring Henry Irving. On 25 and 26 March he met with architects regarding the design of the new London and Harrow buildings but made time to slip into St. Paul's and get another religious souvenir for his mother—the program for afternoon services. He then left for Paris with Chappie Church. From the City of Light he immediately wrote Maria: "Friday night [in Paris] we dined with Nadar. We also breakfasted with him and he has taken my picture. He says he was not satisfied with the other picture."[12]

Nadar père (Gaspard-Félix Tournachon) was as colorful a man as ever entered the ranks of photography. He had taken the world's first aerial photograph—from a balloon—in 1858. He virtually invented air mail by contriving to send messages via carrier pigeon. During the Franco-Prussian War and the seige of Paris in 1870, Nadar escaped over the heads of the startled German troops—again in a balloon. Professionally he was an experimenter. Among the first to take pictures by electric light, he photographed his friends three-quarter length standing under a high skylight against a plain background. His subjects included Napoleon III, Balzac, Dumas, Hugo, Bernhardt, and George Eastman. Although Nadar lived on into the twentieth century, beginning in the 1880s his business was gradually taken over by his son. Paul Nadar, son of the living legend, was Eastman's agent in Paris. With his new Kodak camera, Eastman photographed Nadar fils one morning on this trip standing top-hatted in the Place de l'Opera. In demonstrating the roll holder for Parisian clients, the younger Nadar took some of the first candid photographs—including one hundred shots of a chemist taken at the astounding speed, for the time, of $\frac{1}{130}$ of a second.

The Nadars took Eastman and Church to a production of *Faust*, making a long night of it as the Americans did not rise until 11:00 the next morning. (Eastman's usual European schedule was to bed at 12:30 in the morning, up at 8:00, as compared with the home schedule of a 6:30 A.M. rising. He was living so high on this trip that he gained ten pounds.) As the pattern of intense workdays interspersed with long vacations began to develop, he urged his mother to return with him to Europe that summer, and tried to assure her that "there will be plenty of dividends to pay the bills."[13]

Back in Rochester, Maria was refusing to be mollified or tempted into a more open-palmed attitude. She withdrew into silence and refused to answer his daily missives, so he had to resort to friends to find out was going on back home: "Strong wrote me . . . that Hilbert's vans would form on Ambrose Street tomorrow morning and move to slow and sad music to Arnold Park. . . . He says he don't know as he can ever forgive this last move. I suppose they will feel lonesome but the more I think of it the more I feel satisfied with the move."[14]

"We are wealthy enough now to live in comfort," he insisted to his mother, "and we could not do that according to my ideas in such a little place as 59 Ambrose Street [with its ten rooms]. We certainly cannot spend more than two thirds of my salary alone in Arnold Park. . . . There is no liability of our ever having too little again, and there is surely no reason for trying to save when we now have more than we know what to do with already. The affairs I am engaged in are so large that any difference that we could make in our living expenses would not be visible at the end of the year. So try and get rid of all your economical habits and ideas and just see how much money you can spend with good judgement."[15]

Her silence was beginning to weigh heavily, and this absence of approval from the person from whom he needed it most was beginning to eat away at his confidence. A note of self-justification crept into his letters. "We are going to be *comfortable*, in that house," he wrote defensively, underlining the goal adjective twice, "and I expect it will cost lots of money. Don't hesitate on that account." Although he was telling his mother otherwise, Eastman considered the move to Arnold Park a temporary one. When his mother complained about being moved about and wished that she could be settled in her own house, he mused, as much to himself as to her: "If you want a house all right, but I would advise you to build one. It will give you something to think about. You could buy [crossed out and replaced with] build and pay for a house out of your dividends."[16] For the time being, however, it was the house in Arnold Park that he must make his mother accept, and she was having none of it. She disliked and mistrusted the house and the section of town, and would not be placated. Neither would she lapse out of grudging silence to her son. "A paragraph in Strong's letter," Eastman wrote, "coupled with the fact there is no letter from you gives me great uneasiness." She was making her point melodramatically: "Strong says that you are not going to unpack. I cannot conceive of any combination of circumstances that would oblige us to move again."[17]

There is a comic side to this long-distance mother–son conflict of wills, but a more serious turn was in the offing. Just before sailing for home on 18 April, Eastman wrote a prophetic postscript: "I am afraid you are worrying yourself sick." With his return, the written record is interrupted. George and his mother communicated within the walls of 13 Arnold Park. On 15 July 1890 a letter to George Andrus began "Mother had an operation for cancer (removal of the uterus) performed at the Homeopathic Hospital in this city this morning."[18] Although Eastman had always been able to deal with his mother's series of minor illnesses (he may have believed, and the modern reader is inclined to agree, that these had their source in a mild hypochondria), when she was taken with a serious malady he was badly shaken. The operation was successful— she lived for another seventeen years—but her recovery was slow. Confined to her room for a long stretch of months, and thereafter subject to annual "bad attacks of grippe" (which seems to have been an all-purpose term to describe her various discomforts), Maria was by and large restored to a healthy old age by the ministrations of Homeopathic Hospital's Dr. Lee. Eastman's gratitude was deep. He immediately donated $600 to the hospital, and wrote Lee a thankful note. He did not stop there. After his mother's death he would endow a "Maria Eastman Nurse" position at between $400 and $500 a year, and later build the Maria Eastman Nurses' Wing for the hospital. The strong emotions he felt over his mother's health can be seen in the agitated handwriting of the note to Lee. Rare for Eastman, words are crossed out and others inserted; it took him two drafts to finish.[19]

Eastman was as reticent in his outward emotions as any Scot, but when his mother appeared in a public context he was not at all hesitant to show his feelings. F. W. T. Krohn, who was hired by Walker as a chemist, witnessed an intimate moment between mother and son in 1891. He and Eastman were shipmates and after disembarking in New York City, the two waited in the hotel lobby for Maria to join them. When she did, Eastman gave his mother "a hearty kiss." Krohn was impressed by this sign of devotion to the "sweet, dainty, greyhaired little lady. . . . The simple, natural act was impressive because of its naturalness. . . . A man who loves his Mother like that is sound at heart; he is a white man."[20]

The modern sensibility, conditioned by half-understood Freudian road signs, is apt to put on the brakes, squirm uncomfortably at this kind of display, and then race ahead to interpret Eastman's character in the light of "mother–son fixation" or some other cliché. Eastman's conduct of his life, particularly his decision not to marry, adds fuel. And there is no doubt that his affection for Maria ran deep. His contemporaries knew this well, and many succeeded in getting around the stern and demanding Kodak founder by appealing to his fondness for his mother. No matter how hard a case Eastman was in most matters, he could be reduced to softness by a sentimental reference to when he was "Mrs. Eastman's little boy," or when old acquaintances from Marcellus conjured up word pictures of a three-year-old "sitting on your mother's knee."[21] Even such a fundamentally tactless sort as William Walker indulged: "Truly your mother is a most remarkable woman . . . a standing marvel," he wrote after her cancer operation.[22]

But if Eastman compulsively venerated his mother, he was not alone in his generation. Paul Fussell convincingly and shrewdly points out in his essay, "The Fate of Chivalry, and the Assault upon Mother," that English-speaking males of Eastman's time were heirs of a kind of chivalric tradition that put the mother in the place of the knight's courtly mistress. "Mother is the noblest thing alive," declared Samuel Taylor Coleridge in 1820, and throughout the sixty-year reign of that great mother, Queen Victoria, "it was taken for granted that one's attitude toward one's mother should be conspicuously chivalric, if not reverential"—or, as Krohn would have it, the attitude of a "white man." Fussell demonstrates how the war-mongers of the early twentieth century capitalized on this bent by urging mothers to "Give Your Sons" to the Great War (Mother was never quite the same again after mustard gas and trench warfare, as Fussell shows). A Kodak poster of the time features the Red Cross as "The Greatest Mother of Them All"—and was approved by Eastman since he was head of the organization in Rochester during World War I. Maternal images sent many a Monroe County youth off to the conflict, and bandaged him up if he survived.[23]

Among men of his class and distinction, Eastman's devotion to his mother was the norm. Franklin Delano Roosevelt's mother moved into an apartment near Cambridge to monitor her son's four years at Harvard. Douglas MacArthur's mother similarly ensconced herself at West Point. For neither of these sons were these episodes embarrassing. As Fussell says, "from Mother's omnipresence you suffered no loss of manliness." Among tycoons mother-worship was no less pronounced. John D. Rockefeller Jr. remembered how at the family table his father always held hands with his grandmother as the two gazed fondly at each other and exchanged private pleasantries. Andrew Carnegie waited until after his mother died and he was fifty-one years of age to marry. (Eastman ran into Carnegie, "a grisly little man . . . small bright eyes . . . very free and unaffected in his manners," aboard ship in 1891. The steel maker's younger wife, Eastman wrote Maria, "had taken lots of pleasure with her Kodak."[24]) Eastman's father was as devoted to his mother, Anne Rundell Eastman, as George would be to Maria. In fact, G. W. believed that the cure for the newlywed Maria's loneliness in Rochester would be for Mother to visit "& spend a long time with us." Eastman, his father, and other nineteenth-century men would not have been taken aback by Lord Northcliffe (Fussell's most pointed example), the English newspaper magnate and later an Eastman acquaintance and correspondent: his "mother he always called 'darling,' while his wife was only 'dear.'"[25]

With the move to Arnold Park, Eastman's nest-building and horse-trading instincts in the service of becoming a Victorian gentleman came to the fore. From now on a three-room suite—bedroom, bath, and dressing room—would become de rigueur for the master of the house. He plunged into decorating with a vengeance, writing a series of long, amazingly detailed letters about wallpaper to Harris Hayden, who had wholesale contacts in New York for the benefit of his old insurance colleague. "Mother does not think there is any fun in moving"—a walloping understatement—he explained in a letter to Walker, "but I think there is lots of fun in furnishing up the house. It is a rest for a man compared to building new factories." With each move to rented residences had come more furniture, whole bedroom and dining room suites sometimes, some to be sold if possible—or given away as a last resort—often to a Kodak employee. He liked changing and updating his domestic environment as much as he loved to gear up new camera models.[26]

Maria, the unwilling mistress of the house, now in her seventies and in shaky health, must learn the complex art of Victorian "calling," her son decreed. George Eastman wanted his mother to emulate the fashionable Mrs. William Kimball, wife of Rochester's tobacco magnate. With over one thousand employees in 1884 (compared to the thirty to forty hands at the Eastman Dry Plate and Film Company) the Kimball factory was the city's largest employer. The Kimballs' sumptuous home with a separate art gallery in the Third Ward was the city's largest private residence (and close by Maria's former boarding house at 3 Livingston Park). Calling cards for "Mrs.

George Washington Eastman" were ordered as well as new clothes from the dressmaker. A former Livingston Park neighbor, whose mother had once been better dressed than Maria, began quietly stopping at 13 Arnold Park for bundles of old, discarded clothes. Eastman did not neglect his own appearance, and paid the tailor William Stace in company stock rather than cash; when Stace died, he was worth one-half million dollars. Eastman made many a Rochester fortune in the wake of his swim upward through society's currents.[27]

Equally important was the proper vehicle and coachman, and Eastman pulled out all the stops. In plant area and capitalization, the Cunningham Carriage Factory was the largest industrial enterprise in Rochester as well as one of the largest coach makers in the world. Cunningham now had a customer in George Eastman, who wanted the latest in 1890 transportation equipment. He liked to catalog his carriages by weight: "Brougham, 1185 lbs., Buggy, 290 lbs., Extension Top Phaeton 835 lbs." and so forth. Early Kodak employees recalled that he drove a one-horse, two-seater "trap" to work, parking it in the small shed erected for that purpose. For $475 he bought a new surrey with brass mountings; finding the driver's seat uncomfortable, he sent it back to be raised and padded, along with that of his cabriolet whose springs needed strengthening. As for the horses, he picked them with all the care he would later lavish on automobiles. He was equally determined to sit a good saddle. He took a series of riding lessons at the academy in Central Park, and stabled his personal mounts for weekend and prebreakfast canters.[28]

His interests were not exclusively equine. He purchased a "milch cow," after consultation with dairyman Almon, and added that animal to his stable. Eastman had a near-obsessive craving for fresh milk all his life (and it seems to have run in the family—the very first purchase G. W. made when he settled in Rochester was a milk cow), and when he was deprived, it even entered his dreams. While in the cities of Europe, he wrote home about nocturnal images of strawberries floating in thick, farm cream. Prospective coachmen were interviewed and one was selected for hire—Billy Carter, who turned chauffeur after Eastman began buying automobiles, came to work in the 1890s and remained twenty-three years. Eastman soon had an assistant coachman too—H. D. Stacy. The proper attire—fur collars, gloves, and a coachman's hat—was custom-made by a Fifth Avenue shop in New York City. The barn was enlarged to take in two extra horses as boarders. Indeed, Eastman became so involved with his stable that he once told Andruses not to come for a visit because the horses were sick.

With the move to Arnold Park came a switch from the pool hall to a billiard table at home ("ivory cue tips, small in diameter, no fancy handles but cues very smoothly finished and nicely tapered") and a change from convivial bathhouse hours with Strong to the Genesee Valley Club for after-hours refreshment. When chemist Walter Krohn came for a four-month stay, East-man invited him and Darragh de Lancey, who was putting up the Londoner, over to Arnold Park for Sundays of amusement and play. They played bil-liards in the afternoon, listened to Eastman's new French music box as well as the Edison gramophone (with ear phones) he had recently purchased, then spent the early evening banging away at targets in Eastman's basement where he had set up a miniature firing range. The target was a calling card set on edge, the object being to split it cleanly. Krohn, "more by good luck than good management," fired a shot that flicked off an edge of the card. Feeling triumphant, Krohn handed the rifle to his employer: "Mr. Eastman took the rifle and with his next shot split the card. He then quietly put the rifle away. He had shown that he was not going to be beaten and that was that."[29]

Eastman's instincts for the value of publicity and promotion were always sharply honed, and in 1893 he seized on the opportunity offered by the World's Columbian Exposition in Chicago. In the same year that the Panic had sent the American economy reeling, the Chicago Exposition was meant to steady the nation's economic pins and broadcast good news for its indus-trial future. More than any world's fair before or since, the exposition of 1893 had a lasting effect on its visitors and the taste of the time. As a pre-Hollywood Hollywood, a stage set of reused classical Renaissance forms on a giant scale, this dream city in white plaster was immediately and immensely popular, sounding the death knell for Gothic Revival or Victorian architec-ture and furnishings—and perhaps attitudes. The exposition represented a transfer of power from the old European aristocracy to the new American plutocrats—like Eastman. Henceforth patronage would be the prerogative of the rich rather than the titled as the exposition unveiled an art and architecture of capitalism. A setting of aesthetic leisure fit for a fantasy life was orchestrated by the architects—notably the energetic young firm of McKim, Mead & White—who would come to dominate American architec-ture during Eastman's lifetime.

Augustus Saint-Gaudens, the sculptor who executed many of McKim, Mead & White's commissions, called it "the greatest meeting of artists since the fifteenth century." Aesthete Bernard Berenson said, "We ourselves be-cause of our faith in science and the power of work, are instinctively in sympathy with the Renaissance." Both were talking about the so-called American Renaissance, the reuse of classical or colonial forms in an ordered civic architecture as it burst upon the scene through the Chicago Exposition. A tract of Chicago's swamp and sand had been laid out by Frederick Law Olmsted, the father of American landscape architecture, to be transformed into a Disneyland of the 1890s. Whereas London's Crystal Palace of 1850 had covered twenty acres and had six million visitors, and Philadelphia's Centennial Exposition of 1876 had two hundred acres and ten million people, Chicago dwarfed them both with more than six hundred acres and twenty-seven million visitors. At Chicago's fair, which celebrated the four hundredth anniversary of the discovery of America, George Eastman and others first saw the new fashion in American architecture.

The "City Beautiful" was a brand name invented by Rochesterian Charles Mulford Robinson, city planner, to describe this ordered civic architecture that elicited a sense of civic grandeur through a strongly disciplined city plan. The fair's designers, under the direction and orchestration of Daniel Hudson Burnham, sought to bring classic order out of the Victorian revival eclecticism that had dominated the nineteenth century, including all the houses in which George Eastman had lived since leaving the Greek Revival behind in Waterville. Eastman saw his mission as bringing order to the photographic materials industry, so it is not surpising that Colonial Revival architecture appealed so strongly to him.

Eastman had been busying himself getting ready for the Chicago Exposition as early as July 1891. It was then that he requested an area one thousand feet square: fifty feet on the aisle and twenty feet deep. He bid for the exclusive franchise for photographing the exposition. "It is our desire to make the greatest photographic exhibit that was ever made at any exposition and if granted permission will do a creditable thing."[30] In ads and copy starting in 1892, the soon-to-be-famous Kodak Girl would make her official debut. A $2 per day charge was made by the fair authorities for the privilege of making pictures at the exposition and no plates or film were for sale on the grounds. The amateur had to bring his or her own supplies. This played right into Eastman's—and Blair's—hands. One hundred glass plates "would weigh at least thirty pounds, to say nothing of the weight of the camera," Kodak ads noted. "The Kodak, loaded for 100 pictures, 4 × 5, weighs $4\frac{1}{2}$ pounds. The moral is obvious—*Take a Kodak With You to the World's Fair*."

The exposition's theme of "Not Things but Men" was intended to "commemorate the progress of civilization and be an incentive to further development, not only by displaying the best products of men's thoughts, as shown in material things, but also by bringing together for conference, in a series of Congresses, the leading thinkers, workers and artists of the world." Prominent among the conferences was the Congress of Photographers. "The advancement that has been made in photography, and the processes dependent upon it, within the last twenty years has astonished the artists and scientists of the world," the preliminary address to the Congress of Photographers read, "Its future possibilities are too great for any one to estimate." Eastman served on the Advisory Council to the congress, along with other leaders in the photographic field. They included W. I. Lincoln Adams from Scovill; John Carbutt, Gustav Cramer, and M. A. Seed, plate manufacturers; Professor Smillie of the Smithsonian Institution; photographer William

Henry Jackson; and Edward Bausch and Ernest Gundlach of the photo-optical industry in Rochester. Papers delivered on emulsion photography, photographic chemistry, photo-legal photography, photo-medical photography, amateur photography, photography as an aid to education, instantaneous photography, photographic optics, microscopic photography, astronomical photography, submarine photography, aerial photography and so forth suggest the rapidly expanding frontiers of the field as well as the enthusiastic hopes for its future.

Eastman, whose previous attendance at Philadelphia's Centennial Exhibition of 1876 had roused the inventor-dreamer in him, made his own exhibit a rallying point for amateurs. He meant to dazzle a neophyte audience by stressing the latest Kodak innovations that would make amateur photography easier and more convenient. Retailers advertised the Kolumbus (or Columbus) Kodak, not really a new camera but one of the regular line designated as a promotional item,[31] and along with it, a new, faster film. Daylight-loading film (wrapped in black paper so that it could be loaded into a camera without a darkroom) and noncurling film (which produced negatives that lay flat instead of rolling up tightly like a matchstick) were on display. (Although noncurling film was exhibited, it would be more than a decade—1904—before it was marketed.) Eastman demonstrated how the amateur could be protected from buying old and possibly deteriorated film by presenting Kodak's most recent marketing innovation: date-marked film cartons. He had the Eastman Photographic Materials Company in England send enlargements for a display because "foreign negatives attract more attention." He introduced a positive blueprint paper (blue lines on white ground), asking Chappie Church the usual question: "Will it infringe on anything already on the market?"

He exhibited the No. 4 Kodak camera that had just journeyed to Greenland with Lieutenant Robert E. Peary, who in 1909 would be hailed as the first explorer to reach the North Pole. "Peary Pressed the Button," the ads stated. Twenty-three rolls of film "secured 2,000 first-class negatives," as "the brave explorer . . . fairly outdid himself as a photographer. He not only heeded the advice 'Take a Kodak with you,' but went further and took three."

Eastman visited the fair at least three times, including a trip in May 1893 to arrange a joint contract with Gustav Cramer. For $1,500 Eastman and Papa Cramer erected a building twenty-five feet by thirty-six feet with a twenty-five-foot square showroom and darkroom for changing plates, agreeing to share expenses and accommodations evenly. While Cramer had the exclusive concession for glass plates, Eastman kept that for film as well as the selling or renting of cameras. "We also have the privilege of repairing and exchanging Kodaks," he told Henry Strong, "so that anyone who goes to the World's Fair can be assured of being taken care of in case his Kodak breaks down." He contracted to supply C. D. Arnold, the fair's official photographer, with Solio paper "at a low figure" although the photographic department was free to use albumen or platinum paper from other manufacturers. While Eastman hoped to break even, he gambled that "the exposure will be worth its costs in advertising." His ads stressed that "hand cameras making pictures not larger than four by five are permitted on the fair grounds for $2 a day" and that "the Eastman Kodak Company has purchased the exclusive concession and erected a special building for a free film dark room, available to 'Kodakers.'" He supplied "competent attendants" to assist those who might have trouble with their Kodak cameras and offered to exchange a Kodak camera in perfect working order for any that was not. This was, he said, to assure perfect success to Kodak customers.[32] All of these efforts provided, Eastman told George Dickman, "some indirect benefits, by showing that we keep ourselves in the front pew."[33]

While Eastman was busy promoting the company in Chicago, he was as yet unaware that Strong had begun a financial slide in Tacoma, but his other partner, William Walker, made his presence known. Walker was vacationing in Niagara Falls, and intercepted Eastman, who was traveling back to Rochester from Chicago, at the Buffalo train station. They had a forty-five-minute conference on the platform, during which time Walker tried to enlist Eastman in a hot scheme—investing in a Buffalo paper concern. "I do not know what to think about the paper company," Eastman fudged, as leery of teaming up with Walker again as he was doubtful of the investment. "There is something queer about the ratings. . . . The financial market is in a very delicate condition and it behooves a man to keep his money within reach. You could not borrow $10,000 on a bushel of Kodak stock." Now that the erstwhile partner was retired from the active management, more cordial relations were possible, and Eastman was able to do the Walker family some kindnesses. Eastman took Walker's young invalid daughter, Gertrude, and her English governess along on the train for a visit with his mother: "Gertrude is a splendid visitor," he reported. "She is so easily pleased." Walker was pleased too; he doted on Gertrude.[34]

Creating a nation (and world) of amateur photographers was now Eastman's goal, and he instinctively grasped what others in the photography industry came to realize more slowly: Advertising was the mother's milk of the amateur market. As he did in most areas of his company, Eastman handled the promotional details himself. And he had a gift for it—almost an innate ability to frame sentences into slogans, to come up with visual images that spoke directly and colorfully to everyone. Up to 1892 he relied on his own clear, unadorned copy and sense of showmanship. Two New York advertising agencies—Frank Seaman and J. Walter Thompson—acted as space brokers and advisors. Seaman, a Rochesterian who "married Lillie Huntington and is a member of the publishing firm of Cassell & Co, New York,"[35] especially had become something of an Eastman crony over the years. In 1891 he accompanied Eastman to Tacoma and Yellowstone Park and in 1892 Eastman asked Seaman to go with him to Europe. Eastman was beginning to realize, however, that there were only twenty-four hours in a day and that he would eventually have to delegate the advertising responsibility. He searched for an advertising man, and on 15 March 1892 hired Lewis Bunnell Jones, who had graduated from the University of Rochester in 1890 and was working as a newspaper man in Syracuse. Eastman offered him a salary of "$1,000–$1,200 to start." Forty years later, to the day of his hiring by Eastman, Jones would write his employer's obituary for the national press. In later years Jones would be identified[36] as one of five persons who were most influential in helping Eastman establish and shape the company. By 1893 the "live young man" was running the Kodak show at the Chicago Exposition, and would help Eastman formulate and refine the central advertising image for the company—the Kodak Girl.

In the mid-1880s Eastman had told J. Walter Thompson that "a picture of a pretty girl sells more than a tree or a house" in magazine advertisements. And a young lady, a wholesome outdoor type usually in a striped dress, according to Eastman's prescription, "fashionably dressed, holding a camera," was introduced to America in 1888. Foreign branches featured insets of Kodak Park and George Eastman in their advertisements, but Eastman, essentially a modest (and realistic) person, eschewed such a course in America. "I never use any pictures of myself in our own printed matter, because I do not care about seeing so much of my own likeness."[37] Eventually the English dealers went along with the Kodak Girl promotion. In 1901, when the Girl was introduced in England, the copy read: "This dainty lady, who carries in her hand like a purse one of our neat and inconspicuous Folding Pocket Kodaks, will be used extensively by us for advertising purposes."

By November 1892, when Eastman asked Dickman if he wanted "more than 12 prints of the Kodak Girl" prepared for the fair, the girl had acquired her name. Presumably the nomen was Eastman's creation. As with the Kodak camera, it did not take long for the Kodak Girl ("nameless insofar as the legions of her admirers are concerned," a college magazine swooned) to enter the popular culture. The Kodak Girl eventually moved from poster and newspaper ad to six-foot cardboard cutouts in stores, and finally to a live model in a striped dress who represented the company's products through personal appearances.

The two Kodak Girls who advertised the 1893 Chicago Exposition wore the latest summer frocks with leg-of-mutton sleeves and carried parasols. They posed before the Court of Honor administration building and were drawn by artist V. Perark to the specifications of Seaman, busily creating the image in New York. Magazines were the basic medium for advertising then and while Kodak would be one of the first to use photographs instead of line drawings, in the 1890s half-tone cuts for reproductions were of such poor quality that it was 1901 before the first photographically illustrated Kodak Girl appeared "shooting up the scenery with her Kodak." She would inspire many real-live girls to mimic her garb for fancy dress balls. Thirteen British artists of some renown would work on the Kodak Girl ads. In the 1920s one model of a full-faced girl in a hat would be photographed with George Eastman in Africa. Another would be garbed as a modified flapper in pastel jersey over box-pleated skirt, topped by a felt cloche. Line drawings would feature a tiny, exuberant Kodak Girl in striped dress standing on a huge camera. In Bombay an Indian Girl in a striped dress would stand next to a life-sized cutout cardboard figure (in striped dress). "This figure," Jones would alert dealers round the world, "is a most attractive one, printed in 12 colors, which gives an air of freshness and distinction to the premises in which it stands." The Kodak Girl would live on beyond her creators' lifetimes: In the 1960s the tradition of going down to the sea in stripes would progress to bands of models in princess-style striped suits converging on the beaches of England, Kodak cameras in hand, to snap the bathers there.

Even before hiring Jones, Eastman had identified the family as his principal advertising target. An 1888 ad featured a father on one knee snapping a picture of his little daughter. Eastman knew, early on, as Jones would tell an interviewer in 1918, that "it was the charm of photography not just his little black box that must be sold to the public." If photography was no more than a passing hobby or even if it was "photography for art's sake" as with the original amateurs and professionals such as Stieglitz, the danger existed that customers would tire of it and move on to yet another hobby, shifting their recreational interests perhaps a dozen times. Children, Eastman and Jones reflected, were the "cause of the purchase of a vast quantity of photographic apparatus." Next in importance came travel. Jones, who became adept at pithy, memorable slogans, designed an ad featuring a Kodak Girl in a long, striped dress standing on a windswept cliff, Folding Kodak in one hand and case slung over the other shoulder. "Take a Kodak with you," the caption read.[38]

Almost any slogan—"Springtime is Kodak time," "All outdoors invites your Kodak," "Don't forget your Kodak," "Save your happy memories with a Kodak," or "Have you ever thought how much *you* miss by not having a Kodak?"—could accompany a Kodak Girl. One hard-sell line, "Don't let another week-end slip by without a Kodak," featured a coupon to send in for twenty-five specimen photographs, samples of work taken by different cameras. Another slogan anticipated gifts for people who have everything with "Your friends can buy anything you can give them except your photograph." Jones suggested with undeniable logic that "The snapshot you want tomorrow you must take today." When the word "Kodak" seemed about to enter the language as a common noun standing for camera, Jones and Eastman met this trademark challenge with, "If it isn't an Eastman it isn't a Kodak."

Prince Henry and the Earl of East Avenue

Eastman's bedrock support in all of his industrial and financial dealings came from Henry Strong. Together, the former bank clerk and the erstwhile whip manufacturer succeeded in the burgeoning photographic business where professionals with special technical knowledge came up short. Strong's way with people was a crucial element. Affable and approachable, the gregarious Strong was comfortable wherever people gathered—in a dignified lobby of a London hotel or strolling down Rochester's State Street hailing passers-by. Strong inspired immediate trust; he knew everyone and was universally liked. Consequently, he could get away with armtwisting, peddling Kodak stock to his adult Sunday school class, or enveloping a friend in an exuberant bear hug.

Eastman, of course, would sooner let a patent go uncontested than bear-hug anyone. Taciturn, cautious, shy, and modest—these characteristics of Eastman were often interpreted by strangers as cold unconcern. He needed Strong's expansiveness to humanize the corporate image and the "colonel's" sixteen years of seniority to take the edge off his own callow appearance. Even in his forties Eastman looked at least ten years younger, a condition that he found irksome enough to resort to a variety of hirsute remedies. Portraits of the time show a youthful face adorned by a clump of lip hair that looks almost as if it had been rented for the occasion. It did not help that Eastman usually acted like a withdrawn adolescent in social situations, his eyes cast determinedly to the ground as he talked. The warmth and humor that Eastman could summon up behind closed doors was unavailable to him in public, where his personality was flat, dry, and tough, and he was sensitive enough to know it.

Tom Craig, who headed Kodak's ciné processing and repair department for many years, knew the two men well, and ably contrasted their roles: "You were charmed by Strong, but you depended on Eastman for the things that mattered. When you met Strong and Eastman together on State Street, Strong's hearty 'Hello' could be heard for blocks; Eastman didn't even see you. But if you had a problem, you wouldn't dream of approaching Strong. Eastman was the one who would give you a fair hearing, a decisive answer, and heartening advice."[1]

The bond between Eastman and Strong went deeper than business convenience and strategy. Given their age difference and Eastman's fatherless state since age seven, it is tempting to think of them as father and son. Strong *was* forever attempting to attach Eastman to some available female. Never censorious, he was genuinely concerned that Eastman was not getting as much fun out of life as he should. "Dear Skinny," he wrote in 1888,

> You are a queer cuss, Geo, and I know you never want any sympathy or comfort from your friends . . . but I want you to know that I, for one, appreciate the mountains of care and responsibility that you are constantly called upon to overcome (and you "git there," too) and if I never express it in words, it may be a source of comfort to you to know that I am always with you heart and hand. Never take my silence for indifference. I sometimes think that we do not know each other very well. We surely are neither of us very demonstrative, and Mrs. S. says the Strongs are so queer and I guess she is right. Well, shake old boy.[2]

This may be an attempt on the older man's part to identify with Eastman's inner life, in the hope that he could understand him a bit better. Much of the essential Eastman forever remained a mystery to Strong. Eastman's affection for "my dear pard" is unmistakable, but to assume that Eastman felt a paternal tie with Strong would be an exaggeration; the tone in letters was familiar and jocular, more like that of fraternity brothers. Strong was "Dear Heinrich" (until the World War, when he became "Dear Henri"), or "Old Crazy Man," and sometimes (when Eastman wanted to needle him a little for his liking of a lavish lifestyle) "Prince Henry."

Eastman's loyalty to Strong was steadfast ("I am your friend") despite the many times "Heinrich" would try his patience, but that did not prevent Eastman from showing exasperation and even anger at his senior partner. Strong was often dismayed at the rough treatment Eastman handed out to employees, and would gently remind his partner to "deal gently with Bro Clark now that you have him in your employ" or "Sometimes I think that you are rather hard to please. Did such an idea ever occur to you?" Strong was often enough on the receiving end of the Eastman ire to know what he was saying. Initially Eastman needed the financial boost that Henry Strong gave him. By the 1890s, though, he was well in command of his own business and indeed the whole industry, and could easily have cast Strong aside, particularly after the succession of financial crises Strong encountered. Instead, Eastman chose to keep Strong on as president of the holding company until he retired in 1901; even after that Strong remained vice president of that New Jersey holding company and president of the New York manufacturing company (in Rochester) until his death in 1919.

Beginning in the 1880s Strong was drawn to the boomtown of Tacoma, Washington, and the investment opportunities it seemed to offer. (Old Tacoma was settled in 1852, New Tacoma became the terminal of the Northern Pacific Railway in 1873, and the two were consolidated as the city of Tacoma in 1884.) Strong started with a few rental properties, then persuaded some Rochesterians, including Eastman, to buy property there as well. Then he began looking for loans from his friends so that the latest incredible deal would not be lost. Eastman was skeptical but compliant. "Dear Heinrich," he wrote. "If you would rather borrow of me than Woodbury I will lend you $6,000 at 6% a yr [but] I hope you wont get in the soup with it." The loan was a small price to pay for Henry's bouncy letters, and Eastman intimated as much when he said, "You have considerable Western nerve to claim that you are too busy to write."[3]

Strong's most ambitious deals were for a dry dock, a foundry, and a bank, and he was wildly optimistic about them. "Dear Georgy," he wrote in 1890, "I may be insane but it is a mild attack and I have no fears of a fatal result." But Strong's deals were doomed. In rapid succession the dock and foundry began to fold and the Traders Bank was hemorrhaging in the Panic of 1893. Strong was in serious trouble, which he magnified by borrowing on his Kodak stock and continuing to pour funds (his and others') into these failing concerns. He tried by force of will and hard work to salvage them. Eastman knew that Strong's talents did not lie in administration, and told him so: "If you accept the management of the bank . . . you will be assuming great responsibility in a business that you know nothing whatever about." Eastman's advice, which Strong was slow to accept, was to cut his losses and liquidate. Strong finally conceded: "I have no desire or intention of continuing in the Dry Dock business or the banking business either. . . . You may be able to blow some sense into me yet. I have no taste for battles. I indulge only in cigars." Far from unleashing a fusillade of invective, Eastman counseled him to buck up. He used photographic images to try to help the older man put things, "fast coming to a focus in Tacoma," in perspective: "Keep a stiff upper lip, and do not lose sight of the fact that if the emulsion goes wrong, plates fog, the Solio turns yellow, and the bromide paper blisters, all of these troubles will disappear after a while."[4]

Eastman was annoyed at Strong's wishful thinking that Traders Bank would rally and bail him out, and kept urging Strong to face facts, cut his losses, and get out. But this did not prevent him from propping up Strong's morale with encouraging news about his family in Rochester. He told Strong that a mutual acquaintance saw "Mrs S" at an open window, waved, and had a chat with the sickly woman. He gave Strong's son Harry a job in the printing department but expressed doubts about his industriousness: "Harry wanted the week off to go to a lawn tennis tournament but I wouldn't let him go. Told him if he wanted a vacation he should have taken it before he commenced work. He seems to take it cheerfully."[5]

By the middle of May 1894 Strong began to realize he had lost his investments. Eastman cancelled his scheduled bicycle trip in Europe for 1894, and threw himself into Strong's affairs, trying to salvage what he could. He honored Strong's request to keep his business troubles from his ailing wife. He retrieved Strong's Kodak stock from creditors, took over Strong's Tacoma holdings, and systematically liquidated most of them for what he could get. Eastman himself was considerably short of funds by the end of these transactions, and some properties he found he could not give away. Ironically, by October, the real estate market in Tacoma had settled down somewhat and Eastman found some income starting to trickle back in. "Glory, glory, glory," he wrote, "think of Tacoma paying anything."[6] He held on to those properties for years, and there is some indication that he eventually recouped his own losses. Strong spent the better part of a year winding things up in the Pacific Northwest, but by 30 December 1895, Eastman could tell friends that "the Colonel is hard at work. . . .[He] is all right, but he will not go to work until I put a good carpet on his floor and buy him some new chairs. . . . I think he will like his job." Strong was still president of the Eastman Kodak Company, and to Eastman, "it is a great relief . . . to have him here" in Rochester.[7]

Nothing could daunt Strong for long. Having gone through a financial crisis that would have licked most men, and having recovered with Eastman's help, he pulled himself together. Although he was the first investor and president of the company, he had never been active in its management. Now slightly chastened but still humorous, Strong plunged into the business with characteristic energy, filling the presidential office with acrid cigar smoke and his jaunty presence. "The life of ease such as I am now living," he decided, "can not be improved upon." Eastman maintained the fiction that Strong was recovering on his own. "He pulled out of his western difficulties in good shape," Eastman told an English director. "He still owns more than $1,000,000 of our stock and if we pay dividends, as we expect to, he will pretty nearly clean up everything." No one knew of the debt Strong owed

Eastman and from 1895 to 1901 Eastman had his president just where he wanted him—minding the store while he took off on his bicycle for four-month jaunts through all the capitals of Europe, establishing branch outlets for Kodak goods, reorganizing the companies under an English holding company, and having the time of his life.

During those six years, Strong dutifully wrote his weekly ten-page report ("That is right; I do not lose a wink of sleep, nor an atom of pleasure until I send you word: I think I now have everything in hand and whenever there is a push, I am there to push and push hard") to the traveling Eastman, who kept a tight rein on all the details through a flurry of cables and letters. The presidential epistles, always full of gusto, began with unlikely bursts ("APRIL FOOL!!!!" began one "business letter"), rambled through office details ("de Lancey's film report gave me a *cold sweat* . . . a good subject for you to study when you have nothing else to think about"), and usually ended on a cheery note ("Don't forget to give our love to the Dickey birds!" Strong exclaimed, referring to Mr. and Mrs. Dickman). Henry rolled up his sleeves and found his new-old job quite pleasant: "As I go about from one department to another I begin to feel as if I would like to take off my coat and give them all a lift. I had no idea I would ever feel like working but I seem to take to it like a duck to water. I begin already to dread the loss of my job. I spent a good hour Sunday morning scouring rusty and dirty frying pans and giving orders— 'Do it for the old man.'" Such letters could never replace thrashing out problems in person, however. "You will soon be home to talk it over with all hands. . . . I am glad you realize how unsatisfactory correspondence is when we could come to a decision so much sooner by personal argument."[8]

"Fatherdear," as the three Strong children customarily called their father Henry, very much wanted his son Harry to learn the business. Eastman's past experiences made him reluctant to hire friends or relatives, but eventually he relented in Harry's case. The young Strong was hired in 1894 and worked at Kodak Park mornings while taking chemistry classes at the University of Rochester in the afternoons. Much to Eastman's consternation, Harry was discovered playing football for the university. An ankle injury, however, brought a quick end to that diversion. Harry had no sooner returned to work when he took a day off to attend a tennis match in Syracuse. "I propose to have a talk with him and fully explain my ideas," Eastman told Strong. "No doubt he will buckle down and make a first class man."[9] At Kodak Park Harry was moved around from the printing department to the collodion department and when Jack Hawley, head of the Solio department, took sick, Strong hinted that "Harry would be a good man for the job," but Eastman decided against it. He did find a task commensurate with young Strong's dash and verve during the coating machine trial, when Harry was assigned to move witness Mollie Stephenson from house to house so that her irate father could not locate her and take her back to Buffalo before she testified. Soon Eastman gave up on Harry, who moved on to a variety of other occupations, eventually owning a Rochester car dealership. He died in Los Angeles in 1919, a few months after his father. Henry's daughters, Helen and Gertrude, married and left Rochester. Henry Achilles, Gertrude's husband, was treasurer of the Traders Bank and presumably lost something in that collapse. Helen married George Carter and when Carter's older brother was murdered, George and Helen went to Hawaii to take over the family estate. Carter later became governor of the islands. Strong's wife Helen continued to suffer from ill health until her demise in 1904. Shortly thereafter she would be succeeded by a vivacious, thirtyish, second wife for the sixty-seven-year-old but robust Henry Strong.

Never driven by company affairs like his partner and always looking for variety and excitement, Strong began to chafe under the details and burden of the Kodak presidency. He retired in 1901, and the third act of his life was possibly the most rewarding. He divided his time among old Tacoma haunts; the golf courses of the sunnier parts of the country (his favorite golfing partner was John D. Rockefeller) from Atlanta to San Francisco (where he happened to be in 1906 when the earthquake struck that city); Hawaii with the Carters; and briefer and briefer sojourns in Rochester. There is no doubt that Prince Henry knew how to enjoy life—a lesson that would not be ignored by Eastman once his company had achieved virtual dominance in its industry.

At age forty, in spite of his promise to Maria, Eastman found that a shift in residence was advisable. He had looked around for a suitable domicile for himself, his mother, a growing band of servants, a cow christened "Cora of Sandusky," and Maria's favorite horse Baby, whom she had trained to paw the ground for sugar or carrots. His heart's desire was to build a house from the foundation up. Architect and "Friend Charlie" Crandall had been assigned the task of drawing up floor plans for a forty-foot by ninety-foot "colonial" house, "two stories with attic . . . gambrel roof and port cochere" and the Camera Works had built a model with which Eastman would toy. He studied furnace blowers and drew plans for a two-story "23 by 30 foot conservatory to be used as a palm house and sitting room." He still could not find a satisfactory lot, however, and that frustration, as well as the lack of ready cash caused by Strong's Tacoma debacle, made him postpone. He had already decided against buying his Arnold Park house from H. S. Finch because the lot was too small. Earl Putnam, an old family friend from Waterville, informed Eastman that he was moving to Philadelphia and that his J. Foster Warner-designed house on East Avenue was for sale. Eastman liked the interior layout but not the "dowdy exterior" and he was unable to buy a lot adjacent to the "elephant" for a new stable.[10]

Rufus Dryer, a vice president of the Cunningham Carriage Company, alerted Eastman in England by transatlantic cablegram that the house next to the Dryers' own on East Avenue (and across the street from Putnam's) was for sale. The Soule House, also designed by Warner, was one of the grandest in the city, having cost $250,000 to build in 1892. "House matters seem to be coming to a focus now," Eastman told his mother on 28 August 1894. "The model will be finished when I get home." Meanwhile he also secured options on two existing East Avenue houses: "So you had better make up your mind where you want to live." Apparently Maria chose the Soule House, the price of which was now $100,000. He jauntily told Harris Hayden that "there was no 'nerve' required in buying the 'quarter million' place. It is no longer a quarter million place."[11]

The Rochester architect Warner had been hard at work in his Granite Building office in 1891 when Wilson Soule walked in. "I have bought a lot out East Avenue," the youthful patent medicine tycoon announced, "and want you to design a house for me." Soule planned an extended European stay, granting Warner power of attorney, with the only stipulation being "at least six bedrooms." Warner, age thirty-one, was of the third generation of a family of architects. His father, Andrew Jackson Warner, had designed most of downtown Rochester in the popular nineteenth-century Gothic, Romanesque, or Second Empire Revival styles as well as many of the Italianate mansions on East Avenue and a small job for George Washington Eastman in 1850. His great uncles Merwin and Henry Austin, of Rochester and New Haven, Connecticut, respectively, were responsible for much of the Greek and Gothic Revival look of a still earlier era in those cities. The younger Warner favored the Colonial, Classical, or Georgian Revival styles then sweeping the country and had already designed the Powers Hotel, the "skyscraper" Granite Building, and the Monroe County and Ontario County courthouses in these fashionable modes. Warner, a stickler for high architectural and building standards, had a certain dryness of style, a propensity for bombast, and an autocratic manner that subdued most clients into agreeing with his preferences. With carte blanche and an absentee client, the architect was able to construct one of the finest houses ever built in Monroe County, New York.[12]

The weighty stone structure of irregularly composed masses that rose at 400 East Avenue was imposing in size, substantially built, and enriched by superior craftsmanship and the finest materials. The interior was decidedly eclectic. The barrel-arched vestibule of Numidian marble led into an oak Renaissance hall with a fireplace modeled after a ducal palace in Venice and a frieze of embossed leather. The reception room was Indo-Persian with teak walls, had a ceiling of perforated brass underpainted in red, and panels hung with tapestries. The drawing room was Louis XVI—"white mahogany relieved by delicate moldings in gilt." The library was Byzantine, the dining room Elizabethan with an elliptical ceiling in plaster relief. Six large bedrooms—"one colonial, one French, the others in sycamore, mahogany, birch, and curly maple"—opened off the second-floor hall. So did a sewing room, two chambers, six bathrooms, and several closets. Four servants' rooms, two more bedrooms, and a billiard room occupied the third floor. The Soules with their two young children had less than two years to enjoy the exotic environment Warner had created for them. On the night of 25 July 1894, following a pleasant drive, Wilson Soule became entangled in the reins of a runaway horse and was dragged to his death before the eyes of horrified friends. Pinched for income following the Panic of 1893 and anxious to sell, the young widow accepted Eastman's $100,000 offer, which included five hundred shares of Kodak stock.

The Soule House afforded more outdoor space, which spoke to a quirk of Eastman at the time. The passage of a law allowing the production of oleomargarine distressed him. To insure a regular supply of fresh dairy products, he needed room for cows and "a place where I could do a little flower gardening." There was also a stable "with room for ten horses," which the Eastmans were on their way to filling. The former move to Arnold Park was still fresh in his mind, so "This time I am going to boss the move myself." He sent Maria to New York on October 31 in the company of a friend for a shopping spree. He imported his niece Ellen Andrus to help, and found her a "welcome addition to our small family." The Rochester Carting Company provided a horse-drawn wagon and three men in addition to the driver for a day-and-a-half at the high rate of $25 a day.[13]

Once ensconced, Eastman got down seriously to the bovine business. Cousin Almon was asked for "the best cow in your herd. . . . I spend most of my time nowadays looking for a cow that will give fifty quarts of milk a day and average six per cent butterfat. . . . I think I will go into raising garden truck and peddling milk. . . . What little time I have that is not taken in this occupation is absorbed in building a hennery. I expect to get all of these in shape to resume my normal occupation January 1." When Almon didn't answer immediately, George bought a "muley milch cow," but he told Almon, "I had much rather you pick one but I cant wait. I have got to have plenty of the lacteal fluid right away. . . . If anything happens to this hornless bovine, I will get you to ship your star animal." When he added to his stock, Eastman exulted to Strong, "Now I have got a cow, a cow-cow, a muley cow, and know where I can get another. I bought a common cow because I could not make up my mind to pay for a fancy one." He closed the subject with a bit of understatement: "I am pretty excited about this cow business."[14]

"We are nicely settled in our new house," Eastman told Walker. "For all that it is so large we find it cozy and comfortable." The place was not really satisfactory, though, until he put in $15,000 worth of improvements: herringbone hardwood floors, locks that worked from a master key, sliding doors on the sideboard cupboard, a galvanized iron smokestack, screen door checks, a gun case with Sargeant and Greenleaf locks on doors and drawers, three lightning rods, eight hot bed frames, thousands of bulbs from Holland, two cords of wood from the Rescue Mission for the fireplace grate, and, for good measure, two more "good Jersey cows." A little redecorating was undertaken, too, starting with the Louis XVI drawing room, white mahogany relieved by delicate moldings in gilt being not the Eastman taste. George Ross-Lewis got the commission and the back of Eastman's hand for his suggestions: "It is hardly to be expected that your taste and mine will agree precisely and inasmuch as I am the one who will have to use it, it does not seem unreasonable to ask you to make it to suit me." The drawing room sat until 1897, when Eastman engaged both J. B. Tiffany of New York and the Hayden Company of Rochester to try their hands at turning it into a music room. They, too, failed to produce satisfactory designs, so he refurbished the room himself with chairs from Hayden (returned as unsatisfactory) and a Steinway piano with case by Tiffany (whose designs he rejected as "too rococo").[15]

Eastman's British colleagues could not fathom central heating, but it fascinated Americans. An elaborate temperature control system was installed in Soule House with thermostats in the library, hall, dining room, drawing room, and reception room. Control drafts automatically banged open and closed as the thermostats read the average temperature of three of these rooms. A gas-operated pump, fed by city illuminating gas, was installed in the artesian well. Though the equipment for heating was up-to-date, the owner could but rarely be induced to turn it on. In a burst of 1890s' patriotism, a huge (twenty-foot by thirty-foot) American flag ("best quality") was purchased for a ninety-foot flag pole, which neighbor Rufus Dryer arranged to have painted each year along with the Eastmans' enlarged collection of Cunningham carriages and the fancy court hansom with yellow wheels, which Clarke had happened upon in England while on his butter churn search. Two six-foot by twelve-foot flags for the window poles completed the Fourth of July aspect of 400 East Avenue. Salter Brothers, no longer needed to supply fresh-cut flowers twice each week, now planted the flower boxes that ringed the sweeping veranda.

In the basement Eastman installed a windowless photography laboratory with white tile walls and floor and a shooting gallery (a butler would stand to the side behind a lead shield to set up the targets). For his bedroom he designed a wall of cubbyholes, drawers, and trays within drawers to fit possessions ranging from cuff links to the tall silk hats he wore to the opera or an occasional funeral. He needed little furniture but a new bedroom set for his mother to replace the one he sold to his bookkeeper and a mahogany card table and chairs. The servants' dining table was revarnished and old mahogany chairs and a reed rocker refurbished with white linen cushions. The primary deficiency to the Soule estate was the lack of greenhouses and conservatory. This was partially taken care of when Foster Warner drew plans for five greenhouses—for plants, roses, fruit, forcing, and propagation. (A "winter room" and three more greenhouses were added for a new hobby, orchids, in 1898.)

From England, the Dickmans sent the Eastmans their favorite maid. Sarah Ginger was a comely lass, and purposely chosen for her looks on George Dickman's theory that, "some crabby bachelor says the homely ones will marry the first man that asks her while the pretty ones will be more discriminating." Signals got mixed and Eastman forgot to meet Sarah at the station, but she followed his alternate instructions for taking the trolley to the last stop on University Avenue and walking round the block to 400 East Avenue. "Sarah arrived without mishap, and looked as happy as a bird when she waited on table this morning." Soon Sarah was homesick for Josephine Dickman, however, and returned to England. Dickman's wife continued to be consulted when major household help was needed. A similar situation occurred when Toku, a Japanese valet-butler, came and left quickly. Eastman's first reaction was ecstatic: "a great success . . . made himself popular with the whole household . . . a marvel of neatness . . . only defect is he does not speak English very well . . . understands but enunciation is indistinct." Rochester was just too insular and provincial for these exotic new arrivals.[16]

Burglary insurance was acquired and the Protective Police and Fire Patrol Company engaged to keep an eagle eye on the first home that George Eastman had ever owned. A house account was opened with Alliance Bank with $2,000 and, from then until Eastman's death, that amount was deposited monthly; Alice Whitney was given power of attorney to pay the household bills. At first Eastman answered all inquiries from expectant landscape architects by saying that "our very good landscape gardener at Kodak Park will be laying out the East Avenue grounds." But then someone suggested he contact the superintendent of Central Park in New York City. Eastman took the balance of the day off when Samuel Parsons came on 4 November 1894; Parsons subsequently agreed to "make a plan for planting out my homestead grounds" for $100 plus traveling expenses. Pleased by the result, Eastman asked Parsons to "save half a day to rearrange [the 16.5-acre grounds at] Kodak Park." Plant stock came from Rochester's justly famous Ellwanger and Barry nursery, which specialized in rare and exotic plantings as well as the shade trees, especially elms, which were a particular enthusiasm of East Avenue residents from the 1850s. All Rochester watched what was happening at the Soule House and since most people could not glimpse the goings-on inside, they contented themselves with making remarks about the landscaping. "I notice your man has planted the elm tree in front of your house wrong," one unsolicited correspondent wrote. "The top bends a little towards the northeast. It should be turned exactly around so that the top leans toward the southwest, the direction of the prevailing winds. If it is left the way it is, it will be a one-sided tree."

A housewarming seemed in order so "I had the boys [Hubbell, Dryer, Angle, Church, Woodbury, Platt, Eastwood, and Fenn] up to the house New Year's night for a Scheutzenfest," he told the absent Strong. "The entertainment began with shooting at 7 P.M. We had supper at 9 and at 2:30, the Apollinaris water having given out, the boys went home." Trophies were provided by the host: Bert Eastwood carried off first prize, a silver mounted pipe. Chappie Church received a box of cigars, Walter Hubbell, a pack of playing cards, Rufus Dryer, a penknife. Alas, "John Woodbury had the consolation prize all to himself."[17]

A day in the domestic life of George Eastman at the turn of the century began at 7:00 A.M. as he wound his calendar watch that had been placed face up on the bedside table at midnight. After trotting through his gardens and the neighboring roads astride Jaspar, he breakfasted with his mother and left by bicycle, streetcar, carriage, or sleigh (Billy Carter driving the latter two) for the three-mile trip to 343 State Street. Occasionally at midday he hopped on the University Avenue streetcar and came home for lunch. Following an afternoon visit to Kodak Park, he returned to the office to dictate personal correspondence. On a typical day he wrote for a catalog of Aeolian organs and ordered forty-four reproductions of old master paintings at fifteen francs each from a French catalog, both harbingers of a deep interest in art that would increase with the years. Two decades later Eastman would pay in the six figures for original paintings by these same artists: Rembrandt, Hals, Van Dyck, Tintoretto, Reynolds, Romney, and Lawrence.

He declined a painting by Rochester artist Charles Gruppe but dispatched Harris Hayden to a New York auction in search of a painting he had read about. Clarke was advised that the painting he had bought in Europe the summer before had been set up with six electric lights in a reflector. "It just fills a panel at the front end of the second story hall . . . a fine picture. . . . My mother is especially pleased with it." The Rev. Murray Bartlett was less sanguine: "The first painting I remember in his home was an awful German thing called the Fairy Tale." Charitably, Bartlett thought it came with the Soule House.[18]

His reading matter was eclectic. Eastman subscribed to the *Atlantic Monthly* and ordered from Brentano's the following titles: Kant's *Critique of Pure Reason*, a new edition of Robert Burns, a French dictionary recommended by Dickman, and volumes called *Volcania Eiffel*, *Social Evolution*, *Benjamin Kidd*, *Tile Drainage*, *Irrigation Farming*, and *Furniture*. As he paid the electric bill at the new house, he wondered why Rochester Gas & Electric wouldn't offer the same rate for his house as his office, noting a drawback of living on the edge of town: "Any chance of the voltage being raised at the end of the line? The light is poorer than ever this winter and never has been good. It frequently requires the aid of gas to read by." He was not comfortable with another turn-of-the-century invention, and actually grew to hate having to use the telephone, especially for static-beset long-distance calls. He was forever scolding operators and the telephone company for what he thought was ineffectual service.

Maria would sit in the bay window of the Soule House awaiting Eastman's return from the State Street office. Servants recalled that he was never so animated as when he chronicled the day's happenings to her. After dinner until bedtime he read, wrote letters by hand, and puttered about the estate. Some Sundays Harry Strong would appear for breakfast and the two of them would take "a little spin together to South Park on our wheels with their new pneumatic tires." The cyclists returned from their spins for "a gallon of iced tea, a quart of lemon ice, and cold baths."[19] Regularly on Sundays at 4:00 P.M. Morton Rundel, a second cousin who had boarded with the Eastmans in the very earliest days while attending the Eastman Commercial College, would appear for a game of pool. Rundel, a reserved bachelor, was an artist who ran a paint and framing store to make ends meet. But along the way he bought a little Kodak stock now and then from Cousin George—enough that his 1912 bequest for a "building to house a library and art gallery" grew to more than a million dollars by the 1930s and made possible the main public library of Rochester. More rousing was the ongoing billiard rivalry with Strong, a quick trip to the Adirondacks with Bert and Lily Fenn, or a cycling jaunt with Frank Seaman through the Berkshires.

The women in Eastman's life (all safely married) were beginning to find unexpected tokens of esteem or gratitude appearing after he was no longer there to thank—and embarrass—in person. A silver dish for Josephine Dickman, monogrammed JHD, matched a larger one of the same design for himself, monogrammed GE. Adelaide Hubbell received a new camera and conveyed her thanks: "Walter has gone to church, good boy that he is, and I have torn myself away from the people on the porch . . . to climb to the fourth floor corner room and write this letter. How did you know I wanted a new Kodak? You are as thoughtful and kind as can be and I am glad that in a sort of a way you belong to us." Jessie McNicol, the London secretary, wrote: "I found your kind gift [a music book] too late to thank you in person . . . for the pleasant memento of your visit." Then came a "peace offering in the shape of beautiful roses" for Lily Fenn, whose "naughty husband was telling tales out of school." It seemed that Lily took a roll of film to Kodak Park dressed in her "worst clothes" and Eastman did not recognize her. "The next time I shall wear my best toga and expect your best bow." Tellingly, there were no gifts, and therefore nothing to be misunderstood, to the still available and still gushing Cornelia Hagan. She wrote, affecting the Queen Victoria "we": "Long time since we heard from you and longer still since we have seen you, and fearing you may have forgotten us, will astonish you this morning with an introduction." Replies to the vivacious Hagan remained punctual but cool and businesslike.[20]

Begging letters asking for favors or, more often, money, started trickling into 343 State Street in 1890s only to reach avalanche proportions by the 1920s. Before the turn of the century, this unknown philanthropist could answer each one personally. The Humane Society, established to "prevent cruelty to animals and children," asked for a Kodak camera. Isabelle Hollister wished that "all the friends of the hospital possessed so faithful a memory." Clinton Gibbs lost his legs and wanted "$75 to go to the New York Cancer Hospital." Eastman obliged, and Gibbs responded: "God will reward you for such kindness to a poor sick man." Close friends or favorite relatives did not have to ask: Two hundred dollars went to Ed Hickey in a TB sanitarium. "It gave me much to think about and much pleasure," Ed wrote, "to have such an evidence of your friendship. . . . I accept without even the tribute to my pride of saying 'I consider it a loan.' You are right in supposing that my finances are at a low ebb."[21]

Contrary to some interpretations of the life of Eastman, that he was regarded by the elite of Rochester as a crude upstart, he did manage to maneuver effectively through what "society" existed in Rochester just a half century after it had been a raw pioneer town. Many changes had taken place. By 1890 prosperity was no longer based on flour milling or the canal, the Third Ward was no longer *the* place to live (soon, wherever Eastman lived would be fashionable), nor were the leading families produced by milling wealth. The exception was the offspring of the Moseley and Motley mill families, which maintained their status well into the twentieth century. Motley daughters seemed to favor Eastman cronies. In his years as a bank clerk George had worked with some of the city's future financial leaders and these friendships remained strong for the rest of his life. Bert Fenn, vice president of the Alliance Bank, was a childhood friend and Eastman's staunchest supporter, promoting Kodak stock to one and all. The wealthiest Rochester families were the clannish and intermarried Sibleys and Watsons, scions of the organizers of Western Union. The Homeopathic Hospital was supported, enlarged, and run by Sibleys and Watsons so that they could have the type of care they preferred in an eastside facility near their homes. George Eastman was one of the few outsiders on the hospital board.[22]

Already prominent were the immigrant magnates of the nursery and precision industry businesses. In the 1850s George Ellwanger of Württenberg, Germany, had combined with Patrick Barry of Ireland to produce the "world's most complete nursery" in Rochester. Exemplifying the paternalism of nineteenth-century family companies, Ellwanger and Barry built several streets of houses for their workers, and Ellwanger introduced the Christmas tree to Rochester through his Lutheran church. When Ellwanger's declining health made attendance at Kodak directors' meeting impossible, that 4:00 P.M. monthly institution was adjourned to Ellwanger's spacious home. The Bausches and the Lombs were business associates. John Jacob Bausch, also born in Württemberg fourteen years after Ellwanger, had combined with the German-born cabinet maker Henry Lomb to found the firm that supplied Eastman with lenses. Bausch was also president of the Mechanics Savings Bank. Captain Lomb put Eastman on the Mechanics Institute board while William Bausch of the second generation would soon interest Eastman in dental care.

Eastman was a member of the "right" clubs—the Genesee Valley Club and the Country Club of Rochester—to which other movers and shakers belonged. (When he found he would be in England for most of 1897 and 1898, he resigned from the country club only to rejoin later when Bert Fenn made a determined and largely unsuccessful effort to turn him into a golfer.) He also subscribed to fashionable causes, giving $1,000 to the building fund for the new St. Paul's Episcopal Church that was moving from downtown St. Paul Street, just across the river from Kodak Office, to East Avenue, across the oiled dirt avenue from Marvin Culver's farm. When Eastman urged his mother to subscribe to a pew in St. Paul's and she hesitated, he subscribed for her and told the church to send her the bill. While "not a member of any church" himself, as he tactfully replied to the many letters of solicitation from religious groups, he formed enduring friendships with members of the clergy, ranging from the upright and merry Murray Bartlett, rector of St. Paul's and later dean of the Cathedral in Manila, president of both the University of the Philippines and of Hobart College, to the radical Algernon Crapsey whose questioning of the Virgin Birth would lead to ecclesiastical trial and conviction for heresy. Kodak's closest physical neighbor was the Roman Catholic diocese. St. Patrick's Cathedral and the bishop's residence adjoined the Camera Works and the office building while St. Bernard's Seminary, erected in 1893, and Holy Sepulchre Cemetery adjoined Kodak Park. An elaborately civilized relationship existed between Eastman and Bishop Bernard J. McQuaid, who became Rochester's chief Catholic prelate in 1868 and continued until his death in 1909. Eastman would proudly conduct personal tours through Kodak Park for McQuaid's ecclesiastical guests. Once Eastman politely asked the bishop if the diocesan manure pile could be moved away from beneath his Kodak office window. The dispensation was forthwith granted. McQuaid was a powerful force in American Catholicism, and Eastman recognized an equal in determination and resolve. It was said that the only persons George Eastman would walk downstairs to greet at the office door were his mother and Bishop McQuaid.

Barely forty years old, Eastman could look at the world he had created for himself and feel justified. His business was stretching worldwide, and although shaken at times by economic woes, was proving stable. And he had his mansion and grounds as outward signs of success—the closest thing in a democratic society to an old world earldom.

A Salute for the Czar

Up until the turn of the century, Eastman rode a bicycle to work in good weather and parked it in the basement of the Kodak Office at 343 State Street.[1] If it rained or snowed heavily, coachman Billy Carter delivered him in a one-horse rig. That was not nearly enough pedaling for the energetic Eastman, who was decidedly taken up with the bicycle fad of the 1890s. The decade's great bicycling craze in a way paralleled the public's fascination with pressing the buttons on their Kodaks, and Alfred Stieglitz was not alone in dubbing them both passing fancies. Eastman had a different slant: "Photography is no more a fad than bicycling is,"[2] he maintained. By the turn of the century the bicycle craze was essentially over, while photography was here to stay. But for a while the bicycle completely captured the popular imagination, becoming a staple of the magazines Eastman read and advertised in. Kodak featured bicycles in its ads, most notably one of a handle-bar mustachioed man balanced precariously on his high-wheeler but still determinedly pointing his Kodak at a subject. Eastman started his cycling career on a dangerous high-wheeler until 1892, when local Rochester newspapers told of a man who had ridden his into an overhanging meat hook on Main Street where he was grotesquely impaled. Eastman took a low profile thereafter.

By 1895 more than three hundred manufacturers were producing bicycles; one of these was Albert H. Overman of the Overman Wheel Company, Chicopee, Massachusetts, manufacturer of Victor bicycles, whom Eastman met on a transatlantic trip. "I see your wheels everywhere," Eastman wrote at the start of a long-lived friendship, and he observed that Overman's bike was "decidedly the queen of the wheels in this city. I bought a Columbia because when the craze struck me I found the Victor was 'out of sight'; that is, that all that were in sight were spoken for." Overman offered to provide him with one, an offer Eastman immediately took up. Later Eastman would purchase Victor bicycles for himself and as gifts for colleagues, including his secretary Alice Whitney, and relatives, such as his nephew Royal Andrus.[3]

Bicycle clothes—baggy knickerbockers and sweaters—began appearing at Kodak on dapper advertising man L. B. Jones, whom Eastman photographed as Jones pedaled earnestly over the rough grounds and stubble of the unfinished terrain of Kodak Park, and even on the increasingly sartorially staid George Eastman. During this period, Eastman gave up his beard and toned down his previously foppish wardrobe. Now he went for austere gray and brown business suits, custom made in New York and alternated weekly. He did keep the bright ties, possibly as a reminder that although he was rapidly becoming a business grandee, he was still a relatively young man with many adventures yet in store. And he had one very much in mind. "They are getting bicycles down in this country to marvelously low weights," he wrote William Walker. "Crouch has a bicycle which he intends to use for regular road work that weighs only 17 lbs. You can take it up in one hand and swing it over your head. . . . Such a reduction of weight must add materially to the pleasure of touring." Just getting used to the ubiquitous presence of the Kodak, the world would soon see more than a little of the camera maker and his bike.[4]

By the 1890s Eastman had fixed his life pattern: long workdays, spartan Rochester habits, quiet and bucolic chores (those cows and that gardening), alternating with long, globe-trotting vacations in search of the novel and exotic. As long as his body would withstand the rigor, he would customarily pick one of the most strenuous trips available to a man of his fortune. And when he traveled, he was able to put the squabbles and cares of his business behind him. Whether jaunting through the western United States, over to Europe, or to even more far-flung locales, he was content to leave the day-by-day operations to Henry Strong and Darragh de Lancey—but he was rarely farther away than a telegram, so the final word was always his. His mother did fret during his absences. When a long trip was planned, he would arrange for family members—Ellen Andrus, Almon and Delia Eastman, or Eliza and Auntie Tompkins—to stay with her. From far outposts he would then try to sooth and mollify her apprehensions. Typical is this communication from St. Petersburg in 1896 to Maria: "If the horses die and Charles breaks a wagon and the barn burns down and the factory shuts down and is struck by an earthquake, do not let it worry you. If you feel as if you want me to know about anything cable me. You can cable quite a letter for $10 or $20. . . . If you are the least bit sick, don't fail to get Miss Agnew [the nurse]. . . . Lots of love to you and Ellen." Beginning in 1889, when he took his mother to Europe for the first and only time, Eastman usually planned one long trip "across the Pond to Yurrop" and several shorter ones nearer home during a year. In the 1890s a long trip was two or three weeks; by the 1920s he was away for six months at a stretch. In the early days he was rarely more than a cable away from factory problems and even used his mother as a conduit of business information: "Glad to get the cable that the emulsion is OK," he wrote her from England in 1892. "Just a little worried about Monroe."[5]

A three-week Tacoma trip in 1891 had established the precedent that the business would not collapse if the boss took a vacation. Eastman had contracted with Frank Seaman in New York to do "considerable advertising." Seaman asked Eastman to take "a little vacation" to the West Coast. Eastman begged off; he was "head over heels in work and I do not suppose I ought to leave on so long a trip." Seaman then used the lure of free railway passes: out Canadian Pacific, back Northern Pacific. In September Eastman, Seaman, and "Chappie" Church, the patent attorney, took off. The trio was met by Henry and Harry Strong at Puget Sound and the quintet continued on to Victoria, Seattle, and Tacoma. Eastman's vivid travelogue was interspersed with homey gossip. Cousin Amelia Peet's house in St. Paul—which he had visited in 1888 en route to presenting the Kodak camera to the world—still had "a quiet air of elegance." On the five hundred-mile journey through the Red River Valley to Winnipeg he saw "vast wheatfields, rolling deserts, not a tree for 400 miles . . . peaks bold and rugged, as we ride on the engine through the magnificent Rocky and Selkirt mountains . . . a new experience for me . . . a mile in 59 seconds down along the Columbia River . . . views equal to anything we saw in Switzerland." Seaman and Church were "lively companions," he recounted, but "Harry looks pale, as if he had been up too much late at night."[6]

As the sojourn was nearing a close, Eastman was "up at 6 A.M. to see Seaman off for home. Last night after Strong gave a dinner for eleven we adjourned to the billiard room for a game of pool, Rochester versus Tacoma. Mr. Pickles represented Tacoma, I represented Rochester, the rest of the crowd did the cheering. Each side got two games of 50 points; when we had to quit it was 3 A.M. The wine flowed but I got up as usual at eight, feeling like a bird." Church and Eastman continued to Yellowstone in early October, but were somewhat disappointed to find the area blanketed with snow, the lodge employees all leaving by stage coach, and the park closing early for winter. "I shall not feel satisfied until I have done it over again."[7] He would, several times.

The jaunts through western America were but prelude to pedaling trips through Europe during the rest of the 1890s. "Be sure and write every Thursday," Eastman instructed his mother in June 1892 from the deck of the *City of Paris* as it was leaving New York harbor for Liverpool. Seaman, "an excellent traveling companion," was going along. "We are just passing Coney Island." Never a good sailor, Eastman slept twelve and sixteen hours at a time, just as he had once slept all weekend, only rising to stir the emulsion. The ostensible purpose of the trip was to replace Walker with Dickman at British headquarters, but Eastman had a bicycle trip planned to relieve the tension. A number of associates and friends awaited Eastman at his London hotel. He breakfasted with Haywood Hawks of the Rochester Savings Bank, lunched with Almon and Delia Eastman and took them to Westminster Abbey and the Kodak shop on Oxford Street, and dined with Henry, Helen, and Harry Strong. Following a directors' meeting and dinner, at which it was decided to postpone opening a Berlin branch, Harry Strong, Seaman, and Eastman rented bicycles with "those new pneumatic tyres," henceforth known as "our machines," for a three-week tour. "Mrs. Strong and Mrs. Dickman will go along by train. After we get tired, we can go to Paris," Eastman decided. The cyclists assembled at the Star and Garter Hotel in Richmond, Surrey, Eastman warming up with a solo, ten-mile ride before breakfast. This was his "first time on a safety" bike—the equal-sized wheel vehicle with air-filled tires that was boosting the popularity of cycling. Then Seaman took all three machines in a cab to the outskirts of town, with the others following in a carriage with the baggage. The trio rode for twelve miles, a ride that made Eastman "very enthusiastic, Seaman delighted, Harry tickled to death, and did us all a lot of good."[8]

At Windsor, he took in an art exhibition with Helen Strong and the Dickmans who had come by train. Helen used these three weeks to bother Eastman about his nonattendance at church services: "It was the first time I had seen Mrs. Dickman and I naturally visited with her more than Mrs. Strong. It is the same old story with Mrs. Strong. I do not know if it will be possible to get along with her or not." Eastman had his own ideas about morality, and they did not include ritual and public displays of piety. The daily itinerary through the south of England included from eight to sixty miles pedaling, and the balance by train. When possible, the accommodations for the quintet centered around a sitting room—preferably with a balcony overlooking the town—where the three men and two women could take their meals "en famille." Sometimes these did not meet the ladies' expectations and the cyclists had a longer day than they expected: The thirty-mile trip from Windsor to Rochester, with a stop at a "castle built by William the Conqueror, now an interesting ruin," was to end at lunch followed by a tour of England's Rochester—to compare it with its New York namesake. But while they "met Mesdames Strong and Dickman at 1 PM at hotel with the luggage," and all "did the town" together, the ladies "thought the hotel too poor so went on to Canterbury," twenty miles farther. The cyclists toughed out the first eight miles then hopped a train for the remaining twelve, because Eastman had experienced "my first fall . . . skinned my left arm and knuckle of left hand. Knuckles swelled as if poisoned and I have had to wear a glove which Mr. Dickman gave me."[9]

Soon the group was holed up in Canterbury in the "most comfortable little old hotel that I ever saw." The cathedral was "as handsome as Cologne. You will remember that Thomas a Beckett was murdered here. Romanists all come to the shrine. It is very quaint and curious." The next morning, Eastman, Seaman, and young Strong started out, having planned fifty-eight miles by bicycle, nine by train. After seven miles Eastman's ankles gave out and he had to take the train. He had "worn low shoes so the cords of my heels are inflamed and sore." But he had "bandaged them last night just like the horse. I hope to do twenty to thirty miles tomorrow to Hastings to see Battle Abbey and Normanhurst." Shady lanes, rolling country, and good roads one day were followed by steep hills, hot sun, and rough roads that could puncture pneumatic tires the next. While Helen Strong and Josephine Dickman remained at Stonehenge, the cyclists took off for Ross and a suite with a sitting room that overlooked the bend of the Wye. Over the weekend, the party traversed the Wye in a rowboat and had lunch on the train to Wordsworth's Tintern Abbey—to Eastman just an old ruin of the thirteenth century. On Sunday he capitulated by attending church with Mrs. Strong. Then it was off toward Oxford, back to the London office, and on to Paris with Frank Seaman.[10]

It was time for a breather—"We have been doing nothing quite assiduously since we arrived"—before Eastman had his fill of the cold food at the Hotel Continental. Seaman left for home and Eastman moved into a furnished house on the outskirts of Paris, ten miles from the office. From there he could cycle in by a different route each day, work at the Kodak Société Anonyme Française office from 10:00 until 2:00, and explore Paris for the rest of the day. George de Bedts was in charge then, still in good graces and trying to find Eastman a French cook in Brussels. "Look me up a middle-aged person who can cook and garnish dishes," the boss requested. "We have the best food in the world and it is a shame that we can't cook it properly."[11] While in Paris, Eastman bought a set of pearl-handled dinner knives and fruit knives with solid silver blades. He also purchased a pair of pearl-handled revolvers: one he gave to Frank Brownell, the other he kept for himself—and used in 1932. But he was no longer on vacation: "On the bicycling trip I forget business but in London or Paris it is always on my mind and I don't feel easy."[12]

Not everyone felt easy about the forty-one-year-old Eastman's plans three years later for an even more ambitious cycling tour, in view of the Kodak man's one eccentricity—he did not believe in brakes, thinking them dangerous and preferring to halt his progress by dragging his foot. Dickman, who was not keen on cycling anyway, tried to joke his employer out of this peculiar prejudice in 1895: "In the olden time the vicious were broken upon the wheel, and at the present time a virtuous person is broken on the wheel if he has not a brake. This breaks his journey and if he breaks his neck the heart-breaking news is broken gently to his family."[13] Eastman was having none of Dickman's objections. "Ha! Ha! Ha!" he laughed off Dickman's concern with an allusion to Tennyson: "Brake, brake, brake on thy cold gray stones." Dickman not only proved obstinate, but begged off the trip entirely, and urged Eastman to take Thacher Clarke, "a very jolly companion who is equally at home in French, German, Italian or Greek and most appalling, is enthusiastic about doing 100 miles a day." In the end Eastman got his way, and the party of four cyclists, Dickman, Clarke, Walker, and himself, set off on a tour of Europe in the summer of 1895. But still, the unsympathetic Dickman had to admire Eastman's ambitious itinerary: "That is a splendid scheme of yours to take the railway to the top of the Pyrenees, and then coast down into France. . . . I suppose nothing will break you of your unfortunate habit of implicitly depending upon your foot as a brake."[14]

The European trips gave Eastman the chance to visit the museums and galleries he had missed by not being able to join Third Ward schoolmaster Myron Peck's Grand Tours as a youth. His first purchases of original paint-ings were from local artists; experiencing a cash shortage, he often included a Kodak camera as partial payment for such works. "Am glad you are pleased with the [watercolor] sketch near Leyden Holland," Rochester paint-er Charles Gruppe wrote in 1892, "and can assure you that I am something more than pleased with the Camera." The following year, Eastman bought a sparkling French genre scene, a small oil entitled *At the House of the Field Marshall: Song of War*, by J. Adolphe Grison of Paris. Lacking the necessary $3,000 in ready cash during the depression year 1893, he paid for the paint-ing with sixty shares of Kodak stock. Had he retained the stock it would have been worth $33,000 five years later, an indication that even then, certain aesthetic or luxury items were more important to him than merely increas-ing his fortune.[15] By the bicycle trip of 1895, art catalogs had replaced church bulletins in Eastman's letters home. Occasionally some art criticism crept in: "Modern German paintings are a pretty poor lot. I have seen nothing as good as my Grison. Clarke is thoroughly up in Art & knows almost every picture. I have learned much . . . through being with him." Eastman's European jaunts reveal a more complex man than many of his friends knew. It would later be assumed that his art collection, the only old master collec-tion ever to come to Rochester, had been assembled by decorators and dealers and were "the sort of paintings millionaires buy because they are expensive and bear the right trademark," as architect Claude Bragdon would scold decades later. Instead, the hundred or more paintings and original prints that Eastman bought, sold, or traded were acquired because he liked them and disposed of because he disliked or tired of them. Few would know, as George Selden did, that before he turned to photography, George Eastman had been a Sunday painter.[16]

Checking out Europe from Moscow to Madrid to effect the international organization Eastman now envisioned was planned for the summer of 1896; Eastman, Clarke, Dickman, and A. H. Overman were to participate. Frankfort, Vienna, Warsaw, Moscow, St. Petersburg, Finland, Stockholm, Copenhagen, Hamburg, Berlin, and London were scheduled stops along the route. The Russian leg would be undertaken by only Eastman and Overman, who hoped to sell his Victor bicycle to the Russians. The travelers missed connections, tramped miles across rough country, suffered from dirt, dust, heat, frustration, and exhaustion, munched black bread in peasant huts, attended opera houses, and explored art galleries. Eastman's hidden agenda was to gauge the potential of the European photographic market with an eye to reorganizing the several companies under a single English holding company by floating a large stock issue in London.

By mid-July he was on the Continent and his mother was cabling frantically that he had left home without his nightshirts. "I thought I put an extra one in my steamer trunk," he responded, "but I guess I shall have to do some washing." He bought more in Paris but Maria sent the forgotten items anyway. Now doubly-nightshirted, he and Overman boarded the "Oriental [sic] Express, a vestibule train with a dining car," in Paris and began "not a very hard journey of 25 hours" to Vienna. "There are two splendid art galleries here—the National and the Liechtenstein," he reported from Vienna. He did not care for this European metropolis: "At first impression this city is rather disappointing to me as I have often heard it compared favorably to Paris. The streets however lack the symmetry of the Paris streets with the regularity of their architecture and the town is not nearly so gay, at least at this time of year. But there are many fine buildings and some of the streets are wide and imposing."[17]

Into the hinterlands of czarist Russia rode Eastman, Overman, and the Kodak camera. At the frontier "the officials were all talking at once in German, French and Russian." Thinking this meant trouble with Overman's bicycle, the Americans pulled out pound notes, American dollars, and German marks, but the customs officers wanted thirty kopeks (about fifteen American cents) or nothing. The bikes went in free. Then he spotted an old man in a long black coat who began "jabbering in Polish. Overman thought he was a beggar and tossed him a sovereign but the beggar pulled a wallet out of the folds of his coat and opened it out. Well, in that wallet was enough money to start a bank. He was a money changer! We laughed and I tried my German on him and had him change a sovereign piece so we would have cab fare on hand.

"I used my camera without hindrance in Warsaw and along the road until near Moscow, when the officials stopped me. Cameras are forbidden there without a permit and that takes a month," Eastman observed. "This is the most foreign place I have ever been to. Not a word anywhere that one can read. . . . Strange faces costumes vehicles and buildings. Warsaw is a dusty dirty hot and unattractive town but interesting for all that." If Russian officials were wary of the Kodak camera, the twelve boxes of film in the top tray of Eastman's trunk completely flummoxed them. "After a good deal of talk in German, French and pantomime, I made them understand what it was. And then they *weighed* it and charged me 40 Kopeks (20 cents) for the lot."[18]

Locating an interpreter in Moscow, the trio went on to Nizhni Novgorod "to the great annual fair where people from all parts of the world, especially the far east, come to sell goods. . . . The buildings are mostly brick two and three stories and covering the immense flat at the junction of the Volga and Oka. The streets are wide and paved with cobbles. Here immense quantities of tea are brought from China skins from Siberia carpets nuts raisins from Persia to be exchanged for cotton and woollen goods and all sorts of civilized manufactures. . . . Strange faces Tartars Persians Caucasians Russians hardly a western European in sight. Before we left Moscow we heard that the Czar would be at Nijni so when we looked out of the window of the sleeper at daybreak we were not surprised to see soldiers stationed along the track. . . . They told us it was guarded the entire way. The streets were lined with people waiting to see the Czar go by." For a little extra money, the travelers got a room "on the Czar's route with a good view of his majesty." Breakfasting on the veranda, they peered down on the royal entourage as the czar and czarina passed by in the first carriage. "The Emperor looked up and saw me with my camera and acknowledged the salute I gave him. The carriages were going so fast I probably didn't get anything of a picture."[19]

Back again in western Europe, Eastman and Overman rejoined Clarke and Dickman. Eastman bought in Berlin a large oil painting called *The Fairy Tale*— four feet by six feet—of "two little children in a wood watching a witch" for $1,200 cash. (This was the painting, representing Hansel and Gretel, which Murray Bartlett found so atrocious.)[20] While in Paris Eastman opened an office at 10 Rue Marigan (just one hundred yards from the present office of Kodak Pathé) and engaged a French teacher for himself, two hours each morning for two weeks. Overman returned to his wife and children, summering in Bologna. Dickman was sent home to London to mind the store but not before "Dickman and I went out for a little dissipation."[21]

Clarke and Eastman put their bicycles on the train once more and left for Madrid. "The picture gallery here is probably the best in the world," the museum trotter reported from the Prado. From Madrid the cyclists went on to Toledo, the French border, and the foothills of the Pyrenees. Four days later "we wheeled 44 miles from Bayonne to Orthez and 55 miles on to

Lourdes." Then on to Bourdeaux, to Paris, and back to London. The verdict? "We had a very good time on the wheel, even better than last year." On 24 October 1896 Eastman left for New York to be met by Henry Strong and found himself caught up in a preelection demonstration in favor of the Republican nominee, McKinley, for president. Finally reaching home, Eastman plunged into redecorating the Soule House and saturating his London staff with daily missives, bubbling with plans for the future. "Everything is lovely," cooed a satisfied George Eastman, "and the Goose Hangs High."[22]

While Eastman could see the Kodak goose triumphantly aloft, some thought the golden fowl was beginning to kill them. "Business is booming," Henry Strong, the lover of sweeping phrases, exclaimed, "but the help is dying. Glaser is home sick, McIntyre is on his death bed, Hawley ill, de Lancey will soon break down." Overwork and a furious pace seemed indeed to be claiming many an Eastman lieutenant, and even the commander took note. "It does seem as if some kind of a cyclone has struck us," Eastman agreed. "It would only take the collapse of two or three more to give me paralysis, locomotor ataxia, or some other blooming disease."[23] Hardly a serious worry, however—while colleagues dropped from attempts to keep up with the Kodak tempo, Eastman seemed to thrive on it. Returning from the extended European trip and the edifying detour to the Russia of the czars, he threw himself into his job with all of his energies intact and ready. Play hard, work harder was the unstated Eastman motto, and to it he was ever true. Vaulting two steps at a time to his second-floor office on State Street, Eastman would immediately immerse himself in work so thoroughly that if the faithful Carter had not appeared daily at noon with a home-cooked meal in a shoe box Eastman might easily have forgotten to eat at all. His secretary would often look up from her desk in the late afternoon to find her employer standing there, a look of slight confusion on his face. "Have I had my lunch yet, Miss Whitney?" he would inquire.[24] Eastman was beginning, though, to alter his management style. As he wrote Strong,

> I get up at 6:30, have breakfast at seven, and am down at the office at 7:45. I do not get home till 6:30 and if I have been down to the Park during the day I usually go to bed pretty soon after dinner. If I liked to work this would be lots of fun. Particularly as it does not hurt me one bit. I am as fresh as a daisy the next morning and come up smiling. But my time as a slave is about up and I do not propose to continue any longer than absolutely necessary.[25]

"What makes me mad is that people think I like to work," complained the new Eastman. "I don't think I have ever taken any pains to conceal my dislike for it. I like to watch other people work."[26] Once drawn to every detail, Eastman was delegating more authority. Employees had been used to finding Eastman appearing in their bailiwicks, assuming his usual stance (feet apart, hands in back pockets with thumbs facing out, chin thrust up and out) while listening intently to associates presenting the day's agenda or menu of problems. Now they were seeing less of him. But that did not mean he was losing touch. Confidential formulas for emulsions and the like could not pass from one employee to another without going through Eastman. Projects, such as a new means of casting film base, were initiated by him. Department heads were getting less personal contact with Eastman, but they were not neglected. Pelted with written instructions while he was in town, the targets of a stream of cables (demanding "ALL WRITE"—his code command meaning "keep in weekly touch with me no matter where I am") when he was out of the country, they were ever mindful of their employer's attention. Colleague Frank Brownell's three-hour lunches were noticed and sarcastically commented on. If George Dickman over in England disagreed with an advertising policy, he was "capable of being convinced by reasoning" and by transatlantic cable. "There is therefore no difficulty in getting him to fall into line with my plans." Dickman was not insulated by distance from Eastman's desires, and neither were his people in New York City. It is humbling and wryly frustrating for the modern reader to note that nineteenth-century America had its own very efficient means of instant communication that spanned thousands of miles. A study of Eastman correspondence in the 1890s shows that with five-times-a-day mail deliveries, he could write to his New York manager in the morning, in full confidence that the man would have it on his desk that very afternoon. If the manager was prompt, a reply to Eastman in Rochester could be sent by overnight mail train and be in Eastman's hands the next day. Cyrus Field's Atlantic Cable sent coded messages immediately to "Yurrop," and these terse cables could be followed up by an explanatory letter carried by the Wednesday or Saturday steamer.[27]

Beginning in 1898 employees had access to the boss's ear in a way they had not since the early days. While in London, Eastman heard a talk by John H. Patterson of the National Cash Register Company about the value of employee suggestions. Soon a notice was posted at Kodak Park of monthly contests open to all employees, except management, for suggestions relating to "improvements in product, method of manufacture, system employed, and to the general management of the factory . . . anything, no matter how small. . . . Suggestion slips may be taken home," it was pointed out. Each month six prizes would be awarded: first prize, $20; second, $10; and four honorable mentions at $5 each. Old iron mailboxes were repainted and put up at various sites in the park. During the first year 579 suggestions were received, of which 322 were ultimately adopted. More important than "the immediate practicality or even profitability of the suggestions" was that "men and women working on routine or relatively humble jobs could feel they belonged, that they had a part in the progress and potential of the company." It was the beginning to a far more ambitious program that would take shape in the ensuing years, as Eastman would figure out even more groundbreaking and dramatic ways for employees to feel they had a part in the progress and potential of the company.[28]

By 1897 court actions were going against Eastman. A bromide paper coating suit was denied on the ground that no invention was shown. In England, the courts decided that preference shares, on which no dividends were paid during the years of Eastman's emulsion and other film troubles, were cumulative and shareholders could sue for back dividends. Eastman had Dickman appeal, "suggesting" to shareholders that the company would be "reconstructed" should the appeal be unsuccessful. The decision was eventually reversed, but by then the company had been reconstructed anyway. Eastman shrugged such pettifogging off. "Life would be a dreary waste without a few lawsuits," he quipped, "although I prefer patent suits to plain ordinary litigation." Nevertheless he gradually shifted from patent protection and litigation to innovation, research and development, mergers, and recapitalization, thus staying on the cutting edge of business strategy, ahead of his competitors. Quality of products and honesty in dealing were stressed for pragmatic as much as abstract reasons.

Patents would be maintained for their "moral effect" on the competition, he said, but "the maintenance of a lead in the apparatus trade will depend on a rapid succession of changes and improvements." To do that he organized a new experimental department in the Camera Works. "If we can get out improved goods every year," he decided, "nobody will be able to follow or compete with us." Improved camera models gave people a world of options and kept their wallets out on the counter. We might be tempted to call this "planned obsolescence." But what Eastman had in mind was a supermarket of choices for the customer, a camera model designed for each consumer regardless of age, sex, or economic bracket. Some differences were important, others merely cosmetic, but model changes kept the market humming, and just as important, drove competitors to the edge of distraction in trying to keep up. Eastman had an intuitive grasp of the amateur photographer's desire to possess the latest thing.[29] "No one camera can occupy every niche in the house of photography," the company slogan ran. Eastman's favorite camera was always the latest, the smallest, or the cheapest. For instance the Pocket Kodak, introduced in 1895, measured a tiny $2\frac{1}{4} \times 2\frac{7}{8} \times 3\frac{7}{8}$ inches, making a $1\frac{1}{2} \times 2$ inch negative, and weighing only 6 ounces. Built on Turner's daylight-loading "cartridge system," it was "elegant, artistic, durable . . . covered with fine leather" and cost only $5. Still Eastman believed that the "PK" could be improved: "If the Germans are imitating the Pocket Kodak they are just a year too late. We have completed a new Folding Pocket Kodak which will bowl them out as soon as they get started."[30]

While Eastman was in Europe photographing the czar, the demand for the Pocket Kodak camera became so great that the Camera Works took on a night shift, which was dropped when the demand eased off. When a night shift was set up a second time, police had to be called to keep order among the milling would-be workers as they lined up in the streets of Rochester hoping to be hired at Kodak. Recovery in the economy was coming at an excruciatingly slow pace, but people kept buying cameras and film regardless of hard or boom times. Eastman's business was offering the best employment opportunities in town, now outdistancing the Kimball Tobacco Factory and the Cunningham Carriage Company as the area's largest employer. This would continue into the next century, as Rochester grew to depend on Eastman for the lifeblood of its economy. Meanwhile, he auctioned off all his old stock (particularly the plate cameras that had been sitting in Brownell's Camera Works for more than six months) because it was "getting old fashioned." He had many arguments with his executive employees over this gradual abandonment of glass, insisting that "the film business has the greatest possibilities of profit of any branch of photography."[31]

Brownell in Rochester and George Davison in England were Eastman's camera craftsmen but like Walker before them, they were interested in the camera as a beautiful precision object whereas Eastman just wanted a cheap and simple box that worked well and would sell film. Indeed, he often likened his cameras to the safety razor which, he noted, was practically given away to sell an endless supply of blades. He worried that the No. 2 Folding Pocket Kodak camera was priced too high at $15 and decided, too, that "we must get after the cheap camera men. Heretofore our cheap cameras have been rather too complicated. I am working on one at Brownell's which I hope will fill the bill . . . a film camera pure and simple." When Eastman went to Europe Brownell continued the project. Finally, Eastman's "dream instrument," which Strong called the dollar camera, was put on the market in 1900. It was the Brownie—the simplest and cheapest camera available—then or later.[32]

Even as film photography was taking off in the late 1890s, doubters remained. "The idea that this business is ephemeral has no foundation in fact," Eastman told an English investor. "If the bulk of the pictures taken by amateurs were taken as a mere pastime there would be something in the argument but such is not the case. Most photographs are made for the purpose of obtaining a record which cannot be had in any other way. When the desire for a pictorial record of daily life disappears then amateur photography will decrease, and not until then." In partial confirmation of his optimism, he sold his Kodak camera number one hundred thousand at the end of 1896.[33]

Meanwhile, the British office was humming. Dickman had started a new monthly magazine, *The Kodak News*. The London headquarters were enlarged to the whole of 115–117 Oxford Street in 1895; then in 1897 company headquarters were opened at 43 Clerkenwell Road, E.C. (16,000 feet on three floors) with the Oxford Street shop continuing for retail business. In 1897 two new shops opened at 60 Cheapside and 171–173 Regent Street. By 1897, too, the Harrow factory was in continuous production of negative and positive 35 mm ciné film and the main Harrow building had been extended for additional processing space. Dickman arranged for the first advertisements ever mounted in the omnibuses of Paris and also contracted for one of the first four outdoor electric signs atop buildings at Charing Cross. Not everyone thought the brilliant billboards added to London's ambience, however: "Ha! Ha! Ha!" Eastman commented in characteristic humor. "I can just see that irate Englishman who dont like the blazing ad in Trafalgar Square. Thank heavens we are only one of four transgressors. If it should be decided to make an example of somebody, who will represent our concern, you or I? Or would it be the inventor of the electric sign who would suffer for us all?"[34]

Trading in Europe was extended by the formation of a German company, Eastman Kodak Gesellschaft m. b. H., in Berlin. Kodak Société Anonyme Française replaced the Paris wholesale branch that had opened in 1891. Both were under the direct control of Dickman and the London office that, over the next few years at Eastman's behest, set up wholesale and retail premises in Brussels, Vienna, St. Petersburg, Moscow, Melbourne, Milan, and Lyons. "Norway, Sweden and Denmark ought to be boomed," Eastman continued. Possibly it was Dickman, who had lived in East Asia, who persuaded Eastman at this early date that Japan would one day be the wave of the technological future. The affinity was there: As with Eastman, Japan's strength would in the next century lie in efficient manufacturing rather than basic science. In 1896 Eastman decided to open a branch and wrote director Edwin O. Sage that "the trade ought to be supplied from this end and I think can be better managed by an American . . . might be good opening for George." This was Sage's son who wanted a job with the company, and who represented one of Eastman's perennial problems—the constant requests to find suitable employment for friends and relatives. Against his better judgment he offered Japan to George Sage in 1896, explaining that it would require a prolonged absence of at least five years as he did not intend to put a Japanese at the head of the branch. Young Sage was not interested in that kind of commitment to the company.[35]

Plans for a new one-story, saw-tooth-roofed camera building at Kodak

Park resulted partly from Eastman's growing enchantment with the latest in factory architecture and partly as a ploy to ease Brownell out. When Strong and the rest of the conservative board vetoed Eastman's plans as too expensive and urged him to add on to the existing Camera Works instead, Brownell was kept on. But Brownell continued to be a bottleneck. As camera sales went up and Eastman wanted to lower prices, Brownell had to be satisfied with a smaller percentage of the profits. Brownell's contract was changed to read 5 percent instead of 10 percent of the profits.

Late in 1896 de Lancey offered a position at Kodak Park to Frank Lovejoy, an 1894 MIT graduate who had worked six months in a sugar refinery and two years with a soap manufacturer. Incredulous, Lovejoy refused, but the offer to superintend the celluloid department was repeated. Again Lovejoy declined, "as I had no knowledge of celluloid or of photography or of the Kodak Company. I had never owned a camera or seen a piece of film." At the meeting Lovejoy agreed to come to Rochester primarily because the pay at Kodak Park would be $18 a week as opposed to the $15 he was getting from the soap concern. Several weeks after he was hired Lovejoy met his forty-three-year-old employer for the first time when the keen-eyed Eastman came into the laboratory with a visitor and asked the tall young chemical engineer "with the unruly shock of fair hair, the earnest manner, and the carefully modulated New England accent" to demonstrate that nitrocellulose, when ignited in the open air, merely flamed and did not explode. Eastman soon decided that "Mr. Lovejoy is taking hold fully as well as I expected. He may turn out to be a very valuable manager."[36]

A month before Lovejoy came, Eastman had hired another MIT graduate. When asked by Eastman for names of chemists for Kodak, MIT president General Francis A. Walker (a distant cousin of Eastman) suggested a recent graduate, Harriet Gallup of Chicago. With some difficulty, but with persistence because he was looking for someone who would be as careful in her work as the aging Eliza Tompkins, Eastman tracked her down. Even after she failed to answer his first letter, he contacted Walker again, because "we are favorably disposed toward a woman for the position." Gallup was ultimately found and agreed to come as a works chemist. This was a remarkable step for a woman at the time. More than anything, however, it illustrates Eastman's pragmatism: He wanted specific people for specific jobs, and merit was usually the only qualification. Arriving on the scene in January 1897, Gallup found herself sharing an office and roll top desk with fellow MIT alumni Frank Lovejoy. But romance did not blossom over that desk. Instead, in October 1897, she became Mrs. Darragh de Lancey. Eastman was pleased even though it meant losing his chemist after less than a year on the job. He bought the young couple a silk Persian rug in Paris, sending it home via

Bertie Fenn, who got the honor of paying the duty.[37] Alice K. Whitney's employment as his secretary is another example of Eastman's hiring practices. Most major industrialists of the century typically employed males in that role (so much was this the case, that she regularly received letters addressed to "Mr. Whitney, Secretary") so Whitney's hire was extraordinary, as was the trust and power Eastman invested in her—almost from the day she began working.

Eastman and de Lancey zeroed in on yet another MIT graduate. James Haste, class of '96 and a chemical engineer, came in 1898 to supervise the construction and installation of machinery for the company's initial commercial production of nitrocellulose at Kodak Park and, having passed the test, stayed on as its director. Lovejoy and Haste were thus "catapulted almost immediately into a rapid succession of tasks and responsibilities. From this distance," Lovejoy wrote from the presidential office in the 1940s, "and by the standards that have prevailed since, its seems incredible that the Company could take the risk that . . . was involved in such a procedure. Today, we would think the manager of Kodak Park had gone crazy if he took fledgling college graduates and entrusted to them immediately the supervision of plant operations and control over workmen." Then suddenly, or so it seemed to everyone but Strong who predicted it, at the peak of his frenetic career Darragh de Lancey, the man who always wanted everything done yesterday, burned out. "Mr. de Lancey thinks that he is threatened with nervous prostration," Strong reported, "whether owing to his recent wedding or not I cannot tell. His physician wrote me that such intense and constant application was liable to result seriously and suggested that he had better arrange matters so he could be away one-half day three or four days a week." The last project Eastman and de Lancey collaborated on was the production of celluloid film support on revolving drums instead of stationary tables. With tables a full twenty-four-hour day was required to finish a single coating of film base—a total of 4,800 feet in 200-foot strips. Using this method, the only possible way of increasing production would be to increase the number of film-manufacturing buildings and glass-topped tables. The explosion in ciné and regular film use demanded a continuous coating method. The Blair and American Camera Manufacturing companies bought Celluloid Company film base (produced continuously on a wheel) and coated it on the run. Suddenly these two financially strapped companies who had been after Eastman to buy them out since the early 1890s began to look like attractive purchases. Eastman alerted his private detective, requesting that someone other than Millington himself ("Our friends, the enemy, know you too well") snoop around. Still, so widespread was industrial espionage—Henry Reichenbach loved to brag to Moritz Philipp about all his Kodak "plants"—that within weeks, the Celluloid Company had wind of what was up and was threatening to sue. This did not deter Eastman, except to study

Celluloid's patent with a view to circumventing it and to wonder if Celluloid president M. C. Lefferts might like to sell his company too. It would be two more years, 19 April 1899, before the first Kodak Park wheel was put to use.[38]

The Kodak goose was sufficiently fat to tempt Eastman to make yet another land purchase. Albert H. Overman, the bicycle manufacturer, had invited Eastman to shoot birds at a game preserve in North Carolina several times but the latter could never go. Then in July 1897 Eastman spent four days at Bonnie Brook, the Overmans' New Hampshire farm, doing the cooking for the Overmans and their two sons in exchange for shooting lessons. At that historic meeting, Eastman agreed to Overman's suggestion that the two buy the North Carolina property. The minute Eastman got home he received a hunting "dorg" from Overman and started the Kodak Park draughtsmen at once working on the little hunting shack he called Oak Lodge. Indeed, Oak Lodge would become a site for convalescence, where ailing friends and employees were taken or sent to recover according to that special blend of homeopathy and Eastman health doctrine. Working for Eastman often meant laboring to the point of exhaustion in town and then being hauled somewhere out in the sticks to chop wood and tote water until one "recuperated." The cure was not always to be distinguished from the disease. It is not surprising, therefore, that Eastman's favorite invalids, Josephine and George Dickman, were his first guests in Tarheel country.[39]

11

GE versus Albion's City

Myron Peck, schoolteacher, stockbroker, busybody, and minor Rochester celebrity, who wrote Eastman endlessly, condemning his management of the business, died in 1896. Thus he would not live to see the object of his criticism embark upon expansion plans that required all of the "qualifications" that he considered Eastman lacked—"great executive ability, financial experience, time and careful thought, excellent judgment and complete self control"—plus one more: nerve. Entering this risk-taking phase of his life, Eastman personified the dictionary definition of entrepreneur as "a person who organizes, operates, and assumes the risk for a business venture." During the lean years of 1892 to 1895, English dividends were skipped or partially paid, even for the preference shares.[1] When the English courts held that the preference dividends were cumulative and would have to be paid, Eastman balked: "We are greatly disappointed by this decision and think it unjust." In 1896 George Dickman suggested that the way out of the dilemma was to dissolve the English company and form a new one with increased capitalization. Eastman resisted. It would interrupt regular business and be too costly just to correct a legal error. Still, he kept mulling it over.

Gradually he changed his mind and raised his sights so that by the time the decision was reversed in the courts, Eastman was set on reorganization for other reasons. For three years sales and profits had expanded. Buildings at Kodak Park were going up so quickly that by 1897 more capital was needed. Up to now, the Eastman companies had been privately held, with shares in the hands of a relatively few hand-picked people. Seven Rochester men (Eastman, Henry Strong, Brackett Clark, Edwin O. Sage, George Ell-wanger, Henry Brewster, and John Kent) were the directors and principal stockholders of the American company; six others (Eastman, William Walk-er, George Dickman, Colonel James T. Griffin (chairman), John Pritchard, Andrew Pringle, and Colonel J. Noel Allix) were directors and principal stockholders of the English company. The time seemed ripe for letting employees, customers, suppliers, and the financial public in on the deal, thereby obtaining funds for further expansion and greater profits.

Eastman's "scheme" was to form one huge international company out of the separate companies in America, Canada, Great Britain, and its empire, and the British subsidiary companies in France and Germany. An ambitious goal, and he would capitalize the new company, the plan went, in England for £2.5 million (U.S. $12.5 million), thus more than doubling the current American and English stock holdings. All present shareholders would be "offered the option of selling their shares for cash or exchanging them for Kodak Limited shares." New shareholders would be sought outside the Strong–Eastman circle as the company went public. Then he needed to convince a bank or two that his business was worth such a leap in value. Eastman knew that the promoter and broker of such a business undertaking, if successful, would reap a considerable fortune. He considered gambling for financial independence and power by underwriting it himself. While he had a thriving business and was comfortably well off, he had not yet achieved that magic title, "millionaire."

"The directors, George Eastman not voting, approve," he told Dickman in February. "The affair involves an option to me on all of the stock of both companies. If my anticipations are realized, I shall immediately go to En-gland to obtain the options of the English Company. The scheme is to orga-nize a new company which will take over the options. . . . The difference between the total capital stock of the new company and the amount neces-sary to take up the options will be used in promoting the new company." The British board agreed to issue the prospectus for the new company. Eastman thought he could have the whole thing wrapped up by the New Year of 1898.[2]

Meanwhile, as he told Congressman Henry Brewster, a Kodak director, he would have to carefully weave his way through the legal rules and require-ments in Great Britain and the United States: The American company would continue under its present charter "in order to avoid excessive taxa-tion on both sides of the water." The stock would be almost entirely owned by the new English company, which Eastman thought would facilitate opera-tions in the rest of Europe. Eastman already had almost all the English options (proxies), thanks to Dickman's diligence, and those of most of the American shareholders. From then on he moved cautiously, shuttling back and forth between England and America, feeling his way through the murky waters of British finance. "The bell has been rung and the gangplank drawn." he observed on 6 March 1897 as the ship carrying himself and Walter Hubbell left New York harbor. "My tremendous undertaking is underway."[3]

From the Hotel Cecil in the shadow of Cleopatra's Needle he sallied forth on his bicycle, getting options, including Walker's, and conferring with his solicitors and bankers who, unknown to him, were not taking as sanguine a view of the "amalgamation of the two companies" as that of the Kodak man. Yet, buoyed up because he seemed to have the support of the old shareholders, especially in England, a jaunty Eastman decided "to do it up brown with the Dickmans and finish off in Paris in all its glory." This meant giving black-tie dinners for fourteen every night followed by the theater. Then came three-day weekends in Paris and at Dr. Pritchard's home in Wales, followed by the four-day Easter weekend at the seaside resort of Brighton with the Dickmans and Walkers. Often the dinners were at the Article Club, whose members were "representatives of the largest business houses in each line in Great Britain. We represent photography, of course," he boasted to his mother. In high spirits, Eastman and Dickman sped to Paris for two days of business, Eastman buying a solid silver dinner set with twelve plates and a myriad of serving pieces plus a complete Minton china set. Back in London he gave a gala dinner and theater party for his directors. Then he was off to Hampton Court for the weekend with George Davison, the new assistant manager, and his wife.[4]

At home Maria was confined to her bed. "It was rather naughty of you not to tell me you were ill," her son complained. "If you can find one of those pictures I had Kent's man take of you *profile* view, send by return mail. . . . I had your picture tacked on the wall of my stateroom on the ship so you have not seemed far away." The faithful Ellen Andrus was there, writing Uncle George when her grandmother was not feeling up to it. Maria was well enough to go to Waterville with Almon Eastman, however, to see the ailing Uncle Horace Eastman, George Washington Eastman's last surviving brother. Horace, the man who had declined to lend his nephew funds in 1878 for a dry-plate company, was dying (almost twenty years after he predicted his imminent demise), and his nephew in London reflected: "What a pitiful condition to be in: to have nobody about him that cares for him."[5]

With Eastman in London so much of the time, the Rochester rumor mill took the facts surrounding Eastman's purchase of a rug as a wedding present for the de Lanceys and ground out its latest tale. Hubbell heard that "George is going to be married" from "a prominent carpet dealer," who said that Addie Webster, one of the Motley sisters, now an eligible widow was the prospective bride. Strong wrote Eastman lightheartedly. "I am getting very weary of hearing about your engagement. The subject is as popular and almost as fully canvassed as the coming election. It is, first and foremost,

Mrs. Webster, then Maude Motley, then Mrs. Gould. You have no doubt heard the saying 'Beware of widows.' I would advise that you . . . either deny . . . or acknowledge."[6]

"What a silly lot of gossip is always floating around," Eastman told his mother, goodnaturedly. "Strong seems rather anxious about the reports of my numerous engagements." He wrote in a different vein to Strong, apparently, because the president hastened to apologize: "I find that in trying to be funny I often make mistakes. My reference to those personal matters was by way of a joke and I thought I could see and hear you laugh heartily. From your response thereto I am inclined to think you took it seriously but I trust the effect will be only temporary."[7] Clearly, Eastman was beginning to lose his good-humored toleration of jokes and gossip about his unmarried state. Actually a merger of a different kind—the consolidation of the British and American companies—occupied the whole of Eastman's mind.

On 31 August 1897 he sailed again for London with Chappie Church on the *Saint Paul*. Before settling down to business, he biked out to the Dickmans, then to join the well-known professional photographer Frances ("Fanny") Johnston, and her companion, Mrs. Cornelia Hagan, and finally to see Thacher Clarke's new house in Harrow. He was in England principally to work with Henry Verden, solicitor, who had prepared the option papers to comply with British practice. "I have begun to tackle the financial part of the undertaking," Eastman reported. "It is slow work, but no serious snags. The thing will go easy or not at all."[8]

Once Church was off to the Continent on business, Eastman, feeling restless and blue, packed his bags and checked out of the Cecil, "sent my effects on ahead by cab and followed by wheel," pedaling out once again to stay with the Dickmans. This illustrates two little-known Eastman traits: the wash of melancholy that came over him when friends departed and his imperious assumption that he could simply move in on employees and run their lives. There is no evidence that he was invited by the Dickmans, but once ensconced at Hampstead, he took charge of all extracurricular activities beginning with eight-mile rides before breakfast, even though they had to stop every few yards and knock the mud off their wheels with sticks. Dinners at the Savoy and Article clubs were followed by trips to the theater to see Henry Irving ("good as Napoleon") and Ellen Terry ("getting too old to look at through a glass").[9] Sundays, when the Dickmans went to the local Unitarian church, Eastman stayed behind and wrote long, newsy letters home. His mother wondered why Josephine Dickman was not answering her letters. Had their relationship cooled? To find out, Eastman "went to the Dickmans Sunday for dinner and staid to tea and supper." He had a little trouble finding Josephine alone—while the Walkers were moving to larger quarters, the overworked Mrs. D. had taken in little Gertrude Walker, an invalid, Gertrude's nurse, Mrs. Jones (the Walkers' house guest), and of course Eastman himself, the man who came to dinner and "staid" as perpetual house guest. Wearily, Josephine shrugged off the query. "There is nothing to her fancied coolings," he found. "She dont like to write letters and owes everybody else." Church returned for a while and then Eastman saw him off to Southhampton, which gave the Kodak tycoon another bout with homesickness. So off he went, back to the Dickman domicile and "staid" a little longer. Waiting for subscriptions to the new Kodak company to materialize was tiresome, so he trailed after Josephine when she went shopping, picking up some coachman's gloves and silk socks. "Not as good as yours, of course," he assured his mother, who at the age of seventy-six was still knitting socks for him.[10]

"Our latest coup is Kodak negatives from the Duchesses of York and Fife and Princess Victoria of Wales [sic]. This will help us to get others from the Royal personages. We are going to enlarge them. The Princess of Wales lending her pictures will give a big boom to the show. . . . It will be a grand affair and do much to pave the way to the new company."[11] George Davison was arranging an amateur exhibition with a special section of photographs taken by the Royal family. When the exhibition opened in October, Eastman reported, "Everybody is astonished at its size and extent as well as its beauty. . . . If the Duchess of Teck had not died, the Royal personages were expected to attend en masse on a special day." On another special day, over six hundred friends and Kodak employees did attend. After a special press day, six prominent London papers and many provincial papers published rave reviews. "The exhibit is going to dispose of the idea that Kodaks cannot be used for the highest class of work," Eastman declared with satisfaction. For once though, he felt out of his element. "Dickman and I keep out, leaving to Davison, who is working like a slave and deserves all the credit for organizing." He did not even go to the Oxford Street gallery until the press viewing. Then he cabled L. B. Jones in Rochester to catch the first vessel to London to work out the details for taking part of the exhibit to the Academy of Design in New York City. Jones had already arranged an amateur photography contest that drew 25,000 entries for prizes of $3,000 in gold and Kodak merchandise. The winning entries from that exhibit would now be added to the Royal pictures and examples of the new x-ray photographs. Fanny Johnston was first incensed, then "penitent" (according to Eastman) as she discovered she was ineligible for the Kodak exhibition by virtue of being a professional photographer. Instead, Eastman put her pictures in the loan show, "where the Royalties [sic] are," and used one of her negatives for a reproduction in a "swell souvenir book . . . published in photogravure. . . . So she got a good deal more than a prize in the exhibition." When the London show closed on 16 November, the attendance was 24,700 people in nineteen days or ten times the number of viewers who had attended the Salon and Royal Photographic Society's exhibitions put together in thirty days.[12]

By October 1897 Eastman had been convinced by Strong and the cautious side of his nature that he needed a promoter after all. He narrowed the choice to two, lowered the capitalization to £2,000,000, and pressed on. A prospectus was ready for the bankers by November, but the days of waiting were frustrating for Eastman. As the day of his sailing to America for the Christmas holidays drew near, the brokers and bankers threw him a curve: Unless he could put together a new, more prestigious board of directors, they would not handle his "scheme." In January he returned, bringing Alice Whitney. No one else knew his abrupt shifts of mood from worldwide business deals to dickering with the plumber over a third-floor bathtub. No one else could deal with his habit of dropping one letter in the middle and starting another.[13]

Eastman found "new company matters in quite an uncertain condition. Nothing was accomplished while I was gone towards getting directors and now the time is so short that there is serious danger we shall not be able to fill the board in time." Four days later he had lined up so many stars that it looked like he would have a "surplus instead of a shortage of directors." Sir James Pender, director of the U.S. Cable Company, would act as chairman; Lord Kelvin, most famous physicist of the century, would be vice chairman; the remainder included the Earl of Crawford, president of the Royal Photographic Society; Sir George William des Voeux, former governor of Hong Kong; Sir Henry Munson Wood, Secretary of the Arts; and Leonard Statham, barrister.[14]

To satisfy lawyers, bankers, and potential board members, the normally taciturn Eastman spoke for an hour and a half on the history of the company. Several in the audience were so impressed that they immediately signed up as directors of the risky venture. Eastman remained the skeptic, fully expecting "any little hitch" to come along to "block the whole enterprise." The "fortunes of war," as he called the problematic outcome of these negotiations, he was ready to accept, but as in most wars, this soldier had to spend most of his time sitting around and waiting. January became February, and still no word on whether his plan would be accepted by the bankers and brokers before the April 1898 deadline. By 11 February his tedious ordeal was over. "A $10,000,000 Scheme Fails at the Finish," the *Rochester Herald*'s headline announced. "The stock which people were scrambling for last week at 105 can now be bought at considerably below par." Eastman swallowed hard as he wrote his mother that "I can not say that I am at all depressed."[15]

"The Lord Mayor [of the City of London] is looked up to," Washington Irving wrote in 1817, "as the greatest potentate on earth; his gilt coach and six horses is the sum of human splendour; and his procession, with all the Sheriffs and Aldermen in his train is the grandest of earthly pageants." The pageantry was no less colorful when Eastman involved himself in London finances in 1898, and then as earlier the City of London flourished as the commercial capital of the world. The "City," a square mile enclave of 677 acres in the middle of greater London, was the focus and justification for empire. Side by side within the narrow maze of streets were the major British and foreign banks, the stock exchange, the commodity and metal exchanges. Eastman determined his enterprise should have a London base, regardless of how he felt privately: "As a general thing English lawyers will skin you in every possible manner. . . . The English as a rule are business yentas and it is not safe to turn around without a written opinion from your counsel." For their part the British saw a Yankee upstart with more imagination than good sense. The City viewed the capitalization as unjustified and visionary, and the foreigner trying to float the new company as unscrupulous, outrageous, and scandalous. Typical was this response from *The Rialto*: "Nowadays one is used to hearing of things that take one's breath away, but the latest prospectus of a proposed company that we had seen is perhaps the most marvelous on record. . . . Can anybody in his sane sense look upon 'Kodak' as being worth two millions sterling? Truly the promoter of today regards the intellect of his fellow man as filmy."[16]

Then there was the way he looked—younger than his forty-three years and much more callow than his position as chief executive of a major company would warrant. Indeed many upon first encountering him would assume that he must be the son of the founder of the company. His unlined, apple-cheeked face with piercing blue eyes was disconcerting, as was his Upstate New York accent (nasal, twangy, harsh-voweled, ending each sentence on the up-beat as if it were a question) and American manner of plain speaking and plain dealing. His clothes may have been foppish by conservative City standards—bright ascots and vests, striped trousers or knickers, fur coats, hats, and gloves. And while the management of the Hotel Cecil and later the Savoy, where he stayed on his second attempt to float the company in 1898, may have gotten used to Americans pedaling off to business appointments, there is no telling what the bankers and brokers thought as he arrived by bicycle. Eastman blamed the failure of his deal on British timidity: "Almost all big companies floated during the past year are not panning out as expected and the British public is getting scared. That is to say the brokers and the underwriters are and they affect the minds of the men we need as directors. I have got a splendid board together and thought that they could accept the £2,000,000 capitalization but they finally got scared."[17]

He also suffered from bad press. "Photographic cameras made especially for the dabbler," one report began, citing the "cheap notoriety" surrounding the deal and the "chequered career" of the "Kodak Kid." Understandably annoyed, Eastman went to the *Westminster Gazette* and asked for an interview. The *Gazette* gave him favorable notice. He took it as an opportunity to remind the British of the glories of his company. "Our Rochester factory, which is the largest camera factory in the world, and which it would be impossible for fire to so far destroy as to stop the manufacture of Kodaks even for a single day, has an output of film during the busy season of upwards of 150 miles per week." The interviewer asked him a provocative question: "As an expert would you say that photography as an art is more advanced here than across the ocean?" Eastman answered with diplomacy and a bow to Yankee knowhow: "Treating the question from an artistic point of view, I should say that the English are better photographers than the Americans, but as regards mechanical ingenuity and workmanship, the latter are streets ahead. You have more skilled amateurs; we have more professional workmen."[18]

When his deal fell through in February 1898, Eastman was not yet ready to give up. But by 24 March Eastman could write the principal shareholders on both sides of the water that it had been "decided to go on with the new English company on very much the same lines as before." Support came from Walter Hubbell and Bert Fenn who, almost alone among Eastman supporters and detractors, never wavered in believing Eastman was right in his recapitalization scheme. "All the scheme needed," Eastman stubbornly asserted, "was to be independent of underwriting"—that is, free of the bankers and brokers who proved such impediments.

The Spanish American War broke out in April, making large-scale financial deals even more chancy. Eastman joked about it. "Grim-visaged war has not cut any figure in Rochester yet," he told Dickman. "I think we are all right here but I am afraid that the Spaniards will invade England and pick out the Yanks that are there and hang them to the yardarm." "I am turning my attention to peaceful pursuits," he wrote Walker. "Am now engaged in preparing plans for a green house. When I come to England next will have many garden experiences to compare with yours. Peace extends only to private life, however. In business it is war all the time. Just now we are beginning suits against the Blair Camera Co. and Reichenbach, Morey & Will. We do not always win but when we lose the victory does not seem to have much attraction for the enemy. At least Anthony never got any satisfaction out of winning the coating machine case."[19]

In June Eastman gave Dickman power of attorney to "sanction the sale of the undertaking of the company," and in August the board passed the resolution. By October, six prominent banking houses—two from the United States and one each from Scotland, England, Germany, and France—had agreed to cooperate. In October 1898 an embattled Eastman returned to

London, determined to defeat the City at its own game and float the stock of the company—this time, by himself, as was his original intention. Accompanying him were lieutenants Whitney, Fenn, Hubbell, and Abbott, although the latter two were along on a different Kodak matter. The second major project of 1898 involved the two manufacturers of the best raw photographic paper in the world—Steinbach of Germany, and Blanchet Freres & Kleber of France—who had recently combined to form a Belgian company, The General Paper Company of Brussels. The mission assigned to Hubbell and Abbott was to begin arranging for exclusive North American control of this paper. When the groundwork was complete, Eastman could slip away from his frenetic London life to be wined and dined by the Belgian cartel masters before signing on the dotted line.

As for the stock issue, suspecting informants on the large British staff that had been assembled to handle the flotation, he discharged them all and took over one whole floor in the new office building in Clerkenwell Road. There he sequestered office staff that he trusted for the preliminary work, which included preparing $35,000 worth of newspaper advertising. Early in November he published a new prospectus whereby those who wanted shares would send in allotments. "I do not like the present scheme," he told his mother, "but it will leave me something like a million (in dollars) profit so I do not know that I ought to complain. . . . Most men would think this enough."[20] The new prospectus stressed some additions in the description of the company that Eastman particularly wanted to emphasize, notably experimental laboratories. One apparently naive yet startling item appeared in the prospectus that convinced the City that their instincts about the gauche foreigner were correct: "Mr. George Eastman, who is the vendor and promoter of the company, who is selling it at a profit . . . will also be entitled to the premium payable on the public issue of the ordinary shares."[21] Such things were not done! Actually, they were done all the time, just not publicly stated. Eastman's attempt to float a new company without paying the local toll added to the City's determination that he be stopped. His solicitors had warned that subscriptions from the public would not be binding until the notice of the allotment had been delivered to each applicant. Until then, subscribers could withdraw.

But before the allotment could be mailed, a personal and business tragedy of major proportions befell George Eastman. "DICKMAN IDIOM OPPOSSUM" read the telegram of 11 November, which, the letter following explained, "should be interpreted as 'Dickman dangerously ill. Has successfully undergone an operation.'" The length of his daily explanatory letters to Strong and Maria indicates the depth of his distress. After complaining of severe stomach pain for two weeks, which could only be alleviated by eating, Dickman staggered into Eastman's office one afternoon asking for brandy to allay the pain. An uncertain Eastman administered three drinks, but finding the manager worse rather than better, sent for a doctor. "I got him into the boardroom and as there was no couch, he lay down on the table. His agony was something distressing. Up until that time I had not felt much alarmed." The physician shrugged it off as indigestion or liver trouble, directing the Kodak staff to apply hot cloths to the patient's abdomen—the worst possible treatment for what even then must have been suspected appendicitis. When Dickman staggered off the table, the doctor injected an opiate. Davison was dispatched to check out a nearby hospital, which took no private patients. Dickman would have to go into a ward. "Of course we cannot allow this," Eastman decided. Another injection of morphine and a police ambulance with Eastman aboard drove Dickman home. Four physicians and surgeons, rounded up by Dr. Pritchard, Kodak director, "decided the trouble was either appendicitis or a perforation of the bowels and that an immediate operation was needed." After telephoning for a nurse, the surgical team went to work at 10:30 P.M. in Dickman's own bedroom. By midnight the operation was over but the "doctors were very much depressed. . . . It had not proved to be appendicitis but probably perforation of the bowels. . . . They completely disemboweled the poor fellow, even to taking out his stomach." Eastman offered to stay but there was no place for him. He returned the next morning to find the doctors optimistic and "Mrs Dickman greatly delighted. . . . They are simply astounded at the way Dickman is bearing up. For a man who has appeared to be so easily knocked out, he has shown a wonderful amount of vitality."[22]

"This has been a bad week," Eastman finally decided, with Dickman again at death's door and the flotation scheme up in the air:

> Dickman left us at 9:30 this morning—Mrs D had not quite given up all hope, but I knew the doctors considered him hopeless. . . . I gave Walker £5 and asked him to get flowers. . . . Dickman's loss is a double one: besides being a very able business associate he was a dear personal friend. . . . I do not know what Mrs D intends to do but I suppose she will give up her house to go to America. Dickman had $10,000 life Ins. and about $30,000 in the shares of the new Co. and I had agreed to give him a lot more so she will be in good shape financially . . . with an income of at least $7,500 per year. Last night we were afraid the flotation was going to be a failure—the subscriptions came in so slowly but today has been a good day.[23]

The loss of Dickman's friendly, garrulous charm would wear heavily on Eastman. But on the very day of his death, the business tide turned and the shares were promptly oversubscribed to a degree that would have made capitalization at £12 million easily possible. A two-year campaign had been won. On 23 November Eastman said goodbye to Josephine Dickman and London. After writing his mother one last note about Mrs. D.—"I told her that when she felt like having a good rest that you would take her in and be a good mother to her"—he boarded a steamer for home. "I suppose you will like to know how I am coming out financially after all this worry and trouble," he also wrote Maria. "I shall have the amount written in pencil on the inside flap of this envelope which please destroy."[24] She did, but company records show that Eastman's personal profit from the reorganization was about $969,000. He boarded the ship in a complex of emotions: pride and elation in the success of Scheme versus City, a sense of achievement in his new wealth and power, but in the midst of triumph and elation, the pain of human loss. Dickman's death left a gap in Eastman's personal life that was never quite filled again.

Once he was on the high seas, the London office set to work implementing his final directive, an act that before the turn of the century was unprecedented in American industry. From his personal profit he had set aside $178,000 for the nearly three thousand employees worldwide who had helped to make the coup possible. Frank Crouch and George Davison put the checks in envelopes, the amount calculated by an Eastman formula on the basis of salary, position, and longevity of service. Along with the checks came an explanatory note to the startled employees: "This is a personal matter with Mr. Eastman and he requests that you will not consider it as a gift but as extra pay for good work."[25] It was the first Kodak bonus.

Eastman reached Rochester, skipped up the steps of the Soule House two at a time, only to find his mother in her rocker, knitting away. "We're millionaires now, Mother," he crowed. Without looking up or dropping a stitch, Maria replied, "That's nice, George." She never mentioned the subject again except to say to her nurse, "George's money came too late for me to enjoy."[26]

The era of four-month sojourns in England and Europe, combining business, theater, art museums, and bicycling, ended as abruptly as it began. A certain angst, a kind of world-weariness, seemed to afflict Eastman. He had worked too hard, smoked too much, and his rush of adrenalin had petered out. "I had been falling in love with London but then Dickman's death and my own ill health left me feeling weary and very much out of tune with it. . . . I do not know of anything on earth except some dire distress of the English Co. that would induce me to cross the Atlantic again this year. I want to get rested before I see the place again." Eastman is not saying such things for effect: "You may not believe it," he told Andrew Pringle, "but if the American Aristotype Co. should say to me: 'If you go over to England and back we will give you our business,' I would not look at it. It would be foolish but that is the way I feel."[27]

But out of love with London, he was not entirely out of love with life. He began to rebound and cure his spiritual emptiness with travel. His vacations during the next few years included a week shooting quail in North Carolina; ten days shooting prairie chickens in North Dakota in 1900 with Frank

Seaman and H. N. Higginbotham (head of the Chicago fair of 1893); a six-week trip to Mexico in January 1901 on the rented private car *Grassmere*, with his mother and her nurse, Miss Knorr, Ellen Andrus, Josephine Dickman, and the Rev. Murray Bartlett; then ten days shooting in Nova Scotia in September 1901. In 1902 he engaged the private car *Pilgrim* to take his mother, Miss Knorr, the Hubbells, and the Mulligans to California via Toronto, Winnipeg, Calgary, Banff, Vancouver, Portland, and back through Yellowstone and Minneapolis (to see Cousin Amelia). Later that year he returned to Nova Scotia.

The experience of losing Dickman left him gentler with friends and more considerate of his first managing director, William Walker, whose recent sad letters and actions led Eastman to decide that his former partner "was not responsible for what he says." At the same time he grew more curt and callous with competitors or employees who did not perform. With Walker's retirement and Henry Strong's increasing absences, there were fewer people from the old days around, and consequently, fewer than ever within the Kodak organization who could speak their minds frankly; only one employee, Cousin Eliza Tompkins, still called him by his first name. Into this void briefly stepped Andrew Pringle, board member and art photographer, who felt secure enough to try to take the place of "that splendid Dickman" and "write you private but wholly candid letters. . . . You are the mainspring of our concern and I think you ought to have opinions now and then from someone not an employee. . . . I don't know what you *think*, you are a funny fellow in such matters."[28]

Few ever had much success in guessing what was on Eastman's mind until he acted. In the matter of selecting Dickman's successor, he apparently consulted no one before deciding that the job should be divided between two men. He named George Davison, camera designer and art photographer, as deputy managing director, and F. C. Mattison, another organization man with experience in financial administration and the British banking system, as his second in command. Pringle approved when notified of the decision and attempted to extend the intimacy by sending Eastman some begonias from England for the Soule House, and from that time habitually closed his letters, "My love to all inquiring friends and the begonias." But Pringle was just a stopgap for Eastman. Increasingly the role of confidant was assumed by a former fierce competitor, Charles Abbott. This founder of American Aristotype had refused to accept Eastman's hegemony, had fought him successfully for a place in the photographic paper market, and had earned the Kodak man's respect.

On the other side of the Atlantic was another confidant. Albert O. (Bertie) Fenn, who had been in London during the recapitalization scramble and therefore pressed to lend his banker's acumen to its service, was one of Eastman's oldest and most loyal friends. Coming from humble beginnings before marrying one of the ubiquitous Motley sisters, Fenn was a diamond in the rough, vain about his appearance, but with crude, hard-boiled manners and speech. Indeed, as the Rev. Murray Bartlett, rector of the new St. Paul's Church, now going up on East Avenue, recalled, Fenn and his wife used to chase each other around the house like "a couple of kids." Many Eastman associates felt they were a social cut above the unsophisticated banker. While most Rochesterians who watched their Kodak stock fill their bank accounts to overflowing subsequently bought property in the East Avenue area, Fenn chose to take a lot in E. F. Woodbury's backyard and build a house at 57 Ambrose Street—formed by demolishing two houses, including the one the Eastmans left in 1890. When the Fenns had J. Foster Warner draw up plans for their house, Eastman was particularly impressed with the formal garden designed by Alling S. DeForest.

In appearance Fenn was a horse-faced man with droopy eyes, large ears and nose, and a melodramatic moustache. Always a snappy dresser, he was typically garbed in a checkered jacket, white vest, and bow tie. More outgoing than Eastman, Fenn never developed Eastman's cultural interests, but was proud of his barbarous tastes. They were neighbors in Livingston Park when George was a quiet, thoughtful child, and Bertie a boisterous scamp. As children they matched pennies; as adults, $5 gold pieces. As cashier and operating head of the Alliance Bank, Fenn talked everyone into investing in Kodak stock. "If he had been wrong," said Raymond Ball, Fenn's successor, "there would not be any bank at all." "I hope Mr. Fenn will make the fortune he is after," commented Maria Eastman. "Mrs. Gould tells me he even has the ladies speculating in stock." He did make his own fortune, and that of many others—among them the Motleys and the Woodburys. Eastman wrote in 1923 to F. Colson of Norwalk, Ohio: "I hope you will live many more years to enjoy the stock which you bought on the recommendation of my old friend Bert Fenn. He made many people rich by his advice." People may not have fancied Fenn's crude ways, but they paid attention when he talked money.[29]

A metallurgist who worked for Ward's Natural Science Museum, Charlie Hutchison, was recruited for Kodak in 1899 by the University of Rochester's Samuel Lattimore—the same academic who sent Henry Reichenbach in 1886. De Lancey wanted the young man to start work yesterday but it was only after Hutchison was granted the same salary as at the museum—$12 a week—that he acquiesced. "You won't last three weeks with Stuber," doomsayers predicted, but Hutchison decided he would learn to get along and the three weeks stretched into fifty-one years. "Mr. Stuber was a hard taskmaster but a wonderful teacher," Hutchison said of the blunt perfectionist whose practice of the art of emulsion making verged on alchemy. Part of the new recruit's job was to hide in the emulsion building in hopes of catching an offender suspected of slipping in with a master key and ruining the next day's emulsion. While he was cleaning up between emulsion mixings, Hutchison noticed a stranger, but before he could summon security, the man began to instruct him in the proper way to treat a broom: "When you want to dry a wet broom, don't stand it on its bristles. They'll just crack and dry out of shape. Stand it on its handle and the broom will last longer and money will be saved." Hutchison had just met George Eastman.[30]

Another childhood friend reentered Eastman's life in the late 1890s. Frank Lusk Babbott, born in Waterville during the same month and year as George Eastman, had gone on to Hungerford Institute, Amherst College, and Columbia University Law School. He married Lydia Richardson Pratt of Brooklyn (the family established the Pratt Institute) and settled there in a brownstone decorated by J. B. Tiffany (most likely the reason Eastman later asked Tiffany to decorate his drawing room in the Soule House and design a grand piano case for him). Babbott became a successful manufacturer, director, and officer of the Chelsea Jute Mills. He engaged in law and banking in Brooklyn and New York City but retired in 1891 to devote his life to education, philanthropy, traveling, and collecting art. As a member of the Brooklyn and New York boards of education, he helped organize the high schools of the boroughs of Manhattan and Brooklyn. He was a lifelong trustee of Amherst and Vassar colleges and of the YWCA of Brooklyn, the Brooklyn Academy of Music, and the Brooklyn Public Library. He became president of the Brooklyn Institute of Arts and Sciences (now the Brooklyn Museum), the Packer Collegiate Institute, the Brooklyn Free Kindergarten, and Eugenic Research Associates. A man of wide cultural interests, Babbott amassed a notable collection of oriental art and edited two books, *Classic English Odes* and *John Donne's Poems*. He moved easily in the circle of New York art collectors that included Henry Clay Frick and was a friend of William Rutherford Mead, an Amherst graduate and one of the architects of the Brooklyn Museum. Babbott would receive the Chevalier of the French Legion of Honor and was made a Commander of the Order of Danneborg by the king of Denmark.

In Eastman's eyes, his childhood friend was the epitome of the man of education, culture, and taste. With no trace of envy, Eastman used Babbott as his expert in matters of art, architecture, and furnishings, and found the Babbott children to be models of the younger generation. Babbott's carefully honed and sophisticated tastes ran to panel paintings by Sienese and Florentine primitives and Chinese and Japanese sculpture, whereas the unschooled Eastman preferred the more accessible old master portraits and nineteenth-century Barbizon landscapes. Babbott gently tried to influence

Eastman's selections—including a failed attempt to interest the Kodak man in acquiring Winslow Homer's *Gulf Stream*. Babbott introduced Eastman to art collectors and collections, architects, dealers, and decorators, among them Widener, Frick, Knoedler, Duveen, Cottier, Tiffany, Mead, and Mrs. Havemeyer. The process produced a sprightly correspondence that attested to Eastman's belief that the self-educated man with access to books and experts could be as art-adept as one with more formal schooling.[31]

New friends appeared as well. On one of Eastman's transatlantic trips Dr. Edward T. Mulligan and his wife Mary were looking over the passenger list for fellow Rochesterians. Spotting a "Mr. George Eastman," they introduced themselves. Mulligan was a rumpled hulk of a surgeon, said to resemble the back side of an elephant; Mary Mulligan was petite and vivacious, hostess to Monday afternoon salons for the Rochester intelligentsia.[32] While old friends were not dropped, the Mulligans were the first of a cultured and fun-loving set that gradually came to surround Eastman in the new century. Edward Mulligan belonged to the venerable and literary Pundit Club, whose members wrote, read, and listened to scholarly papers. In the early 1900s Eastman was persuaded to join Pundit (although he had already turned down the equally distinguished Fortnightly Club) and wrote two papers for presentation—one on photography that he sent to Thacher Clarke for proofing—before resigning. Thereafter, on Pundit nights, Eastman and Mary Mulligan played bridge with another couple. Eastman regularly attended the Mulligans' soirees and when he built his mansion, Mary Mulligan would become his envied hostess. "King George and Queen Mary of the Palace," tongues would wag, implying a more intimate relationship. Mary, like Josephine Dickman, was able to put the awkward Eastman at ease. The Mulligans and Eastman became a constant group as the Dickmans and Eastman had been in England, and as the Martin Johnsons, the George Nortons, and the George Whipples would be for Eastman in later years.

Returning from his extended honeymoon with the former Harriet Gallup, Darragh de Lancey continued to disintegrate under the enormous pressure brought on by the nature of his work, the personality of his boss, his own volatile personality, and perhaps the chemicals he worked with daily. On 10 March 1899 he resigned but agreed to work one-third of the time until Eastman found a replacement. "De Lancey is on the ragged edge of nervous prostration," Eastman worried. "His physician recommends he sever all ties with his job. . . . His is a very peculiar case, but I have no doubt as to his loyalty."[33]

Eastman again turned to Harris Hayden, his former boss in the insurance company, offering him $5,000 a year. "I want to divide de Lancey's duties so Kodak Park can be run by a first class methodical businessman without a technical education. . . . What is needed there now," he told Hayden, "is business ability and the ability to keep the heads of the technical branches pulling in harness together. I have got to make a pretty prompt decision."[34] Hayden once again turned Eastman down. An ad in the *New York Herald* turned up no satisfactory candidates. Meanwhile, the man who was increasingly filling de Lancey's shoes was quietly proving that right under Eastman's nose was a capable replacement. Frank Lovejoy's friendly manner was beginning to soothe some of the old antagonisms at Kodak Park. But Stuber, who nominally reported to the Kodak Park manager, protested that Lovejoy was too young and inexperienced. For a year Lovejoy held the job without the title. Lovejoy, a Frank Merriwell type, was quiet without being timid, warm without being effusive, serene without being naive. Lovejoy's first project was to continue developing a method of producing continuous film by pouring raw, liquid dope onto a broad-rimmed, slowly revolving wheel or drum.

"I think you had better send for Alward," yet another of the company's detectives or industrial spies, Eastman had told Moritz Philipp in July 1898, "and ask him to go over to Newark and see if he can find out who made the Celluloid Company's wheel for casting film support. . . . If he is unsuccessful in this he had better approach the man who left us and is now in the employ of the Celluloid Company." M. C. Lefferts, president of Celluloid, got wind of this and threatened to sue, so Eastman instructed Alward to lay low, even though he believed that the Lefferts–Stevens patent could be shown to be confined to the hopper that distributed the dope. Experiments continued quietly at Kodak Park. De Lancey had a prototype cast and tested in April 1899, but for months the quality of film base coming off the wheel varied widely. While it would take two more years for wheels to completely supplant tables, the park force grasped that they were poised on the brink of a new era of film making. With the help of new recruit Perley S. Wilcox, mechanical engineer and recent Cornell University graduate, who had worked with similar mechanisms in the meat-packing industry, Lovejoy continued to refine the experimental wheel after de Lancey's departure in June. The problems with the "wheel scheme" were myriad (although the heavier-based ciné film was more easily made that way), but Eastman remained the optimist, knowing that success would quantitatively and qualitatively improve the output of film. "When we can make the film continuously we can compete with glass plates as to price. Then we will do some business. It makes me tired the way business is hanging fire this year." When success finally came, labor costs were cut by four-fifths.[35]

Then the film went bad once again. Lovejoy blamed the emulsion; Stuber blamed the dope, especially as it came off the new wheel. To prove that the dope was not at fault, Lovejoy coated Stuber's emulsion on glass, an inert support, and the result was the same. Eastman decided that Stuber had transferred his feud with de Lancey to Lovejoy.[36] Finally in June 1901 Eastman noted, "The film that is being turned out [on the new wheels] during this heated term [93°] is of much better quality than that made on the tables from the same emulsion." That being the case, Eastman ordered shutting down the film tables forever. A year before that historic Kodak day, however, Eastman announced that Lovejoy's "services as assistant manager of the Kodak Park works during the past year have been highly satisfactory to the Company." Lovejoy could now "draw a salary at the rate of $3500 . . . with promotion to the position of Manager of Kodak Park Works."[37]

"It is a fine, elegant office, exceedingly pleasant and convenient," Eastman reported to Strong in Hawaii. "Everything seems to fit itself into the place intended very nicely." Eastman's office was moved in the spring of 1899 from the original building into a new two-story building that fronted it and now filled in the lawn and garden space to the sidewalk. With skylights, "handsome brass work," a marble staircase bathed in soft light, a city and a factory phone, a kitchen and double dumb waiter off Eastman's suite, roll top desks, gaslights in the offices, and electric lights in the shipping room, it represented the latest in office architecture and furnishings. "Something effective but not elaborate," Eastman had told J. Foster Warner. What he got was effective, but also "too fancy for my tastes" and a far cry from the massive masonry of Kodak Park buildings. "I am glad the picture gives you the idea the building is substantial," he wrote Davison. "As a matter of fact the front is mostly glass and galvanized iron painted. It's really a rather handsome building considering its flimsy construction. The only part which is substantial is the basement which we built fireproof to protect our records."[38] The painted cast iron front topped by decorative finials and fronted by a wrought iron canopy turned its face toward downtown Rochester and put Kodak even more firmly on the city map: "There is going to be a whacking big parade here on Fourth of July and we are going to decorate our new office. The light colored facade will lend itself to flag decoration very gracefully." That gave one neighbor an idea: "Bishop McQuaid called upon me this morning and suggested that the name of Vought Street be changed to Kodak Street. He said that many times his visitors find that the street car conductors and others do not know where Vought Street is but that everybody knows where the Kodak factory is."[39] It is a measure of Eastman and McQuaid's power that city fathers granted their wish.

While traveling through Iowa in June 1900 on the *Grassmere*, the private Pullman car Eastman often rented, he received an unwelcome telegram: "EXPLOSION NEW DOPE BUILDING TRACY KILLED NO OTHERS SERIOUSLY INJURED OTHERWISE DAMAGE SLIGHT NO FIRE." George Tracy, twenty-eight-year-old graduate of the Sheffield Scientific School and superintendent of the film department, "was experimenting toward the elimination of electricity from the film as it comes off the wheel, . . . using an electric stove. . . . The film touched the stove, ignited, and finally communicated fire to the dope vapors. . . . Mr. Tracy was . . . hurled across the basement and instantly killed. . . . It was the first fatal accident that has ever happened in any of our works and of course we feel badly about it. . . . We now have on foot experiments looking to the prevention of any repetition of this accident." A year later fire broke out in the film base scrap house, spreading to the nitrocellulose building. Before the newly organized Kodak Park Fire Brigade, with reinforcements from the city, could isolate and control it, three firemen perished. "The loss of life was shocking, considering the trifling character of the fire." More than ever Eastman pondered fire safety and what he could do to further safeguard his workers.[40]

In a reference that had its roots in film making or gardening, Eastman remarked in 1899: "I am on the lookout for two new chemical engineers and have appointments with four or five recent graduates. . . . I intend to keep a good stock of this material on hand." He was impressed with the "stock of material" recruited from MIT—especially Darragh de Lanccy, Harriet Gallup, James Haste, and Frank Lovejoy—and asked Lovejoy to have the annual reports of "Boston Tech," as MIT was still called, sent his way. His interest in education was primarily as a source of more efficient employees. Lacking formal education himself, he became demanding of sheepskin bearers: "The technical men at Kodak Park must . . . make a record in order to hold their jobs. If they do not, they are not any better than uneducated men; in fact, not as good because an educated man who is not efficient is a spoiled man." Late in life Eastman looked back wistfully and expressed the wish that he had possessed more formal education, but if the lesson of his life means anything, it is that self-education can bring a person a long way.[41]

But Eastman's chief educational interest lay closer to home than Boston. "The Mechanics Institute has no endowment," the letter of 14 March 1899 to community leaders from the institute's president began. "Possibly it has not occurred to you that it is the only place in the city that enables persons who work with their hands to acquire an education which is practical and to increase their earning power."

"What is the present estimate of the indebtedness?" Eastman inquired. "$12,000," was the reply. "Then I will give an amount equal to one-half of what you can raise before May 1, 1899." The institute set its goal at $8,000 in the prospect of receiving another $4,000 from Eastman. Warming to this new project, Eastman offered to build the institute a much-needed all-purpose building with classrooms and laboratories to replace its scattered housing. The offer consisted of $200,000 to purchase land sloping down to the Erie Canal from behind city founder Nathaniel Rochester's house and to construct a building that would be "turned over to the Institute board when completed, free from encumbrance." The final cost came to $250,000. The gift was to be anonymous but word got out. The "Eastman Building" was a another opportunity for Eastman to immerse himself in construction details and to apply some of his pet theories about factory construction ("I am a great believer in the saw tooth factory scheme"[42]—a method of so configuring a roof as to capture the most natural light). Whenever a new structure went up at Kodak Park, Eastman would sketch out a plan before letting architect Charles Crandall draw up the elevations for contractor Thomas Finucane, recommending sturdy, simple, and economic materials and "mill construction of the slow-burning type." In preparation for the Eastman Building of Mechanics Institute, he "went with Foster Warner to Buffalo to look at some fire proof construction. . . . The delay in getting plans out is because the lighting, heating and ventilating are very elaborate and require a good deal of work on the part of the architect." The dedicatory brochure for Mechanics Institute paid homage while explaining the benefactor's rationale. Warner was learning to adapt to his client:"While adhering to the original plan, these suggestions made by Mr. Eastman were adopted by the supervising architect, Mr. J. Foster Warner." Warner was instructed that a competition would be held for the exterior design of the building, and "that you will prepare the necessary drawings and specifications." In the end Warner was allowed to put his stamp on the entrance and façade. This odd procedure would become the Eastman modus operandi for succeeding architectural projects.

Community leaders were enlisted to serve on the House Committee chaired by George Eastman. Rochester women, including Maria Eastman, organized raffles, entertainments, demonstrations, readings, concerts, flower displays, refreshments, exhibits, dances, and costumed tableaus for a week-long fair instituted to raise money to buy furniture for the new building. These activities and their hostesses were the precursors of the lavish entertainments in Eastman's future and indicative of the way in which Rochester society, a tight and circumscribed entity, would, along with Eastman, throw itself into community projects.[43]

The Power of
Combination

■ ■ ▪ ─────────────────────────────────────

By the turn of the century Eastman's wealth was estimated at $425,000 a year: $25,000 from salary and the rest from 20,000 shares of Kodak Limited stock. His success at dominating the various segments of the industry meant that other, less efficient firms would suffer. He began to attract enemies along with money, but his competitors' envy was alloyed with the realization that Eastman was the only figure with enough power to organize all aspects—paper, plates, cameras—and keep them from going under when the economy faced a depression. While dealers chafed under the restrictions imposed by Eastman's terms of sale, they did see their profits increase. Most photographic companies were still single-product firms in overcrowded sectors and as such were subject to vicious price wars. Eastman had the film, ciné, and film camera sectors zipped up through patents and constant innovation. The main option for smaller companies was to merge or be acquired by one of the giants. Eastman had already consummated two such consolidations when he bought the Western Collodion Paper Company in 1894 to cover the collodion alternative (an acquisition that essentially failed) and the Boston Camera Company in 1895 to obtain Samuel N. Turner's daylight-loading film patent.[1]

In 1898 a handsome, well-equipped plant across the Genesee River gorge, about halfway between Kodak Office and Kodak Park, became available. Financial backers of the Photo Materials Company, who originally thought the "traitorous trio" of Reichenbach, Passavant, and Milburn could equal or better Eastman's success, in the end had to rid themselves of the former

Eastman employees, and persuade their erstwhile boss to help them. The trio had attracted $125,000 in capital to construct elaborate and enviable production facilities in which to make their Kloro paper, Trokenet cameras, and celluloid sheet film. They overran their budget, however, and stockholders had to put up $80,000 more. Continuing to lose money, they abandoned camera manufacture and sold most of that machinery but continued making Kloro. Photo Materials remained outside paper and plate pools, selling their paper at a very low price, a strategy that paid off in the short run but was eventually devastating as the company's profit margin evaporated. One after another the "conspirators'" services were dispensed with, a vindicated Eastman told his directors. Reichenbach left in 1897 and, after Eastman refused to hire him back, joined with two other Rochesterians to form a new company called Reichenbach, Morey & Will. As for the others, "The chemist [Passavant] died and the traveling man [Milburn] became a dissipated wreck. . . . Finally the stockholders decided to close up or sell out."[2]

Responding to urgent pleas of the Photo Materials stockholders, Eastman obliged by buying a majority of the company's stock and bonds on the property at a bargain price.[3] In 1898, foreseeing that he might need more space if his "tremendous undertaking" panned out, he foreclosed the property mortgage and so acquired the building that would in 1911 be named the "Hawk-Eye Works" in honor of a camera that had originally been marketed by Samuel Turner but was acquired by Eastman (by way of Blair's temporary ownership as head of the Boston Camera Company). Eastman kept the pressure on Reichenbach, whose new partners, John Morey and Albert Will, and their attorney, George Selden, pleaded with Eastman on a bicycle trip to drop his coating machine suit against them because they were not infringing his patent. Look, said Eastman, "Why not just stop using the machine?"

"We might as well get off the face of the earth."

"No, you can use the Sarony-Johnson machine which Mr. Reichenbach testified was just as good."[4]

By mid-1899 Reichenbach, Morey & Will had not left the earth, but, just as good for Eastman, had closed the doors on their rival enterprise. Then Henry Verden, English solicitor, reported that "this man Rickenback [sic]" had resurfaced in London where he was to be the chemist for a new company in which William Walker had been approached to take an interest. Eastman was not worried: "He has betrayed every person who has been in business with him . . . and he probably now regards Europe as his last ditch. . . . Besides being unfaithful he is visionary and unpractical . . . and one of the most convincing talkers that I ever met."[5]

Three more companies were purchased during 1899 and moved into the Photo Materials Building. The Kodak optical branch was moved there from the Camera Works in 1913, going on to fill the building and several additions. Vastly expanded during World War II, the Hawkeye Plant is still in use.[6]

Thomas Blair finally got his wish. If it is true, as Oscar Wilde said, that there are only two tragedies—one is not getting what one wants, and the other is getting it—Blair had it both ways. For eight years he had hovered over the photographic battlefield, threatening (with suits) or cajoling Eastman to buy out one or the other of his companies. Eastman resisted; the companies were money-losers and would add nothing to Kodak's technology, he said. Although Blair's fertile and inventive mind had led him to buy up patents and start a new company almost every time he had an idea, he could never manage one once it got going. Instead, he would sell out or turn the management over and move on, popping up serenely in Europe and then Massachusetts, offering to swap influence, legal testimony, or patents. In the early 1890s Blair had interested millionaire Darius Goff into becoming the major stockholder of the Blair company. Blair then started the European Blair Company in imitation of Eastman's branch there. Inventor Samuel Turner left the Blair company and founded the Boston Camera Manufacturing Company to supply European Blair with goods. In 1895 Eastman bought out Turner to obtain his daylight-loading patent but was unable, because of contractual stipulations, to also get David Houston's front-roll patents, which had been licensed to Turner. Meanwhile Goff and his board fired Blair, who went back to England until his source of supply was cut off by Turner's sale. In 1896 Blair returned to the United States and started the American Camera Manufacturing Company in Northborough, Massachusetts, to supply his European company with cameras and film. William Walker urged Eastman to buy Blair out in 1896. But "Blair is small potatoes," Eastman said. "An annoying flea," Strong agreed, "ever on the jump but never doing harm."[7]

Upon returning from Europe on a steamer with Blair in late 1897, Eastman entertained feelers to buy the American Camera Manufacturing Company. By then Blair had the exclusive license to use Houston's two focal-plane patents. Since the departure of Blair and Turner, Darius Goff's Blair company had virtually stagnated; yet this company owned a patent on a new film that, instead of Turner's red window, had a perforation that operated a counter, thus avoiding the Turner patent. Eastman's purchase of both companies could increase his patent protection and circumvent expensive litigation. The complexity of Eastman's "schemes" confused and amused Strong. "It is proposed that Blair continue manufacturing film and Buckeye cameras," Strong mused. "We consider his film a direct infringement and were . . . commencing suit. We are now the owners, practically, of that company and must continue making the infringing article and furnishing it to the trade. This seems rather inconsistent. . . . Blair pays a . . . royalty to Houston. Houston is suing us on his patent. We are making the cameras here in spite of him, and by becoming the owners of the ACMCo., we would be making the same line of goods and paying [Houston] a royalty."[8]

By February 1898 Eastman was the majority stockholder of the American Camera Manufacturing Company. David Houston, the North Dakota farmer whose patents were central to this deal he knew nothing about, called at Kodak Office, encountering Strong because Eastman was in England: "He was bound to pound his side of the story into me," Strong reported. "Thought it greatly to our advantage to negotiate a settlement to . . . buy him out root and branch. His previous offer of $100,000 is now reduced to $75,000. . . . I told him I knew nothing and regretted that Mr. Eastman was not here to pay him proper attention." Then Houston popped next door to Frank Brownell's office and "tried to talk himself into a tour of the Camera Works. The old snoozer thought he was going to play a sharp trick."[9] An agreement was signed in Chicago on 4 March 1898 with Blair, Anthony, Eastman, and Houston. Eastman bought two Houston patents outright but insisted that Houston's previous assignments of inventions and letters patent to Blair be included in this new contract. Houston signed but second thoughts gave him a sleepless night on the train back to Hunter. Later, Houston took the matter to court but lost.

When it became clear that Eastman would move the American Camera Manufacturing Company to Rochester, Blair was "invited" (Eastman's quotes) to come along as an employee. Blair declined to come and asked to purchase back one of the buildings. Eastman agreed, as long as Blair signed a contract that he would not produce cameras or film. Blair's new company, the Whiting Manufacturing Company, was incorporated to make cash registers. Nevertheless Blair owned a movie machine patent that Eastman was not interested in—"We make no kinetographic claims"—and did go on to develop a move projector in the years with Whiting. But in 1914 Blair would testify, "My occupation was a manufacturer. At present I am largely a farmer."[10]

The Blair Camera company from Boston and Pawtucket was the next arrival, but the machinations for that acquisition were not quite so complex. Darius Goff had been trying to get Eastman to buy him out for seven years. Goff, who had invested about $150,000 and was watching it trickle away, owned the patents on a perforated film system which, "although it was not very successful in their hands, might fall into other hands which would make it more successful," Eastman decided but continued to feign indifference. "I hope you will not say anything to Mr. Goff," Eastman cautioned Blair in April 1898, "to lead him to think we are anxious to have his company. I have grave doubts myself as to whether it would be a wise plan even if it could be purchased at a reasonable price. So long as I feel that way about it I do not want to be drawn into negotiations." But a year later, on 15 April 1899, Eastman paid Goff 7,280 shares of Kodak Limited stock for the Blair company, including a film plant in Pawtucket and a camera works in Boston, both removed to Rochester. Blair cameras—Hawkeye, Kamaret, Weno, and Hub—would be continued in production and used "to help cover the field and keep out competitors. . . . We are going to have quite a little camera factory" in the Photo Materials building, Eastman exulted to George Davison.

Goff had had his treasurer, Charles Ames, overestimate their inventory, putting its value at an inflated $20,000. Immediately suspicious, Eastman had Brownell check it out, and he brought the value down to a more realistic $16,000. But Eastman did ask the Blair treasurer to come to Rochester and manage the Photo Materials building. Ames proved an excellent hire, eventually rising to vice president of Eastman Kodak. But he and Brownell rubbed each other the wrong way during the Blair inventory controversy, and their feud continued for years. A ruggedly independent and loyal sort, Ames always felt that Eastman had ruthlessly run Blair out of the photography business.[11]

Eastman also stuck into the now bulging Photo Materials building the small firm of Palmer and Croughton, makers of albumen and baryta coated paper, while sending partner John Palmer off to Toronto to open Canadian Kodak Limited. Palmer could not find a suitable rental property there, so Eastman said, "Why not build?" As plans for the King Street building were drawn, Palmer was the recipient of Eastman's architectural ideas and amendments to the original design: "Enlarge the manager's office by pushing the partition in to the steno room . . . leaving just enough space for a cabinet of stationery. . . . West wall should be pilastered heavy enough to carry the load. Then you will have a heavier, handsomer building. . . . The brick arches over third story windows are to be laid plain without the projection of the keystones, arched lines of pediment over from door to be changed to straight lines. . . . Partition around closets in lavatory should be marble."[12] Simple, heavy, handsome, fireproof, with nothing spared in the plumbing—vernacular factory architecture, an indigenous American mode that has received little notice from architectural historians, was getting some creative input from George Eastman.

"The Rev. Goodwin ghost is up again," Eastman informed lawyer Moritz Philipp in September 1898. Hannibal Goodwin had finally triumphed in his patent quest. Between the filing date of 2 May 1887 and 12 September 1889, when an interference was declared with applications filed by Eastman and Henry Reichenbach, Goodwin's application had been revised and amended seven times, mostly at the suggestion of the Patent Office. Goodwin's vague directions for flowing a solution of nitrocellulose over a smooth surface were again rejected by five different patent examiners in 1892, 1895, and 1897. But Goodwin's attorneys filed an appeal to the three examiners-in-chief, who reviewed the case on 8 July 1898, reversing prior decisions and clearing the way for the issuance of the patent by September. In the reversal the examiners noted, first of all, that Goodwin's numerous changes and additions all fell within his original specifications (not surprising, since they were so vague); second, that Eastman had testified in the first interference that he and Reichenbach had not obtained a satisfactory film until 1888; and third, that both Goodwin and Edward Weston, chemist, had submitted affidavits that a film satisfactory for photographic purposes had actually been produced. Therefore, "this applicant, as far as the record before us discloses, is the first inventor of the successful photographic film pellicle."[13]

With patent in pocket Goodwin began his campaign in the press to charge Eastman with using, without authority, a process belonging to Goodwin. It was, the reverend declared, "a foundation patent in the film business, and owing to the scope of its claims it is believed to occupy a controlling position in regard to other patents." The Eastman Kodak Company, he and his lawyers maintained, had been "obliged to acquiesce in the decision awarding priority to Mr. Goodwin, a subsidiary patent only being granted to his opponents."[14] Again Eastman rejected these implications, chastising the photographic journals for trying to "force us into fighting our patent suits in the newspapers." Nevertheless Eastman answered the charge in the *Kodak Trade Circular* of September 1901:

> The facts of the matter are that Goodwin, after he had learned of our success in perfecting a process for the manufacture of rollable transparent films, and after we had successfully marketed such films, raked up an old application which he had sleeping in the Patent Office, copied into it a lot of matter he obtained from us, and then tried to raise the issue in an interference proceeding. After a hot fight we made him show up what he had in his original application, and obtained a decision from the Commissioner of Patents which put on him the burden of proving that he had first made the invention. . . . Goodwin did not attempt to support this burden . . . and decision of priority was made in favor of Reichenbach, our assignor. Afterwards Goodwin disclaimed our process under oath. . . . We do not think Goodwin ever had any workable process for making a transparent film. . . . We have never heard of his using it.[15]

After waiting over a decade for the other Goodwin shoe to fall, Eastman at least affected not to be worried. "There is absolutely nothing to be feared from Goodwin," he told George Davison. "If he brings suit against us, it will be greatly to our advantage because it will have a deterrent influence on would-be competitors. I am really very sorry that Mr. Goodwin has not got a good strong patent, because if he had I am pretty sure we could get hold of it and add it to our collection."[16] This confidence was echoed in a statement he gave to a Rochester newspaper:

> Before Mr. Goodwin can make any use of his alleged invention he will have to invent a method of casting his film support, all the methods now in use being patented. If he succeeds in doing this he will then be unable to market his film because the public will accept only daylight cartridges and these are covered by the patent issued to Samuel N. Turner [in] 1895, and owned by this company . . . [which] makes more than 90 percent of the film that is manufactured in the world. Our business does not depend on one patent or process but has been built up through many years of laborious experiment.[17]

Privately Eastman fumed: "It is preposterous that any man can come into the business at this late date with one patent and control it. . . . It is absurd." Despite his unruffled public demeanor, Eastman had Moritz Philipp's detectives keep tabs on the Reverend Goodwin. One of them reported back to Eastman from Newark with news of an event that would change the whole complexion of the Goodwin affair. After reporting that the Rev. Dr. Goodwin was getting ready to manufacture sensitized film, had erected a building just outside of Newark, and imported an emulsion maker from Europe, detective R. A. Adams added: "For five months Goodwin has been laid up with a broken leg." In the summer of 1900, a year after he had organized the Goodwin Film and Camera Company and borrowed $10,000 from a friend to build the film plant in Newark, Goodwin was injured in a street car accident from which he never recovered. He died on 31 December 1900. The following June Eastman received a letter about the Hannibal Goodwin estate and alerted Philipp that "if the Goodwin patent is coming on the market we might be willing to pay a small sum for it."[18]

Further evidence that Eastman was about to sweep the photographic field was the new attitude of his oldest rival, the Anthony company. At the same time that Eastman was mopping up all the complexities of the many Blair deals, in November 1899 he was considering an overture by Anthony that he purchase the company. The mere entertaining of the notion of selling out to an old nemesis indicated that the Anthonys were in financial straits. Eastman, however, declined. Then, before Eastman could purchase the Goodwin patent, he saw his archrivals obtain it instead. Frederick and Richard Anthony, nephew and son respectively of the late Edward, joined forces with W. I. Lincoln Adams of Scovill and Adams in July 1901 to purchase 51 percent of the stock of the Goodwin Film and Camera Company. The remaining stock was owned by Goodwin's wife and the friends who had financed the manufacturing venture. In August Frederick Anthony offered Eastman the Goodwin patent for $1 million, half cash and half stock, with the veiled threat that if settlement was not reached, he would sue. "That seems like a large valuation," said Eastman. "Why do you consider the Goodwin patent so valuable?"[19]

"We have been advised that you infringe it," Anthony replied, "and there is the prospect of a large recovery from you. Secondly, there is the right to work a valuable process." Eastman's rejoinder was: "I don't see how the Goodwin patent can protect anyone in the manufacture of any salable film at the present time. . . . We are only looking for someone to sue us under that patent. . . . Now we have renewed hopes. . . . It would be regarded as a friendly act," Eastman concluded. Anthony tried another tack: "Wouldn't the patent be valuable to you as an article of manufacture?" Eastman thought not: "I don't know of a more flagrant attempt to get something that does not belong to him than the one by the Rev. Goodwin: He had been fumbling away with his application with no prospect of getting anywhere with it, when we came out with something definite; he had attempted to grab it by importing claims into his specification that would cover us." Anthony reminded Eastman that Goodwin had beaten him in the patent suit. Certainly not, Eastman said: "You have been misinformed. We certainly beat him in the interference. Satisfy yourself by examining the records." Following this hardboiling and stonewalling, according to Eastman, the two "shook hands and parted on the best of terms." Although Eastman coolly affected an air of disinterest, in the end it would mean one of the greatest defeats of his life.[20]

And so the Goodwin patent had proved useless to Frederick Anthony as a bargaining chip. In December 1901 the Anthony and Scovill companies, formerly the industry leaders and keen competitors but now reduced to secondary status by their own lethargy and Eastman's aggressive manufacturing and marketing, officially merged as a holding company to pursue a second course—a lawsuit against Eastman. Richard Anthony was president, Frederick Anthony was vice president and treasurer; W. I. Lincoln Adams, former president of Scovill, and Thomas W. Stephens, banker and president of the Columbia Paper Company, were among the board members. The merger combined chemical, collodion paper, film and plate camera companies, a jobbing contract with Hammer Dry Plate, an option to buy a DOP producer, and the potential for film production through the Goodwin patent. Having seen what Eastman accomplished by covering the field, the Anthonys, Adams, and Stephens prepared to follow his lead. The major weakness of the new combine was lack of capital, but that they hoped to remedy through the Goodwin suit. Oblivious to the evidence that a noose was drawing tightly around the neck of his company, Eastman had some fun kidding Kodak's competitor about this merger. The *Kodak Trade Circular* of January 1902 sported: "No longer will 'Down with the Trust' be the burden of their song, but, pinning to their shirt front the jewels of consistency and accompanied by the doleful strains of their trade organs, they will sing in seductive tones, 'Down with the other trust.'"[21]

Unmanufactured film was no threat, Eastman knew. But one of the Anthony & Scovill board's first decisions was to manufacture in the old Monarch paper building in Binghampton, New York. The film plant was organized not with production profits in mind but merely to produce film quickly by the Goodwin process so suit could be filed. The first roll of Ansco film came off a crude wooden machine in December 1902 and within a week Eastman, Lovejoy, and Strong were served with subpoenas as the Goodwin Film & Camera Company filed suit for patent infringement. Eastman immediately retaliated by filing suit against Anthony & Scovill under the Turner patent on the daylight-loading feature when the first Goodwin and Ansco cameras hit the market. Then he told Philipp to demand an apology from the rivals who he felt were flagrantly infringing Kodak trademarks: "We would like to publish a letter from such a concern that will be humiliating enough to show that they cannot do this sort of thing with impunity, or else put them to enough expense to impress upon them the same thing."[22]

Anthony & Scovill retaliated twice, in 1903 and 1904, by having sympathetic dealers file complaints under the Donelly Antitrust Act, which declared any agreement or combination creating a monopoly in manufacture, production, or sale illegal in the state of New York. This caused considerable handwringing in Rochester but in both cases the charges were dismissed after lengthy hearings. Despite these machinations, as financial burdens increased, the Anthonys tendered two more offers to Eastman in 1904 to sell both Anthony & Scovill holding company and Goodwin Film & Camera manufacturing company. This way Eastman could have a monopoly and raise prices, Anthony suggested. Eastman replied scornfully that he was trying to lower prices, not raise them. Next, Anthony offered to stop litigation and give Eastman a license under the Goodwin patent if he would reciprocate with a license under the Turner patent. Again Eastman refused. Samuel Turner was on a $100-a-month retainer from Kodak. Eastman told Philipp that he would double Turner's salary if the Goodwin case was won. Turner must be kept occupied in New York, however, since "he will demoralize the help if he comes to Rochester." As a last resort, Eastman suggested, "set him to work compiling a history of photography." But the Kodak suit against Anthony & Scovill for infringing the Turner patent failed both in the federal district court in 1905 and in the court of appeals in 1906, for want of "inventive novelty."[23]

Buoyed by these decisions, Anthony made a third and final offer and was again spurned. By 1907 both Richard and Frederick Anthony and W. I.

Lincoln Adams had left the company. The new president was Thomas W. Stephens, with banking interests holding the company's notes. The company was reorganized as the Ansco Company, taking as corporate name the trademark it had used for film and cameras. Stephens continued to prosecute the Goodwin patent, the company's only major asset, though not without considerable expense. Eastman, too, was spending between $3,000 and $4,000 a month on legal counsel, but he could better afford it. As late as 1912 Eastman was convinced that Ansco was "up against a stone wall." This kept him deaf to suggestions by Philipp of an out-of-court settlement to end this worrisome case.

The Defender Photo Supply Company of Rochester was founded in 1899 by former employees from Photo Materials and New Jersey Aristotype, to introduce Argo paper, a lower-quality brand of gelatin DOP aimed at the professional market. By 1908 the company had secured about 10 percent of the total paper market and after Eastman Kodak, whose sales that year were $3,058,058, was the largest paper manufacturer in the country with sales of $422,083.[24] In June 1909 Frank W. Wilmot, a former Kodak employee but now president of Defender, approached Eastman "as a last resort" to buy the one-third of its stock a disgruntled stockholder was selling. Eastman countered that he would buy only if he could have 60 percent. The deal was made, with the five other principal stockholders chipping in the balance. In 1911 Wilmot approached Kodak to make film for them that they would sell under their trademark Vulcan. Wilmot's reasoning was that

> the Ansco Co. were discriminating against us, that is, they would say to a dealer in a veiled way, "If you don't sell our paper, we won't sell you film." The effect on us was, it made it harder for us to sell our paper. They would take our dealers from us on the strength of that. They were able to supply the film and we were not. We made only plates and paper, no film. As to why we went to Eastman for Vulcan, when we were handling the Ensign film, manufactured in England and sold through Gennert, we could make no money on Ensign film, as discount was not large enough.

Although "the trade guessed where the film came from," as Wilmot later testified ("any user would know it, because it was the best film on the market") the deal was never publicly announced. Upon investigation for antitrust violations, the federal government in 1913 insisted that Eastman sell his stock to someone outside the Eastman Kodak Company—he did, to George D. B. Bonbright—and that the Kodak name appear on the Vulcan packages.[25]

"The vast majority of our dealers and customers are happy with our restrictive policy" of discounts to dealers who sell only Kodak products, the *Kodak Trade Circular* of February 1900 sought to demonstrate. The company had taken a poll of the some 2,500 dealers, and of the 320 ballots returned, only 10 were opposed. Despite the *Circular*'s poll Eastman admitted that "Our action . . . meets with the almost universal condemnation of the dealers, but the policy is selling Kodaks. Eventually the dealers come around when they see their sales increase." Eastman told Davison how to do it: "We always precede any change of policy by some kind of missionary work to prepare the minds of the dealers. First, get the concurrence of as many influential people as possible by private conference. . . . Conciliate by asking whether such a concession would not give him practically every thing that he is fighting for." But remember, he added, "The only time you can ever get the rebate system in force is when the market is free from competition." Until then, dealers would work hard enough pushing Kodak products to justify their discount. Better to give it to the public or use it for advertising, Eastman reasoned.[26]

Eastman saw a kind of social Darwinism determining the fate of the photographic industry, and he was confident that he was poised on the right side of natural selection with film. In 1920 he recalled: "When we first began to make transparent film I had a conversation with Papa Cramer. . . . He said to me 'Well, this may be all right for amateurs but you surely do not expect professionals will ever use it.' I replied: 'Oh yes, we are going to drive out glass plates altogether.' He smiled and said it would not be done during his lifetime. . . . We had to work hard about twenty years before we could make a film that would satisfy the professionals and it has taken about five years since then to convince them that we could do it. The fight is now over . . . [although] I missed my guess by about thirty years."[27] The *Circular* echoed the seeming inevitability of the company's success: "It is the old story of the survival of the fittest. The hand has survived the 'stand' camera. And of hand cameras the Kodak is the fittest."

The turn of the century found Eastman, in his forty-sixth year still a baby tycoon, in the full flush of his powers and virtually unstoppable in attaining his industrial aims. His genius at consolidating businesses and centralizing power put a relentless pressure on his competition and his continuing emphasis was on innovation, quality of product, and vigorous salesmanship. Always Eastman's greatest fan, Henry Strong thought that since he had proved himself "an expert promoter," Eastman should not stop until the entire world of photography had the Kodak stamp: "I would like to see you next take hold of Dry Plates and put through a grand Consolidation of Plate Makers which if you get under our control the same as paper will leave no more worlds to conquer. . . . This ought to be enough to keep us from the Poor House . . . and make us willing to give a chance to the Rising Generation."[28]

Eastman had moments of Napoleonic fever. In a letter to his mother from Paris he wrote: "You may remember that some time ago I told you that if I set about it I could probably get control of the photographic business all over the world—Well I have been talking with the representatives of the powerful German ring who control most of the business over here and *they* proposed to me that I should do it, and that they would come in and help it along." Furthermore, "they seemed to think . . . that I am the only one who can do it." But, he suddenly remembered, "I was looking for less rather than more responsibility." Only a few years earlier members of the German "ring" had cold-shouldered Eastman when he asked to be the exclusive importer of its unique raw paper stock, but now members were in earnest: "They think they see in the steady advance of the Kodak Co. an avalanche that may overwhelm them—and they want to get on top of it instead of under." Plans were already in motion to combine paper, dry-plate, and camera interests. It only remained for him to assume the leadership in these various segments, gathering them under the banner of the Eastman Kodak Company.[29]

The paper wars of the early 1890s had ended, but an uneasy truce was in effect. Raw paper prices went up but Kodak could not raise prices for fear of being undercut by other sensitizers. Eastman's attempts to organize the dry-plate and paper sectors through the Merchant Board of Trade in 1894 had failed. Eastman's coating machine suits were thrown out on the ground of no invention in 1896. Fixing prices through pooling arrangements was declared illegal, but mergers and acquisitions were not. A different strategy was the logical next step. The General Paper Company of Brussels, a raw paper cartel formed by the merger of Rives and Steinbach, provided the model. It was to corner this valuable market that Charles Abbott of American Aristotype and corporate counsel Walter Hubbell accompanied Eastman to Europe in the fall of 1898. At the very moment that "the great company event was finally upon us" in London, Eastman received a cable from his surrogates in "Frankfurt-am-Main, that the General Paper people had captured the last concern that stood out of the paper deal." As soon as Kodak Limited was successfully floated, Eastman slipped away to complete the paper deal with the new Belgian cartel.

That tripartite arrangement made Kodak and American Aristotype the exclusive American agents for the General Paper Company and gave the two companies discounts on paper used for their lower-priced fighting brands. Kodak and American Aristotype agreed to use only Gepaco raw stock for ten years. Abbott agreed not to make gelatin POP, thus clearing the way for Eastman to boost Solio prices and profits. In return, Eastman agreed not to make collodion paper, thereby "sacrificing" a segment of his business on which he had lost $30,000 in 1898. Even so, under the trust laws, as Eastman explained to his directors, "no combination could be formed between [any other] company and the Kodak Co. as regards prices. The whole manufacture must be in the hands of one concern."[30] The formation of the raw paper cartel got Eastman and Abbott thinking about ways they might develop the American paper market by controlling this crucial foreign supply and still not running afoul of American antitrust laws. Abbott, former fierce competitor, was now feeling vulnerable because his collodion chloride POP, still the industry leader, was threatened by the rising sales of new papers, notably the Nepera Chemical Company's Velox. Unlike Eastman Kodak, American Aristotype was a single-product firm. "I found Abbott very nervous over the paper situation," Eastman reported, but since he was deep in the details of reorganizing his companies, "I do not feel like undertaking any great additional burdens; unless a very good thing can be figured out, I shall not encourage it."[31]

Elsewhere on the paper front, small firms were redoubling their frantic efforts to bootleg European paper through the black market. A New York woolens dealer operating as middleman in the black market offered foreign paper to Eastman by mistake. Eastman and Gepaco were able to plug that leak. American manufacturers scrambled to supply raw paper as well. "I never saw such spotty stuff," Eastman snorted. "I hear on all sides it is a failure." In the back of his mind was the nagging thought that some means of price maintenance had to be found in this disorganized mess to insure profits to the manufacturer and quality to the consumer. And Abbott continued to press: "Mr. Abbott seems rather anxious to form a paper makers trust; that is, have us form a paper company and buy out the American and New Jersey Aristotype Companies and the Nepera Co., and possibly the Lithium Co." Fearing that Abbott might combine with paper companies other than Kodak, Eastman began to warm to the idea. He also liked Abbott's relatively low valuation of American Aristotype—$750,000—for the purposes of merger.[32] In developing the plan, Eastman decided against having either the New York company or the British holding company acquire the paper producers, suggesting instead that George Eastman and associates buy the paper companies out and form an outside holding company, with the proviso that Kodak Limited have the option to purchase the combine within three years. Abbott and his associates, Ralph and Porter Sheldon, would be kept on for at least five years. Eastman planned to invest $300,000 himself, looking forward to a possible personal profit of $800,000.[33] The English directors were suspicious but Eastman was able to demonstrate the excellent financial condition of both companies. The English board formally approved on 18 June 1899, eventually invested in the deal, and agreed that Eastman should act as promoter and underwriter.

Meanwhile in Brussels, Louis Goffard, manager of the General Paper

Company, watched with interest. He was still loathe to cut off Gepaco's other good American customers and remembered Eastman's verbal promise that he would supply a limited amount of paper or buy out selected companies that might experience hardship. Goffard cabled a conditional response: "WE WOULD ACCEPT WITH PLEASURE THE NEW COMBINATION BUT SHOULD LIKE TRANSACTION WITH NEPERA SETTLED FIRST."[34]

The officers of the Nepera Chemical Company in Yonkers, New York, were Leonard Jacobi, president; Dr. Leo H. Baekeland, secretary; and Albert G. Hahn, treasurer. Hahn had trained as a photochemist at Cornell and the Belgian-born Baekeland at the University of Ghent before emigrating to the United States in 1889 to work for the Anthony Company. By 1893 Baekeland was with Nepera, marketing his newly developed Velox paper. Velox was gradually adapted by amateurs for contact prints and by early 1898 had begun to affect sales of Kodak's Solio paper. In response, Eastman had Stuber investigate what he called "Velox formulas" and in 1898 Kodak introduced Dekko paper to compete with Velox.[35]

The version of the purchase of the Nepera Chemical Company that has come down in legend was first given wide circulation in Eastman's obituary in the *New York Times* and continues to be related thirdhand. This appealing story begins with Dr. Baekeland offering Velox to Eastman for $100,000 and Eastman refusing, only to later pick up the phone and ask Baekeland to return and discuss the deal. Baekeland spent a sleepless night on the train to Rochester and the next morning was ushered into Eastman's office. "Baekeland, I will give you $1 million for that damn paper, and not a penny more," Eastman was supposed to have offered. Baekeland said later had his knees not been locked, he would have fallen flat. "I looked at Mr. Eastman and said, 'Well that is a very valuable paper, but I will let you have it.'"[36] The version that emerges from Eastman's correspondence is that "the taking of [Nepera] into the deal was a necessity because they controlled the bromide paper situation. Without them we could not get the agency from Steinbach. . . . Gepaco insisted on it." On 12 June 1899 Eastman traveled to Yonkers, where he met with Leonard Jacobi, "the principal owner of the Nepera Chemical Co. He was in a very intractable mood and demanded $750,000 for his business."[37] On the basis of its 1898 profits, Eastman figured Nepera was worth $500,000 at most. But Jacobi insisted that Velox sales were growing so rapidly that the profits of the first six months of 1899 must be used instead. Eastman dickered with Jacobi for three days, finding him so tough that Eastman's casual and latent anti-Semitism surfaced. "Mr. Jacobi, who is of Semitic origin, with all the characteristics of his race, evidently thinks the combine must purchase his business at his own price but I think we can attain our object . . . by the expenditure of much less."[38] (Eastman's prejudice, which seems largely the product of ignorance and provincialism, was not as mean-spirited as that of Thomas Edison, nor as virulent as that of Henry

Ford, but if a Jew proved just as hard a bargainer as himself, then out it would pop. In later years, when he would deal more with people of varied cultural backgrounds, his attitude improved.) In the end, Jacobi held out for his price, $750,000. Baekeland's share of this, even if one counts the $15,000 worth of General Aristo stock that he as well as Jacobi and Hahn each received, does not amount to the fabled round number of $1 million. Eastman showed great deference toward Baekeland, asking him and Hahn (but not Jacobi) to remain as consultants. When Baekeland chose instead to spend two years at the Paris Exposition of 1900, Eastman volunteered letters of introduction. Baekeland may have hoped to stay on with Nepera as chief photochemist, but Eastman apparently had come to believe that bright young chemists were easier to come by than lifelong loyalty to the Eastman Kodak Company. Consequently Simon Haus of the Kodak Park emulsion group was named chemist.

In August 1899 Eastman's roundup of the paper producers took final shape and barely kept ahead of antitrust laws then passing through Congress and the state legislature. Palmer and Croughton of Rochester was the first to be enveloped, followed by Kirkland Lithium Paper Company of Denver. Kirkland was a minuscule outfit, but with it came the talented Frank Noble, who was sent to Chicago to open a wholesale house and then rose through the Kodak ranks. Serving as both promoter and underwriter for the new General Aristo Company, Eastman assumed all risks and profited handsomely, acquiring options on the American Aristotype, New Jersey Aristotype, Nepera Chemical, and Kirkland's Lithium Paper companies. The deal was put together so smoothly that when a huffy telegram appeared— "THE NEW YORK TIMES IS THE LEADING MEDIUM OF FINANCIAL INTELLIGENCE AND WE SHALL GREATLY APPRECIATE IT IF YOU WILL FAVOR US WITH AN ORDER FOR THE ADVERTISEMENT OF THE ARISTO CO AS APPEARING IN ROCHESTER PAPERS"—Eastman could ignore it.

Abbott, who had initially promoted the combine, was the only member of the board not associated with Kodak, controlling approximately one-third of the capital stock. Eastman invited Abbott to visit Rochester, because he already envisioned the gregarious supersalesman assuming Strong's duties as alter ego, arm-twister, and source of levity. This might cause some displacements, notably of Sam Mora, head of the salesforce, whose talents Eastman acknowledged but who had delusions of grandeur about being Eastman's heir apparent. Yet he appreciated Mora's efforts—"considerable ability as an office man, a hard worker with good habits"—because he knew that sales were so central: "People who have an itching to manufacture the goods do not understand what they will encounter when they try to sell them."[39]

"The success of the General Aristo affair is astonishing," Eastman admitted. "The books closed two days early [and the new company was] subscribed three times over." Kodak became the sales agency for the General Aristo

Company—the name was a nod to the most popular paper—with an option to purchase it within three years. The new combine took up its headquarters in the overstuffed Photo Materials building. Factories remained at Kodak Park, Jamestown, and for a time, Nepera Park. Kirkland Lithium in Denver was closed as was New Jersey Aristotype. With the merger, the General Aristo Company controlled 95 percent of the photographic paper produced in the United States. Yet this virtual corner on the market would last only a decade. In 1908 Eastman Kodak, which had exercised its option in 1902 and purchased General Aristo, controlled only 69 percent. In the interim, American paper mills began to turn out satisfactory raw stock. As incandescent light became generally available, developing-out paper (DOP) finally caught on. Almost as soon as the shares in the new company were placed, Abbott's Aristotype paper and Eastman's Solio began their very gradual decline. Because Velox was strictly an amateur paper, Joseph Di Nunzio, makers of the best platinum paper, was purchased in 1906, and Artura, makers of paper for professionals, came into the fold in 1909. Unwittingly, Eastman tied his own hands with the Gepaco deal by promising not to develop other paper sources, engage in experimentation, or start his own paper mill for ten years. When the contract was up in 1909, he renewed it under duress and a few years later was very glad to get out from under and start producing his own paper at Kodak Park.[40]

Eastman had just mopped up the acquisition of all these new papers—Velox, Azo, Aristo—when the perfect use for them appeared: photographic postcards. Originating in Austria in 1869 and introduced to the United States in 1873, postcards began carrying pictures about the time of the Columbian Exposition of 1893. Because regulations permitted only the name and address of the recipient on the face of the card, any message had to be scrawled across the face of the photograph. The situation changed in 1903 when postal authorities in Great Britain and Europe began to allow, as George Davison informed Eastman, "half the front, where the address is put, to be used for writing communications upon." Eastman was quick off the mark. "It looks as if there might be a big future in postal cards," he alerted Ralph Sheldon of General Aristo, "and we want to have a full assortment." And so the new combine was well prepared to meet the frenzied demand for postcards once the United States Post Office followed the European model in 1907, allowing cards to be likewise divided down the middle.[41]

"The idea of the new dry plate and camera combines," Eastman told his directors in 1899, "doubtless have their [sic] origin in the success of the General Aristo Co." Too caught up developing its basic product, film to keep up with the latest technologies in the company's original product, dry plates (and emulsion formulas are cumulative), Eastman Kodak in 1900 held less than 10 percent of the dry-plate market. After failing to produce better plates, a logical move would be to acquire a good dry-plate company; still, Eastman had remained aloof from Strong's urgings and from earlier attempts to organize the sector until pressed into service at end of the century. One reason was his conviction that dry-plate photography was a dying sector; the only question was when. To help its demise along, he had invented and patented in 1890 a double-coated film that he called first Geloid, then Pelloid (having rejected Elloid and Gelak as "liable to be mispronounced"), and finally Kodoid (or simply "N.C.," for noncurling film). Even with a new name every few months Eastman's pet film had a rough time with buckling, dust settling, streaks, spots, and the back coating dissolving into a slime.

Between 1899 and 1901 the dry-plate companies themselves, encouraged by Eastman and Abbott, struggled toward the formation of a combine under the aegis of an independent promoter. That effort failed. Early on Eastman offered financial and organizational assistance and, as with paper, to act as sole agent. "I do not expect that this proposition will work immediately but it will be put to soak," he told Strong.[42] Then at the Paris Exhibition of 1900 Eastman and Gustav "Papa" Cramer agreed that "the best way is for Messrs. Seed, Cramer, Hammer [the three St. Louis giants] and Stanley [of Massachusetts] to pool their concerns in a new company, which should be formed to buy them out." In August 1901 Eastman and Abbott went to Boston to begin talks with Stanley Dry Plate. While Eastman tarried with the widow Josephine Dickman for a week at her summer residence in Gloucester (after her husband's death, she had moved to the Boston area), Abbott stayed in Boston and entered into negotiations with that "great pair of yankees," the Stanley twins. Even though Francis Stanley had a new, all-consuming interest in his Stanley Steamer automobile and Freeland Stanley was in poor health, making them both anxious to sell the dry-plate business, there were, as Abbott reported, innumerable complications.[43] It would be 1904 before the Stanley Dry Plate Company of Newton, Massachusetts, was finally taken in under the umbrella of the Eastman Kodak Company. Meanwhile, Eastman also purchased the Standard Dry Plate Company of Lewiston, Maine, obtaining two excellent chemists for Kodak: Milton Punnett and his nephew, Reuben Punnett.[44]

Despite the growing success of roll film, many professional and serious amateur photographers still preferred plate cameras. In 1899 five Rochester camera companies had joined forces to form the Rochester Optical and Camera Company, or "Carlton's camera combine," as Eastman called it after the company's manager, W. F. Carlton. Initially Eastman was approached indirectly and he indicated that he was not against the combine. But when it attracted much favorable attention he began to worry that a formidable rival was in the making. He informed Carlton that he had changed his mind and that Kodak now considered Carlton's combine an antagonistic entity. The way out, Eastman proposed, was to make Kodak the combine's exclusive

trade agents. Predictably, Carlton was not happy with this proposal so Eastman moved to option number two, informing his board that "we shall proceed at once to fight the combination by putting out plate cameras. We have
kept out of the plate camera business for many years but the best time to take
issue . . . is before they are fully organized." Eventually Eastman and Carlton worked out a contract only to have a howl of protest go up from the
dealers that undermined the whole scheme. Except for the Premo, its best
line, "Carlton's camera combine" would not be much of a success, losing as
much as $100,000 a year. In 1903 Eastman acquired it for $330,000 and
changed the name back, for simplicity's sake, to the Rochester Optical Company. In 1907 it became the Rochester Optical Division of the Eastman
Kodak Company and in 1918 the Rochester Optical Department. The factory became Kodak's Premo Works from 1912 to 1921, when the combination of a court decree and the fading of the plate camera brought the Premo
line to an end.[45]

   At Abbott's suggestion and with his aggressive assistance, Eastman began
buying up stock houses in June 1902, just a month after the purchases of the
Seed and Standard Dry Plate companies were completed. The network of
Kodak outlets thus established were forerunners of the chain-store system of
selling soon to become universally popular. In England Eastman set his
sights on the Ilford and Imperial companies, on the Continent on a Dresden
paper company and even Lumière, and on becoming the agent for Agfa, a
giant German aniline syndicate. First, he told his lieutenants, "we have to
satisfy ourselves . . . that we are not going to run against a lot of prejudice
against trusts." And so, these propositions were "put to soak" until Abbott
could be dispatched to investigate.[46]

The revolution begun in 1888 when the Kodak camera made photography
accessible to anyone who had $25 was completed in 1900 when the Brownie
camera made photography accessible to anyone who had a dollar (and fifteen cents for film)—the ultimate in democratic photography. "Plant the
Brownie acorn and the Kodak oak will grow," said trade circulars about
Eastman Kodak's phenomenal new marketing tool. The idea was George
Eastman's, the realization Frank Brownell's, Eastman's master craftsman of
the Camera Works. The name was not a bow to Brownell but to Palmer Cox,
the Canadian illustrator whose Brownie characters cavorted through the
pages of popular magazines. Beginning in 1901, a year after the Brownie
camera was introduced, Cox-esque elves emblazoned the Kodak carton and
advertisements.[47]

   While it is not known whose idea it was to call the new Kodak camera
specifically aimed at children a "Brownie," it is well known who had the final

say. Eastman wanted to reach people "the same way the bicycle has reached them."[48] The main feature of the Brownie camera was its calculated average-ness. Designed to make average pictures in average light at average speed with film of average sensitivity, it was deemed perfect for starting children on a lifetime of shooting pictures and, therefore, using film. For a dollar the child also received a fifty-four page booklet with instructions on time exposures, flash photography, developing film, and making prints. For no dues the youngster could sign up as a member of The Brownie Camera Club, enter all its contests, and regularly receive the free Kodak Art Brochure. More than one fine arts photographer began his or her career with a Brownie.[49]

Eastman saw the first Brownie cameras produced in 1900, then he and Charles Abbott, now vice president and second in command at Kodak, took off for the annual meeting in London leaving Henry Strong in charge. The first batch of five thousand Brownies sold immediately with reorders piling up. Strong ordered another thousand, then ten thousand, and in a few weeks, twenty thousand. Japan wanted two thousand, London more than doubled that request. The Brownie camera brought a record thousand additional hands to work in the Camera Works. Some dealers felt a dollar camera was beneath both them and amateur photography and at first cold-shouldered the Brownie. As the little box disappeared from their shelves, however, they found themselves simultaneously reordering and in competition with the corner drug store, which was also selling Brownie cameras.

"Picture ahead. Kodak as you go," sloganized Lewis Bunnell Jones, Eastman's adman, showing that "kodak" was still used, even by the company, as a verb or common noun meaning camera. Kodak cameras were on the march, going off to war and other adventures. From the trenches in Cuba in 1898, William Dinwiddie reported in *Harper's Weekly* about "pitiful scenes around the field hospital and our men in action." Even so, "the Kodak box has served as a pillow at night during the advance on Santiago." During the Boer War reports filtered back of one "very cool noble" who, when captured and robbed, "blandly turned over his field glasses, his pistol, his purse, and his pony [but] clung to his Kodak camera through it all and cheerfully snap-shotted his captors." In 1901 "the victim of a stage coach holdup insisted on photographing the highwayman while his rifle was leveled at the driver" and natives of Mandalay and the Hawaiian Islands snapped the tourists with their Kodaks. In 1904, when the Dalai Lama fled from his Tibetan palace, he brought his Kodak camera with him.[50] All were "Kodak freaks," a term coined in a 1905 trial in definition of this emerging breed of humanity. "Wherever they go, and whomever they see, and whatever place they have come to," the transcript read, "they have got to have a Kodak along for the purpose of getting pictures."[51]

"The Witchery of Kodakery" was the elegant phrase L. B. Jones used to convey photography's magic to the consuming public. Jones—dark, lanky, gregarious, debonair—saw advertising as a craft emerging from its heavy-handed tub-thumping beginnings. At first Jones wrote his ads to please Eastman. Then once, after Eastman returned from a trip, he summoned Jones. "These ads are better than usual. How do you explain it?" asked Eastman. "Maybe because they were written for the public instead of for Mr. Eastman," Jones replied. Eastman handed the pile over. "From now on I don't want to see any ads until they're printed." With free rein Jones came up with: "Picture ahead! Kodak as you go!" When certain dealers started selling goods from other manufacturers but calling them "Kodaks," Jones wrote, "If it isn't an Eastman it isn't a Kodak." During World War I Jones crafted one of his most brilliant exploitations: pictures of the young men of the American Expeditionary Force in the trenches of France looking longingly at "The picture from home."[52]

With a new century, innovation replaced patent protection and managers replaced craftsmen as the primary means of staying ahead of competitors. Eastman ruefully told an inventor who was trying to peddle new coating machinery that getting a patent is tantamount to giving competitors a pattern to copy: It is just too hard to catch infringers and to make the charges stick. Just as Eastman was pioneering in mass production while Henry Ford was still learning to be a machinist, he was now changing and adding camera models long before the idea of planned obsolescence hit the automotive industry. Brownell, original and titular head of the Camera Works, lacked the entrepreneurial vigor and marketing sense to come up with enough model changes to suit Eastman. He was not always a good manager either: Employees remembered a hot temper and the goods always backed up. Still, Eastman liked Brownell and with characteristic directness, proposed a solution: He would buy Brownell out for $150,000 and divide the position— William Gifford from American Aristotype would be business manager and Brownell the head of the experimental department. Brownell's "selling out" was profitable and his new job as design expert appealing and lucrative at $12,000 a year (at a time when Frank Lovejoy, manager of Kodak Park, earned $6,000).[53]

The Gifford switch was typical: Although Eastman claimed that top management of the various companies he bought was not kept on because "we have found that the switch from top man to employee does not work," this was a convenience to slough off those he considered undesirable. When he wanted a man, he simply shifted him to a different division. Thus, Gifford went from American Aristotype to the Camera Works; Frank Noble from Lithium paper to manager of the new Chicago branch; Charles Markus from president of Benjamin French Company, Boston, to president of

Sweet, Wallach & Company, Chicago; Milton Punnett and his nephew Reuben Punnett from Standard Dry Plate to the Ashtead factory in England (obtained though the purchase of Cadett and Neal) and back to the Blair company when the pair found they did not care for England; and Charles Abbott from president of American Aristotype to the inner sanctum as vice president of Eastman Kodak and Eastman's heir apparent. Sometimes Eastman erred, as in not finding an assignment for the talented chemist Leo Baekeland who, as part of the sale of Nepera Chemical, had signed a contract agreeing not to reenter the photographic-materials field for fifteen years. During this period of corporate consolidation Eastman was looking for good managers rather than talented chemists. Without this career frustration, Baekeland might not have gone on to combine phenol and formaldehyde to make the first synthetic resin, bakelite, and thus launch the plastic age.

Before the 1902 switchover at the Camera Works, Eastman had been hounding Brownell to find "some scheme of keeping track of tools that would work similar to our map scheme of keeping track of traveling men."[54] When Brownell procrastinated, Eastman devised a method of drawing the outline of each tool on the wall behind its peg. Pleased with the "scheme," he would adapt it for his tools at home and at Oak Lodge and for the cutlery he packed in picnic basket after picnic basket. Like the tools and the wandering salesmen, internal routing, records, and bookkeeping presented problems. Eastman hired a consultant, one Mr. Hewitt, to straighten out his billing system—a system similar to that which Eastman's father had taught. The expert Hewett, who had put in systems at National Cash Register and Studebaker, soon succumbed to nervous prostration and returned to Indiana for a long rest, sending word that "this business was the most complicated that he had ever tackled" and questioning whether Kodak's system of billing could ever be made practical. Eastman persisted, straightening it out to his own satisfaction in the face of doubts from Henry Strong, who agreed with Hewitt. Yet the perfection in products, service, quality, and methods he sought would continue to elude him. For instance, as soon as the billing system seemed to be improving, a film thief got loose. Boxes of film were being sold in Manhattan at half price. The thief turned out to be a Kodak Park employee, shipping the stolen goods to a friend. The employee was immediately fired, but because of his tender age, Eastman did not press charges.[55]

Kodak's first brush with strikes and unionization came in 1900. The International Machinists Union of the National Metal Trades Association tried to increase and standardize wages in metal-working shops. Because Kodak was not a metal-working shop and used machinists only as "a side issue," the company took no part in union negotiations. A minority of the machinists in the Camera Works and several more at Kodak Park were involved. Eastman directed Lovejoy and Brownell to have the essential machining done by outside contractors so that if a strike materialized, work would go on without a hitch. After the strike was broken, some of the striking machinists were rehired without repercussions. Eastman saw a union representing employees akin to an organization of employers he might join voluntarily; in either case he was not about to permit an outside group to dictate company policy. In 1903 the firemen in the Kodak Park power plant struck. Wages and hours (seven days a week) were not princely, but because they were standard, Lovejoy and Eastman decided the strike was unjustified and simply moved other men into the boiler room.[56]

Since smoking factory chimneys were the symbol of prosperity in the iconography of early-twentieth-century business, it was only fitting that Kodak Park have "the highest stack that is connected with the earth in this part of the United States"—higher than the Statue of Liberty or Flatiron building in New York and one hundred feet higher than the Powers Building in Rochester.[57] To carry off the noxious fumes from the nitric acid plant, two round radial brick stacks 366 feet high were built, with their German builders guaranteeing that "it will carry fumes so high that they will not be detected from below." Acid rain, the effect from high-flying pollution on the Adirondack mountains to the east, was, of course, not understood at this time, but in building his chimneys as high as possible, Eastman was using the best technology available to preserve Rochester's air.

A. W. McCurdy, Alexander Graham Bell's personal secretary, had come up with an intriguing gadget in which exposed film was placed on a spindle with a celluloid apron in a little, metal-lined, oblong box filled with a developer. By turning a crank the film was drawn through the developer, then washed and fixed. "Now amateurs may themselves accomplish every step of picture-making . . . without once straining their eyes beneath the feeble rays of a ruby lamp," promotional literature stated. After McCurdy had overcome several design "bugs," Eastman purchased the patents and marketed the device amid panegyric testimonials from Alexander Graham Bell (written during an April 1902 visit to Eastman's home), Thomas Edison, George Eastman, Lady Kelvin (who received the first developing machine to come off Brownell's assembly line), and sundry professional photographers at the Buffalo convention of 1902. The 1902 production of developing machines was about 14,000, doubling during the next year, and going on to much larger totals during the life of the patents. The parade of new products continued. In 1903 alone two spinoffs of McCurdy's invention, developed by Kodak staff, were marketed—a ciné developing mechanism and one for the commercial processing of roll film—both necessary for the development of large-scale photography but both primitive in terms of modern equipment. The same year the famous 3-A Kodak camera appeared, a relatively large folding camera producing $3\frac{1}{2}$ by $5\frac{1}{2}$ inch negatives, which settled into a standard size for snapshots to this day. And one of the few tangible assets in the purchase of Rochester Optical was the famous Premo Film Pack: "An ingenious hybridization of roll and sheet film, it provided twelve films in a pack only a little thicker than a conventional double plate holder." A simple adapter made film packs usable in plate cameras, and they remained popular for many years, in spite of their high cost.[58]

The familiar yellow box that even today almost jumps off the shelf into the customer's hand made its appearance about 1906, tradition having it that Eastman chose the color. About 1915 someone in the advertising department thought it was time for a change and blue boxes had a brief fling receding into dealers' shelves. Then the yellow box returned—for good.

Ever since the advent of small, light cameras there had been considerable interest in kite photography. Eastman joined the crowd trying out various kites, particularly at Oak Lodge, and studying ingenious shutter-releasing devices. Employees remember him on the factory roof releasing his kites, almost blown away by sudden gusts. In 1909 he turned down one inventor's design for a kite camera as "too complex for amateur use" and in 1914 he did not share Thacher Clarke's enthusiasm for Paul Boucher's semiautomatic Aerophote camera in which one yank of a lanyard advanced the film, set the shutter, and made the exposure. Yet his interest in the nascent phase of aerial photography persisted, evident from "official" aerial views of Kodak Park, which also began in 1909 and were clearly labeled as kite photos. Eastman realized that the implications for Kodak went far beyond mere postcard scenes of "our plant."

Pilgrimages to Rochester by hopeful inventors seeking audiences and financial backing were increasing geometrically but few saw their brain-children reach the market; most innovation still came from within. In 1902 Eastman examined E. J. Rector's Ikonoscope home movie camera and projector. Rector had brought the cost of film down by slicing standard 35 mm ciné film in two, making 17.5 mm film for amateur use. Eastman was lukewarm about camera lenses and film too slow to make movies indoors in winter, however. Rector should return during the summer, when he could film Maria Eastman as she walked through "the Garden of Eden on East Avenue," as Strong called the Soule House grounds. (Rector returned in 1906.) The next home movie machine Eastman considered, in 1908, was Edison's. A deal was struck whereby Edison granted Kodak a permit to make household machines and sell them through Kodak dealers. They were too complex and expensive to catch on; amateur movie making would have to wait for the simplified machines of the early

1920s and a method of processing the film by reversal of the negative image. Eastman's lack of enthusiasm for home movies stemmed from both the complexity of the machines and the safety factor associated with the use of the volatile nitrate film. The first mention of a less flammable film in Eastman's correspondence came in 1899 and thus began a long, convoluted, thirty-year search for a resilient, durable safety film base. City governments, notably in Berlin and Paris, cited the potential dangers of nitrate ciné film; should even an inferior safety film appear on the market, all nitrate might fall under a swift and drastic ban. Still, as he told his Paris manager confidently, "there will be a considerable lapse of time between the 'invention' of a non-inflammable film and its introduction in any quantity to affect us." That confidence changed when there were intimations that first Pathé, then Lumière, and then Bayer were coming out with a nonflammable ciné film. In 1908, after several years of research and development, Kodak did produce an acetate film that was deemed generally satisfactory and thought to be the world's first commercially viable safety film. (It burned, but at the relatively conservative rate of brown paper.) Eastman's plan was to send out safety film to customers as if it were regular film, that is, "without their knowing about it. It will only be after we find that it goes all right that we shall announce it." But so many problems developed that Eastman had to admit that "the trade does not like our acetate film as well as nitrate film."[59] Acetate film continued to be thin and weak, tending to warp. The status of various patents and the extent to which new films infringed kept cryptic transatlantic cables flying between Eastman and Clarke. Most important, acetate film cost half a cent more per foot than nitrate film. And with the company's increased size and reputation for tested quality, Eastman was becoming more conservative: "We make it a rule not to change any of our products without testing in every possible way." So after two years of marketing, the initial experiments with NI film were declared a failure.[60] Still, he knew he was sitting on a time bomb. "It is understood that celluloid [meaning the nitrocellulose base made by the Reichenbach formula] will decompose and spontaneously ignite," he wrote. "It is very dangerous stuff and ought not to be left around in any shape in the factory."[61]

The NI film had been introduced stateside only. Although the Edison licensees (Motion Picture Patents Company) saw an exclusive contract for safety film as a way of squeezing out the Independents, the municipal codes outlawing nitrate film that the Edison people were banking on never materialized. Neither exhibitors nor the public really cared whether movie film was hazardous or not; all they wanted was movies. So nitrate film—strong, resilient, transparent, long-lived, but highly hazardous and volatile—continued to be used for commercial motion pictures with safety supposedly built into theaters by making the projection booth fireproof. Acetate cellulose film would be developed first for industrial, medical, educational, and home use, where the safety factor was most crucial, but would not come into general use for ciné or regular film until the 1940s. When in 1911, for example, Edison "perfected" his home Kinetoscope and asked Eastman if he would be interested in selling it through Kodak dealers, Eastman agreed, with the proviso that the film be acetate. As with many other photographic advancements—dry plates, film, color, motion pictures, instant photography, and three-dimensional photography—the potential for making nonflammable film was obvious long before it evolved into a practical, commercially viable product.

Eastman was ecstatic about the 1914 proposal of R. J. Gaisman, inventor of the Auto-Strop razor. He had asked his staff to devise a way for amateurs to identify or date snapshots as they were taken, a perennial problem, but those theoretical scientists were having "little or no success" when in walked Gaisman with "the solution delivered and practically ready to go." The invention consisted of a narrow slot in the rear of the camera that the photographer could open and then write his or her message on the red backing paper.[62] Legend maintains that Gaisman walked out of Eastman's office with a check for $1 million; the story probably grew from Eastman's estimate, voiced on several occasions, that had the inventor accepted payment on a royalty basis, he would have netted a million. Actually, Eastman paid $10,000 on the spot and offered $300,000 outright, effective January 1915. In addition, he gained a correspondent: Dozens of letters to Gaisman extol the virtues of Gaisman's Auto-Strop razor, which Eastman not only used but often bestowed as a gift to friends. (He even wrote a testimonial for Gaisman but squawked when Gaisman printed it more than once and with his picture.) Eastman saw the Autographic feature as a sensational patent purchase, the basis of a whole new system of photography which, with the Turner patent declared invalid and Ansco busily marketing Buster Brown cameras to compete with Kodak's Brownie cameras, could be publicized and demonstrated and protected from imitation. Autographic cameras in various models and at various prices were featured in Kodak catalogs for the next seventeen years, the life of the patent and coincidentally, the remaining lifetime for George Eastman. But, like the developing machine, the Autographic device never really caught on with the public; to the consternation of their descendants, most amateur photographers (including, ironically, Eastman himself) remain oddly reluctant to identify their snapshots, no matter how easy the camera manufacturer makes it for them.

Something was definitely out of sync in England. The London shop looked spick-and-span and the Harrow grounds as beautifully kept as Kodak Park.

But from Harrow, Abbott reported seeing spots, scratches, and blemishes on the bromide paper. No wonder that the goods were not selling. And Harold Senier, superintendent, had been hiring his relatives and wasting materials. Simon Haus and assistant were quickly dispatched from Rochester with instructions "not to socialize with Senier or his satellites" and to report their findings directly to Eastman. "I have never seen a dirtier work room than the coating plant at Harrow," Haus wrote. He reported glaring departures from standard emulsion-making practices and lax supervision. Eastman cabled Davison to get Senier's resignation and put the Americans temporarily in charge of the all-out effort to clean house, literally and figuratively. The big shakeup took the props out from under Davison, whom Eastman had never liked. Haus hated England, but Eastman wanted Haus at Harrow and kept him there by raising his salary and telling him there were no openings commensurate with his talents at Kodak Park, and by other compliments and cajolery. Finally during the Great War, a decade and a half after he began complaining about his outpost, Haus was brought back to Rochester because the British were offended by his German name, accent, and manner. After the war Eastman sent Haus back to Harrow—as "Mr. House." In addition to Haus's shoring up management at Harrow, Kodak sought to refurbish its image to customers. Eastman had great respect for Davison's flair in making the English shops the most picture perfect of any in the world and his knack in staging photography exhibitions.[63]

In spite of the efforts of the reliable Haus and Davison's design aptitude, in the early 1900s Kodak goods were not selling well in England. Davison was a poor manager of time, resources, and personnel. He placed heavy orders for film one month and none the next, throwing Kodak Park into a tizzy. (As a result, however, Lovejoy devised a method of refrigerating film so that it would keep longer, thus solving a major seasonal employment and layoff problem.) Davison's primary sales tactic was to cut prices to compete with Lumière's cheaper film and inexpensive German cameras then flooding the market. That drove Eastman wild; he wanted to stress mechanical and optical innovations and superiorities and keep prices up. Davison was also alienating the powerful English dealers with his rigid and militant policies. Be more conciliatory, let the dealers think you are backing down, then they will fall in line, Eastman counseled. Davison had opened a Kodak Limited branch in Australia in 1900 but the veteran firm of Baker and Rouse, which had formerly been a Kodak agency, was running rings around it. Finally, Eastman found Davison a crashing bore. "This noon we are all going out to the Davisons to spend the afternoon," he wrote his mother. "It's a deadly place but it can't be helped." The differences accelerated, and in December 1907 Eastman wrote Davison that he was coming to England in February "to see if I can

do something to get the European organization into more effective working shape." He asked for Davison's resignation, noting that

> I am not unappreciative of the fact that you have always done your level
> best for the interest of the concern. I only think that you have not the
> faculty for selecting and managing men that is required to make the
> most out of the organization. Personally I much regret to propose
> the severance of our relations after so many years working together. . . .
> The business, as far as the distributing part of it, is in a most unsatisfac-
> tory state and I think the only way to tackle the problem is through new
> hands.[64]

Eastman then asked Davison to fill the board vacancy created by the death of
Lord Kelvin in 1907; he remained a director until 1913 when Eastman felt
his extracurricular activities as the editor of an anarchist newspaper was a
conflict of interest. (Even so, he found Davison's efforts "rather wishy-washy.
If I were going to be the editor of an anarchist paper I think I should get
some ginger into it.") Davison, who had been "a humble second division Civil
Servant in the Exchequer and Audit Office"[65] before joining Kodak, had
plenty of Kodak stock to live comfortably in retirement. When the Bolshevik
Revolution erupted in Russia, he espoused that cause and when he died in
1931 Eastman called Davison's a "misspent life."

William Gifford was made managing director of Kodak Limited in 1908
with the faithful Frank Mattison continuing as deputy managing director as
he had served Davison. When Gifford retired in 1919, Mattison, a kindly,
grandfatherly type, became managing director and even though he suffered
from pernicious anemia and was not given long to live, continued in that
position until 1927 and then as chairman until his death in 1943. Gifford
and Thomas Baker in Australia now became Eastman's long-distance confi-
dants while Gifford, his wife May, and daughters Katherine and Louise
became close personal friends.

Just as the big British holding company was settling in, the Boer War in
South Africa loomed and the British government levied a 5 percent income
tax on British-owned, foreign-based companies. Eastman filed an appeal.
Because Kodak Limited was Eastman's creation, the London brokers refused to push the sale of Kodak stock. Three-quarters of the ordinary and
half of the preference stock was held in the United States and American
stockholders were not pleased. General Aristo shareholders particularly
would have had little reason to favor assimilation into a British company. Yet
a drastic change would alienate the new British directors. Eastman put a
decision on hold for a year, then decided to reorganize the company (for the
final time) under a holding company based in corporation-friendly New

Jersey. Kodak Limited would return to being an operating and production unit, as the Eastman Photographic Materials Company had been, with its capitalization tailored down. Shareholders would be given equivalent holdings or bought out. The British board would become American-dominated. In "estimating the amount of capitalization necessary to take in all of the people that we have contemplated," Eastman made a rough breakdown:

Kodak	$19,642,000
American Dry Plate Makers	4,335,000
Willis Platinum Works	1,230,000
Ilford Dry Plate Work	2,410,000
Dresden Paper Makers	4,000,000
	$31,617,000

In October 1901 the Eastman Kodak Company of New Jersey, capitalized at $35 million,[66] was incorporated "to acquire the stock or absorb the various manufacturing and selling corporations known as Kodak Limited, London; Eastman Kodak Company, Rochester; the General Aristo Company, Rochester; the Eastman Kodak Societe Anonyme Francaise, Paris; and Kodak Gesellschaft mit beschrankter Haftung, Berlin." Specified were factories at Rochester, Jamestown, Nepera Park, and Harrow; headquarters in Rochester, London, Paris, and Berlin; branches in New York, Chicago, San Francisco, Liverpool, Glasgow, Brussels, Lyons, Milan, Vienna, Moscow, St. Petersburg, and Melbourne. When the offering was quickly oversubscribed, Eastman and Strong sold some of their common stock to meet the demand. Even so, it was necessary "to cut everybody down a little, to make room. . . . There is no chance to make money on this scheme," Eastman decided. The original plan called for the New Jersey corporation to take over the Rochester operations, dissolving the New York company. Problems of real estate, taxes, and transfer of tangible and intangible property proved so complex that Eastman had the New York company continue as the operating company and made the New Jersey company strictly a holding company, serving as financial clearing house for all Kodak enterprises, receiving and paying dividends to shareholders. Rochester never knew how close it came to losing its principal employer. Following this last recapitalization the "directors deem it a fitting occasion to give the shareholders some account of the company's progress." With the addition of American Aristotype, Nepera Chemical, Photo Materials, and Canadian Kodak, Limited, there were now eight associated companies instead of four, four thousand employees on the payrolls of the various companies, 118 traveling men, new depots in London and Berlin, and "improvements bound to be epoch making to photography: Non-Curling film, Kodoid plates, the Daylight Developing Machine, and the Rochester Optical Company Premo Film pack."[67]

For the first time Eastman assumed the title of president of one his companies. Strong continued as president of the New York operating company until his death and was made first vice president and treasurer of the New Jersey corporation. Walter Hubbell was second vice president and secretary and Alice K. Whitney, assistant secretary, a remarkable position for a woman in this period. Of the British members of the 1899 Kodak Limited board, only Sir James Pender and Lord Kelvin appeared on the New Jersey board. The new corporate structure was approved in England in November 1901, over the reservations and strenuous objections of Henry Verden, solicitor, and certain of the directors who (correctly) saw their power slipping across the Pond. Approval came from the American board and shareholders in December and shares were issued in July 1902. For that first annual meeting and the start of the New Jersey company Eastman arranged to have his most distinguished English director present. William Thomson, First Baron Kelvin of Largs, the greatest British physicist of the 1800s, the greatest of teachers, arrived for a tour by private railroad car to New York, Niagara Falls, Jamestown, and Rochester. Maria Eastman gave a luncheon for Lady Kelvin at the Genesee Valley Club while her son hosted one for the baron. The excuse to bring corporate headquarters back to American shores was the taxation. Yet the appeal eventually succeeded. In 1904 Eastman cut the English directors' fees to bring them in line with those of the American directors. Howls went up: "I had no idea Sir James [Pender] and Pringle relied so heavily on these fees for living expenses," said Eastman in mock amazement. He then offered selected employees a stock option plan. His goal was a lean, aggressive, rapidly growing worldwide concern. He could maintain that delicate balance between the American and English companies, using figures to prove whatever point he was making to whichever group. He could say in truth that "the approximate number of shareholders is 3,300 of whom 2,200 are European" when trying to impress British stockholders with how British the company was. Or he could call attention to the fact that four-fifths of the shares were held by Americans (notably Eastman, Strong, and Walker) when arguing that corporate headquarters should be in the United States. More than one personal fortune was founded on such opportunities as the 1902 stock option plan, and the precedent was set for future employee benefit programs more definitively than in Eastman's arbitrary gifts of 1898 out of personal profits. With the stock so much in demand now and so tightly held for investment, he decided not to pay the $1,500 fee to list on the New York Stock Exchange. For the nonce (until April 1905), the London Exchange would do.[68]

Eastman never could understand the fear of bigness and monopoly that was gripping the country at this time. His only goal, he said, was to serve the consumer better and this he was manifestly doing, evidenced by the reduction in price of Kodak cameras from the original at $25 in 1888 to a much better model seven years later for $5. "How about that statement [in *Photographic Life*, a Nepera publication]," he asked, chuckling, "that the Lumière Co. is the largest photographic manufacturer in the world?"[69] He could afford to laugh; he knew he was number one, the Alpha and Omega, the key figure in the growth of the American photographic industry, a shrouded symbol of power, head of the corporate tribe—loved, hated, feared, respected. The specter of the Goodwin patent and the serious problems the acquisitions of the past decade would eventually cause him lay in the future. For now, he and his company were riding high. He had "effected a major refinancing and reorganization of the photographic industry without recourse to outside banking and investment interests," and the opportunity was too rich not to have the last laugh on his English board and managing director. The yokel from upstate New York, who had first come to London hat in hand with a little plate-coating device to peddle, had emerged a couple of decades later as the ruler of Albion's photography world.

"As a photographic and financial center it appears that little London is not in it with great big ROCHESTER," he wrote.[70]

Crazy about Color

■ ∎ ▪ ━━━

"If we could devise some simple process for making color photographs," said George Eastman laconically but prophetically in 1904, "it might have quite a vogue."

During the last twenty years of the nineteenth century the photographic process had been pushed forward, popularized, simplified, and improved—often through Eastman's impetus—to the point where the next major advances would not be finalized until after his death. These would be primarily in color photography and safety film, both possible during his lifetime and both objects of his unflagging attention; yet both would need thirty years from inception to perfection. In 1904 he was totally ignorant about color photography. The time had come to investigate. His goal was to whip color photography into such shape that "the amateur can get good results."[1]

By 1911 he knew enough that, invited to talk on the evolution of color photography, he produced a paper in language lay persons could comprehend. Eastman singled out James Clerk-Maxwell, who in 1861 rigged up a trio of magic lanterns to project a multicolored image by the additive method: three separate negatives shot through colored filters, then made into three positives that could be projected. In his 1868 patent, Ducos du Hauron outlined most of the possible processes of color photography, both additive and subtractive. Subtractive processes, in which unwanted colors are absorbed, achieve purer, crisper, and more intense color, with less loss of light than additive processes, but subtractive processes are more difficult to manufacture.[2]

The process that would be marketed under the name Autochrome was already fifteen years old, when, in 1904, the Lumière brothers began dying starch grains in three separate lots, sifting them onto glass plates prepared with a tacky coating, pressing the starch grains flat, and filling the interstices between the disks with lamp black. Projected or illuminated from behind, they were quite beautiful in a soft-focus way. Eastman was concerned: "I have no doubt but that Anthony will try and make a coalition with Lumière," he brooded,[3] the premonition goading him into action. But no such coalition materialized and the French firm would not market its plates until June 1907, giving him a three-year respite. The Lumières, Eastman had to admit when he saw the first Autochromes, had done for trichromatic photography what Daguerre did for monochromatic photography—produced results.

Spurred by the Lumière brothers, the Agfa and Rotograph companies in Germany, the Finley company in England, du Hauron in France, and Eastman at Kodak Park worked on similar projects. In 1904 Eastman engaged John K. Powrie and Florence Warner of Chicago to demonstrate their process, which followed the known patents and additive processes. The Powrie–Warner method seemed to Eastman both cheaper and better defined than others he had investigated, as well as "beautiful when thrown on a screen by magic lantern."[4] The negative plates were used in an ordinary holder and camera with yellow filter. Then positives had to be made in another camera, so it was not yet the carefree system of Eastman's dreams. The exposure was too long for snapshots and while the projected color was rich and beautiful, the hottest, most powerful arc lights were needed to project the transparencies.[5]

Eastman directed Frank Lovejoy to provide help and facilities for Powrie and Warner's demonstrations and construction of machinery. John Huiskamp of the Seed Company—by now a subsidiary of Eastman Kodak—was imported from St. Louis to work on the project.[6] "I am in a fair way to make a contract with this man for his process for the world," Eastman mused at the height of his euphoria. Powrie and Warner toiled away at Kodak Park, meeting with the usual delays, but when they finished their demonstrations, Eastman did not exercise his option. Difficulties in getting uniform results was the major problem, and Eastman was always adamant that uniform results precede mass production. Then, too, Moritz Philipp had advised that the Powrie chromatic plates infringed patents that would have to be purchased too. "Miss Warner sailed out in a huff," but returned when Eastman assured her he had not lost interest. He mollified her by treating her to "a little history of the non-curling film," which took fifteen years to bring to perfection. While experiments continued at Kodak Park, Thacher Clarke was working his own "Premo film scheme" at Harrow. Eastman applied for a patent for Clarke, encouraging him to continue investigating other color processes, old or new. Simultaneously, F. A. Fifield of Canadian Kodak made color screen plates by piling and cementing sheets of thin celluloid, dyed red, blue, and green, then slicing off sections to use as the emulsion support. Early color investigations were so unsystematic and available staff so small that sales managers and corporation counsels were augmenting the experimenters and so-called specialists. Eastman himself devoured the *British Journal of Photography*'s monthly digest of color patents and Clarke's translations of salient German and French articles.[7] Processes of development were complex enough that Eastman envisioned his old adage, "You press the button, we do the rest," becoming operative once more. Color photography in 1904 was about at the point that black and white was in Daguerre's time: A moving object could not be recorded.[8] Eastman's concentration on amateurs instead of studio professionals was economically sound: Eventually more than 70 percent of color photographs would be taken by amateurs. Meanwhile, he put his one experimental chemist at work on a reversal process—making the negative into a positive by bleaching the silver. Having only *one* experimental chemist was beginning to bother him too.

When the Lumière brothers marketed Autochrome plates, Eastman saw them as "a great success as far as publicity is concerned," but breathed easier because "they are not panning out profitably." Because they were glass plates and had to be viewed by transmitted light, their application was narrowly limited to lantern slides. Still, Lumière had a better manufacturing process than Powrie. The next year, 1908, the elder Lumière brother and his New York agent and interpreter, Jules Brulatour, "floated in here . . . and wanted to know if I would consider a proposition to buy out the Lumière operation." The unlikely trio then crossed the Atlantic together to size up the situation. Eastman found financial chaos—"the wives of the sons and father all take a hand in the management . . . so no definite hard-headed policy is maintained"—and did not exercise his option. (The initial contact with Brulatour, however, blossomed into a business association and friendship as the suave Frenchman became Eastman's agent for Kodak motion picture film.)[9]

Hand-colored prints and lantern slides were the rage when Eastman, the Mulligans, and Frederick Monsen—photographer, guide, Indian expert— spent six weeks in Arizona during the summer of 1909. Monsen colored Eastman's slides for him to project for friends "in the colors of nature" when he returend to Rochester. Wallace Nutting, Kodak dealer, worked up a thriving business coloring platinum prints by hand, and Eastman could see nothing on the color photography horizon that would interfere with this business for many years.[10] Still, he never let an opportunity slip to investigate a new color theory: The hope was always that the next process would be the answer.

In 1910 a prototype color laboratory was established at Kodak Park under Emerson Packard, MIT graduate. In preparation Eastman started a collection of color samples "of historical value" from the Lumière, Omnicolor,

Heliochrome, Dufay, Thames, Kunstseide, and Deutsche Raster Gesellschaft companies. Eastman instructed Packard to devise his own filter screen
that would overcome the difficulties of the Powrie and Fifield methods and
still not infringe Lumière's Autochrome.[11] Concurrently, Clarke optioned
patents for a two-color process from German chemist Carl Spath, and investigated a granular color screen worked out by Rudolph Ruth, a concert
cellist.[12]

"During my [recent] twelve weeks in Europe, my longest absence for
many years," Eastman wrote in April 1910, "I spent a good deal of time
on new developments in color . . . which I hope will develop into something commercial."[13] Once again Eastman felt threatened, this time by two
German companies—Neue Photographische Gesellschaft and Vereinigte
Kunstseide Fabriken. Fearing that their patents would delay marketing the
Spath process, he instructed Clarke to pay Kunstseide's asking price. Rather
than risk infringing, "I would cheerfully buy them out. . . . Do not be afraid
of the money . . . just get the option." He conducted fading tests on
Kunstseide film by hanging strips in his office windows, one exposed to the
sun and the other to north light, examining them weeks later by microscope.
"Fugitive dyes are going to be a serious feature," he predicted. And so they
would be. Also, a process that worked well for its inventor would fail misera-
bly at the hands of another, equally skilled operator. To semioutsiders such
as Darragh de Lancey, Eastman crowed about how Packard and Spath and
others were "enthusiastically engaged . . . producing color negatives and
positives on film." But—and this was a big but—they could only be viewed by
transmitted light.[14]

Clarke reported on the Berthon reversal patents of 1908. "I do not see
how any reversal scheme can be practical for making moving pictures because one must have duplicates," Eastman wrote, "and the process is not in a
stage where we can deal with the A. G. F. A."—the German dye manufacturer and rising film competitor that would henceforth be known by its
acronym.[15] And so in 1910 the Berthon process (which would be purchased
by Pathé in 1914 and Kodak in 1926) was put on hold.[16] Processes and
inventors did move around. Carl Christensen, the Dane who initiated the
collodion chloride POP process in the 1880s, had a color process Kodak
investigated and abandoned only to have it used to manufacture Agfacolor
film. The complexity of color was such that competitors were no more successful than Eastman, although rumors abounded that other companies
were about to market color plates, cut film, or ciné film. "When you think
that even with the simple process we propose," Eastman said, "there are two
printings and three dyeings, a slight error in any one of which operations
will spoil the result, it becomes evident that we must get a greater uniformity
of action in all of these operations. . . . Color experiments are being pushed
and good progress is being made but the more I see of the job the more I

realize that it is a difficult one and will take time." By October 1910 he told Stuber that the color department was ready to begin experiments with emulsion.[17]

Eastman anticipated two separate color processes, one on nitrate film for cartridge use and the other on acetate (safety film) for motion picture projection. For ciné films, which were discarded as they wore out, fugitive dyes would not be so much of a drawback but for snapshots in the family album, "dyes that faded or darkened . . . would be out of the question."[18] Spath was brought to Rochester, but his results were flawed. While contracts with outside inventors and experts provided for all available technical help there came that moment when Eastman decided the process was hopeless and summarily dismissed the hapless expert. Like most inventors, Spath was convinced that given enough time, his process would work; uninvited, he returned to Rochester months after his 1913 dismissal. "Very injudicious of you to come without knowing whether I had changed my views," a short-tempered Eastman observed. "It is useless for you to experiment further at Kodak Park and there is no advantage to an interview."[19] Only occasionally did he despair, as when, in 1911, he sent Clarke a one-sentence letter: "What is the use of our going on with color photography experiments?"[20]

"He was crazy about color," Charles Edward Kenneth Mees, the first director of the Kodak Research Laboratories, would decide. "He had a true amateur's love of color." So anxious was Eastman to be the first to market color film for amateurs that he introduced it too soon, according to Mees: "The sensitizing dyes known before 1930 wandered badly." In 1906 the blunt and peppery Mees, smitten by science at age ten, had approached the British firm of Wratten and Wainwright, then a father-and-son dry-plate operation, and was offered the opportunity to buy into a partnership.[21] In 1909 Mees visited Rochester to meet the enigmatic great man of photography, and two years later Eastman returned the compliment with a further purpose in mind. Legend has it that while spending the Christmas holidays of 1911 in Europe, Eastman was entertained by Dr. Duisberg, head of the Bayer Company. After expounding about Bayer's research staff of several hundred chemists, Dr. Duisberg asked, "And how many research chemists do you have, Mr. Eastman?" Eastman allegedly told Clarke: "If Bayer can afford a research staff, we can." Apocryphal though the details may be, in January 1912 Eastman was in London offering Mees the opportunity to plan and head a unique research laboratory at Kodak Park.[22] In the back of Mees's mind was the desire to return to research. So when Thacher Clarke called to say Eastman was coming, Mees was receptive—intrigued even. He set conditions, insisting that Eastman buy out Wratten and Wainwright, perpetuate its most significant products (panchromatic plates and filters), find places in

Kodak Limited for its people, and continue with its contract to establish a Hungarian dry-plate factory. It was not an expensive proposition for the world's largest photomaterials company. When the taciturn Eastman acquiesced, his chief description of the American company to Mees was: "You will like Lovejoy."[23]

Mees the scholar and theoretician and Eastman the practical manufacturer viewed a research laboratory from different perspectives. Eastman saw Mees as "a practical manufacturer of color plates, . . . the highest authority in color photography in the world," and the new chemist's job as supporting his own aggressive research in color photography.[24] For Mees, the main thrust of the enlarged Research Laboratories would not be color photography or solving the eternal practical problems but basic research into the nature of the photographic process and the formation of the photographic image. He was intensely curious as to how the latent image becomes the developed image, why gelatin emulsions were much more sensitive to light than collodion emulsions, and so forth. He did not know whether research so conducted would eventually lead to new or improved products of commercial value to the company. He insisted to Eastman that nothing of commercial value should be expected to come out of the laboratory for ten years.

Eastman was willing to be patient and spend the money he had begrudged Powrie and Spath: He had more confidence in Mees and the team he was assembling. "Your job," he told Mees, as he had once told Reichenbach, "is the future of photography." Besides, he was in an expansive mood in 1912 when Kodak stock was selling for $500 and paying juicy dividends and he was establishing the wage dividend, trying to build low-cost housing for Rochester, making his first big gift to MIT, and giving another big gift to the Universiy of Rochester. Mees arrived permanently in August, followed shortly thereafter by other Englishmen, notably Samuel Sheppard and John Capstaff. The new Research Laboratories would have a distinct English accent but would also have Eastman's personal stamp for the remainder of the decade. It marked a new beginning, an infusion of energy, talent, and experimentation into the company at a time when it could have grown fat and complacent. Despite Eastman's anxieties about the giant German corporations, the competition seemed far behind. When in late 1911 the attorney general began investigating Kodak as possibly violating the Sherman Act, Eastman listed his principal photographic competitors as the Ansco Company at home and the Ensign Company abroad, neither of which was much of a threat in terms of amount of goods produced.

Pathé, Eastman reported to associates in January 1914, "is about to bring out a color process which will revolutionize the industry. . . . Invented by a man named Berthon . . . the colors are in the film, reproduction is simple . . . finished positives costing scarcely anything extra for color . . . and projected by any machine with trifling alterations . . . on the market in four months."[25] Eastman stepped up in-house efforts and by the fall of 1914 John Capstaff had devised a two-color subtractive process that produced seductive portraits but unsatisfactory colors for landscapes. Known by a new trademark—*Kodachrome*—the negatives were taken through red and green filters and transformed directly into positives. A mirror in the camera reversed one of the negatives so that the two-color positives could be superimposed face to face as a completed picture. The picture still had to be viewed by transmitted light but in addition to its being used as a lantern slide, an ingenious illuminator—a shadow box with electric light inside—made wall-mounting and table-top viewing possible. Marketing of the new process was held up by the outbreak of the Great War in August 1914 and the sudden unavailability of red photographic dye from Germany (defects plagued domestic dyes). The lengths and expense to which Eastman went to obtain even a precious ounce of Complementar Rot dye through Sweden illustrates his dogged commitment to get Capstaff's Kodachrome on the market.

Professional photographers were the obvious target for Kodachrome but J. M. Mock of Rochester, Eastman's personal portrait photographer of the period, was one of the few who responded and spent $500 to fit up his gallery. (In return, Mock received the meager three-days' supply of dye Kodak had on hand.) Medical photography was considered another market and Kodachrome plates were sent to Rochester General Hospital. Only a Brooklyn surgeon, Dr. Beers, head of a large New York laboratory, seems to have used the plates to graphically record certain skin ailments. The complicated operations involved in developing this new subtractive process limited the use of the Capstaff Kodachrome to a few experienced and pioneering professional photographers.

Eastman himself had great fun with the new Kodachrome process; innumerable associates, cronies, and visitors were photographed. Ellen Dryden was invited "to get your picture taken for George's Christmas." He collected pretty young women and children in red or green dresses—Eleanor Eastwood, Mary Mulligan, Victoria Powers, Margaret Woodbury, Nell Newhall, little Miss Sibley, little Miss Lindsay—and kept these in his office. He stepped behind the camera to record George Eastman Dryden, Josephine Dickman, and probably many others. Copies were sent to the grateful sitters—including Darragh de Lancey and William Walker. The portraits were viewed at Rochester's Memorial Art Gallery during November 1914, where the show was declared "splendid"[26] by Eastman. The private view for a select nineteen Kodak men[27] and their familes was followed by the public opening, when 2,800 persons crowded into the little museum after which the thirty-two photographs were favorably reviewed by the newspaper's art critic.[28] But in March 1915 fifteen Kodachromes were shown at the Royal Photographic Society and that report was less glowing, complaining that "the correctness in colour-rendering was much inferior to that of the three-colour process" but admitting that "the results were sufficiently encouraging to justify the assumption that a slight improvement in colour-rendering . . . would be satisfactory for many purposes." The same photographs were shown at the San Diego and San Francisco Panama Pacific Exhibition of 1915. "Do not call them colored photographs," Eastman admonished Ellen Dryden, having just mastered the distinction himself. "They are quite a different thing—*color* photographs."[29]

"Invention is primarily the art of getting out of trouble," declared Leopold Damrosch Mannes in 1952. "The trouble with color photography is that the more you tell a layman about it, the less he understands," pronounced Leopold Godowsky Jr. in a talk at the George Eastman House in 1956.[30] The textbook history of inventions features successful inventors: Eastman, Edison, Ford, Whitney, and others who emerged victorious. Countless early struggles are forgotten; frustrated experimenters and tinkerers never appear in the histories even though these efforts, too, are part of the story. So it would be with color photography. The resolution, although Eastman would not live to see it, began in 1922 when two youngsters called on him in his suite at the Murray Hill Hotel in New York.

Earlier, in 1916, Godowsky Jr. and Mannes, both sixteen years old and sons of well-known musicians, became acquainted as classmates and amateur photographers. Like Mees they disliked school sports but instead of cleaning chemistry labs to escape, they found solace in playing sonatas and taking, developing, and printing Brownie snapshots together. Upon seeing an early color movie with its limited spectrum, they decided, in the all-things-are-possible haze of youth, to improve upon its process in their school physics laboratory. The boys built a camera with three lenses that combined the primary colors by means of projected beams of light—basically what Maxwell had done, but they didn't know that and exuberantly reinvented the wheel. Godowsky went on to study physics and mathematics at Berkeley and Mannes to receive a degree in physics from Harvard—so much for later tales that color film was invented by two musicians who didn't know enough science to realize that it was impossible. They renewed their friendship in New York through musical interests. Impressario S. L. (Roxy) Rothafel, who consulted on the Eastman Theatre, loaned them use of his projection booth at the Rialto. Their first pictures were dark and fuzzy. Bouncing back from many disappointments, they switched from multiple lenses to multiple-layered film, from the optical to the chemical approach of treating film with layers of emulsions, from an additive process to a subtractive process. They made the right decisions. Soon they were producing, in bathtubs and sinks in their own homes, double-layered plates on which part of the spectrum could be photographed—a feat other photographers had attempted from the beginning. But their parents, musicians all, tired of the chaos and declined to finance further experimentation. Desperate for funds, the young men finagled that interview with Eastman in 1922. He received them courteously and listened to them sympathetically, Godowsky told a *New Yorker* magazine interviewer in 1956, and "[Eastman] said he would see what could be done about the money situation, but [we] never heard from him again." (By 1922 Eastman, age sixty-eight, was having regular spells of forgetfulness. He had greeted innumerable color experimenters, listened to their rhapsodic tales, looked at their beautiful results, but found them all lacking in practicality. Besides, the Eastman Theatre and School of Music were now occupying his attentions as Kodak Park once did.)

Mannes next contacted Robert Williams Wood, head of the experimental physics department of Johns Hopkins University, who put him in touch with Dr. Mees. Mees agreed to provide the moonlighting scientists with "whatever equipment and other supplies, prepared according to their specifications, they might need for their experiments, and he proposed that, in return for this assistance, they visit him in Rochester from time to time to keep him posted on developments."[31] Godowsky and Mannes considered this manna from heaven and throughout the 1920s the musicians took out forty photographic patents and continued their experiments in rented laboratories in New York. Some financial backing—less than $20,000 in a loan—came through banker Lewis L. Strauss, later chairman of the Atomic Energy Commission. Meanwhile Messrs. Mannes and Godowsky Sr. complained that their boys were not practicing their music. Also, while bankers thought the boys weren't devoting enough time to experimental photography, photographic experts hinted they should stick to their music—through which they continued to earn support for their scientific careers.

As George Eastman passed his seventieth birthday in 1924, company officials were even more anxious to introduce a commercially viable color system during his lifetime. On 18 April 1926, en route to Africa and nearing Port Sudan on the Red Sea, Eastman wrote a remarkably prescient letter to Lovejoy. "Last night, as I lay in my berth, I dreamed a dream," the letter began. Mees, according to the dream, had come across a new full-color process that could be used easily by movie amateurs. Eastman described the process in detail, the steps by which it was to be produced and marketed, and even the advertisements that announced it. He forecast gigantic sales with a drain on inventories of film, cameras, and projectors. A modification of the Berthon process,[32] which Eastman had earlier found wanting, was acquired by Kodak in 1925 and considerable effort expended at Kodak Park to develop it as a three-color amateur process. Film could be made reversible—negative to positive—through a process developed by Capstaff and was thus relatively inexpensive to the consumer. It was reasonably easy to make, being embossed on the support side with a corrugated surface that formed minia-ture images of the filters on the emulsion. But it was still the old additive system of light-absorbing filters, making mandatory very bright illumination through a special projector. Despite this major drawback and against the advice of Mees, who felt color photography was not ready to be marketed, in 1928 Kodak introduced a 16 mm film for home movies under the name of Kodacolor, a trademark that would be later used for an entirely different color-print process. Home movie aficionados tried it and most returned to black and white.

At the same time, Capstaff, whose reversal process made amateur black-and-white movies possible in 1923, continued to work on a two-color "Ko-dachrome" process for professional motion pictures. He set up his studio in a loft over the Eastman School of Music and, in an early use of incandescent rather than arc lighting, shot visiting luminaries. The premier showing of Capstaff's Kodachrome motion pictures was at the opening of the Eastman Theatre in 1922. Eastman liked what he saw and sent Capstaff on to Holly-wood with special camera, film, and processing equipment. Still, the old limitations of good flesh tones but inadequate color for scenery, plus a blind-ing, hot light level, brought Capstaff back home, disappointed. While in the movie capital Capstaff shot a number of shorts and contracted with Fox for a full-length feature that was never made. He never gave up, and into the early 1930s, a Kodachrome section with several employees was maintained in the Research Laboratories. Even for professional motion-picture photography, Capstaff's two-color Kodachrome gave as good results as any two-color pro-cess available in the 1920s, including one by the Technicolor Motion Picture Corporation. About 1932, however, Technicolor, Mees would write, "worked out its three-color imbibition process . . . a triumph of technical skill . . . that gave results superior to any two-color process and grew rapidly in public favor."[33] Technicolor was fine for Hollywood, but much too complex and expensive for amateur use.

Out of these machinations wholly new concepts were born. Mees saw Mannes and Godowsky's work on a subtractive process as a possible solution for amateur color film. By 1928 the Research Laboratories had extended the range of sensitizing dyes and adjusted the emulsions so that dyes would no longer wander easily from one layer to another of the superimposed films. In 1930 Mees suggested that his protégés move to Rochester to continue their work. Mannes and Godowsky accepted, while warning Mees that they were hardly cut out for small-town Rochester life—although Mannes would meet his wife there. At Kodak Park they became known as "Man and God" or "those musicians." At the Eastman School, where they played chamber music with the faculty, they became known as "those color experts." Around town people who heard them play in the Eastman Theatre with the Rochester

Philharmonic Orchestra wondered what Kodak was coming to, hiring a violinist and a pianist to do scientific research. The newcomers made things worse at the park by timing their plate developing by whistling, two beats a second to, say, the Brahms' C-Minor Symphony. (They worked in total darkness; watches with radium dials might fog the plates, they claimed.)[34]

When the Depression hit, jobs were thrown in jeopardy. Mees had assured Mannes and Godowsky that there would be no hurry to invent anything and they were reveling in investigating the broader aspects of color photography under ideal working conditions and having dozens of experienced technicians and emulsion makers with doctorates in chemistry and physics working with them; still, as belt-tightening started, seemingly unproductive research looked more and more suspect. Under tremendous pressure, with Mees, by then a vice president, stalling the other departments, Mannes and Godowsky developed a two-color film that the amateur could use as easily as black-and-white film.

Mannes and Godowsky considered this film but a stepping stone to a three-color film that could reproduce all the colors of nature, whereas Mees, under pressure now from other directors, saw it as a stopgap money maker and ordered the manufacturing department to gear up. That was enough of a deadline to get the musicians to solve the three-color riddle; perfectionists both, they continued to plead for time to make improvements but again Mees overruled. "If he hadn't, we'd probably be at it to this day," Godowsky admitted in 1956.[35]

The name "Kodachrome," registered in 1914 for that earlier, now moribund process, was brought out and dusted off. On 15 April 1935 Kodachrome motion picture film went on sale, followed in short order by Kodachrome film for color slides. Byzantine in its complexity of development but breathtaking in its clarity and color, here, at long last, was the color film that George Eastman had envisioned for amateurs to use in any camera.

IV

The Upstate
Lorenzo at Ease

The Garden of Eden

As the century drew to a close Eastman turned from frenetic trips abroad to homegrown pleasures: gardening, automobiling, housebuilding, music, even a touch of metaphysics. The immediate causes were undoubtedly world-weariness brought about by Dickman's death and his mother's increasing age and problematic health. But soon he was playing as hard as he once worked and enjoying it more.

Maria Eastman in her seventies and eighties loved her son, her flowers, her relatives, her church, her friends, her horses, her servants, and her travels—in approximately that order. She was jaunty, she was quick, she was serene. Kodak gave George Eastman a zone of high-tension work in which he thrived, but Maria gave him a zone of quiet civility within which he could plan his pleasures. She was forever reassuring her son in case his brash "schemes" did not pan out. As she wrote to him in London in October 1898: "I do hope your most sanguine ideas will be realized but there are so many things to be reckoned with that I hope you wont be too disappointed if things don't turn out quite so well." When things turned out she allowed herself a moment of pride in her son's accomplishments, characteristically expressed in a roundabout way: "Mrs. Leighton thinks I failed in bringing you up, ta ta," Maria wrote to her only surviving child. "I think I have reason to feel quite satisfied with the results up to this time whether owing to my bringing up or not." When George was away, his mother led an active social life, ran the estate, visited Kodak Office and Park as if she were in charge, kept her plants in the engine room where they were the most pampered flora ever, took spur-of-the-moment trips to Oak Lodge with butler Shirley Tompkins, and made little digs in her letters pointing to her son's long absences or his failure to write. Mornings coachman Billy Carter drove her to Highland Park, south of the city; afternoons they went to Seneca Park, north of the city and across the river from Kodak Park. Most afternoons she took a nap, but not before sitting in the bay window and checking out the movements of the neighbors. "Everything looks very pleasant after the elegance of the Astoria," she concluded, revealing her preference for home over the elegant hotels where her son sometimes ensconced her. "I like to stay home where I can be cared for without troubling anybody else."[1]

In 1901 Eastman engaged a sculptor, Effie Stillman, to do a bas-relief likeness of his mother in plaster and then sent medallions struck from the likeness to friends and relatives.[2] In 1902 he made a lantern slide ("which can be thrown on a screen") of his favorite picture of Maria, offering the well-known artist Robert Lee MacCameron $300 to $350 to paint her portrait. MacCameron obliged and the portrait became Eastman's favorite rendering of his mother.[3] The last letters exchanged between George and his mother were dated 1903. As her health deteriorated—"Mother has been threatened with the return of the trouble she had ten years ago"—he took no more long trips. From 1903 until 1908 he stayed close to home.

The music and the metaphysics were fostered by a new neighbor, the Rev. Murray Bartlett. The rector of St. Paul's Episcopal Church was only twenty-six in 1898 when the church was moved from St. Paul Street in downtown Rochester to East Avenue and Maria Eastman became a parishioner. His later titles included dean of the Cathedral of Manila and president of two institutions of higher learning. Even early in his career Bartlett was self-confident enough to call the son of his new parishioner, "George"—in spite of being eighteen years junior to the Kodak empire builder.

Until his marriage in 1903, Bartlett dined with the Eastmans every Sunday and spent the afternoon before Morton Rundel and other guests arrived at 4:00 for billiards and music, listening to player rolls on "one of those Aeolian organs that you had to pump." Bartlett decided that Eastman had good records—Beethoven's Fifth Symphony and some waltzes of Strauss—and was clearly embarked on educating himself in this area. Soon Eastman was researching organs for his future dream house and, finagling an invitation to a house in Buffalo with such an organ, took Bartlett and Beecher Aldrich, organist for St. Paul's, along to look it over.

While Bartlett and Eastman listened to music, they discussed metaphysics. Eastman was not generally interested in books, but he did carry pocket-sized volumes of the Roman Stoic philosophers, especially the *Discourses of Epictetus*, a former slave, and works by Marcus Aurelius, a former emperor.

Highlighted by one of those exclusive green pencil marks was this passage in that well-thumbed *Meditations of Marcus Aurelius*: "Short then is the time every man lives, and small the nook of the earth where he lives; and short too the longest posthumous fame." These philosophers counseled adherence to duty and a strict ethical life, without hope of personal immortality. They also taught that everything that comes into a life through individual achievement does not primarily belong to that person. Bartlett and others decided that Eastman evolved his philanthropic philosophy from these works.[4]

In March 1899 Eastman ordered two of A. H. Overman's new "chainless" bicycles, the Spinroller Victor for himself and the Spinroller Victoria for Alice K. Whitney. When Overman couldn't fill the secretary's order, Eastman insisted on an "interim wheel . . . so she won't have to walk to work." Whether Eastman stopped by 100 East Avenue on his bicycle for Alice Whitney on his way to work is not known but several years later, when he had a small two-seater automobile with a rumble seat, the neighbors watched each morning for him to pick her up—by then she was living on Barrington Street, a short block from Eastman House. Since neither Alice nor George wanted to ride in the rumble seat, there sat the chauffeur.[5]

The Victor would be his last bicycle because he was developing an extraordinary interest in horseless carriages. Two months earlier he had inquired of the Pope Manufacturing Company about "one of your Mark II lot 3 Columbia electric carriages" only to find that Rochester Gas & Electric power could not be converted easily to charge the electric car. Meanwhile, Albert Overman's bicycle factory went through bankruptcy. Eastman was a stockholder, but the loss of this small investment did not faze him. Overman then prepared to manufacture steam automobiles, pressuring Eastman to order one. Eastman did order a Victor car in 1898, mostly to help Overman out. What he really fancied was the Stanley steamer; the factory in Newton, Massachusetts was run by the same twins who headed the Stanley Dry-Plate Company. But the Stanleys suddenly sold out to two entrepreneurs who immediately quarreled and split the business into two factories: One produced Locomobiles and the other Mobiles—both based on Stanley designs. So that Overman would not know of his defection, Eastman ordered his Locomobile runabout in Harris Hayden's name and had it delivered to Nepera Park. "I do not wish to order this machine in my own name on account of my friendly relations with Mr. Overman," he told Hayden. "If I have an opportunity I am going to get a [Locomobile] in the meantime," he finally confessed to Overman, "and when I get yours I will let somebody else run the [Locomobile]." Overman was so slow in delivering that Eastman already had the Locomobile long before his Victor was ready. When the Victor finally came, featuring boot, phaeton top, and mud guards, and was given a trial run, Eastman dispatched an eight-page missive listing in minute detail every defect. "I am sure you will take this letter in the spirit it is written. . . . I am only interested in your success and it is my duty as a friend to tell you that I think you are on the wrong road."[6] Thus began a small crack in the relationship of the Oak Lodge partners, which widened geographically in 1902 when Albert sold his American business and the Overmans moved to England where the automobile market was "more advanced." Eastman then bought out Overman's share in the North Carolina shooting preserve and also purchased another hundred adjoining acres. They parted friends, saw each other in London, and occasionally corresponded.

Eastman bought two Locomobiles, one a runabout seating two persons and having no top, and the other a surrey seating four and having a canvas canopy which could be stretched across the top. Meanwhile, the Stanleys resumed production and Eastman ordered one of their new runabouts, also run by steam from a boiler under the front seat. (It got up five hundred pounds of steam in five minutes and went up hills lickety-split.) Then came a White steam car, with a rear entrance and tonneau.

The Stanley twins (identical down to their teetotaling) handmade their first steamer in 1897 after inspecting one from France; two years later they began turning out two hundred steamers a year for carefully screened customers, still resisting mass production. When the Stanleys originally moved from violins to cars they brought over elements of the instrument craft. They refused to employ pattern-makers, for instance, whittling the precise wooden forms for casting automobile parts and bodies themselves, and encouraged their mechanics to assemble the cars as each thought best.[7] Eastman, apostle of standardization and mass production, did not know that the Stanley he drove for thirty minutes at Joe Mandery's Rochester Automobile Company was not the same as the one he had ordered. He did, however, request a double acting brake and suggest that the Stanleys use a De Laval turbine, then settled back to fume while the twins took until January 1902 to deliver his new toy. Too "snowy and cold" to try it on the roads, he "fired it up once and gave it a turn around my yard" only to find a major flaw: "Am sorry you did not put a double-acting brake on it. If the chain should break on a hill I do not see what would prevent one from taking a trip to the other world."[8]

When he was able to install a charging panel at home and at the office, he turned to electric cars, vowing to "wait until experience has demonstrated and remedied the probable defects of gasoline machines" before buying one. "The electric automobile is a peach," he said in 1902, "and if the Edison battery is a success, you will not need to bother with horses any more." The Edison battery turned out to be a failure. Henry Ford (who venerated Edison) found the battery too weak in 1912 for gasoline cars, and in 1915, after he tried to manufacture an electric car especially for it, he still found no success.

By 1903 Eastman had six automobiles registered: a Baker Electric, a cab, two Locomobiles, a White steamer, and a Winton. Aware of the hazards of the side-winding starting crank, he had stuck to steamers and electrics, resisting the "gas car fever" until 1903 when he purchased the Winton. Then he had to report to Abbott that "Your Uncle Ebenezer had a close call when he went out to start the Winton," and gashed his eyelid when the crank shattered his right eyeglass. After washing the hemmoraging lid in the horse trough, he stole into the house, tip-toeing past his mother to call Drs. Mulligan and Ryder who came immediately, dressed the wound, and sent the patient to bed. Maria learned about the accident the next morning. Despite the accident, Uncle Ebenezer decided "that the Winton is proving a greater success than I had any idea of. This year's pattern . . . has a much larger and more Frenchy looking body." Shaking off his injuries Eastman went out the same evening, to make a call. "A call on whom?" Abbott wondered. The next day at the office the mystery deepened: "I have not explained the cause of my accident to anybody and you would laugh to see the curiosity it has excited."[9] It appealed to Eastman's sense of mischief to appear in public all banged up, offer no explanation, and leave people to speculate.

With the arrival of these "self-propelled carriages" having the seats, body, and appurtenances of horse-drawn carriages, collapsible tops and side curtains which could be buttoned in place if it rained, Eastman's play hours entered a new phase. No longer were he and his friends confined to a twenty-mile weekend bicycle trip to Lake Ontario and back. With a car, or in Eastman's case, a whole caravan of cars, the men could don their khaki suits, the women their long linen dusters, and everyone a pair of goggles, then off to Waterville they went for a picnic with Almon and Delia Eastman, or for a whole weekend of picnicking ("I cooked seven meals on the road," Eastman wrote Ellen proudly in 1914), bedding down at the O-te-sa-ga in Cooperstown or the Yama-no-uchi (Yama Farms Inn), Frank Seaman's new Japanese-style place in Napanoch, New York. Extended automobile trips gave Eastman the opportunity and excuse to indulge his love for tinkering and gadgets. He began to design, maintain, and improve upon picnicking gear including stoves, bakers, thermal cups and plates, tents, cots, and picnic tables. This equipment could be piled into a second or third or even fourth car, making for a splendid parade as the vehicles tooled onto East Avenue for a weekend adventure. Coachman Billy Carter was sent to driving school and Maria Eastman soon became "one of the most enthusiastic automobilists you ever saw."[10] Horses would be kept, but as pets; Eastman still liked a horseback ride before breakfast and, until the day he collided with a bicyclist, to drive a small one-horse "trap." Then he switched completely to cars for transportation.

Happily all his accidents were minor, and in his opinion (shared by nearly every motorist before and since) always the other driver's fault. But there were enough of them that it seems clear that despite his mechanical bent, he was a poor driver. Indeed, when Strong was offered a ride, the president first walked up to the "Four Corners" of Main and State Streets to buy some life insurance. That tickled Eastman. And when the two went putt-putting off through South Park and it became apparent that the car had no brakes (or the driver didn't know how to use them), Eastman headed straight for a flower bed.

The first automobiles were rich men's toys and early motoring was high adventure—mechanized pioneering for and by the wealthy. Eastman entered into the spirit as he and three friends solemnly established the "Office of The East Avenue and Suburban Automobile Touring and al fresco Lunch Association and Barge Canal Bridge Club, Limited" which letterhead declared "George Eastman, Roadmaster; J. H. Stedman, Pathfinder; H. W. Sibley, Enumerator; and E. G. Miner, Demonstrator; and further that this club had "splendid constitutions, All gone by-laws, and No rules."[11]

Not everyone shared Eastman's enthusiasm for the automobile. *Harper's Weekly* in 1902 complained about "the multiplication of accidents in the public highways," proposing facetiously that "a troop of minute-men armed with rifles shall stand on street corners and pick off automobilists as they pass, much as the minute-men of '76 picked off the offensive redcoats." Eastman disagreed. "I believe that automobiling is destined to be a great benefit to this country in many ways," he told an Albany legislator in 1902, "and I think we ought to be very careful about adopting repressive measures against it . . . as they have in England." Eastman was such a booster that without his consent the local Automobile Club elected him its president in 1901. He refused the honor with a reply that became standard: "My time is so much occupied . . . and I do not believe in accepting office under such conditions."[12]

Finally there came a lull in the frenetic purchasing of motor wagons because, as he noted to friends, "I am not expecting to buy any new automobiles this year. I am blowing my money in on the house." But he could still tool about in the five automobiles he already owned; in the end, only Kodak got short shrift: "Between automobiling and house building I do not expect to give much attention to business this coming summer."[13] Eventually he settled on Packard touring cars and limousines (by 1910 he had purchased his eighth Packard) and it was not difficult to place the "trade-ins." The previous year's Packard could be handed down to his niece Ellen, or shipped to England, where the managing director might use it between Eastman visits. In 1909, when he sailed to Jamaica with the Mulligans, the 1908 Packard went along. In the 1920s he purchased a Cunningham luxury car, made by some Rochester friends and equipped with his own special steamboat auto whistle to scatter the pedestrians, livestock, and lesser autos.

As early as 1899 Eastman sought "to get an active secretary, on whom I can throw some of the details which I now attend to." Harris Hayden was his first choice, but after hiring Hayden, who then didn't look so good, Eastman's appreciation of Alice Whitney's talents grew geometrically. It was probably no accident that Hayden's resignation and Alice Whitney's appointment as assistant secretary to the New Jersey corporation came in the same month: June 1901. From that date on, her duties increased. She was given power of attorney to pay all household bills while Eastman was away and access to his personal bank accounts. During Eastman's absences she wrote the "pep talks" to traveling salesmen and added coy postscripts to his letters. Coy her public persona was not. Impeccably garbed in severe black or crisp navy with starched white cuffs and collar, she was tough, discreet, intelligent, wily, soft-spoken, highly respected, and all business. Insiders bowed and scraped when she glided through the halls. Outsiders writing to "A. K. Whitney, Secretary, Eastman Kodak Co.," assumed she was a man. Although she methodically recorded every other executive's salary in the precious letterpress books, hers (and Frank Crouch's) is nowhere to be found. She was amply rewarded by stock options and invested her earnings in lots in Brighton and when that property was broken into building lots, the street running through the subdivision was called Whitney Lane.

By the turn of the century Eastman had surrounded himself with a cadre of women, who were able to supply him with some of the friendly intimacy that he might otherwise have derived from marriage. It is a tribute to Eastman's companionable personality that, almost to a woman, they enjoyed being his domestic satellites and thrived under his attentions. In September 1899 Mrs. Josephine Dickman and Mrs. Harriett Dana, a Hampstead neighbor of the Dickmans, arrived for the first of what would become at least an annual visit. Eastman planned a jaunt of escorting the two widows to New York for the "Dewey Parade of Land and Sea" and asked both Frank Seaman and Harris Hayden about the availability of seats "so we don't have to climb a tree." Seaman offered a boat on the Hudson but Eastman accepted Hayden's offer of a bleacher stand on Riverside Drive. The first mention that Eastman enjoyed cooking up anything except emulsions occurred fifteen years after the fact. In 1914 Frank Seaman reminisced: "I was especially pleased to see Mrs. Dickman again—I had not seen her for over fifteen years. I could not see that she had changed at all, in fact she looked even younger and fresher and more attractive than the last time I saw her in dear old London. We talked about you and your dinner that evening and regretted that we could not get a picture of you cooking it."[14] Shortly after that unkodaked event, more evidence pops up in Eastman's correspondence that by 1900 at least the master of the Soule House had begun to putter around the kitchen in his usual methodical way. "When I master every method of cooking eggs," he wrote Overman, "I am going to tackle another branch of cooking."[15]

With overnight satchels and heavy trunks, seven travelers—Murray Bart-lett, Josephine Dickman, Ellen Andrus and her friend Elizabeth Treadway Mather, Maria's nurse Miss Knorr, and the Eastmans—boarded the Pullman car *Grassmere*, rented especially for the railway journey to California in 1900. "We are not going for our health but for fun," Eastman decreed. Fun they apparently had—at San Diego, Coronado Beach, Los Angeles, Pasadena, San Francisco, Salt Lake City, Denver, Colorado Springs, Manitou, Mon-terey, and Yosemite. Miss Knorr later reported that "Mr. Eastman never once raised his voice in anger nor put on the airs of a millionaire. You wouldn't know he earned more than a dollar a day."[16]

For a time, it seemed that Ellen Andrus might break down under the pressures of the role both she and her uncle wanted her to take up. In 1890 Ellen had entered Wells College in nearby Aurora, New York. Eastman not only paid her tuition but provided her with a monthly living allowance. He may also have paid, in whole or in part, the tuition of her bubbly friend and roommate, Evangeline Abbott (familiarly called Nell), who would become an Eastman favorite and orbit about him for the rest of his life.[17] Ellen and Nell became frequent weekend and vacation visitors who flitted in to eat oysters, bake chocolate cakes, and help Uncle George move into the Soule House. Nell called him "uncle" as well, and generally assumed the role of an extra niece. The two young women provided amusing and distracting company for Ellen's grandmother, Maria Eastman, particularly when Uncle George was in "Yurrop" for long stretches. Unfortunately, the young Ellen was af-flicted with a shy awkwardness that made her appear bovinely passive in social situations. As a result, she always felt overshadowed by the pretty, vivacious, and often flirtatious Nell, who found it a snap to charm her ersatz "Uncle George." Upon graduation from Wells in 1894 Ellen wanted to work in a hospital, presumably as a nurse. Her father in Cleveland, George An-drus, felt such a job was beneath her and Eastman did not approve of this career ambition. He told Ellen that tying herself down this way would pre-vent her staying with her grandmother during his extended European stays. This kind of male manipulation of a young woman's life was, of course, commonplace for the era, but that did not mitigate the effect on the victim. For the young Ellen it was a severe personality crisis. Overcome by guilt in the wake of Eastman's protests and demands ("Of course grandmother is my best friend," she wrote), Ellen took to her bed in the Soule House for a month. As puzzled by Ellen's "nervous prostration" as he was by Darragh de Lancey's earlier breakdown, Eastman nevertheless tried to help. He made reservations at Lake Placid, "where the air is recuperative," for "an invalid and her [step]mother," Merie Andrus. "Miss Andrus is not consumptive," he assured the hotel. When Ellen returned, she took to her bed for several more weeks, this time with mysterious stomach pains.[18]

Ellen adored the uncle she found intimidating, so psychologists would not find it too surprising that she married a man very much like Eastman in both background and personality. George Dryden of Cleveland was a childhood friend of Ellen who had left school at age of twelve to go to work, rising steadily in the rubber business until he owned his own profitable hoof pad and tire concern—first for carriages and then for automobiles. Like Eastman, Dryden was a successful, self-made man—fiercely independent, plain speaking, and staunchly Republican. There were some differences. Dryden was coarser than Eastman, highly vocal in his allegiance to the Almighty, and devoted to the consumption of hard liquor, while Eastman was diffident toward both. Dryden was well launched in his career by the time he and Eastman, the latter senior by fifteen years, met for lunch at the Chicago Auditorium shortly after the engagement was announced. Eastman later paid for the elegant wedding of 20 June 1901. "You are wonderful!" Ellen gushed. "I had no idea a wedding was so expensive," she said in awe after pricing bridesmaid's dresses and tents for the reception. Ellen wanted her uncle to be best man but he waffled. "I would do anything for Ellen," he told his mother, "but this is a little out of my line." In the end he hired a private railroad car for himself, Maria, Josephine Dickman, and Murray Bartlett (who performed the ceremony) and apparently spent the weekend as both best man and good sport. Following the honeymoon at Bar Harbor, the newlyweds stopped at the Soule House and the two Georges went for an automobile ride. Later, Eastman remarked, "That husband of yours doesn't talk much, does he?" to which Ellen replied, "Funny, Uncle George, but that's exactly what he said about you." They were, of course, sizing up each other. A few years later Eastman suggested that Dryden and family settle in Rochester where Eastman would build them a house next door to his own. Dryden bristled at the thought of giving up his work and friends to be a rich man's nephew, just as he bristled fifty years later relating the incident to Beaumont Newhall, director of the George Eastman House of Photography. Later Eastman told Ellen, "That husband of yours is all right."[19]

The Dryden marriage produced two children. George Eastman Dryden, called Eastman, was born 8 June 1902, and Ellen Maria Dryden, called Sister, was born 14 August 1904. Marriage and a family did not keep Ellen from spending plenty of time in Rochester. "It seems funny to hear a kid crying around the house," Great Uncle George confided to Frank Babbott in 1902 when Eastman Dryden made his debut, "although I must admit he is not addicted to this habit to any great extent." As the children grew older, tutors were hired to keep young Eastman and Sister's studies up to snuff during extended visits to Rochester. One of those tutors was a medical student named Albert David Kaiser. Kaiser went on to write a book, *Tonsils, In or Out?* on a subject that would come to fascinate Kaiser's new friend, George Eastman. In later life Eastman would always take a physician or surgeon along on extended trips, and even though he was a pediatrician, Kaiser became one of

Eastman's regular medical companions and consultants. When the children were at home in Kenilworth, Illinois, Uncle George found with amazement that he missed them. "I yearn for another visit with you and the kids," he wrote Ellen, adding, "Give Sister my love. I was certainly overwhelmed by her growth and pretty manners." He never stopped bossing them around either. "Stop letting those children ride Western saddle—If they are taught to ride English, they can always switch." English or Western, there was a photographic use to be made of the children's activities: "Send a negative of Eastman and Sister on horses so I can make a lantern slide."[20]

Eastman had been generous with gifts of Kodak stock to Ellen and Royal Andrus when they were young and later he gave stock to Ellen's children. These Christmas and birthday presents from a man whose first savings account was still intact were meant to be cherished and saved, of course, as a nest egg or hedge against hard times. When in 1900 Royal Vilas Andrus secretly and foolishly sold his Kodak stock, undoubtedly to pay off one or more of the debts he had already incurred in his early twenties, it began a pattern that would repeat throughout Royal's life—making him the undisputed black sheep of the Eastman–Andrus brood. Royal was constantly in debt, going through money, asking for more. It was not a lifestyle guaranteed to please his benefactor, who felt used—and there were few things Eastman hated more than to feel that he was being taken advantage of. "I do not know what can be done for Royal," he told his mother in 1901. "I fear nothing at present. He will have to feel the pinch of poverty for a while I expect. Surely it does no good to give him money or pay his debts. . . . Two or three years of adversity may give him more reasonable ideas of life."[21]

Eastman tried to deal with Royal only through his father, George Andrus, brother-in-law, George Dryden, or second cousin, Edward Eastman, who screened Royal's solicitations before either denying them or passing them on to Rochester. Shortly after his marriage to Ellen, Dryden told Eastman in amazement that the twenty-four-year-old "boy" had no sense of money and would have to be carefully monitored and kept on a strict allowance. Twice Eastman agreed to bail him out only to discover that "after sending you this money for this specific purpose, you failed to satisfy me that you had paid any of the debts." Royal kept digging himself a deeper and deeper hole so that when he approached his uncle on a business deal he received the reply that "with this [former] transaction in memory I would not be justified in allowing the Company to enter into any business relations with you for the reason that you might play the same trick upon it." Men like Dryden and Eastman who managed money and their affairs with precision had no comprehension of those who did not or could not. Several times Royal tried coming to Rochester and pleading his own case, but he rarely got by the receptionist at Kodak Office. Still, Eastman bailed his nephew out of a fair number of disasters. The nephew had enormous trouble holding a job. At one time or another he was a railroad inspector, a concrete salesman, a tungsten lamp salesman, a Sears Roebuck salesman, and a Todd Company salesman. For a time he worked for George Dryden in the rubber business. Despite every blandishment Royal could concoct, the uncle steadfastly refused to hire him, either in Rochester or one of the Midwest branches. "Royal knows perfectly well that I would not put him in one of our concerns," Eastman told his Chicago-based Edward Eastman in 1909.[22]

Royal married Elina in 1904, letting the news of the liaison gradually filter out. The next year, he was "threatened with consumption" and asked to be sent to Arizona to recuperate. Consumption would be followed by rheumatism in 1907 and syphilis in 1911. Although Eastman regularly sent relatives and friends on geographical cures, the only kind available in 1900 for such diseases, with no questions asked, he insisted that a doctor examine Royal each time before funds were forthcoming. And while he paid for an operation and sent Royal and Elina to Hot Springs, Arkansas, in 1905 and 1907 with compassion—"Am very sorry you are in such bad shape and hope you have now reached the turning point"—and sent the nephew a winter overcoat in 1907 "which may enable you to get through the winter without buying a new one," as the disasters, physical and financial, piled up, he became decidedly less sympathetic. For a time Uncle George tried the positive approach—congratulating Royal for every new job or promotion and continuing his $40-dollars-a-month allowance through thick and thin, even raising it periodically. He tried letting Royal pay off his debts out of the allowance and then he attempted to have Royal send him a list of the debts while deducting "ten dollars and remitting the balance to you." Next he put Royal on a budget, accounting for every penny of his allowance before the next installment came. But Royal had very creative accounting procedures. Elina had no clothes, he wrote, "not even underwear" and the couple had no furniture: "Elina has been using a packing box as a dresser for years."[23]

In 1909 Royal discovered his wife in a compromising situation with a male boarder, and asked Eastman for advice. Elina also wrote, pleading for a second chance. "Go slowly and do not act while you are in the heat of passion," the uncle counseled. "It depends upon you, and you alone, what you will make out of your life. Nobody can make a good reputation half as fast as they can make a bad one. I think I have always shown a disposition to help you but the amount . . . will depend a good deal upon how much you are willing to help yourself." To Elina he wrote: "From all I hear you have exerted a good influence on Royal and it is a great pity that you have betrayed him. Thinking that you may need ready money to tide you over until you can adjust yourself to such conditions as may be necessary I enclose check for $50." But Royal did exactly what Eastman feared: He left his job and descended upon sister Ellen for the duration. "This affair is no justification for sitting around and doing nothing," his uncle wrote. "As I intimated in my last, I shall not be disposed to send you any money unless you show a disposition to help yourself." In 1911 Eastman had a new concern: "Let me know the result of Royal's Wassermann test," he wrote Dryden.[24] Royal kept reforming, promising to do better with a sincerity that was probably felt at the moment: "Misunderstandings and deceit have brought unbelief in your past and I am through forever with that method of treating with you. Believe me Uncle George." Irresponsible and procrastinating, a malingerer and malcontent who lacked the strength of character to be completely dishonest, Royal let his family down time after time. Perhaps Eastman had Royal in mind when he said, as Marion Gleason remembered it, "I am glad I never had any children. This house seems to me just perfect. If I had brought children up in this atmosphere and permitted them all the luxuries I enjoy, they might have been worthless. If I had enjoyed this luxury myself but deprived them of it they would have hated me."[25]

Health problems continued to plague Kodak people. Attorney Walter Hubbell, who was four years older than Eastman, had a "nervous breakdown" while teaching his famed Hubbell Bible Class for men of the First Baptist Church, which he had founded in 1892. This put him out of commission for several months, and posed the intriguing question: Why did so many people around GE seem to break down? Today we might question whether environmental pollution was involved, especially because of all the dangerous chemicals. In 1909 Hubbell was "taken with a dizzy spell," as Eastman explained to Strong. "He is in bed today although feeling much better. Mulligan says he thinks it is a nervous breakdown." A similar episode occurred in 1911, at which time Eastman helped carry his old friend out of Genesee Valley Club. In 1916 Eastman and Hubbell were en route by train to Chicago. The travelers returned to Rochester, where Mulligan did not agree with an earlier diagnosis of pneumonia, but thought it was another "nervous breakdown." Eastman kept Hubbell on as his "outside" counsel (with James S. Havens serving as "inside counsel" until *his* death in 1926, another case of a mysterious illness striking) and between these spells, Hubbell gave good service and was someone Eastman trusted totally.

Another key employee, Reuben Punnett, had "rheumatism," so Eastman sent him to a suitable curative springs. Most worrisome, Charlie Abbott, second in command, was not a well person. In the winter of 1904–5, Abbott's "quinsy-gout" got much worse, so Eastman reserved a private railway car and sent him to Oak Lodge again to partake of its miraculous curative powers. The medical reports of January and February 1905 concerning a lodge-bound Charlie, too sick to even hobble around on his crutches, were not encouraging, yet Eastman was not expecting the "great shock and blow" of 2 March 1905 which he had to relay to Strong: "MR ABBOTT DIED AT OAK

LODGE LAST NIGHT SUDDEN ATTACK NEURALGIA OF THE HEART." "My
loss . . . was not confined to the business side," Eastman wrote Hedley Smith
in France, "We had grown to be close personal friends and I feel very much
broken up."[26] Besides the personal loss, Abbott's death affected Eastman in
two other ways. Eastman found himself with two houses (he was already
building his dream house) and Kodak found itself without an heir to Eastman's authority. The Soule House, which Eastman had hoped Abbott would
buy, would remain vacant for two years. It was not, Eastman admitted, a
house just anyone would buy. He even offered it to William Walker and his
new bride, Harriet Dana, friend and constant companion of Josephine Dickman. But the Walkers decided to settle in Great Barrington, Massachusetts,
on an impressive country estate called Brookside, located on acres of rolling
Berkshire foothills. Finally, in 1907 Andrew Townson, a member of the
management of the Sibley, Lindsay & Curr Company department store,
bought the Soule House. Townson's children would use the Eastman-
designed cubbyholes not for top hats and cuff links, but toys.[27] At work
Eastman suddenly found himself taking back administrative responsibilities,
particularly for the foreign business, which he had recently delegated to
Abbott. The stock that had been given to Abbott to qualify him as a company
director now went to Frank Lovejoy, who was transferred in 1906 from
Kodak Park to Kodak Office where he became Eastman's top assistant. James
Haste succeeded Lovejoy as manager of Kodak Park.

At about the time of Abbott's death Eastman started carrying around in
his pocket two small books of the ancient Stoic philosophers, not richly
bound and printed like those he was buying for his handsome personal
library, but ordinary reprints that bore the marks of much handling and
reading. At the time of Eastman's death there was still a marker in the
Meditations of Marcus Aurelius at this statement: "The art of life is more like
the wrestler's art than the dancer's, in respect of this, that it should stand
ready and firm to meet onsets which are sudden and unexpected."[28]

The House That George Built

Despite his distaste for personal notoriety, as the twentieth century dawned Eastman made plans to build the largest private home ever constructed in Rochester. At four stories (including the attic but not including the basement) and 42,000 square feet, it would surpass the house built by Hiram Sibley of Western Union—until Eastman's ascension to wealth, the richest man in the history of Monroe County—and that built by William Kimball, Rochester's tobacco magnate.[1] Its pipe organ would be more magnificent than Kimball's and its art collection more prestigious. Surrounding the house would be formal gardens with lily pond and several pergolas, a cut flower garden, a rose garden, a peony garden, a vegetable garden, a rock garden, an orchard, a grape arbor, four greenhouses and a palm house, horse and cow stables and barnyard, a carriage house, a poultry house, workhouses and a repair shop, and a boiler room with a generator that serviced the entire estate. The mansion itself would stand in withdrawn majesty, set well back from East Avenue on its practically self-sufficient urban farm behind a luxurious screen of landscape plantings. It sent out a double message: "See how rich men live," and "Keep a respectful distance."

In 1902 all Rochester watched what was happening to the property in the name of a mysterious "Mr. Abbott" at 350 East Avenue (the address would be altered in 1912 to 900 East Avenue when the street was renumbered). The land was surveyed and large trees uprooted, only to be planted elsewhere on the eight-and-a-half-acre parcel. Even larger trees—huge elms, eighteen inches in diameter, guaranteed to live for two years—were brought from

Buffalo by canal barge and horse-drawn drays. Smaller trees were cut down and neatly stacked for firewood. Marvin Culver and his wife, the previous owners, were allowed to stay in the farmhouse for some eighteen months until house, barn, and outbuildings were carefully dismantled; the wooden parts split, sawn, and neatly stacked; the foundation bricks chipped of mortar and put aside. The contractor had orders from the architect who had orders from the mysterious owner that "any stone or brick taken from . . . the large frame house, frame barn and sheds, and brick barn, including foundations . . . if properly cleaned and approved as in suitable condition by the architect may be used in the new work."[2]

Stakes marked out a large rectangle, the long side parallel to East Avenue but set back some hundred yards. An even longer rectangle was staked perpendicular to the first one, forming a giant "L" among the old orchards. Horse-drawn shovels began scooping out the 12,500-square-foot cavity to receive the basement foundations of "Mr. Abbott's" house of 37 rooms and 13 baths. Observers noted that Adam Friederich and Sons, general contractors, operated the shovels. J. Foster Warner, architect, visited the construction site to confer over a sheaf of blueprints with Friederich and Alling Stephen De Forest, landscape architect. Yet little could be construed from the information Warner imparted to questioners. "Yes, a Mr. Charles Abbott of Jamestown owns the lot," is all Warner would say.

In January 1902 Eastman sent his usual precise order to Messrs. C. Keur & Sons, Hillegom, Holland, for $239.75-worth of spring bulbs—1,000 each of Roman hyacinths, freesias, and paper white hyacinths; 300 L'Innocence hyacinths, 100 Czar Peter hyacinths, 500 single tulip Kezerkroon, 500 Rose Liusante tulips, 500 King of Yellows tulips, and 250 Pottbaker white narcissus—a nostalgic reminder of cycling through the tulip beds of Europe a decade earlier. As delivery approached, he advised that the bulbs should be sent to the greenhouses at 350 East Avenue instead of 400. "Just before I left on a six-week trip to the Canadian and U.S. Pacific Northwest," he wrote in June 1902, "I sold my house to Mr. Abbott, the vice-president of our company and purchased a lot on the same side of the street about one-quarter of a mile nearer town." To spare himself "notoriety," the lot was purchased in the name of Charles Abbott (as land for Kodak Park had been purchased in the name of Brackett Clark) so that only a small in-group knew the identity of the real owner. Since Abbott was preparing to move from Jamestown to Rochester to take up his new Kodak duties, he was the logical choice for front man.[3]

Eastman paid $100,000 for the lot, "284 feet on East Avenue and about 505 feet on Culver Park. Mr. Culver . . . feels that he is giving it away," Charles Thoms, real estate agent, told Eastman. Walter Hubbell thought Eastman was paying too much but the semianonymous purchaser wanted that lot badly. He had considered another and found it wanting. "I have concluded to take the Culver property," he informed Abbott. "On looking over the Ely property I found that there was not room enough in the rear . . . to arrange the stables and greenhouses. . . . While there are no such magnificent trees on the Culver property as on the Ely, the land lies much better and can be laid out to great advantage. . . . I omitted to say that the deed . . . will be drawn in my name. People have an idea that you are the purchaser and I have not announced to the contrary, proposing to leave it gradually filter out." On 3 July he presented a letter with sketch to J. Foster Warner: "I hand you herewith the ground floor plan of the proposed buildings on the Culver property. I shall be glad to have you submit sketches for these buildings, it being understood they are to be without expense to me and that I am to be left free to the selection of an architect. You are not to be bound hard and fast by the plan I sent you. It merely embodies my ideas as far as they have evolved up to the present time." A similar letter went to twenty-seven-year-old Alling De Forest, who, after completing a two-year course in freehand and mechanical drawing at Mechanics Institute, had been a draftsman in a landscape architect's office. Then for ten months De Forest worked for the prestigious Olmsted Brothers in Massachusetts, successors to Frederick Law Olmsted, who started the profession in America.[4]

De Forest had recently designed formal gardens for Walter Hubbell and Bertie Fenn (both lived in Warner-designed houses built in 1901). De Forest was "to make a preliminary general plan for planting my new place for $100, it being understood that if I decide to have you make detailed working drawings, you will do so and superintend the work for the sum of $400 in addition." Eastman had already sited the house on "a general plan of the grounds . . . showing the proposed outline location of the new buildings," and ordered a topographical map drawn. Eastman and De Forest located the house close to the east boundary, leaving almost half the property, running from East to University avenues an undisturbed meadow with border planting. In 1914 *Town & Country* magazine would laud "this breathing space" as "priceless. . . . It introduces the quality of scale," the prominent magazine stated. "It . . . bestows a sense of open country, which is, indeed, remarkable when we remember that it is all within the limits of the city." When Eastman returned from his western vacation six weeks later, Warner agreed "to perform full professional services (including supervision) for your new residence . . . for five percent . . . excluding part of the interior fittings." Warner's own work would amount to $328,187.85, which would not include fittings and furnishings ordered through the interior architects and designers or the organ.[5]

Eastman enthusiastically accepted Frank Babbott's offer to act as design consultant and had an immediate assignment for his childhood friend. Now that "my general plans are pretty well studied out, but before deciding upon them finally, I would like the criticism of an independent architect; that is . . . to consult someone high up in the business just as I would some specialist in a difficult case of law or medicine. I have had a quarter scale model of the house made and some things have cropped up upon which I would like to get the opinion of an architect who has made a specialty of colonial architecture. Do you happen to know any such man and do you know whether architects ever render services in such a capacity?"[6]

Babbott had an ace up his sleeve—William Rutherford Mead, fellow Amherst graduate, who along with his partners Charles Follen McKim and Stanford White was architect of the new building for the Brooklyn Institute of Arts and Sciences (now the Brooklyn Museum), of which Babbott was president. Of the three partners, Mead was the level-headed businessman, serving as office manager and balance wheel—applying a stimulus to the dilatory McKim or a cautionary brake to the exuberant White. (As Mead himself said, "I prevent them from making damn fools of themselves.") From years in an engineer's office, Mead could supply the technical scrutiny to ensure that a building was sound. Eastman, too, believed that engineering and a floor plan was where all building started and that "architecture" was just applied decoration.[7]

McKim, Mead & White were the architects who popularized the Colonial Revival through the World's Columbian Exposition in Chicago in 1893 where Eastman had first been exposed to this new fashionable architecture on such a grand scale. By 1894 he had a plan and a model for a "colonial" house by Charlie Crandall. The period was one of social and cultural transition with self-made millionaires like Eastman rising quickly to the fore. Within a few years after amassing their fortunes, those millionaires began determining the directions whole communities would go. Within this shifting social climate there arose a pervasive psychological need for the anchor of a clear architectural authority and adherence to tradition. McKim, Mead & White, by now the most celebrated firm in the country, satisfied this need. Eastman's life can be seen as a striving toward clarity, order, and simplicity as well—whether it be in furnishings, camping equipment, or photographic components. He was naturally drawn toward an architecture that espoused these qualities along with functional arrangement, structural soundness, and visual pleasure.

Reaching for roots deeper than the imported Georgian architecture of the colonies, to the sources of that style—Renaissance Italy and Classical Rome—McKim, Mead & White developed an urban architecture of monumental classical façades. While true colonial precedents such as Mount Vernon were too diminutive to provide those qualities of scale and assuredness desired in public architecture or for the palatial statements of the nouveau riche, the firm demonstrated how a native classicism reaching back to Thomas Jefferson could be fused with sophisticated elegance, great taste, and modern construction techniques to form a splendid new architecture for a new century. McKim's Boston Public Library (1888–95) was said to be the first public building in the country derived from (French) Renaissance sources. (Similarly, Warner's Monroe County Courthouse [1891–96] was reputed to be the first public building modeled after an Italian palazzo.) Although Mead gave less of his time to actual designing than his partners, he was noted for his innate feeling for scale, proportion, and timely criticism. And so as Mead tinkered, critiqued, and tuned up Warner's plans and elevations, scale and proportion came to the fore.[8]

Three weeks later, Eastman wanted Mead "to pass on the drawings . . . to come up here for a day to look at the site, examine the model and plans, and give Mr. Warner his criticism and suggestions."[9] The main staircase would be the place Eastman, Warner, and Mead converged. Taking accurately reproduced colonial balusters and handrails (which Warner had earlier used for the Hubbell house, but there confining the stair to a narrow corridor as in a vintage colonial house), Mead designed a monumental double stair, as found in his firm's public buildings, and made it the centerpiece of the house. The stair is surrounded by airy space, with light pouring from the oculos above and the glass-roofed conservatory behind. The surrounding hall is paneled and painted a warm creamy white. Engineering that light-splashed flying staircase by means of a full-scale model became a major project for the architects.[10]

The "Dutch colonial" silhouette of the gables at either end of the Hubbell house as well as the way the rear wing meets the main house were also used for Eastman House in much larger scale. Eastman watched the progress of his lawyer's house closely enough to advise Strong by letter how it was proceeding after Hubbell had finally decided he wanted a "colonial" house in preference to any other style.[11] Although there is no direct evidence, he probably expressed approval of certain features and the overall look of Hubbell's house, directing Warner to do the same, only larger, since he was the president of the company. Eastman was much taken with palatial houses dubbed "colonial," a generic term for anything reflecting early America. He admired the house of Nelson Curtis, manager of the American Photographic Paper Company in Boston, as being "a very symmetrical and well thought out example of the colonial style."[12] And professional architects of the Colonial Revival such as Charles A. Coolidge of Boston would admire Eastman House because its owner "had taken our native Colonial architecture as a theme and carried it on to a higher development, . . . a sensible and patriotic thing to do."[13] Accuracy as to scale was not part of the Colonial Revival: No actual colonial building, not even a church or statehouse, was as big as Eastman House. Friends found the size astounding. "Knowing what you do now," Hermann Dossenbach, orchestra and quintet leader, inquired in 1915, "would you build it this large?" "Twice as large," Eastman shot back. Frank Seaman, after congratulating his old client "on the artistic and homelike atmosphere you have created," added facetiously, "It must bother you a little to take care of a friend or so who drops in for the night unexpectedly; to provide for such an emergency, you ought to build on an addition."[14]

The four-foot by six-foot model of the house was built at the Camera Works,[15] then Kodak photographer Ben Cline snapped its picture and that of the Culver farm so that a montage could show the house in situ. In lieu of elaborate renderings, Eastman sent this montage to Mead, as well as to friends, designers, and suppliers.[16] The model came with two entrance porticos for Eastman to try: one a semicircular arrangement of columns with balcony above of the kind Warner used for several other Rochester homes; the other a pedimented portico with columns, which was both a giant version of the Eastmans' Greek Revival house in Waterville and a near copy of the portico on the White House in Washington. Perhaps to echo a scene of his youth or to establish his pecking order on Rochester's "Avenue of Presidents," Eastman subconsciously chose the latter.

Mead was asked to design and subcontract the five major public rooms on the main floor, which meant separate architects for the inside and the outside of the house, one operating out of New York, the other on the scene in Rochester. Such elementary tasks as lining up the doors on one set of blueprints with those on the other set kept the mails humming. And while the New York brahmins employed "draughtsmen" and a battery of secretaries to answer the correspondence, Warner hired only "draftsmen," and used a battered typewriter to peck out messages on penny postcards. On 30 December Eastman "had a long interview with Mr. Meade and Mr. Warner. He [Mead] is a very charming and not in the least offish man," Eastman concluded with a certain amazement. "I shall be back the first of March," he told Warner as he left for Europe on New Year's Day, "which will be time enough to let the main contract. Let the granite and steel as soon as the bids can be obtained. I believe that none of Mr. Meade's suggestions altered the granite except to widen the dining room extension and lengthen the front steps. . . . When giving the order, the bricks in the Root house should be mentioned as standard."[17]

Since the building of Eastman House (1902–5), the legend that McKim, Mead & White were the architects grew steadily, a case of the more famous name getting the credit. In 1979, however, the long-missing plans and elevations were found in the engineering department of Kodak Park, a fitting repository for the blueprints of a man who believed that all architecture was engineering. They were clearly signed by Warner. Correspondence at the New-York Historical Society further clarified the relationship between the local and national architects, an unusual but apparently successful one from the client's viewpoint, because he would use it again for the Eastman Theatre and School of Music.[18]

Ground was broken on 1 April 1903, and by the middle of May the cellar excavations were finished and the foundation walls were one-third of the way up to grade. By July "the kitchen part of the house was up one story, the steel beams for the first floor set and the concrete floors being in." The house was built, furnished, and occupied from back to front, service wing to public rooms, familiar to unfamiliar, according to the methodical specifications of its owner. First came the greenhouses and palm house, planned and built by Hitchings who had just finished extending the greenhouses at the Soule House. When the kitchen and dining wing was completed in June 1905, a year late because of a long-winded quarrel with the New Jersey company over its slipshod manufacture and installation of the generator that would run the whole estate (and some wildcat strikes in the building trades), Eastman and his mother moved in. During the next four months, July to October 1905, the major rooms of the first floor were completed. George Eastman moved into his new house with his eighty-four-year-old mother in July 1905, a few weeks after Henry Strong married a new thirtyish wife in Tacoma.

While Eastman House was under construction kibitzers watched a four-story steel and concrete bunker rise, complete with fourteen-inch thick walls and a roof of reinforced concrete, as solid and fireproof as any building housing "homemade cotton" (nitrocellulose) at Kodak Park. For a while construction was held up by the brick situation. Eastman had sent Warner and a photographer to Buffalo to see and photograph the Root house from all angles, including "the Delaware Avenue gable. . . . What I want more particularly from these negatives is to show the color of the brick and the manner of laying to get the variegated color effect. Therefore, I want the negatives taken on a cloudy day with orthochromatic plates."[19] But then the architect couldn't find anyone to make the bricks to specification. And that bothered the boss: "The thing that is troubling me most now is the getting of brick for the new house. The concern that made the brick I want failed two or three years ago and the other concerns that have been trying to make them so far have failed. It looks now as if I should be able to build the foundation and then have to wait for two or three years until I can start a brick yard and make the brick myself." But Warner persevered in the search and was soon able to locate a source of cream-colored Roman bricks that were "an exact match of the Root brick."[20]

"We have just begun to get brick in large quantities," Eastman told Mead, "seven carloads having been shipped . . . , so I now expect to have the house ready for the roof October 1 [1903]."[21] For that concrete roof, after rejecting the suggestion of a red tile roof, "what I am looking for is a shingle tile that will look as much like old weather-beaten shingles as possible." Frank Haddleton, Kodak engineer, brought the first shipment from the car yards, but a displeased Eastman sent them back. Then he organized his own crew to set up shop on the property to hand-split and shave 25,000 running feet of spruce bolts brought in from the Adirondacks. Two dilatory workmen, Jacob

Consler and Michael Nolan, installed the 135,000 shingles on the house, carriage house, covered walk, cow barn, and stable. Consler and Nolan were each paid $2.25 a day—an average salary, as other workmen received $2.10 to $2.70 and a foreman $5.00 per diem. But Consler and Nolan made the mistake of trying to borrow $50 against their wages and then "failed to prosecute their work . . . with promptness and diligence. . . . Such neglect and failure is sufficient ground for me [Warner] to terminate employment," the architect warned. "I hereby notify you . . . three days." But a compromise with built-in raise was worked out as Nolan "Rec'd of George Eastman $50 advance on services to be worked out at $2.50 per day."[22]

As with many businessmen who want Mies van der Rohe for the office but Michelangelo at home, Eastman slipcovered his concrete and steel house, inside and out, with the decor of earlier periods. The house would be a study in contrasts, since Colonial and Federal Revival settings surrounded twentieth-century amenities such as the dozen-plus bathrooms, twenty slave clocks run off a master clock, and twenty-one intercom telephones.[23] Not unlike the eclectic mishmash of the Soule House, the reception room would be designed in the style of the eighteenth-century Englishman, Robert Adam, as would the low-relief plaster decorations on the ceiling of the living room. (The Adamesque formal reception room, mandatory in 1905, would go out of style and be transformed by Bacon into a new book room or "little library" in 1927.) The dining room was to be Georgian with a gothic ceiling; the billiard room (with modern table designed by Bacon) was to have Tudor leaded glass containing painted glass medallions (designed by Bacon) featuring a modern history of transportation.[24] But although the rooms would borrow from many pasts, Eastman considered them comfortably modern, which they were in 1905. He was not looking backward with nostalgia. The past was represented by a boarding house and poverty (probably worse in his mind than the reality had been). The future was bright and boundless: Science and technology would solve the age-old problems of sickness and poverty. The new house with its miraculous gadgets and "scientific" lighting, power house, elevator, switchboard, charging board, phonographs, and motion picture projectors was a way of leaving the dusty Victorian age behind. Priceless antique furnishings were not sought, despite Babbott's pushing objets d'art from estate sales. Copies were fine in most cases such as the dining room ceiling and when it darkened to the color of old ivory he liked it even better. "It cost $20,000 to have that ceiling copied and nearly thirty years to achieve that perfect color," he proudly told Kodak employee Ben Cline who came to photograph the public rooms for an article in *Music Digest* in 1927.[25]

Eastman's sketches and Warner's plans and elevations of the colonnaded mansion, which might be described as center-entrance southern colonial on a colossal scale, showed a library and a living room (two large, identical rooms, twenty-one feet by thirty-five feet, with back-to-back fireplaces) east of the entrance hall. At the last possible minute Eastman "decided to throw the library and living room into one," as he told Mead. Warner obliged, redrawing one large library, thirty-five feet by forty-two feet, with fireplace against the east wall and a chandelier in the center. But the proportions of this cavernous salon, sometimes called the living room and sometimes the library by Eastman, were wrong from the beginning: The ceiling was simply too low for the "acres" of floor space caused by "throwing" two rooms into one. It became a challenging space to furnish too. Eastman did not worry much about the proportions, although he never viewed the room with the enthusiasm he had for the reception and billiard rooms. The reception room, with its celadon green-striped silk walls on which he would hang watercolors and prints, he pronounced "just about perfect."[26]

The proportions that bothered him always were those of the conservatory— thirty feet by thirty feet and over twenty feet high. The room was almost a cube and represented a typical Foster Warner touch. Warner houses had square, sky-lit, marble-floored garden rooms as their central feature. But if Warner was a "square" person, Eastman was "rectangularly" inclined and that room would distress him for the next fifteen years.[27] As it filled with rugs, drapes, wicker furniture, and pot upon pot of flora, it took on the aspect of a steamy jungle. Yet at least one guest would marvel: "I do not quite know how Mr. Eastman made that house so homelike. The conservatory with palms and pipe organ, where we had our meals, might have been a room in a palace or a hotel, yet it was somehow 'homey.'"[28] Other guests concurred that it greatly resembled the lobby of a small hotel.

West of the conservatory but east of the porte cochere (the entrance used for all but the most formal of occasions) were sited the elevator, telephone booth, men's washroom and ladies' powder room, housekeeper's office, butler's pantry, servants' dining room and kitchen. The elevator, still in service in the 1990s, was a new Otis 1903 model but the second-hand motor was a gift from Hiram W. Sibley, who took it from his mother's house. (Contrary to legend, the elevator was not installed in response to Maria breaking her hip in 1904: It appears on Warner's 1902 plans.) In 1927 he commissioned Ezra Winter to do paintings for the elevator.[29] The powder room and men's room were furnished with as much care as the public rooms—Bacon's sketches for a vanity were redrawn twice to Eastman's exacting specifications.

While he did not blink at spending $11,000 on the woodwork of the front hall, Eastman kept a tight rein on petty economies. "I am told," he wrote Warner, "that the hand pressed rosettes on the railing of the main deck and front entrance will cost about fifty cents a piece. I do not think that way up in the air anyone could ever tell . . . the difference . . . from the pressed rosettes at five cents a piece."[30] In general, though, only the best materials and craftsmanship were sought by the exacting householder. Window glass, including skylights, was the finest Belgian photographic glass available, shipped from the Seed Dry Plate Company in St. Louis (by then owned by Eastman Kodak). Paneled and floored in teak, the billiard room was finished with fine carpentry, its panels "joined" and its floor sealed with wooden butterfly joints of the sort once used on the decks of wooden ships. When workmen began using a mechanical sander on the floors, Eastman not only could not bear the noise; he rejected the results. Soon the workmen were down on all fours with spokeshaves—this did impart a unique finish that accented the grain of the parqueted oak and butterfly-joined teak.[31]

Once the interiors were underway the letters fairly flew between Warner and Mead. Warner did most of the writing and frantic telegraphing. Mead answered most of the mail (that to Eastman with great deference) but also assigned as liaison from his office Burt L. Fenner, who had attended the University of Rochester and MIT and had been a draftsman for Warner for several years before joining the New York firm. Fenner's job was to accompany Eastman on his visits to various suppliers in New York, facilitate his decisions, and revise the drawings as needed. Warner's messages to Fenner centered around the problems of having two different sets of architects working hundreds of miles apart. At one point he found that the ceiling beam plans for the main hall did not line up with those for the pilasters; at another juncture he was stymied in constructing the dining room mantel because he did not know where Fenner's employers had put the electrical fixtures. Coordination difficulties were a daily concern: "In order to make no mistake in the final bringing together of the Silver Safe Doors with the hinging of the Secret Doors in the wainscoting in the Dining Room, I am sending you a sketch of present conditions," Warner wrote. But an equal number of memos back and forth between Rochester and New York were taken up accommodating Eastman's constant revisions. "While plans show double swinging doors from the butler's pantry to the dining room, I think a single door is better," Warner wrote, "but Mr. Eastman wants double swinging doors from the dining room to the covered walk." But soon: "Please disregard my letter of yesterday." Then, "Re the opening from dining room. Mr. Eastman now thinks squareheads on covered walk side will look better than paneled lunettes." Eastman was poking into nearly every detail of design, substituting mirrors for glass doors under the stairs, changing the size and location of the conservatory floor registers, and enforcing his preferences in greater matters: "Mr. Eastman wants to avoid an outside vestibule . . . wants bronze and glass outside doors with inside wooden doors to always stand open winter and summer except when house is closed at night."[32]

Once the shell of the house was under way, Mead had six decorating and furnishing firms submit proposals, bids, and renderings for the public rooms. Bidders included Tiffany Studios, with whom Eastman had battled over his grand piano and drawing room decor in the Soule House; the

Hayden Company of Rochester, which had picked up the pieces in the Soule House when Tiffany failed to please but also failed to come up to Eastman standards; James Wingate; Phillip Hiss; Thomas Wadleton; and A. H. Davenport. Eastman again rejected Tiffany: Rene de Quelin's rooms "are too heavy, especially the billiard room, and neither is colonial enough to meet my values." Hayden would be given a second chance—allowed to make the interior mahogany doors—until Eastman learned that the doors would not be made in Hayden's Rochester plant and cancelled the order. Hiss was given the contract for the hardware and marble floors of the conservatory, but a prolonged fight developed during that installation. Wadleton, well known for his massive furniture designs for the New York City University Club (whose architect was Charles McKim), was given the contract for Eastman's dining room paneling.[33] Eastman liked to visit Wadleton's studio and admire the pickled oak paneling[34] in progress; but when house construction was delayed a whole year, Wadleton sued to have Eastman take the paneling off his hands or pay for fire insurance.

The primary contract for decorating and furnishing went to A. H. Davenport and its chief designer Francis Henry Bacon,[35] an old archeology colleague of Thacher Clarke. Bacon struck just the right chord with Eastman. "You are right," Eastman told him, "in thinking that I prefer simplicity in the designs for the library, reception, and billiard rooms and that I do not care for glass doors on the bookcases." Eugene Glaenzer of New York constructed a model of the garden for $125 with Eastman's caveat that "I have no intention of spending any large sum of money on the garden, for the reason . . . that it would be out of scale with the exterior of the house, which is very simple."[36] Similarly, De Forest's most elaborate plans for the garden were rejected in favor of a formal garden half the proposed size. Trusses and girders for the huge living room ceiling came from the Rochester Bridge and Construction Company. The vacuum sweeping system, with engine in the power house and fabricated to Warner's specifications, led to outlets in all rooms and halls, three outlets in the barn, and a separate branch to the billiard room. Warner designed two special brushes: one for the horses and one for the organ. An enormous wet battery was installed in the powerhouse, controlling the alternative in case city electric power failed.[37]

In the living room a green Axminster rug specially woven to almost cover the floor, green plush drapes and portieres, creamy woodwork, and green silk damask wallcoverings set an elegant tone. From Bacon's detailed sketches, Eastman ordered a round oak table of great size and presence to put under the chandelier, which so dominated the space as to give the house the distinct flavor of a men's club. Large sofas and easy chairs, a book table, a carved walnut chest, a mahogany writing table, bookcases, a card table and study table, as well as an assortment of occasional chairs and a French tea table were arranged with the fashionable haphazardness and mixture of periods and patterns often seen during this Colonial Revival period. The Steinway grand piano was moved from the Soule House, with Bacon designing new legs for it.

A disagreement arose between Eastman, who wanted a cellar floor of creosoted rounds such as were then used on streets off East Avenue, and Warner, who insisted upon concrete. The architect got his concrete but it was a hollow victory. Except for projects then on his drawing boards, Warner would receive no more Eastman commissions. This may have been accidental, since Eastman always liked to make a change, whether in camera design, the positioning of a painting, or in housekeepers and architects. Still, Warner always blamed the cellar for his subsequent neglect by Eastman.[38] On the other hand, those who pleased Eastman often were rewarded. He made a surprise cash gift to Charles King, Warner's assistant, and a $5,000 donation to Amherst College in honor of William Mead and Frank Babbott.[39]

Moving in on time was contingent upon the installation and proper operation of the electric generating plant for the organ, elevator, vacuum system, pump, and the rest of the estate. More than one hundred telegrams, memos, and letters flew among Eastman Kodak engineer Perley S. Wilcox, who tested the engines for Eastman; president Gardiner Sims and testers of the Marine Engine & Machine Company; and various consultants who backed up Eastman's contentions of undue smoke, odor, and noise. The patience that Eastman displayed in his own field as he waited thirty years for the perfection of NI film or color film is not seen in the year-long agony surrounding the "generator affair." "As to the outcome of this affair," he told Sims, "I realize you feel pretty sore about it, but I cannot see that it is in any way my fault that you have not been able to furnish outfits to fulfill the contract. . . . I am not tearing out and replacing the engines just for fun. In fact, it is something of a mortification to me to replace these outfits as they form the only exception to the rule which has been that everything installed in my new house has worked satisfactorily."[40]

Beginning in the early hours of 26 February 1904, a two-day, multimillion-dollar conflagration destroyed downtown Rochester. Miraculously it took no lives. But the contents of the Sibley, Lindsay & Curr department store in the Granite Building were destroyed; henceforth Rochesterians would date happenings as occurring before or after the Sibley Fire. "The fire got wholly out of control and if there had been any more than a very light wind," Eastman wrote, "perhaps it would have come as far as the Camera Works, there being no other fireproof building between us and the burned section."[41] Warner's office was also in the Granite Building, which was gutted but structurally "fireproof," so survived—a lesson not lost on Eastman. Besides plans and elevations for "A House for the Hon. Mr. George Eastman," Warner had plans for a new Eastman Cottage for Boys at the Rochester Orphan Asylum and an Eastman Laboratory of Physics and Biology for the University of

Rochester on his drawing boards. All would be redrawn and built.

Far more devastating than the Sibley Fire, which was covered by insurance and remembered chiefly as a jolly holiday, was the blaze that struck the Rochester Orphan Asylum in 1901, when twenty-nine children lost their lives. The board of trustees abandoned plans to rebuild on the grim old site and purchased land high in the suburban hills, retaining Warner to design a whole new campus with one- and two-story cottages and halls surrounding a central flower-bedecked green. In concept, such an cluster arrangement for orphanages was ahead of its time. Eastman took his job as president of the orphan asylum and chairman of its building committee seriously, accompanying Warner and other trustees to similar institutions for planning pointers. Confiding to friends that he was sorry to have his big house finished, he decided to build a small one to see if he could make it "just as perfect." He soon found, as he told Ellen Dryden, that he could "get just as much fun out of" masterminding all the details—playroom, porch, storm encloses, wood finishes—of the Eastman Cottage for Boys for $11,414 as he did out of building his own house for thirty times as much.[42] After her Illinois house burned, Ellen caught the building fever giving Uncle George the opportunity to build a house, at least in his head, all over again. "If you want my opinion in detail I will proceed to give it." And so he pelted her with handwritten notes and seven-page theories about window sills, radiator grills, porte cocheres ("ugly at best"), wood paneling ("if you could see Mrs. [Isabel Stewart] Gardner's famous house in Boston you would realize what a comparatively useless thing 'fine finish' is anyway"), and beamed ceilings ("there is no reason why ceilings should be broken up with beams"). Even more than his earlier directives to architects, these daily missives of July 1905 represent his crystallized thoughts on house building, now that he had finally gone through the process start to finish.[43]

If the Eastmans had moved into their new house on schedule, that is, during the summer of 1904, Maria Eastman would not have tripped on the dining room rug in the Soule House one morning in January 1905. At first her son stubbornly refused to believe she had broken her hip and would be permanently incapacitated. For months Billy Carter carried Maria everywhere—up and down stairs and to the car for her daily ride. Finally, as they were getting ready to move, Eastman ordered a specially designed "reclining rolling chair . . . with pneumatic tires and ball bearings. . . . If you can fit two light carrying bars under the seat so that they can be detached," he instructed, "do so. The chair is for an invalid who weighs only about 90 lbs. and it would be convenient to have these bars for lifting the chair up and down stairs. Also please protect the hubs with rubber caps so that they will not mar furniture or door casings."[44] When the wheelchair came, Eastman couldn't bear to look at it straight on. Maria's nurse, Miss Knorr, who had been let go after the Mexican trip in 1901, returned. The thought that the accident might not have occurred had the nurse been on constant duty may have added to Eastman's gloom. Carter's kindnesses were not forgotten; he stayed on as chauffeur for many more years, long after drunken antics similar to his would have gotten another employee fired. Then one night Carter met Eastman's train in so inebriated a condition that the boss put the chauffeur in the back seat and drove himself home. The next morning Carter was pensioned at full salary.

While the house was still under construction Eastman had four friends for supper in the big east living room. One of these was Victoria Powers, wife of Walter Powers but also a constant companion of J. Foster Warner. "We sat on nail kegs," Mrs. Powers recalled, "ate off boards laid on barrels, and the cooking was accomplished in the fireplace. . . . I can vouch for his being a good cook: I never ate better beef steaks."[45] As the date of the housewarming dinner approached—it was first scheduled for 30 September 1905, then switched to 7 October because Eastman decided he needed a two-week vacation at the end of September—he had still not found the right oriental carpets for the hall. And so he borrowed carpets from New York ruggers John Keresey and Kent-Kostigyan for the housewarming, to be photographed for the souvenir booklet and placed therein alongside the menu and the songs the Kodak contingent would sing after dinner. ("You should fill that house with children instead of Kodak men," sniffed one of the one thousand recipients of the booklet.[46]) For months after the festivities Eastman still could not come to a rug decision even though Babbott, Bacon, the Rochester collector and expert William Ellwanger, and all the New York rug merchants had sent their choices with explanatory treatises. Returning yet another batch of carpets because he had yet again changed his mind and "now wanted Persian," he quipped to Bacon: "Perhaps you think it is wonderful how flexible some people's minds are."[47]

Eastman's pipe organ would serve as his alarm clock. Exactly at 7:30 A.M. on weekdays and 8:00 A.M. on Sundays his bedroom door opened and he descended the grand stair enveloped by the strains of the great organ, which surrounded the conservatory and whose echo could be heard through the oculus and all the way up to the widows walk on the roof. As early as December 1902 Eastman was "thinking some of putting an organ in my house but if I do I shall have to put it at the head of the stairs in the second story as I have not allowed for a special room. I really have not gone very far with the idea."[48] After corralling Murray Bartlett and Beecher Aldrich to try out various house organs with him, he wrote to several manufacturers. He then learned that the Aeolian Company's new music for its self-playing attachment had double the number of notes found on any other music and that it did not fit the self-playing attachments of other makers. Deciding that he was in over his head, he hired Professor George E. Fisher, organist of the Lake Avenue Baptist Church in Rochester, to assist in the purchase and installation of an organ for the conservatory that Eastman had been dreaming about and planning for more than a decade. In the way of further investigations, Frank Seaman took Eastman and Fisher to inspect Andrew Carnegie's organ and Frank Babbott took them to see Henry Clay Frick's, both in New York City. Because of its superior self-playing attachment, Eastman and Fisher settled on an Aeolian, Opus 947, with fifty-six stops, considered the Rolls Royce of house organs. By October 1904 the pair were in New York inspecting a finished organ. On 19 August 1905 Eastman sent the Aeolian Company "a check for $30,319.25 to cover your bills for the organ and music." The horseshoe-shaped console in the conservatory had three keyboards and a two-and-one-half octave pedal clavier. The pedal, great, choir, and echo organs were installed in the two-story space, with the swell organ in another space on the second floor—about one thousand pipes in all.[49]

The organ, which one visiting organist called "a tonal and mechanical wonder . . . the last word in organ building and in many respects absolutely unique," would go a long way toward satisfying Eastman's strong urge to tinker. It also gave him plenty of opportunity to horse-trade and bicker with tradesmen, one of his favorite occupations. Despite a contract with Aeolian to keep the organ in tune and repair for $200 a year, there would always be something wrong with it, whether true or imagined. Eastman wanted perfection and anything less was not acceptable. He contemplated "seeing if some other organ builder can remedy the defects" or "relinquishing the use of the organ except to accompany the quintette," but in the end always appealed to Aeolian to come and fix the instrument. Finally he decided that the way to deal with the organ problems was to enlarge his giant mechanical toy. In 1917 Archer Gibson, an organist from New York, consulted on additions. Gibson counseled: "I feel certain that what you have in mind requires a rather extravagant plan. Where one's own home is involved one always ultimately regrets purchases in the way of art objects that are *less* than *exactly* the thing we have in mind."[50] Eastman readily fell in with Gibson's suggestions.

After adding almost ten feet to the conservatory in 1919, a new four-manual Aeolian solo organ with seventy additional ranks of pipes was added to the original instrument, installed over the dining room in what had been Maria Eastman's bedroom (and since her death in 1907 the billiard room). Both organs were playable from one reconstructed console in the conservatory. The original organ opened into the conservatory from two sides of the second floor. The new organ opened from a third side, enveloping the room in sound. An echo organ was on the third floor and spoke through the oculos into the stairs. Ten extra speaking stops, some normally found only on theater organs, were installed. Purists shuddered at the sounds of locomotives and thunderstorms reverberating throughout the house. By 1918 Eastman was convinced that the organ needed a greater body of tone and contracted at about $47,000 to overhaul the old south organ and put in some additions, which practically added a new organ, called the "north organ." "I did not want the biggest organ in the country," Eastman reminded the Aeolian Company, "but I wanted the best for its size."[51] Fisher would be Eastman's personal organist from 1905 to 1919. In a typical year in Eastman's early music programs, the agreement with Fisher would be $1,200, "your duties being to officiate at the organ at the Sunday and Thursday concerts during the season of forty weeks . . . ; to play in the morning for an hour twice or three times each week, for an hour one evening each week when I am at home during the season; and for any extra recitals that I may desire that do not interfere with your previous engagements."[52] In addition to the organ solos at the Thursday and Sunday concerts, Eastman also hired the Dossenbach Quintette. Hermann Dossenbach, the leader, was a local violinist who had been introduced to Maria Eastman by Adelaide Hubbell and may have played for the Eastmans in the Soule House. When Dossenbach organized an orchestra that debuted in 1900, Eastman gave $1000 on behalf of his mother as a "patroness." Dossenbach also had a string quartet that played regularly at the Lake Avenue church and was on occasion augmented to quintet by Theodore Dossenbach, brother of the conductor who also played the violin.[53] When Harold Gleason succeeded Fisher as Eastman's organist beginning in 1919, he surveyed the situation at 900 East Avenue and later wrote in awe: "As far as I know, he was the first and last person in the United States to maintain such an elaborate musical establishment in his house."[54]

In 1907 the silver cord was severed. "When my mother died I cried all day," Eastman told friends. "I could not have stopped to save my life."[55] Bert Eastwood called at the home and found Maria Eastman's son gloomily looking out of the window. He turned as Eastwood entered as though to catch a sob in his throat or to conceal the emotion on his face. He swallowed hard and facing Eastwood said, "It's all right now."[56]

Confined to a wheelchair since her fall, the frail old lady became bedridden for three months during the spring of 1907, developed bronchitis, "and is slowly losing ground," Eastman wrote on 2 June. "I am much worried about the outcome." Cousin Henry H. Eastman of Chicago, upon hearing this wrote to George on 12 June, his words showing that the cult of mother devotion was unabashed and thriving in the Eastman clan of 1907:

> Soon you will be called upon to lay your Mother away; She your guardian, with whom you have had the sweetest communion of all your life, and in your devotion to her there can be no sweeter recollections ever come to you than of that companionship of a loving Mother and of your

devotion to her which was fully reciprocated as only a Mother could. With her passing, she the last of that large family of Uncles and Aunts, the last link of that generation of our Fathers and Mothers will have been severed.

Maria died on 16 June. The next morning George cabled thirteen relatives,[57] all of whom except Henry and Almon Eastman were recipients of regular stipends from Cousin George. Eastman even cabled George Dryden, perhaps in response to his mother's wishes, to "OUTFIT ROYAL AND LET HIM COME TO THE FUNERAL."[58]

"Beautiful floral tributes" were sent from the State Street offices and Kodak Park and "out of respect . . . the offices and factory were not opened until 9:00 o'clock, two hours later than the usual opening time." Services were at St. Paul's, the Rev. Murray Bartlett officiating. The funeral train to Waterville carried a male quartet in addition to family and friends. Maria Kilbourn Eastman was buried in the family plot next to her husband and daughter Katie. Although Eastman was an outspoken advocate of cremation as opposed to burial, believing that cemeteries cluttered the landscape, he did not carry out this principle in respect to his mother. "I am glad the dear body was not cremated," wrote Cousin Mary Eastman Southwick. The monument, which he also claimed not to believe in, had been in place for years so he was not inconsistent when he wrote Almon: "I think on reflection that the inscription . . . had better read 'wife' instead of 'widow.' While the latter is technically correct, the dates on the monument are sufficient." Upon returning to Rochester, he immediately sent Billy Carter to the Packard School for Chauffeurs, then left for "my little [600 mile] trip to the east"—two weeks in the Boston area—conducting some business and probably staying with Josephine Dickman.[59]

Maria's estate totaled $102,856.31, roughly four-fifths in cash in three local banks and the remainder in tax-free bonds. Her personal effects, valued at about $1,500, included her Russian sable muff and storm collar, three diamond rings, six pins or brooches, three watches (one of which her son would henceforth carry in his pocket), and a gold thimble. After bequests totaling $4,350 to seventeen servants, including the two butlers Shirley Tompkins and Solomon Young and chauffeur Billy Carter, and bequests totaling $17,500 to eighteen relatives, eight from the Kilbourn side, eight from the Eastman side, Amelia Kilbourn Eastman Peet, who was both, and Merie D. Andrus, the remaining $81,000 was left to her son George, who was the sole executor. He in turn gave $40,000 outright to Ellen and "thinking you would be interested to know the disposition of your grandmother's estate," he told Ellen in July 1907 that "I have $40,000 in bonds in one of my safe deposit boxes which are marked: 'property of Royal V. Andrus.' If anything should happen to me they would be turned over to him but in the meantime, until he shows a steadier inclination, I intend only to make him payments out of the income received from same. . . . Of course I shall not communicate any of these facts to Royal." This secret bequest would later exacerbate the relationship of nephew and uncle, but for now he did write Royal that "in looking over Mother's things, Ellen and I have selected for you some little keepsakes and she will take them when she goes back to Chicago."[60]

In the days following Maria's death Ellen's children were both comfort and subject for the ever-vigilant amateur photographer, Great Uncle George. "THE CHILDREN ARRIVED SAFELY TODAY," he cabled George Dryden about ten days after the funeral. As he once had pursued and snapped Royal and Ellen in the backyards of Ambrose Street with his first Kodak camera, he now captured Ellen's children around the hydrangea pots, lily pond, and brick walkways of the formal garden on East Avenue. "I am sending you a picture of two children," he alerted dealers and photographers worldwide, "which I took in my garden on a cloudy afternoon to show the results photographed with one of the Kodak automatic shutters and star-shaped blades. I have never been able to get such full exposures as this under such conditions before and I do not think they could be got with anything else but a curtain shutter working at a very slow speed." For the amateur photographer, the children were cuddled by Uncle George and even posed in Maria's wheelchair, indicating that while her son would always revere her memory, he had no veneration for the hated artifacts of her old age.[61]

From Oak Lodge to Tuskegee

"Who really knew George Eastman?" wondered John Slater, University of Rochester professor, in his biography *Rhees of Rochester*. "Portrait painters put on canvas his clear-cut features and keen gaze. They painted what they saw; but they . . . could not show in one face both the parsimony that grudged unnecessary postage and the generosity that gave millions for Negro education. They painted Mr. Eastman, not GE."[1]

Oak Lodge was the North Carolina retreat where Mr. Eastman became GE, the place he went each fall, winter, and spring for recreation and rejuvenation. Located thirteen miles from Enfield on the coast, one hundred miles south of Richmond, it originally consisted of twenty acres purchased in 1897 by Eastman and Albert H. Overman from H. Spooner Harrison, farmer and postmaster, who lived in Ringwood and owned the adjoining plantation, Rocky Hill. In 1902, when Overman left for England, Eastman bought out his share in Oak Lodge. In early days he sometimes went for six weeks at a time but in later years it was usually three two-week visits over Thanksgiving, right after Christmas, and at Easter. On those occasions an office wag remarked that "the Eastman Kodak Company is in North Carolina."

By 1912 the property had grown to 2,500 acres of Halifax County owned solely by George Eastman, much of it in unspoiled timberland. Eventually he owned 2,900 acres. The property might have grown even larger, except, as he told a real estate man, "There was a time . . . that I would have been glad to buy the Threewitts' place but it was spoiled for my purpose when the timber was cut."[2] Living in this pine grove were about two dozen squatters.

Instead of evicting them he built new cottages for them, refurbished their existing cabins, hired them to work and manage the plantation, and had them pay rent in five-hundred-pound bales of lint cotton, the number of bales contingent on how many horses the tenant owned rather than the price of cotton. "No record is kept of the products. My foreman receives a salary of $100 a month and is allowed one-half the products raised for my own consumption, such as poultry, hogs, etc. none of which are ever sold by me."[3] The tenants also grew corn, tobacco, sweet potatoes, and peanuts, which provided them with some income. Eastman's cotton, collected as rent when he arrived for his first autumnal visit, was stored in a shed for two or three years if necessary until it brought a good price. "There is nothing I enjoy more than motoring except my visits to North Carolina," the owner declared in 1907. And when Henry Strong wrote of the social whirl and rounds of golf with John D. Rockefeller he was enjoying in Augusta, Georgia, Eastman responded: "I would not trade the restfulness and freedom of Oak Lodge for all the millionaire society that was ever bunched in Augusta."[4]

Eastman and Overman built their lodge a quarter mile from a spring (or "branch," in local parlance), where a large oak tree lent the place its name. The lodge itself was centered on the edge of a clearing by a beautiful pine forest. Neither it nor any of the numerous plantation buildings had a drop of paint on them.[5] There were six beds on the ground floor with cots upstairs in two rooms for servants. Male guests, if they wanted to eat, had to work. They put on new roofs, mixed cement, and installed sanitary conveniences and plumbing fixtures under the direction of foreman George Eastman. On his own Eastman built wooden seats around the trunks of the larger trees. He took a boyish pride in churning out "the best butter in Halifax County," all patties duly stamped with the ubiquitous monogram "GE." At first water had to be carried in from a nearby spring until Eastman made concrete hydraulic rams to bring in first drinking water and later bath water, naming each ram after a guest. (The trails were named for the guests, too, as in Maryadelaide Avenue.) Once the rams were finished, he directed the guests to use up the concrete by practicing "tree dentistry": Whenever a decayed area of a tree was spotted, it would be cleaned out and the cavity neatly filled with concrete. This plethora of concrete also led to the idea of replacing the platform around the lodge with concrete steps.[6]

Oak Lodge was a hospice for sick and grieving friends or employees, beginning with the ailing Dickmans in the 1890s. Florence S. Glaser, Eastman's first employee, who had bad lungs, and Sam Mora, sales manager, whose wife had died suddenly of appendicitis, were both dispatched to the lodge to recuperate. Charlie Abbott was sent twice, and the second time he died there. Young Louise Gifford, diagnosed as tubercular, was sent with her mother and nurse to spend the winter in The Pines, the guest cottage originally built to house the Dossenbach Quintette during its 1908 sojourn.

The principal treatment for TB in those days was to put the patient out in the coldest, most bracing air possible and hope for the best. "The porch," Louise's father had reported from damp and chilly England, "has been *life* for her!" And so in 1910 Eastman built a sleeping porch on The Pines for Louise.[7]

Oak Lodge was a simple place. From a recessed porch one entered a large square living-dining room with massive fireplace and a framed photograph of George Dickman on the wall. Two bedrooms, with bath between, opened on each side. The women lived on the left side, the men on the right. The bedrooms were heated by drum stoves and at dawn tenant Julia Burt entered the women's rooms and made up the fires (the men made their own) and a little later returned with small cups of hot coffee. At dawn Eastman's butler—at first Shirley Tompkins, later Solomon Young—entered the men's rooms, as he did Eastman's bedroom suite in Rochester, closing the windows while saying "Good morning, Mr. Eastman." At the lodge Eastman and guests wore hunting clothes all day long, the men in khaki knickers and laced hunting boots. Invariably Eastman was the first to rise in the morning and had already enjoyed a horseback ride before breakfast. When a wild turkey hunt was on the agenda, however, he borrowed Anna Hubbell's alarm clock so that 4:00 A.M. would not find him napping.

Those who did not appear at breakfast promptly heard a sharp, reminding knock. Breakfast was leisurely, with the coffee kept hot in the fireplace, and the butler bringing in endless pancakes and sausage prepared by Katherine Lovely, a cook from Rochester who accompanied the houseparties. The kitchen and more servants' quarters were across a long hall, on the stark white walls of which hung dozens of tools. Each had its particular nail or hook, its silhouette definitively outlined in blue chalk.[8] Lunch was usually a picnic. In the morning the men went out to shoot quail that had been imported, bred, and stocked throughout the plantation by Henry Myrick, while the women were driven by buckboards, each pulled by two horses, to one of several appointed spots by a "branch" in the woods. Earlier, one of the Myricks had driven out and put a tarpaulin over the chosen spot, set up chairs and a table, and lit the fire so that by the time the picnickers arrived there was a fine bed of coals for cooking and a dry spot for dining, even in the rain. Eastman cooked the steaks and chops, baked a johnny cake or simple pastry, and settled the coffee grounds with powdered egg. Once he asked Henry Myrick to lay out a trail for the guests to walk from the picnic site to the river. As so often happened, he did not give specific instructions and Myrick blazed such big chunks out of the trees that Eastman was staggered. The next day the guests were engaged to take pails of paint along the whole trail to cover the scars on the Avenue of Magnificent Blazes.

Flowers and music followed Eastman to North Carolina. Rows of yellow and white asters and of roses both red and yellow surrounded the lodge, while white, yellow, and red honeysuckle vines (the same Kodak colors as in his Rochester garden) climbed over the outside of the house and red ramblers grew on fences. The porch was equipped with wooden swings and a rod from which a canvas awning was extended to shelter it from the sun, and here the guests sat in the afternoon and evening. Trees were purchased in profusion: 240 elms "ordered from the best nursery" were planted forty feet apart with another 240 Carolina poplars between. Mulberry, walnut, butternut, and pecan trees were acquired and hedges of California privet, osage orange, and Japanese quince set out.

Then there were the dogs that he and George D. B. Bonbright raised at Mumford, New York, to be sent, after training by John Hunt, to Horn Point or Oak Lodge. There were so many of them—about nine at a time—that he bought five hundred pounds of Ideal dog biscuits, three hundred pounds of Shredded Wheat, two hundred pounds of Spratt's dog cakes, five cases of canned meat, and fifty cheap dog whistles all at one crack. He also had his own recipes for sixty gallons of mange dip with ingredients to be added to make it a flea dip. These setters and pointers all had names (Dick, Don, Muff, Belle, Kate, May, Billy) and when a favorite one like Jack died "of that awful disease the hogs have," as Enfield's Mr. Bobbitt reported, there was general mourning.

At 6:30 in the evening, everyone got to "rest" for a few minutes, before appearing for dinner at 7:00 P.M. The men simply donned sports jackets, but the women, once a week or so, surprised them by wearing evening clothes. "I can best testify to his love of music by recalling the many times I changed those grand opera records during the course of a meal," wrote Anna Hubbell.[9] "The Aeolian and Gramophone came in for a fair share of attention," Eastman told Frank Seaman in 1903, "although our 'choir' [of guests] furnished most of the music." Not all the music was canned. Often a dozen or so little children from the local Eastman School (which he caused to be built in 1919) came to sing, or the musical director of the Joseph Keasbey Brick Agricultural, Industrial and Normal School[10] led a mixed quartet in singing spirituals. Although he brought a small piano along, Eastman liked the singing better a cappella.

Sometimes the party, even members of the Dossenbach Quintette who came along from Rochester to provide musical evenings, went hunting raccoons at night. On nights when there was no hunt, dancing, a group sing on the porch or before the fire, auction bridge, or silent movies filled the evening hours. Eastman considered bridge a better game than poker despite his legendary prowess at poker, based on stories from shipboard days of the 1890s.[11] In early years, short films were ordered by the dozen from the Edison Manufacturing Company of Orange, New Jersey, with such intriguing titles as *S.S. Deutschland in a Storm*, *Ducks Bathing*, *Allentown*, *Pa. Duck Farm*, *Fun in a Bakery*, *Old Maid in the Drawing Room*, and *Dull Razor*. Once the

Eastman Kodak Company started putting out its own Cine Kodak cameras for amateurs, however, the guests were required to act out charades while the host filmed them; the reward was a finished reel as a highly prized keepsake. Long after the guests had gone to bed, Eastman might stay up developing the film.[12]

Eastman and guests would leave Rochester for Oak Lodge in the evening by flower-bedecked private train car with six rooms. The car was rented from the Pullman Company; Eastman never owned nor wanted to own his own car. The company supplied a cook and porter while Eastman's own butler acted as waiter. During the wait in Washington the next evening, shad roe and oysters, racks and hind quarters of lamb, rib roasts and pot roasts of beef, porterhouse steaks and corned beef, as well as heads of lettuce would be brought on board in ventilated barrels. This fare would be augmented by the home-grown victuals at Oak Lodge. The Myricks raised cows, chickens, turkeys, and pigs. "The home-made hams were delicious," Solomon Young told an interviewer in 1940, "and Mr. Eastman was fond of home-made sausage ground from the meat of [pedigreed] White Chester and Spotted Poland hogs." He also "liked the hickory-smoked bacon made from these hogs." In order to facilitate the sausage making, Eastman devised an advanced abattoir, or "hog murdering outfit" which, he told friends, "any hog in the county would be honored to enter."[13]

Eastman and guests were met at the Enfield station by Henry Myrick with riding horses for those that chose to make the thirteen-mile trip that way (usually just Mary Mulligan and Eastman) and a buckboard pulled by two horses for those who did not. The residents who gathered to watch this plutocratic entourage being put together found it difficult to reconcile this image with the group that did all the plumbing and cementing of trees. The hog-murdering outfit was only one of the projects Eastman visited upon Oak Lodge. Earlier, in 1914, when he started "a little dairy of Holsteins," he built a silo, leaving the size to the International Silo Company because "I am a novice in these matters." In 1904 came the alfalfa project. The growing of Sudan grass, clover, soy beans, millet, vetch, rust-proof oats, field peas, and corn soon followed. In 1918 came the poultry project, in which the breeding of turkeys, geese, ducks, and chickens, complete with incubators, was initiated, and the bee project, complete with a "thoroughbred queen," drone traps, two-story hives, and a honey extractor "for beginners in beekeeping." In 1919 came the cotton gin, along with "a potato digger for harvesting the peanuts" and a sawmill for cutting the timber. Milk reports from Henry were initiated in the 1920s. Eastman kept up with his reading by ordering pamphlets on "Pig Management," "Bee Disease," "Brooding of Chickens," "Strawberries," "Ducks," and many more from the Department of Agriculture.

The comforts of home came slowly: screens, an Aeolian player piano, one of Frank Seaman's gramophones, a telephone (but Eastman still had to go into Enfield for long distance), a refrigerator, and a radio set in 1922 placed on top of the bookcase (with antenna parallel to the clothesline and high enough "so that in shooting clay pigeons we will shoot under the wires"). At Oak Lodge he loosened up, or as Anna Hubbell described it, "during these vacations . . . business cares were dropped and he entered with a boyish enthusiasm into all sorts of serious and foolish pastimes. . . . The more juvenile his guests behaved the better he liked it." In Rochester his late entry into active social life had made him ill at ease in company. He made almost no "small talk," although he could speak fluently if really enthusiastic about a subject. He enjoyed being with people who were not in awe of him, and if they were jocular, he responded in kind. His wealth and bias toward business tended to make him serious and restrained at home, but away from Rochester he did not have to maintain the dignity of his position. He ordered "a phonograph for outdoor use, to give great volumes of sound" and "some brass band records." He ordered dance records from Alexander Moore at Edison's and announced that he was going to learn "to dance the two-step without having to count to myself as I step."[14]

Oak Lodge was a new neighborhood for Eastman, populated by Southern whites very much unreconstructed, the first generation to grow up following the end of the Civil War. The landowners were gracious and hospitable people—the Harrisons, who had a large vineyard at Medoch, two miles from Oak Lodge; the Williamses; and Mr. Bobbitt—who watched over Eastman's property and were there in a minute if you needed them, such as during the crisis surrounding Abbott's fatal attack. Eastman sent Mrs. Harrison hundreds of chrysanthemum plants the way he showered orchids on Rochester women. He wrote letters and sent Brownie cameras to little Mary, Tissie, and Louise Harrison the way he wrote letters to Sister and Eastman Dryden or little Florence (Flossie) Fleckstein, daughter of a photographer in San Francisco, or sent cameras to other small friends. Louise had her own magnolia tree picked out at Oak Lodge and Eastman labeled it as such. Louise was a favorite of both Eastman and his mother. Frank Macomber found himself revising some "previously conceived impressions of GE" when the Macombers and Eastman went to call on the Harrisons between embarking from his private railroad car at Enfield and arriving at Oak Lodge by horseback and buckboard. As they approached the Harrisons' house "the door flew open and a little tot of four or five summers ran out on the porch calling 'Uncle George, Uncle George' . . . threw herself into his arms and kissed him affectionately as he carried her into the house. During the whole visit," Macomber recalled, "she sat in his lap and . . . told him all the news of her young life, to which he responded with interest and amusement." The next year, as the *Grassmere* approached Enfield, Macomber asked if they would stop to see

Louise. At first Eastman said nothing, but when Macomber repeated the question, he said tersely, "Louise died this winter" (of complications from the measles).[15]

The Eastmans were of Yankee abolitionist stock, and they were from Rochester, a city where Frederick Douglass had found support for his publication of his newspaper, *North Star*, and where a progressive tradition in race relations was strong. His Dixie acquaintances did not know that Eastman had entertained Booker T. Washington in his home for dinner. But the Harrisons, the Williamses, Mr. Bobbitt, and other Tarheel neighbors sensed that the Northerner Eastman would need some guidance in observing some unwritten Southern rules. They cautioned him, first of all, not to pay his black help more than the going rate. They became concerned when he chose, instead of hiring a white overseer as was the local custom, to have the Myricks act as managers of all his properties. They objected, basically, to his system of self-reliant black tenants. As self-appointed spokesman, Paul Garrett of Norfolk wrote to express these concerns. Eastman's polite answer reassured the white neighbors, "who have always been very friendly and obliging," that he had no intention of interfering with the region's peculiar institutions ("the white man's burden") but made clear that he had "no sympathy with those who try to exploit the colored man. . . . I want to deal liberally with these people," he quietly insisted. He welcomed their advice, admitting he had "no theories in regard to the solution of the negro problem." But he was not going to be pressured into hiring a white superintendent. He soothed their concerns about the radical move of having a black foreman by explaining that he had "not tried to keep the three of four white tenants" originally on the property; thus the objection that whites would never submit to black supervision was irrelevant. Echoing Garrett's phrase, he said blandly that "I have never discovered in the Myrick family any inclination to become 'smart niggers'" but that if problems did arise, he wanted to hear about them and was sure they could be smoothed over.[16] Eastman displayed no crusading fervor to right injustices. Instead there was the touch of the clever politician who has two, possibly contradictory goals, but is determined to meet them. He wanted to keep his North Carolina idyll in peace with his white neighbors, and wanted to continue his fair and humane dealings with his black tenants. By such trimming as in his words to Garrett, he accomplished both. The Myricks stayed as overseers.

At Oak Lodge was "a Negro family of three generations," Eastman told Murray Bartlett, "of which the man of the second generation acts as foreman of the property and selects the tenants, all Negroes."[17] Primarily they were members of the large Myrick, Carroll, Hedgepath, and Burt clans, plus Clarence Wiggins, who, when Eastman purchased the Weller property in 1903, pleaded that he not be evicted. He was not. Eastman first met Aunt Fanny (a former slave) of the first generation of Myricks when Overman had her cook for the visiting hunters, then camping out on the partners' twenty acres. Eastman liked her food. Later on he decided that "Fanny is an ideal lady's maid of the old style." When he wanted some work done on the place, Overman recommended Uncle William (another former slave), who Eastman soon decided was "as good as gold." Upon learning that Aunt Fanny and Uncle William were married, and that "Mrs. Harrison says they are the best house servants in the County of Halifax," Eastman hatched the management scheme for Operation North Carolina that so upset the neighbors.[18] "There are only negroes on the place but that is merely an accident," he told a neighbor. "I am not undertaking any premeditated sociological experiment. It seemed unnecessary to drive all the tenants off the place so I let them stay there and they are looked after by a negro foreman who has proved very capable to manage them and grow the feed I have to have for my horses. . . . Of course I aim to have only decent negroes . . . and try to influence them a little in the way of keeping their places in order but further than that I do not undertake to do."[19]

It was Aunt Fanny and Uncle William's son, Henry Myrick of the second generation, who became the foreman. "He was a common farm hand when I took him but he is developing into a good all around manager," Eastman said with pride, "and it is interesting to note the influence on the surrounding Negroes that can be exerted in various ways through such a man. I do not attempt any startling innovations but just try to steer them gently in the way they should go."[20] Every year or so there was a new Myrick, son or daughter to Henry and his wife Mary, until by 1917 there were fourteen living children (out of eighteen born) in the third generation, not counting cousins. Visitors found that some bore amalgams of familiar names. Edward Mulligan Myrick, Ellen Dryden Myrick, Pearly White Myrick (named for the Harold Gleasons' maid), and Shirley Eastman Myrick.[21]

"I will leave the wages of the laborers to your good judgment," Eastman wrote Henry Myrick after the latter succeeded his father as foreman. "I know you are anxious to be fair with the men and at the same time will not waste my money. You will also bear in mind the fact that I do not want to set a pace for wages that will embarrass my neighbors." The shipping department at Eastman Kodak regularly sent Henry preaddressed, prestamped envelopes in which to mail his regular reports. Henry's reports, written in pencil on inexpensive, lined note paper, were addressed to "Mr. Eastman Dear Sir." Eastman's weekly replies, whose salutations "Henry Myrick, Dear Sir:—" changed later to "Dear Henry:—" but whose closings were always "Yours truly, GeoEastman," were, among other things, attempts to get Henry organized like a Kodak employee.

> Henry: I think you had better make a practice of inspecting the Ford
> machine twice a month to see whether it is getting any moths in the

upholstery. Take a whisk broom and brush it out and if there is any sign
of moths spray it with the liquid which you have for the purpose. . . . Put
this letter on the top of your file and read it over every week until all the
specific directions are carried out. . . . I am sending you by same mail a
calendar upon which you can enter your work each day and at the end of
each week tear off the sheet and send it to me in the stamped and
directed envelopes. . . .

[*Handwritten postscript*] Keep all the letters that I write you in the file,
the last one on top, under the cover; leaving on top of the cover for
occasional reading any that the directions in which have not been fully
carried out.[22]

All this organization did not always apply to the boss, however. Eastman
regularly left his umbrella, his glasses, his razor strop, and his movie camera
at the lodge. One might think these items could have been replaced in
Rochester, but he was bent on Myrick sending them back. And to Y. A. Spivey
of Ringwood he admitted with resignation that "when I was clearing out my
pocketbook I found your check in payment for the rent of the land you had
last year. . . . I must confess that I do not treat my Oak Lodge affairs in a very
businesslike way." Eastman *said* he wasn't undertaking any premeditated
sociological experiments nor was he trying to influence his tenants except in
trying to introduce a little more order into their lives, but of course he could
not keep his mind off improvements. The first thing he did was to build them
spic-and-span new cabins.

Even before Frankie Myrick, sister of Henry, pointed it out, Eastman
could see that the Myrick, Carroll, Wiggins, and Hedgepath children were
not receiving much schooling in the dilapidated one-room building that was
the Enfield colored school. As the Hampton agent noted in 1913, the school
over which Frankie presided as sole teacher was in session only five months of
the year. Eastman decided to deed the county three acres of land in the
middle of his estate and pay for one-half the cost to build a five-room school
with separate building for manual training. He immediately put Rochester
architects Gordon & Kaelber to work on the plans. In the building of the new
schoolhouse, Eastman reminded A. E. Akers, superintendent of the Halifax
County Schools, that "My offer stands also to any additional equipment in
any department which is necessary to make this a model practical negro
school. If there is anything in the project that is impracticable I shall be glad
to have your views." Akers was not keen on the economics of a five-room
school and what he considered Eastman's grandiose plans. He cautioned at
one point in the discussions: "Believing as I do in negro education as well as
education for others, and knowing the situation as I do, I feel it would be
much safer . . . to go slowly than to attempt to do too much in one community more than we can do in other communities." But Eastman got his way. In

the end, the school cost $14,872, of which Eastman paid $7,777, the county building fund $5,095, the state loan fund $1,000, and the Julius Rosenwald (president of Sears, Roebuck) Fund and the black community $500 each.[23] Disappointed that the construction moved along so slowly, Eastman returned in January 1920 to take charge himself. He made a tentative plan for the workshop, which could be constructed west of the new schoolhouse, suggesting that "the old schoolhouse would very nearly supply the materials except the shingles." He planned the ventilation system. The 140 movable seats that he ordered "will permit the use of the two rooms which have a folding partition for community purposes, which I believe will be helpful in many ways," he wrote Akers. "I am a firm believer in the proposition that if we can get the negroes more interested in their community life the labor situation can be much improved in any locality such as that around Ringwood."[24] On a smaller scale, Eastman was trying to do what he did in Rochester: Make the community a better place in which to live and work.

The principal of the Eastman School was Frankie Myrick. Staffed by older Myricks and attended by younger Myricks but open to all black children within walking distance, the Eastman School in Enfield went up at about the same time as Eastman School in Rochester. It also coincided with the startup of Eastman's tonsil clinic in Rochester, "to do 400 cases per week," as he wrote Akers. And since he was determined to remove every diseased tonsil from children in Rochester, he naturally felt he had to do the same at Oak Lodge. In December 1920 he took his personal surgeon, Dr. Edward Mulligan, to North Carolina to examine the children in both the white and colored schools at Ringwood and send the report to Akers and also the state board of health. By early 1922 he proposed to Dr. G. M. Cooper, the state health officer, that he would be willing to pay half the expenses of the operations for the children from Oak Lodge. "Such acts make a powerful influence for promoting harmonious race relations," wrote William G. Willcox, chairman of the board of trustees of the Tuskegee Normal and Industrial Institute in 1921. When it was time to hire a teacher for the industrial department, Eastman offered "to pay half the cost of the equipment of the workshop, including a Ford Runabout for the teacher." A similar deal was made when the supervisor of agriculture for the school was hired. Meanwhile, Ellen Dryden furnished the articles for the sewing department and Adelaide Hubbell and Mary Mulligan the articles for the domestic science class.

Eastman kept close tabs on the school and when things needed some correction he expressed himself. "I was rather disturbed when I visited the school last to see the disorder in the domestic science department," he wrote Frankie Myrick. "The desks were out of line and very dusty. . . . The utensils were not hung in their places; there were grease spots on the table, and the general order of the room was distinctly untidy. I think this is the room which above all should be kept in a spick and span condition *by your pupils.*

They should be taught neatness and order. I have asked Henry to have Richard put clothes hooks and shelves in your closets . . . and look over the doors and make sure they are in good condition. . . . You should have him fix the places for all the utensils that are to hang on the wall, marking the outline of each one, and then insist upon the utensils being put back every time they are used."[25] Despite the reprimand, Eastman had great respect for Frankie and was highly disturbed when he heard Akers was thinking of firing her.

> I have heard with regret that you are thinking of discharging or trans-
> ferring Frankie Myrick. I am too firm a believer in the fundamental
> principles of administration to attempt to exert any influence which I
> may have with you to modify your decision, whatever it may be, but I do
> want to say that I am sure you have no more loyal and sincere worker
> than Frankie Myrick; and that her influence, and the influence of her
> family, in regard to school matters in that vicinity are all to the good. She
> first got me interested in the project of building the new school, so I feel
> that she has been instrumental in doing much good. As to her ability as a
> teacher, and the ability to handle those under her, of course I know
> nothing.[26]

Akers had found Frankie "failed to get along well" with the teachers she herself hired. "Last year I sent her of my own choice two teachers from Hampton Institute and they left in February, assigning as their reason that they could not get along with the principal. I suggested . . . that I make the farm agent principal and make all teachers accountable to him . . . [but] Frankie insists that she wants to be principal or that she does not want to teach in the school. So far as her individual work is concerned, I think she has made a success. . . . Though I have not made up my mind definitely . . . I shall reach a decision soon," Akers wrote on 8 June 1923. And on 17 June Frankie wrote to Eastman from Tuskegee Institute, where she had gone to recruit more teachers: "It is true I did thank you in advance but the joy that comes from having things adjusted in my *favor* forces me to say, thank you, to you again."

The Eastman Community School of Halifax County, North Carolina, continued to thrive at least through the lifetime of its founder. Two more rooms were added in 1925; a library of three hundred volumes was formed through money raised in the Oak Lodge community and donations of books, magazines, and newspapers by Eastman and his friends. A piano was purchased, again with everyone chipping in. In 1926 the practice of serving a hot lunch daily was started, using the corn and tomatoes canned during the summer. "At first they didn't like it much," the farm agent reported, "but it is hard to get enough for them now." In 1926, 212 students were enrolled with an average daily attendance of over 200.

Eastman winked at his rule about not giving to "church work" when Frankie Myrick told him "that the Ivy Church people [including many Eastman tenants] want to build a new church near the schoolhouse and would like to trade their present site [on land Eastman owned] for a new one." He was agreeable, telling her he would select a site the next time he came to the Lodge. He had in mind a lot one hundred feet by two hundred feet on the opposite side of the main road near the woods, asking only that the parishioners submit their plans for his approval. He was also willing that the church people "use the schoolhouse for their services until such time as they can build a new church."[27]

Booker Taliaferro Washington, two years younger than Eastman, was born into slavery. Still a boy after the Civil War, he worked in a salt furnace and in coal mines in Malden, West Virginia. He attended mission schools but was largely self-taught. For three years (1872–75) he attended Hampton Normal and Agricultural Institute, newly founded by the American Missionary Association for the purpose of educating blacks and Native Americans, and headed by Samuel Chapman Armstrong, former brigadier general of a black regiment. At Hampton, Washington learned to be a brick mason but was such an excellent speaker that he turned to teaching, first at Malden, then Washington, D.C. In 1879 back at Hampton he organized a night school and was in charge of the industrial training of seventy-five Native Americans. His projects were so successful that in 1881 Armstrong, who had been born in Hawaii and educated at Williams College, selected Washington to organize and head a black normal school in Tuskegee, Alabama. Washington soon made the new institute into a major center for industrial and agricultural training, and in the process became a national figure.

It was at Atlanta in 1895 that Washington made his famous compromise speech, urging blacks to accept their inferior social position for the present and to strive to advance themselves through vocational training, self-education, economic self-reliance, and by striving to be efficient workers. More militant blacks, such as the writer W. E. B. Du Bois,[28] strongly opposed Washington for what he considered quiescent tactics, but many other Americans, both black and white, found Washington's program to their liking—including George Eastman. Eastman certainly endorsed efficiency, self-education, and economic self-reliance—for everyone, not just for blacks—and it was probably this aspect of Washington's views rather than his endorsement of the status quo that most appealed to the budding philanthropist. (Eastman liked to maintain he was not a social reformer at the very moment that he was creating or endorsing some forward-looking program.) Robert Moton, Washington's successor, liked to compare Tuskegee's "work and spirit . . . to that of the Eastman Kodak Company, which I think is one of the world's wonders from many aspects."[29] Judging from the reaction of other blacks who wrote to Eastman in 1924 when he made the largest-ever gift to Tuskegee and Hampton institutes, the majority would have been in Washington's rather than Du Bois's camp at that time. The Rev. James E. Rose of Mount Olivet Baptist Church in Rochester, for example, wrote that while most African Americans realized "that there should be in this country no place for a school or university distinctly for Negroes, regardless of the system of training pursued, . . . the practical man faces a situation as he finds it and . . . sets out to do the best he may under the circumstances. . . . Our earlier friends in the North, perhaps, made a mistake when in the days immediately following the close of the Civil War, they founded schools and colleges of only higher learning for the Negro in the South [e.g., Howard, Fisk and Shaw universities, Morehouse College at Atlanta], forgetting that he was a child of the soil and a son of toil. . . . The Negro, having always labored with his hands, needs as much now to be taught the dignity of labor as to labor skillfully."[30]

Eastman replied that he had read this letter carefully and said that he agreed with Rose's "fundamental proposition"; he then added:

> Tuskegee and Hampton are doing the outstanding work in this line and are encouraging a lot of imitators who will extend the work which is basic. There is plenty of room for such institutions as Howard for higher learning. The proportion of negroes who are fitted for this higher learning is very small just as the proportion of white people is also small. I believe there are a lot of white boys who are being put through college who ought to be put to work and thus make room for those who are better fitted for a college education.[31]

The first contact between Washington and Eastman apparently came with the latter's perusal of *Up from Slavery*, Washington's autobiography, published in 1901. Eastman ordered it from F. N. Doubleday, Page and Company; his copy is autographed, probably during Washington's visit to Rochester.[32] He was impressed and asked for a Tuskegee annual report, then sent a check for $2,000. Washington was stunned and quite naturally pursued the association with vigor. Perhaps because Washington was its most noted graduate, Eastman also gave generously to Hampton Institute. As he gradually evolved a kind of quota system for his charitable donations—so much for health, so much for culture—he decided to limit his contributions for black institutions of higher learning to Tuskegee and Hampton. When Hattie Strong, now busily spending Henry's money to start many charitable ventures of her own, appealed to Eastman for a contribution for a "negro orphan asylum" in Atlanta, he responded that "I hate to do it but I guess I will have to turn you down. . . . I gave Booker Washington $10,000 a spell ago, which is my whole colored appropriation for the season 1908–1909."[33]

Sometimes Eastman sent Tuskegee and Hampton unrestricted gifts and other times he responded to appeals for a particular project. In 1914, for example, he gave Washington $5,000 specifically to build a veterinary hospital, an area in which, with all his cows, he had obvious interests. "The building is going up a little slower than it otherwise would," Washington wrote, "for the reason that we are having all the work done by students and in this way we are giving them the practice, and in the end we shall have the benefit of the building." In May 1915 Washington sent Eastman "a picture of the scene attending the Dedication of the Veterinary Hospital, which you so kindly and unexpectedly gave us." The program of twelve "dedicatory exercises" included such topics as a talk on "How the Live Stock in the South can be Improved by giving the Colored Boy Veterinary Science." On 8 November 1915 he wrote Dr. Washington that "I have read your annual report and also your treasurer's report and make you the following proposition: If you will raise enough money to pay all of your debts . . . and add two hundred and fifty thousand dollars to your endowment fund, I will give you the sum of two hundred and fifty thousand dollars for your building fund." He picked out the four buildings and "'the Barns, etc.' mentioned under the head of 'Special Needs,'" to which he wanted his money applied. "This does not," he cautioned, "include item No. 5 'Building for religious purposes,' as I am not interested in that sort of work."[34]

Washington's unanticipated death six days later intervened, and Eastman immediately wrote that while his offer was made "before I knew Dr. Washington was sick, I had been thinking of the matter for some time and would have written the letter just the same after his death as I think it is a good time for the friends of the Institute to get together and demonstrate that it is not going to be allowed to fall back on account of its great loss." The gift was listed as an anonymous endowment. "Major" Robert Russa Moton, another graduate of Hampton, succeeded Washington in May 1916; his initial letter to Eastman about "fitting these boys and girls for efficient service, that is fitting them to meet the conditions as they are," indicates that Moton strove to emulate his predecessor.[35]

In 1916 trustee William Schieffelin suggested that a department for teaching photography be established at Tuskegee as "a new outlet for creditable employment of talented colored men and women." As head of its new photography school, Tuskegee officials had in mind "Mr. C. Marion Battey, a colored man with good education and character, [who] has had experience in various branches of photography and is familiar with the technical work, legal and commercial photography, as well as portraiture and other artistic branches." C. E. Snow and H. M. Fell of the Eastman Kodak Company vouched for Battey's professionalism and he was hired. Eastman and Charles Ames approved Battey's list of materials and supplies at greatly reduced prices and Eastman personally donated $750 toward their purchase. "You have a large investment in the enterprise," wrote William G. Willcox, chairman of the board of trustees, who knew the identity of the anonymous donor. "Tuskegee Institute represents in a marked degree the moral and educational leadership of the Negro race. . . . The faculty and trustees need the encouragement and advice of our best citizens in meeting their problems and a visit from you would be greatly appreciated." Eastman did give some advice to Moton when the latter called on him in Rochester but he never did get to Tuskegee. Rush Rhees went in 1921, perhaps in Eastman's stead, to the Founder's Day exercises and dedication of the new trades buildings and was able "to listen to warm words of appreciation of you and your worth."[36]

Although Eastman's largest gift to Tuskegee before 1924 was the $250,000 given in 1916, his annual contributions, which started at $2,000 at the turn of the century and grew to $10,000 by 1911, were not accompanied by the usual caveat that his identity not be revealed. As soon as word filtered out that this Northern millionaire was donating to Tuskegee, other Southern schools and colleges, both black and white, began soliciting. He did respond to Hampton President James Gregg's annual appeal with $2,000 and regularly hired agricultural experts from Hampton Institute to help the Myricks with their farms. In fact, one of Hampton's agents planted the seed for a better institute that would come about six years later. In 1924 Hampton and Tuskegee combined in a fundraising effort and so would share equally in Eastman's major gift then.

On the other hand, many other Southern schools, black and white, received Eastman's stock reply: "I am doing all the southern educational work that seems practical just now." In turning down requests, many of which were for an "Eastman Hall to replace the building that burned," he was motivated to keep from "scattering" his money, explaining that he liked to "bunch" it for the greatest effect. As he told the trustees of Fisk University in 1912 and Howard University in 1919: "I am doing all I care to in the line proposed by subscribing to the Tuskegee Institute; therefore I do not see my way to meeting your wishes." Even unsuccessful applicants got a lecture on fire safety, however, and occasionally Eastman changed his mind as when, in 1923, possibly to placate that aggressive philanthropist Hattie Strong, he suddenly sent a $5,000 check to Howard University "for your medical school." In 1929 he built and equipped a dental department for Meharry Medical College in Nashville for $200,000. "Unless you have tried to raise money for Negro education you cannot fully realize how much I, personally, appreciate your generous gift," the president of Meharry, John J. Mullowney, wrote on that occasion. "It is so very hard to interest the average man of means in the Negro's needs."[37]

Not every door opened on demand to the Kodak King. The laws of segregation in the 1920s were as intractable as those of South African apartheid in the 1980s. When Julia Burt became ill, Eastman was sure his connections at Johns Hopkins in Baltimore would assure her swift treatment there. But the director recommended that because "We only have a limited number of beds in our colored wards and we have a waiting list of patients who ought to come into the Hospital but who we have been unable to get in for weeks, . . . I wonder if it would not be better for her to go to the Watts Hospital at Durham or the James Walker Memorial Hospital at Wilmington?" Segregation of course was not limited to the south in the 1920s. One of Rochester's leading hotels refused to accommodate a black Episcopal bishop. Rather than community leaders protesting such blatant discrimination, the odd solution proposed was to build "a YMCA for the colored men of our city," the argument being that "such a building will eliminate such humiliation." Eastman was favorably inclined to give such a building until former mayor James G. Cutler investigated and found there were only eight hundred blacks in Rochester, which was not considered enough to support such a building. Eastman did contribute to a YWCA branch for colored women and to two black orphan asylums when solicited by Mary Mulligan and Hattie Strong. Within Eastman's own purview discrimination was banned. As he wrote one concerned Rochester parent:

> I have received your undated letter concerning your daughter Freda Small, a member of the Eastman Theatre Ballet Class. You certainly must be mistaken in fancying that there has been any discrimination shown against her on account of her race as that would not be tolerated for a moment. I have referred your letter to Mr. Eric T. Clarke, manager of the theatre, and I am sure if you will see him the matter can be straightened out to your satisfaction.[38]

There was the case in 1907 of Ivoe de Calesta, a twenty-eight-year-old West Indian by birth, who was fluent in Spanish, French, and German. De Calesta "worked his way through the University of Rochester and now has charge of the order and advertising departments of the Rochester Optical Co. [a Kodak division by now]. He is honest, tactful, energetic, ingenious, and said to have very good judgment. His prospects in this country are much hampered," Eastman told George Davison in England. "The prejudice against people with negro blood is growing in this country and is a great handicap in business. My impression is that this prejudice does not exist in England and in some countries on the continent." Eastman wanted Davison to "make use of this man and work him up to a branch managership. . . . Our need of good men is so great that I would like to see him in a place where he would not be handicapped . . . by his Ethiopian features." Davison replied that Eastman was misinformed: Prejudice was everywhere, including Europe, and the geographical solution would not work. Frustrated, Eastman left the man in his present position while instructing Davison to continue to search for the right situation. "I do not know that I ever ran across a case where I felt so strong a desire to help a man overcome race prejudice as I do in this one," he concluded.[39]

Eastman's annual contributions to most charities remained unchanged from year to year—for example, in 1900 he gave $15 to the Needlework Guild, $100 to St. Mary's Hospital, $100 to the German Home for the Aged, and in 1930 he was still giving the same to each. But when a cause caught his interest, he increased the amount without urging. His annual gift to Tuskegee began at $2,000 about 1901; in 1903 he gave $3,000, in 1905 $7,000, and in 1912 $10,000 (in response to Washington's plea for an endowment fund; Tuskegee's acknowledgment was often to send a box of "sweet potatoes, grown on our farm, which I hope will reach you for Thanksgiving dinner").

Then, on 1 December 1924, Eastman gave approximately $2.2 million ($271,000 in cash and nearly $2 million in Eastman Kodak common and preferred stock) to Tuskegee, "by far the largest single contribution that has ever been made to Negro education," noted Clarence Kelsey, chairman of the then current Hampton–Tuskegee campaign. Hampton received a similar amount. Because of the escalating value of the stock and the matching gifts his contribution called for, about $9 million would "ultimately be made available for this work," Kelsey said. In explaining his choice of beneficiaries out of the many outstretched hands available, Eastman said:

> Almost the entire attention of educators has been thus far devoted to the white race but we have more than ten per cent Negro population in the United States. . . . The only hope of the Negro race and the settlement of this problem is through proper education of the Hampton Tuskegee type, which is directed almost wholly toward making them useful citizens through education on industrial lines. These two institutions are no longer experiments. Through many years of trial they have proved their ability to turn out men and women who mostly go back to their homes and serve as centers of influence for better living. The amount of work that these institutions have been able to do in proportion to their field is small. They need a lot more than I have offered them and I hope that others will realize their importance and deal liberally with them.[40]

Dalliance

■ ■ ·

He showered her with uncommon presents, typically things *he* liked: cows,[1] butter churns, hot water pans, picnic sets, music lessons, geological survey maps, or a roof for her Packard. Occasionally more conventional gifts were sent: Pomeroy champagne, caviar, Christmas turkeys, handkerchiefs. He turned to her for companionship particularly in time of sorrow and he looked to her for help in practical matters such as finding the right housekeeper. She exerted tremendous influence over his activities, exposing him to intimate string quartets in the European tradition as well as to large public concerts and the opera. She trotted him around to see some of the great private art collections and houses of the day—notably those of Joseph Widener in Philadelphia, Henry Clay Frick in New York, and Isabelle Stewart Gardner in Boston. She took him to his first aviation meet.[2] She encouraged his philanthropies, especially those concerning MIT and preventive dentistry for children. When they were together they spent hours taking photographs of each other and their respective homes and gardens. The pictures she took of him or someone took of the both of them show a rare mellowness of expression, a letting down of the guard. The pictures he took of her show a tender regard for his subject not always present in the rest of his 13,000 surviving snapshots. Of course if he could capture her off guard he would snap that picture with gusto too.

During the eighteen years between the death of her husband in 1898 and her own death in 1916, Josephine Dickman appeared in his correspondence, as both subject and recipient, more often than any other woman—except during those early years when his beloved mother was still alive. During that time she was more Maria's correspondent and confidante than George's. "Their house is lovely," Eastman told his mother in 1895, "and I found Mrs. D. expecting us and just as jolly and charming as ever."[3] He encouraged her to buy Ivy Hill, the adjoining property to Oak Lodge, and she "was so much interested that she wanted to go over to Ivy Hill the second time and actually did some figuring on how she would rebuild the house but finally it came to nothing."[4] "Finally it came to nothing" was how many friends looked at the affair, if that is the proper term. Perhaps the spark was missing, these same people decided. "Only once," said Nathaniel Myrick, the second butler, "did Mr. Eastman seem about to provide his house with a mistress. She was a prince. When she came to visit the staff was alerted days ahead and all were nervously aware that nothing short of perfection would satisfy the master of the house while his lady guest was present. Everybody jumped. But we were disappointed in our hopes. Mrs. Dickman came and went and there was no announcement. Several years of this wore down our anticipation as the romance just seemed to fritter away."[5]

Since the days of the Washington widow, Cornelia Hagan, and the elementary school principal who sat on her Arnold Park porch in hopes of getting acquainted with the taciturn and eligible Mr. Eastman, young women had been honing their wiles as their designing mothers pushed and primped them, but all efforts were met with a seeming indifference on Eastman's part. Yet most people who knew him best saw this uncaring attitude as part of the façade behind which he usually hid his deepest feelings. In reality, he cared intensely about a great number of things. When asked in later life why he had never married, Eastman explained that as a young man he was simply too busy building his business. There can be no doubt, however, that George Eastman was never too busy with photography that he could not find time for travel, expanding his knowledge of the world, and pure adventure. Probably closer to the truth is that he found personal independence to his liking from an early age, and that inclination grew with time into a settled habit. Perhaps it could even be called a fixation. Eastman was never one to relish being beholden to the preferences of others; he could be kind and thoughtful to his friends and relations, but invariably, he was the one in charge. His was the power of direction, and he was loath to cede it to anyone. Throughout the correspondence of a lifetime, through every incident of his public and private careers, there is no evidence that Eastman ever considered seriously the prospect of marriage and a family of his own. All ideas or suggestions in this regard came from others, never from him. Added to this insistence on personal freedom was his chronic shyness, which seems to have made intimate relationships very difficult for him always, and which manifested itself in an impenetrable public mask (and often a private one as well) and a chilly demeanor. In all, George Eastman seems to have been almost congenitally unsuited for a permanent domestic life.

The unsettled married life of his own parents was no advertisement for wedded bliss, and the pathetic, scapegrace character of his nephew Royal Andrus might have made Eastman think more than twice about giving up hostages to fortune in the form of his own offspring. At any rate, the early loss of his father led to an unusually strong bonding with his mother, and when Maria Eastman died, he may have thought (with some relief, perhaps) that it was too late for him. George Eastman was finally orphaned at the age of fifty-three.

Whenever the life of a confirmed bachelor is considered, there are those who are quick with the cliché, and Eastman's reputation has not been spared the occasional rumor (though not in print) about his sexuality over the years. In at least one instance—a 1980 television interview with Marion Gleason in which she claimed he had made a sexual advance when the two were making a transatlantic crossing alone together with adjoining staterooms and sharing a bath—there seems to be no question of his heterosexual inclinations. Unfortunately for those who would psychoanalyze Eastman over chasms of time and space, there is absolutely no evidence of a secret sexual life, no proof that he carried on outlaw liaisons, dangerous or otherwise, with members of either sex. Few lives are as well documented as Eastman's; fewer have been attended more closely by contemporary observers; fewer yet have been subject to the purview of inhabitants of four continents over nearly fourscore years. It is simply beyond all reason that a sexual life could have been kept hidden for a lifetime of seventy-eight years and for more than a half century beyond the grave. Was George Eastman less subject to sexual stirrings than is usually accounted "normal"? Was he, as we post-Freudians like to say, "repressed"? No telling. What we can say, on the basis of real evidence, is that the inscrutable George Eastman enjoyed more loyal and enduring friendships with members of both sexes than most people, that his affinities were passionate, that he cared deeply about what happened to people when they were alive, and that he mourned them acutely when they were gone. Nothing illustrates these qualities better than his relationship with Josephine Dickman.

She was a rarity in the early twentieth century—a financially independent woman. The death of her husband George in 1898 left her bereaved but not bereft. George Eastman saw to that. Josephine lived on the dividends from the generous allotment Eastman gave her when her husband died. "She will be well fixed," Eastman told his mother in 1898. "I told her," he added, "that when she felt like having a good rest you would take her in and be a good mother to her." In writing the Farmers Loan and Trust Company in her behalf, because "she was in somewhat of a quandary as to the appointment of an executor of her will," Eastman referred to Josephine Dickman as "a large owner of Kodak stock"[6]—so large, in fact, that for several years Eastman, Henry Strong, William Walker, and the widow Mrs. Dickman thought it best to form a stock syndicate, keeping a large preponderance of Kodak shares together as a hedge against a great block of stock flooding the market at one time and depressing the price.

Perhaps she suffered from the affliction of the age—"consumption," that is, tuberculosis—or at least the fear of it, because upon returning to the United States after years of wandering and living in hotels, she settled near her childhood home of Fitchburg, Massachusetts, in nearby Petersham, a resort area high above the swampy lowlands that were believed poor for one's health. Between 1908 and 1910 she built an immense home for herself, naming it "The Ridge." Off her bedroom was the required sleeping porch for breathing deeply of the crisp air that was believed to ward off or cure the dreaded TB. She furnished The Ridge with pieces brought from England and Europe, agumented by New England antiques and reproductions. Conversational groupings of eclectic chairs were casually strewn throughout her large living room or salon along with vases of informally arranged flowering branches atop the grand piano, bookcases, sideboard, mantle, and tables. The living room of Eastman House took on this same studied, lived-in look in photographs taken in 1912—in contrast to those of 1905, where a few overstuffed pieces stood awkwardly about. One can only guess at how much cross-fertilization of ideas there was between the two house builders. As an obituary in a Boston paper (and reprinted in Rochester) noted after Josephine's death, "The delightful house she built there was full of her own magical atmosphere, and the hours spent with her by the fireside or in the gardens which were her joy and pride."[7] After her death, her estate was found to be worth more than $1 million, the bulk of which ($750,000) she left to her nephew and godson Caryl Parker Haskins to receive when he reached twenty-five. (Young Haskins, whom Eastman referred to as "the little chap," would go on to become a research scientist, author, and educator, heading the Carnegie Institution of Washington [1956–71]. The Ridge remains prime residential property in Petersham.)

She adopted Eastman's interests in automobiling, picnicking, and cows. She kept a "fleet" of motor cars at The Ridge,[8] of which the Packard—as at Eastman House—was king. She followed his recommendations in the acquisition of cattle and picnic sets. This led him to present her with cows, churns, and a picnic set that he spent months designing and several pages explaining to her how it all went together. The set included his hand-crafted pantry and kitchen boxes, a fire grate, a dishpan bag (another Eastman invention), a custom-made baker (for biscuits and gems), little bundles of specially cut wood for making fires, the same hot-water thermal pans that he spent years trying to get Abercrombie & Fitch to produce in quantity and market, and a canopy to attach to her Packard to form the picnic tent at stops along the

automobiling route. He offered his mixes and recipes with hesitation, however, because "I should not presume to send such an accomplished cook as
you a recipe without a request" but ended his letters on an eager note: "If
there is any further information that you want, command me."[9]

They gave to each other's favorite charities: "Mrs. Dickman has requested
me to forward the enclosed check as her contribution to the Red Cross fund
for the relief of the earthquake sufferers in Italy." While in Rochester in
1915, she purchased and presented to the Memorial Art Gallery of the
University of Rochester, on whose board Eastman served (1912–32) a portrait of a young woman by the contemporary American artist Douglas Volk.
In 1913 Eastman enclosed "my check for $5000 for the [groundbreaking of]
Lowthorpe School" of Landscape Architecture, Horticulture and Gardening for Women at Groton, near Petersham in Massachusetts. "I hope you are
successful in raising all the money you want but do not take too much upon
yourself."[10] Josephine's health was a persistent worry: The constant toothaches of the early days in England had been replaced by the worry of her
friends over an unidentified operation in 1910 and a serious and sometimes
debilitating heart condition.

Music was a favored pursuit of both of them. She was a trained singer; he
felt the world should be populated with trained listeners. One summer when
she was in Rochester he had her take music lessons (of an unspecified nature)
with his personal organist, George E. Fisher.

When Maria Eastman died, letters of condolence poured in from relatives
and associates around the world. Only the Drydens and Josephine's cables
read, "ARRIVING TONIGHT AT SIX." Following his return from Waterville and
Maria's obsequies Eastman was absent from the office, off for two weeks to
Boston—"My little trip to the east," he called it in a letter to Strong—and that
is all we know about that. Arriving home, he threw himself into a frenzy of
geological surveying, ordering Massachusetts maps of Warwick, Winchester,
Fitchburg, Petersham, Belchertown, and Worcester for her; and New York
maps of Hamlin, Ontario Beach, Caledonia, Honeoye, Brockport, Rochester,
Macedon, and Canandaigua for himself.[11] In October 1907 Josephine accompanied him to Oak Lodge ("a bully good time," Eastman reported to Strong) to
join the Hubbells and the Mulligans and the six musicians who would soon
have their own cottage there. Then she came for Christmas 1907, went back to
Oak Lodge in April 1908, to Wyoming with Eastman and the Eastwoods in
August (for "the best trip" and "the longest vacation I ever had," Eastman
reported to Moritz Philipp and Frank Seaman), and to Rochester again for
Christmas and Eastman's New Year's Day party with the Drydens.

In the first decade of the century, Josephine traveled extensively with Mrs.
Dana, the widow who became William Walker's second wife, and then with
Miss Parker, the niece of her doctor and a former schoolteacher. She kept
apartments in New York, had a summer place at Gloucester, Massachusetts,

and winter quarters at the Cambridge in Boston and the King Edward Hotel, Toronto, where Dennison Dana lived. Brussels was a favorite watering spot. While in Boston or Petersham she was attended by her chauffeur and butler, R. A. Chase. Keeping track of Josephine's whereabouts kept Eastman's head whirling. One December 23 he wired frantically: "WHERE WILL EXPRESS PACKAGES REACH YOU WEDNESDAY NIGHT?" He became miffed if he was not the first to learn of her movements: "I was greatly surprised to hear that Mrs. Dickman and Mrs. Dana had arrived as I was under the impression that their boat was a slower one." Sometimes he had to wire ahead to find out where to telephone her. And sometimes those wires had the connubial ring of a long relationship:"HAVE YOUR TRUNKS BROAD STREET STATION NINE SUNDAY NIGHT. . . . WILL CALL FOR YOU AND PAGIE AT BELLEVUE STRAT-FORD BETWEEN TEN AND TWELVE LEAVE TWELVE FIFTEEN."[12]

Some of his letters to her were typed at the office and entered into the letterpress books but many end with "I will write you by hand tomorrow" or "I will telephone you tonight" and there are no originals or copies of these. Considering Eastman's phobia about the telephone, his frequent references to their vocal contacts are remarkable: "I was talking to Mrs. D. by telephone last night"; "In talking with Mrs. Dickman, she thought . . . "; "Mrs. Dickman tells me . . . "; "I was just talking with Josephine over the telephone . . . "; "I WILL CALL YOU IN NEW YORK; WILL TELEPHONE YOU FROM BELMONT ABOUT NINE TOMORROW." That he was willing to put the hated instrument to his ear, argue with long-distance operators, and patronize the despised Bell System for the sake of Josephine Dickman are in themselves testimony of his regard for her.[13]

She was often at her New York apartments during his frequent visits to the city and sometimes accompanied him back to Rochester, particularly while his mother was still alive. Some summers she came to house-sit and mother-sit while he went off camping with his cronies. On more than one occasion she brought her brother, Caryl D. Haskins, and his family for a week's stay. Rochesterians "knew" vaguely that Eastman saw a woman in New York and this "knowledge" may have been indirectly the source for one character in the novel *By His Own Hand*, Henry Clune's *roman à clef* about George Eastman published in 1952. Despite her physical frailties Josephine was able to handle the rigorous vacation schedules that Eastman arranged. "I think the best trout fishing I ever had was above the Jam Rapids in Quebec," he decided with satisfaction. "The two trout caught by Mrs. Dickman weighed $4\frac{1}{2}$ pounds each." From Jackson Hole in 1908 he took to reporting to friends that "Four weeks of the time was spent camping. Mrs. Dickman was able to ride twenty or thirty miles a day when we were in the mountains." Around the campfires Josephine would sing and once, when distant coyotes decided to accompany her, Eastman doubled up in uncontrolled laughter.[14] Before leaving Rochester they were photographed separately: she in her white lace summer dress in a wicker chair looking pensively out of the conservatory window or poised with a cue stick above the billiard table; he in a dark suit lying on his side on the black leather sofa. When they reached Chicago, the first leg of their trip, they stayed with the Drydens and were photographed again. In Wyoming and later at Oak Lodge they were photographed together—fishing, in camp, on horseback, on the porch swing. The Wyoming scenario was repeated in 1910 on a fishing trip to Labrador and in 1913 on a rented yacht bound for the Caribbean, but always there were other couples—the Macombers, the Mulligans, the Hubbells, the Eastwoods, the Drydens—along as companions. Eastman liked to turn his own camera on her when she was poised with bow and arrow, about to shoot billiards at East Avenue, lounging on the cushions in his conservatory, regally posed in a Jacobean chair in Eastman House, displaying the fish she had caught, picnicking with friends, standing in a canoe with a fishing pole and looking for all the world like she was about to capsize, or lolling about the woods in a lace and organza frock with other women friends, thereby creating a serene composition. Considering his shyness, perhaps all this photographing was a way of making love without making love.

The years immediately following his mother's death, from 1908 to 1913, which coincided with his most concentrated friendship with Josephine, could also be called the Summertime of George Eastman—the most relaxed and contented years of his life. "My garden has been a dream of beauty this summer," he said in 1908. "Kodak stock has been soaring to the clouds lately," he said in 1909. "I am doing the best I know how to enjoy life," he said in 1910.

Housekeepers were a perennial problem. The Dickmans had sent the Eastmans Sarah Ginger, a comely English housekeeper, in the 1890s but she became homesick, so the Eastmans muddled along with a dozen house servants and grounds attendants but no overall manager. With the new house in 1905, Frank Babbott sent his own Mrs. Bainbridge, the emergency housekeeper he employed when his wife and infant child died in childbirth in 1904, but Mrs. Bainbridge was unable to manage tactfully and was let go when mutiny threatened. Panicked by the thought of his rudderless estate running amuck for lack of a manager, Eastman put in a cabled S.O.S. to Josephine Dickman, asking her to travel all the way from Minneapolis to Buffalo and then on to Rochester to interview the prospective candidates. One Mrs. Conkling got the nod. After seven years with Mrs. Conkling, Eastman felt he needed a change and hired Miss Osgood from Boston. "She is a maiden lady of uncertain summers," Eastman mused, "businesslike, and a good deal of a Boston blue stocking."[15]

Two years later it was again time for Josephine to find yet another housekeeper. This time she sent her friend, Marie (Molly) Cherbuliez, "American about 42—trim but not too good looking," as Eastman described her. (Miss Osgood went on to become housekeeper to John D. Rockefeller Jr., receiving an excellent reference from Eastman, who explained that he just liked to change housekeepers now and then.) Miss Cherbuliez was the last housekeeper he would employ; she was with him for seventeen years and would have a bearing upon his life and upon his death.

Molly Cherbuliez was living in New York when Eastman put out his latest feelers. "Before I'd live in the house with an unmarried man, I'd have to see him," she told Mrs. Dickman. She found Eastman "very pleasant, very nice," but when he asked her to take the position, she told him, as Harris Hayden and William Walmsley had decades earlier, that she didn't want to leave New York for provincial Rochester. Instead of taking offense, Eastman suggested she think it over. That evening he telephoned her with what he regarded as the ultimate concession: "Miss Cherbuliez, I want you to become a member of my family." She capitulated and came in February 1915.

At first she had reservations about Eastman. He was cold, he was sarcastic, he could "skin you with a look," he was very sensitive and quick to take offense. On the other hand, she found him "upright mentally, morally, and physically," and an "honorable man who never said a word against anybody." She was able to maintain her equilibrium mainly because she was not intimidated by him. Gradually she learned what certain others had: that he had a natural contempt for bootlicking, but could not escape it. He admired people who stood up to him, although he made it as difficult as possible to do so. Occasionally she found ways to penetrate the icy reserve, and in the end grew to admire and respect him.

Many of Molly's responsibilities fell outside the usual job description for a housekeeper. Once Eastman had prepared a speech that he planned to read to a group of prominent people who would be gathering at Eastman House. His audience was to be seated in the conservatory while he, flanked by radio microphones, would address them from the heights of the stairway landing. Molly was asked to read the speech from the landing while he seated himself in the conservatory to see "how it sounds." "Sounds fine," he decided. "You read it tonight."

Molly ran a tight ship, keeping forty people in line, hiring and firing them, plus handling the full-time job of pleasing her difficult boss. The house was like the company and Eastman with his logical mind and instincts for management probably regarded it as "Operation East Avenue." He was constantly alert to any trace of inefficiency or lack of sound economy. It was almost physically painful to him to run across waste, and as a result such an encounter usually meant that someone would soon be unemployed. Nor was he satisfied merely to eat the bovine output of milk and butter; Molly was required to submit a report on which appeared the beast's name along with the amount of milk she had given that day, the amount of butter fat, number of pounds churned, and so on. Another time she was given a three-year project of counting and logging all the roses so he could decide which varieties produced best. But when he planted some peach trees and presented Miss Cherbuliez with a little black book, Molly said after a moment of stunned silence, "All right, Mr. Eastman, but don't expect me to count all the grapes on the arbor."

Miss Cherbuliez did not endear herself to other women trying to gain access to Eastman. Everyone had to go through her (or Alice Whitney if the office route was chosen) and she protected her charge with such vigor that she earned herself the sobriquet "Dragon Lady." While Eastman was active and in good health, there were ways to circumvent his keeper; later, as he withdrew more and more behind the walls of the steel and concrete fortress he had built, the Dragon Lady's power increased tremendously. During the years of his illness (1927–32), George Eastman changed greatly and became at last a vulnerable human being, his housekeeper decided. His physical weakness evoked sympathy and affection in many, including Molly, as his austere integrity had never done. He became gentler and more dependent but he never quite made the shift to a contemplative life: Occupation and activity had filled all his days and when he was deprived of these he substituted hours of radio music, reading, driving, and movie-going several times a week. Molly always remained loyal to her friend Josephine Dickman. "That gossip about Mr. Eastman and Mrs. Mulligan is ridiculous," she said in 1950. "Mrs. Dickman was the love of his life. I think she would have married him if she'd been well." Did that mean that Eastman had asked Mrs. Dickman to marry him? "Miss C. suddenly became silent," the interviewer recorded.[16]

In the fall of 1916 the usual group was getting ready for its annual trek to "God's country" in North Carolina. Ellen Dryden received a letter in early December:

> I wonder if you have heard of Josephine's sudden death Nov 28th at the Copley-Plaza Boston. She had been feeling very well that day and had been out in her car that morning and the last thing she did was to buy some little Thanksgiving trinkets for the Oak Lodgers. She had luncheon in the public room and along in the afternoon went to lie down. A little while after her companion Miss Parker went to look in on her. . . . I am doubly glad now that I went over from Greenfield that evening early in October and dined with her.[17]

Abandoning his guests at the lodge, Eastman had sped to Boston for the funeral, "set for two o'clock. The best I could do was to take a train from New York arriving at 2:21 . . . and at the chapel at a quarter to three." Miss Parker had sent an automobile to Back Bay station and kept the organist playing those forty-five minutes until "Josephine's good friend, Mr. East-man" arrived. After the services he "had a good long talk with Miss Parker about Josephine's last days," returned to North Carolina, sent the guests and servants home by private railroad car, and worked out his grief at the kitchen stove. "Dear Ellen," he wrote: "Here I am staying on all alone at Oak Lodge. . . . You would have laughed to see me cooking my meals, Aunt Fanny acting as scullery maid . . . roast turkey, warmed up turkey, creamed turkey, cold turkey, sausage, grilled chicken, broiled quail, oyster milk stew, oyster cream stew, fried oysters, bread, baking powder biscuits, gems, muf-fins, cream toast, boiled eggs, oatmeal, coffee, salad, etc."[18] Months later, upon being asked by her executor if he would like to "select some articles from Mrs. Dickman's personal effects," Eastman replied, "I think I would prefer the picnic outfit which I sent her about three years ago. Some of my pleasantest remembrances of Mrs. Dickman are associated with camping and picnicking and I believe I would rather have these articles than anything else which she possessed. . . . I think Chase would know all about this out-fit. . . . The loss of Mrs. Dickman was irreparable to all her friends, among whom I was always proud to include myself."[19] After his death, Eastman's wallets were examined and a list made of their contents. They read like chapters out of his life. Among the personal effects found was a vignette portrait of Josephine Dickman in a folder with protective tissue.

War and tuberculosis, the twin scourges of the 1910s, touched Eastman in a personal way through the daughter of his London manager.

Louise Gifford's condition was deteriorating. She had been slated to go to a sanitarium in the Swiss Alps, but when war broke out on the Continent the family decided on Saranac Lake in the Adirondacks of New York State. May Gifford accompanied her daughter to get her settled but then returned to England to be with her husband, leaving Eastman, who had given the pair his stateroom and was now just a few hours from Saranac, *in loco parentis*. At the Trudeau Sanitarium, Louise married Arthur Purvis, and the honeymooners moved into a cottage of their own. Eastman was unable to attend the wedding but sent Kodak stock as a present. Louise, "your grateful and very loving B. B. G." (for Ba-by Gifford, Eastman's pet name for her), danced around the cottage with her "very first little slip of paper," before making Eastman feel guilty by sending him "my photograph in that most important garment—my wedding dress. My pictures always look slightly like a dying sheep—and I wish especially that this was an exception—particularly for you, who really should have been here."

Christmas 1915 found Eastman sending her a more frivolous present —probably chosen by Josephine Dickman, for whom lorgnettes were a signature—to which Louise responded on 22 December:

Of course I *couldn't* wait until Christmas and therefore simply ripped off its papers the minute it came—It is quite the loveliest lorgnette I have ever beheld and when I think that it belongs to me! Really I have spent almost the entire day in playing with it and tho' I know the glass in it is only plain I *assure* you I can see twice as well through it! My ambition now is to wear it at Covent Garden and stare haughtily through it at my English fellow-country women.[20]

In almost the same mail Eastman received a telegram from the sanitarium— "PREPARING YOU FOR SERIOUS NEWS . . . : ANOTHER BLEEDING WITH HIGH FEVER . . . WEAK HEART SYMPTOMS . . . WITH OCCASIONAL SHORT BREATHING ATTACKS THAT ALARM HER. HAVE REASSURED HER AND NOT TOLD PURVIS MY FEARS"—and so he sped to Saranac. Louise did indeed rally to live another five months, writing him often with forced cheerfulness about "our little flat," her mother's "bad rheumatism," how "so many people come to Saranac too late" to be cured, of hopes for a trip to England that summer, and how "our friends *will* write us and say, 'Cheer up, the winter will soon be over etc.' We are not in any hurry for the time to pass and consider our Life here almost perfect for a year's honeymoon!"[21]

"What a comfort you have been to Louise," said Josephine Dickman in May 1916, then herself hospitalized. "You must be glad." May Gifford confirmed this when she wrote shortly after her daughter's death: " I hope the years will give—if there be years—many chances for long and less sad talks of the little girl we love. Even that dreaded day . . . I can recall without bitterness and it will blend into the memories that are only sweet."[22]

By war's end Eastman had not only institutionalized his former functions at Kodak; he had become something of an institution himself. His influence over the cultural, economic, and political life of Rochester was considerable, and in most cases definitive. Yet he recognized no contract to appear in public, and the fact that he chose not to lent an aura of mystery to his image of unequaled wealth and power. He went to some lengths not to ingratiate himself with small talk or to suffer small talk from others. He refused to bore the younger generation with platitudinous speeches or to have his biography recorded by any of the eager reporters now clamoring to do so.

For the first time since Charlie Abbott died unexpectedly in 1905 there was a vice president of Kodak other than the outside attorney Walter Hubbell. Indeed, facing his own mortality at the age of sixty-five, Eastman ended forty years of his own sole, autocratic rule of the Kodak company by appointing five vice presidents, thus establishing a chain of command and providing at least some semblance of an order of succession. If Eastman had died or been incapacitated between 1905 and 1921, when he held all reins of authority, his company might well have split into various component elements. More and more Frank Lovejoy, now a vice president, began assuming the responsibilities of general manager, the catchall phrase from the 1880s that had been one of Eastman's own titles for four decades. "At last," he told Edward Bausch, son of the founder of Bausch and Lomb who shared an 1854 birthdate, "we are both of us getting to the age where we can look with complacency and satisfaction on letting the young men do the work. I'm trying to fix it so that I will have to come down to business only about every second rainy Thursday."[23] That was more a wish than reality, since it would take almost another decade before Eastman could afford to take such a diffident stance, but at the end of the century's second decade, Kodak was humming along relatively smoothly, so Eastman began looking outward to other projects.

Meanwhile, Hubbell's health was questionable after his "nervous breakdowns," and his partner, Fred Goodwin, had not, Eastman decided, done well with the decade-long telephone suit. While not wishing to dismiss his old friend, he augmented his legal counsel by hiring James S. Havens in 1918 to work out the consent decree with the government, the eventual result of which was favorable to Eastman. In 1919 Havens hired a young law clerk from Hubbell's office, Milton Robinson, whom Eastman immediately steered into doing legal aid work for Kodak employees. This did not sit well with outside lawyers but represented yet another free service Kodak provided for its employees. Havens was in poor health; after a lengthy illness he died in 1926 at age sixty-eight. Hubbell lived on into his eighties, dying only two months before Eastman in 1932 but these lingering illnesses of his two once-brilliant attorneys preyed on Eastman's mind. To be alive and yet not fully alive was a condition he wanted to avoid. Meanwhile Robinson, almost by default, became Eastman's personal lawyer, inheriting as it were the task of writing and rewriting Eastman's will every few years, adding codicils as conditions changed. The amounts of bequests were always left blank in the wills Hubbell, Havens, and Robinson prepared. Eastman filled them later in private before signing the document in the presence of three Kodak witnesses. Miss Whitney would then hand each witness a $10 gold piece for his services.

By 1919 Eastman's social contacts had broadened to include more than just the old guard of the Hubbells, Mulligans, Eastwoods, Bonbrights, Sibleys, Watsons, and the rest. A dual standard of behavior—one for the business world, another for the social world—evolved as well. As he told Marion Gleason, "Yes, one has to be hard, hard, in this world. But never forget, one must always keep one part of one's heart a little soft."[24] As a new crowd with the irresistible energy of youth came to the fore, Eastman embarked upon a second adolescence—or, one could argue, the first adolescence that was denied him by circumstance. He had no sons and a less than satisfactory relationship with his only nephew, Royal Andrus, but two young men entered his life in 1919 who grew to feel a filial affection that bordered on devotion for the aging Eastman. So did an irreverent and fun-loving young woman who was not impressed by his mythic status and briefly captured his heart.

Dr. and Mrs. Audley Durand Stewart came to Rochester in 1916, and in 1919 he became an associate in the aging Edward Mulligan's office. In 1920 Stewart joined an Eastman camping trip to British Columbia as the official physician, Eastman having decided that henceforth he would have one along (Mulligan begged off because of problems with diabetes, and his feeling that he was too old to cope with another strenuous Eastman "vacation"). Eastman, his butler Solomon Young, and young Stewart exchanged scarcely a word on the first lap of the journey. When George Dryden joined them in Chicago, tongues loosened, and Stewart began to enjoy his initiation into an Eastman camping trip where all was prescribed down to the way the beds were made and the dishes were washed. Not only did the gregarious Dryden bring Eastman to life; a visit to the Chicago office of Eastman Kodak gave Stewart a glimpse of the Eastman business style. By the time they got to British Columbia Stewart had learned that Eastman sucked an orange in bed before arising at 7 A.M. and made his bed in a carefully prescribed way, but could also be surprisingly informal and lacking in self-consciousness. As the train was passing through a deserted section of Kansas, it was suggested that Eastman step from his private car and have his picture taken in his pajamas. He nonchalantly rose to the challenge, decked out as he was in Jules Brulatour's latest gift—a bright orange silk-trimmed outfit with acid green at the neck and sleeves.

When interviewers sat down with Stewart in 1954 they found him still quite emotional in reminiscing about Eastman. "I loved him like a father," he told Beaumont Newhall, Oscar Solbert, and Roger Butterfield over lunch at the Genesee Valley Club.[25]

Harold Gleason, twenty-seven, was organist and choirmaster of the Fifth Avenue Presbyterian Church in New York City, when a young man appeared in the organ loft in January 1919. Introducing himself as Arthur Alexander, he said he was George Eastman's music advisor and had heard the organ as he was walking down the avenue. Would Gleason be interested in moving to Rochester as Eastman's private organist? Eastman was gearing up for his next megaproject. During the previous year he had purchased a music conservatory and presented it to the university; made a codicil to his will that left his mansion to the university for use as a music school; dismissed George E. Fisher, his organist of fourteen years, because Fisher was endorsing products in advertisements and identifying himself as Eastman's organist; enlarged his music room at home by almost ten feet; and installed a second organ in his mother's former bedroom. Gleason went for an interview. Eastman was impressed that he had been director of the Boston Music School Settlement. Gleason in turn was impressed with the two-story conservatory, the two organs on the second-floor opening into the conservatory, the one-hundred-plus ranks of pipes, the echo organ on the third floor that spoke into the stairwell, the male quartet that often sang, and the string quintet that regularly played for Eastman and his guests.[26]

"I played for about twenty minutes and stopped, not wanting to overdo it," Gleason recalled. "Then his voice sounded over the bank of flowers in front of the console, 'Please play some more.'" Eastman offered Gleason a salary considerably less than he was receiving in New York. Gleason declined and rose, indicating the interview had ended. "However, the stern look I had noted changed to a faint smile and he said, 'I think we can do something about that. I will increase your salary, and you can also teach organ at the Institute of Musical Art.'" Gleason moved to Rochester on 1 May 1919 with his wife and young son. The relationship with Eastman soon filled a gap. "I never had a father," Gleason explained later. "He never had children. I was twenty-seven [Eastman was sixty-five] and I felt from the outset that he was a father figure." Gleason never had a formal contract, although Eastman out-lined what was expected of him in a letter. He was to play the organ for an hour during breakfast each morning, 7:30 on weekdays and 8:00 on Sundays. "At exactly 7:30 his bedroom door opened, and I would begin to play as he came down the stairs to the music room." Gleason learned to vary the repertoire according to Eastman's mood and he found he could gauge it by the way Eastman spoke to Solomon Young, his butler. Wednesday evenings after dinner and Sunday evenings Gleason was to accompany the string quartet. Purists might object to these strange arrangements for organ, piano, and strings but Eastman would say quietly, "They forget the music is for me, not them."[27]

Eastman made a point of introducing Gleason to his guests. When Prince Gustav-Adolf and Prince Sigvard of Sweden, sons of the crown prince, came to stay at the house, Gleason promised he would practice saying, "Your royal highness." Eastman replied, "Oh, I think that's too formal. We'll just call him 'Prince.'" Gleason was astounded, but knowing his employer to have a some-what offbeat sense of humor, refrained from pointing out that the salutation was akin to hailing a dog. He was even more amazed when Eastman ushered Gustav-Adolf to the console and said, "Prince, I want you to meet my organ-ist." The prince stiffened visibly, then relaxed and smiled, holding out his hand. "How do you do, Prince," said the organist with as straight a face as he could muster.[28]

In her eighties Clara Louise Werner Ward was a figure of enormous pa-nache, presence, and bosom. Her resonant voice and deep, rippling laugh rolled up from her toes to command the attention of all. Her retinue of courtly admirers, mostly young and male, included Andrew Jackson (Jack) Warner II, son of architect J. Foster Warner. In the 1920s Jack Warner was Eastman's music ambassador, the man who was sent to London and Europe to interview or clinch the deal with prospective conductors or musicians for the new Rochester Philharmonic Orchestra. In the 1930s, 1940s, and 1950s Jack Warner, music critic for the Gannett newspapers and a bachelor, would sashay down the aisle of the Eastman Theatre in tails, spats, and velvet opera cape, with Mrs. Ward, known to all simply as Clayla, on his arm. Every few yards the glittering couple would pause as Clayla bestowed her blessing on the latter-day patrons of the orchestra.

When Harold and Marion Gleason first came to Rochester in 1919, Eastman's car was frequently seen parked in front of the late Judge William Werner's house on Oxford Street. The esteemed judge of the state supreme court had known Eastman socially and on a community level. But Eastman's car was parked on Oxford Street while he visited with one of the judge's three lovely daughters—Clara Louise (Clayla), Caroline (Kyrie, who would marry newspaper tycoon Frank Gannett), and Marie—who had been groomed by their lovely and fun-loving mother to be social successes. The first memento Clayla kept from her father's friend was a printed card that arrived in December 1913 and said simply:

Mr. George Eastman will be happy to see *Miss Werner*
Dancing

The same card went to dozens of debutantes in similar privileged homes up and down East Avenue and the fashionable side streets off it. The party of 2 January 1914 followed up a fabulous ball of the night before. The next Eastman memento Clayla kept and cherished from her father's friend was a cryptic postcard from Eastman, vacationing at the Augusta Country Club on 25 February 1914:

The Hyena is still grinning and the ground covered with snow

Upon completion of her schooling and several more years abroad, Clayla Werner returned to Rochester and renewed her friendship with Eastman. "He seemed like a lonely little boy seeking a companion who really understood him." she recalled after his death. Never one to spoil a good story by too much veracity, Clayla nevertheless saw personality traits others confirmed. "One could only go so far with him. Then a compartment locked in his mind and one couldn't get any further. Consequently, he was not thoroughly appreciated by women even though he was at his best with them and very interested in the feminine point of view. But he kept his thin lips closed against gossip. I don't think any friend ever knew what he thought of any other."

One day he asked if it would be "too terrible" if she came Saturday mornings for breakfast at 900 East Avenue. Clayla went, spending a pleasant hour each week in animated conversation over the organ. Clayla's friend, Charlotte Whitney, daughter of Eastman's old banking and biking colleague, Warham Whitney, was invited too. But Fannie (Mrs. Warham) Whitney was estranged from Eastman because she had always given a New Year's party and considered it "her night" and also because Eastman pressured her to increase her contribution to the War Chest to the extent that Mrs. Whitney gave nothing. So Charlotte was forbidden to go to Eastman House and Clayla went alone. The more time Miss Werner spent with Mr. Eastman, the more she felt he was going through a second adolescence. Clayla found that she was calling her new friend "George" to his face, as he had requested, but "Mr. Eastman" in secondary references because of his mythic status.

She noted that "Mr. Eastman could be remarkably persistent in getting what he wanted, even if it was a very trivial matter." One memorable evening he wanted to hear violinist Andre Polack, protégé of Mary Mulligan, but Polack had not brought his violin with him to the Mulligans. So the three of them—Polack, Eastman, and Clayla—took off in the car with Eastman at the wheel, "backing and filling and generally being inept as a chauffeur. In spite of his inventive cleverness, he was rough on cars, jamming the brakes and grinding the gears as he drove, and playing the devil with the machine. Here he was, on the loose, although he was over sixty." Once the violin had been procured, the trio realized they had no accompanist, so they stopped again and got one out of bed at the Sagamore Hotel before proceeding back to 900 East Avenue for champagne. "While searching for the keys to the wine cellar, Mr. Eastman suddenly said, 'Oh *she's* got them.' So he shouted upstairs until Miss Cherbuliez came trotting out, hair in paper curlers, breathlessly exclaiming, 'Whatever is the matter?'" Later, over champagne, Mr. Eastman looked at Miss Werner and murmured, "'Clara Louise, if I were younger, I'd elope with you.'" To which Miss Werner replied, "'Imagine what some of your lady friends would think.' At that, Mr. Eastman fairly roared with laughter." All of this was probably the champagne talking. Yet weeks later, according to Clayla, on another hair-raising drive through one of the parks Eastman had given to the city of Rochester, "he proposed that they consider seriously the matter of eloping."

"Although she really felt devoted to him," recalled Mrs. Ward in 1940, speaking of herself in the third person, "she considered that they should give it long and serious thought." But, she added, he "never did he force the issue," admitting instead that "I would have nothing but gain while you have your whole life ahead. There would be twitterings and whisperings because I am old enough to be your father." Miss Werner felt that the twitterings and whisperings and censorious glances had already begun, particularly when a friend sauntered up to her at the Rochester Horse Show and remarked, "Everyone is expecting you to marry George Eastman soon." Clayla's letter to George cooling the flirtation does not survive. But his response of 26 December 1919 does: "As I have come to know you better I have grown more and more fond of you and I want you to know that I welcome your friendship more than I can say. If the new year allows me to see you oftener, it will be just so much happier." Many people were surprised when, in 1922, Clayla married the widower Hawley Ward, who was head of Ward's Natural Science Center that turned dead animals like Eastman shot into trophies for the wall. Eastman threw a lavish prenuptial party for them with American Beauty roses lining the stairs. Everything that could possibly be shaped into a heart—the hors d'oeuvres, the rolls, the decorations—was.[29]

In place of Saturday breakfasts of strawberries and cream with Clayla, Eastman soon instituted Saturday luncheons with four matrons in their early thirties who, as Marion Gleason would have it, were "under the control of their husbands." (She was one of the four, along with Marion Folsom's wife and the wives of the dean and faculty of the new medical school.) With this new arrangement, Eastman was not likely to find himself "engaged" again. Rush Rhees called them "an extra set of nieces," thinking of Ellen Dryden who joined the group when in town. And since lobster was very often served, they soon became the Lobster Quartet.[30]

Frozen Music: GE and His Architects

In George Eastman's outer office was a large flat cabinet of the kind usually found in an architect's office—full of blueprints for buildings planned, currently under construction, or recently erected. "One of his greatest interests," wrote Marion Folsom, who occupied an office adjoining this architectural anteroom, "was the careful scrutiny of these plans, which very often resulted in important changes." From his post, Folsom saw (in the ubiquitous green pencil) such comments as, "I don't like the way the draftsman makes his R's."[1] If he had been born in more affluent circumstances, it is possible that Eastman would have pursued architecture as a career.

Even as an amateur, Eastman was an inspired contributor to factory architecture, one of the unheralded and unrecorded contributions of America to world architecture. He may never of heard of Louis Sullivan (although one of his architects, Claude Bragdon, wrote extensively about Sullivan), but he adhered to Sullivan's famous "form follows function" dictum for factory buildings and pragmatic projects such as the School of Medicine and Dentistry of the University of Rochester. For more aesthetic projects, such as his mansion or the Eastman Theatre and School of Music, he employed nationally known "slipcover" architects after he and a sympathetic local architect had worked out the plans together. The plan and program was the important part. Then if an academically trained Beaux Arts architect wanted to add a fancy cornice or a Gothic tower to hide the elevator shaft, that was all right as long as it did not interfere with the plan and if costs were kept in check. His other contribution to factory architecture was landscaping. Having spent his first six years in a nursery of roses and fruit trees, he knew instinctively that no building was complete until it was landscaped. Kodak Park was one of the first industrial parks that made full use of landscape architecture.

The metamorphosis of the Kodak Office building during George Eastman's lifetime began in 1882 when the Eastman Dry Plate Company bought a plot of land behind 343 State Street and opened a four-story basic brick factory building designed by Charlie Crandall (who was paid in stock). The skylighted fifth floor was added in 1888 to accommodate the new processing division, where women made prints from negatives taken with the new Kodak camera. A sign "OFFICE" by an inauspicious side door was the only indication of where the headquarters might be. The building stood on Vought Street, basically an alley, a half-block from State Street. As business expanded, the property toward State Street was acquired and shacklike outbuildings were demolished for a parklike square of grass, bushes, and a tree in a circular flower bed. This modest Garden of Eden was enclosed by a wrought iron fence. A walk now led to the office door where flower pots stood and a brick wall topped by flower boxes hid ugly appurtenances on the new (State Street) front of the building. Emblazoned on this façade were inscriptions tracing the company's history. "THE EASTMAN DRY PLATE CO." was superseded in 1884 by "THE EASTMAN DRY PLATE AND FILM CO PHOTO-GRAPHIC MATERIALS," which by 1889 read

"You press the button, we do the rest"
KODAK
THE EASTMAN COMPANY
KODAK
PHOTOGRAPHIC MATERIALS

Finally in 1892 "EASTMAN KODAK COMPANY" replaced "THE EASTMAN COMPANY." Inside, Eastman's desk was a standup affair in one corner, similar to one he had occupied at the bank. After a few years his corner was partitioned for privacy and eventually a rolltop desk was installed in the center of a fairly large room. The standup desk in the corner he kept always and when he tired of sitting in a swivel chair, he stood up to write his checks or conduct other serious business.

In 1892 the "Kodak Crystal Palace," or Camera Works, again by Crandall, was built across Vought Street from the office but flush with State Street. Six stories and a high basement had twenty-six windows each ten feet square on every floor to let in enough daylight for the camera makers. Although steel construction was beginning to be used in Rochester, the Camera Works stuck to masonry with brick walls three feet thick at the base. The building was connected to Eastman's office-factory across Vought Street (soon to be re-named Kodak Street) by a bridge on the fourth level.[2]

For the dawn of a new century, Eastman had J. Foster Warner design a new two-story office to replace that flower-bedecked and grassy fenced-in plot in front of the original office-factory. Warner used leaded glass between classical pilasters on three sides for a light and airy ambience. On the roof stood ten carved pinnacles joined by a filigreed balustrade, centered on a fancy flagpole base featuring a carved shield with "EKCo" emblazoned. A cast iron and glass porte cochere led from the front door to the street so that visitors need not carry umbrellas. Warner wanted the world to see that the Eastman Kodak Company had arrived and now faced the world with more than a factory building, but Eastman thought the construction "flimsy" and the decorations overdone. By 1904 Warner's construction was already being called the "old office building," as Charlie Crandall returned to design a new six-story building, 68 feet by 190 feet, north of the office. The top four floors matched the Camera Works to the south (also designed by Crandall) while the bottom two floors were united with the 1900 building in a façade of heavy striped brick and stone pilasters under a cornice. Warner's pinnacles and filigree were replaced by a simple balustrade and his front was obliterated by Crandall "to conform to the new." Inside, offices and reception areas were shifted and a new front door created in a massive split pediment in the center of the new façade. Two years previous Crandall had been highly unhappy that Warner was chosen to design Eastman's mansion, but he now had his chance.

Business was booming in New York City in 1906. The Kodak manager received a raise and was told to look for larger quarters. Finding nothing that pleased Eastman, a building was bought and demolished on West 23d Street to be replaced by a new eight-story structure, designed by McKim, Mead & White, William Kendall in charge. It would be one of the last to be designed during the lifetimes of all three original partners. (Stanford White was mur-dered that same year, 1906; McKim died in 1907.) The firm's emphasis on both street-level glamour and visual interest can be seen in the plate glass façade with three double doors on the first two floors and a delicately filigreed eighth floor. As was his practice, Eastman chose the ash cans and wire glass for the transoms, worked out the plumbing, and specified the pioneer use of armored concrete in New York City. As delicate as it appeared, the New York office was built like a bunker, so impervious that it was the only McKim, Mead & White building designated a bomb shelter during World War II.[3]

Meanwhile in London, managing director George Davison commissioned George Walton, noted Scottish architect and designer, to embellish the new Kodak Limited offices with ultramodern carpets, wall designs, lamps, and windows. Walton was the first to treat the "hoarding"—the wooden fence surrounding a building under construction—as a work of aesthetic significance. Walton started with the Clerkenwell Road offices, and then was commissioned by Davison to design new Kodak shops—in London in the Strand, Regent Street, and Brompton Road; in Glasgow, Brussels, Milan, and Vienna. Walton brought a lightness of touch, color, delicacy, and charm not seen before or since in Kodak buildings. The shops were featured in contemporay periodicals; long gone now, they continued to illustrate his work in architectural histories.[4] Eastman acknowledged in a diffident way that Walton's designs were attractive but he was more concerned during this period (1901–7) with Davison's lack of administrative talents, his continuing guerilla warfare with dealers, and his involvement with that anarchist newspaper.

By 1910 the Clerkenwell headquarters were outgrown and William Gifford, managing director, was told to scout for a new location. Eastman liked a lot on Kingsway, a new street just being cut through, and a ninety-nine-year lease was signed on the spot. Eastman sketched his ideas and dictated his specifications for Sir John Burnet, renowned architect of the British Museum, but Sir John's first plans were not up to snuff. Eastman then gave his sketches to Gordon & Madden in Rochester, who produced just what he wanted, and these plans were sent to London for adaptation. The Kingsway building was an immediate success, with Burnet (rather than Gordon) widely praised and published for its simple elegance, its lavish fittings and use of materials, and its new business architecture based on utility—the start of "having use determine form rather than vice versa."[5] Fifty years after it opened in October 1911, Kodak House, Kingsway, was still being cited by architects as forward-looking for its time. The interior was described in the November 1911 issue of the *British Journal of Photography*, beginning with "the first floor, where are situated [the reception gallery], the chief executive offices, counting-house, and correspondence departments." This floor ("second" in the United States) "is gained from the street level by a staircase of Greek marble, the walls of the entrance hall and first floor being of Italian statuary marble, decorated with pilasters of blue marble, and presenting, in conjunction with the wrought-iron balustrades and matt-silvered electric light fittings, a most ornate appearance." The layout of this head office (for a staff of three hundred, seven hundred more being at Harrow), wholesale headquarters, and retail store, shows the balance maintained by Eastman between the amateur and professional segments, the emphasis on quality, efficiency, and order, and the concern for the customer. The second floor housed invoicing and dealers' stock departments. The third floor contained a full-size cinematograph theater, plus a developing and printing room for ciné film. Advertising and export departments were up a floor, along with the technical department and a fully fitted darkroom. The fifth floor accommodated an elaborate professional showroom, with stock rooms of professional plates and papers adjoining; a sixth was added above the coping in 1926. The street level contained shipping and receiving departments, and the large and lofty basement stocked immense crates and cases of films, plates, papers, and apparatus from Rochester, which passed through these vaults on the way to European customers. Harrow was not neglected: Eastman supported Simon Haus in starting the Eastman Library there, which held both instructional and recreational books. Even with an ocean between them, foreign managers could not do something so simple as start a library or lunch room without the Eastman approval.

The plan for a fourteen-story office tower that would be the tallest building in Rochester was worked out in 1911 by Eastman and Kodak engineers. The tower replaced the original five-story building and "You press the button, we do the rest" was gone forever. Five local architects or firms—Crandall, Warner, Claude Bragdon, Gordon & Madden, Hutchison & Cutler—were invited to submit drawings for the façade.[6] At the last possible moment, Eastman decided to make the tower sixteen stories. The design by George Hutchison and Howard Cutler featuring a heavy overhanging cornice to block the view of the elevator shaft was chosen, but Eastman was never happy with it. He contacted William Kendall of McKim, Mead & White to "work out some difficulties we need help on." Kendall obliged. William Mead heard of the goings-on and wondered why he had not been contacted sooner. "I decided it would not be politic for the company to ignore local architects," Eastman explained, "so I instituted a competition which resulted in five or six of the principal ones submitting designs." Rather than pit the famous firm against the locals, Eastman had McKim, Mead & White do the interior treatments of the executive offices on the top floor and the connecting corridors from the street to the elevators. The reception area would remain in the Warner/Crandall front building until it was demolished in the 1950s.[7]

The complex continued to grow in a haphazard manner, new buildings joined to old with levels that did not always match. Kodak Office added Building No. 10 in 1924 (situated north of Crandall's 1904 Building on State Street, it is a massive five-story yellow brick structure with twenty-three windows across the front on each floor). After thinking about the cornice on the 1912 office tower for fifteen years, Eastman wrote Edwin Gordon in 1927:

> I have always considered the design of our State Street office building weak and unsatisfactory; also that the heavy overhanging cornice was a structural mistake. Since the development of step-back style in New York City I have wondered whether it could be adapted to our building. Sometime when it comes handy I wish you would speculate on it a little. Not that there is any prospect of our doing anything about it in the near future but I am curious to see how it would look.[8]

Gordon & Kaelber did some speculating on paper, and in 1929 Eastman had another idea: "Have you seen a picture of the tower of the Grand Central

Building in New York? It in general reminds me of the tower in the design for the alteration of our office building but I am inclined to think it is better. Will you please get a photograph of it and compare it with our design and let me know what you think?"[9] The New York Central Building north of Grand Central Terminal (today the Helmsley Building) had just been completed in 1929. Designed by Warren & Wetmore, it culminated in a great pyramidal roof topped by an elaborate cupola—the perfect punctuation mark for the long canyon of sober apartment houses on Park Avenue. Gordon & Kaelber modified their design: Three new floors now culminated in a pyramidal roof topped by a cupola to mask the mechanical systems.

Eastman's office was for a time on the second floor over the entrance in the 1899 Warner-designed two-story building. It was moved to the sixteenth floor when the Kodak Office tower was built in 1912 and to the nineteenth with the addition of 1930. Georgian paneling, a round dining table, Minton china for luncheons, a kitchen, his rolltop desk, and oriental carpets completed a suite facing north and east. On a clear day one can see Lake Ontario ten miles north and those with vivid imaginations say they see Toronto. Alice Whitney held forth from an adjacent desk while a nearby vault contained the sacred letter books. Al Franck, messenger, was once dispatched from here to pick up theater tickets. Returning, Franck decided the floor was too beautiful to step on and was busily leaping from one carpet to the next when he inadvertently performed the splits at the feet of the boss who burst out laughing. "I hope the show tonight is as good," said Eastman.[10]

Eastman's successor on the nineteenth floor, William G. Stuber, would retain all of Eastman's furniture, equipment, and pictures, including photographs of his friends and trips. Stuber's single addition was a picture of Eastman himself, perhaps the large crayon portrait made after the Nahum Luboshez negative made in the London office in 1921, Eastman's own favorite and the stock corporate photograph of the company founder.[11] But when company directors presented that portrait to Eastman for his office, he responded, "That's all right to hang up after I'm dead. I don't think I want to look at it now."[12] The visitor to Eastman's office was invariably struck by the small four-inch by six-inch glossy print of the new campus of MIT on the Charles River, the only tangible evidence of the $20 million Eastman had bestowed on that institution.

Eastman first met the thirtyish Edwin S. Gordon about 1897 when the latter came to the Soule House as J. Foster Warner's assistant to work on the palm house and greenhouses. Gordon's mother had wanted him to pursue an artistic career and began his training as soon as he was old enough to hold a pencil. She died when Gordon was ten but he had already decided to be an architect. Gordon's father thought the profession so overcrowded that he persuaded his son at fifteen, after a year at the Rochester Free Academy, to take a factory job as an assistant janitor. When Gordon was eighteen his father relented and secured him a job as unpaid office boy in an architectural firm. In 1891 Gordon formed his own firm with two contemporaries, Claude Bragdon and William Orchard.

Bragdon, a year older than Gordon, was born in Oberlin, Ohio, where his father was "an excellent and forceful [newspaper] writer, but a poor businessman." He, too, drew prolifically, "published" a "magazine" at age eight, and built a model theater for the plays his sister "produced." Both his sister and his mother considered him a genius and he would come to agree. He graduated from high school in Oswego, New York, as class valedictorian in 1884, the year the family moved to Rochester (their eighth move in twenty-two years). Bragdon, too, started in a nonpaying position in an architectural office but disliked his employer's work and the long periods of inactivity so began moonlighting as a cartoonist. He was soon discharged for mocking leading citizen Daniel W. Powers' art collection. Bragdon drifted in and out of jobs until he hit his stride as chief draftsman for architects Charles and Harvey Ellis. Put in charge of the construction of the Stein-Bloch building and knowing nothing of construction techniques, he located an engineer who did. When Ellis failed to pay Bragdon for several weeks, he moved on to New York and then to Buffalo for two years, working as a draftsman. He dabbled in theosophy, Eastern religions, and the occult, returning to Rochester in 1890 to find "a happy city, predominantly youthful."[13]

Since both Gordon and Bragdon were immensely talented with the pencil, the small firm of Gordon, Bragdon and Orchard subsisted by entering competitions—for the Carnegie Library in Pittsburgh, Copley Square in Boston, a courthouse for Baltimore—reaping prize money but never a major commission. They won $2,000 for a city hall design for New York City, but had to sue to collect it. The contrast between the partners during the four years of the firm's existence (1891–95) is instructive. Bragdon called it his "purple cow period . . . a time when life did not make sense and nothing seemed important." Besides the architectural competitions, he designed advertising posters for *Harper's*, end papers for publishers, and bookplates for friends, and wrote articles for architectural journals. With Harvey Ellis he organized the Rochester Society for the Arts and Crafts. His naive exuberance annoyed professionals, but Bragdon was on his way to becoming "The Upstate Leonardo."

Gordon, having married at twenty-one, was more serious and focused. To make ends meet he taught classes in drawing at the Mechanics Institute four evenings a week. He watched Eastman's photographic business grow and, according to Bragdon's autobiography, Gordon and his wife subsisted happily all one winter on cold potatoes secure in the anticipation that he would one day garner all the Kodak King's architectural commissions. When the partnership broke up so that Bragdon could have a *Wanderjahr* in Europe, Gordon, who knew as little about construction as Bragdon did, "soon realized that my need was a better knowledge of construction," as he puts it in his modest, unpublished, three-page autobiography. So he approached the autocratic J. Foster Warner, whom Gordon describes as "an architect of great ability, whose knowledge of planning and construction is exceptional," and spent the next seven years as Warner's draftsman. This gave him "an unusual training in the fundamentals of the architectural profession . . . stressing the importance of a practical and workable plan as a basis for all things in connection with a good building." This was Eastman's credo too. In 1902 Gordon and William Madden, another employee, asked Warner for partnerships; Warner agreed to make Gordon a partner but not his friend, so both left and the firm of Gordon & Madden was born. It lasted until 1918 when Madden retired; before that, in 1911, the firm took on William G. Kaelber, born in 1886, who became Gordon's partner in 1918. In 1908 Gordon had his first Eastman commission—for the Horn Marsh Gun Club ("Norfolk bungalow," Gordon called it), the Virginia "duck shooting proposition" of Eastman, James Sibley Watson, and the Bonbright brothers.

Eastman immediately plunged into planning every detail of Horn Marsh—from the gun room to the caretaker's sitting room to the fly screens. He reversed Gordon's floor plan and instructed him to keep the entrances of both the kitchen and furnace cellars "in the court formed by the main building and kitchen extension. The windmill should also be shown on the plan in this court."[14] The other partners were indifferent to these details; a rough shooting box was all they wanted. Once the bungalow was built, Eastman lost interest; if he visited Horn Point once during the year, that was a lot. It was not nearly as interesting as Oak Lodge, where there were cow barns, silos, saw mills, cottages, schools, and offices to be built, alfalfa and clover to be planted, quail and partridges and cows and dogs to be imported, tenants to be educated, medicated, and launched. Eastman had Gordon produce the plans for the North Carolina buildings. Small and modest, only slightly more than log cabins and nary a drop of paint on any of them, they marked the beginning of Gordon's practice, one that would grow with Eastman business until between the World Wars it was the largest and busiest firm in town.

Another Eastman-inspired commission for Gordon in 1908 was a major addition to City Hospital, soon to be renamed Rochester General.[15] Eastman gave the money to build it and the architects, Gordon & Madden, wrote thanking him for the honor of designing it. The firm became architects for the Rochester city schools and Gordon achieved national recognition for his one-story schoolhouse built around a courtyard-playground that allowed natural light to enter two sides of every classroom—a concept that was widely copied, particularly in California. In 1915 Eastman had two new projects gearing up: the Rochester Dental Dispensary and the new Rochester Chamber of Commerce building. Gordon & Madden were named architects of the dispensary and so pleased Eastman with their practical, step-saving, U-shaped plans and inspired use of skylights that allowed the second-story operatory to be flooded with natural light, that Eastman requested these plans be followed when the five European dispensaries were built fifteen to twenty years later.

Architects for the Chamber of Commerce were Foster & Gade of New York City and Claude Bragdon of Rochester. John Gade was son-in-law to Hiram Watson Sibley, businessman and heir to the Western Union fortune. Gade maintained a Rochester as well as a New York office. In 1913 his firm designed the University of Rochester's Memorial Art Gallery for Gade's wife's aunt, Emily Sibley Watson; the design was almost an exact copy of Charles Follem McKim's design for the J. Pierpont Morgan Library in New York. Bragdon was the local supervising architect for the art gallery, but had no input into the design. Rush Rhees recommended the Gade–Bragdon team to Eastman. Perhaps because he was already thinking of building a large music hall for Rochester and wanted to compare architects, Eastman acquiesced in the choice of Bragdon, then at the height of his reputation, and the New York firm. But Gade was more businessman than architect, as even the large Watson-Sibley clan admitted, and indeed would eventually leave architecture for the diplomatic service.[16] And Gordon had prepared sketches for the Chamber, whether at Eastman's request or on his own, which he sent Eastman with the note that "the Chamber is welcome to them. I also am taking the liberty of offering a few suggestions." Eastman green-penciled some of Gordon's suggestions including the location of the kitchen and, "on the exterior, we suggested an adaptation of the Classic which would recall the colonnades and porticos a type of colonial residence peculiar to this locality. Personally, I would prefer a concrete structure as the most modern construction and I know it can be made architecturally beautiful."[17]

Gordon had one run-in with his client and patron in regard to the dispensary. While Eastman was out of town, the architect highlighted the carved ceiling of the portico in bright colors, the better, Gordon thought, to enhance the depictions of animals in the floor tiles. When Eastman saw it, the color rose to his cheeks and he shouted abruptly, "Gordon, you know I don't like vivid colors!" The ceiling was repainted white and never mentioned again. What Gordon did not know was that Eastman was simultaneously disagreeing with Bragdon over the painting of the Chamber ceiling in color.[18]

Gordon and his partner Will Kaelber got along with Eastman by going along, a facility that both Bragdon and Warner lacked. Whereas Warner advised strongly against using creosoted blocks for the basement of Eastman House, and got his way, Kaelber was skeptical about Eastman's cutting his house in two but agreed, once the deed was done, that the proportions were much better. Warner and Eastman got along well enough on the Eastman

Cottage for the Rochester Orphan Asylum in 1906, probably because both were working toward a common cause, but he never received another Eastman-related commission until the Rochester Savings Bank built its Franklin Street branch in 1924. That lavish and jewel-like temple to commerce was finished in 1928, a year before the stock market crash wreaked its fury on the economy. Warner was associated again with McKim, Mead & White whom Eastman first brought to Rochester in 1902, and Ezra Winter, an Eastman protégé who did interior paintings, mosaics, ceilings, and decorations for the bank and Eastman Theatre and School of Music. Although Eastman declined to be a member of the building committee, his clout with his old bank of prephotography days was tremendous. As Edward Harris, chairman of the bank's board, wrote McKim, Mead & White in 1924: "Mr. George Eastman, who is not a member of the building committee, has made a suggestion that . . . Mr. Warner, who is more readily available, . . . make rough sketches for study and criticism which will be submitted to you for your suggestions."[19]

Again the long hand of Eastman was reaching out and the famous New York architects were being asked to follow his unusual procedures in which they were merely the "decorators." Only in Rochester did an obscure local architect get first crack at the plans with McKim, Mead & White asked merely to make "suggestions." In the case of the bank, Eastman silently approved of the selection of Warner, so Warner's claim of an irreparable break with Eastman over the basement floor was exaggerated. Eastman *did* break with his architects, beginning with Charles Crandall who did not get to design the East Avenue mansion even though he had prepared all earlier plans and models. "Your office is too small," said Eastman matter-of-factly to "Friend Charlie," while admitting he was "sorry for old time's sake."[20]

The versatile Bragdon, besides being an architect and accomplished draftsman, was the designer of interiors, furniture, stage sets, and light shows; editor of Louis Sullivan's *Kindergarten Chats*; an articulate raconteur and popular lecturer; exponent of mystical yet mathematical theories of light, decoration, architecture, and the "fourth dimension"; theosophist and translator of Ouspensky; prolific writer of books and magazine articles dealing with his own theories on all of these; and self-proclaimed genius. "I did not *choose* to enter the profession of architecture," the prodigy records, "but found myself in it without effort. I was a 'natural.'" The Upstate Leonardo became a cult figure in his own time; even today, the designation "Bragdon-designed" can sell a house or object when other merits are not apparent. Any melding of this megalomaniac and mystical personality with that of George Eastman was doomed from the start, as Bragdon himself acknowledged. "Profoundly dissimilar in character and outlook," he wrote, "it was inevitable that Eastman and I should break with one another, though I had for him the greatest liking and respect."[21]

Bragdon's years as an architect seem marked with a certain difficulty in making a living but unlike Gordon, who was satisfied with scraps and leavings because he was convinced that one day Eastman's architectural business would be his, Bragdon was less patient. Indeed, he felt deeply an estrangement from Eastman, of the sensitive artist poised against the one-dimensional businessman. Possibly from the lack of significant public commissions through several more partnerships, Bragdon turned to domestic architecture. His big chance came in 1908, when he won the competition for the New York Central Station in Rochester. The grand and spacious station, which opened to great fanfare in 1910, drew upon the machine age and specifically the locomotive for its ornamental features. It remained his masterpiece, embodying his aesthetic theories that "the appeal of any work of art consists in the perfection with which it not only obeys, but publishes and proclaims certain laws . . . musical, numerical, geometrical."[22] Eastman and Bragdon came to know one another in 1906, when both served on a citizens' committee to "select from the designs submitted, the one most suitable" for public monuments honoring the Grand Army of the Republic.[23] They became better acquainted in 1913 after Bragdon and Warner were chosen local architects for the new YMCA building, for which Eastman was the principal donor. Bragdon's tasks were designing the auditorium and the exterior elevations.[24] As he noted in a letter to his wife: "I am learning a great deal by this experiment. I believe it's to prepare me for a greater problem—perhaps a music hall for Geo Eastman! He'll surely build one, and I think he'll give me the job."[25] When Bragdon was chosen for the Chamber commission he was absolutely intoxicated with the possibilities of the Eastman connection: "I'm going to convince Eastman that I'm THE man in this job. Gade saw me as a tame cat on the art gallery and Jackson saw me as a tame cat on the YMCA. I'm a lion when roused and I'm roused. They are eliminated so far as design is concerned and they know it. Me and George."[26]

The outstanding feature of the building was the lofty wood-paneled Grand Assembly Hall on the third story, "wherein a dinner for a thousand people could be served." Bragdon wanted to finish it in the manner of the Doge's Palace in Venice: "the walls panelled, without constructed or applied architecture, with decoration of colour and gold in the ceilings and practically nowhere else."[27] He knew all along that he was battling uphill in trying to introduce so much applied ornament. Indeed, Eastman insisted it be left out of the contract and discussed when the room was otherwise finished. Bragdon was knowingly playing cat and mouse: "I am not willing to raise the issue now, but I will raise it later when I am better prepared and better fortified. In this game I have now the advantage and mean to keep it."[28]

For the next year all went smoothly for the architect. He had the friendship and backing of architect and former mayor, James Goold Cutler, now president of the Chamber of Commerce: "J. G. . . . did reach [Eastman] by telephone and guardedly suggested that in matters aesthetic I was a safer guide than Gade." He had Eastman's attention: "My tomorrow's interview with Eastman is likely to be important. There is the change in the Assembly Hall to talk over, the interiors, and the business arrangement between him and us. Don't fear but that I shall stick for all rights and privileges. I need everything I can get." Eastman had put off a decision on the ceiling but was fair in the matter of Bragdon's compensation and even generous in his praise: "Eastman is all right—he's pleased with everything—I can see that. . . . He told JG that he likes it—particularly the recessing of the front." He liked Bragdon's revised sketches for the assembly hall too.[29]

"I've had a 'terrific' Monday, but triumphant," Bragdon wrote his wife. "There's no doubt in my mind but that I'm in right with Eastman. . . . Gade's tactics are perfectly futile and foolish—They all know who furnishes the brains for this problem and if anything vital comes up they always send for me."[30] When the plaster ceiling was "in the white," Eastman and Bragdon met to discuss its further treatment. As the architect recalled in the autobiography he wrote in 1938, he "reminded Eastman of our former conversation . . . and told him it was now time to let the contract for the decoration. 'How much will it cost?' was his first question. I told him that it would probably cost from five thousand dollars to twenty thousand, the difference depending upon the eminence of the artistic talent employed. He ruminated for some time. 'I could give an ambulance to France for five thousand dollars. I like the ceiling just the way it is—I think I'll leave it that way,' he finally said." "I was dumbfounded," Bragdon records, "particularly as I knew how impossible it would be to make him understand the way I felt." The architect protested that had he known he would have designed the whole room a different way; as it stood now "colour is now the only thing which will prevent it from looking meagre and bare." But as with Gordon's portico ceiling for the dental dispensary, Eastman was opposed to color. His exit line hit Bragdon's "supersensitive ear" as "little short of blasphemous": "'You architects are full of expensive notions; engineering is all there is to architecture anyway.'"[31]

As the Chamber project was winding down, Lewis P. Ross, Eastman's neighbor to the west, died, leaving his house jointly to the University of Rochester and to his sister, Helen J. Clark, wife of George Clark, son of Brackett Clark and an original Kodak stockholder (after Eastman's death, the *largest* Kodak stockholder). Eastman began the complex negotiations to convince both parties to sell and in 1916 bought the property for $45,000. He demolished the house and outbuildings and asked Bragdon to design a garden. The bay window of Eastman's much-used sitting room (the former billiard room) had always been close to the Ross property line and acquisition of the property gave him the chance to create an intimate garden that could be viewed from that window and also from the porte cochere. Eastman's own

bedroom suite overlooked that property as well; when the house was originally sited by Warner and Alling De Forest in 1902, he had them place the
major gardens where his mother could see them from her bedroom and
sitting room windows. Now he was to have a garden of his own and in the
1920s he would spend much time in his new Sunken Garden.

Bragdon was convinced that he was selected because Eastman suffered
from a success complex. As the architect explains in his autobiography: "In
his *Fault of Angels,* Paul Horgan puts this highly characteristic speech in the
mouth of the character drawn evidently from Eastman: 'I am interested only
in success.' This perhaps accounts for his choice of me, for by that time I was
a successful architect."[32] A more likely interpretation is that Eastman was
always looking for a change, for something new, whether it be in housekeepers, paintings, camera models, automobile models, furniture location,
interior designers, or architects. Yet his architects all felt there had to be a
reason for their selection, and a smoking gun if they did not get the next job.

Nevertheless, Bragdon was eager to prove himself capable of tackling the
big music school job that was speculated about in Rochester circles. In addition to a sunken garden, Eastman wanted a loggia on the far property line
that would serve as sight barrier to the next house along East Avenue.[33] He
also asked Bragdon to design a chicken house, peony garden, laundry drying area, and four new greenhouses for the Ross property. "George was in
this morning," Bragdon wrote his wife. "He found something he liked in the
Lutyens book and we had quite a visit. I showed him photos of sound and
light and he seemed interested. I'm going out to his house tomorrow morning."[34] Eugenie Bragdon would have understood Claude's several trains of
thought. Bragdon was not a landscape architect: While he had produced
plot plans for certain of his more modest dwellings, Alling De Forest usually
designed the gardens accompanying a Bragdon house. And indeed Bragdon's West Garden is more static and less interesting than De Forest's dynamic crisscrossing of paths leading to a sunken oval lily pool in the East Garden.
In 1916 Bragdon must have been surprised to find himself asked to design a
garden to replace a massive East Avenue "stone dowager" and complement
the most baronial mansion of all. He met the challenge by pulling out books
in his library. On his visit to Bragdon's office, Eastman was drawn to the
gardens of Hestercombe, a landscape layout of Sir Edwin Lutyens (1869–
1944), fashionable and highly original British architect with classical lean-
ings. Young Lutyens' gardens were designed in collaboration with middle-
aged Gertrude Jekyll and the pair produced perhaps the epitome in the
English landscape tradition.[35] Bragdon's second reference was to his own
sound and light productions; Eastman eventually turned him and others
with similar schemes down flat. Bragdon was scandalized and asked Eastman
how he could give millions to music, about which he knew little, and nothing
to an art of light, about which he knew a great deal. When Eastman replied

with a version of his famous dictum about what you do in your leisure time determines who you are, Bragdon interpreted that as meaning that "his benefactions for the promotion of music were in the nature of insurance against industrial unrest."[36] Bragdon is not alone in interpreting Eastman's philanthropies as a hedge against the revolt of the masses yet there is little in the day-to-day evolution of his music plans for Rochester to support this cynical view. What Bragdon did not know was that Eastman was being bombarded regularly by begging letters from Mary Hallock Greenewalt, a relative of the duPonts of Delaware, who claimed to have invented color music and sound and light shows herself (and that Bragdon had stolen the idea, another instance of an idea being in the air and several "inventors" appearing on the scene simultaneously).[37]

Bragdon went to work adapting Hestercombe to the West Garden of 900 East Avenue: Lutyens' diagonal axis was squared so that the paths and sight lines would start at the porte cochere and bay window of the sitting room and terminate at the west boundary of the Ross property, where Bragdon had designed a triple-arched loggia based on the orangerie at Hestercombe. (As is evident from his drawings, in the redesign from orangerie to loggia, the architect was able to incorporate many of his pet theories of geometrical proportions that he expounded so completely in the New York Central Station.) To the insult of the Chamber ceiling was now added the injury of potatoes in the garden. After the garden was finished, its architect was deeply offended to hear secondhand that his client had plowed up his new garden. Eugenie, he records, "when she learned that Eastman had planted potatoes, purely as a war-time gesture, in the sunken garden I had designed for him, said: 'Claude, if we starve, you shall never work for that man again.'"[38] What Eastman recorded was: "I am plowing up my lawn and planting all the open space and also the open space on the Ross place to potatoes and onions. I made up my mind that this year my gardeners could be better employed in hoeing potatoes than in cutting grass."[39]

But the myth that the garden rather than the lawns and open spaces were plowed up persisted, in part because Bragdon's autobiography was published while Eastman's letters were not. In the 1980s Eastman House released the statement that "the sunken garden . . . was torn up by Eastman in 1918 and replanted with a victory garden," despite the evidence of correspondence, photographs, and De Forest's 1921 survey plan that none of Bragdon's design features were touched until after Eastman's death. The combination of ceiling and potatoes has given rise to the further myth that Bragdon left Rochester and architecture forever in 1922 because of Eastman's vindictiveness. While it is true, as one commentator notes, that "Bragdon's practice was diminished after his quarrel with George Eastman,"[40] the architect himself seems to have made no such accusations until fifteen years later. A 1918 letter suggests a different reason for his moving on to New York

City and a new career in the theater as a scenic designer: "The war has practically put an end to my architectural practice, . . . but fortunately I have a few thousand dollars still coming to me on the Chamber. . . . Besides, . . . it is the rich people who should do the worrying. It is the greatest good fortune, in these days not to be caught in the debacle of the Aristocracy. I hear the rattle of the tumbrils."[41] In 1937 Bragdon confided "the darker side to the Eastman story" in a letter claiming that Eastman literally drove him out of Rochester. The architect went on to claim that he had always been the architect of the Gensee Valley Club and that Eastman, as president, had offered the club $50,000 not to hire Bragdon. Bragdon was not willing to have this story recorded in 1940 when Frank Lovejoy and Oscar Solbert were gathering material for a new biography of Eastman that would "humanize" him. "All of the anecdotes and reminiscences of mine in regard to him which I care to have appear in print are contained in my autobiography," Bragdon wrote Lovejoy. Whether Eastman actually did pay off the Genesee Valley Club to deny Bragdon the commission cannot be verified. Building committee and board minutes show Bragdon never did any work for the club during this time span and that Eastman never contributed $50,000 to any building drive.[42]

"What has happened in the matter of the School of Music?" inquired architect Burt Fenner of his former colleagues, Gordon & Kaelber, on 1 July 1919. "We are all much interested in knowing whether it is going ahead." Fenner was still with the nationally prominent firm of McKim, Mead & White, whose man on the job he had been during the construction of Eastman House, and he kept in chatty touch with his Rochester acquaintances in hopes that the famous New York firm would land another Eastman project. By 1919 William Rutherford Mead had retired to Maine, where he remained in consultation with his firm, the principals of which now included William Mitchell Kendall and Lawrence Grant ("Larry") White, Stanford's son. Fenner soon learned to his dismay that "Mr. Eastman with Ed Gordon and Will Kaelber . . . has been at work . . . over plans. They have visited theaters and music halls all the way from Boston to the Mississippi River," Fenner wrote to senior sage Mead, "and have gotten all the practical details of the auditorium construction worked out to the last inch, but the result is an abominable plan which is architecturally impossible. If they had only gotten us into it at the start," Fenner sniffed, "I am sure we could have saved the situation. Even now Kendall and I are both satisfied that we can revise the plan so as to make it architecturally possible and at the same time meet all the practical requirements."[43]

Having determined that the modest Italianate house of the DKG Institute of Musical Art, which Eastman purchased in 1918 and presented to the

University of Rochester, was not suitable for his grand plans for music in
Rochester and that he did not want to wait until his own demise turned his
mansion into a music school and thus miss the fun of planning and building,
Eastman had gone looking for suitable lots. By the summer of 1919 he had
selected a site—the most attractive one available—several blocks east of the
business district on Main Street and a half-mile west of the university campus. Best of all, it was on a trolley line. Coincidentally, the area was once a
grove of trees near which Eastman had climbed George Selden's attic stairs
for lessons in wet-plate photography. Surveying the sylvan scene in the
1870s, the bank clerk had pronounced it worthy of a painter's palette; forty
years later the grove was nearly gone and in its place, spanning Main Street,
stood Gibbs, Swan, and Grove streets as a pleasant residential neighborhood
of frame houses and an apartment building. Buying up the houses was easy
but the owner of the apartments demanded what Eastman considered an
exorbitant price, and so, refusing to pay the "baksheesh," he had Kaelber
redraw the plans for the large auditorium so that it fit the remaining trapezoidal plot.

Most important was positioning the grand entrance on the very corner of
the plot, which was not a right but an oblique angle. Eastman saw this wide
sweep as ideal for a marquee and entrance to be seen by both street car riders
on Main Street and motorists there and on Grove and Gibbs streets. But the
positioning automatically skewed "the axis of the auditorium at an angle
which is not a right angle to the most important facade" and this is what so
bothered McKim, Mead & White. "Architecturally it is extremely difficult to
obtain a satisfactory treatment of a facade which bends around a corner,"
they grumbled.[44] They were classicists, of course, and thought in terms of
symmetry, not of form following function, nor as the layman Eastman did
of attracting the largest crowds, nor as modernists such as I. M. Pei would, of
fitting the building to its trapezoidal lot. Furthermore, they did not like the
elliptical corner lobby with its low ceiling that appeared on the Eastman–
Kaelber plans and felt that a 3,500-seat auditorium was much too large for
Rochester. They foresaw crowds being throttled and disoriented as they
entered and left the auditorium, particularly in the area behind the orchestra seats.

The delay in contacting the New York firm was calculated. "They are the
best *decorators* in the country," Eastman once explained cavalierly, "but I
wouldn't let them *near* the plans."[45] Why? "A floor plan is an engineering
proposition, and must take precedent over the architecture in any commercial scheme." Thus, as Eastman told Larry White, "It is a set policy in all my
building operations to work out the plans myself with all its details before
calling in an architect." White, who had inherited his father's facile sketching
talents and interest in classical detail, had never heard of such a policy. The
Eastman Theatre and School of Music was to have been the first major

project for which he would be chief designer and he was anxious to salvage it
if he could. For his part, Eastman wanted White and his colleagues primarily
to insure that "a house of this size would not be 'barney' in character," as well
as "to make the entrance foyer gay, bright, and beautiful," the second balcony "warm and rich in color, and beautiful in proportion and details . . . and
in every respect just as attractive a place to sit and safe to walk in as the main
floor," and to plan for "indirect lighting throughout so people can walk in
without stumbling." It was not the kind of secondary decorative assignment
the prestigious firm was accustomed to tackling. Indeed they "felt justified in
asking a substantial sum for our services. I do not believe anybody can
criticize a professional fee of $15,000," Fenner confided. "If we can bring
some architectural order out of the present chaotic plan, that service alone
will be worth all that Mr. Eastman will pay for it." But Eastman decided
$12,000 was what decorating skills were worth. "The Eastman matter is a
troublesome one," Fenner reported to Mead. "With the plan Kaelber has
developed it will be exceedingly difficult to get adequate architectural treatment for the Court Auditorium and its approaches. We submitted an alternate plan. . . . Mr. Eastman was skeptical in the extreme and said he was
unwilling to sacrifice anything whatever to architecture either as to seating
capacity or service arrangements. . . . He said he would build a perfectly
plain brick barn if he felt he could thereby bring music to the largest number."[46]

As with the Kodak camera, the "largest" was also the magic number to
Eastman. The New York architects, he felt, were engaging in elitist thinking;
their view was "the old-fashioned one that the chief effort should be to please
the occupants of the best seats," Eastman told Frank Babbott. "Of course, it is
this class who support concerts and operas but they are not the ones I am
after in my scheme." Worst of all, the McKim, Mead & White plan "used the
very corner of the plot, which is one of the most important in the city, for
service stairs and elevator. . . . We had a mighty nice interview but I suppose
right down in their hearts Messrs. Kendall and White think I am a pretty
headstrong proposition and I think they are letting their art interfere with
utility."

"Like most laymen he regards architecture merely as applied decoration," Fenner complained to Mead. "He says that if we admit the possibility of
his plan . . . we can design a satisfactory auditorium, chamber music hall,
entrances, and a good exterior. All of which we admit we can do. He fails to
see the point when we contend that still the building will be architecturally
poor."

"He did make one important concession," Fenner wrote. Because East-
man was just leaving for a six-week trip to the Rocky Mountains, McKim,
Mead & White were allowed that time to whip their proposition into order.
Meanwhile, Fenner would go back to the man who originally introduced

Eastman and William Mead. "I shall try to see Mr. Babbott and . . . ask him
to advise. Kendall, Richardson, and I all feel that rather than accept the plan
as it stands and the responsibility for it which would certainly be placed upon
us by the public, we would withdraw from the work." In the allotted time,
mid-August to October, the New York architects prepared a plan "which,"
they wrote, "equals yours but is structurally more direct and straightforward." Eastman did not agree and would hear nothing about decreasing the
number of seats or giving up "the spacious stairways and ramp from the
mezzanine to the second balcony." He conveyed his objections in a letter that
ran for several pages.

> I could not help feeling when you left me yesterday afternoon that you
> did not realize what you were up against in endeavoring to change the
> floor plan. . . . It may be that 3,500 seating capacity is a little ahead of its
> time. . . . The seats are expected to yield $150 per annum. If the capaci-
> ty is reduced only 200 the receipts would be reduced $30,000. Cap-
> italized this would mean $600,000. . . . If it turns out we are unable to
> fill the house . . . rather than cut it out I would erect a semi-permanent
> curtain to cut off the upper third or half of the gallery. I cannot think
> that the . . . axis of the auditorium is a matter that will ever be noticed
> by the public. . . . I, myself, much prefer the elliptical lobby to the
> circular one.[47]

"You may think we have gone too far in offering to do more work and then
if he does not like it, offer to retire and waive all claims to reimbursement,"
Fenner reported to Mead, "but Mr. Eastman took the position . . . that there
had been a perfectly distinct understanding . . . that we were to go
ahead . . . unless we could devise a plan which contained every single detail
of arrangement which his plan showed. He felt we had failed to do so. . . .
They think our plan is impossible from an operating point of view. . . . Mr.
Eastman's attitude was and still is perfectly courteous and friendly. . . . We
are therefore going ahead . . . but without much hope. . . . Eastman is such
a big factor in Rochester that people do not argue with him but accept what
he says as law. I doubt whether his own friends dare to advise him honestly
when they think he has made a mistake and if we were to decline further
association with his work, I think it would be a very great surprise to him and
possibly make him reconsider."[48] Instead, it was the New York architects
who were in for the surprise. Eastman impassively listened to their arguments, watched them walk off the job, had them return their drawings, then
"summoned" William G. Kaelber, and, at this crisis moment, plunged into
another enormous undertaking: the cutting in half of his four-story concrete and steel home in order to enlarge the conservatory by nine feet four
inches. He then turned to another matter that had long occupied his attention: the swift and orderly removal of every diseased tonsil in Rochester.

Only after the successful completion of the Great Housecutting Caper and the Great Tonsillectomy Marathon did he return to his long-range projects of establishing a first-rate music school and a first-rate medical school in Rochester.

Whenever Eastman was really worried about something, he invented another complex situation on which to expend his energies. In 1898, while anxiously awaiting the London decision over his international expansion plans, he discovered a batch of glass plates on which the emulsion had gone bad. Most business heads would have delegated the recalling of the defective plates. Not Eastman. He had to chase down every single piece of glass himself, even if it was after midnight before he found the offending piece. Then in 1913, after the government began its all-out trust-busting suit and Judge Hazel held that Kodak had infringed the Goodwin patent, Eastman threw his mammoth New Year's party for nine hundred people and decided to crack down on the rubber band situation: "My dear Crouch," he wrote the office manager, "The rubber bands that are mostly used in this institution are very bad. I think that a proper cooperation between the purchasing department and the laboratory would get us a rubber band, perhaps of a color peculiar to ourselves, which could be relied upon." Eastman joined in the search by writing George Dryden to see if a man who manufactured tires could not also come up with a better rubber band. So it is not surprising that while waiting until the New York architects saw the error of their ways, he decided to correct what he considered the major blemish of his house, the square conservatory.

Charlie Crandall had been instructed to design a twenty-five-foot by thirty-foot conservatory in the house of 1894 that was never built. When Warner put a thirty-foot by thirty-foot two-story conservatory in the house of 1902 that was built, Eastman was skeptical. For seventeen years he brooded about this tall square room that had an entirely different feeling of space than the oblong room that he had always envisioned. When he needed a project to take his mind off the impasse, he summoned William G. Kaelber, his current architect, to draw plans for enlarging the room to thirty feet by forty feet without in any way reducing the size of the adjacent rooms or changing the lines of the exterior. That was a daunting challenge. The only way this could be accomplished, Kaelber advised, was to cut the house cleanly in two, through concrete and steel, from cellar floor through roof slab, and move the entire rear half of the house back ten feet. All right, Eastman said, do it. Then he decreed that he must be able to use the house while the work was being accomplished although dinner might be served in the hall during the time that the dining room was inaccessible. Kaelber designed flexible tubes that could carry heat, electricity, and water from one half of the severed house to the other. Although the architect told Eastman that he was "foolish to conduct such an expensive operation to get only nine feet of extra space," when the deed had been done, he admitted to Eastman that he had received a lesson in architectural proportion. Kaelber's partner, Ed Gordon, was so impressed with the "education and pleasure" value of the project, that he declined to send a bill for his services.[49]

One bonus of the enlarged conservatory, and perhaps another reason for doing it, was a new organ and more space for Eastman's musicale guests. "The old organ has been rebuilt and some additions made, which are located in the room that was Mother's over the dining room," he explained to Babbott, while inviting his old friend to come up to hear Archer Gibson, famous New York organist, play that new organ. "The main change in the organ is to give it more stops with the heavy rolling cathedral tones. I am going to make quite a feature of the music this season."[50] The other bonus was a chance to redo the conservatory furnishings. Francis Bacon had been after Eastman for years to get rid of his old wicker furniture and what everyone but Eastman considered an execrable hanging basket planter cum chandelier with brown silk fringe, ivy dripping over the edge. But Eastman loved that fixture; it hung directly over his breakfast table to provide the scientific lighting he so desired but retracted when the conservatory was set up for other purposes. He gave the decorator commission to Elizabeth Averell Rogerson of Arden Studios, New York, and kept the fixture.

McKim, Mead & White, having reduced their fees "below what we think our services are worth," returned in 1920 at the urging of Frank Babbott to finish the limestone façade and interior decorations of the Eastman Theatre and School of Music. The resumption of the project coincided with Eastman's return from a three-week visit to Japan. As a condition of their return, Eastman issued a directive that all publicity was to state that McKim, Mead & White were "not responsible for the plans."

The name of the complex was not yet settled, however. "What would you think," Eastman asked Rush Rhees, president of the University of Rochester in 1921, "of calling the school the Academy of Music and this [music] hall the Academy of Motion Pictures, that title to go on the frieze over the portico, the advertising name for motion picture purposes to be Academy Theatre?" During construction, the hoarding exhibited these names. But Rhees and the university trustees saw advertising purposes better served by "Eastman Theatre." Once the donor, who had always maintained that the only thing he wanted to see his name on was the company he founded, was convinced of the financial soundness of their notion, he acquiesced. Building strikes delayed construction so the school opened its temporary doors to students on 14 September 1921 amid the clatter of riveting and hammering. The theater was only a steel frame and classes were held on the third and fourth floors of the school, the only finished areas.

The Beaux Arts-trained Lawrence Grant White pleased everyone with his Palladian façade, although a national magazine dismissed the effort cavalierly with "A $17-million school of music is . . . somewhat grandiose for a town of Rochester's size."

"The dignity of a public institution is emphasized rather than the gaiety of a theatre," reported *The American Architect* of 23 February 1923 in an article Eastman liked well enough to order several dozen copies to distribute to his friends; the article described the building as follows: "An order of Ionic pilasters, broken at the two entrances by engaged columns of Vermont marble [the color, by a curious coincidence, known as "Eastman green"] serves to give unity to the main facade." Topping the façade was the inscription, crafted by Rhees but expressing Eastman's objective: "For the enrichment of community life." Very little escaped Eastman's attention. Of A. W. Hopeman, general contractor, he inquired, "Would it not be well to have some extra tile laid on the flat roof so that they can weather in case they are needed for repairs. If we are to put in a few spic and span new tiles some day . . . it would ruin the beauty of the roof." And when Babbott suggested that Eastman have his portrait painted for the lobby, Eastman had his own suggestion: "Would it not satisfy your portrait aspirations if I should be sculpt'd heroic size for one of the figures on the roof, with a camera in one hand and a horn in the other?" Inside, the effect of the oval lobby, which the New York architects deplored but agreed to decorate, and the other public rooms to which they added their inimitable touch was akin to the decor of an ocean liner. Twelve *Psyche and Cupid* panels celebrating that ancient Greek myth were printed in fifty shades of gray for the lobby and mezzanine. Based on drawings by Jacques-Louis David, the woodblocks were commissioned by Napoleon and first cut and printed in 1814 by Lafitte. Reprinted only once, in 1923 at the behest of classicist Lawrence Grant White, the blocks have since been dispersed past recovery.[51] Francis Bacon, on his own now instead of head designer for the Davenport Company as he had been when Eastman first hired him in 1905, designed the furniture and furnishings.

From a gilded sunburst in the coffered, domed ceiling was hung one of the largest chandeliers in existence. It weighs two-and-one-half tons, and is fourteen feet in diameter and thirty-five feet tall. It consists of 585 lamps, 20,000 pieces of glass and crystal from Europe held by steel cables capable of supporting 10,000 tons (after Lon Chaney's *Phantom of the Opera* came out in the 1920s with its famous scene of a chandelier crashing down on an opera audience, a second chain, heavy and conspicuous, was added to dispel the fears of moviegoers).[52]

Larry White had fun with his own special "problem in architectural astronomy." "On the ceiling is an annular band decoration in which the signs of the Zodiac occur in twelve circular panels," White wrote to Robert Burnside Potter, astronomical expert. "I feel sure that some captious scientist will remark that they are not properly oriented as was the case in the ceiling of the waiting room of Grand Central Terminal. Assuming a person is lying on his back and looking up at the ceiling, on what compass bearings would Aries appear and should Taurus be to the right or left of it?"[53] *Interlude*, a jewel-like painting by Maxfield Parrish, was purchased for the landing of the stairs leading to the loges and Eastman declared it a "peacherina." Also in the mezzanine was a "beautiful allegorical painting of the Renaissance period formerly in a well known collection."[54] Eastman bought it from Stanford White's estate through his son. Eight murals were commissioned of Barry Faulkner and Ezra Winter for the side walls beginning at the level of the loge. Painted in the full flush of the romanticism of the period, Faulkner's murals on the right represent *Religious, Hunting, Pastoral,* and *Dramatic Music* while Winter's on the left represent *Festival, Lyric, Martial,* and *Sylvan Music,* all posed against Italian landscapes. Winter immortalized his friends, including architect Will Kaelber on horseback, as models for the paintings. The murals also occasioned a row between the Rochester and New York architects on a basic level: design versus acoustics.

In his new design White wanted to raise the theater ceiling and standardize the coffers. "Unless it will really be a great improvement," Will Kaelber wrote, "we . . . are informed by Dr. [Floyd R.] Watson, the acoustical expert [from Urbana, Illinois], that this is the ideal ceiling height from the standpoint of acoustics. . . . Also, the more the coffers are varied in pattern the better. . . . We do not wish to appear to be dictating . . . merely passing along suggestions," Kaelber continued. Next came an argument over how many square feet of sound-absorbent surface in the form of quilted felt panels were needed. "I cannot agree," Kaelber wrote, "that it is well to defer the felt panels until such time as the need is demonstrated. Should we wait and the hall be bad, nothing that we could do to change the conditions would ever catch up with the story of our failure to produce a good room from an acoustical standpoint. The auditorium must be correct acoustically, or as near as possible, the first night that it is used by the public."[55]

To create the illusion of a massive stone-walled Medici palace but still have the advantage of modern acoustics, White ordered a composition board called Zenitherm ("looks like stone, works like wood; waterproof, inert and durable; installed by carpenters not masons," read the ads). Those interior walls of Zenitherm are so eye-fooling the skeptic must touch to confirm that the coldness of real stone is absent.[56]

The acoustics versus design conflict raged for some time. White was appalled at suggestions that gilt-tinted felt be applied to the ceiling and even more aghast at the idea of placing the Faulkner and Winter paintings on stretchers with springs to prevent buckling and felt behind them: "Absolutely impractical!" he thundered. "For best results, paintings should be made in place on a plaster wall as with the great Italian mural paintings. Next best is to mount the canvas on the wall . . . but the slightest wrinkle will absolutely detract from the effectiveness of mural painting." As an alternative White suggested "panels of felt covered with velvet hangings which can be removed if not needed."[57]

The Eastman Theatre, still one of the largest concert halls in the country, was initially pronounced as acoustically one of the best. Paderewski, who played on 15 November 1922 at one of the opening concerts, called it "the finest temple of music" in which he had ever tickled the ivories. Recent conductors have deemed it less than perfect.[58] Its original dual function as both movie theater and concert hall meant that compromises had to be made that affected both roles.

In the Eastman School of Music, a wide corridor or "promenade" ran the depth of the lot on two levels, forming a connecting link between the school and theater that could also be used for receptions. The walls of the school's upstairs corridor were lined with a gray cloth, "forming an excellent background for exhibitions of paintings . . . to afford city artists an opportunity to show their work without charge." This exhibition space would mark Eastman's only foray into public visual art.[59] The Subscribers' Entrance remains the carriage entrance to the mezzanine, the "Diamond Horseshoe" of the Eastman Theatre. A beautiful elliptical stair rises to a richly furnished lobby. Construction delays meant that this entrance was not used until several weeks after the theater opened.

Just a day before that event, a tour of inspection convinced Eastman that the two rear corners of the balcony were not adequately lighted by the enormous chandelier that hung from the center of the ceiling. But the electrical fixtures throughout had been designed and specially constructed by E. F. Caldwell & Company, who had designed the fixtures for his mansion and whom McKim, Mead & White considered the premier producers of electroliers in the country. Obviously there was no time to get a Caldwell fixture and "can't" was not a word in Eastman's vocabulary. Within hours an ingenious artisan was rigging up two ordinary corrugated metal wash tubs with chains for hanging. For decoration he used a two-inch rope along the bottom rim. From a nearby florist came a *wreath immortelles*, which was draped from the upper rim, while a plaster pineapple, left over from the theater ceiling, were fixed to the center of each tub bottom. Gilded and wired, the tubs were installed as a temporary solution. Amused by their incongruity but amazed at their effectiveness, Eastman decided not to order regular chandeliers from Caldwell.[60] Eastman was no sentimentalist but that emotion triumphed fifty years later when the Eastman Kodak Company undertook to restore the faded elegance of Mr. Eastman's theater. Public sentiment demanded that the golden washtubs remain and they did. Also at that grand reopening of 7 January 1972 every seat was occupied but one. In another bow to sentiment, Eastman's chair—number 48 in first row of the mezzanine along the right aisle—had been restored and recovered but not renumbered.

George Todd accompanied Eastman during his eleventh-hour inspection tour on Labor Day Eve 1922, and there was a lot of shifting around of furniture to achieve the effect most sought. When the lobby seemed satisfactory, there was one console table left over. Eastman looked around, spotted a mirror or two on the side walls and decided to place the table under one of them, remarking that it would make a handy place for women to lay their purses while looking in the mirror to adjust their hats or apply lipstick. "It takes a bachelor to know all about women," Todd was heard to murmur.[61]

In all some 2,500 blueprints were drafted and between five hundred and seven hundred workmen employed to create the Eastman School and Theatre. This phase brought its creator more pleasure than the massive public acclaim that followed in its wake. The process rather than the product was always the exciting part. As a labor of fun as well as art, the theater has aged gracefully. Restored to its original elegance, it remains one of the magnificent concert halls of the nation. A poll of architects in the mid-1980s named it Rochester's most beautiful and architecturally significant building—despite the presence of works by Frank Lloyd Wright, Louis Kahn, Harvey Ellis, Pietro Belluschi, and I. M. Pei and despite the continuing fact that postconcert crowds still bottleneck when trying to leave via Mr. Eastman's elliptical lobby.

The Platinum-Mounted Farm

In 1920 Charles Carpenter, Eastman's chauffeur who succeeded Billy Carter when Carter retired, was killed in a tractor accident at a household staff picnic. Eastman, out of the country at the time, was visibly shaken when told at the train station about the accident. Harvey Padelford, a young man from nearby Canandaigua and Great War veteran, had recently come to Rochester to find work as a taxi driver, heard of the vacancy, and applied through Molly Cherbuliez. "This is a year-round twenty-four-hour-a-day job," said Eastman. The interviewee was hired with the warning: "Harvey, you have the name of being a fast driver. Don't have any accidents."

The daily routine of the 1920s for Harvey began as the side door under the porte cochere opened about 7:45 A.M. and Eastman emerged. Once in the car, he pulled a Lucky Strike from his pack while Harvey paused at the end of the driveway and watched in his rearview mirror until the cigarette was lit and then drove on. The chauffeur had rigged an electric lighter, operated on a cord to serve the rear seat of the car. Eastman preferred lighters to throwaway matches; he studied the mechanisms of different lighters and experimented with various fluids. Gasoline caused too much smoke. Eastman also tinkered with his automobiles. He concocted a handle to be screwed on the door under the rear window so he could pull himself out of the rear seat and alight quickly. Hating to be waited on, he would not let Harvey open the door for him. Harvey kept his boss apprised of what was happening around town during the morning ride. When Eastman learned, for example, that it was hard to get onto the public golf course in South Park, he had another course laid out and opened. He was pleased, he told Harvey, that the only charge to the public at Durand–Eastman Park was for lockers. Once Eastman asked Harvey how many stop lights there were in Rochester and the chauffeur spent the morning at city hall so he could report that there were seventy-four. What use Eastman made of this information is unknown.[1]

The route went by St. Joseph's Church where, unknown to the priests, Eastman pulled out his mother's small, plain watch and set it by the belfry clock. Eastman had had George Dryden make a rubber washer that fit the watch stem to keep it from falling out of his vest pocket, so he could avoid wearing a chain. When the watch needed adjustment, it was Harvey's job to take it to E. J. Scheer's jewelry store on Main Street. But one morning the clock in the church tower was not working and the good fathers were startled to find George Eastman on the doorstep of the rectory. Upon hearing that there were no funds to repair the clock he ordered them to "Fix it and send me the bill. That clock is as important to Rochester as the Kodak Company is."

On mornings when he did not stop at the Eastman Theatre to check the receipts of the previous night, the Eastman car pulled up to the front door of 343 State Street at 8:00 A.M., the one cigarette having lasted the trip. The morning run complete, Harvey went home and got busy putting the cars on the turntable to be washed and tended to. Harvey often found himself a collaborator with Eastman in various ad hoc enterprises. For example, when a stranger wrote to Eastman letting him know that he was incorrectly displaying the American flag in front of the house, with the blue field to the right instead of the left, Eastman could not simply switch the flag about. Instead, he made a project of it. Harvey was sent for a copy of the American Legion Flag Code of 1924. The pair huddled over the illustrations in it, pondered the rules and regulations for flag displaying thoroughly, and then framed the illustrations and hung them in the garage for staff to use as a guide when the flag was brought out on patriotic holidays and hung from the portico.[2]

Just before noon Harvey drove Solomon Young, head butler, to Kodak Office with the makings for Eastman's lunch. Late in the afternoon Harvey would get a call on the direct line from the office to Eastman House. On this trip he was forced to speed, because one time he happened to arrive just as Eastman was stepping out of the Kodak door. From then on, Eastman liked to brag that he only had to put on his hat and come down from his penthouse office and the chauffeur was there. Before arriving at Kodak, Harvey would have glanced through the evening paper and picked out items for his boss to read on the trip home. Harvey rarely drove the boss to friends' homes. Most often they came to his place, but when he did go out—to visit the Mulligans, Ranlets, Nortons, Whipples, Todds, or Simon Stein—he walked or drove himself in the Packard Eight or dark blue Cadillac roadster. Sometimes, though, Harvey drove Eastman and businessman George Todd around all evening long while those virtual twins in looks and interests discussed the Chamber of Commerce, Eastman Theatre, or new River Campus of the University of Rochester. There were other spur-of-the-moment assignments for the two-tone green Lincoln, or two-tone green custom Cunningham that had cost $12,500, or the Packard Imperial limousine with the extra seats designed by Eastman.

Padelford was Eastman's factotum—the man for every occasion. One night at 11:00 came the command, "Take me to Kodak Park." The odd couple headed for the cafeteria, slid their trays along the rails, sat at a table, and solemnly ate. "How is it?" asked Eastman. "Fine," Harvey replied, "Just fine." Apparently there had been complaints, and nothing would do but that the Kodak King and his squire should check out the menu.[3]

Despite the damask walls, embossed plaster ceilings copied from European manors, and velvet portieres with gold braid, the general impression of Eastman's home was one of spaciousness, restraint, airy lightness, and spare, clean lines, particularly when compared to the Victorian excesses of neighboring houses. The cavernous living room was used for large-scale entertaining and community planning sessions during Eastman's thirty-year reign as Rochester's wealthiest, most powerful, and most influential citizen. Musicians who played there twice weekly dubbed it "the grand salon." The Steinway grand was there. A string quartet named "Kilbourn" drawn from the faculty of the Eastman School of Music would perform Sunday evenings for 100 to 125 guests, culled from a rotating list of 1,500 friends and acquaintances, Kodak employees, university and Eastman School faculty, and distinguished visitors. If those invited had not replied by the day before the concerts, Molly Cherbuliez telephoned them. Eastman greeted the guests at 5:00 P.M. sharp; they were then seated in canvas camp chairs set up in the living room. The musicians slipped in by the porte cochere, scooted up the side stairs to the motion-picture room to tune their instruments, and in winter warm themselves before the fire and their descent to the main floor, kept frigid because Eastman liked it that way.

The first two leaders of the Kilbourn Quartet, Arthur Hartmann and Vladimir Resnikoff, departed after fallouts with Eastman. The next, Joseph Press, succumbed to pneumonia in 1924. The fourth, Gustave Tinlot, was concertmaster of the Minneapolis Symphony Orchestra when contacted in 1925 on behalf of Eastman. For the next seven years Tinlot was first violin and director; Gerald Kunz, second violin; Samuel Belov, viola; and Paul Kefer, cello. The Kilbourn Quartet's final concert was given Sunday night, 13 March 1932, less than twenty-four hours before Eastman's death. Eastman's yearly contract with each musician ran forty weeks, from the last week of September when the Eastman School (where the musicians taught) opened for the year until late May. When he was away, the quartet played for friends like the Hutchisons, the Mulligans, and the Hubbells and thus drew year-round salaries. The Dossenbach Quintette had played on Thursday evenings from 1905 to 1919, but the new Kilbourn Quartet came on Wednesdays because the Philharmonic concerts were switched by Eastman from Wednesday to Thursday to avoid interfering with midweek services in Rochester's Protestant churches. Wednesdays Eastman and twelve to twenty dinner guests gathered for cocktails before a warming fire in the sitting room; the musicians donned black tie, with dinner guests similarly attired. A single concert at 8:30 featured works performed the previous Sunday complemented by ensemble and solo pieces. The time schedule was as strict as if the ensemble was performing on a national radio network rather than in a private home; if the musicians were not ready promptly, Eastman would press a button that rang a buzzer on the third floor and all would scurry down. If they finished five minutes before the full hour and a half, Harold Gleason would note the next day that Mr. Eastman had noticed this. As Sunday afternoons turned to dusk in late fall, the men would turn on the little lamps over their music stands and sometimes during intermission one or more might neglect to turn off his light. Without a word Eastman would quietly step up and turn it out himself. It was not so much that he felt the waste of a penny of electricity, Tinlot decided, as that his orderly mind needed to have such details attended to properly.[4]

Nicolas Slonimsky has written that Eastman "admittedly had no knowledge of music, and could well emulate President Ulysses S. Grant in his famous, if possibly apocryphal pronouncement, 'I know only two tunes: one is Yankee Doodle, and the other isn't.'"[5] Howard Hanson, director of the Eastman School of Music from 1924 to 1964, saw things differently, claiming that Eastman's "unusual passion for music" was unique in his experience. "He desired it in an elemental way, like food and water and air. He did not probe or analyze; he merely listened. Nor was he impressed by the statements of the 'musical intelligentsia.' Of all his many interests, art and music were the only things he did not pursue or dissect intellectually. He knew instinctively what he liked or disliked, in music as well as painting. I can't imagine anyone with his sensitivity to music being tone deaf," Hanson argued. "Being tone deaf is like being color blind. This man was extremely sensitive to music."[6]

The wine cellar of 900 East Avenue was not heavily stocked; Eastman apparently had no favorite wines nor was he a connoisseur of liquors. He had champagnes, sherry, port, and sauternes in very moderate supply, recalled

Molly Cherbuliez, keeper of the wine cellar keys. While he indulged himself where food was concerned, he was almost abstemious when it came to alcohol, perhaps recalling his father's weakness.[7] Ever the gracious host, he might sip a cocktail with his guests before dinner and a little Pommery champagne during the evening—as little as possible, Cherbuliez noted, and she never remembered him having a drink when alone. He was inclined, in her opinion, toward asceticism in his habits, an unusually clean-minded and clean-living man. Guests such as Eugene Goosens, director of the Rochester Philharmonic Orchestra, observed that one got the obligatory two glasses of champagne and then "the supply automatically ceased, and the rest of the supper was carried on to the accompaniment of ice water."[8]

Then Prohibition slowly descended upon the country, first through bills that prohibited the manufacture of distilled liquor, wine, and beer, and finally in 1920 in the form of the Eighteenth Amendment to the Constitution. "Don't you think it advisable to get a dozen or two of some liquor for purposes of cooking?" Molly asked as the year of grace before final enactment was running out. He had her purchase a modest six bottles of cooking sherry and six bottles of brandy. Eastman believed in observing the letter of the law at his Sunday musicales or other large gatherings, serving "Prohibition beer" made in compliance with the Volstead Act (although when George Dryden sent him "medicinal spirits" he served it discreetly to close friends). He refused to patronize bootleggers, but when one of his New York lawyers, J. J. Kennedy, sent him a "formula" for peach wine, he "made a half batch of your wine and it turned out mighty well as to flavor but it is a little muddy. Can you give me any suggestions as to clearing it up?" Such formula mixing in his latter years started him reminiscing about his "many years of preparing the emulsion when I did the cooking myself in a small room."[9] When asked for his opinion of Prohibition, his was not the response of other industrialists like Henry Ford, Harvey Firestone, Julius Rosenwald, Walter Chrysler, and Charles Schwab in opposing repeal in the late 1920s. He found himself "more in doubt than ever as to the net results of prohibition."

Decorative pieces at Eastman House were mixed the way they would have been on a real baronial estate, suggesting that several generations had already lived there. This was true of Eastman's art collection as well as his furniture. In the living room, three priceless old master portraits by Rembrandt, Frans Hals, and Anthony van Dyck hung on the green silk damask of the fireplace wall, the first backdrop a visitor would see from the grand entrance hall. On the side walls above the bookcases and between the windows, Eastman hung contemporary Barbizon landscapes and genre scenes. On the west wall, the only one a visitor could not see from the hall, he hung his "instant" ancestral portraits—paintings of his parents by Philip de Laszlo from 1850 daguerreotypes that replaced, in 1927, the Rolshoven portrait of his mother.

In October 1904 Eastman had engaged Julius Rolshoven through Josephine Dickman to paint a large portrait of a seated Maria Eastman, the second of at least four portraits of his mother. Rolshoven came for a sitting and to measure the space—above the bookcases and beneath the cornice on the wall opposite the fireplace in the library/living room. Then Maria broke her hip and the portrait had to be finished from photographs. "One has to live with a painting for some time to gauge all its qualities," Eastman said tentatively when he first saw the painting. "You had better come and retouch," he decided finally in August 1906. "As a picture it has received a good many compliments but as a likeness of my mother it is at present a total failure."[10]

Although Eastman's art collection is most familiar because of its old master portraits (the only old master collection ever assembled in Rochester), more than two-thirds consists of paintings and graphics produced during his lifetime. The majority are landscapes and rural genre scenes; of these, the works of the conservative Barbizon school of mid-nineteenth-century France, and of their Dutch and American followers, make up a significant portion.[11] Some were purchased while he lived in the Soule House, while others can be traced to his involvement, through Babbott, in the Painters and Sculptors Association and later the Grand Central Art Galleries, where dues entitled sponsors to a painting or sculpture by an American artist, determined by the luck of the draw. Several of the bronzes that adorned his public rooms came in this way, while the paintings often became Christmas presents for Ellen Dryden. The "witch picture" from the Soule House hung for years in the front hall of 900 East Avenue until replaced by a Tintoretto portrait of a Venetian doge. The great burst of art collecting began when Eastman House was built and continued until the walls were full. Although he never stopped collecting, visiting galleries, trying out works (in 1928 he had ten throughout the house at one time), and horse-trading his paintings for new ones, he considered his collection limited by the wall space available. He often turned down a "lovely little picture" because he already owned something by a particular artist and "I think the one Corot which I have is enough for my small collection." When a new work came, an old one usually went. He did, however, own two or more works by Raeburn, Romney, Reynolds, Millet, Anton Mauve, and Jacob Maris. Eastman was used to making up his mind quickly: "My whole business life has been based on making decisions, not withholding them," he once said. "More time and business are lost by a delay in making a decision than in making the wrong decision." But in building and decorating his home and choosing his philanthropies and art works, he took months, years, even decades to cogitate and decide.

Thanks to Babbott and Josephine Dickman, Eastman had been trotted around to see principal private art collections of the East Coast—those of Henry Clay Frick, Joseph Widener, and H. O. Havemeyer. Babbott introduced Eastman to Italian and Netherlandish Primitives and to Japanese art, both of which the Brooklynite collected, but Eastman decided he preferred eighteenth-century British portraits to the earlier European works. The only Japanese objects he collected were netsukes. Babbott also introduced Eastman to that spectacular art dealer Lord Joseph Duveen, whose career was built upon the observation that Europe had art and America had money. Two vases were the only things Eastman ever purchased from the legendary con man. But while Eastman made his own decisions, buying what he and not some friend, art dealer, or decorator liked, he had a fear of paying more for a painting than it was worth. Babbott's real value to him was double-checking that the art Eastman chose bore the right trademark and was not overpriced. His taste was comparable to that of other millionaire American collectors at the turn of the century. In order to demonstrate their appreciation for the arts, they wanted paintings that were not only of great aesthetic quality, but also dignified and noncontroversial in subject.

Fifty-five paintings and prints from his collection were in the house at the time of his death and thus became the property of the University of Rochester. Eventually most would be moved to the university's Memorial Art Gallery.

The formal gardens of Eastman House were planned to be viewed from inside. From the bay of the living room, one looked out to a terrace garden, then the eye was led down a long vista crisscrossed with gravel paths, designed in 1902 by Alling De Forest. Triangular beds between the paths were planted with a brilliant show of bulbs—"Just now the garden is ablaze with Darwin tulips," Eastman wrote one early June day[12]—followed by a summer show of annuals and perennials and finally the winter "bones" of the garden: evergreens and paths. The diagonals give the De Forest garden a liveliness and a flow, an element of surprise as to what is coming next, making it wonderful for strolling. By contrast, the West Garden by Claude Bragdon is more static. The garden at Hestercombe had this kinetic energy because it, too, used diagonals, but Bragdon changed the axis to make it straight, square, and predictable. Neither Bragdon nor De Forest had formal training in landscape architecture; indeed, there was very little available at that time. Despite his consciousness of a lack of formal education and his self-derogatory description of himself for the American Society of Landscape Architects—"No medals, no degrees; however there are many growing monuments as a result of my labors"[13]—De Forest, unlike Bragdon, was totally focused on this profession.

The central feature of De Forest's formal outdoor court enclosed on two sides by the L-shaped house and the other two by a colonnaded pergola and stone balustrade, was a sunken oval lily pond (containing goldfish sent by William H. Walker). The east—west axis to the pond coincided with a bay that had been added to the long latticed ambulatory that connected the dining room to the palm house and greenhouses beyond. In that bay of the covered walk or loggia, Eastman liked to stage intimate summer dinners, the gardens softly lit with Roman torches and perhaps a string quartet sequestered somewhere. On that same axis, across the lily pond was a covered and colonnaded pergola where a larger dinner party could have tables set. "The loggia that connects the house with the greenhouses is open to the garden in summer and enclosed in glass in winter," Eastman told *Town & Country,* "thus protecting the [rare forms of] English ivy which covers the walls and ceiling."[14] He kept the palm house stocked with tropical plants and the orchids he began to import in the 1890s. He continued to import orchids from England and bulbs from Holland up until his death. Even after his passing Alice Whitney Hutchison sent in the annual bulb order at the request of Rush Rhees who, as president of the university, was then living in the house in compliance with Eastman's will that the house be maintained as it was during his lifetime for ten years following his death. For this he provided a $2 million endowment, the income of which should have equaled his yearly house expenditures, or $80,000.[15]

Beyond the palm house were five greenhouses fronted by a long bowling green that extended to the old-fashioned rosery, where Eastman had a "rose bush growing . . . which was raised from a slip taken from a bush given to my mother when she was a little girl and lived on Paris Hill, Oneida County."[16] He had roses, too, from a root sent to him by his distant cousin Arthur Colgate of Manchester, New Hampshire, which had been set out by their common ancestor Ebenezer Eastman in 1773.[17] These family roses were soon joined by 650 other rosebushes, whose blossoms Molly Cherbuliez was asked to count in her three-year logging project. Eastman had De Forest plant a hedge of crimson ramblers along his neighbor Lewis Ross's fence "extending from the clothes yard north . . . 50 ft."[18] In 1924 he added Hybrid Tea roses that the Rochester Parks Department had bred by crossing the *Earl of Warwick* with *Constance* and registered as *George Eastman* with the American Rose Society in June 1923.[19]

The cold frames, cutting gardens, and vegetable gardens were all effectively hidden from the living room bay because they were on a lower level and behind a stone balustrade with garden bench. East of the formal gardens was the long vista of lawn with shrub border for croquet games and visiting children to frolic and be photographed in. The roadway from the cow stable to University Avenue was bordered by ten apple trees, each of a different variety, Northern Spy, Jonathan, and Golden Russet being the only ones that would sound familiar to modern ears. For the orchard of 1904

Ellwanger & Barry planted blackberries, currants, and four varieties of raspberries as well as eight pear trees, including Bartlett and Seckel, eight plum trees, and eight peach trees, again, one each of different varieties. An elaborate, colonnaded grape arbor, designed by Warner in 1907 and centered on a charming, unique garden with rocks (as distinguished from a true alpine rock garden), was the punctuation mark and culmination of the series of east gardens. (Today it forms the forecourt of the George Eastman House International Museum of Photography and Film.) To the west stood the compound containing the horse stable, stable yard, poultry house, scratching shed, boiler room, engine room, and compost yard, and a cow stable for the five resident Jerseys. A semicircle of silver poplars defined the fields and cowpasture extending to University Avenue.

That was the way De Forest planned it on 11 November 1902 and the way it was essentially completed. But no sooner had the dust settled and the stickers been removed from the dry-plate glass windows than Eastman began tinkering. In 1907 he replaced the casual, unobtrusive, and welcoming gravel paths with more formal brick, because he didn't like to have the gravel raked every time it had been disturbed by footsteps. Next he acquired two antique Venetian well curbs and fitted them as fountains. Planting plans highlight red, yellow, and white tulips—Kodak colors rather than the delicate pastel shades common to traditional gardens. The Eastman gardens took on the heavy, massive, men's-club aura of the living room. In 1917, when the Ross property was added to the west and Bragdon was engaged to design a formal garden there, the greenhouses were moved to that side too and a drying yard and peony garden added by De Forest who, nineteen years after his original plan, had been rehired to record the completed estate on plans and provide extensive new planting lists. The gardens were a source of joy and pleasure not just to Eastman but to passers-by, who often wrote to tell him so or to ask if they might look at them more closely or paint them. Usually he said yes.

Upstairs and downstairs at Eastman House there were eight maids and two butlers; a pantry girl in charge of dishes and silver; a houseman to vacuum, do the windows inside, and mop the marble floors with kerosene and cold water until they shone; and a maid for the maids. The latter came in every day to clean the maids' bedrooms and bathrooms, change their beds, set the table in the servants' dining room, and clean up after them. She also worked in the dairy, separating the cream from the milk, churning the butter, and stamping each little pat with the "GE" monogram designed by Tiffany's. Most of the maids were Irish so Molly Cherbuliez threw a big party on St. Patrick's Day and a big Christmas party, letting each member of the staff invite so many friends. The maids received $14 a week, which was considered good pay, because it included room and board, laundry and uniforms, and shoes, all of which were white.[20] Molly had her own dining room on the first floor (which was a corner of her office just inside the side door), an expansive sitting room on the second floor, and a bedroom on the third just off Eastman's "playroom" where he kept his home movie equipment and installed his "museum" of trophy heads. The maids also slept on the third floor. One of the downstairs maids waited on Miss Cherbuliez.

The help, which decided they were not classified as "help" in Eastman's eyes since "everybody was very dear to him if you worked for him, something precious and valuable," loved going to Oak Lodge. Their eyes popped at the private railroad car with its blue "velvet" rug, its mahogany furniture, and their own brass beds. They boarded their special compartment at bedtime but did not pull out of the New York Central Station until 2:00 or 3:00 A.M. Occasionally Eastman had business at the White House or Justice Department in Washington, where they changed trains, and the help, except for Young, who stocked up on lobsters and meats at the public market, had three days to explore the city on their own.[21]

At Eastman House the maids waited on the women guests. While the men breakfasted in the conservatory with Eastman, the women had trays brought to their rooms whenever they buzzed and called down through the intercom system—rarely at the appointed breakfast hour downstairs. The maids pressed the guests' clothes, helped them dress for formal affairs, and packed for them. Dinner for the help was at noon and then, to borrow a phrase, their work was done. The maids sat in their dining or sitting room playing cards and reading the morning paper. They could stroll through the grounds, or go "up town" to window shop (while the boss was working his tail off at the office) as long as they were back for supper at 5:00. The maids straightened up the ladies' rooms after they left for the day, turned down the beds, pulled the drapes, left lights burning in the bedrooms, and placed pitchers of ice water on the dressers. The butlers took care of the men as well as answering the door and telephone. All in all, Eastman House was an ideally run hotel.[22]

The staff each received three to four weeks of vacation. Two or three maids might take off to Boston together. They also got in-house vacations if Eastman was gone, say, from three to six months. Marie Cherbuliez would then let loose the reins, and toot off to New York herself. But they all worked like beavers at housecleaning time; when all the extras came in to wash the paint, the regulars would do the fine work and settle up the house again. The help was not given keys but had to ring for John Ginann, the night watchman, to let them in. Isaac Ven de Sande, a Dutchman, was the houseman; Philip Ham, the electrician; Chauncey Chapman, the carpenter. Fourteen to sixteen men worked outside under Camiel DeSmet on gardens, shrubbery, greenhouses, chickens, and cattle. The gardeners were usually Belgian and the Japanese delegations that came through acknowledged that even in

Japan they did not have chrysanthemums as huge as the ones Mr. Eastman raised. Sam McCleary took care of the cows.[23]

Terry Ramsaye came in 1927 to interview Eastman for a feature article in *Photoplay*, boarding the Empire State Limited at 11:30 P.M. to arrive in time for breakfast. Eastman normally sent a chauffeur to meet his guests—"Any Red Cap can point out my car," he would tell them—but reporters had to take cabs. When Ramsaye was ushered into the conservatory he found Eastman, "a crisp and wiry 74, might be any age over 50," at breakfast. The host was "cautiously cordial," saying "on time, let us sit down," even though the reporter was three minutes late. Ramsaye apologized anyway, citing a taxi driver who "didn't know where Eastman lived," but Eastman "rose to the sally" and mentioned the taxi strike that brought new drivers to town. Dressed in a "dark business suit of gray, his slightly sprightly vest and really merry scarf set off with a great plum of iridescent black pearl," Eastman had already eaten part of his grapefruit, his coffee was poured, and a scone was buttered. He added some "very yellow cream" to his coffee and gazed contemplatively at the banked drift of flowers. The coffee was excellent to the third cup and then a humidor of cigarettes appeared. From his breast pocket Eastman produced "a slender onyx holder, with a trick ejector tip, gold and delicately ornamented." He fitted the cigarette with care and leaned back. Little was said during the breakfast so Ramsaye reported that "Eastman is definitely the world's best listener," but that gave the reporter a chance to size up the mansion and the man. Eastman, Ramsaye's lead says, was "discretion personified—a crystallized, hard, dry, seasoned success, entirely surrounded by millions and discipline." Looking around, Ramsaye saw a house "redolent with extreme comfort, glamoured with magnificence, yet a restrained magnificence, a subdued splendor. Eastman lives with the grandeur of a rajah, but a very careful Puritan rajah." The journalist saw Eastman as the "last great Yankee American," a throwback, even, to the nineteenth century.[24]

Ramsaye had come to Rochester once before, in 1922, to interview Eastman for "a romantic history of the motion picture" because, as Ramsaye's editor, James Quirk, wrote to Eastman, "You are as familiar with the beginning of pictures as any man in the world . . . especially the remarkable development in photography and photographic materials with which you have played such an important part."[25] Quirk further suggested that Eastman or Kodak finance a photography museum to preserve "early pictures which will some day be of real historical interest." Eastman declined to found the museum but invited Ramsaye to come to Rochester. "He is probably the best posted man in the world on the history of the movie art," Eastman decided, and thus "would not make any mistakes as to important facts."[26]

While they talked in the sitting room after breakfast the mail arrived and

Eastman methodically opened each envelope with a paper knife. (Personal letters addressed to 900 East Avenue were torn up as soon as they had been answered, while those sent to the office were methodically filed by Alice Whitney and thus survive to this day.) On the mantel were seven photographic likenesses of his mother, whom Eastman told Ramsaye was "the only woman of importance in my life," and one (borrowed) daguerreotype of his father. Ramsaye wandered into the library where he noticed Keyserling's *Book of Marriage* and "a scattering of periodicals ranging from *Ainslie's* and some pulpwood magazines to the *Political Science Quarterly*." The reporter fingered a massive map table with a curious top of "waxy soft orange tint" and a voice from behind said, "I shot that table myself"—it was rhino hide.

"Let's go and see my guns and playthings," the host suggested and up the grand stair they went and on for another flight to the third floor and the motion picture room, trophy room, gun room, and workshop laboratory. "An arsenal of shooting rifles stands ranked against the wall, everything from squirrel rifles to great double-barreled English elephant guns, ready to hurl steel case slugs with a 5000 pound impact. Also there are wall cases with trout rods, each in its groove and niche, gay with silken wrappings and bright with varnish. And there are rods of greenheart and lancewood, bearing the marks of hard service." A great round table was covered with native African weapons—"hand-hammered iron arrow heads, once coated with poison, spear heads, still too sharp to handle carelessly, war clubs and amulets and charms. . . . All about are vases made from elephants' feet, mounted heads of Rocky Mountain goats, Alaskan mountain sheep, and the skins of bear and puma."

In the motion picture room, Eastman projected films he shot with his Cine-Kodak camera, including one of a rhinoceros charging him in British East Africa. "Too close for comfort," observed Ramsaye. "I was too busy with the camera to notice it at the time," was the reply. "Now we will see where I have the most fun of all," said Eastman, taking Ramsaye into his workshop and darkroom. Ramsaye noted the enormous developing sink in the middle of a large room, "equipped with a greater array of photographic apparatus than will be found in most professional establishments." One corner was for carpentry—a heavy bench equipped with vises and clamps and stools. "On the wall are tool cases," Ramsaye observed, "all in typical Eastman apple-pie order." Ramsaye drifted to the window to survey the estate as Eastman told him, "I got the last large tract, the last remnant of a farm, inside the city. . . . You see I keep cows and chickens here." Ramsaye decided that "it is a sort of platinum mounted farm . . . a setting as improbable as a ranch in Central Park." During his stays in Rochester Ramsaye felt he saw the private man, the real Eastman, as opposed to the persona the public glimpsed. The world knows Eastman, Ramsaye said, as a stern and exacting materialist who demands discipline and excellence from himself, his company, his products, and his customers. "It is all neat, concise, elegant," Ramsaye concluded. "The company reiterates the man."[27] What sets the Ramsaye biographical article apart from all others, including Carl Ackerman's book-length biography that Eastman thought was too long, was that the subject liked it (even without vetting it and correcting it before it was printed—his usual condition for an interview). To "My dear Ramsaye" he wrote: "I have just read, with a good deal of interest and some amusement, your sprightly article on yours truly. I think it is by far the best one that has evolved. Of course if forced I would have to admit that it is overdrawn but I cannot help but like it just the same."[28]

34. Between 1902 and 1905 a grand "colonial" house, solid as a steel and concrete bunker, rose on East Avenue, Rochester's unpaved "Avenue of the Presidents." Full-grown elms were brought by Erie Canal barge and horse-drawn drays to complete the landscaping. Cream-colored roman bricks matched those of the Root House in Buffalo, while the windows were of the finest Belgian dry-plate glass available. (GEH)

35. Of five major gardens surrounding Eastman House, the East Terrace, seen
here from the living room in 1905, is the oldest. By 1907 the gravel walks, which
Eastman thought a bother to rake, were replaced by brick. In 1912 the fountains
were superseded by antique Venetian well curbs. At left is the covered walk—open
in summer for parties, closed in winter to protect the English ivy—that leads from
house to palm house. Beyond are greenhouses, rose garden, cutting garden, and
grape arbor with rock garden. At right is the pergola for summer dining and an
ancient apple tree from the original Culver farm. Smokestacks reveal how close
the property is to industrial Rochester. (GEH)

36. On 31 October 1919 the conservatory, as seen from the dining room, is set for Eastman's breakfast. Behind the bower of flowers the organist will play on the Aeolian, beginning as Eastman descends to the landing—behind flowers and organ. Eastman's favorite retractable and "scientific" light fixture, awash in ferns, appears above the breakfast table. (GEH)

37. On the third floor of Eastman House, Francis H. Bacon of the Davenport Company created a playroom for Eastman. Here Eastman stored his fishing equipment, mounted his hunting trophies, kept toys for visiting children, decorated a tree at Christmas, and showed movies to his friends. Here, too, the members of the Dossenbach Quintette and later the Kilbourn Quartet, gathered to tune their instruments before a musicale on the first floor. (GEH)

38. Maria Kilbourn Eastman—at age eighty-five, with great grandchildren, Ellen Maria and George Eastman Dryden—broke her hip shortly before moving into Eastman House in June 1905. She was confined to a wheelchair for the remaining two years of her life. (GEH)

39. George Eastman and Josephine Haskins Dickman at her home, *The Ridge*, in Petersham, Massachusetts, 1910. Josephine was the widow of George Dickman, manager of Kodak Limited. From Petersham Eastman and Mrs. Dickman joined a group for two weeks fishing in Labrador. (EKC)

40. Evangeline (Nell) Abbott Newhall and Eastman wash and dry camp dishes during a Canadian trip in 1912 while Albert B. Eastwood rolls up the tent. Nell was Ellen Andrus (Dryden)'s roommate at Wells College in the 1890s and a special favorite of Eastman. (GEH)

41. Eastman's gift of ambulances to France during World War I brought him the privilege of touring the trenches at Rheims in 1916. (GEH)

42. At his North Carolina retreat, Oak Lodge, Eastman tests a new camera, designed to allow the photographer to compose a picture on ground glass without losing the convenience of roll film. The No. 4 Screen Focus Kodak camera, considered the ancestor of all modern folding roll cameras, was introduced commercially in 1904, the year after this picture was made. (EKC)

43. A hunting party rests at Oak Lodge after a day in the field. Eastman (*left*) knew each dog by name. His guests (*left to right*) include Walter Howard, Francis S. Macomber, Albert B. Eastwood, and unknown. (EKC)

44. Eastman has his camera and tripod set to record an important milestone in the history of the Eastman School of Ringwood, North Carolina. Perhaps the occasion is the 1919 opening of this neighborhood primary school for the education of African-American students, which Eastman built on land he gave the county from his Oak Lodge holdings. (UR)

45. Because of the precarious state of his own teeth and gums, and the pain he remembered his mother enduring, preventive dentistry for indigent children worldwide became one of Eastman's priorities. Here a dentist checks a North Carolina student in December 1921. (GEH)

46. The electric announcement in *The Tech* on 10 January 1920 that "EASTMAN IS 'MR. SMITH'" ended two decades of speculation as to the identity of the anonymous donor of the new Massachusetts Institute of Technology campus. (MIT)

47. The only evidence in Rochester that Eastman was the donor of the MIT buildings was this 4 × 6 photograph that hung on his office wall. (GEH)

48. Eastman's gift to the Hampton-Tuskegee Endowment Fund in 1924 was reported in the national press as "by far the largest single contribution that has ever been made to Negro education." His choice of Tuskegee and Hampton was due in large part to his friendship with Booker T. Washington. (GEH)

49. Shortly after obtaining a copy of Booker T. Washington's autobiography, *Up from Slavery*, in 1902, Eastman began making annual unsolicited gifts to Tuskegee. Later Washington approached Eastman for more specific purposes, such as a building or funds supporting a course in photography. (GEH)

ROCHESTER, N. Y   4A-H1725

50. At Eastman's behest, all frivolous details are absent from the seamless complex of the University of Rochester's School of Medicine and Dentistry, Strong Memorial Hospital, and Rochester Municipal Hospital. The one exception is the hospital's porticoed entrance, which housed a paneled waiting room as memorial to Eastman's old partner, Henry A. Strong, and his wife. (postcard)

51. The Eastman Theatre, "erected MDCCCCXXII for the enrichment of community life," featured popular movies such as Rodoph (sic) Valentino in *The Young Rajah* to help pay for that community enrichment. (EKC)

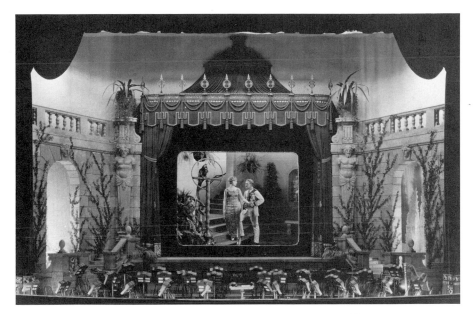

52. Architect Lawrence Grant White designed two sets for the Eastman Theatre. The set pictured here is a Hollywood-inspired one for motion pictures with pit orchestra rising mechanically in the foreground to accompany the films. The other, more traditional and sedate set, was for once-a-week concerts by the nascent Rochester Philharmonic Orchestra. (EKC)

53. Kilbourn Hall of the Eastman School of Music is a five hundred-seat acoustical gem for chamber music. (EKC)

54. The Budapest Chamber Orchestra salutes Eastman in 1928. (EKC)

55. In October 1926 opera singer Mary Garden performed at the Eastman
Theatre and posed with Eastman on the steps of Eastman House. (EKC)

56. Eastman and Thomas A. Edison recreate their starring roles in the birth of motion pictures: Eastman holds the continuous film he first produced in 1889 that Edison adapted to motion picture use. The two met in 1907, again in 1924, and here in 1928 at Eastman's "Kodacolor" garden party introducing a color motion picture film. (GEH)

57. Employees at work in 1920 in the much more sophisticated research and development laboratory that was opened in 1912. (EKC)

58. In 1925 Eastman (*center and seated*) retired from active Kodak management. Now chairman of the board, he is flanked (*left to right*) by William G. Stuber, president, and Frank Lovejoy, vice president of manufacturing. Standing (*left to right*), Lewis B. Jones, vice president, sales promotion; James Havens, vice president, legal department; Marion Folsom, Eastman's assistant and secretary of this management advisory committee; C. E. Kenneth Mees, director, Research Laboratory; James Haste, manager, Kodak Park. (EKC)

59. Eastman's favorite photograph of himself was made in London in 1921 by the Russian photographer Nahum Ellan Luboshez (1869–1925), who became a Kodak demonstrator and received a medal of the Royal Photographic Society for improving x-ray photography. The Luboshez portrait remains the corporate image of Eastman.

60. Eastman and Alice K. Whitney, his only secretary, at their adjoining desks on
the top floor of Kodak Office in the late 1920s. (GEH)

61. During the 1928 safari in Africa, Eastman posed with his guide and this Kodak Girl signboard. (EKC)

62. "The Kodak King at Kodok with His Kodak" is how photographer and explorer Martin Johnson titled the series taken during Eastman's 1928 safari at this tiny post office along the White Nile in the Sudan. Eastman created the sign from a strip of deck chair canvas, tracing dinner plates for circles. Pictured (*from left*) are Martin Johnson, Dr. Albert D. Kaiser, Eastman, and Osa Johnson. (EKC)

63. The Society of the Genesee, which honored Upstate New Yorkers annually, had long courted Eastman without success. Finally, in 1931, Thomas J. Watson (*right*), the dynamic founder and president of IBM, persuaded him. Eastman's only caveat was that his niece's husband, George B. Dryden (*left*), be seated next to him. That way, the tired Kodak King explained, he would not have to engage in superfluous small talk. (EKC)

64. Because William S. Paley of CBS broadcast a program of organ and choral music from Eastman House on Christmas Day, 1930, Eastman escaped to Evanston, Illinois, with the Drydens. Photographs from later years show a contemplative Eastman. (UR)

V

Philanthropy
under a Bushel

Mr. Smith Goes
to College

■ ■ ▪ ─────────────────────────────

"I am not interested in higher education," Eastman stated flatly in 1898 to two young women. They were soliciting funds to enable themselves and other local women to attend the small Baptist college for men that since 1850 had called itself by the courtesy title, University of Rochester. Eastman's unyielding answer was but a recast of his reply to the many religious appeals now crossing his desk: "I am not interested in church work." He had the self-made man's indifference toward formal education, believing that the most useful training came through trial and error and the rugged individual pitting himself or herself against experience. Any notion of higher education as edifying the mind and imagination he found flighty and untrustworthy. "You may not be interested in education now, Mr. Eastman," the bolder and more prophetic of the two women said, "but you will be."[1]

The University of Rochester had been without a president since David Jayne Hill, whom Eastman considered "a cold fish,"[2] left in 1896, later to become Assistant Secretary of State in the McKinley administration. During the four-year interregnum during which the president's chair stood vacant, the all-male board of trustees felt pressure to admit women from crusading feminists, Rochester mayor and university trustee James Goold Cutler, and a bequest from anthropologist Lewis Henry Morgan earmarked for women's education. The trustees agreed in principle that women could be admitted once supporters had raised $100,000. Without the help of men of considerable wealth like Eastman, the fund merely inched toward its goal, even after the trustees agreed to reduce the required amount to $50,000. Then suddenly, two months before the inauguration of a new president in 1900, Rochester feminist Susan B. Anthony pledged her $2,000 life insurance policy to complete the women's "dowry."

The new president, Rush Rhees, believed strongly in what was called coordinate education on the model of Barnard or Radcliffe as opposed to coeducation—that is, even on the same campus, women should be taught separately from men, learning subjects tailored to the lives they led. Women, he wrote, had "distinct and in some particulars quite different interests, aims, and traditions." After prolonged hesitation, Rhees, a forty-year-old professor of New Testament interpretation from Newton Center, Massachusetts, had accepted the invitation to become the university's third president on the same day that he married Harriet Seelye, the daughter of the president of Smith College (for women). Rhees thought that he was coming to head a well-off men's college with a comfortably remote possibility of admitting women. Instead, he found himself with thirty-three young women enrolled and a huge debt to retire.

For the inauguration on 11 October 1900 the new Alumni Gym, designed by J. Foster Warner, was bedecked in dandelion yellow,[3] but was not yet paid for. The faculty of the little university numbered 17, the student body 157. The endowment was less than $1 million. The three other buildings, also not paid for, included a library with a meager 35,000 volumes. Among small colleges, and even in its own city, the university enjoyed no very great prestige. But unbeknownst to all, one of the great academic executives of the twentieth century had just come on board. Although George Eastman's great-grandfather had also been a Baptist preacher, he adhered to a humanistic interpretation of life, shunning organized, sectarian religion. Yet the slowly unfolding friendship (it would be twenty-five years before they addressed each other by their first names) between the modest, erudite Baptist preacher-educator and the shy, agnostic industrialist is surely the principal reason that the University of Rochester would become the largest beneficiary of Eastman's wealth.

Eastman and Rhees met in 1902, if not before, when Lord and Lady Kelvin came for their grand tour of the United States and the world-famous Scottish scientist and inventor spoke at a university assembly. Despite a painful attack of neuralgia, Lord Kelvin outlined the obligations of educated men, which, contemporary accounts held, brought cheers that "could have been heard half-a-mile away." Eastman was probably in the audience along with Walter Hubbell, class of 1871 and a trustee of the university. Rhees did not approach Eastman until after J. Foster Warner had drawn plans for a biology and physics building. Lewis P. Ross, trustee and also chairman of the Mechanics Institute trustees and Eastman's neighbor to the west, had written sarcastically to Rhees: "If you could possibly, instead of designing new plans, discover either a gold mine or a bank-note factory, it would probably accelerate the erection of such a building as we need." Rhees had already tried soliciting John D. Rockefeller, Andrew Carnegie, Mrs. Russell Sage, and others, but these philanthropists responded only through layers upon layers of advisors. Rhees then perceived that his gold mine might be closer at hand—and Mr. Eastman employed no front men. The president and Mrs. Rhees called at 900 East Avenue to personally alert Eastman that $150,000 was needed to build and equip the laboratory. Eastman offered $10,000. As the Rheeses were leaving, Eastman called them back. "You're disappointed, aren't you?" he asked. "What did you expect?" "I had hoped," Rhees replied, "that you might give the whole building." "Well, I'll think it over," said Eastman.[4] The next morning a check for $60,000 to cover the cost of construction appeared on Rhees's desk, because, as Eastman told Walter Hubbell, "Dr. Rhees let me alone." Years later Eastman would boast, "Dr. Rhees never asked me for a cent." Rush Rhees's report of the incident to his trustees read: "Mr. Eastman, entirely on his own initiative, without any solicitation either direct or indirect on my part . . . increased his pledge to $60,000." In a defensive addendum that Rhees loved to quote after the Eastman sums had rolled into the many millions, the donor cautioned, "This is the last I shall do for the university."

Two years after this gift to end all gifts, however, Rhees had to report that "work upon the new Eastman Laboratories has been delayed beyond all anticipation." The trustees were deeply embroiled in a controversy as to whether the façades of new buildings should be "colonial" or "collegiate gothic." The donor of the Eastman Laboratories was not happy that his name was afixed to the building but cared more that the structure "will be a modification of the so-called mill construction of the slow burning type" and that "the partition walls throughout are fire proof" and that the "floors be built of heavy Georgia pine timber" than what the façade looked like. Finally, the trustees "retained the services of Messrs. Heins & LaFarge of New York as consulting architects to collaborate with Mr. J. Foster Warner . . . who had nearly completed the plans for the interior construction of the building." The New York architects' façade for the new physics and biology building turned out to be an ornate treatment of the main entrance to Warner's rather plain, vernacular, brick building. Rhees also seized the opportunity to have Heins & LaFarge draw up a master plan for the campus in which six to eight new buildings would be added to the existing four, including an art building and separate dormitories and classroom buildings for men and women. Unlike his predecessors, Rhees did not regard dormitories as sinks of iniquity; he wanted to change the thrust of the university from a strictly local institution for day students to a residential college drawing students from all sections of the country. Although Rhees was convinced that a professional school, such as a law school or music conservatory, had no place in this university without adequate endowment, in 1904 he accepted a gift of rare musical manuscripts from Hiram Watson Sibley. With this seminal Sibley Music Library in mind, he told Heins & LaFarge that "it might be well to bear in mind a possible building for a music school—though that is in the somewhat distant future." The architects sketched a music building on the long-range plans. Rhees also had Warner thoroughly renovate the university's Sibley Hall, donated by the Western Union magnate in 1876. A steel balcony or gallery was added to increase the shelf space by another 35,000 volumes. Rhees considered the library the heart of a college campus.[5]

Although the original gift for the Eastman Laboratories was accumulating interest at 4 percent, it was not enough to offset the rising costs brought on by the two-year delay in the construction. So Eastman sent another check, this one for $15,000, explaining his actions by anticipating Rhees's words: "I am very glad to send you this without any solicitation on your part, either direct or indirect, because . . . I am so well pleased with the result of your efforts to get a suitable building without undue expense." A master key was turned over to the benefactor "for the oftener you visit it the deeper our satisfaction." (The key remains attached to Rhees's letter in the archives of incoming correspondence.) Eastman reluctantly consented to his name on a small bronze tablet, courtesy of the class of 1904, with an inscription devised by Dr. Rhees: "This building given by George Eastman is dedicated to the study of life and energy for the larger knowledge of truth."[6]

Invited to become a trustee, Eastman declined, and was appalled at the suggestion that an honorary degree be bestowed. "I am sorry," Frank Babbott wrote. "I would like to see some recognition of your work." "The reason I refused the degree from the Rochester University," came the reply, "was that I do not care for that sort of thing. Besides that I am not a professional man and I have a feeling that such degrees should only be conferred upon professional men. I told Dr. Rhees I got more satisfaction out of the offer than I would out of the degree itself."[7]

Despite Eastman's satisfaction in his first major gift to the university, he reiterated that it would also be his last. Yet Eastman was, perhaps unconsciously, strongly influenced by personalities. Rhees had such a positive effect that Eastman found himself giving in to liberal education in spite of his loudly proclaimed views against it, while Ross, president of the board of trustees of Mechanics Institute, proved to be a negative force through his inability to keep the budget balanced there or to find a strong manager of the Rhees type. And perhaps Eastman was beginning to become interested in education of a more liberal stripe. The opening of the new Eastman Laboratories coincided with the completion of Eastman's house, and his desire to honor William Mead and Frank Babbott for their part in making it a success. What about a $5,000 gift to Amherst College, which both Mead and Babbott (and incidentally, Rhees) had attended? The honorees were touched when the Eastman Lectures in Science were established at Amherst. Ellen Dryden asked for a contribution to Wells College and Uncle George responded with $5,000, on the condition Ellen give it under her own name, not his. That same year he also gave $5,000 to the Lowthorpe School of Landscape Architecture for women, a favorite charity of Josephine Dickman, and another $5,000 to Tuskegee Institute.

Meanwhile, Rhees had been successful in his overtures to the Andrew Carnegie Foundation. In 1905 the steel magnate's representatives offered $100,000 to erect an Applied Science Building on the condition that the university raise an equal sum for endowment and reverse the denominational test imposed in 1892 on the choice of trustees, officers, and faculty. (Carnegie, like Eastman, refused to give to any sectarian purpose.) It took three years to meet the conditions and it would be 1911 before the building was ready. Because courses in mechanical and chemical (but not civil) engineering were planned, a "source highly friendly to the University" suggested that Rhees spend the 1908–9 academic year abroad "observing technical education in England and on the Continent." A purse was put together to enable six Rheeses, including the three children and a grandmother plus a nurse, to travel comfortably. The "source highly friendly to the University" was not identified but since Eastman put up most of the money, was highly interested in technical education, and was at that very moment proposing to Rhees that Mechanics Institute merge with the university under his strong management, one could draw conclusions.[8]

Then in 1912 Amherst College was without a president and rumors were rampant that Rhees was a candidate. "Any alumnus finds the highest honor in the serious consideration of his name in connection with the presidency of his own college," Rhees allowed. Amherst had a complete plant, a considerable endowment, and no acute financial problems. Also, there were no women on campus. "The fact that Amherst College is not coeducational constitutes a strong attraction to a man of my convictions," Rhees stated bluntly. He then put all his cards on the table and listed the conditions to be met if he were to consider staying at Rochester:

> 1. Provision for some increase in the faculty, and for definite increase in the scale of salaries. . . . 2. We ought to take immediate steps to establish our work with women on a co-ordinate basis. . . . I told my friends here that I was quite ready to believe that after careful consideration they might deem the first of these needs impracticable of realization and the second of them undesirable; that if this should be their judgment, I feel it my duty to reply that if Amherst wants me I will accept.[9]

Gentle pressure relentlessly applied. George Eastman offered $500,000 if an equal sum was raised. The Rockefeller-supported General Education Board pledged $200,000 and the remaining $300,000 was raised in the nick of time, primarily from alumni who were delighted to be rid of coeducation. Quickly, Susan B. Anthony Memorial Hall, with kitchen, lunchroom, gym, and social room, and Catharine Strong Hall, the academic building with classrooms and auditorium, named for the $100,000 pledged by Henry Strong in memory of his mother, were erected. "Perfect parity"—separate but equal—was the doctrine. Everyone was happy except some of the women students.[10]

It is sometimes maintained that George Eastman discriminated against education for women, his 1898 refusal to contribute to the feminist cause and this 1912 support for the nullification of coeducation being cited. But in the first case he was still genuinely opposed to contributions to all liberal education and in the second case he was following the advice of his expert, Rush Rhees. If Rhees thought it best to teach the women in separate classrooms (some subjects being too delicate for a mixed audience), so be it. Yet Eastman willingly paid for Ellen Andrus's four-year liberal arts education in the 1890s and continued his support of Wells College after her graduation, albeit anonymously by a convoluted scheme calculated to avoid "the holler." And in 1924 he would give $1.5 million to the University of Rochester College for Women—without solicitation. More accurately, it seems that neither Rhees nor Eastman, nor most educators of the period, saw coeducation as either desirable or the wave of the future.

If 1912 was a turning point for Rush Rhees at the University of Rochester, John Slater, Rhees's biographer, also saw it as a watershed in the spiritual life of George Eastman, then age fifty-eight. "He grew more in the remaining twenty years, intellectually, aesthetically, generously, and humanely, than in all his previous life," Slater maintained.[11]

Eastman's interest in education in 1912 was not wholly academic. His own customers, he decided, needed training in modern methods of making, processing, presenting, and selling photographs. So Kodak had established a Traveling Professional School in selected cities to give portrait and commercial photographers intensive courses with modern materials and equipment. In 1912, too, Eastman discovered that Jack Robertson, now head of the Camera Works, had been personally helping certain young workers take evening courses at Mechanics Institute. Eastman broadened this by establishing a special company fund with the proviso that the students take the courses seriously enough to complete them. But 1912 was perhaps most notable, as it related to education, for the beginning of Eastman's career as the mysterious, glamorous, and generous Mr. Smith.

The Massachusetts Institute of Technology was a small land grant college founded in the 1860s by geologist William Barton Rogers and commonly known as Boston Tech when Eastman first contacted faculty members there in search of an engineer to supervise the construction of Kodak Park. Darragh de Lancey, class of 1890, became that engineer upon graduation. Even before de Lancey hired Frank Lovejoy, James Haste, and Harriett Gallup out of MIT, Eastman was moved to write to Dr. Thomas N. Drown, the professor of analytical chemistry who later recommended the quartet, that "I have a great deal of confidence in the material you turn out at your institution."[12] For the next two decades Eastman quietly perused annual reports from MIT.

Like George Eastman, Richard Cockburn Maclaurin, born 5 June 1870 in Scotland and inaugurated president of the Massachusetts Institute of Technology in 1909, was a man of boundless optimism and enthusiasm for his work. Unlike Eastman, he was a specimen of openness and charisma. "When I first came to Technology," Maclaurin recalled later, "and had time to take observations, I found that the Institute was in the doldrums. It was clear that someone was needed to give it a real push." (All the new president wanted was a whole new campus.) Maclaurin's dreams were verbalized in his first annual reports. Sometime when I'm in Boston, I would like to meet this man, Eastman told Josephine Dickman. He said the same to Frank Lovejoy. One or both got in touch with Maclaurin. Primed, Maclaurin took the initiative and wrote to Eastman about how, because MIT's enrollment was just beginning to grow, one-half of its graduates had been out for less than ten years and were therefore not in "a position to help in any very large way financially."

"A recent communication from Mr. Frank W. Lovejoy suggests that you may be ready to lend a helping hand," said Maclaurin, getting straight to the point. The institute had recently purchased a fifty-acre site along the Charles River for a new campus. Of the $750,000 purchase price, $500,000 had been donated by T. Coleman du Pont, president of the MIT board of trustees and alumni association. But no building fund was in sight. In his letter to Eastman, the president then launched into a description that showed an acute awareness of Eastman's views that all architecture should be a variation of the slow burning brick barn or factory building.

"I should gladly visit Rochester," Maclaurin concluded. Don't come *here*, Eastman decided. People would wonder what was going on. A more neutral, anonymous place, the Belmont Hotel in New York, was best for the first meeting. On 5 March the two met for the first time and the next day Eastman dispatched the culmination of twenty-two years of careful thought: "In confirmation of our conversation in New York yesterday, . . . I am prepared to give the Institute, as a building fund, the sum of two and one half millions of dollars; the money to be used exclusively in building suitable buildings for the Institute on the new property which has been acquired." Eastman was more interested in the overall design of the campus than in architectural details.

> No conditions are made as to the architecture of the buildings to be constructed but this subscription has been made after listening to your expressions as to the inappropriateness of the Institute indulging in

any extravagant architectural features and the desirability of getting breadth of effect, more by the proper grouping and general design of the buildings than by elaborate details. One of the objects of this subscription is to enable the Institute to lay out and treat the undertaking as a whole, thereby possibly getting better results than if the buildings were erected at widely different dates.

In a single day, Maclaurin had found his Santa Claus, a stranger who wanted to help, as Carl Ackerman has noted, and did not even want public recognition in return. With the formal letter of 6 March came a personal note: "I am sending you the enclosed letter so as to justify you in altering your plan of campaign for raising money among your alumni but I should prefer not to have it made public, or my name mentioned, until I see you again. . . . No time has been specified for the payment of the money but it will be ready any time that it is needed."

Maclaurin always felt that his most significant career achievement was the raising of money for MIT, especially from Eastman. "At this [initial] meeting," he would write, "as at many since, I could not fail to be impressed with his capacity to go to the heart of a problem quickly and see immediately what the main points are and to keep to those points in later discussion. He was interested in Technology's problems, but made it clear that his continued interest would depend upon its problems being tackled in a bold way and in a liberal spirit. . . . He likes things done well," Maclaurin concluded, "but does not think they are done well unless they are done economically."

By the next day, 7 March, Eastman "acknowledge[d] receipt of your letter of yesterday" with an attitude even more firm about keeping his identity secret as long as possible. "I think it very likely the source of the gift will gradually filter out and all those who have any right to know will know but in the meantime much of the fuss that is made over such a gift will be avoided if the name of the donor is not announced." So, when Maclaurin informed his executive committee about the gift, the largest in the history of the institution, he announced that the donor's name was "Mr. Smith, just Mr. Smith."

The alias caught the public's fancy and caused wide speculation. While avoiding "all the holler" was certainly a motive, Eastman thoroughly enjoyed the ensuing guessing game that ran through the nation's newspapers plus society and education circles. Two New York millionaires, each strongly suspecting the other was "Mr. Smith," met for dinner one night to have it out but separated with only renewed respect for each other's bluffing power. In other cities men and women claimed either to be the elusive Mr. Smith or to be married to the same. No one suspected George Eastman who, at age sixty-two, was unknown nationally as a philanthropist.

"I have seen some of the clippings from the Boston papers . . . of the attempt to locate the donor," he told Maclaurin on 3 April, "and found them very amusing. The matter has quieted down now so that it looks as if the secret might be kept for some time yet, perhaps indefinitely." Eventually nine people knew the identity of Mr. Smith: Dr. and Mrs. Maclaurin (and his secretary), Josephine Dickman, Alice Whitney, Frank Lovejoy—and Seward Prosser and Benjamin Strong Jr., president and vice president of Bankers Trust, New York, respectively—and Mr. Smith himself, of course.

Eastman directed Bankers Trust to make provisions for continuance of the plan in the event of his sudden death, which "might cause delay in our plans and because I want to get all of my matters in good shape before leaving on vacation." Thus, "I do not see why you should not take all the time necessary to perfect your plans before building," he told Maclaurin. "It is not often that an old institution has a chance to plan an entirely new outfit. And it is evident that there is an opportunity to obtain a high degree of efficiency in the layout." Deciding to put some extra funds "at the disposal of the Institute, to draw upon when needed . . . , I am enclosing my check for one million."

Writing checks for $1 million was as much fun as quibbling with workmen over one hundred cents. Maclaurin interpreted Eastman's gifts to MIT as his opportunity to get considerable sums of money (for that time) into effective action for the benefit of the whole country. Eastman wanted MIT to gain world leadership in its chosen field, Maclaurin said, and through his gifts he and the institution would achieve that goal. Once Maclaurin indicated to intimates that Eastman would lose interest in MIT, as he had lost interest in Mechanics Institute, if it did not strive for the highest things. More than one commentator has noted Eastman's "success complex": Achievement was everything and failure was not to be tolerated. As with latter-day foundations, Eastman gave to MIT in proportion to its ability to raise money from other sources, thus keeping Maclaurin from depending on him entirely.

He suggested, but did not insist upon, McKim, Mead & White as architects of the new complex. However, Maclaurin and his board (which did not know Mr. Smith's identity) chose Welles Bosworth. That was apparently all right with Eastman: In June 1913 Eastman increased his subscription by $500,000, "making it three million total."[13] Construction got underway but so did the World War. Eastman had other matters on his mind. Then, in February 1916, Maclaurin hastily penned a note to warn Eastman that "Mr. A. D. Little, a member of the corporation of this Institute, is going to Rochester today in the hope of seeing you and interesting you in a project for strengthening our Department of Chemistry." Eastman didn't mind. He listened attentively to Little's plea for money "to educate chemical engineers to cope effectively with industrial problems," a theme that was close to Eastman's heart. He gave Little a tour of Kodak Park, and a few days later, a check for $300,000. Little was so overwhelmed that he was "quite unable to express my deep sense of appreciation of your splendid generosity toward the Institute of Technology." This time, MIT was allowed to identify its benefactor, a move designed to deter any guessers from getting too close to the truth.

That summer Eastman "drove down to Boston . . . as the guest of Mrs. Dickman to hear the presentation of 'Siegfried' in the Harvard Stadium." "I will reserve Saturday morning to go over and look at the buildings," he told Maclaurin. Ebullient at what he found, he shared his excitement in a panegyric to Frank Babbott, who was ignorant of Mr. Smith's identity:

> The building is all under one roof except the central feature at the back of the court, which contains the small auditorium and library on top . . . perfectly splendid in every way, monumental in character, magnificent in size, and thoroughly appropriate; [constructed of reinforced concrete, faced with Indiana limestone, and . . . not a bit of carving anywhere except on the fluted pillars at seven portals on the interior of the court, which is almost big enough to contain the Harvard medical building. . . . I do not suppose so much talent has ever been employed on working out the detailed arrangement of any building before. The rooms as lighted just about as well as any factory building without interfering with the architectural effect.[14]

Never one to miss the opportunity to start a new project as an old one wound down, upon leaving the MIT campus Eastman went to see Benjamin Forsyth for an hour's talk about the Forsyth Dental Institute on the Fenway in Boston. But Mr. Smith was not finished with MIT. For eight years following his initial gift he added to various endowments and causes, usually with an emphasis on buildings, until the total reached almost $20 million. And always the letter of intent closed with, "I make the same request in regard to not disclosing the source."

When the MIT buildings opened in June 1916, throngs descended upon Boston for a week-long celebration. The public announcement at a banquet of Mr. Smith's latest gift was linked by telephone with similar celebrations in thirty-six other cities. Because of his $300,000 gift as Mr. Eastman, Mr. Smith was invited to attend the Rochester banquet at the Chamber of Commerce, which he had just finished building. He cheered Mr. Smith to the rafters as loudly and enthusiastically as the rest. The alumni presented to the absent "Mr. Smith . . . where'er he is" a volume of drawings of the new buildings that Maclaurin accepted and promised to deliver forthwith. Then in May 1918 Maclaurin received a note with the hint of every college president's dream—unrestricted funds in the form of "$400,000, $4\frac{1}{2}$ percent bonds of the Third Liberty Loan issue."

Together Maclaurin and Eastman worked it out that the bonds would be applied to endowment, the income to be used "for the general purposes of the Institute during the war . . . and thereafter, for the development of courses in chemistry, chemical engineering, and physics; the principal to be available at any time for adding to the main building . . . my intention being that the main building shall continue to represent the funds furnished by me." Maclaurin next made a secret visit to Rochester in June 1919 to plead for more endowment funds. Again Mr. Smith was receptive. Following breakfast at 900 East Avenue Eastman confirmed "my oral offer . . . [to] give the Institute, for endowment purpose, 5,000 shares of Kodak common stock, providing the Institute raise an additional three or four million. . . . The time limit is December 31, 1919. In case the sum is not raised I will donate a lesser number of shares, in proportion to the amount raised." With the donation of Kodak stock, the cat was out of the bag.

The $4 million was easily raised but perhaps at the expense of Richard Maclaurin's health. Rushing to meet the end-of-the-year deadline, he continued soliciting right through an attack of grippe and exhaustion. On the eve of the celebratory banquet at which he was to announce the identity of MIT's great benefactor, Maclaurin suddenly died. It remained for General T. Coleman du Pont to rise and deliver Maclaurin's posthumous speech, the last sentence of which was: "Mr. Smith is George Eastman."

Eastman was hard-headed in his magnanimity as he assumed the role of philanthropist. "The rich man never gives anything," he said. "He only distributes part of his surplus. The credit to him lies in the distribution of that surplus." But he was determined to merit that credit and to make a lasting difference during his lifetime. The wise use of his money preoccupied him. During World War I, he expressed a variant of that thought during a rare speech he agreed to give to sell war bonds in Cathedral Hall at the request of his friend and neighbor, Bishop Thomas G. Hickey, Bernard J. McQuaid's successor. "A rich man should be given credit for the judgment he uses in distributing his wealth, rather than in the amount he gives away." Both Hickey and C. E. Kenneth Mees would later recall that Eastman's burning desire was that the money he distributed "should do good and not harm." This was why he investigated so thoroughly and gave so much personal attention to the organizations that received his gifts.[15]

So imbued with the work ethic was Eastman that once the day-to-day functioning of the company was in the capable hands of such lieutenants as Lovejoy, Stuber, Whitney, Haste, and Mees, he spent more and more time "putting my money to work." When asked for the reason for his munificent gifts, he told a *Rochester Times-Union* reporter: "All I'm trying to do is to work out my own salvation." At first he talked about "charitable work" in a diffuse, general way but as he began to focus on certain areas of interest and decide how much of his philanthropic budget would go to each, he would write about "my work in this area." Certain areas, such as "church work," he declined "not because I have any lack of respect for religious enterprises or lack of appreciation that they form a very necessary part in our life but simply because I cannot subscribe to any of their various beliefs."[16] As he clicked off projects or felt that his money had done as much good as it was going to in a particular field, he would say prophetically, "My work [in this area] is done." In May 1925 he stated succinctly his philosophy of life as he had lived it in a talk he gave at Kodak Park: "By working seriously and effectively in our work hours, much can be done to enable us to make the most of our leisure hours. What we do in our working hours determines what we have in the world. What we do in our play hours determines what we are."

Unlike his contemporaries and acquaintances Andrew Carnegie, Henry Ford, Murry Guggenheim, James Duke, Julius Rosenwald, or John D. Rockefeller, he did not establish a foundation to be administered by trustees after his death and in perpetuity. "Men who leave their money to be distributed by others are pie-faced mutts," he declared in 1924 as he signed away the bulk of his fortune to four educational institutions and gave another $9 million in Kodak stock to company employees. "I want to see the action during my lifetime."

Eastman was modest to the point of anonymity: Even the list compiled by Kodak in November 1932 estimating his philanthropies at $68 million (not including the $25 million estate that went primarily to the University of Rochester at his death) covers only the best known. When the *New York Times* asked for an interview in 1920, immediately after he was revealed as the mysterious "Mr. Smith," he responded that he would "make an appointment but I should tell you in advance that I am very much adverse to making any statement as to my policies in regard to philanthropies."[17] The *Times* published an article entitled "Philanthropy under a Bushel."

It was virtually impossible to exercise influence on the direction of his gifts. Friends, such as Albert Eastwood or Walter Hubbell, were often approached to intervene with Eastman in behalf of a cause. They usually refused because they knew their influence would carry no weight; unless Eastman was wholeheartedly in sympathy with an undertaking, he would give nothing.

He believed that those with large fortunes had different responsibilities than those with modest means. Small givers could take care of individual cases; certain things could only be done with "large bundles of money." The "power of direction" that his wealth gave him meant that he could create institutions that would outlive him the way foundations outlived the other philanthropists. Instead of "taking care of" the teeth and tonsils of one indigent child, he could "clean up" a whole city the size of Rochester or an area of a megacity such as London and still have produced a pilot project that other cities around the world could emulate. This was better than "scattering" his money, which was not infinite, in a helter-skelter fashion among those individuals who wrote the most convincing begging letters. Yet from this well-conceived plan and philosophy of philanthropy the myth arose, at least among his Rochester friends interviewed after his death, that Eastman was interested only in institutions and not individuals.

Newspapers in the 1920s attempted to keep a running box score of his major gifts as they became known, based on the information Alice Whitney could piece together from his correspondence and personal checkbook (over which she held power of attorney in his absence). Up through 1916 his philanthropies amounted to $2,026,600, with the largest recipients being the University of Rochester ($575,000), General Hospital ($500,000), the YMCA ($287,500), the Hahnemann Hospital ($100,000), city parks ($91,500), Homeopathic Hospital ($76,600), Friendly Home ($58,000), Children's Shelter ($43,000), and the YWCA ($28,500). Obligations, partly paid, included the new Chamber of Commerce Building ($500,000) and the Rochester Dental Dispensary ($1,250,000). At this time the massive infusion of millions of dollars for MIT, which would have led the list, was not known. By 1924 the total was $58 million, with Eastman listed as fifth among U.S. philanthropists after John D. Rockefeller, $575 million; Andrew Carnegie, $350 million; Henry Clay Frick, $85 million; and Milton S. Hershey, $60 million. James B. Duke, with $41.5 million, was sixth. At the time of Eastman's death his gifts were initially reported as $69 million, although as the amount of anonymous giving was recalculated, that number was placed closer to $100 million. His estate, originally thought to have been in the neighborhood of $10 million, was found to be more like $25 million, most of that accruing to the University of Rochester as residuary legatee.

Eastman's primary target was education, including medical, musical, technical, and liberal arts, because, as he told a reporter who asked, "The answer is easy. In the first place the progress of the world depends almost entirely upon education. Fortunately the most permanent institutions of men are educational. They usually endure even when governments fall."[18] The University of Rochester, situated as it was in "the town I am interested in above all others," would receive the most, $50 million, followed by MIT with $20 million. He would also give to Hampton and Tuskegee institutes, Howard University Medical School, and Meharry Medical College, all educational institutions for blacks. Cornell University, the Stevens Institute of Technology, the Rochester Athenaeum and Mechanics Institute (now Rochester Institute of Technology), the Brooking Graduate School of Economics and Government, and the Harvard Business School received substantial sums. He would also establish a visiting professorship at Oxford University, a lecture series at Amherst College, and music scholarships at the University of Iowa.

Next to education in interest and dollar amount came health and welfare, with the emphasis always on prevention. Six pilot projects of preventive dentistry for indigent children would be established in Rochester and five

European capitals with the expectation that their success would cause other municipalities to undertake similar ventures. Rochester hospitals were generously supported: Eastman would build a whole new complex for Rochester General Hospital, nurses' wings for the Homeopathic (now Genesee) and Hahnneman (now Highland) hospitals, establish the Maria Kilbourn Eastman Nurse scholarship in both of the latter hospitals, and persuade Henry Strong's daughters to underwrite a teaching hospital for the medical school that he was building. Eastman would head and be the lead giver to the Red Cross, the War Chest, and the Community Chest. He was president of the Rochester Orphan Asylum and gave the major challenge gifts to the building funds of the YMCA and Rochester Friendly Home (for the aged). At an unpopularly early stage he supported national movements in eugenics and birth control.

There were more exceptions than most people realized to his rule about giving money in "big chunks" to institutions rather than small bites to individuals. If any of Eastman's first cousins or their offspring, the children, grandchildren, and great-grandchildren of his fifteen now-deceased aunts and uncles, needed help, Eastman opened his pocketbook. Coping with the Copes was typical. Tommy Cope, who spent so much time at the Waterville homestead of Aunt Maria and cousins Ellen, Katy, and George, married three times and had seven children. Eastman educated the youngest two, Frances and Helen, and the four children of Tommy's son, Walter Cope.[19] Eastman immediately set up a procedure whereby Frances, and later the other five, would write to him when a tuition payment was due and Alice Whitney would send the checks. In between, they were to write and let him know how they were doing, a requirement he would make with David Hochstein and other "individual cases."

Active participation became part of the projects he subscribed to. Sound judgment, astute advice, and keen interest were as important as the money. But by 1900 he could no longer screen all the requests that came pouring in. Because Alice Whitney saved every last scrap of paper addressed to him, it is today possible to see that a preponderance of requests (and an occasional threat of blackmail) came from crackpots and soldiers of fortune. Answering all the begging letters was taking up more and more of his time and he found himself apologizing for a short and definite "No."

Obviously such elaborate attention to each single "individual case" became impractical as both the company and Eastman's reputation as a philanthropist grew. And so he began looking for ways to institutionalize both the health and welfare measures he thought he owed his employees and the private acts of charity that by the early 1900s were too numerous for him to screen individually.

Edgar Long, investment counselor, wondered in 1917 why Eastman didn't hire a "Secretary of Philanthropy, a man who would stand in the same relation to you and your various generous benefactions as [Frederick] Gates does to Mr. John D. Rockefeller" and offered his services "to follow your benefactions to make sure that [your money] is wisely used and properly spent." But Eastman was reluctant to let the process go out of his hands completely—he had no wish to set up a Rochester counterpart to the Rockefeller staff at 61 Broadway—and besides, fifteen years earlier he had engaged "a competent woman who investigates such appeals."

Helen Arnold was the secretary and treasurer, that is, the only paid staff member of the Society for the Organization of Charity of Rochester, New York. Members paid an annual subscription of $150 to this modest institution, founded by a few prominent Rochesterians and maintaining offices in three sections of the city with office hours weekdays 10:00 A.M. to noon. The board and Arnold then dispersed the funds to needy cases that came to their attention. In 1905, a few years after Eastman joined the organization, he had the bright idea of referring cases to Arnold along with a check for $500 every now and then to cover the needs of the organization.[20] Arnold obliged and soon was Eastman's one-person charitable foundation, investigating many of the begging letters he received while he continued to supply her with the grants to cover those she found worthy. Arnold retired from the society in 1912 but not from Eastman's informal employ.[21] Though lame and in poor health herself, Arnold continued to act as Eastman's agent and investigator to the extent of going to New York to investigate the building of model tenements there, in anticipation that Eastman would do the same in Rochester. An unemployment crisis in 1908 due to industrial layoffs (but not at Kodak) led community leaders to start to organize one hundred local charities and religious organizations (but not including Catholic Charities) into a new umbrella organization, United Charities. This absorbed the old Society for the Organization of Charity, which became its Rehabilitation Department and later the Family Welfare Department.[22]

Eastman took no direct or official part in the formation of United Charities (under the directorship of William Kirk of Brown University) but he paced its drive as largest giver and agreed wholeheartedly with the philosophy of combining multiple appeals into one and eliminating overlapping services.[23] Despite some progress in checking duplication of effort, United Charities would lack the staff and leadership to effectively bring all Rochester charities under its umbrella. The older charities particularly went their own ways. It would take the formation of the Patriotic and Community Fund in 1917, commonly called the War Chest, of which Eastman would be president, and the War Chest's successor, the Community Chest, to bring to charitable work in Rochester the same expert and businesslike administration that Eastman demanded at Kodak.

"Pull" Is a Verb

◼ ◼ ▪ ▪ ─────────────────────────────────

The management of the Eastman Kodak Company and the groundbreaking employee relations established by its founder are Eastman's strongest suit. His critics point to his harsh treatment of competitors during the 1890s, including his industrial spying, but even they concede that inside the Big Yellow Box, the employee who toed the mark was richly rewarded. Conversely, those who didn't—such as William H. Walker, Henry Reichenbach, George Monroe, Walter Butler, George B. Selden, Sam Mora, George Davison, Harris Hayden—were treated as harshly as any competitor. Still, if GE can sound a little too good to be true when viewed only through his slogans and pronouncements, it is well to remember that not only were these codified as policy by his immediate successors, but they have been energetically revived in the 1990s during one of Kodak's darker periods financially, by the first CEO who did not rise through the ranks. If the Eastman life versus the Eastman legend is fuzzy in this area, it may be because Eastman instinctively knew that ideas and legends can be the most powerful tools a leader has, and pragmatically he made the most of them. What he did behind the scenes in individual cases may not always live up to the legend.

The kind of employee Eastman wanted was partially determined by the kind of employee he did not want. One day the widow of an old friend called looking for a job for her college graduate son who had been spared the hard knocks of life. The young man had no "pull," the mother complained. "He has his oar in, but isn't getting anything worthwhile." Eastman's answer was that the young man, "when he was a little fellow, had nothing to do but play.

Your idea . . . was to safeguard him and save him from the rough corners of this world. You pampered him; he had no chores to do. . . . He didn't have to . . . fill the wood-box for his mother. . . . Our cities are full of steam-heated incompetents, looking for somebody with 'pull' to do their 'pulling' for them. . . . 'Pull,' much as I regret it on your boy's account, Madam, is not a noun; 'pull' is a verb."[1] A variation on that crisp aphorism, which extolled the value of "push" in the achievement of success, was first quoted in 1917 by Joe Mitchell Chapple in his weekly *Personal Interview Letter Series*, conversations with business leaders. It would continue to be attributed to Eastman.

Eastman thought that early hardships made him realistic about life, helping him develop independence and initiative. He had strong opinions about nepotism from his early experience at the bank that shaped his philosophy in dealing with employees. Soon he was saying things like, "If anybody *alone* decides whether a man is to be promoted it is the man himself."[2] Or, "the past and continued prosperity of our Company is not due to the value of a patent or an invention. Quality can only be secured by extreme skill and alertness not only as individuals but as an organization." This was a sea change in business philosophy from the nineteenth century, when patent protection was everything to Eastman. The Goodwin suit proved to him that patent protection could not keep a company healthy. Only people could. "An organization cannot be sound unless its spirit is," he said. "That is the lesson the man on the top must learn. He must be a man of vision and progress who can understand that one can muddle along on a basis in which the human factor takes no part, but eventually there comes a fall."[3]

The Eastman Kodak Company would be a meritocracy, with future leaders trained by current ones. "The ideal large corporation is one that makes the best use of the brains within it,"[4] Eastman decreed. "No one merits promotion in his work until he has trained the man under him to take his place." Future presidents were not sought by headhunters; from 1880 to 1993 they rose through the ranks. This made it difficult for people to enter the company at the middle-management level. "We try to fill all positions by promotion," Eastman told one applicant. "I have run across young men who, like yourself, I should like to get into the Company but it is almost impossible to do it except at the bottom without lessening the esprit de corps of those who are in line for promotion." In the closing years of his tenure, a journalist would describe him as "a modest, direct man in his seventy-fifth year, a person without any frills. . . . His business has reared its own staff of executives, and smoothly runs itself with that minimum of supervision which is the principle of its founder."[5]

"As labor conditions grow more difficult, it will be greatly to the advantage of the Company to be a leader not a follower," he warned Strong in 1912. "Our employees are well satisfied and loyal and the new [Wage Dividend] plan can only make them more so. . . . I do not know of any [business] that depends more upon the good feeling and faithfulness of its employees." He had ideas about Social Security before it became a popular phrase, even though the problem of employment and wages in his own industry was not a serious one. Because the business was new and expanding, he had always been able to pay wages equal to or higher than those prevailing in the marketplace. This led to grumbling by those in older Rochester industries such as shoe and men's clothing manufacturing, which were not expanding but were convulsed by devastating strikes. The absence of labor unions at Eastman Kodak confounded labor organizers, who called it reactionary and repressive, and filled outside executives with wonder and envy. His reputation for fairness was such that he served as arbitrator in a strike of Rochester masons against contractors over the matter of wages—with his judgment accepted by both sides. A paternalistic aura overtook Kodak Park as ubiquitous posters admonished safety on and off the job and display cases featured the latest Suggestion Box winners. The employee's every recreational desire was gradually being met through gyms, auditoriums, shooting galleries, bowling alleys, camera clubs, baseball teams and stadiums, and the like. One result was that during Eastman's lifetime the company boasted one of the lowest employee turnover rate of any major corporation—about 10 percent per year.[6]

In lieu of labor contracts Eastman tried to anticipate rather than react to labor's demands and the absence of work stoppages attest to his success. At the turn of the century a series of accidents—the collapse of a building under construction, the accidental electrocution of a worker, heart attacks on the job—led Eastman to consider ways of preventing and meeting emergencies. At first he personally assisted widows and families of victims but as that became impractical he pressed his directors to set aside $1 million (half in 1909, half in 1910) for a permanent Welfare Fund. "The interest on this fund," he told James Haste, manager of Kodak Park, "is to be used in relieving employees who need help, either on account of sickness, or old age, or any other cause. . . . We have so far dealt with each case on its merits and charged the expense up to the product. In view of the fact that our earnings may not continue to be as large and that the age and number of our employees is continually increasing, I thought it wise to put aside a good bunch of capital."[7] The Welfare Fund began three years before the New York State Workmen's Compensation Act was passed. As one of the first such funds in the country, it anticipated sick pay, disability payments, pension, and hospital benefit plans.

Altruism was not Eastman's only motive in setting up seminal employee-benefit programs. As he explained to William Hall Walker, who was grumbling about such measures because they cut into dividends, "There are four directions in which the payment of big dividends could operate to the disadvantage of the company: 1. The stimulation of competition. 2. Attracting the attention of the government during this period of excitement about the Sherman [antitrust] Law. 3. The effect upon our employees. 4. The effect upon our customers. . . . The third objection we are endeavoring to take care of through our wage dividend and welfare fund."[8] And so Kodak was one of the first concerns to adopt the idea of wage dividends and pensions— about forty years ahead of most companies.[9] Eastman conceived the dividend (now called the annual "Kodak bonus") not as income to be spent, but as reserve for workers' later years. But it became evident that not all workers had the discipline or compulsion to save that Eastman did and thus reached retirement age without sufficient resources to provide for themselves properly. When Frank Babbott inquired how he had arrived at the formula for the 1912 wage dividend plan, the childhood friend replied:

> I have examined all of the propositions in this line that I could find, and I do not believe in putting any string on the money. The employee is either entitled to it or he is not. If he is entitled . . . he should not be treated like a child. . . . The way our dividend is fixed the employee has a very live interest in the prosperity of the Company and he does not run the risk of losing capital as he would if he bought common shares. Very few employees are capitalists and if they have any extra money what they should do with it first is to buy a place to live in. If, on the other hand, they are extravagant and want to waste the money, the Company has no right to use any force to prevent them. As you know, I do not believe in anything that favors patronage. The majority of the employees are keen enough to see through it and it makes them sore as indeed it should.[10]

"The scheme involves everybody on the payroll," Eastman told Strong, "except officers of the New Jersey Company which means Miss Whitney, Mr. Noble, Walter Hubbell and me. It does not include you either, partly because I cannot find that you have any salary."[11] And so, beginning 1 April 1912, every Kodak employee received a "two percent dividend on his wages of the past five years. . . . I do not really see anything else to do," Eastman declared in mock despair. "If we do not devise some other way of using the money the shareholders will begin to kick at having such big dividends crowded on them."[12] With minor alterations, Eastman's wage dividend plan remains in effect. "You can talk about cooperation and good feeling and friendliness from morning to midnight," he told the *New York Times* in 1920, "but the thing the worker appreciates is the same thing the man at the helm appreciates—dollars and cents."

By 1910 the price of Kodak stock was soaring—selling at $500 and more— and the two retired partners, Strong and Walker, were making a killing. Eastman released them and Josephine Dickman "from the syndicate arrangement," while noting that "it is not likely that I shall ever want to sell any Kodak stock, at least while I am managing the business; so if at any time you want to sell you can do so without thinking of me." Eastman found it more satisfying to quietly donate his stock to educational institutions like Tuskegee and MIT or with modest fanfare to his employees. Without any personal heirs on whom he wished to bestow the bulk of his estate, he distributed $80 million to public institutions during his lifetime and $25 million more through his will. Had he held on to the capital and invested it, he might have died worth $200 million or $300 million. When Strong wondered why Kodak stock was not always listed on the exchange, Eastman admitted, "I do not keep much track of the stock market." By 1910 he had basically lost all drive to accumulate. His money was sitting around in various banks earning little or no interest or finding its way to his favorite educational and charitable enterprises. But even these took second place to the industry he had built and his greatest pride now was that it enabled a great many people to earn a living. He thought first of those people in distributing the fruits of that business in gestures that said "well done" to employees.[13]

Equal opportunity employment was not a concept of Eastman's time, but there is evidence that he was moving in that direction. Women were hired as chemists from the days of Eliza Tompkins and Harriet Gallup de Lancey; Alice Whitney was one of the most powerful figures in the company. He believed in giving people a second chance. In 1917 Vincent Love, Convict No. 28,798 at Auburn State Prison, was pardoned by Governor Charles Whitman on Eastman's pledge to help "this man who has borne his punishment for eleven years in a satisfactory manner. I am pleased to confirm . . . that we will give him a job so he can become a self-supporting member of the community at once."[14] Employing the handicapped won his approval. After the Eastman School of Music opened, Rush Rhees called his attention to a blind piano tuner, and Eastman immediately telephoned the director of the school, "suggesting that he consider this application. It would be a highly desirable thing to employ such a young man." Employment possibilities for needy students and scholarship students at the school was another concern: "Among the positions that might be filled by students are running elevators, vacuuming apparatus, part of the janitor work, ushering in Kilbourn Hall, ushering in the [Eastman] Theatre, running motion picture apparatus, office detail work, piano tuning, etc."[15]

Eastman constantly worried that the price of Kodak stock was too high for the ordinary investor, particularly a Kodak employee. He then told Strong an anecdote about a manager whose business went sour during his regime so that its stock "was within the reach of the humblest purse. I am considering now whether I cannot do some work in this direction myself. The Welfare Fund is the first step; the Wage Dividend the next; and if we can only find a third step we will begin to show some results. What will it be?"[16] That third step came in 1919 when Eastman was sixty-five. He had thought to leave, at his death, a large block of Kodak common stock so that it could be acquired by employees. But, "as I have given up on an early demise," a new plan was devised. He donated ten thousand shares of the common stock he held, one-third of his holdings, contingent on the setting aside of an equal block of unissued company-held stock. Kodak people were eligible to buy at par stock equal to 2 percent of their total earnings. Par was $100 and the current market price $575; hence the gift had an immediate market value of $5 million to employees. Proceeds from the sale would go into a Welfare Fund created for the benefit of all the employees. The only adverse comments on the plan came from lower-bracket wage earners, who found it difficult to scrape together an amount equal to 2 percent of their earnings. However, Eastman was set against gift stock, believing that it would be immediately sold and not foster a sense of proprietary interest in the company.

"I wish to donate that stock," he told his board, "but the plan should not end there. It has advantages which are valuable to the Company and stock-holders . . . and I feel very strongly that the Company should make it possible to continue the plan and enable future employees . . . to look forward to the enjoyment of a similar privilege upon a common basis. . . . This can be done if the Company will set aside a portion of its unissued common stock . . . for sale at par."[17] In explaining the reasons for the stock dividend distribution plan of 1919 to *System* magazinne, Eastman said:

> Because we are alert to employee's personal finances they are alert to ours. . . . The past and continued prosperity of our Company is not due to the value of a patent or an invention. Many competitors make the same kind of goods we do. . . . We have no controlling patents. We have to depend upon quality, which requires painstaking research, constant scrutiny, and improvement of the smallest details. Quality can only be secured by extreme skill and alertness. . . . Sharing profits secures alertness [and] loyalty, too. In the last twenty years, for example, almost none of our valuable executives or technicians have left our organizations.[18]

A copy of the letter to the employees went to Strong (Walker having died in 1917), along with one of Eastman's last letters to his old partner, dated 12 March 1919. Strong would die in July of that year and for some time previous was too ill to carry on his end of the once-vigorous correspondence. "If you do not feel like writing get Hattie to send me a line once in a while," Eastman's last handwritten postscript read. "Young and vigorous as I am, I hate most awfully to write a letter myself in long hand. If it were not for Miss Whitney, I am afraid even you would hear from me mighty seldom. Don't worry about the load on my shoulders. The steering machine is so interesting that I seldom think about the chances of running off the road." The bulk of the letter informed Strong of a new program for dealing with employee grievances: "We are . . . meeting with the representatives of the employees, with an idea of devising some plan whereby grievances can be handled without friction. Inasmuch as we are already on such good terms with our employees and this enterprise is not undertaken under duress, we hope in a year or so to make the Company stand at or near the top in industrial relations."[19]

And so, as Marion Folsom would observe years later, while Eastman was a conservative in politics and economics, intellectually he was profoundly radical.

Although in the nineteenth century Eastman did all of the hiring and firing, by 1900 he was sending out many letters to the effect that he had nothing to do with the hiring of employees, and he made that point particularly clear to friends such as the mother of the young man with no "pull." There were times, however, when he broke his own rule. In 1912 he wanted the man he considered "the greatest expert on color photography" so badly that he not only went to England and hired C. E. Kenneth Mees, but also agreed to buy Mees's company (including a factory in Budapest Eastman had no need for) and to establish Kodak's new Research Laboratories that Mees was to head on a much more theoretical, less practical basis than Eastman originally envisioned. Two years later he decided he wanted a graduate of the fledgling Harvard Business School for the commercial side of his business. And so he dropped in to see the dean.[20]

Marion B. Folsom, who had graduated from the University of Georgia at eighteen and was now slated to graduate at twenty-one with highest honors, was minding his own business in the small library of the Harvard Business School one afternoon in May 1914, when he was summoned to the dean's office and told that upon faculty recommendation, an appointment had been set for him to be interviewed by Eastman the next afternoon at the Hotel Touraine in Boston. The dean was of course terribly anxious to enlist Eastman's financial support for the business school, which had only been in operation since 1908. Folsom, who up to that moment planned to return to Georgia and enter his father's business, then returned to the library to look up the Eastman Kodak Company in the financial books. "The information was meager, especially when compared with the railroad reports," Folsom recalled in 1968. It was enough to show a prosperous and growing company, but Folsom was surprised to find that Eastman as founder was only listed as treasurer and general manager, not president. Small in comparison with modern corporations, the company was considered a large concern for 1914 with about seven thousand employees in Rochester and ten thousand worldwide.[21]

In the hotel room the next day Folsom faced a sixty-year-old "in the prime of health" who told him a little, very little, about the work he wanted Folsom to do except that it would be in Lovejoy's office. Eastman asked almost nothing about the student's courses, interests, or background. But, Folsom recalled, "I was impressed with Mr. Eastman's frank, direct manner and friendly attitude, and with the general brevity of his speech." Folsom himself was a soft-spoken, mild-mannered, almost mousy man of few words and no visible vices. On 8 June 1914 Eastman alerted Harvard that "Mr. Folsom has accepted the position I offered him and I shall be glad if you will kindly put in writing what you told me about his record and any information you may have about him." Young Folsom went off to Europe for the summer as planned, but with letters of introduction to the manager of Kodak branches concerning "a young man who is going to join our business staff in the fall. Mr. Folsom has had no experience in our line up to the present time but I should like to have him take advantage of his visit to Europe and see our [London, Paris, Berlin] establishment and bespeak for him your kind attention," Eastman wrote Mattison, Harries, and Janson. Like Eastman, Folsom left Europe just as war was breaking out and on one of the last ships. Meanwhile he had accepted Eastman's offer and agreed to start in October at $100 a month.[22]

A person could not help "liking Mr. Lovejoy from the first encounter," Folsom decided after his new boss had driven him around town to find a place to live and ensconced him in a small adjoining office. He saw little of Eastman for the next three years except for an initial encounter in his "very impressive suite," during which he "suggested I not let it be known he had personally hired me." Folsom honored this agreement until the history of the Harvard Business School was written by a faculty member, divulging "how I was selected for employment by the Kodak firm."[23]

The company Folsom encountered in 1914 was "a simple organization with few titles. Frank S. Noble, a director in charge of most of the commercial activities, had the title of assistant treasurer, and the only vice-president was a practicing attorney, Walter S. Hubbell, who was also secretary and general counsel." Top executives handled a wide range of activities with no staffs other than secretaries. It was a company whose foreign branches felt the brunt of war three years before this country entered it, and Folsom's first job was to collect statistics for Lovejoy on the changing conditions of the worldwide organizations. In 1916 the company adjusted wages to meet the increase in the cost of living based in part on a cost-of-living index for Rochester that Folsom prepared. On the assumption that the emergency was temporary, the first increase was put in a separate pay envelope.[24]

Simple organization notwithstanding, "it was the Kodak Company that formed Folsom," Joseph Alsop concluded in a 1955 article for the *Saturday Evening Post* about the man sometimes called the father of the Social Security system, who was then the new Secretary of Health, Education, and Welfare in the Eisenhower cabinet. Alsop continued: "One must try, therefore, to understand the company in order to understand the man. In particular, one must try to understand the greatest single influence in Folsom's life, George Eastman, whom Folsom to this day always calls 'Mr. Eastman' with a perceptible tone of reverence."[25]

In 1914 Folsom, a Georgia Democrat and ardent admirer of Woodrow Wilson, was thrown into a hot bed of Republicanism that was especially hostile to Wilson because of the antitrust case still pending against the company. Folsom recalled overhearing Eastman and Lovejoy the November morning after the 1916 presidential election, when the results were still in doubt. Wall Street was betting odds on Hughes, said Lovejoy. Eastman, who was a presidential elector for Hughes, as he had been for McKinley in 1900 and would be for Hoover in 1928, replied with satisfaction, "Well, money talks."[26] As the early optimism faded into gloom, Folsom, like Brer Rabbit, kept his own counsel.

In May 1917 Folsom entered officers' training camp, subsequently saw service with the AEF, and upon discharge in 1919 was asked by Lovejoy to return and organize a statistical department. Because undergraduate business schools were being organized in colleges all over the country with few persons with graduate degrees available to teach, he also had offers to join the faculties of the University of Georgia, Georgia Tech, and Emory University in Atlanta. At age twenty-seven, he was offered the deanship of a new school at the University of Georgia. But Folsom claimed in 1968 that he "never regretted the decision to return to Kodak, although I was sorry to leave the South."[27]

Few corporations had centralized statistical departments, but Lovejoy sent Folsom to visit one that did, the American Telephone and Telegraph Company, right after he rejoined Kodak in July 1919. Within the year Eastman decided Folsom and his statistics were such a good thing that Lovejoy would have to share them. Indeed, in inventing a title, "probably unique in industry," Folsom said later, and in moving Folsom's office from adjacent to Lovejoy's to adjoining his own office, Eastman was effectively taking over Folsom. (On the other hand, someone finally had a toe into Alice Whitney's private fiefdom, a listening post inside the inner sanctum.) Lovejoy wasted little time before commandeering Albert K. Chapman, who had founded the development department immediately after the war, to become *his* assistant. Eventually, both Folsom and Chapman, assistants to the two principal managers of the company, would develop their own staffs. Meanwhile Eastman sent a GE-signed memo to eighteen executives, and to plant and department managers, which began: "I have appointed Mr. M. B. Folsom Statistical Secretary to the President, to organize a department in which statistics regarding all phases of the business will be centralized. This department is intended not only to collect statistics for my own use but also to be of assistance to all executives."[28] Not only was Folsom's job to summarize the voluminous reports now coming to Eastman and to develop monthly graphic charts comparing sales and trends with previous years, but also to chart the attendance at the Eastman Theatre relative to the movie being shown during a particular week, and to prepare an organization chart of all the household staff of 900 East Avenue and list their functions.

Folsom soon discovered that some of the oldest and presumably most secure employees, such as Lovejoy and L. B. Jones, were actually terrified of the boss. Folsom suggested that the company substitute a more complete annual report for the four-page format that had been in use for twenty-five years. Lovejoy and Jones okayed Folsom's draft and dummy, which included glossy pictures of the various plants and a colored one of the new store in the Place Vendome, Paris, but declined to present it to Eastman. It's up to you, Folsom, they said. So he did it, and the dragon proved to be a pussy cat. Eastman made one correction—changing the word "agriculture" to "horticulture" as was correct in context—but then approved in toto the draft of a greatly expanded annual report.[29]

The one-man company became less so in 1919 when Eastman was sixty-five—late in a corporation's history for staff functions to develop. Price, Waterhouse & Company was asked to present a plan for reorganization and its study questioned the wisdom of such highly centralized control as exercised by Eastman and Alice Whitney with so little staff assistance. Eastman may have agreed in principle: Since the beginning of the century he based many company decisions and actions on what might happen "in the case of my death." And at the time, decentralization seemed the wave of the future: Pierre S. du Pont was doing it with his company as was General Motors. But Kodak was deeply mired in an antitrust suit in which the Justice Department was seeking to dissolve the corporation by breaking it up into autonomous divisions, each with its own staff. Eastman was arguing with considerable vigor that such a breakup would destroy the coordination of research and the sequence of production of photosensitive emulsions.

Rather than play into the hands of the Justice Department, whose demands Eastman considered unreasonable, the major suggestion of the study was rejected. Instead, five vice presidents were created, each with his own area of responsibility. Lovejoy was named vice president in charge of manufacturing, Stuber of photographic quality, Noble of sales, James S. Havens of the legal department, with Hubbell remaining as the company's outside counsel. Between 1919 and 1925, when he actually retired, Eastman gradually withdrew from the active management of the company by devoting himself to outside activities, principally the establishment of the Eastman Theatre and School of Music. Alice Whitney received no new title but since

everything cleared through her, including employee relations and philanthropies, her power remained undiminished.

In 1909 Congress passed the Corporation Excise Tax, a thinly disguised
income tax that the Supreme Court declared constitutional. Then Congress
and the states approved Amendment 16 to the Constitution. The first federal
income tax went into effect on 1 March 1913, providing a one percent normal
tax on incomes, plus a surtax of 6 percent on incomes above $200,000.
Eastman joshed to Strong: "Miss Whitney made up my income tax report. It is
too early yet to know whether she has to go to jail or not. How I am ever going to
raise the money to pay the tax I do not know." During World War I, the normal
tax was increased from 6 to 12 percent on individuals with the surtax as high as
65 percent on incomes in Eastman's bracket. He then began switching his investments to tax-free municipal bonds. Still, in 1918 he paid about $1.5 mil-
lion in personal federal income tax and began declining to make investments,
no longer on the grounds that he did not invest in any enterprise outside photography, but "on account of the Income Tax." In 1921 he told the Reverend
Paddock in Idaho whose school for indigents he had long supported that
"Taxation nowadays takes more than two-thirds of my surplus cash."[30]

Certain minor suggestions of the Price, Waterhouse study were immediately adopted. A new department of customer service and correspondence
was set up. Partly in response to a postwar slump in morale among workers,
limited neither to Kodak nor Rochester, a health, welfare, and industrial
relations department was conceived. For once no one inside the company
seemed qualified.[31] W. H. Cameron of the National Safety Council was
finally hired in 1919 with Dr. Charles Eaton, consultant on industrial relations, engaged to work directly with Kodak superintendents and foremen,
educating them in the most modern techniques of management. The next
year, *Kodak Magazine* was founded, edited by employees, and the new catch-
word "quality" was established—a word that would remain the company's
primary stated goal to the present day.[32] Unlike other American corporations of the period, such as Du Pont, which was founded as a gunpowder
company and whose leaders were denigrated as "merchants of death," Kodak maintained its image as the benign purveyor of pleasure and happiness
through amateur photography.

Like other American corporations of the period Kodak became the developer of two suburban housing projects. Meadowbrook, comprising ninety-
eight acres in Brighton (where Eastman as a teen held mortgages), was
developed by the Kodak Employees Realty Corporation. Six- and seven-
room houses with attached garages sold for $10,500 to $16,500, mostly to
rising Kodak executives. In the suburb of Greece near Kodak Park, Koda-
Vista with more modest homes was developed for worker housing. The
Kodak Grammar School, later renamed the Kodak Union Free School, was
also established in Greece.[33]

In 1921 Rochester and Kodak were hit with a postwar depression. Benjamin Seebohm Rowntree, British Quaker philanthropist, lectured in Rochester about unemployment insurance. Folsom heard the lecture and discussed it with Eastman, who made the extraordinary leap of instructing Folsom to prepare a scheme of private unemployment insurance for Kodak. In the end the plant managers and supervisors objected mightily to the scheme and the depression lifted. But Folsom continued to study the mainly European literature on social welfare, "certainly an odd pastime for a coming young executive," Alsop commented, "until he became one of the handful of American experts in the field." About that time retirement became a problem at Kodak. Because working for Kodak was widely considered as the best employment in Rochester, most of the workers who started with the company in the 1880s and 1890s stayed on and on. But by the 1920s even they had begun to retire. Eastman had strong feelings about "these young jackanapes who want to put Old Bill on the street after forty years" but also strong feelings about pensions being a reward for improvidence and a penalty on self-reliance. "It got so none of us dared mention pension plans to Mr. Eastman," Folsom told Alsop. "And then a friend of his whom he couldn't very well throw out of his office happened to tackle him on the subject." Eastman invited Folsom to meet this friend, Walter Forster, insurance agent and "the fastest talking man in America." Soon Eastman, who had always held that with good wages and the substantial annual bonus the company had done its part, and it was up to the individual to take care of retirement, asked Folsom to find out what other progressive companies were doing.[34]

The plan finally recommended to Eastman provided for a retirement annuity, life insurance, and total disability benefits. It was inaugurated 1 January 1929. The purpose, as Eastman wrote in a cover letter, was "to provide, more liberally and reliably . . . an income for old age, a proper protection for disability, and life insurance." He also decided that Kodak didn't know anything about the insurance business and that the plan could be better managed, and with fewer hazards, by the Metropolitan Life Insurance Company. The 1929 plan represented a culmination for Eastman of the advances made since his unexpected sharing of his own personal profit from acting as promoter in the 1898 reorganization of the company in London as Kodak Limited. "A comprehensive program of industrial relations has now been established," he wrote his "fellow employees in the Kodak Company." His work in that area was now done.[35]

Pension and retirement plans were not unknown in American industry, but they were uncommon. Businessmen tended to regard them as evidence of managerial softheartedness and softheadedness. The Kodak plan, prepared by Folsom, turned out to be fiscally conservative, hailed by the *Atlantic Monthly* as an important advance, and withstood the test of time. Soon Folsom was called to testify before the United States Investigation of Unemployment and named to advise the New York State Legislative Committee on Unemployment. In 1930 the Eastman Kodak Company, with seventeen other Rochester concerns, formulated plans for unemployment insurance. Some, including Kodak, actually put the plans into effect. Eastman was interested first in Kodak employees, then in Rochester workers, and finally in workers all over the nation. If Rochester could hammer out a workable plan, he thought, it might guide the legislators in Albany to adapt it.

Folsom went on to become one of the architects of the Social Security measures adopted by the national government several years after Eastman's death. Ruminating in 1968, Folsom said: "I have often wondered how Mr. Eastman would have reacted to Social Security measures. . . . I am inclined to think his views would have been [that] . . . as a result of the depression, governmental action was necessary and that the contributory social insurance was far better than relief measures to prevent destitution. . . . In spite of the opposition of the great majority of business people, . . . Mr. Eastman did approve the Rochester Unemployment Benefit Plan, adapted in 1931." Folsom's own conclusion to his years of close association was that "Mr. Eastman was the only man I ever knew who started out a conservative and ended up a liberal."[36]

My Hometown

"Back into the community he is putting some of the fortune made by the Kodak Company," interviewer Arthur Gleason told his readers. "Two-thirds . . . of his public gifts have gone to his home town of Rochester. His idea is to make Rochester a better place for the community to work and live in. This means health, enjoyment, artistic development."[1]

Rochester was never a prototypical company town, although its successive nicknames derive from whatever industry was dominant at a given time. "The Flour City" of the early nineteenth century reflected the mills on the Genesee; after midcentury the more decorous "Flower City" was attached, in deference to the growing nursery trade. By the early 1900s it was definitely "Kodak City" remaining so to the present. Eastman's lifelong love affair with Rochester—he skipped over his birthplace of Waterville to call it "my home town"—is unique in the annals of American communities. In few other places has a man, a company, and a city been so closely identified. For all of this century, between one-fifth and one-third of all residents have been dependent on the area's largest employer for a major portion of their income, but Eastman's and Kodak's influence have been wider than that.

The University of Rochester (now the area's third largest employer), its School of Medicine and Dentistry, its Eastman School of Music, its attractive River Campus at a bend of the Genesee, and the Eastman Dental Center are obvious community assets that would not exist without Eastman's money and vision. The city's level of health care, its governmental efficiency, its libraries, and its museums—all directly or indirectly owe their existence to the same man. The Rundel Building that houses the Rochester Public Library was built with Kodak stock bought by Morton Rundel, Eastman's distant cousin. Rundel's death in 1911 went nearly unnoticed until it was found that he had bequeathed to Rochester a sum for the construction of an art gallery and library. Litigation kept the Rundel funds in limbo until 1933, when construction of a library building (an art gallery having been built in 1913 by Emily Sibley Watson) was begun as a means of stimulating building trades during the Depression. The Rundel fund then totaled about $1 million. The Strong Museum, opened in 1982, was also built with Kodak stock originally purchased by Eastman's Ambrose Street landlord, Edmund Frost Woodbury. That stock was passed to his only son, then to his only grandchild, Margaret Woodbury Strong, who founded the museum and bequeathed some $80 million in that stock to it.

Blake McKelvey, former Rochester city historian, noted in 1987 that "Rochester's golden age may have been from 1905 to 1925 when George Eastman spent some of his money. We haven't had that same degree of creativity since then."[2] Roger Butterfield, who extensively researched Eastman's life in the 1950s in preparation for a biography that he never completed, found that "George Eastman's life and Rochester's development during much of the first half of this century were so intertwined, and often interdependent, that the story of one is an explanation of the other."[3] While Eastman's business, cultural, and philanthropic interests were worldwide in scope, Rochester was the hub of all three. His leadership in community affairs came to flower during World War I and the postwar period. After the war he emerged as the city's dominant leader in practically every aspect of community life. His sense of social responsibility developed gradually and knew few bounds.

Cynics maintained that his generosity was just a calculated effort to keep the skilled labor force from becoming restless and moving elsewhere, and indeed he carefully underscored the pragmatic motive for his gifts in many of his public pronouncements. Yet the cloak of anonymity that initially surrounded his gifts—"philanthropy under a bushel," the *New York Times* called it—suggests that he derived pleasure, for its own sake, from watching Rochester prosper under his silent regime. Having no immediate family on which to lavish his excess wealth and believing that unearned wealth only spoils heirs, Eastman nominated Rochester as his major legatee. He once defined a citizen's duties as first, keeping himself solvent; second, supporting his family; and third, supporting his community.[4] If Kodak can be considered his surrogate "wife," his community became his extended family.

Earlier philanthropists such as Andrew Carnegie invented the concept of welfare capitalism, that combination of ambition and idealism that made it a self-imposed duty to give gigantic fortunes away while one was still alive. Eastman was a follower in that sense; indeed, he admitted to John D. Rock-

efeller that he considered the old Standard Oil tycoon "the foremost philanthropist of the age and have admired the wisdom with which your vast wealth
is being distributed."[5] But Eastman so personalized his philanthropic projects, from conception through execution, that he stands apart. He attended
to the details of philanthropy himself rather than hiring a squad of bureau-
crats. He concentrated his efforts in Rochester, where he could personally
supervise everything on his way to and from work. Except for his contributions to MIT, Oxford, Tuskegee, and Hampton, he rarely just threw money
at a project and let others make the decisions. As long as he stuck to noncontroversial gifts, such as park land, a Chamber of Commerce building, hospital wings, or paying off the debt of the YMCA, his gifts were gratefully
received. The recipients may have squirmed to be so beholden to a rich and
powerful dispenser of favors, but they did not refuse the bounty. Only when
he tangled with what could be turned into a political controversy (a new city
hall, low-cost housing for the poor, the creation of the city manager system to
replace an elected mayor), or when he thought he could deal with tempera-
mental artists the way he dealt with engineers, did he run into trouble.

The publicity inherent in philanthropy made *him* squirm: "I understand
that the YMCA people have a crowd of money raisers who go at it in a raw
sort of way." He preferred that his philanthropies stay sub rosa: "I object
seriously to having my name used in any prominent way with this campaign."
His shyness kept him from receiving thanks or compliments graciously: "I
do not want every time I pick up a paper to see something about 'George
Eastman's munificent gift,'" he wrote a newspaper editor. "The fun is in the
game rather than the mostly unintelligible holler about it," he told cousin
Almon. He arranged to be out of town—preferably on the other side of the
world—whenever anything connected with his name was announced or
dedicated: "I deeply appreciate the honor and deeply regret that it is wholly
impossible for me to accept." Invitations to testimonials to his bounty made
him forthright: "I should be embarrassed beyond measure on such an occasion and do not feel I could go through with the ordeal." Yet if the cause was
one that could be helped by his physical or public presence, such as a Red
Cross or a War Bond Drive, he would come out of hiding, accept a chairmanship, ride on a float, make a speech, or even lead a parade of six thousand
Kodak workers down Main Street.[6]

In 1900 it seemed that technical education would be Eastman's chief philan-
thropic target. His earliest substantive gift, his earliest community board
membership, his earliest gift of a building were all connected with the
Rochester Atheneum and Mechanics Institute (now Rochester Institute of
Technology). It might have remained his sole interest. Unfortunately for
RIT, but fortunately for MIT and the University of Rochester, where strong

leadership inspired Eastman to make large unrestricted gifts, he became disenchanted with the management of Mechanics Institute in the early 1900s. Four superintendents ran the various divisions as separate fiefdoms, reporting to citizen committees and the board rather than to a strong administrator. There was no endowment; the institute lived solely on annual contributions and was accumulating a hefty debt. After the announcement of Eastman's $200,000 gift in 1900, trustees sought but failed to get an endowment that would put it on a par with Pratt in Brooklyn and Drexel in Philadelphia. The institute conferred no degrees, sending students to the University of Rochester for academic subjects. Lewis P. Ross, shoe manufacturer and Eastman's neighbor, was for a time president of both the university's and the institute's board of trustees. Ross suggested to Eastman about 1902 that the university and institute combine. This solution was never acted upon.[7]

In 1910 with Eastman as board president, the highly recommended Carlton Gibson was brought in to "put the institute on scientific basis" as its first president. With the outbreak of war in 1914, Gibson asked for a brief leave to go to Europe with Herbert Hoover and distribute food. Then he asked for an extension to that leave, and then another, and another until finally in May 1915, Eastman asked for his resignation. Gibson's indignant ten-page response ("Here I am feeding the starving . . . " etc.) was buried deep in Eastman's correspondence, with only Gibson's dignified resignation released to trustees and community.[8]

By 1917 things were back to where they had started. "An educational institution travels on four wheels—the trustees, the faculty, the student body, and the alumni," one unhappy Mechanics Institute faculty member wrote Eastman. "This is well shown by the developments at the University of Rochester in the past few years while at the Mechanics Institute at least three wheels are off the ground. Neither the president nor at least three of the four superintendents has the confidence of the faculty, the student body, or the alumni or the informed general public."[9] Application was made to New York State to make the institute a public trade school. When this, too, failed, suggestions that the institute combine with the university under President Rush Rhees's administration were revived, but again came to naught in 1924.[10]

Eastman's other early community commitment was as board member (1892), special building committee member (1904), and president (1901) of the Rochester Orphan Asylum.[11] He took the job seriously. He ordered the coal (off season for better rates), insect screens, and gas fixtures ("absolutely plain black, simple fixtures, like those in the Country Club"). He pressured J. Foster Warner to get out specifications and sent for the masons, carpenters, plumbers, heaters, and painters. He instructed Warner to "make drawings for the two long tables for the dining room, and have information as to the height and kind of chairs most suitable, also the size of beds required. . . . I would like to have the drawing made for the four wheeled truck which is to be used in carrying dishes from the kitchen to the dining room." He traveled to observe similar institutions in action, became enmeshed in the building details for the Eastman Cottage for Boys, read reports on foster homes, and passed on the adoption of children. "I have already said all I can for you to the managers of the Orphan Asylum," he told one applicant for the position of matron, "You will readily appreciate the fact that I cannot dictate to them whom they shall employ."[12]

It was a "fun" job, especially since Mary Mulligan and other vivacious young ladies were so involved in the women's committee there. (Mrs. Mulligan was also a trustee of the Mechanics Institute and the Rochester Symphony.) But after the fire and the building of a new and model campus of fire-resistant brick cottages atop the beautiful Pinnacle Hills, much of the challenge was gone. Eastman remained as trustee until June 1919 when, as head of the new Community Chest that planned to finance the asylum and other charities and investigate any complaints, he resigned for reasons of conflict of interest. "Of course you will understand," he wrote, "that this action does not indicate that my interest in the Asylum is on the wane."[13] The Hillside Children's Center now looks much as it did in Eastman's day though with additional buildings; the main difference is in the clientele: Today Hillside deals with few orphans but many children from broken or dysfunctional homes or those dealing with the more contemporary problems of drug abuse and teenage pregnancies.

Thanks to the many nurseries in the "Flower City," Rochester had become a city of parks. Eastman was an original supporter of efforts to create a zoo there. In July 1901 William Bausch decided to raise $25,000 for a building and small collection of caged animals at Seneca Park on the Genesee (an Olmsted-designed park). Eastman agreed to contribute $1,000, "providing you can get subscriptions of $20,000." Bausch did. Music in the Parks was organized in 1901, with Eastman contributing $250 annually, earmarked "for Sunday concerts." Theodore Dossenbach, brother of Hermann Dossenbach, the leader of Eastman's quintette, conducted the Rochester Park Band that was known as one of the finest military and concert groups in the country. By employing the quintette twice a week and hiring Dossenbach's Orchestra and the Park Band to play at his large entertainments, Eastman partially subsidized local musical efforts during the first two decades of the century. He became involved in the extension of Maplewood Park across the river from Seneca Park at the urging of Roman Catholic Bishop Bernard McQuaid and Elizabeth Farrar, who suggested he "create the Maria Eastman Parkway where a desert of rubbish exists. Anyone who has done for Rochester what you have," Farrar wrote, "should have his name on the parkways

and gardens as well as the public buildings his munificence has erected."
Eastman contributed $5,000 in April 1905 for the city to purchase the prop-
erty. His name stayed off but when the area was graded for a pond and
building, the park commissioners presented Eastman with two "very symmetrical" American elms and a white ash for his new East Avenue estate.[14]

At the urging of his friend Alice Peck Curtis, in 1908 Eastman purchased
a tract of land adjoining the city's new Cobb's Hill reservoir the municipality
was then constructing. The city had previously purchased sixty acres of land
and Eastman added thirty more acres at a cost of more than $50,000. It took
more than three years to develop the park, despite Eastman's protestations.
The city also wanted to build employee housing in the middle of the park.
Eastman counterproposed that the city "buy the gun club property, which is
for sale, and utilize the house there which is already built and the rear of
which is thoroughly screened from the bank above by trees." He concluded
his gentle suggestions to Mayor Edgerton for the aesthetic betterment of the
area with, "Thanking you for your courtesy in asking my opinion," which,
considering he was paying the bill, was the least the city could do.[15]

Dr. Henry Strong Durand, Mary Mulligan's brother, lived in an old stone
house on 270 acres of orchards, fields, and woodlands, with 4,000 feet of
beachfront on the shores of Lake Ontario—arguably the wildest, hilliest,
most dramatic and secluded terrain in the county. In Durand's own words,
he "induced Mr. Eastman to purchase over 200 more acres [for $50,000] for
presentation." Eastman and Durand made their agreement in February
1906. In 1908 Durand left for Mexico and wild times (he was reported dead).
Meanwhile, Eastman was left to dicker with the city to accept the property in
February 1908, build a pavilion, and improve and macadamize roads "not
later than August 1, 1910." He had to persuade eight property owners to
part with their lands. Then he had to prevent the city from building a
cesspool for sewage on the park land in 1910. During the five years between
the first visit to Durand's property and the opening of a new city park, he
escorted caravans of friends to the beach for cookouts and campouts. Eastman wanted to call the project Durand Park, but was talked into allowing his
own name to be affixed as well. On 14 October 1911 a band concert and "a
little repast in the way of a clam bake" was held for Eastman and his friends
by the park commissioners. The next spring the park officially opened with a
May Day Walk to make the public "familiar with Durand–Eastman Park and
all that has been done."[16]

In October 1912 the park board and Chamber of Commerce formed the
Rochester Zoological Society (Eastman not attending: he had jury duty),
"taking the liberty, without consulting you," a spokesman wrote Eastman, "of
naming you as Treasurer . . . , trusting that your interest will lead you to a
favorable consideration of their action." But the new treasurer declined his
post. In 1913 the Zoological Society took over two hundred acres at Durand–

Eastman and the supervision of $3500 worth of wild animals and birds then in the park, proposing to stock it with more fauna. Eastman agreed to all this but since everyone thought that Durand had met his end in Mexico, he of course was never consulted. Resurrected from rumored demise, he arrived in Rochester in January 1915 "and found that the City, ignoring all protests of my servants, and without a word of explanation, had appropriated the northern end of my reservation for a Zoo, and had cut down almost all of an apple orchard which I had there. I was greatly amazed," Durand wrote the mayor, "but was assured by [the park commissioner] that the arrangement was only temporary." Durand closed his Rochester house in 1916, leasing his property to the city with the agreement that responsible people should live in and care for it, using the income. He sold all his farm equipment, and moved to California.[17]

By 1915, 141,300 deciduous trees and 7,250 evergreens had been planted in the new park, including a special nut grove of 140 walnut, chestnut, and butternut trees. In January 1920 Eastman learned that 200 adjacent acres were available from the estate of Miss Alcesta F. Huntington, and wrote Mayor Hiram Edgerton that he "would be glad to know to what extent the City would be interested in the acquirement of the property." The mayor referred the question to Commissioner Riley who was not interested, so the Huntington property passed into the hands of a private developer. At this point Durand roared back into town, found that "the Huntington land is lost to the city forever," that the city had destroyed or allowed his buildings and orchards to crumble, and that "the Zoo still flourishes on my property." Eventually he sent the mayor a bill for all damages plus "unwarranted and unlawful seizure of my land for the purposes of a Zoo" and retired to Paris to live until his actual death. Eastman visited him in Paris in 1926 en route to Africa with Durand's cousin, Dr. Audley Durand Stewart. Eastman also wrote a letter of introduction for Durand's daughter Margaret, who wished to be an opera singer, to the manager of the Metropolitan Opera Company, of which Eastman was a director.[18]

In 1923 Eastman and Durand did buy and donate to the city a small adjacent woodland for $8,700, with "Dr. Durand" noting to "Mr. Eastman" (apparently they never did arrive at a first-name relationship) from Los Angeles that "if our chief executive shall be able to bring about the completion of the artificial lake system, that we also may include ourselves among the proud and satisfied" and that he hoped "that this cooperation has produced something which shall be worthy to rank with the best of your many good works for the advancement of civic life."[19] Eastman demurred that "you may be assured that I was glad to join you in putting the finishing touches on the Park property. You are entitled to the big share of the credit for it all and I hope you will be able to forget your unpleasant experience . . . and take full satisfaction in the knowledge of what a great thing you have done for the city. I am sure that the appreciation of it will steadily grow in the minds of Rochester's citizens."[20]

From 1894 the Chamber of Commerce had its headquarters on the top floor of the thirteen-story Commerce Building built by tobacco magnate William S. Kimball—who once was Rochester's major employer, built its largest house, and owned its finest art collection. With a new century Rochester had a new tycoon who wanted to outdo Kimball in all these fields. Many times a delegate to the national convention of the Chamber, Eastman offered in 1915 to build the local chapter a new building.

The president of the Chamber was George Todd, an engaging man-about-town who inherited a thriving business of check-writing paper that thwarted would-be forgers. Todd was a Eastman lookalike. Both he and Eastman (and Frank Gannett, another Rochester tycoon) developed round, prim "have" faces with wire-framed glasses as they aged. That gaunt, hungry, swashbuckling look was gone forever. So identical did Todd and Eastman appear that when Todd took his wife for a spin in their roadster, people talked about Eastman having a new interest. They lived a few blocks apart and Eastman often walked over to the Todds on a summer evening, tapping his way with a walking stick, or he hopped in his Cadillac coupe on a winter evening to confer with Todd. The Chamber building cemented the friendship and brought national acclaim to its donor: "Such an imposing Tennessee marble structure, located in the heart of the city, and devoted exclusively to the city's exploitation and welfare, does not fall to the lot of every city—for George Eastmans weren't born every day." Thus stroked the *National Magazine*.[21]

The Great Hall of the Chamber would be headquarters and forum for Eastman's new project, the War Chest (which later became the Community Chest). At the completion of the new building Eastman gave a dinner to the men who had worked on the structure. His speech was characteristically brief: "I told them, when we decided to build, that we wanted to have the best material, and have it right, and naturally the best work has been done. I have looked over the building, gentlemen, and I think the highest compliment I can pay you is that I am not disappointed." He then sat down. There followed a week of revelry, with notable American and English speakers as headliners each day. Lord Northcliffe, head of the British War Mission, stayed at 900 East Avenue, and addressed the group "in his breezy, but matter-of-fact manner." (The next summer he took Eastman for his first airplane ride.)[22]

Less sanguine was Eastman's attempt to build a grand new civic center. In 1924 controversy erupted over enlarging city hall. From Kamloops, British Columbia, Eastman masterminded the scene, directing architects Gordon & Kaelber to prepare sketches of a new city hall, a public library, and an opera hall seating 6,000 to 8,000 to be built over and around the Genesee River in downtown Rochester. He authorized the architects to offer $500,000 for the vacant Kimball Tobacco factory building on an island plus 63,000 square feet of river bank land. Meanwhile Mayor Clarence Van Zandt had secretly secured an option on the tract across the abandoned Erie Canal from city hall and pressed to build an annex there. Angered at what he considered the mayor's duplicity, Eastman went public with the startling announcement that he had purchased the old factory building and would lease it to the city for four years without charge for use as a city hall annex. This would allow officials to have a leisurely discussion of civic center plans. He further offered to give the property to the city if it fit in with their civic center decision. His offer stimulated a host of civic center schemes, amateur and professional, plus offers and suggestions of other sites. Succumbing to pressure the mayor accepted the factory and turned it into a city hall annex with the public library occupying the entire first floor. But he kept the site across from city hall too.[23]

In 1929 Harland Bartholomew, a consultant from St. Louis, took charge of city planning in Rochester. While Eastman's contacts with Bartholomew were cordial, his usual enthusiasm for new projects was absent. When Eastman suggested an architectural competition for the civic center, Bartholomew gave him a six-page reason why this idea was not practical. Despite his squabbles with architects, Eastman had always given local firms his business. Bartholomew favored opening up the field to outside firms. By this time Eastman's health and enthusiasm for life were on the wane and the civic center, which he did not contribute to further during his lifetime or provide for in his will, did not get the usual Eastman endorsement. A civic center would not be built until the 1950s, and then it was never completed.[24]

The Young Men's Christian Association drew Eastman's attention and largess in 1904. He had previously declined to serve on the board of the YMCA, but he offered to help retire the organization's debt of $60,000 by subscribing $20,000 on the condition that $40,000 more was raised from the community. Other gifts totaling $43,193 from 116 people, with the next largest being $5,000 from Hiram W. Sibley and $3,000 from Joseph T. Alling, were added and the debt was successfully erased. In 1912 Eastman was again approached by Alling, YMCA president, this time to contribute to the $750,000 building campaign for new downtown facilities that would include two gymnasiums, one for men and one for boys, a swimming pool, a lunch room, separate club rooms for men and boys, reading rooms, educational classrooms, a small auditorium, and from 250 to 300 sleeping rooms. In addition, the mortgages on the old "Railroad Y" building and the new "Y" club house in South (now Genesee Valley) Park would be paid, a camp site on a Finger Lake purchased and equipped, and branches built in four residential sections of the city. Although Eastman noted that he had "never been wholly satisfied that the only thing the YMCA lacked was a new building," he subscribed $250,000 on 31 December 1912 on the condition that the whole amount ($750,000) be raised by 1 July 1913. The Strongs were the next largest contributors at $50,000, and Hiram W. Sibley third with $25,000. Despite Eastman's reservations and his not being a member of the building fund committee, when Sibley left for Europe in June 1913 he wrote Eastman: "I am perfectly willing to leave the whole thing in your hands to do with as you think best." Both Eastman and Sibley had hoped that the building would include a concert hall, but none was included. It seems fair to deduce that this was one of the forces leading to the Eastman Theatre five years hence. During World War I Eastman subscribed $100,000 toward the war work of the YMCA.[25]

Because Eastman paced the YMCA and United Charities drives of 1914 he was automatically solicited by the Young Women's Christian Association, the favorite Rochester charity of Hattie Strong and national charity of Abby Aldrich Rockefeller. Eastman subscribed $25,000 to the local fund of 1913 with the stipulation that "$75,000 additional is subscribed."[26] In the 1920s he subscribed $25,000 toward the debt of the national board, primarily because Mr. and Mrs. Rockefeller Jr. both wrote personally asking for his support. There were years, 1927 being one of them, that Eastman pledged to contribute $10,000 to the national YWCA as "one of ten," only to learn from Abby Rockefeller that "we were unable to secure the pledges of ten people."[27] There is no record that he withdrew his contribution.

Even though pioneer feminist Susan B. Anthony was received and respected by crowned heads and international statesmen, she and the suffragist movement were ridiculed and opposed by the Rochester press and the citizens of her native city. In the first popular test of the women's suffrage amendment in 1915, Rochester men voted against it 18,000 to 13,000. But it was not only men who opposed women voting. Among those active in the antisuffrage movement were Eastman's friends Emily Sibley Watson, who founded the Memorial Art Gallery of the University of Rochester and the David Hochstein School, Mary Mulligan, Elizabeth Harper Sibley of the Harper publishing family, and her daughter-in-law Georgianna Farr Sibley, active in the international YWCA. These were the female community leaders of Eastman's time, and he followed their lead, contributing $250 to the antisuffrage cause and declining to give to the suffragettes nationally when solicited by the wife of New York banker Frank Vanderlip. He did contribute regularly to more traditional charities, such as $1,000 to the Women's Educational and Industrial Union, which was formed in 1917 "to further welfare work in the community."[28]

Some women felt threatened when Eastman spearheaded the organization of the Rochester Patriotic and Community Fund (commonly called the War Chest) to increase the number of contributors and do away with the multiplicity of appeals. A lengthy letter from Alexander Lindsay, dry goods merchant, Kodak director, and perhaps fifteen years Eastman's senior, warned that "Some of the ladies feel that the joy is going to be taken out of their Christmas work by the yearly appeal and the Chest ever ready to supply the needs. . . . They want to hold onto the . . . various little societies and associations which are gathered together for good work and . . . there should be no interference . . . even if your Chest should be full to overflowing."[29]

One of the strangest chapters in the history of Eastman's municipal gifts was his "model tenement" project. It never came to fruition, but remains a reflection on the working of the Eastman mind. Cynics decided his objective was merely to clear nearby slums and provide cheap and temporary flats for his workers, thus saving the property for future company expansion. From his penthouse office he saw mainly ramshackle frame houses, outbuildings, and board fences, the area having hardly changed since junk and kindling wood yards stood between that first factory-office building and State Street in 1882.[30] But the property he purchased or considered was in several locations, not all contingent to Kodak buildings. Even with adjacent property, the motive was more complex.

Unlike social reformers connected to churches or temples, who thought of Rochester as a city of homeowners, detached houses, and neat lawns, Eastman as observer of human nature believed that not everyone could be or wanted to be transported to the suburbs. It was, he said, "to relieve the condition of the people who cannot be induced to move into the outskirts that my enterprise is directed."[31] After all, this was the same neighborhood that his mother had been so loathe to leave in 1890 for the fancier address of Arnold Park. By providing substantial, four-story apartment buildings of the same cream-colored brick as his own home and office tower, with separate entrances for each tenant and green space on all sides of each building, he would be improving the neighborhood where he worked not just for himself but for those who wanted to live there. And despite his disclaimer, in reference to Oak Lodge particularly, that he didn't dabble in sociological experiments, the evidence suggests otherwise.

As early as 4 October 1901 Eastman was requesting more information from the "Secretary of the Charity Organization Society of New York City" about "plans for tenement houses." The next intimation that something was afoot comes a decade later in a letter to Dr. Elgin R. L. Gould, president of City and Suburban Homes Company, New York City, which begins: "Having read . . . in the current . . . *Review of Reviews* concerning your model tene-

ments and being somewhat interested in the subject I write this to ask whether it would be agreeable to you to put me in the way of examining some of
your buildings? I expect to be in New York . . . and would ask you to address
your reply . . . in care of the Hotel Belmont."[32]

During the next two months Eastman visited Gould's various New York
projects—Junior League House, Hotel for Women at 78th Street and East
River; several Model Apartment Estates on the upper east and west sides of
New York; several Model Apartments for Colored People on West 62nd and
63rd Streets; and the suburban Homewood in Brooklyn. "Tenement" was
not yet a pejorative term; the properties were designed to create an income
of 5 percent for their owners but were also constructed in line with the
building and fire codes of the day to replace slums. Eastman began poring
over Gould's annual reports. These were spanking new properties in the
hands of an original owner, not an absentee slum landlord. It seems obvious
that there was little profit motive to Eastman's interest.

As usual, he ran this new project by his oldest friend and confidant, Frank
Babbott, noting the "interesting hours" spent with Dr. E. R. L. Gould looking over some of their tenement houses. "Do you know anything about this
aggregation of capitalist philanthropists who have invested between six and
seven millions of dollars in trying to give working men more than they
deserve?" he inquired of Babbott.[33] He then alerted Gould about his one-
person foundation of the past decade, Helen Arnold, "who knows a lot about
housing conditions of the poorer classes. . . . I should like to have her see
your buildings. . . . If you have no objection, I will send her down to New
York." Eastman recommended Arnold for "her wide knowledge of existing
conditions in Rochester and her ability to judge how far those conditions
would be remedied by such buildings." And so Helen Arnold, the expert he
trusted in this field, came out of retirement and with supreme effort in spite
of physical disabilities, went to pass on the tenements. On 7 June 1911
Eastman, then "engaged in court in a case in which the company is interested," heard "quite an enthusiastic report" from Mrs. Arnold. And so,
Eastman told Babbott, he had "some intention of putting up the money
necessary for the trial." With that, he moved into action. He asked George
Dryden to locate "an apartment house built around a court opening on the
street" that he once noticed in Chicago so that a photographer could be
dispatched with "a No. 3A Kodak and roll of film to make the negatives for
me."[34] The very next day he purchased two State Street properties, one
"adjoining our office and camera works" and the other "in the next block,"
persuading Babbott "to have these properties deeded to you and to have you
execute quit claim deeds, back to me in one case and to the company in the
other, not to be recorded at present." Next he bought 188,000 square feet
adjacent to the rose garden in Maplewood Park and across the Genesee from
Kodak's Hawkeye plant. At eight cents a square foot, this was, Eastman said

proudly, "the cheapest property that I know of in Rochester." Two young lawyers in Hubbell's office, Messrs. Kaelber and Platt, were listed as the incorporators and directors for the first year.

In December 1911 Eastman placed the matter in Lovejoy's hands and went off to Europe for six weeks. While there he talked tenements with Sir John J. Burnet, the architect of Kodak's new London building on Kingsway and designer of Workman's Dwellings that replaced slums in London, Birmingham, Manchester, and Liverpool. Soon he was reading pamphlets, journals, and papers about "Workmen's Dwellings," "Meeting the Question of Overcrowding the Ground," and "Housing and Town Planning," all supplied by Burnet. Then he was writing the architect of the London Council, W. E. Riley, and "visiting the housing enterprises of the Council, lodging houses, tenements, and cottage dwellings."[35]

Meanwhile in Rochester Hubbell was obtaining building permits and writing the fire marshall in the names of Babbott and Kaelber. Lovejoy kept Eastman apprised of the surveying of the property and disputes with owners of adjacent land in daily missives to London, always assuring his boss that "Of course Mr. Hubbell has phrased his letters in such a way as not to indicate the owner or the location of the property." By March 1912 Eastman was back in the Rochester saddle, making decisions on everything from concrete and steel to "projections of the pilaster cornice." All seemed to be going along smoothly, with Gould putting the finishing touches on "plans for the tenement houses" and Eastman thinking ahead to a "Grand Opening of the Model Tenements" at which the "public would be invited to come and look."[36]

But there were rumblings as contractors began clearing the land in the spring of 1912 and word leaked out that Eastman was planning to erect four-story apartment buildings in those parts of the northeast quadrant of the city that he referred to as the "Italian," the "Polish," and the "Hebrew" districts. The designations were accurate: This was where the newly arrived immigrants from southern and eastern Europe settled—in dilapidated and overcrowded housing that was the best they could afford but also had the redeeming solace of being near relatives and countrymen speaking the same tongue and observing the same customs. Eastman's critics wanted him to sponsor a model village in the suburbs, but instinctively and immediately he said no; such a project must be tackled where the people live. Eastman had discovered, or knew in his bones, a basic fact about city housing: that no matter how many old houses are torn down, tenants try to stay in the same neighborhood to be with family and friends.[37]

The first attack came from the Rev. Mr. Edwin A. Rumball of the Unitarian Church, "who is the editor of a small leaflet . . . called *The Common Good*," Eastman told Gould. In his thirty-two-page monthly journal devoted to social and civic reform, Rumball denounced the construction of multifamily dwellings instead of single houses and any program that provided housing for only 230 families instead of "seeking the Common Good of the whole city." He further stated that "model tenements destroy the fundamental elements of the home." Joining the chorus of condemnation were the voices of national experts on the housing question. Charles Mulford Robinson, a Rochester landscape architect and proponent of city beautification who had gone on to become the first professor of civic design at the University of Illinois and a leader of the "City Beautiful" movement (a phrase that he coined), was among the opponents of the Rochester tenements. Eastman's plans coincided with the appearance of a new "City Plan for Rochester," written by the Olmsted Brothers, the most prestigious landscape architects in the country. That report concentrated on cosmetic beautification, and Eastman's tenements did not fit.[38]

Then the opposition shifted its objections to fire escapes, an easy way to catch Eastman up: He wanted fireproof Philadelphia fire towers (stairs inside fire doors—like tall buildings today) not just because they offered an excellent, smoke-proof escape route but also because the people could not toss out garbage or hang out wash in plain sight as they could with fire escapes. But the city code insisted upon fire escapes. Nor was the Building Code Commission moved by Eastman's arguments that fire towers were safer. The doors on the landing might be left open, said J. Foster Warner, chairman of the commission. The commission dug in its heels at making exceptions, even for Eastman, and the project dragged on and on.

On 6 June 1912 Eastman's proposal was officially turned down by the city. From time to time other developers of model tenements continued to contact Eastman and he always showed some interest. But by 1925, he had just about given up. "There is no opportunity as far as I know to develop the scheme in this locality at the present time," he wrote, "but I shall not forget it."[39] The inner-city apartments were never built. The land purchased near Kodak Office eventually became the site of company expansion and parking lots. In May 1915 Eastman deeded the property adjacent to Maplewood Park to the YMCA as his contribution to its drive to establish branches in each section of the city. "After having made possible our whole building project, this extra gift of what is universally regarded as the ideal lot for outdoor athletics" was gratefully received, as chairman James G. Cutler wrote. Ironically, the square, cream-colored brick exterior of the new Maplewood Y, designed by Claude Bragdon, strongly resembled the unbuilt model tenements. In a sense "the Rumball crowd" won. But it could also be argued that the poor lost.

Future forays into housing by Eastman and his company would be limited to the suburbs: Koda-Vista, in the nearby town of Greece, for Kodak workers but not limited to them; and the Meadowbrook subdivision of ninety-eight acres in suburban Brighton.

A lifelong Republican, Eastman contributed warily and sparingly to the national party, $250 to $1,000 a year, or about what he would give to a small Rochester charity. He was a presidential elector three times—in 1901 for McKinley and Roosevelt; in 1917 for Hughes, who lost to Wilson's bid for a second term, and in 1929 for Hoover. He was chairman of the electors in 1917 and 1929, bringing home the ebony and gold gavels as souvenirs. In 1929 he made a twenty-line speech. He admired Theodore Roosevelt, but hated Grover Cleveland and especially Woodrow Wilson, under whose administration his antitrust troubles came to a head.

The Republican boss of Rochester was George Aldridge—on a first-name basis since boyhood with Eastman, who recommended Aldridge to William Howard Taft for a federal job (to no avail) and for a while did favors for him. As he began to see Aldridge as essentially operating machine politics, the favors stopped. In 1905, for example, Eastman declined to advance a Kodak employee at Aldridge's request. Eastman then switched to supporting locally the Good Government movement founded by Joseph T. Alling. Gradually he came to believe that better results could be achieved on the municipal level through nonpolitical means. Movements aimed at citizen reform of the boss-dominated politics of Aldridge in traditionally Republican Rochester began in the 1890s. Of concern was the fact that Mayor Aldridge was blatantly ignoring civil service laws by filling posts of truant officers through political patronage. In 1894 Aldridge was appointed State Superintendent of Public Works; although he exhausted the $9 million budget for completing the Barge Canal so that Governor Black discharged him, he remained a power in Rochester. Watching Aldridge's machinations with misgiving were some loyal Republicans and active religionists such as Alling, a paper manufacturer, president of the YMCA, University of Rochester trustee, and Bible study teacher. He enlisted Walter S. Hubbell, Eastman's chief counsel and another Bible class leader; Clarence Barbour, minister of Lake Avenue Baptist Church and later president of Brown University; and Isaac Adler, member of a men's clothing firm and a leader in the Jewish community. Encouraged by the National Conferences for Good City Government, these four and their adherents who believed that civic affairs were everybody's business organized clubs in each ward and in 1896, with Democratic help, elected a mayor. The "Goo Goos," as the opposition press branded them, had a brief moment in the sun, but soon their leader Alling was being called "narrow, clumsy, offensive, egotistical, and a political boss" himself.[40]

Eastman, busy with company affairs, often abroad during the 1890s, and, as Paul Horgan would note years later, "having no concern with those powers which a political machine can bestow,"[41] must still have been aware of the strivings of his friends to take government out of politics and make it as aboveboard and economical as possible. One event of the 1890s influenced the drive by Eastman in the 1920s to remove municipal government from the realm of politics: The White Charter, drafted by the dashing and impulsive Governor Theodore Roosevelt, greatly increased the elected mayor's powers. Aldridge took advantage of this new charter and got his hand-picked mayoral candidate, Hiram Edgerton, elected no less than seven times. And although Eastman had no use for partisan politics, the boss was an old enough friend that the two regularly exchanged recipes for bran muffins and other trivial marks of ancient friendship.

In 1902 Eastman sent a copy of the report of "the Boston Conference for Good City Government, 1902" to Henry Brewster, cigar merchant turned bank president, Kodak director, and congressman, referring particularly to "the uniform system of municipal accounting" other cities used. Nonpartisan, nonprofit, private organizations to research and investigate the management of public business, making city governments more efficient and effective were springing up; Eastman became a member of the Philadelphia-based National Municipal League. Contacts between Rochester and the Bureau of Municipal Research in New York City began in October 1911 when the Rochester board of education asked for help in installing a complete system of expense accounting. In May 1912, if not before, Eastman wrote for "circulars showing just what your Bureau is, its scope, organization, and the manner in which it is maintained." He began digesting and ruminating upon this material much as he had with annual reports from MIT fifteen years earlier. He investigated the Municipal Government Association, also based in New York, but decided that the bureau offered the best program for Rochester.

"What do you think about the Municipal Research scheme?" he naturally asked Babbott on 20 January 1913, noting that he had "agreed to furnish some money to help do some State work." The same day he wrote Frederick Cleveland of the New York bureau that he was "encouraged to believe" that Rochester would "welcome a Bureau of Municipal Research." He invited Cleveland to "talk the matter over with the Mayor, Mr. Edgerton," and promised financing. In October 1914 Eastman contributed $1,000 toward a $25,000 fund to pay for a report to the state constitutional convention on how city "departments are organized and what each man employed is doing."[42] He pulled out all the stops. Frank Lovejoy, president of the City Club, scheduled a luncheon for three hundred "to bespeak of Cleveland's proposition for municipal research your favorable consideration." Anticipating that the bureau might be "charged with being controlled by a few givers," Cleveland said, "the first step should be the selection of a board of trustees only one of whom makes any contribution to the work and all of whom are men of such repute for disinterested public service and independence of thought as to leave the staff entirely free for the pursuit of the work along scientific lines."[43] With Edgerton's permission, Eastman directed Cleveland to survey Rochester. He lined up a board of eleven with himself as president. "HAVE

AGREED TO FINANCE BUREAU OF MUNICIPAL RESEARCH TERM OF FIVE YEARS WILL YOU SERVE?" he cabled an impressive list of business leaders.[44] Young Leroy Snyder, who had been with the *Indianapolis News* and came highly recommended by Eastman's friend Robert Lieber of that city, was among those applying for the job of director. Snyder had also been affiliated with the bureau in New York City. He had some misgivings about working for the only bureau of the few then operative in the country that was financed by one man. At his interview, he asked how the money was to be handled; Eastman replied, "I want the board to manage just as if the money had been left to them." Snyder was hired in May 1915. Eastman may have dominated the bureau by his character, Snyder said later, but he didn't force people to agree with him.[45]

Charles Mulford Robinson badly wanted the job, although he was noted as a city planner and "idea" man rather than as an administrator.[46] Eastman believed local government should be run like a business, removing it from both politics and overidealism. Besides, Robinson had crossed Eastman on the tenements; apparently he was never seriously considered for the job. He was older than Snyder, too, and Eastman always favored the promising younger man. Eastman had earmarked James G. Cutler to be vice chairman of the trustees, but Hubbell warned that Edgerton "expressed a very decided preference for the election of [James Sibley] Watson . . . since . . . Cutler was too bombastic and apt to interfere in other people's affairs."[47] Eastman knuckled under, even though he once said of the president of the Security Trust Bank and co-owner with Eastman and the Bonbright brothers of the Horn Point Gun Club in Virginia, "Watson has the ability and the leisure but he never exerts himself and in my opinion [he is] practically useless."[48] Trustee meetings were scheduled for the spacious living room of 900 East Avenue or at the Genesee Valley Club.

The survey by the New York bureau concluded tactfully that "Rochester's government is superior to that of any other city" but still suggested improvements. From the start the Rochester bureau's suggestions for municipal housecleaning and improved services were practical and nonpartisan. They included tighter budgets, stricter regulation of city contracts, a standard salary schedule for city employees, more efficiency in street cleaning, better fire safety, improved garbage collection, auto-driven snow plows, asphalt repair of Rochester's omnipresent potholes, selection of playground directors, continuous water-meter reading, and safety conditions in Convention Hall Gallery, a city-owned property.[49]

United Charities and Catholic Charities had always been separate organizations but with a bureau plan for Catholic representation on the board of the United Charities integration began. By 15 August 1915 Eastman was able to

report to Murray Bartlett that the new bureau was "meeting with excellent
success. The administration is adopting its recommendations right and left
and our small staff of experts . . . work to get improvements in shape for
adoption. . . . The Bureau works very quietly and doesn't blow any horns. If
the Administration does not later on 'buck' against the program . . . instead
of having the 'best governed city' in the United States we will have an ideally
governed city."[50] As for his own part, Eastman told those who asked that he
was "thankful to be able to help and quite willing for city officials to get any
credit." He also kept up a steady, gentle pressure on Aldridge, stroking the
politician continually so that the old boss would be convinced that the bureau
was not a threat to him. "My dear George," he wrote,

> Herewith I am sending you . . . a report of the Bureau on street clean-
> ing . . . merely because I want to have you know just the kind of con-
> structive work that the Bureau is doing. There is no "fireworks" about it
> but just plain methodical work. Please read it through carefully. From
> talks with Mr. Edgerton I know how necessary it is to have a lot of men on
> the payroll of this department who cannot do a full day's work, it being
> better to have them earn something than to put them in the poorhouse,
> but I think this report shows clearly that even they can be so instructed
> and organized as to be much more efficient without taxing their powers.
> With kind regards, George[51]

Eastman continued to press Aldridge as the 1918 street car situation
makes clear. A Price, Waterhouse report concluded that the five-cent fare
must be raised. "The Administration has committed itself so positively in
opposition," Eastman wrote Aldridge, "that it may be difficult to change its
attitude but I do not see for the life of me why it is not in a position, especially
in view of the recommendations of the Taft–Walsh Commission, to pass the
buck to the Public Service Commission, which is in a position to handle the
matter without prejudice of lawsuits and local bickerings. It must be recognized sooner or later that the victory of the city in the lawsuit over the
contract is an empty one. The only power it gives the city is to throw the street
car company into bankruptcy. The city cannot get blood out of a stone and
there is no way of getting good service . . . except by allowing a revenue.
Cannot something be done that is constructive instead of destructive?"[52]

The administration of the Department of Charities was studied in 1916
and a reorganization recommended through a charter change that included
eliminating the title "overseer of the poor" for the Commissioner of Charities. In 1918 the bureau unanimously voted to "organize a committee [with
United Charities] to deal with the problem of illegitimacy," an indication that
real problems were not being swept under the rug.[53]

In addition to founding and financing the bureau, Eastman opened doors
for Snyder. He lined up the president of Cornell to offer "the cooperation of

our engineering college with some of the work which the Bureau is under-taking."[54] Snyder went to 900 East Avenue often, so that he and Eastman could "talk over government matters and the whole social situation. "At the time," Snyder recalled in 1940, "there was a great deal of social unrest." Eastman had enormous interest in municipal government and the whole local social situation and willingly gave Snyder all kinds of time to present and discuss problems. At the end of a session Snyder would rise to leave, and if Eastman was not pressed for time, they would continue the discussion for an hour or more. Social unrest and the then current Russian Revolution were popular topics. Eastman became interested in the Open Forum as a safety valve for the views of the discontented, and even more, in the city manager plan as a "scheme" to give all groups proportional representation in government. Proportional representation, the system of electing mem-bers of a legislature designed to give each political party a share of seats in proportion to its share of the total vote cast, was a new concept in Eastman's time. It permitted the representation of groups normally excluded by ma-jority politics, such as Socialists and Communists. Opponents argued, how-ever, that the system offered a haven for extremists, but Eastman supported it wholeheartedly. He also felt it was all right for some countries to "try the communistic experiment." Russia being so far away made it the ideal place and he said he didn't care if the revolution came to the United States as long as he could keep two things—a bathtub and a Ford car.[55]

Once during a problem session with Snyder, Eastman remarked, "I like to deal with people who are hard to handle." He believed in "scientific" govern-ment for Rochester, Snyder said, the way he believed in "scientific" music, camping, or film making. The correspondence indicates that Eastman regu-larly started the director working on something new, that he carefully super-vised the way Snyder was handling a sensitive matter such as the suspected dishonesty or negligence of the police force, and occasionally came down rather hard or him and then apologized: "If you were not an idealist I should not think as much of you as I do. If I have seemed to criticize you lately it is because I am probably inclined to the opposite point of view and have felt that you were worrying over the future so much that you might take your eye "off the ball" as the golf cranks phrase it. If I was mistaken forgive me and have confidence that I will discover my mistake."[56] On 20 March 1919 Snyder wrote Eastman that he had been "offered an opportunity to engage in business of such a nature that I have concluded that I owe it to myself and to my future to take advantage of it." The job was in his old newspaper field and the raider was a dynamic young Frank Gannett, who had arrived on the Rochester scene the year before to buy the *Evening Times*, a paper partly owned by Boss Aldridge and the *Union and Advertiser*, another afternoon paper. Buying two papers out of five extant in Rochester and merging them gave Gannett a circulation and advertising niche. On 12 March 1918 the first

Times-Union was published and the Gannett Newspapers were on their way to empire.

James W. Routh, who had been in the employ of the bureau since its inception, succeeded Snyder. As he had with Snyder, Eastman loaned Routh money to buy a house. No pressure to collect on these loans was applied until the man left to take another job; then the dunning letters appeared that began, "I should like very much to get your loan off my books." At Eastman's behest Routh plunged into studies of "Commission Manager cities."[57] By 1920 Eastman was underwriting the bureau at $40,000 a year. That year, too, Routh made a speech in which he said that "many officials in City Hall are solid ivory from the neck up," a remark not calculated to endear him to Aldridge and Edgerton. When Routh was dismissed in early 1921, Eastman insisted that he "did not have in mind your unfortunate speech . . . but your furnishing the article on City Government to the *Times-Union* without consultation with the Bureau while you were still in its employ."[58] Eastman gave Routh a half-hearted recommendation, telling him that "I shall be very glad to see you located in a place where you can make the most of your training and experience and it would probably be better for me to give you a general letter of recommendation than to have to reply to pointed questions about your ability to get along with others, or about your loyalty to your employers. I feel that you are lacking in both of these qualities."[59] On 7 April 1921 Stephen B. Story, a staff member originally from the New York bureau, applied for the position of director, and on 9 June was elected.

The bureau drew Eastman increasingly into the mainstream of civic reform and more. "I too am learning something about politics," he told George Dryden in 1927 during the fight to establish the city manager form of municipal government, a bureau recommendation. "Fortunately we amateurs have been able to line up on our side some disgruntled politicians. . . . No doubt we will have a hard fight." They did but they won. "I suppose we shall have to call you Boss Eastman now," Will Hays, United States Postmaster General and movie czar, wrote when the plan was voted in. "If I were twenty-five years younger I might have some fun with the political situation," Eastman responded, "but at my age the idea of being a political boss does not appeal to me and I have been careful to keep out of real politics. The only thing I am interested in is the City Manager plan and I think we have that cinched."[60] He wanted proportional representation as well as the city manager form of government included in the 1924 charter since both were means of removing partisanship from politics, but it was discovered that proportional representation was illegal in New York State.[61]

Not wanting to show favoritism among the city's newspapers, which were beginning an intense competition, Eastman arranged a meeting at his house with all five editors in September 1921. "My idea . . . is to discuss the advisability of going into the matter on a purely community basis, without any attempt on the part of any one newspaper to get any individual advantage out of it."[62] The *Democrat & Chronicle* "is the organization paper," Eastman explained. "The *Express* is a Republican paper and the *Herald* independent with Democratic tendencies—at any rate 'agin' the organization. All of these men think it will take considerable time to educate the people."[63] Several months earlier he had invited Aldridge to meet Professor A. R. Hatton of Western Reserve University, the man pushing the "city manager scheme of government."

A commission form of municipal government consisting of an appointed professional manager working alongside an elected common council and mayor (whose powers are greater when no city manager is in place) developed at Galveston in 1901. A City Government Plan Committee was formed March 1923 at Eastman's urging. He funded visits by Stephen Story, new bureau chief, and W. Earl Weller and other staff members to twenty-four other cities that had adopted or rejected city manager or commission forms of government. Eastman sounded the start of the campaign in December 1924. Rochester, he said, "is well started on its way toward being the finest city in the world to live in and bring up families. . . . All that I can see that it needs now . . . is a civic center and a modern system of municipal government."[64] By 1924 over three hundred cities were using the plan and Eastman finally went public in his support:

> For some seven to eight years I watched the development of the City Manager plan. I was attracted to it from the first because it is the one almost universally used in the management business . . . watched it . . . thinking some hidden defect might develop when applied to city business. No such defect has manifested itself. I feel that the time has come when the most conservative persons can approve it with safety. I am satisfied it will enable the city to get better service.[65]

With that Eastman entered the fray. A City Manager League was formed, sponsored by the Women's City Club under Alice Peck Curtis, which brought in Emily Knuebuhl from Cincinnati to organize volunteers to campaign door to door getting petitions. Eastman paid her salary. Then in 1927 he admonished the Federation of Churches that "Your group is one of the most powerful in the city and your members can do a tremendous lot in educating their parishioners in regard to this opportunity and the simple way in which they can take advantage of it. *Will they do it?*" he underlined, then added: "This letter is not confidential but it is not for publication because it is not wise to have too much Eastman in this campaign."[66]

"The [Republican] Machine has consistently opposed the Manager Charter from the beginning," he noted. By 1929 he could report to Dan Pomeroy, Republican state chairman, that "we have had the worst example of corruption by the organization in the recent primary that has been brought to light in many years. They have even resorted to the voting of dead men and men in the penitentiary."[67] Then Harry Bareham, Aldridge's successor as boss, claimed to Eastman that for fifty years "the Republican party has been charged with the administration of the city's government" and asked "Does the City of Rochester mean anything to you? Is its welfare worth fighting for?" Eastman replied, while also declining to contribute to the local party anymore:

> Your organization does not seem to realize that the people of Rochester have taken away from you . . . the duty of managing the city's government. . . . Recent occurrences in the primaries demonstrate in my opinion that there are too many of the old crowd of politicians around you to make it safe to trust the organization with the business affairs of the city, and I believe that it will be wise if you keep your hands off the situation. . . . As your letter is on a matter of public interest I am sending a copy of this to the morning [organization Republican] paper.[68]

Hearst's *Journal* and many political leaders remained openly hostile. Snyder, now special assistant to Frank Gannett, wrote a series of articles supporting the movement. Gannett as editor endorsed the plan wholeheartedly and was ready to pull out all the stops. Eastman had gotten Gannett to drop the subject in 1921, telling him that "his previous editorial had been inopportune," as he wrote Aldridge in November 1921, and that a better way was his own gentle massaging of the boss. Aldridge died unexpectedly in December 1921 of a heart attack, but Eastman did not forget Gannett's earlier acquiescence and in 1927 wrote:

> I will never forget the part that you have taken in this great affair. The public spirited way in which you gave up your plans to let me work with George Aldridge was a most notable act and I never miss a chance for making it known. George Aldridge had such a prejudice against the Times-Union that it would have no doubt lengthened the fight but you knew perfectly well that in time the City Manager idea was sure to win out over his opposition. You therefore deliberately sacrificed the prospect of a victory the credit for which would all have gone to the Times-Union. I cannot recall any other case where a newspaper has done such a public spirited thing.[69]

Eastman built the same kind of loyalty in civic staffs as he had at Kodak. When the new charter passed he invited those who had worked with him to his house and presented each with a check. "It is pleasant always to receive money that is not expected," one recipient wrote, "but the thought that you have been pleased is even more pleasant. We all want to please you, Mr. Eastman, not because you pay us but because we like you. That is awkwardly expressed but you will understand."[70]

Eastman inexplicably refused to endorse LeRoy Snyder for mayor. Instead, the first mayor under the new council-manager form of government in 1928 was Joseph Chamberlain Wilson, former alderman, city assessor, treasurer, comptroller, jeweler, and a director of the Haloid Corporation (which his grandson of the same name would head during its transformation into the Xerox Corporation). Stephen B. Story, director of the Bureau of Municipal Research, became the first city manager on 1 January 1928. His successor, W. Earl Weller, who had been with the bureau since 1923, found himself a frequent visitor to 900 East Avenue during the last four years of Eastman's life. Weller was completely taken aback by Eastman's abrupt telephone manners, particularly his disconcerting habit of hanging up without saying goodbye. But his visits to Eastman's home were more relaxed and pleasant, even though he came on official business such as presenting the bureau's quarterly budget to Eastman, who would look it over, ask a few questions, then initial it "OK GE" in green and write a check for the whole amount. Once Weller suggested that Eastman invite City Manager Story to lunch twice a month to keep abreast of what was going on in the city.

"No," said Eastman, "that would make me the political boss of Rochester."[71]

Manifest Destiny

"The manifest destiny of the Eastman Kodak Company is to be the largest manufacturer of photographic materials in the world," George Eastman confided to Henry Strong in 1894, "or else to go to pot."[1] By the turn of the century that destiny was thoroughly manifested and Eastman then found himself with a new set of problems. Two protracted litigations would occupy him and his attorneys, particularly Moritz Philipp and Philipp's partner, J. J. Kennedy, during the first two decades of the twentieth century. The decisions, when they finally came, were both by the same presiding judge, John R. Hazel, and were consistent with the fear of bigness, monopoly, trusts, and restraint of trade then gripping the country. The first of these litigations, *Goodwin Film & Camera Company v. Eastman Kodak Company*, had been building since 1887. After a decade of legal and out-of-court maneuvering, the Goodwin patent suit brought by the Anthony & Scovill Company on 12 January 1903 was finally decided on 8 August 1913 and an out-of-court settlement made on 21 March 1914, the same year that Eastman's antitrust problems came to a head.

It was a matter of pride to Eastman that his company had been first on the market with transparent film. He never could bring himself to cover the alternative by buying "this straw patent," even though he had bought every other patent that might apply to his business. The other problem involved the continuing problem of what to do about the Anthonys. Since 1898 the company under its various presidents and names—first Anthony, then Anthony & Scovill, and finally Ansco—had been willing and anxious to sell out

to Eastman, but Eastman was unwilling to buy, even as a minority stockholder, particularly once antitrust sentiment began to build. As late as 1912
Eastman was convinced that Ansco was "up against a stone wall." This kept
him deaf to suggestions by his attorneys of an out-of-court settlement to end
this worrisome case.

When the "long-drawn out Goodwin suit" was finally argued before Hazel
on 5 January 1913, Eastman appeared jubilant. "I AM GLAD STEVENS PUT
HIS PRICE TOO HIGH FOR SETTLEMENT," he cabled from the Caribbean,
where he was cruising on a rented yacht with ten friends for six weeks. But he
admitted that "If this case should go against us it would be a most serious
thing. I should have no fears if it were not for the present attitude of Judges
against big corporations."[2]

During the winter and spring of 1913 Kodak Park was instructed to find a
way to make film that would not infringe the Goodwin patent in case an
injunction to stop production was issued. Film in stock houses around the
country was sent to England, where the Goodwin patent did not apply.
Eastman and Philipp wrote statements in case the worst materialized. Since
Kodak made 90 percent of all U.S. film, an injunction would "absolutely
stop . . . camera users and motion picture men all over the world. . . . To
deprive the hundreds of thousands of Kodakers of the use of their cameras
would cause untold hardship and annoyance," Eastman declared.[3] Out-
wardly, Eastman kept up a cheerful face, telling jokes about how terrible
Ansco film was and assuring customers that regardless of what the decision
was "there is no likelihood of the production of the Kodak Company being
interfered with." Privately he said that change was slow because "we like to
have a year's trial to make sure that little differences do not crop up which
bother our customers." In the end even changing the formulas proved futile,
so broadly would the courts interpret the Goodwin patent as covering any
film poured and flowed.[4]

The key issues considered were whether Goodwin's modified claims of
1895 were equivalent to those of the original 1887 application and whether
Kodak's use of some camphor absolved it from infringement. Judge Hazel
decided that less than 40 percent of camphor made a process fall under the
broad and vague claims of the Goodwin patent and that the solvents in the
original application and final patent were equivalent. Then, "Mr. Colfax met
me on the dock with the cheerful news that the Goodwin suit had been
decided against us." During the dark days following Hazel's decision of 13
August 1913, Eastman shared his fears with Gifford in London. "There was
a sensational article in the *Sun* yesterday stating that we were liable to pay
somewhere between five and twenty-five million dollars. If this should prove
to be the case and the Government should succeed in their suit to dissolve us,
what will be left of the Kodak Company?"[5]

Thomas W. Stephens, president of Ansco and a banker by trade, continued to pursue a settlement out of court. Eastman said any proposition must come quickly, as he was leaving for a six-week trip to the Sierras. Kodak attorneys appealed the Goodwin decision and again Eastman, Kennedy, and Philipp "had a hunch that we will win." But the three-man judicial board agreed with Hazel while also picturing Goodwin as the poor, aged clergyman facing "the five examiners who improperly deprived him of his rights during these eleven years . . . truly an extraordinary and deplorable condition of affairs. . . . The long delay and the contradictory rulings of the Patent Office would have discouraged an inventor who had not a supreme faith in the justice of his cause."[6] Eastman Kodak then applied for a stay of injunction, which gave the company time to market $150,000 worth of infringing film. Although it was stated in the press that Eastman planned to take the case all the way to the Supreme Court, his lawyers and bankers convinced him otherwise. Because the decision covered all Kodak film ever made, it was considerably more serious than it appeared on its public face and could have wiped out the business. "The situation was very dangerous," Eastman admitted to Thomas Baker in Australia, "so we settled by the payment of a large sum of money."[7]

Judge Hazel, then trying the government antitrust suit against Kodak, slyly asked Kennedy how much Kodak had to settle for but Kennedy replied that it had been agreed not to disclose the amount. "I suppose you had to pay them as much as $1 million," said Hazel, continuing to fish for information.[8]

"We had no idea that the court would go to the extreme in interpreting the patent," Eastman wrote Strong in Hot Springs, Virginia. "The situation looked so serious that through the kind offices of Mr. Benjamin Strong of the Bankers Trust Company, who advised us to settle at any cost, I got in touch with Stephens and after he stuck for six million dollars [and Eastman countered with $3.5 million], we settled at five million cash money which happened to be just the amount of money which we had stowed away on certificate of deposit in the Bankers Trust Company. Everybody who knows about the real merits of the case is simply amazed at the attitudes of the courts. I am about as pessimistic as anybody but even I never dreamed of such a situation. Of course all of this is on the dead quiet. We do not want the Ansco crowd to ever know what they missed. Well, that is over. Now the only thing to do is forget it."[9]

Ansco's financial speculators had a field day. In addition to Kodak, all other film manufacturers[10] owed Ansco their pounds of flesh. Ansco retired its debts, paid 100 percent dividends, and constructed a cellulose nitration plant (which was an economic disaster). Once the remaining eighteen months of the patent term expired the speculators disappeared with money in their pockets and Ansco returned to its pre–Goodwin settlement economic plight. Fritz Wentzel, who came to Ansco from the photographic laboratories of Germany, found that Ansco in the 1920s with its five hundred employees made a good first impression until the narrow and weak line of products and aging production facilities became equally apparent. "Ignorant as I was of the financial status of the company and the conditions behind this glittering facade, I was confident of a brilliant future for Ansco and myself."[11]

The settlement was hailed in the press as a victory over trusts but the amount was not public knowledge. The *Wall Street Journal* estimated that the sum paid was $1,850,000. Stephens and Eastman both "declined to disclose the amount of the settlement."[12] Eastman's $5 million covered all previous Kodak film sales and licensing rights for the brief remaining life of the Goodwin patent.[13] The out-of-court settlement, though painful, was considerably easier to live with than a court decision that might have put Eastman under the crippling necessity of producing without a license. He kept the amount out of the next annual report, possibly because he paid it out of his own pocket and possibly because he felt that the less stockholders knew about the company's close shave, the better. "Five million dollars," the *Rochester Herald* announced five years later on 21 May 1919, in the first accurate report of the final figure, "the price which the Eastman Kodak Company . . . paid in settlement of a claim for patent infringement, has gone astray, according to allegations made in an action just begun to compel an accounting." Unfortunately for Ansco stockholders and employees, the allegations were correct. Banker Stephens and cronies had taken their profits and run.

One book, *Photography and the American Scene*, by Robert A. Taft, published in 1938, became the bible of photographic history and is still widely used as a reference. A great work otherwise, it is biased in its complete espousal of the Goodwin side of the film controversy. It is likely that the Eastman Kodak Company refused to give Taft access to documentation that would have shed a different light on the matter. If so, it was a public relations error. Indeed, Eastman's summation in 1914 of the Goodwin decision looks more accurate than Taft's today: "The decision was merely a sentimental one in favor of an aged widow who had in fact a ninth interest in the recovery against a big corporation."[14]

Judge Hazel was well acquainted with the photographic industry and the Eastman Kodak Company, so Eastman was not unduly surprised when a summons from the U.S. government arrived.

The early 1900s saw a powerful effort on the part of manufacturers to monopolize industries (witness the formation of the Standard Oil Company of New Jersey in 1899, the United States Steel Corporation in 1901, and the International Harvester Company in 1902). The growth of trusts was an outcome of the factory system, which made it cheaper to produce goods on a large rather than a small scale. Since fierce competition for raw materials and markets resulted in lower profits, the corollary seemed to many industrialists that the elimination of competition would stabilize prices, lower operating costs, and raise profits. But then federal and most state governments passed laws forbidding monopolistic combinations of capital. For example, the Clayton Act and the creation of the Federal Trade Commission, both passed in 1914, put further teeth in the Sherman Act of 1890.

During the "trust-busting" administrations of Theodore Roosevelt, William Howard Taft, and Woodrow Wilson, the courts tried many cases, finding some trusts, including Standard Oil and the American Tobacco Company, to be illegal. Other companies signed consent decrees, agreeing to refrain from illegal practices. Still others, such as the Shoe Manufactury, were exonerated. Trusts, and their opponents the "busters," provided early-twentieth-century America with its greatest social and economic public issue. However, not all citizens were on the side of the antitrusters. In towns such as Rochester, dependent on one industry for its livelihood, workers and their families interpreted the government's actions to break up companies as a threat to job security. At the height of the government effort, the name of Woodrow Wilson brought no applause in Kodak City.

Kodak's dominant position in the industry drew attention to its fair trade and exclusive dealership policies. Anthony & Scovill and several supply houses instigated, in 1902 at the state level, the first serious antitrust charges, requiring Kodak to prove that the companies it had acquired were not competitors. In 1904 Kodak was exonerated of all charges. A 1904 suit, again instigated by Anthony & Scovill, asked for annulment of the corporate charter, and again the charges were dismissed. Lulled into complacency, Eastman became confident that company practices could stand scrutiny.

But as the decade progressed he became increasingly worried about the growth in popular sentiment against trusts and the small army of photographers, dealers, and unhappy competitors bent on proving that Kodak was violating antitrust laws. In 1904 the *Chicago Tribune* noted that "drastic and comprehensive measures are about to be taken by the amateur and professional photographers of the country in order to protect themselves from what they characterize as the unjust and illegal discrimination and the stifling of competition by the so-called photographic trust." The formation of an American Photographic League was conceived as a national movement under the direction of the Rev. Henry Mason Baum and headquartered in Washington. Its object was to fight Eastman and Kodak policies through massive publicity and a boycott of Kodak goods. According to Baum, the league did not recommend "the goods of any other manufacturer, agent, or dealer." However, since, as the attorney general discovered in investigating the case, "the defendants, as a holding corporation, carry on upward of 90 percent of the photographers business in the United States," a boycott often meant going without photographic goods. Baum patterned his movement on the Free Camera Club of England, which had given George Davison problems and was perhaps the real reason that Eastman asked Davison for his resignation as managing director of Kodak Limited. The English group's "crusade resulted eventually in compelling the photographic trust in that country to abandon its efforts to control the market," Baum noted to the *Tribune*. In a shoot-the-messenger action similar to the dismissal of Davison, Eastman fired Sam Mora, his aggressive sales manager who was thoroughly unpopular with independent dealers. The reason given for Mora's dismissal was that he was acting too much like an heir presumptive while the reason given for retiring Davison was his active espousal of the politics of anarchy.[15]

By 1907 the Hearst papers were in full cry against the "Kodak Trust," noting how Kodak "controls a score of the leading manufacturers of photographic goods, all of whom formerly were bitter rivals. Acting together these corporations have induced nine-tenths of the retail dealers of America to join in a boycott of all independent makers. As a result the corporation is doing ninety per cent of the photographic supply business of the nation. By similar policies abroad they have risen to a dominating position in Canada, Great Britain, France, Australia, Belgium, Germany, Russia and Austria, and are making strides toward the establishment of the first world trust."[16]

In 1907, perhaps in response to such criticism, Eastman modified his sales policy, requiring Kodak dealers to market the company's products exclusively to one in which patented Kodak goods had fixed prices. Other U.S. trusts of the period dominated American markets in oil, steel, sugar, and so forth, but as the *Boston American* stated, the Eastman Kodak Company was in fact the first to dominate world trade in its field. This was more the result of Eastman's early aggressiveness and eye for international markets, from 1879 on, than any international companies that he bought or controlled. The tough policies he followed in competition or mergers were common to industries of the period. Eastman's instincts were to stay within the law and he took it as a personal affront when his actions were questioned as illegal. Similarly, charges that he was using his monopoly to keep prices artificially high cannot be sustained as he regularly passed on to the consumer the savings that came through increasing efficiency and mass production. And his stated confusion as to exactly what the law required seems genuine. "We don't understand the Sherman Law," he often said. "I would like to see the man who does."[17]

Even before that admission, under the administration of William Howard Taft, the Eastman Kodak companies of New Jersey and New York had been investigated and exonerated by the Antitrust Division of the U.S. Department of Justice. "The Wickersham investigation was most searching," Eastman wrote, referring to Taft's attorney general, "and was entered upon in a spirit which was anything but friendly to us. . . . The only way to meet such an inquiry was by giving free access to all the books, records and other historical data of our business." Anyone who thought such documents might prove embarrassing would certainly have destroyed them. In 1912 Eastman was still supremely confident; the Goodwin decision the following year shook that confidence to the core. Eastman thus agreed to the government's proposal for restructuring the company, "not because it was alleged that we had actually violated the law, but because it was deemed by the Attorney General advisable that we modify the terms in the interest of freer trade relations."[18]

Wanting to score some political points for the dying Taft administration, Wickersham urged Kodak to delay implementing the changes until a consent decree was signed. Eastman agreed to allow the trial to go over to the next administration, which, as it would turn out, would be a much more unfriendly one. After Woodrow Wilson became president in 1913, the government began an all-out trust-busting suit against Eastman Kodak. Wilson's own views concerning the dangers of monopolies and trusts were made clear while he was still president of Princeton University. The petition, *United States v. Eastman Kodak Company*, was filed on 9 June 1913. As the antitrust proceeding got under way, Eastman warily wrote Gifford that "all of the counsel, and in fact everybody who has investigated the case, are confident of winning against the Government, except perhaps the writer of this who, in light of recent experience [with the Goodwin suit] has great fear that the courts will be prejudiced."[19]

In order to set up a defense tailored to the government's offense, Eastman hired W. S. Gregg, formerly of the Department of Justice, who had worked on similar cases and knew the government's attitude and stratagems. To Rush Rhees he agonized with a touch of cynicism that "the position of the Government in regard to our case is . . . in effect, 'If you have been built up in violation of the law, it is not sufficient to reform your evil practices. You must be dissolved. If you cannot be dissolved, you must be destroyed; and we hope we can prove that you have been built up in violation of the law.'"[20]

For nineteen years, from 1902 until 1921, Eastman's mood alternated from the optimism engendered by early dismissals of the case at the state level and the relatively friendly federal investigations under the Taft administration to the deep pessimism brought on by vigorous assaults of the Justice Department under Wilson. The final, indecisive chapter would be written by the Great War, which mellowed the attitudes of public, government, and company alike. By then Kodak's main competitors would be German companies such as Agfa and dissolution would have benefited the foreign "enemy" more than any domestic competitor.[21] The hearings themselves alternated between Buffalo and Rochester. The subpoena listed sixty-two companies acquired by Eastman Kodak between 1892 and 1912, of which twenty-two were manufacturing companies that had been moved to Rochester. The question was, Why were they acquired and did that acquisition constitute an illegal monopoly in any or all branches of the trade? The decision would be based on Judge Hazel's interpretation of the Sherman Act as construed by the Supreme Court in recent cases against Union Pacific Railroad, and the International Harvester, Standard Oil, and American Tobacco companies. (The latter two were ordered by the Supreme Court in 1911 to dissolve.) When the hearings were over in 1915, Judge Hazel posed the question as primarily "whether the defendants were simply beneficiaries of the natural expansion of the photographic art and the business of manufacturing and selling photographic materials, and of the conspicuous skill, industry, and sagacity of Mr. Eastman . . . and whether the merging of the various enterprises was merely supplementary to an established business first in the field, and not for the purpose of protecting it; or whether indeed the defendants are guilty of forming a conspiracy or device to correl or concentrate the business with a view to monopolizing interstate trade or commerce by the adaptation of unfair methods which tended to . . . diminish or destroy the business of their competitors."[22]

Of the ten camera-manufacturing companies Kodak acquired, three had been started by Thomas Blair who, had he possessed Eastman's "conspicuous skill, industry, and sagacity," as Judge Hazel put it, might have been a more serious competitor. Indeed, in the 1890s Eastman considered Blair, not Goodwin, his most serious rival in film. U.S. attorneys, with access to Kodak files including minutes of directors' meetings, put into the court record that George Eastman had once said, "The Blair Company owns and controls the only competing system of film photography at present in existence." Blair also had the exclusive license for some of Houston's patents; on the witness stand Eastman explained: "I had been making cameras from 1894 to 1897 carrying the film in front of the focal plane without any license from Houston. . . . Blair had a contract with Houston, and it was that contract we wanted to get rid of. . . . Blair had certain contracts with Houston which prevented Houston from dealing with us. We therefore had to deal with Blair." There was no coercion in acquiring the Blair Camera Company, Eastman testified; Darius Goff was delighted to sell. "He had got into it about $140,000 and it was all to the bad. Not a ghost of a show for him to save any of it except through sale to us. We paid him in shares of the company and he still holds them; about 900 or 1,000, so you will honestly say that he made a big winning in his deal with us. I cannot honestly say that we lost anything either."[23]

In his "Opinion" of August 1915 Judge Hazel agreed with government lawyers that amateur photography started with the perfection of the dry plate but not with their contention that the next step forward was the Blair–Turner Bulls Eye camera of 1894. He conceded that the greatest impetus to modern photography was the Eastman–Walker roll holder of 1884 and the Kodak camera of 1888. But he held, too, that Eastman's purchase of the Blair

Camera Company with its advanced Hawk-Eye cameras and film system did give Kodak greater control over the business. Still, Judge Hazel found nothing coercive or illegal in any of Eastman's dealings prior to the turn of the century—but that, he said, was just the beginning, "and it can scarcely be doubted that such acquisitions were the nucleus from which arose the intention to bring other companies manufacturing and dealing in photographic supplies under its control."[24]

The judge enumerated the company's raw paper contracts, its acquisition of paper, dry-plate, and plate camera companies as well as supply houses and employment of terms of sale as indicating the intent to monopolize. Defining such "intent to monopolize and restrain" was, Eastman maintained, a subjective judgment not entirely separate from "the power of this popular uprising against trusts." But "it is a thing that has to be now taken into calculations by anyone whose business comprises any large part of the total output in any given line."[25]

"Eastman Kodak Company controls . . . between 75 and 80 percent of the entire trade . . . and has accordingly obtained a monopoly thereof,"[26] Judge Hazel noted. Having thus defined in percentage terms what constitutes a monopoly, the judge continued with a line of reasoning that seems to negate that such a definition can be made. He said there was no legal limit "to which a business may grow," unless "acquisitions of property . . . are accompanied by an intent to monopolize and restrain interstate trade by an arbitrary use of power resulting from a large business to eliminate a weaker competitor, then they no doubt come within the meaning of the statute."[27]

> In view of the fact that the majority of the plants were dismantled and the business concentrated at Rochester it is evident that they were not actually required by the defendants but were acquired with an idea of monopolizing trade. Considering next the conditions imposed on dealers in relation to price and the exclusive handling of Eastman products, that the business of the defendants increased in magnitude as a result of such restrictions, which operated to drive out competition, is to me too plain for controversy.[28]

Judge Hazel's decision thus rested on his interpretation of Eastman's intentions. Eastman's explanation of his "acquisitions of the various companies" and the primary cause of the "increase in magnitude" of his business was naturally different. When asked why, in the light of his statement that "from 1885 down to the present moment we took the position publicly and generally that we were pushing film cameras in preference to plate cameras," he would still buy up plate camera and dry-plate companies, his answer was that the company's aim was to cover the photographic field.

"Our line of plate cameras was an absolute failure," he confessed, "and we wanted to furnish plate cameras as well as film cameras to those who wanted them." As for dry plates, "we devoted our entire time to the manufacture and exploitation of film photography and we bought the Seed Company because the art of making dry plates had progressed beyond us. Seed had the best emulsion in the world and we bought it more to apply it to films than any other reason."[29] Eastman was not being entirely accurate. The correspondence indicates that it was only *after* the purchase of the Seed Company that William Stuber, Kodak's chief emulsion maker, discovered that the dry-plate emulsion could also be used on film and was actually much faster than Kodak's film emulsion. One by-product of preparing for the lengthy trial was that the history of the photographic industry was recorded as Kodak attorneys collected evidence, then primed Eastman on his testimony. For instance, the models of each camera and patented apparatus assembled for the trial were kept for decades afterwards in a Kodak Patent Museum. And, as Eastman's testimony makes clear, the state of emulsion making in 1913 was not much in advance of what it had been in the 1890s when he ruefully contemplated starting a "Praying Department" to help the emulsion along:

> The exact cause of the extreme speed in emulsion is not known. Emulsion making is largely empirical, but the great experts have succeeded in making an emulsion that is very uniform. It is easier to make emulsion for glass plates than it is for film, because glass is quite indifferent to emulsion; it has no effect chemically on emulsion, whereas film has. . . . The necessity for greater uniformity in film is not that film cannot vary and still make good pictures, but that the man who uses it expects to get exactly the same results under all conditions.[30]

Emulsion was the reason given for acquiring the Artura Paper Manufacturing Company too: "The Artura formula, in its constituents, was exactly the same thing as what we were using, and yet we could not make Artura paper; we paid a million and a quarter dollars, practically, for that formula."[31] Trade secrets did not necessarily come with the purchase of formulas, and even today they are guarded more jealously than patented items whose components are publicly stated. As for the quantum leap in business, it was due, the defense maintained (and it would be hard to disagree), not to squeezing out competitors but to the growth of the film business, particularly ciné film, and the fact that try as they would no other company could make film as good as Eastman Kodak's.

Philipp, Kennedy, and Gregg were unsuccessful in seeking a settlement out of court. As the government's suit dragged on for twenty-seven months, competitors became emboldened by Kodak's apparent vulnerability and the outcome of the Ansco–Goodwin suit. Eastman's old supplier, M. C. Lefferts of the Celluloid Corporation, threatened to sue because he learned that

Kodak had been using a variant of its old wheel-coating idea for film base. Eastman successfully fought Celluloid's plea for an injunction but the prospect of another court battle attempting to justify himself and his company to a hostile world made him "tired." A year before the case was scheduled for trial, Eastman settled out of court, writing Lefferts a check for $1.25 million on the spot. It may have been less costly and psychologically bruising than a long court battle, but it hurt so much Eastman couldn't bring himself to write the amount in a letter to Strong. "I'll tell you when I see you." In two other cases, he chose to settle for relatively small amounts but most of the efforts by small companies were so far-fetched they could be ignored.

Judge Hazel's decision of 24 August 1915 charged the company with intent to monopolize through raw paper contracts, acquisition of paper, dry-plate and plate camera companies, supply houses, and its terms of sale. The court's solution, as Kodak counsel James S. Havens explained it, was that "to satisfy the law there would have to be some division of the business of the defendant corporation among two or more competing companies, but what division should be made was left for future decision."[32]

Alice Whitney cabled the news: "DECISION GOVERNMENT SUIT AGAINST US" to Eastman at the Panama Pacific Exposition in Los Angeles. Later she wired Gregg's summary and interpretation: "VERY VAGUE," Gregg thought, but generally the company seemed all right in production and distribution of cameras as well as film, both regular and ciné. Appeal to the Supreme Court should reverse the decision and buy a few years' respite from dissolution action. Eastman was more glum: "Can't see how anyone can get any consolation out of it," he wrote Miss Whitney. Hazel "certainly intends to force some kind of dissolution if he can." Still, life would go on, and in the next sentence he launched into a critique of the San Francisco Exposition ("clever and beautiful but not so satisfying as the San Diego as a composition"). Alice agreed that it was a glum time but her ironic humor surfaced: "I went uptown this noon and ordered a blue blue gown,"[33] she said, in a play on words that evoked the popular fashion color called "Alice Blue." Later, Eastman would summarize the decision: "Judge Hazel gave us sixty days to formulate a plan to bring the company into conformity with the decision. We worked hard to devise a plan that would satisfy the Government but when it was presented they turned it down; refused to make any suggestions for bettering it; and finally refused our application to submit the whole matter to the Trade Commission for adjustment."[34] The appeal to the Supreme Court was filed on 8 March 1916. This bought them several years to figure out how to comply with Hazel's decision without destroying the company. The climate had change over twenty years and so did certain judicial interpretations. Judge Hazel acknowledged that Kodak had dropped its line of "fighting brands" in photographic paper—Crespa, Nepera, and Vulcan—in 1911 in line with the government's changing interpretation of antitrust legislation. After the Clayton Act was signed by Wilson on 14 October 1914, counsel advised Eastman to terminate the agreement with Thomas Edison and the licensees of the Motion Picture Patents Company. Eastman immediately gave Edison sixty days' notice.[35] In refusing to sign a consent decree to break up film manufacturing into two or more separate companies, Eastman was banking on attitudes softening too. Dissolution was what really worried him. The government wanted Kodak to split the manufacture of film into separate competitive companies and even "show a new company how to make film the same as we make." Impossible, Eastman maintained; it would mark the end of the Eastman Kodak Company.[36]

James Havens, counsel, and Louis Antisdale, Rochester newspaperman, went to Washington to negotiate with the Justice Department but "failed to get any modification of the demand that the new company should be put in the way of manufacturing film," Eastman reported to Kennedy two weeks later. "Havens told them that the requirement was so unreasonable I would not consent to it. . . . He thinks they are afraid to make any reasonable settlement of the case. . . . I am glad the attempt has been made because it cannot be said that any stone has been left unturned to settle the case."[37]

Meanwhile Eastman brought certain other of his activities more in line with what the government seemed to be requiring. In 1917 he resigned from the American Fair Trade League.[38] Although Kodak would not drop fair-traded articles until the 1940s, it is obvious that in the teens the government was already looking at such practices as being in restraint of trade. Stopped by antitrust laws from the buying of competing companies, Eastman stepped up the pace of Kodak's production of materials or supplies necessary for basic production. By the end of 1917 the new paper mill was in operation and a gelatin factory under construction. A cellulose acetate plant was purchased in Kingsport, Tennessee, in 1920, and the Lake Ontario pumping station was in operation. Eastman was even considering buying a coal mine. "If we do this," he quipped, "we need only buy a silver mine and an optical glass factory to make a symmetrical organization. . . . If the Supreme Court will hold off long enough, it will have quite an establishment to split up."[39] The long years of litigation effectively silenced the already reticent man and his company. Eastman always disdained what he called personal notoriety ("So far I have successfully avoided being written up," he said once with pride) and the inaccuracies of lazy reporters. In 1912, for instance, he fumed at the *New York Sun* as he reviewed a proof of an biographical article that was "so full of errors that it seems to me unfit for publication":

For instance . . . Mr. Henry A. Strong was never known as Major . . . he was never president of the Rochester Savings Bank; . . . he was not my employer. There never was any dog episode. The first Kodak could hardly be called cumbersome. Professional photographers never spread rumors about my financial standing so far as I know. . . . I never used fibre for camera boxes. . . . I never was forced to borrow money to exploit my inventions and neither I nor the Company has ever borrowed any money except on very special occasions for short periods. I have never been pressed for money to buy clothes or advertising or anything else. Dr. Mees is not a German. My house is not in the country; it is not at East Rochester; it has not even approximately one hundred rooms; the statement in regard to my dining to the strains of my orchestra, to draw it mildly, is incorrect.[40]

But now there were new and compelling reasons to avoid being written up. In 1916 Samuel Crowther of the Wildman Service interviewed Eastman with the understanding that he and his attorneys might read the article before publication. When they did, Eastman had to cable: "COUNSEL FORBIDS PUBLICATION INTERVIEW. . . . PLEASE DO NOT USE ANY OF IT."[41] The repercussions of this decision would continue for decades, even after Eastman's death. Major roadblocks would be put in front of would-be biographers in terms of access to information. Even biographies of Eastman and histories of the company that were initially commissioned by Kodak would end up unpublished. In 1974, the same year that Eastman Kodak officials decided not to publish a biography of Eastman the company had commissioned Lawrence Bachmann to write, *Financial World* magazine, which had its own problems getting information, commented: "While there are companies that are nervous and unhappy when being grilled by financial analysts, Eastman [Kodak], thanks to whom Aunt Sally is forever enshrined in the family album without her teeth, has elevated corporate reticence to a new art form.[42]

Eastman's gamble paid off. Beginning about 1915 when the appeal was filed the government's attitude began to change. As World War I heated up, Kodak, now considered a chemical as well as a photographic industry, was bringing into America profits that had been almost exclusively German. "And for this," Eastman told the Rev. Murray Bartlett, "the Government is trying to break us up, make us less efficient. It seems to me the joke is on the country, just as much as on the company. Twenty-five years from now, this phase will be looked on with the same derision as our 'free silver' experience. By that time damn foolishness will no doubt be directed into some other activity."[43]

In 1918 the government postponed the case for reasons connected with the war. But at the same time officials snubbed Eastman's offer to set up a school of aerial photography, possibly for fear of accepting favors from "the Trust." Plan after plan was presented by Kodak but none were accepted. In 1920 Eastman was still trying to satisfy the government without committing corporate suicide. "We offered the Government everything they had a right to ask and more than they had a right to expect," he said. "They didn't accept, I believe, because the representatives we dealt with didn't have the courage to take responsibility for a fair compromise." Even competitors such as Ansco sensed that drastic dissolution of the Big Yellow Box could hurt rather than help them. Eastman, too, mellowed over the twenty years that the government was poking its nose into his business. For example, in 1920 as Ansco continued to have financial difficulties, Eastman wrote to banker Daniel E. Pomeroy, later an Eastman safari companion:

> We realize that we cannot be without competition and that any disaster coming to our largest competitor would be a disadvantage to us. To prevent this is the sole motive actuating us to offer assistance along the lines indicated. . . . If the difficulty is in the manufacture of the product, particularly in the manufacture of sensitized goods, the management of this Company could not in justice to its stockholders give to a competitor the results of more than twenty years' experience and what has cost this Company millions of dollars in research and experimental work.[44]

The longer he could hold the government at bay, Eastman felt, the better his chances. When a steel decision came in March 1920, attorney John Milburn remarked, "The decision shows that when they see that on the whole a concern should not be broken up they find a way not to break it up, and, as you say, that is encouraging." In 1921 the case was settled after Kodak signed a consent decree agreeing to sell three plants and equipment and the trade names involved and to drop certain brands of equipment. "What is known as the Folmer and Schwing-Century Division is to be sold," *Kodak Magazine* told employees in March 1921, "including the trade names Graflex, Graphic, and Century. . . . Similarly we are to sell the Premo factory and equipment and the trade name Premo." In the end Kodak Park, the Camera Works, and the Hawk-Eye Works were not affected "and the organization of our sensitized good department remains intact."

The trade name Artura was sold, and with it the formula for Artura platinum paper. Alfred Stieglitz would complain in 1924 that he couldn't get platinum paper in this country because "Eastman had ceased making it" and then would thunder: "Have I not earned the right to have that platinum paper made if I cover the cost? Even if it is the law not to make it? . . . If I had been a madman I might have been tempted to go to Rochester, and do some harm, because of my feeling for photography."[45] But Artura, apparently the only platinum paper made in the United States, was sold to the Defender Company that Eastman had divested his stock in, so that Stieglitz should have been railing at that Rochester company instead of at Eastman.

The Standard, Stanley, and Seed dry-plate names and formulas were sold. So, too, was the American Aristo plant at Jamestown. However, products marketed under those names that originated in Kodak factories after the original purchase could still be produced and marketed under new trade names. Two years was given to make the sales and then the properties would be put up at auction. In the meantime the factories would be operated "to the fullest possible extent." Artura paper was supplied up to the moment of the sale. Meanwhile, since the "avowed object of the Sherman law is to provide for the widest possible competition," Kodak would start immediately making paper and plates "to compete with the brands that we part with." The company was prohibited from coming out immediately with competing cameras. "The sale of any of our factories was the one thing the company endeavored to avoid in making this settlement," the employees were told, "but after the most strenuous efforts . . . the Government refused to yield. . . . It was made clear . . . that the sale of any of our factories would result in the separation . . . of employees . . . who would necessarily lose benefits derived from wage dividends and stock distribution and many other features peculiar to the Kodak organization."[46]

Divested of dry plates, plate cameras, platinum paper, and Aristo POP— all of which were in the dying sectors of photography in 1920 and amounted to only a fraction of business—Kodak was not severely hampered. The evolution of the company, even without the decree, would arguably have been in the same direction. But the *Kodak Magazine* analysis was correct in that the real losers were neither the company, Eastman, nor any high-placed executive, but the employees of the divisions that had to be sold.

> It was hoped that this consideration would appeal to the Government, and we believe that in a measure it did, but the representative of the Government felt that under the terms of the decree of the District Court they had no option but must insist upon some division of the manufacturing plants. . . . Although the terms of the settlement are severe and . . . unwarranted, still in many respects we shall presently be in a better position than ever to go on with our development of photography, many elements of doubt and uncertainty having been removed.[47]

Privately Eastman echoed optimism. "While we are very careful not to brag that the settlement is a favorable one," he wrote Gifford, now retired in Florida, "as a matter of fact the Company is not likely to be much damaged. Portrait films will . . . supersede glass plates within two years. We are not prevented . . . from using any of the formulas which we are to disclose. . . . We already have an improvement on Artura which has never been marketed. . . . We hope through the new paper we can retain 80 or 90 percent of the business. . . . It will simply take a little time to overcome the inertia of the photographers. They are slow to change anything."[48]

Eastman liked to present the face of gloom and doom to the public, however. "A decree dissolving the Kodak Company has been issued since you left," he wrote newspaper editor Ernest Willard. "If you had your money all in Kodak you might not be able to get back to Rochester, something I should regret very much." To Babbott, he was more honest: "As you will have seen by the papers, we have withdrawn our appeal in the Government suit and have made a settlement, . . . the final details of which . . . were settled in Washington this morning. . . . [It] is not wholly satisfactory but we decided it was better to settle than to take the chances of the appeal."[49]

Despite the continuing battle and his disgust at having government lawyers tell him how to run his business, Eastman had behaved throughout with exemplary patience and tact. In 1920 he paid back $335,389.76 in war contract profits, stating he didn't want to make money off the government on such work. And then, about the same time, while in Italy he was about to purchase some expensive Venetian glass that he really liked. The proprietor began outlining ways Eastman could get around paying the duty. "You mean cheat the government?" he asked, and out he stalked.[50]

Over There

■ ■ ▪

GE was profoundly unmarried.[1] His primary love relationship was with his work. His passion for Kodak became a major reason for keeping marriage at a distance, as he himself frequently explained. Perhaps, too, the memory of a father who struggled to establish himself in two occupations while shuttling his family between two locations, and who then died at an early age deeply in debt, was the example that made him focus solely on vocational goals. And by the time he had enough money to place himself and his mother forever out of the reach of poverty, the thought did nag him that women were mainly interested in him for his wealth and position.[2]

As is usually the case with bachelors, he had to explain himself more frequently than his married male friends. According to Marian Gleason, a woman forty years his junior who entered his life in 1919 as the wife of his new organist, he did much of his explaining to her. She believed that although he may have been sexually distant, "there was some hunger in him for women, for the most part wholly controlled." She said that he confided to her the details of a unrequited love affair of the 1890s with a married woman that began on board a transatlantic steamer. This brief affair allegedly ended when the cuckolded husband sued and collected $50,000 from Eastman. His mistrust of women began with this episode, she believed. Gleason further asserted in interviews that the woman in question came to Eastman House once and that those in the know followed the events of the evening with great interest but no resolution.

Marian Gleason apparently talked frankly enough with Eastman during the last decade and a half of his life to enable her to say that he was normally amorous but for various reasons, including the fact that he was quite shy, he kept himself under rigid control, suppressing these feelings or expressing them only toward those he could not marry. Gleason told interviewers and would-be biographers of Eastman—André Maurois in 1940, Roger Butterfield in the 1950s, Lawrence Bachmann in the 1970s—and a general television audience in 1980 that in 1928 when she went to Europe to accompany Eastman home after his last African trip, he made a sexual advance in her direction, which she rebuffed.[3]

In addition to these uncorroborated anecdotes is the tradition that has come down in the Mulligan family to the late twentieth century that Mary Durand, a Rochester beauty of 1890, had two persistent suitors, George Eastman and a medical student, Edward Mulligan. Miss Durand chose Mulligan and they were married in 1892.[4]

And then there is Gertrude Strong Achilles's story of Eastman losing track of an early love when she left Rochester to study music in Europe. On 2 December 1927 he received a handwritten letter from a Susan F. Brown that could lead one to agree that such a young lady did exist and that she never forgot George Eastman. (His letters to his mother in the 1890s mention a "Miss Brown" or "Miss B.") His 1927 reply was not dictated to Alice Whitney, but answered by Eastman by hand, at home. Apparently Susan Brown telephoned him after receiving his reply (which has not been preserved), and Eastman visited her in Pasadena. In September 1930 she came to Eastman House en route to New England. The morning she left, she also left him a note on *900 East Avenue* stationery. "This is to say good bye again. . . . For parting is so especially sweet sorrow this time that I could say it until tomorrow and then it would not be enough. . . . Good bye again dear dear George Eastman. Believe that I am always more truly yours than you would understand."[5]

There was an aspect of Eastman's personality that enjoyed what in his era were considered feminine pursuits—music, art, flowers, gardening, cooking, or washing the dishes on camping trips. He was interested in women's clothes, read *Vogue* magazine regularly, and enjoyed chatting about babies with younger women friends. This from a gun aficionado who stalked elephants and grizzlies and endured privations in the wild with a cheerful machismo.

A bachelor's life meant terrorizing the kitchen staff Sunday mornings after breakfast by regularly arriving for a session with the pots and pans. The staff's amusement at his puttering was countered by their annoyance at his invasion of their domain. His "bring me this, that, and the other" was answered with unenthusiastic obedience and mutterings that "his biscuits were like bullets." He turned out pies, cakes, biscuits, and muffins the way he once produced photographic emulsions.[6]

A bachelor's life meant presiding every Wednesday at an elegant dinner for twenty, enjoying his role as host and more than holding his own in the dinner conversation. It also meant diffidence toward family-oriented holidays. "Forgetting that it was the 4th of July I tried to call you but the janitor explained why you were not there," he wrote E. P. Snow, Kodak's New York manager. People assumed that Rochester's leading citizen would be fully engaged on holidays but one woman was pleasantly surprised when she invited him to Thanksgiving dinner only to have him eagerly accept. Bachelor or not Eastman could recollect some memorable events, some happy, some sad, of the twenty-six Christmas holidays he spent while living in Eastman House.

The happiest Christmases were when the Drydens came to Rochester, helped the housekeeper decorate the tree, and then opened presents by its warm glow. Sometimes, Ellen's college roommate Nell Newhall came for Christmas with her husband Charlie and small son Watson, because, as Uncle George said, "we need at least three children in the house to keep it going. Besides, the merchants here are beginning to notice that I am not ordering any supplies lately."[7]

There were bittersweet Christmases involving young Louise Gifford; the prescribed treatment for her tuberculosis was a rest cure and bracing fresh air to heal her infected lungs. Eastman made the guest cottage at Oak Lodge in North Carolina available to Louise, her mother, and a nurse, for the Christmas of 1910 and the rest of the winter of 1911. He spent several weeks there himself building a sleeping porch for Louise, because Louise's father had remarked that "the porch is Louise's lifeline." The treatment bucked her up temporarily. "Louise never looked better," Gifford reported when his wife and daughter disembarked from the *Kaiser Wilhelm II* in Plymouth. Eastman spent the next Christmas with Louise and her family in Bournemouth on the coast of England, finding that "Louise is getting on splendidly. She . . . is able to take long walks, three or four miles a day."[8]

The following year, 1912, Eastman as chairman of the *Eastman & Gifford Entertainment Committee* was happily planning a giant wedding for Louise's sister Katherine to be held in his house and garden, which would also be a reception for their parents. In April he submitted to Katherine in England "samples" of wedding invitations and fancy boxes "to be used as favors for the bridal table, the box for the girls to contain cake and those for the men to contain cigarettes; these also to serve as place cards." Architect Edwin Gordon designed dancing and dining pavilions that included a "kitchen and band stand." At Eastman's behest, Katherine went to Tiffany's and picked out a Steinway piano as her wedding present. He personally selected and ordered a menu of "Crab Flakes Escaloped in own shells, Breast of Squab,

Guinea Hen Saute, chicken and lobster salads, individual creams, fancy iced cakes, and bon-bons." The Dossenbach Orchestra and Park Band were engaged. But the illness and death of the groom's father cancelled plans for a extravagant wedding and reception at 900 East Avenue. Eastman put Gordon's plans in his architectural file at Kodak and brought them out for the 1913–14 holidays for an even more lavish affair.[9]

The biggest party ever held at Eastman House occurred on New Year's night of 1914, when 1,200 invitations were sent out worldwide. More than 900 attended, "without any crowding," Eastman told Thomas Baker, Kodak's representative in Australia who sent regrets. Gordon's temporary "dancing pavilion was built over the brick terrace adjoining library and music room" (living room and conservatory) to the east of the house. The east porch was also enclosed and connected with the dancing pavilion so that the dancers could dance from the conservatory right around to the farther end of the porch. There were two platforms for musicians, one occupied by the park band in their white uniforms and the other by a string orchestra of about forty pieces.

A supper room seating 256 and with another small orchestra was built between kitchen and carriage house "with entrance from the covered ivy walk which you will remember runs from the dining room to the palm house." Alternating throughout the evening, the orchestra and band played one steps, two steps, waltzes, and tangos with such titles as *Hitchy Koo, Ramshackle Rag, Good Night Nurse, Snooky Ookums, When the Midnight Choo-Choo Leaves for Alabama,* and *In My Harem.* "If it is any inducement to you wicked Brooklynites," Eastman wrote Babbott and his college-age children, "the Tango will not be prohibited at the forthcoming party. We are very broad minded up here and . . . kindred modern steps have been modified so as to at least pass police censorship."[10] Art dealer Carmen Messmore of M. Knoedler & Company sent up a luscious painting of *Salome* to further enhance the ambience of the grand ball.

Guests were dropped at the porte cochere entrance, went up the side stairs to leave their wraps, then promenaded down the grand staircase to be greeted by Eastman and his hostesses: Josephine Dickman, Nell Newhall, and Rochesterians Mary Mulligan and Eleanor Eastwood. Ellen Dryden, recovering from surgery, could not stand in the receiving line; however, Uncle George made sure she did not feel forgotten. Her Christmas present that year was a long and expensive rope of pearls that became her signature thereafter. The day before the party, Eastman had his friend Victoria Powers walk down the front staircase so he could judge how the lighting effects would be on the night of the ball. Next he consulted her as to the best place for him to receive his guests in the lower hall. "This all sounds simple, but it was not, and it would be some time before he was satisfied," Mrs. Powers told Oscar Solbert, first director of the George Eastman House, many years later.

"But I could not help but notice on the night of the ball how all confusion was avoided as he received his hundreds of guests just by this planning."[11]

According to oral tradition, Eastman gave a second party on the night of 2 January 1914 for the young scions and debutantes of Rochester's leading families and, according to some sources, the children of privilege wrecked havoc on Eastman House. Apocryphal or not, Eastman's New Year's festivities of 1914 turned out to be a pre-Waterloo ball.

As the guns of August 1914 began to rumble and communication with all continental branches except Paris was cut off, Eastman sped to England to complete contingency plans. Business was so poor that the Harrow force was cut by two-thirds, Kodak Park's by one-third. "We are doing the best we can to give all of our employees something to do and hope that if things do not get any worse, we will get through the winter without any great distress," he wrote to Ernest Janson, the manager of Kodak in Berlin.

"I was never so glad to get home. . . . London was such a sad, gloomy place."[12] On the overbooked liner *Campania* Eastman insisted that Louise Gifford and her mother take his cabin while he bunked below with two strangers. During the first confusing months of the conflict that is today called World War I, Eastman maintained a strict business policy of impartiality toward the belligerents: Eastman Kodak had branches and representatives on both sides. He authorized Ernest Janson, the Berlin manager, to pay four hundred marks each month to the German Red Cross; in return he requested the help of the German Red Cross in locating Kodak employees, and certain Frenchmen such as Maurice Kleber of the Rives Paper Company who was a prisoner of war. Eastman sent David, Prince of Wales, later Edward VIII, and still later the Duke of Windsor, a check for $5,000 and personally contributed to French and Belgian relief funds. He told Gifford and the other European managers that "it is our intention to pay wage dividends to the men who have joined the colors on the same basis as if they had been on the payroll for the full amount of their wages."[13]

London's role in supplying and controlling Kodak branches in Germany, Austria-Hungary, and Turkey was now *verboten* by the German kaiser. Janson in Berlin could order direct from Rochester, but the goods could only be shipped in American vessels. One supply pipeline went from London through Sweden, where Nils Bouveng of Haselblad played a major role, and then to Archangel and into czarist Russia, where "the trade is brisk," Eastman reported. Over somewhat the same route vital German chemicals reached Rochester until they were cut off by the British blockade. Eastman estimated he had about a year's supply of gelatin, glass, and paper. Yet the eventual effect of the war was to end Eastman Kodak's reliance on Europe for raw materials, particularly those from Germany. Over the objections of those who thought the war would be over in a few weeks, Stuber stockpiled huge amounts of high-quality gelatin. (In 1930 Kodak would acquire an American glue company, and today, the purest gelatin in the world and the largest quantity outside of the Jell-O Division of General Foods is made at Kodak Park.)

The German invasion of neutral Belgium and sinking of the *Lusitania* on 17 April 1915, in which three Rochesterians were lost, raised Eastman's hackles. "Very likely," he wrote Thomas Baker in Australia in June 1915, "by the time you get this, the United States will have severed relations with Germany. The country is wrought up over her submarine exploits and is . . . gradually waking up to the fact that this war is just as important to us as it is to England." After that initial falloff, business was good, thanks partly to the tremendous domestic demand for motion picture film. The men in the trenches of France coveted the Kodak Vest Pocket camera for snapshots. There was a boom in Russia for Kodak cameras and film. Eight months after the war began, the company's revenues had increased dramatically. By January 1916 the company and Eastman personally had $4 million invested in British, French, Russian, and Italian war loans and had determined to withdraw all company funds from Germany. The government's antitrust suit and Judge Hazel's ruling against the company in 1915 did not alter Eastman's emerging role as superpatriot but it did shape his reaction to the government's continuing refusal to accept his offers of aid: "It may be that the Government is afraid to accept favors from one of the so-called trusts. Of course, we are not paying attention to such discrimination but are trying to help where we can." He predicted that "the time is coming when business men will be treated better than hobos by the administration."[14]

While President Wilson adopted a policy of "watchful waiting," Eastman was in favor of a more belligerent "preparedness," and eagerly plunged into home front activities. For the first Liberty Loan drive, he subscribed $2.5 million, believing this a patriotic duty rather than an act of charity. Feeling an obligation to set an example, he emerged for the first time into the limelight as chairman of the New York State Division of the United War Campaign ("I am chiefly occupied this afternoon in figuring out how much I shall assess on Waterville," he notified Cousin Almon) and as chairman of the Rochester Home Defense Committee. He rode on a Liberty Loan float that read "NOW—ALL TOGETHER! PRY THE KAISER OFF THE EARTH" as it cruised along East Avenue in front of his house.

He accepted the chairmanship of the Rochester Red Cross. Under his vigorous guidance, Rochester oversubscribed to the Red Cross campaign by pledging three times its quota, the highest percentage of any city in the country. Even old William Hall Walker received an earnest phone call and followup letter on 10 June 1917 urging him to help Rochester meet its $1 million quota toward the national $100 million fund. "Our duty," he reminded Walker, "to jump in and help the people who have almost exhausted themselves in fighting for us is too plain."[15] Like Strong, Walker gave $50,000. A month before, the Walkers had journeyed to Rochester to attend the dedication of the Rochester Dental Dispensary, fully expecting to spend some time with its donor, and were nonplussed to find that he was out of town. In November 1917 Walker died. "Poor old fellow," Eastman commented. "He never got much joy out of his wealth." (Although Walker maintained a palatial establishment [Brookside, in Great Barrington], a Stanford White townhouse next to the Rockefellers, and gave generously to Stevens Institute of Technology and Eastman's Rochester causes, he grumbled as he wrote his checks.) The next year, Harriet Dana Walker, who had inherited Walker's wealth, declined to contribute to Rochester's War Chest: "Gertrude and I have decided we will make our contribution here in Great Barrington, as we wish to identify ourselves with all the interests of our town."[16] It was an argument with which Eastman had to agree.

He encouraged Kodak employees to attend a military preparedness camp in Plattsburgh, New York, "for up to four weeks, without deduction from pay other than an amount equal to the sum received by them for military services." Eventually a thousand of them would see service in the American Expeditionary Force. In June 1916 he engaged a military band and agreed not only to march with but to lead six thousand people in the great Preparedness Day parade through the streets of Rochester. Rain poured on the parade and women employees were given $1.50 each for rain damage to their clothing.

In July 1916 Eastman received government permission to go to England on business. He wangled an invitation to visit the trenches at Rheims, wrote a check for $100,000 to Alice Whitney to put his affairs in order in case of his death, and came home with a souvenir piece of blue glass from Rheims Cathedral and a report: "It was very quiet in that sector and I was . . . impressed by the matter-of-factness with which people just inside the firing line were living their lives and carrying on their occupations without paying attention to the noise of the shells."[17]

Eastman and Mary Mulligan organized and directed a group of sock knitters, or rather Eastman organized and directed "My dear Mary" on how to achieve top efficiency and mass production in her task. He recommended the following procedure: "1. Confine your instruction . . . to women who will agree to teach regularly, form groups, or work in the shop. 2. Use your main instruction room for this purpose only. 3. Use your second room as a practice room. See that these women are in pairs or groups and as soon as ready, let Eleanor Eastwood take them, . . . you furnishing teachers for oversight." And so forth. "Mary took her sock knitting machine to the Lodge and knit fifty-six pairs," Eastman proudly reported to Ellen. That did not make Mary the champ. "Eleanor's department turned out 1789$\frac{1}{2}$ pair." The grand champs were the city firemen, with "an average of nineteen pairs a day per machine." With records like these and the need for 111 knitting machines, the sock-knitting chapter and other activities soon outgrew headquarters. Eastman made arrangements for the Red Cross to move into the building then occupied by the Home for the Friendless, an institution serving widows and children. Then the home, which had planned to move to its new building in December (and be renamed The Friendly Home), put off the move until the following May. "But your uncle got after the trustees," Eastman told Ellen, "and they have been very nice about expediting things." Part of the persuasion took the form of increasing his pledge to the Friendly Home by $50,000 (his original contribution was $8,000). After moving the home in a hurry, the trustees also voted to accept men as clients; tradition makes this an Eastman stipulation too.[18]

As President Woodrow Wilson prepared to run for reelection on the platform of "He kept us out of war," Eastman grumbled about "our weak and vacillating course in international affairs. . . . The failure of President Wilson to gauge the significance of the great conflict is simply amazing. He has succeeded in anaesthetizing a large body of our citizens, but they are beginning to recover, and the pending campaign will . . . show that the great war is simply and solely a conflict between democracy and military world despotism."[19]

"As for Henry Ford, he makes me both sick and tired," Eastman wrote in a double-barreled denunciation of Ford's efforts to achieve peace in his time by visiting the belligerents on his Peace Ship. Despite the high pressure and belligerent patriotism, Eastman did not fail to respond to the human suffering caused by the war. When four employees of Kodak Gesellschaft were killed in action, Eastman told Janson, the Berlin manager, "You may continue paying their wives what is necessary up to one half of their salaries. . . . We feel great sympathy with the people of all the countries which have been drawn into this terrible war and can only hope it will come to a speedy end so that they can take up their accustomed occupations."[20]

When Mortimer Adler, a Rochester clothing manufacturer, approached Eastman for aid to Jewish refugees from eastern Europe, Eastman "listened silently, then wrote a check for $5,000." It was Adler's first meeting with the industrialist, whom he gauged to be "addicted to understatement and brevity but possessed of unusual mental lucidity. He [Eastman] demands performance and has little patience with subterfuge," Adler judged. This was the beginning of a mutually pleasant association between Eastman and the large Adler family, which ran the Adler-Rochester clothing firm. It included Isaac Adler, a lawyer who was solicited by Eastman to be a trustee of the Bureau of Municipal Research and later became a city councilman; Simon Adler, assemblyman in Albany; Elmer Adler, fine printer in New York City and collector of fine printing; and Mortimer Adler, who was associated with Eastman in the beginnings of the Community Chest.[21]

By the time the United States entered the conflict in April 1917, Eastman and his company had backed the Allied cause with $8.5 million in addition to heavy war taxes in England, France, Italy, Russia, Canada, and Australia, and Eastman's personal contribution to many relief causes and to the American Hospital in France. Kodak ads featured an American soldier on foreign soil looking longingly at "The Picture from Home." Within days after war was declared, Eastman notified Assistant Secretary of the Navy Franklin Delano Roosevelt that the company was prepared to supply the government with cellulose acetate for weatherproofing airplane wings and unbreakable lenses for gas masks. When Roosevelt called for individuals to loan their binoculars, telescopes, spyglasses, and navigation instruments as "Eyes for the Navy," Eastman collected all of his, including one of special significance: "I am sending you today . . . a pair of Bausch & Lomb binoculars. I shall be glad if these glasses can be returned to me at the close of the war as they were a gift from my friend Edward Bausch. My name is engraved on the frame." In December 1917 Roosevelt would call Eastman to Washington and arrange for Kodak to reorganize the government's binocular business because the company having the contract had fallen down in deliveries and quality.[22]

Eastman also offered to set up a school of aerial photography at Kodak Park. "This offer was turned down [by the Secretary of War] on the excuse that they could not send men away from their camps for instruction. This of course was rubbish," he told Alexander Lindsay, "but nevertheless the offer was turned down and forgotten." The rejection was a bitter pill. "Prejudice against the big concerns seems to have cut quite a foothold in the Signal Corps," he wrote to MIT's Richard Maclaurin. It could just as easily have been a case study in the proliferating confusion that marked the mobilization of the AEF. Seven months later the government "attempted to start a school at Langely Field, and . . . discovered that they were up against it and turned to us for help. We reminded them of our previous offer, but the officers then in charge had never heard of it. There was not time left to teach the teachers [as per the original offer], so we made them an offer to take 1000 men at a time and lend them about fifty of our experts to help with the teaching. They jumped at this offer and have shown the greatest activity in preparations for establishing the school." With the government's approval of Eastman's package, three existing schools of aerial photography—at Cornell, Langely Field, and Fort Sill—were consolidated at Rochester.[23]

"We had a great deal of difficulty in finding out what the Signal Corps wanted in the way of cameras," Eastman remembered later. Aerial reconnaissance was a brand new craft; in 1914 men went up in balloons and reported the enemy's position to the artillery by telephone. By October 1917 the men could take along cameras loaded with special film. The first aerial cameras used glass plates exclusively "because they [the Allies] have been unable to get photographic results required on films. This is partly because they have been trying to use the ordinary camera films, which are quite unsuitable for the work. They also have been unable to handle the films mechanically." Kodak developed "an automatic film camera which will make fifty exposures, six inches square, in succession, and which are equal to anything that can be taken singly with glass plates." By the time the Signal Corps accepted Eastman's offer to set up a school, the camera had already been tested at Curtiss Field in Buffalo, at Pensacola, at Langely Field, and on a flight from Washington to New York.[24]

The next year, 1918, Clarke's son, Dr. Hans Thacher Clarke, who joined Kodak Research Laboratories in 1914 as director of the department of synthetic chemistry, and Dr. Leon Lilienfield, Austrian chemist, established the first large, synthetic organic chemical laboratory in the country at Kodak Park. Chemical research had long been stymied in industrial and university laboratories by German control of fine and experimental chemicals. When Eastman made his public gift of a chemical engineering laboratory to MIT in 1916, he received numerous requests to bring more of this kind of research to American shores. By 1921 Kodak's department of synthetic chemistry furnished more than one thousand different chemicals to American and Canadian markets.[25]

For the duration of the war Eastman agreed to the request of Herbert Hoover, world food administrator, to "forego all profit on [motion picture film] which we shall require during the progress of our [the Food Administration's] activities"—this despite the fact that prices of raw materials for film had skyrocketed. Silver was up 90 percent, gelatin 100 percent, bromides 800 percent.[26] Through Jules Brulatour, formerly president of Lumière in New York and now Kodak's distributor of motion picture film, the company agreed to assist in the distribution of motion pictures to American military camps in France. By the time of the Armistice on 11 November 1918, 38 percent of the company's business was in war contracts.

On the home front, Eastman at first kept his greenhouses running so as not to throw men out of work, but eventually transferred the men and closed the greenhouses to conserve coal. He moved the potted fruit trees and palms into the conservatory along with large vats of water to supply humidity. Soon the conservatory was as dense and steamy as a jungle. This bothered the servants much more than it did the master. "Of course my household is observing all the injunctions as to meatless and wheatless days and in the conservation of sugar," he advised the Liberty Loan Committee.

He directed Henry Myrick at Oak Lodge "to grow plenty of corn and beans, chickens, hogs, and turkeys [as] almost everybody seems to think there will be a general shortage of food this year." To Henry Strong, whose salutation had changed from the Germanic "Heinrich" to the French

"Henri," Eastman divulged that he was "plowing up my lawn and planting all of the open spaces . . . in potatoes and onions. I made up my mind that this year my gardeners could be better employed in hoeing potatoes than in cutting grass."[27]

The February 1918 issue of the national *Red Cross Magazine* printed the poem "The Holy War" by Rudyard Kipling (who had married Caroline Balestier, a Third Ward neighbor of the Eastmans in the 1860s), and Rochester's Roman Catholic Bishop Thomas Hickey flagged Eastman's attention to its negative reference to the pope. Eastman quickly wrote the magazine "that it is unwise to . . . needlessly antagonize any of the elements upon which the Red Cross is depending for support. The Catholics here . . . have given . . . their whole-hearted cooperation and while the Bishop is broad minded . . . it will make it harder to work up enthusiasm among his people during the next drive."[28] By the time the next drive came, only a month after the Kipling brouhaha, Eastman had the unprecedented vision of combining all war and charitable drives into one, including the Catholic and Jewish charities. Cooperation in fundraising was relatively untried when, in 1917, dozens of war relief agencies burst on the national scene with appeals. Out of the confusion that followed, organizers in Columbus and Syracuse combined appeals into one War Chest. When, in March 1918, Eastman was preparing to head the annual May Red Cross campaign, he invited ten key Rochesterians[29] to his living room to discuss a War Chest. "Much to my surprise," he reported, "I found that already there was a general demand for combining at least all the war charities in one drive and instead of turning the idea down it was voted to have a larger meeting and investigate further."[30] Of the twenty-seven Rochester charitable organizations, only the Red Cross and YMCA argued against the proposal, saying that as large, well-known organizations with efficient fundraising apparatus in place, they could raise more money separately. Eastman then wrote a letter "shadowing my resignation as Chairman of the Red Cross," with the prediction that "the common peepul will decline to be dictated to."[31]

On 7 May 1918 a committee of three—Eastman, Hiram W. Sibley, and Roland Woodward of the Chamber of Commerce—organized the Rochester Patriotic and Community Fund, Inc. (commonly called War Chest). Eastman was named president, Mayor Edgerton his honorary associate, and University of Rochester president Rush Rhees chairman of the budget committee. The goal was fixed at $3.75 million, which included $488,335 for thirty-six local charities. The seven-day campaign organized by Harry P. Wareham, who would be director of the Community Chest for twenty-seven years, surged over the top to $4,838,093. Eastman's own subscription was $600,000. His reasons for such vigorous support of this new cause went beyond the usual motive of efficiency.[32]

"The principal advantage I see in bunching all the charity funds is that it is bound to get interested a great number of people who do not now subscribe to any of the charities," Eastman wrote Strong. "We ought to get anywhere from 50,000 to 100,000 subscribers . . . and when the . . . war fund is gradually done away with there will be a big number whom will remain as contributors to the local fund. Be prepared to come across with $125,000," Eastman warned Henri in Augusta, taking some poetic license with his arithmetic, "which is only double what you and Mrs. Strong gave to the Red Cross a year ago."[33] To work on the campaign, Eastman released his two personal assistants, Frank Lovejoy and Marion Folsom, probably the most community-minded men at Kodak. A special speaker was imported from New York, put up at the "Chateau Eastman," and slated to speak in the Great Hall of the Chamber of Commerce after Rhees and Woodward had warmed up the gathering and led "the way to 'impromptu' remarks by some of the prospects from the floor."

> What we want to get into the minds of these people is that they ought to give, give, give, and that the standards of giving that have heretofore prevailed are inadequate. We have some notorious slackers in this town, some of the rich men and rich women who have given during the last year amounts of two or three thousand dollars when they ought to have given twenty-five and in some cases one hundred thousand dollars.[34]

Daily luncheons for all the campaign team captains were organized at the Chamber with little pep talks "trimmed down to the uttermost limit," Eastman explained. "Everything is going to be on a time schedule to the minute, the idea being to have the team captains eat their luncheons, make their reports and get out on the warpath without delay. . . . Dr. Rhees in his usual happy and direct manner will explain the budget committee. . . . It will be more work to keep things down to this snappy program than it would be to let the fellows talk."[35]

Eastman and his cohorts collected "lists of contributors to all the funds during the past year [and] were simply shocked at the number of slackers," he told Ralph Sheldon, now head of American Aristo in Jamestown. "We went out with a campaign to smoke them out." All the large Kodak shareholders, many of them former employees or wives, sons, or daughters of original officers and investors—Harriet Dana Walker; George and Daniel Clark, sons of Brackett; Pauline Abbott, widow of Charlie; Harry Strong, his sisters in California and Hawaii and his uncle Augustus Strong; artist Ada Howe Kent, daughter of photographer and first Kodak vice president John Kent; Laura D. Hawks, sister of Haywood Hawks; attorney Moritz B. Philipp; Darragh de Lancey; Darius Goff, former owner of Blair Company; and Thomas Finucane, the contractor who was always paid in stock because Eastman had so little cash, and many others—received Eastman's armtwisting letter softening them up for the door-to-door canvas by seven thousand workers. The company would not be making a war dividend, he noted, even though "a law has recently been passed giving the directors power to do this. . . . Company administration still believes . . . that the War Fund should come from individual subscription." Eastman stressed the profits Kodak was making from the war that were making its shareholders wealthier.[36]

"We are trying to get the War Chest subscriptions lined up from the top and the bottom and then squeeze the center," Eastman told Henri. "We hope to get Bausch & Lomb for $300,000 and want to get you for $150,000 or $200,000." Eastman's new quota for Strong was up from the $125,000 of two months previous and the handwritten postscript to this particular four-page epistle read, "If you love me wire 200 George." Eastman offered to publish his income tax return (his salary in 1918 was $100,000 a year) and let the other members of the committee determine the amount of his contribution. He tried to get government officials to release the returns of the "slackers." "It would be worth $500,000 in the next drive," he told the head of the American Red Cross. "It was done during the Civil War, so there is a good precedent."[37] "The campaign ended up in a blaze of glory," Eastman exulted to Cousin Almon in June 1918. "A few of the ultra conservatives go so far as to say that we raised too much money but I reckon it will all be needed. The prod the slackers got was hard . . . but there are still some left. Their hides have not been pierced yet but we hope to get them next year. I never had more fun in working out anything in my life."[38] By July 1918 Eastman and Rhees were spreading the gospel to other cities through "a proposition to organize a National War Chest Information Bureau."

Unlike scores of war chests founded on Rochester's model, this one did not disband at war's end. Instead it became the Community Chest, a title coined, according to Rochester tradition, by Eastman himself. Instead of the usual one hundred philanthropists of prewar days of United Charities, there were over one hundred thousand contributors. By 1921 forty-nine local charities were included in the Community Chest and its slogan, "Rochester always goes over the top," was literally true. In 1924 a separate Council of Social Agencies was formed that included voluntary nonprofit and tax-supported health, welfare, and recreation organizations. Eastman continued as the formidable head of the Community Chest for another decade, giving the "slackers" the usual sharp prod.[39]

On 7 November 1918 the nation was gripped by false reports of an armistice. Eastman telephoned Bert Eastwood in Washington, who asserted that "the Red Cross had received confirmation straight from the Secretary of War." Alice Whitney spread the news to a group on the Kodak Office elevator "going down to lunch. . . . One of them threw up her hands and yelled 'Ain't it swell?'" Then the whistles began to blow and "the populace would not pay any attention to denials" coming in to the newspapers. At six o'clock, "everybody having left the office," Eastman hopped in his Cadillac coupe "and started up toward the Club. It took me nearly an hour [instead of ten minutes] to get through the crowd of hilarious people." At his club and later his house Eastman found himself the authority and justification for people popping corks to celebrate. "You will have to straighten out . . . the whole canard," Eastman warned Eastwood, "or you will not be able to come back to Rochester." When the armistice actually came on 11 November, Eastman found to his surprise that the previous "unrestrainable spontaneous outburst of the people" to false reports had not "taken the edge off . . . the mob desire to take advantage of the occasion to have a hilarious time. . . . You had to look very closely to realize the difference."[40]

On 2 July 1921 the war with Germany was declared officially at an end by presidential proclamation and Eastman had company auditors make a final check of all war contracts. Earlier, in 1919, he had cancelled or refunded $152,461.43 on all cost-plus government contracts with a note beginning, "It is not our intention to make any profit whatever out of these materials." On 3 February 1922 he refunded $182,770 more that had been "paid the Eastman Kodak Company on war contracts in excess of the contemplated profit provided." President Warren G. Harding and the Secretary of War acknowledged that "Your action in this matter is most refreshing." Simon Haus was sent back to England, with Eastman renewing his contract for five years. His name was changed to House and Gifford put on notice: "Simon agrees to stay only three years in Europe. After that we are to provide for him at home. If any individual opposes him, don't hesitate to use the big stick. He is the only man qualified to supervise manufacturing in Europe." At long last the Jansons were out of Berlin and after several months in a sanitarium, returned to their native Sweden. In addition to back salary, Eastman sent them $20,000 in war bonds for devotion to duty. Gifford, too, was worn out by the war and asked to retire to Florida for the rest of his days; Eastman reluctantly agreed.[41]

Eastman celebrated war's end with a lavish New Year's party, the first since the ball of 1914. Singer Richard Bonelli burst through the portieres between dining room and conservatory in a Pierrot costume "singing the prologue to Pagliacci." Eggnog was served from bowls in the billiard room and front hall during intermission. "Then we unrolled a motion picture screen down over the portieres and had some war pictures, the machine being on the stair landing where the quintet usually plays." Organist Arthur Alexander accompanied the movies by watching them "in a small mirror over the console." At the stroke of midnight Pauline Bonelli sang "Ave Maria," Rush Rhees spoke for four minutes, and the entire group sang "Auld Lang Syne." Next came midnight supper. "Fifty were served at small tables in the dining room and about eighty in the library. While the people were at supper the whole lower hall was cleared of carpets and made ready for dancing. You never would have recognized the house with the white marble floor showing."[42]

The next year he told his Waterville cousin Almon Eastman that he was "giving two parties, one New Year's eve for a couple hundred grownups and one New Year's night for about 160 children all ages from about thirteen to eighteen or nineteen." For 31 December 1919 "we expect to pull off" a private, nonadvertised production of "the little opera 'Secret of Suzanne,'" which was brought in from New York. *Suzanne* was a forty-five-minute production starring singers from the Metropolitan Opera Company, for which Eastman was now a director, augmented by bit players engaged by Ludwig Schenck, conductor of the Rochester Symphony. New Year's night was a dance for "boys and girls of Ellen Maria and Eastman [Dryden]'s ages."[43]

With the psychological pressure of wartime production of trench periscopes and aerial machine gun cameras removed; the closings of the School for Aerial Photography and the cellulose acetate aeroplane wing dope plant, both at Kodak Park; and the exit of the naval contingent working on providing ships with protective coloration as a means of frustrating German submarines (for which a new word, "camouflage," was coined), Eastman detected a slump in the morale of Kodak workers. This, coupled with the perceived threat from the new International Workers of the World (or "Bolsheviki," as Eastman called them) in other industries, which apparently never materialized at Kodak, led Eastman to decide that a fresh approach to his workforce was needed. A whole new department of industrial relations was started under W. H. Cameron from the National Safety Council, with Dr. Charles Eaton as consultant. Another legacy of the war returned: Lieutenant Albert K. Chapman, who set up a special project for developing and manufacturing equipment used in aerial photography at the Research Laboratories, had so impressed everyone that Eastman urged Chapman's superiors in Washington to expedite his discharge. In the short term Chapman became Lovejoy's assistant; in the long term he became president of the company. Talk of a factory in France was revived and perhaps one in Russia, if that country settled down to a free enterprise system. But while many were experiencing a certain postwar letdown, Eastman was renewing himself on all fronts.

He began turning his mind to peacetime pursuits. This time it would be dentistry, medicine, and music in a big way. A whole new "scheme" for bringing music and movies to Rochester and the world was hatching in his mind and would occupy his total attention and tremendous energies throughout the 1920s the way that Kodak Park had occupied him during the 1890s.

Kodak Man
to Be World's Doctor
and Dentist

■ ■ · ────────────────────────────────

"Eventually the poor will be able to chaw their food as well as the rich," said George Eastman, contemplating what he had wrought in establishing six dental clinics for indigent children around the world.[1]

That Eastman, a bachelor, had an abstract interest in children is evident from his long-term involvement in the Rochester Orphan Asylum and from his support of the Children's Aid Society, Children's Shelter, Children's Playground League, Playground and Recreation Association of America, and the National Child Labor Committee. And in 1913 Judge George Carnahan solicited Eastman for help in building a Children's Shelter. Carnahan told Eastman that if he wasn't interested to say so quickly. "But I *am* interested," Eastman countered. "What is your plan?" Carnahan returned with a plan and Eastman quietly wrote out a check for $43,000, the entire amount needed.[2]

The health of children interested him enormously. He frequently asked Dr. Albert Kaiser, pediatrician, how this or that disease common to children might be controlled. In Alaska with Eastman Kaiser began examining Eskimo children living in a Christian orphan mission. Most of the children had tuberculosis, and Eastman immediately began clucking about a church that would remove these children from their native habitat within the Arctic Circle, exposing them to the white man's diseases. Kaiser noted that much sanitary education was also given, and Eastman concurred. But he stuck to the theory and lesson of the Rochester model tenements—that transposing people to strange places far from their natural home was contrary to nature and hardly ethical or "religious." In Africa, while Kaiser examined the children, Eastman photographed them. And Kaiser thought Eastman's provision of medical and dental facilities for children may have been the result of a suppressed desire for children of his own.[3]

Eastman talk was straightforward; he assumed that any child could be a Kodak photographer and could understand anything plainly put. And so he never patronized. Take Teddy Marceau, son of photographer Colonel Theodore C. Marceau. In December 1909 Eastman sent "a high speed Graphic camera for Teddy, which please hand over to him with his other Christmas things and greatly oblige." Teddy received a letter by the same post:

> This is a camera with which you can take moving objects no matter how fast they are moving, athletic sports, automobiles, animals, and all that sort of thing. And furthermore, by using the finder with the mirror set at an angle of forty-five degrees you can take pictures of people unawares. . . . I used one of them on a trip to the Hopi and Navajo Indian country last summer and photographed dozens of Indians without their knowing it. I enclose some of my own pictures.[4]

He rarely sent adults examples of his own photography. On the other hand, he was not interested in being taken advantage of by children, as this note to one in Kansas makes clear: "I think [your letter] must have been written without your mother's knowledge as I am sure she would not approve of your asking strangers to buy clothes for you and your sister. Talk with her about it and she will explain why your request should not be made or responded to."[5] He was at his best with children and never felt the need to put on his icy public mask with them. With Clara Lieber, daughter of an Indianapolis Kodak dealer and theater owner, Eastman played the gracious host, took her to Kodak Park, then "for a ride . . . in the morning, to the Horse Show . . . in the afternoon, dined with me alone, and then went to the movies with Mrs. Mulligan and me. . . . She is one of the loveliest girls I have ever met."[6]

The small boy who played in front of Kodak Office received a "Hello, Sonny" as the Kodak magnate came and went. The tag stuck and as an octogenarian, Sonny was still "Sonny." His chauffeur lived in an Eastman tenant house near 900, so the children played in the gardens where Eastman chatted with them during postbreakfast searches for a boutonniere. In a favorite anecdote, the chauffeur's daughter was asked if she knew Mr. Eastman and answered, "Oh sure, he lives in my back yard." On Halloween neighborhood boys came for trick or treats. Eastman treated them to cider and doughnuts, then solemnly canvassed the group, asking each his name. "Ah yes, I know your father," he would say, his blue eyes boring into the boy. Few windows were soaped at Eastman House.[7]

Marion and Harold Gleason arrived in Rochester in 1919 with one son and eventually had four. As each was on the way, Eastman would sternly quiz the parents about whether this new person would "clutter up the world." Yet he was unfailingly kind and gentle with each boy, stooping to tie a shoelace or asking Young to cut the child's meat. Kodak photographer Charles Turpin, who worked for the company for "38 pleasant years," was often sent to take pictures when the Eastman clan gathered. Once, when Turpin had been shooting in the garden, he saw a little girl run up to Eastman. He took the child in his arms and when a sudden shower came up, piggy-backed her into the house.[8]

At age sixty-nine he had a typical grandparent's view of children—"I do love to see their little faces," he said, "and then I do love to see their little backs"—which may be why his relations with them were always fresh and sparkling. The children he knew best were his grandnephew and grand-niece. A halcyon time in his life is how Eastman Dryden remembers visits to Eastman House; his great-uncle made 900 East Avenue a magic place for the young. But despite his memory of Eastman as "a beautiful person," Eastman Dryden experienced the taskmaster side of that character too. Once Uncle George washed his mouth out with soap for the dreadful things he had said to his little sister. When Eastman Dryden went off to Cornell and Ellen Maria to Wells College, they spent many weekends with their friends at Eastman House. "This morning as I was eating my breakfast," the great-uncle reported to Ellen Dryden in 1921, "Eastman blew in and said he was going to stay over night. . . . I did not notice that he was worn out by the holiday dissipation." Perhaps the most poignant communication of this period was the telegram that arrived from young Dryden in 1920: "PASSED ENTRANCE EXAMINATIONS CAN I COME TONIGHT AND HAVE BRACES PUT ON TEETH?"[9] Chances are the youth got his wish.

Other people's children were easier to deal with: Dental care did not turn them into house guests. So it is not surprising that Eastman's favorite project, the one he said gave him the best return on his money, was the establishment of dental clinics to care for the teeth of children of indigent parents up to the age of sixteen at the cost to the family of a nickel per visit. Unlike projects that never got off the ground because of the political controversies they stirred, the dental clinics brought him satisfaction to the end of his life. "Dollar for dollar," Eastman told Cyrus Curtis of the *Saturday Evening Post*, "I got more from my investment in the Rochester Dental Dispensary than from anything else to which I contributed."[10]

Preventive dental care for children was all but unknown until this century. Children, if they were lucky or had a good diet and genes, might hope to keep their teeth into their mature years. More likely, decaying teeth or receding gums would begin in early adulthood and the toothpuller would be visited. "Teeth extracted with or without pain," was a common advertisement in the 1800s. As a young matron Maria Eastman faced sleepless nights brought on by devastating toothaches. Dentists were itinerant practitioners whose principal work was the excruciating extraction of teeth with turnkeys. (Forceps were not yet invented.) In 1888 Maria sat in her kitchen chair while the toothpuller removed fifteen of her teeth without the aid of anesthetics. "I never forgot the terrible pain she endured before and after," her son said later.[11] Eastman endured similar bouts stoically and was wearing a $24-set of ill-fitting dentures when he first met Dr. Harvey J. Burkhart, the mayor of Batavia, New York, and a practicing dentist. Burkhart inferred that Eastman had earlier suffered from gum disease and thus lost teeth when he was relatively young. He made a comfortable, good-looking set of padded dentures, opening up Eastman's bite so that his chin and nose would not meet as in so many toothless countenances of the period. "Let's pull out all the kids' teeth, governor, and make plates for them," cackled Eastman in a euphoric burst. "I've never been so comfortable!"[12]

And Eastman money was itching to be spent. "If a man has wealth, he has to make a choice, because there is money heaping up," he told *Hearst's International Magazine* in 1923. "He can keep it together in a bunch and then leave it for others to administer after he is dead. Or, he can get it into action and have fun, while he is still alive. . . . It is more fun to give money than to will it." And so he told Burkhart: "You want to get hold of these children early. If you keep their mouths in good conditions you will help their digestion and general health for the rest of their lives. It's better to work on young people. . . . We old fellows are nearly through."[13]

The first free dental clinic in the United States was started by the Rochester Dental Society in 1901 at City Hospital but discontinued after two years.[14] Then, in 1904, Captain Henry Lomb, cofounder of Bausch and Lomb, donated $600 for instruments and appliances for a clinic at Public School No. 14. A charter was obtained from the State Board of Charities. At first relying on donated time by Rochester dentists, Lomb then paid the salary for a regular dentist up until his death in 1908. Shortly after the No. 14 clinic was established, Lomb, the same who first interested Eastman in supporting the Mechanics Institute, persuaded Eastman and William ("Billy") Bausch, son of the other founder of Bausch and Lomb, to join him in furnishing a second clinic in another school where children in the immediate neighborhood could be treated. In 1909 Eastman was one of ten who contributed $200 a year toward the maintenance of the Free Dental Dispensary of the Rochester Dental Society. Eastman would broaden the idea to pilot clinics in key cities around the world to demonstrate the importance of early dental care. For one who made occasional noises about the evils of socialism, Eastman was about to embark on his own great experiment in socialized medicine.

In 1913 Nelson Curtis, the paper manufacturer who supplied raw stock for Velox, sent Eastman pamphlets about the Forsyth Dental Infirmary under construction in Boston. In 1914, while visiting Josephine Dickman, East-man slipped off to look over the infirmary construction incognito. "During the rest of that year," Ackerman reports, "Eastman reflected upon the possi-bilities of a similar project in Rochester without revealing his thoughts to anyone."[15] The Boston clinic was the first such experiment in centralized dental care for children in the country, and perhaps in the world. A second visit to the clinic confirmed his commitment. That same spring of 1915, a committee of citizens and dentists chaired by William Bausch proposed more free clinics in locations throughout Rochester. Eastman greeted the proposal with his usual protracted silence and voluminous reading. Four months later he presented his own solution: a centralized clinic with trained hygienists, paid by the city but under the control of an independent board of trustees. The hygienists would visit the schools twice a year and refer the serious cases to the clinic. With the proposal came the offer to build the clinic if these conditions were met.

Among his readings was a report to the Carnegie Foundation on medical education in the United States prepared by Abraham Flexner. Flexner's survey concluded that "graduates . . . are lamentably lacking in knowledge and technique and need a postgraduate training before they go into general practice." If this was true for fledgling doctors, Eastman reasoned, it would also apply to fledgling dentists. A centralized clinic would provide this post-graduate year. Another argument for a single clinic was that "it is necessary to have as operators young, immature dentists who cannot be allowed to work without first-class supervision." Critics saw Eastman's central clinic as a monument to himself and his sudden (to the outside world) interest in den-tistry as a marketing device to sell x-ray film and plates. Sensitive to the second charge (the first he considered silly since he was opposed to monu-ments), Eastman had Ackerman refute it in a long note that began: "He had long since made it a definite policy not to mix business and philanthropy."[16] (Nevertheless, the income per year from the dispensary doing x-ray work for Rochester dentists at reasonable rates would amount to about $54,000.)

In July 1915 Eastman sent Edwin Gordon, architect, Dr. Burns, dentist, and William Bausch to Boston to meet Thomas A. Forsyth. Gordon came home with pictures of the Beaux Arts Forsyth building, which he carefully pasted in his growing Eastman-projects scrapbook. The architect's first ren-derings, entitled "Suggestions for the Rochester Dental Dispensary" and featuring a limestone façade with classical pilasters and red tile roof, are strongly reminiscent of the Boston clinic. The name, chosen by Eastman, would remain until after his death.[17]

The second condition of Eastman's proposal, "trained dental hygienists," possibly suggested by Harvey Burkhart, was controversial too. "At that time," Burkhart would write, "this was regarded in the light of an experi-ment and many doubts were expressed about the wisdom of creating a new vocation for women." Eastman had no doubts, and lobbied mightily in Albany to obtain legislation to amend the state charter to legalize the practice of oral prophylaxis by young women. As a result the School for Dental Hygienists of the Rochester Dental Dispensary, opening in 1916 in borrowed rooms of the university's Catharine Strong Hall, was the first such school to be established by legal authority. The city charter had to be amended to permit the city to contract with the dispensary for prophylactic work in the schools.[18]

The third condition was "a corporation to be managed by trustees . . . to provide for the raising of . . . not less than $10,000 yearly for five years." Bausch organized the board of fifteen trustees, who each agreed to contribute $1,000 a year to the operation of the dispensary. Eastman proposed to "build and equip a suitable central building and contribute . . . $30,000 per year for five years." Then, "if the institution is . . . performing its mission satisfactorily I will endow it with . . . $750,000. If . . . $40,000 is not enough for running expenses . . . I will furnish the same proportion of any additional sum."[19] In the publicity Eastman's name was not mentioned and the clinic was incorporated as the Rochester Dental Dispensary on 26 October 1915 for the prevention and cure of diseases of the ear, nose, mouth, and throat. Eastman wrote the budget for the first year and then resigned as a trustee and officer of the corporation on 8 November 1915 to take effect upon election of a director. The choice of a director was left to the trustees, hardly one of whom had not heard about that wonderfully comfortable set of teeth. Harvey Burkhart was the unanimous selection.

On 15 October 1917 the doors of the new dispensary opened. The functional, U-shaped building of rough-textured brick with white Venetian marble trim patterned after Italian Renaissance architecture, two stories plus basement, restrained yet handsome in proportion and detail, had cost Eastman $402,972.88 for property, architects, models, and construction. For the dedication, the dental society furnished the music and flowers, and Eastman the fifty-cent luncheons for five hundred guests. He managed to be out of town for the dedication. He got wind that the state dental society had appropriated $500 as a testimonial to George Eastman. "I don't want any loving cup," he told them sternly. "I wish you'd take the money and buy something for the dispensary instead."[20]

The second-floor "operatory," a large room with floor-to-ceiling windows along the two long sides and space for sixty-eight operating units specially designed by the Rochester-based Ritter Dental Company, appears amazingly light, airy, and modern in vintage photographs. Thirty of the thirty-seven motorized units installed in 1917 were given by the daughters of the late Frank Ritter of Rochester, who invented the modern dental chair. They were designed by Otto Pieper, engineer, with tips from Eastman, and served as models for the manufacture of similar units elsewhere. Later, Eastman and

Burkhart would devise an improved dental cabinet with a washstand at one end and a sterilizer at the other so that the operator did not have to waste steps by leaving to wash his hands or to sterilize instruments.[21]

The most notable feature was the children's waiting room provided by William Bausch. Here oak brackets were carved in the form of elephants, sheep, and dogs, and the oak paneling had animal figures sculpted in high relief. Above the paneling are whimsical murals by Clifford Ulp, head of the art department of Mechanics Institute, depicting Mother Goose scenes of "Goosie Goosie Gander," "Sing a Song of Sixpence," and "Little Jack Horner" (in a corner, of course). Behind the drinking fountain was a ceramic mosaic wall in bronzed tiles with frogs and lily pads. In the center of this large and cheerful space was a handsome aviary with live birds. The room represented Bausch and Eastman's effort to encourage the children of Rochester not to fear dentistry. The birdcage would become the logo for Eastman dental clinics and when more were built in Europe, they had birdcages in the waiting rooms.

The east wing contained the research department, a museum of both animal (some shot by Eastman) and human skulls illustrating dental formations, and the library of the dental society. The west wing had the x-ray and photographic departments, and rooms for special examinations and root canal work. The mezzanine was arranged as a children's hospital for oral surgery patients. Besides the main operatory, the second floor contained the orthodontia department to the west, extracting and oral surgery rooms to the east. The basement with panic lock was given over to the kitchen and lunchroom. Twenty to thirty dental interns every year each had their own chair, equipment, and patients. Standard surgical, x-ray, research, and laboratory techniques and procedures were put into operation.

Work was limited to children under sixteen, although if the family income was $5 per week or less, the children could come until they were twenty-one.[22] To insure appreciation of services, a charge of at least five cents per visit was made. In 1920, in consideration of one thousand shares of Kodak stock from Eastman, reduced rates were extended to children of Kodak employees. The children were also examined for nose, throat, and mouth defects. Burkhart wrote that "an astonishingly large number had hypertrophied tonsils and adenoids to such a degree as to cut down nasal respiration to a point that very markedly interfered with the normal development of the jaws."[23]

For routine dental care, prophylactic squads were galvanized and dispatched to the public and parochial schools with portable chairs, instruments, sterilizers, and lantern slides proselytizing oral hygiene. (The city paid for this.) Toothbrush drills were de rigueur. Followup cases were referred to the dispensary. To train the squads as well as the hygienists who worked at the dispensary, Burkhart engaged two instructors at $100 a month, an assistant to teach the toothbrush drill, a social service worker, a matron, and a principal. Nineteen hygienists graduated the following June from that first short course, thirty-six the second year, forty-one the third, and fifty-five the fourth. Tuition rose accordingly from $60 the first year to $105 the fourth. Pamphlets, printed in English, Italian, Yiddish, and Polish were sent to parents, instructing them to bring their babies to the dispensary as soon as the first tooth appeared and keep them on the rolls for followups.

Within a few years the dental department reported the advantages gained by standardization of filling materials and methods made possible by the centralized clinic. The department of orthodontia reported even more miraculous results: "Not only were the appearance and comfort of many children improved," Eastman said, "but improvements in speech were obtained by widening the arch, and frequently children who were below normal mentally were helped by the removal of nerve pressure usually found in a crowded jaw."[24] In 1921 Eastman himself, ever the tinkerer and inventor, would go back into the Camera Works and design a special orthodontia camera for the "remaking of faces," as he called the straightening of teeth with the hope of improving a person's appearance. The unit led to a new department— dental photography. Next to tonsillectomies, "remaking faces" seemed to be his primary interest. Pictures were taken periodically of the front view and profile of patients' faces. With the Eastman camera there were no variations in position or size; orthodontic progress became strictly comparable. Instead of waiting five years to endow the dispensary with $750,000 as he had promised if the institution lived up to expectations, Eastman decided to make it a nice round $1 million after just three years.

"The tonsil clinic . . . is the one thing that really interests me nowadays," said Eastman in 1921. The oral surgery department of the dispensary had been established to deal with parts of the mouth other than teeth—"cleft palate, harelip, and most notably," Dr. Burkhart wrote, "defective nasal respiration caused by enlarged tonsils and adenoids." Operating three days a week, the oral surgery department with eighteen beds also "removed tonsils and adenoids when symptoms from these parts seemed to have a direct bearing on dental work." In addition, "during the routine examination of Dispensary cases, many were found to have diseased tonsils which were not strictly obstructive, but which were detrimental to the children's good health." Children with infected tonsils and adenoids were thought to be more susceptible to infectious diseases; removal of the culprits would prevent whooping cough, measles, scarlet fever, rheumatism, heart disease, and kidney disease. "Many children can't breathe, can't digest, can't grow or learn because of the poisoned excretions from diseased tonsils and adenoids." George Eastman, with his great respect for scientific experts, was no skeptic. If the doctors said tonsils caused illness, then, by George, he would remove every diseased and enlarged tonsil from every Rochester schoolchild. "If we do what we ought to do," the publicity stated, "what an example Rochester could set before the world! Will we do it? Will we rid our children of tonsils and adenoids? Of course we will!"[25]

Special clinics were set up at the dispensary and scheduling put on a scientific basis. Albert D. Kaiser organized and supervised the history taking and medical exams; Edward S. Ingersoll was the chief pediatric laryngologist, with three other surgeons doing the bulk of the operating. Children were brought in during the late afternoon, given supper, and shown a movie picked out by Eastman, operated on in the morning, and sent home the next day. Those who had no transportation were picked up by taxi or by the free transport provided by the Women's Motor Corps of the Red Cross, supervised by Eastman's good friend, Netta Ranlet. As the "operable cases of tonsil and adenoid defects reached an alarming total" the small clinics began to have waiting lists. An emergency clinic was scheduled for every day and in rooms throughout the dispensary. Two hundred operations a week were scheduled for seven weeks. "As a matter of record," Eastman reported proudly, "it may be stated that operations were performed on 1,470 children without a single fatality."[26]

The public campaign was heartily endorsed in the newspapers, shop windows, "going-to-the-hospital" posters, and lantern-slide shows in movie theaters, and from the pulpits of the city. Physicians at Johns Hopkins, Cornell University Medical College, and the University of Rochester department of physiology, to say nothing of George Goler, the city's health officer, concurred that "the benefit from tonsillectomy is a change for the better in growth and development of the child." Schools and agencies such as the Rochester Orphan Asylum agreed that there had been "an increase in weight, considerably fewer sore throats, and many more smiling countenances because the aggravation has been removed. . . . All the children recovered quickly, with no set-backs."[27] Donations of toys, games, and phonograph records represented a new concept of making the hospital experience less scary for the patients.

The following winter an even more intensive tonsil clinic was organized (3 January to 15 April 1921) by Goler and Ingersoll with the cooperation of the dispensary and four city hospitals.[28] The surgeons and "x-ray men" were sent to the Rockefeller Institute to learn about "new tonsil treatment" from Dr. Simon Flexner. The planners met at 900 East Avenue and "Mr. Eastman spoke briefly of the great desirability of continuing the campaign begun last summer for the removal of diseased tonsils and adenoids," the minutes recorded. "The tonsil clinic . . . is running finely," Eastman said after this incredible happening was underway. "The only thing that worries us is getting consents from the parents. Out of the 18,000 children that have been diagnosed as needing the operation we have only 7,500 consents, which, at the rate we are operating, will only give us fodder until the first of April; so we are working every scheme to get after the parents."[29]

More than any other single incident, the tonsillectomy marathon reflects the arbitrary power an individual once wielded over an entire community. No other Rochesterian before or since could have closed all the schools for half a day and moved their population en masse into a makeshift operating theater where 7,833 sets of tonsils were summarily removed. Eastman may not have fully understood the extent of his influence and power. He thought he was just doing his job to promote good health among children, starting in Rochester.

Eastman's pleasure in the smooth operation of the dispensary and his conviction that proven results were evident led him to establish clinics in five European capitals where Kodak had substantial branches: London, Paris, Brussels, Rome, and Stockholm. He was delighted to share his research and growing expertise with other tycoons casting about for philanthropic ventures. A similar dental clinic was endowed in 1930 on East 72nd Street, New York City, by Murry and Leonie Guggenheim.[30] A few days later Eastman boasted to Lord Riddell (who was spearheading a clinic in London that Eastman was financing) that Guggenheim was going to spend $25 million to $30 million on his New York clinic. "I look for a blossoming out of the idea in the next few years. Julius Rosenwald spent a day with me last week and before he went away he announced his intention of tackling Chicago."[31] Rosenwald, chairman of Sears, Roebuck, was also slated to build a clinic in Berlin (one reason Eastman did not "tackle" Berlin himself was his antipathy to the Germans left over from the war years). Rosenwald died before the clinic could be started and his children, watching the growing persecution of Jews under Hitler, had no stomach for continuing the project.

Eastman's enduring memory of the British he knew so well in the 1890s was that they all seemed to have bad teeth.[32] England was the scene of his first triumph in photography, so why not also the initial European site for his newest enthusiasm, dental dispensaries? Lord Riddell, president of the Royal Free Hospital in London, agreed to add an Eastman Dental Clinic for $1 million that would serve four of the neediest districts of London. When that cornerstone was laid on 30 April 1929, Eastman was characteristically four thousand miles away at Oak Lodge. Burkhart and Frank B. Kellogg, former Secretary of State, represented him. The prince of Wales and the prime minister came equipped with long speeches and bad jokes about the value of teeth and Eastman's "great gift of this clinic," at which the crowd of three thousand laughed and cheered. The clinic was opened on 20 November 1931 with the United States ambassador, Charles E. Dawes, making the principal address and soon five hundred treatments a week were being performed.[33]

On 4 June 1929 following conversations with Cesare Sconfietti, Italian consul in Rochester, Eastman offered to build a similar clinic in Rome. Mussolini's government, he insisted, must provide maintenance. By 22 August the agreement was signed in Rochester through a special Italian representative. Again, the clinic was to be a "demonstration center which will be competent to care for, and as far as possible rectify, the teeth of all the indigent children in the city of Rome up to the age of sixteen."[34]

In 1930 applications were received from Stockholm and Paris for similar institutions and from Brussels in 1931. The Paris cornerstone was laid 29 July 1935 and the building was dedicated 21 October 1937. It was sited on a large new park and playground, on the Rue George Eastman. The Stockholm clinic was the result of Eastman's friendship with Nils Bouveng of Haselblad and later Kodak Limited (who supplied the rare red dye for Capstaff Kodachrome plates and film in 1914). The cornerstone in Stockholm was laid on 30 April 1933 with the crown prince officiating. The Stockholm clinic and school for hygienists was dedicated 25 April 1936 by Crown Prince Adolf and Princess Louise.

"The choice of Brussels is a sentimental one," Eastman said, and the sentiment went back to the early days of World War I when Belgian employees bravely kept company books and records out of German hands. The cornerstone of the Brussels clinic was laid 20 October 1933, and the building was dedicated 31 July 1934 by Leopold III. The dedication was the last public function attended by the beautiful and popular Queen Astrid before she was tragically killed in an auto accident. During World War II German authorities requisitioned the Brussels clinic, using it to perform head, jaw, and facial surgery on their troops. The building was plundered, and after the war, hob nail boot marks were still evident on the floors. The Brussels clinic is the only one that is now moribund.

Gifts of dental clinics to European countries did not sit well with those who believed charity should begin at home. The Men's Bible Class of the First Church of Christ in Grafton, West Virginia, for example, debated the merits of Eastman's gift of the Rome clinic and a spokesman wrote, "If you have money to give away why not give it to spreading the Gospel? . . . Why not pay it to your workers in wages? . . . Why not give it to your country where you made same? I told the class you would not answer. Will you?—Yours for America First (P.S. Loan on this church of $8,000)." Remarkably, Eastman did reply in great detail, "chiefly because of the economic and social questions that you raise."[35]

In 1910 Abraham Flexner startled medical and educational circles with his scathing report on the weaknesses of *Medical Education in the United States*. Chief of these, according to Flexner, who was not a physician himself, was the American emphasis on the trade school-style apprentice training of physicians rather than on a scientifically based program in which medical school staffs devoted themselves exclusively to instruction and research. Of the nearly 150 medical schools he reviewed, only five were praised. On the basis of the report, the Rockefeller-supported General Education Board put him on staff in 1912 and by 1917 he was the board's secretary and chief executive, empowered to spend millions for the improvement of medical education in the United States.

Flexner's objections centered on whether the faculty of medical schools should accept fees for seeing patients or should be completely salaried. It was a question that would occupy medical reformers for a generation (roughly 1905 to 1930) before the economics of the situation made it moot. In 1910 idealism was in the ascendancy. "There is no inherent reason why a professor of medicine should not make something of the financial sacrifice that the professor of physics makes," Flexner declared in his Carnegie report.[36] Even so, for salaries to be competitive, funds had to come from somewhere. With $100 million from John D. Rockefeller, Flexner had the clout to make or break a medical school. He planned to effect his reforms through the reconstruction of existing institutions and the creation of new ones. Flexner encountered little difficulty arm-twisting the smaller schools to adopt "clinical full-time," as the system was called. Johns Hopkins, Yale, and Washington University reformed according to the Flexner formula. But Harvard, Columbia, and Cornell, though hungering for Rockefeller money, all had prominent practitioners doing their clinical teaching. These schools, Flexner decided, were not "half as much interested in scientific medicine as in the persons who held posts from which they would have to be dislodged. . . . So for the moment New York [City] seemed impossible."[37]

Flexner decided "that the situation might be taken in the flank" and looked upstate. Albany and Buffalo had medical schools loosely affiliated with universities and Syracuse had one that might be raised to what Flexner considered "a true university level." His first proposal was to close the Albany and Buffalo schools and throw all the support to Syracuse. But he came to feel that Syracuse could not provide either the adequate leadership for reorganization or the local funds to match the Rockefeller grant. Meanwhile Harvey Burkhart, concerned about legitimatizing the Rochester Dental Dispensary, read in September 1919 of John D. Rockefeller's intentions to give $100 million for medical education and wrote to the General Education Board of the "need for an improvement in dental teaching. . . . It seems to me that if dental departments might be organized in strong medical colleges, it would greatly improve the output."[38]

One day at about the same time, Flexner turned to his Pullman car companion, Dr. Wallace Buttrick, president of the General Education Board and a former classmate of Rush Rhees. "I said to him quite casually, 'The University of Rochester is a modest but good institution, isn't it?'" Buttrick agreed, calling Rhees "a fine college head." "'It has occurred to me,'" Flexner continued, "'that if we could help to plant a first-rate medical school there, perhaps New York City would wake up.'"

"'Why Rochester?'" Buttrick wondered.

"'Rochester has a clean slate; and besides there is Mr. Eastman.'"[39]

The Eastmans originally espoused homeopathy. Founded by Dr. Samuel Hahnemann of Leipzig about 1800, the homeopathic theory was that a drug that will produce certain disease symptoms in a healthy person will cure a sick person who has the same symptoms. Homeopaths also believe that small doses of a drug are best and in an era of aggressive treatment (mercury, arsenic) this moderate therapeutic system at least caused little harm. The years 1880 to 1920 were the heyday of homeopathy in Rochester. Hahnemann (later Highland) Hospital opened in 1889 in the former home of Judge Henry Selden, father of George the automobile man and Eastman's first patent attorney. Dr. Bigelow, head of the hospital, had been Maria Eastman's personal physician but once refused her a house call. As long as Bigelow was associated with the hospital, Eastman refused to make a contribution. The Homeopathic (later Genesee) Hospital was started by the families of the Western Union partners, Hiram Sibley and Don Alonzo Watson. After his mother's death in 1907, Eastman built a nurses' wing for the Homeopathic Hospital in her memory. (This was the hospital where she had successful surgery for uterine cancer in 1890.) As soon as Dr. Bigelow was gone, he built a nurses' wing for the Hahnemann Hospital too.[40]

Then there was City Hospital. In the 1850s the Female Charitable Society sponsored concerts by Jenny Lind and lectures by P. T. Barnum to raise funds to get it started. Finally, the Common Council donated a cemetery as land but it was 1857 before the graves were removed and 1864 before a four-story brick building opened. The first board of managers was entirely female. Tents were erected on the grounds to treat the wounded during the Civil War. Three outbuildings were added over the years—a nurses' home, a maternity building, and a children's pavilion. Eastman was approached in 1908 to help enlarge the facility. He agreed, with stipulations, to pay $500,000 of the $800,000 total.[41]

"There is nothing that I am more interested in than public health," he told New York governor Nathan Miller in 1922 when asked to chair a statewide committee. "But I am already so tied up with public (mostly local) matters that it would be useless for me to try to take on anything more as it would simply result in my neglecting the things I am committed to."[42] Eastman's goal was nothing less than producing in Rochester "one of the healthiest communities in the world." In 1921 the *Democrat & Chronicle* quoted him as

saying that "the time is near when it will be possible for the poorest family in
Rochester to have the benefits of all that modern medicine and surgery
afford in the treatment of cases of sickness and in preservation of health. . . .
There are many people in Rochester who haven't the means to send their
sick friends to such medical centers as Baltimore, Rochester, Minn., or Boston for treatment by specialists," Eastman continued, and soon, he maintained, "no such need will exist, for treatment of equally high order will be
obtainable in this city."

Lauding city health officer George Goler for his "safeguarding of public
health" by groundbreaking and widespread preventive measures, Eastman
noted that "there are two distinct phases to activity in behalf of public health.
First is disease prevention, in which the city physicians and school nurses
play an important part. Second is the placing of the most effective curative
forces within the reach of all citizens, regardless of their financial status."
Eastman then became acutely interested in the nutrition classes for sickly or
underweight children conducted by Dr. William R. P. Emerson of Boston.
Emerson originally approached Eastman for a financial contribution, casually sending him some books on nutrition. Eastman read them at breakfast,
then invited Emerson to come and stay for a while so that he could set up
classes in Rochester—particularly at Hillside Home (formerly the Rochester
Orphan Asylum). Mrs. Beckley, president of the Hillside board, had breakfasted with Eastman and "expressed herself as greatly interested in the
nutrition problem and desirous of seeing [Emerson's program] properly
worked out at the Home." But the superintendent was dragging his heels.
Eastman decided that "that can be easily corrected." After the super got "the
right slant," as Eastman put it, and Emerson assigned one of his people to
Hillside to oversee the feeding, Eastman sent personalized reports of the
program's progress to Boston. "One of the girls, Eleanor King, has since
come up to full weight and was I understand in the graduating class." When
Emerson's program was written up in the bulletin of the Tuberculosis Association, Eastman dispatched those bulletins to friends and acquaintances.[43]

George Eastman was primed for Abraham Flexner's ideas.

Forty-eight hours after his conversation with Buttrell, Flexner had an invitation to breakfast with Eastman. It was not the first time a medical school had
been suggested for Rochester and Rhees had already been approached,
offering cautious hope with the caveat that "medical education is the costliest
form of professional training, and the University is not interested in undertaking such work without resources sufficient to make that work unques-
tionably of the first class." Rhees refused to approach Eastman himself but
did arrange for the interview. At the appointed breakfast, Flexner outlined
his proposal in detail. Eastman listened so quietly that Flexner was uncertain

what kind of impression he was making. When noon came, however, and Eastman pressed a button for lunch, Flexner began to think he was making progress. At 4 P.M. Eastman announced that he had to go to his office but invited Flexner and Rhees to dine with him.

"I am interested in your project," Eastman said in the sitting room after dinner, "but in these recent years I have given away thirty-one million dollars. . . . I can only spare two and a half million" (out of a needed $8 or $10 million). Flexner left, but a few days later was summoned by telegram to return. This time the offer was $3.5 million. Eastman wanted it settled before he went to Japan. If Eastman's interest in higher education was a gradually growing commitment, his interest in the health field was spontaneous and comfortable. It was only a few weeks after the first meeting before a handwritten note invited Flexner to lunch at Kodak Office. "I'll give five million dollars, including the dental clinic valued at one million, if the Board will give five million." Flexner accepted with alacrity and retired to New York to report to his board. He had no authority to make such an agreement, and Eastman had no authority to give away the dental clinic, endowment and all, as he had placed the clinic in the hands of an independent board. But as others have noted, a man in Eastman's position has means of getting his way.[44]

That was 15 March 1920. The Rockefellers, operating by committee, could not move as fast as Eastman alone. Eastman's steamer for Japan left 10 April and the GEB did not meet until after that. But on 22 March, based on hearsay that "the executive committee members are all very appreciative of my offer . . . and are of one mind," plans were made for Rhees to go to Johns Hopkins, which was to be the model for the new school, confer with its head, and bring back its superintendent to "look over the situation here and help decide on locations. The options on the real estate will be obtained before any news of the project leaks out," Eastman wrote. "On telegraphic advice of my arrival in San Francisco May 30th Dr. Rhees will call a meeting of his Board and then of the Dental Dispensary Board and invitations will be sent out in my name for a dinner given by me to the members of these boards and the trustees of all the local hospitals and their staffs, at which the announcement of the enterprise will be made." And so was it done. By June Eastman could report that the dinner "was pulled off successfully. . . . Flexner made an excellent speech. There is no doubt but what we will get full cooperation from the local doctors." The selection of a dean was left to Rhees, with Flexner submitting names. Funding for a teaching hospital was left up to Eastman.[45]

The press produced banner headlines, running Eastman and Rockefeller photos side by side. Eastman wrote to John D. Rockefeller Sr. about how proud he was "to have my name associated with yours in a philanthropic enterprise." Then he tipped his hand: "For many years I have considered you the foremost philanthropist of the age and have admired the wisdom with which your vast wealth is being distributed."[46] Carnegie, Ford, and Edison would all get the back of his hand at one time or another. Henry Strong's contemporary and old crony from the Augusta golf links was Eastman's model. As for "Flexner the Fleecer,"[47] Eastman could not help but admire his ability to attract funding. Eastman, of course, loved every minute of the sparring and when Flexner jokingly asked him if he could have a job at Eastman Kodak, he replied, "Yes, with the highest salary ever." Their friendship and correspondence lasted to the end of Eastman's life. Flexner would be instrumental in helping Eastman build a dental clinic in London, and on one more occasion Eastman would not flee in time and the highwayman would hypnotize him in 1927 into establishing a professorship of American studies (complete with a George Eastman House for the professor) at Oxford University.

The funding of the hospital had been in the forefront of Eastman's mind since 2 March 1920, weeks before he and Flexner had reached their agreement. In the past he would have put the request for donations first to his old partners, Henry Strong and William Walker, but they were gone now, so he turned to Strong's children. Gertrude Achilles had homes in Ossining, New York, and California and Helen Carter lived in Honolulu. While Eastman had not seen either in some time, he approached them annually to contribute to the Rochester Community Chest, which Helen always did and Gertrude usually declined in favor of "giving where I live." From crude sketches the 250-bed hospital was estimated to cost at least $1.5 million. Ideally the three Strong children—Gertrude, Helen, and Harry—could each have provided $500,000. But Harry Strong had died in California in the fall of 1919 just a few months after his father, leaving a wife and two young sons, Alvah and Pritchard. Eastman explained the situation, sent the sisters a subscription form suggesting $750,000 from each, "payable as the money is needed . . . only out of money paid to me in excess of $1,500,000 from my fathers estate," and "binding only in case my sister shall subscribe an equal amount upon the same terms within six months."[48]

Gertrude and Helen did not jump at the opportunity to memorialize their parents as Eastman proposed. Gertrude was cross with Eastman because he had neglected to write her a year earlier when her father died. She was uncertain, too, as to the extent of her inheritance, having encouraged her sons to become teachers rather than businessmen with the assurance that they would always have backup funds. None of her four children was earning more than $5,000 a year. She had just bought a California ranch. She did not live in Rochester, had not been born there, and was snubbed on the infrequent times she visited. On 19 July, citing six reasons, Gertrude said no. But she still fretted that if she and Helen did not give the hospital, her stepmother Hattie might, and this she did not want. For Helen, the timing was wrong because of her deep commitment of funds to a dental infirmary for Honolulu.[19] Eastman, of course, had cultivated *that* interest.

On his way to Japan in April, Eastman stopped to talk further with Helen, leaving her with plenty of information about dental clinics. At some point Eastman proposed to donate Harry's share anonymously, and this offer may have been the clincher. Months of uncertainty passed during which Eastman visited Gertrude personally to reassure her about her inheritance[50] and her relationship with her stepmother Hattie. It was a classic case. Gertrude's parents, grandparents, and great-grandparents had made fortunes in Rochester and Eastman proposed that the Strong heirs repay the community with a tangible memorial. Gertrude wanted no part of a project in which she and Hattie appeared as equal partners. To which Eastman countered: "Have you ever thought what might have happened if Hattie had been a scheming or designing woman, with an ambition to get control of all of your father's property? The last years of his life he got to depend on her so absolutely that it seems as if she might have influenced him against his children in almost any way if she had wanted to."[51] Something in his appeal got through to her, because on 12 August 1920 Eastman had good news for Rhees: "I was much surprised this morning to get a letter from Gertrude Achilles enclosing her subscription for the Memorial Hospital. I had about given up hope." He started thinking ahead. "If this affair goes through and we get Helen Carter's signature we must not fail to use it as a 'prod' with the Rockefeller crowd. I do not suppose Flexner would have any idea of our using a prod so early in the game." Helen did sign, and Gertrude pressed for Eastman's name to be included on the dedicatory plaque but he stalled with: "We will decide about my name being on the plaque at a later date. . . . If you insist . . . I shall be only too happy . . . only I do not think I deserve it." Better than fame or even winning the game with Flexner was the satisfaction of giving Rochester the best: "The affair will be so financed and staffed that there is no question but what the hospital will be one of the most distinguished in the world and second to none unless it be Johns Hopkins."[52]

One of Eastman's goals when starting the Rochester Dental Dispensary was to have a school for training dentists connected with it, but Harvey Burkhart had always put him off, insisting that such training must be associated with a first-rate medical school. In the end, whether because of his own sensitivity or Burkhart's political skills, Eastman asked only for "full cooperation" rather than the corporate union of the two institutions. Such a union would have subordinated the proud and prickly Burkhart to a new dean twenty years his junior.

In October 1920 George Whipple, pathologist, researcher, director of the Hooper Foundation in San Francisco, and dean of the University of California Medical School there, took it for granted that his career would keep him permanently in California. So when Rush Rhees's letter arrived asking Whipple to come east with the view of heading a new medical school, he cooled the enthusiam by citing his own opinion about California's prospects. Whipple explained that research, not administration or developing a laboratory or building a medical school, "is and always will be the field of greatest interest to me." Rhees was not daunted by the refusal. Whipple was the unanimous first choice of Rhees and both Flexners, and thus of Eastman, for the post of dean of the new medical school. "Far from closing the case," he said, "it intensifies my impression that he is the man we ought to get." Eastman told Rhees to stop writing letters and go get his man. Instead of purchasing a train ticket for Whipple, he bought one for Rhees.[53]

In California Whipple faced both educational and financial difficulties. The forests left by George Hooper to provide endowment for his Hooper Foundation had not yet paid any income and the University of California refused to liquidate the lands while simultaneously cutting out all annual appropriations. If Whipple stayed, fundraising would have taken more and more time from research. In Rochester, by contrast, "they now have $10 million available," Whipple noted after Rhees had successfully changed his mind, "no strings tied to the gifts, and the desire to develop a school of the type of Hopkins. . . . The trustees expect President Rhees and the dean to develop the policies of the school and determine the choice of men for the various chairs in the medical school faculty." The die was cast. On 25 February the university trustees unanimously appointed Whipple dean of the new school and professor of pathology. In early April Whipple accepted the appointment to begin 1 July 1921. Rhees, Flexner, and Eastman had won. "From all we can learn he is the man best fitted for the job of organizing the faculty of the new Medical School that there is in the country," Eastman wrote Frank Babbott.[54]

As part of the agreement Rhees assured Whipple that the medical school was to be physically a part of the university with buildings and grounds paid for out of income from the Eastman and Rockefeller gifts. Whipple stipulated that he must have executive control of the medical school's affairs, that facilities for his own research into the disease of pernicious anemia were to be provided as soon as possible, and that adequate hospital facilities were to be constructed to remain under the control of the medical school. The latter had already been provided. Whipple cautioned Rhees that he "intended to attend one or two scientific and administrative meetings a year, but no more. I hoped that he would permit me to decline local invitations for talks or membership responsibilities on committees when they would interfere with my work, although from the standpoint of the trustees and interested citizens it might appear that I was selfish and lacking in civic interest. I told him that meeting important people at dinners, club meetings and the like took much time and energy and definitely interfered with my work on the following day."[55] In his reserve, single-mindedness, no-nonsense approach, and lack of small talk, Whipple was much like Eastman. The two would get along famously.

Whipple's notions of utility, efficiency, and economy dovetailed with those of Eastman. Backed by his powerful ally, Whipple sketched out a floor plan resembling a "tic-tac-toe" board with walls of concrete block and brick that so integrated hospital and medical school that it was hard to tell where one ended and the other began. So high was the energy level to get the new complex in operation that construction was started before floor plans were complete. Gordon & Kaelber were the architects with McKim, Mead & White to design the memorial entrance and lobby of the hospital. Beaux Arts-trained classicist Lawrence Grant White immediately designed a decorative cornice to unify the entire medical center and Eastman just as quickly lopped it off the plans, saving $45,000. "I would much rather see that money," Eastman told Rhees, "if it is going to be spent for decorations, used on the main college buildings where it is perhaps desirable to get a somewhat different effect. I do not think from any point of view that it is undesirable to have the hospital very plain. . . . Unless they [the New York architects] will abandon the classic and produce exactly what they were told, namely an outstanding example of simplicity and economy, I would cut them out of the job altogether and get somebody who will do it."[56]

Standard one hundred-foot units of uniform width and fenestration were designed, and details of walls, plumbing, and equipment left for a later date. When borings showed a layer of quicksand, foundations were placed on concrete piles. Pipes and conduits were left exposed to reduce maintenance. As the concrete was poured for the frame of each wing, the wooden molds were moved to the next wing. Corridor walls and partitions were formed by three rows of hard-burned bricks for a mop-board with gray sand-lime brick above, all removable if necessary and all eminently cleanable. Walls and ceilings were left unpainted except in patient rooms. The cost was fifty-seven cents per cubic foot. Ten acres of floors, one-and-one-half miles of corridors, and two thousand windows went up in four instead of the projected five years. The building functioned beautifully for the next forty years and remains in use as the university medical school even after a new Strong Memorial Hospital was constructed in the 1960s. Eastman's contribution was the exceptional fire protection the complex enjoyed through interlocking water mains, sprinklers, and standpipes; explosion controls in the x-ray units; and special units to house explosive or inflammable materials. Blueprints were altered to take advantage of Eastman's profound knowledge of how to fireproof a building. And when fire underwriters inspected all U.S. hospitals following a Cleveland catastrophe caused by incinerating nitrate film x-rays, only Strong Memorial Hospital passed the test.[57]

A visiting Viennese professor commented that the building was a barn, and all the professors boys. The visitor was right: The professors were all in their twenties and thirties. Whipple wanted young American men to mold in the image of the medical school because he felt they would be adaptable, familiar with American ways, and team players rather than individual stars. He created nine departments headed by full professors, including the dean, plus the hospital director as head of the tenth department. He began by filling positions in anatomy, physiology, and pathology—all departments for more than a century; bacteriology, which had been around for forty years; internal medicine (incorporating radiology and psychiatry); surgery (including opthamology, otology, orthopedics, and urology); and pediatrics. He decreed that obstetrics and gynecology as well as biochemistry and pharmacology be taught together and not separately as at Johns Hopkins.[58]

Just as the Eastman School of Music brought a wholly new cultural group to Rochester, the new medical school attracted a class of professionals hitherto unseen in the city by the Genesee. The feeling that important and historical innovations were about to occur was infectious, as was the enthusiasm. "The years after World War I were fabulous times for the university," its historian wrote.[59] Thus George Whipple, like another Eastman protégé, Howard Hanson, was given the rare opportunity of creating a significant institution from scratch. Both took full advantage of this, putting their stamps so indelibly on the schools of medicine and music that well into the 1950s succeeding university presidents found themselves faced by fiefdoms holding valuable Eastman endowments over which they could exercise but minimum control. "The medical school has fully justified all expectations," Abraham Flexner decreed in 1940, citing Whipple's "fundamental discovery which subsequently led Dr. Minot of Harvard to use liver extract in cases of pernicious anemia" as "alone enough to justify the Rochester school."[60] For their work, Minot and Whipple would share the 1934 Nobel Prize in medicine.

When Flexner first approached Eastman, the University of Rochester's total endowment stood at $4 million. As plans for the music school and medical center progressed, Rhees considered how the College of Arts and Science might keep pace with new demands, as well as with the two new schools. He had already proven himself a master builder and fundraiser. The Eastman Laboratory of 1904, the Kendrick dormitory of 1911, and the Memorial Art Gallery of 1913 had been results of his quiet persuasion, as were four other new buildings, two of them dormitories committed to creating a "coordinate college for women" erected between 1912 and 1915. But there was still no auditorium or adequate library space. Sibley Hall, built by Hiram Sibley, Sr. in 1876, once "one of the most commodious library buildings in the country" and enlarged in 1903, was pinched for room again. Rhees wanted more dormitories: "A strong college cannot be a local institution," Rhees said. "Local men . . . must meet here many men from other communities and states." To enhance the medical school, more undergraduate science facilities and equipment—at least for the men, who were perceived by Rhees and Whipple as more likely than the women to pursue a medical career— was another objective. Whipple's acceptance of the post of medical director had been contingent upon adjoining university and medical school campuses.[61]

And so Gordon & Kaelber sketched the new medical and science buildings sitting cheek by jowl with the ten existing structures on the twenty-five-acre urban campus in downtown Rochester, close to the Eastman School of Music. The fit was too tight. The choice seemed clear: Buy up expensive real estate in what was perceived to be a deteriorating section of town, or move to the suburbs. *The Campus*, the weekly publication of the College for Men, described the decline: "Old alumni tell of apple orchards . . . before the Prince Street Campus was adorned with apartment houses and factories. It is the blended odor of boiling cabbage and of soft-coal smoke . . . slumbers interrupted by freight traffic on the New York Central, and students . . . taking on a soot-speckled appearance. . . . Commerce and over-population are pressing closer . . . but in Monroe County there are plenty of open spaces remote and of scenic beauty."[62]

Another factor that influenced what presidential reports confidentially called "The Removal Project" was the status of coeducation, which had not been solved simply by the matriculation of women. Although Azariah Boody originally wanted to donate his land for a women's college, and the great anthropologist Lewis Henry Morgan bequeathed funds for that purpose, university presidents steadfastly opposed overtures toward coeducation. In response to Rhees's strong bias, the trustees created a College for Women as a separate part of the College of Arts and Science. On land donated cater-corner to the main campus, the Susan B. Anthony Hall with gym and social room began to rise, with funds for salaries and construction quietly matched by Eastman (he who presumably was not interested in either education or the advancement of women). Henry Strong gave an adjacent women's classroom building in memory of his mother, Catharine Strong. But the separation of the colleges was never quite complete. *The Campus* even ruminated in 1919 about "Rochester Becoming a Women's College; Men to Petition Faculty to Keep Coeds in Their Own Buildings."[63]

It was the other self-made George—Todd—who like Eastman had no tie with the university or any other institution of higher learning, and James Havens, Kodak's outside counsel, who suggested purchasing the Crittenden farm for the medical school and the almost contiguous Oak Hill Country Club site for a new men's campus. The ninety-acre golf course on the rolling hills of a former Algonquin village in the great bend in the Genesee had served at various times as a prosperous nineteenth-century farm, a loudly smelling glue factory, and the infectious disease or "Pest House" hospital.[64]

"Mr. Todd made two contributions," the alumni magazine would say when it was all over, "one sleepless night and $100,000. As noteworthy as was the latter, the former was probably more significant for it was during the sleepless night that he first dreamed the dream of a new college on the rolling acres of what was then the Oak Hill site."[65] "I want to tell you about a great idea," Todd would begin, buttonholing everyone from the university trustees to the Oak Hill Country Club officials. Critics, Eastman among them, pointed out that the site was a cul-de-sac, bounded by the river, Genesee Valley Park, and picturesque Mount Hope Cemetery, with a noisy and dirty railroad traversing, all making future expansion difficult. Eastman, probably more than anyone, had a stake in the development of an integrated urban campus that included his new music school and theater. Yet he consistently defended the opinions of those "experts"—trustees and administrators—who knew the situation better than he.

The faculty, consulted in an advisory capacity only, was not in favor of segregation of the sexes. One winning argument was the cost of city real estate versus a suburban site. Whipple favored the move. He opposed the center city locations proposed and was unconcerned by the awkward separation caused by the railroad. The intrusion might present problems to architects laying out the campuses, but the railroad to Whipple meant convenient and cheap delivery of building materials and coal for a power house that could be built at the crossings to serve both campuses.

The news broke as 1921 began, taking Rochester "by storm," *The Campus* noted. Alternative sites were immediately proposed. Hiram W. Sibley, a downtown resident, envisioned a cultural district of which the Eastman School and Theatre would be the "crowning glory." (Sibley lost out, but today such a district exists, centered as he hoped on the school and theater with the crowning jewel of a new building housing the Sibley Music Library.) His son Harper favored a bluff overlooking Lake Ontario. Many spoke for the Pittsford site, which the university would purchase to exchange for the river perch of the country clubbers. (The boundary of the Pittsford site was named Kilbourn Road, legend has it, for services rendered by Maria's son.) The owners of five hundred acres on Irondequoit Bay off Lake Ontario, four miles from center city, offered to sell. Too far out, countered Rhees; the president's decision was Oak Hill, also four miles out, or nothing.[66]

A few weeks earlier, hot on the heels of the disclosure of the gift of a teaching hospital from Henry Strong's daughters, had come the announcement that Henry's widow, Hattie, was giving the university $200,000 to construct the Henry A. Strong Auditorium on the Prince Street Campus. Within a month it was confirmed that the "present site of the college was to be abandoned" for Oak Hill with its "country atmosphere," room for "spacious dorms, tennis courts, golf links, and the Genesee for varsity crew." Strong Auditorium would be built there as well.

On 18 February 1921 *The Campus* announced—some thirty-five years prematurely, as it turned out—that "both colleges for Women and Men will move." Gordon & Kaelber's earliest plans for the River Campus (there would be forty-seven sets before the final decision) confirm that not only were a women's dormitory and classroom buildings contemplated on the new campus, but an art and architecture building as well as a law school. Since by the terms of Azariah Boody's will a portion of the old campus would revert to his heirs if not used for educational purposes, a preparatory school under university management was proposed for Prince Street. Almost immediately stumbling blocks appeared. The faculty, which had opposed the "segregation" of the sexes, also showed little enthusiasm for the preparatory school concept. The heart of the argument for those proposing coordinate education was that "certain subjects should never be taught to a mixed audience," but on the other hand "the building of two new identical classroom buildings seemed an unwarranted expense." Then there was the delicate situation whereby only if the women remained could the university, in Rhees's words, "keep sacred the gifts of generous friends of the past, such as Sibley Hall, the Reynolds Laboratory, the Eastman Laboratories, the Carnegie Building, Catharine Strong Hall, the Anthony Memorial, and in particular the Memorial Art Gallery."

When it became apparent that a major fundraising campaign was in the offing, George Todd agreed to head a committee. Rhees outlined three plans: a $5 million, $7.5 million, and, most hesitantly offered, a $10 million plan. Then, from a chair of Todd's spacious drawing room where the committee had gathered came the quiet dry voice of George Eastman: "I think we'd better run up the ten million flag and see what we can get."[67] Behind the endorsement was a confidential offer to match any contribution, up to $2.5 million, that the General Education Board would make. "For instance," Eastman told Rhees, "if it is willing to chip in $2.5 million, I will do likewise. As this $10 million is mainly to buy clothes for the baby it has left on our doorstep, I hope the Board will recognize the reasonableness of the suggestion. If I had known his baby was going to grow so fast I should probably have told Flexner to take it back home in the beginning but it is such a pretty baby that one does not want to give it up now without a struggle to help support it." When the board declined to give more than $1 million—and that with the stipulation that it must be matched five to one—Eastman chipped in $2.5 million anyway. The board's hesitancy delayed the start of a citywide campaign but after several years in the planning, at least one false start, and no professional fundraising guidance, the "Ten Million in Ten Days" campaign of 1924 was launched. On 14 November 1924 Eastman entertained 125 top

Kodak stockholders at his home and gave the pitch that he would repeat in person and by letter for the next ten days: "From the Kodak point of view, I consider it highly desirable to have a good college here, not only to help train good men, but also to make Rochester an attractive place for Kodak men to live and bring up their families." Although its goal was met by some inspired juggling of figures, the campaign remains a remarkable feat. "The greatest community project ever undertaken in behalf of higher learning," trumpeted *The Campus*, immodestly, "was brought to a successful close."[68]

Eastman was pleased by the campaign results: "We are all set now to develop our university on the broadest lines and make it one of the outstanding universities in the country," he wrote. "By that I do not mean the largest but one of the highest rank in all the fields which it has entered." On 1 December he paid up his pledge for $2.5 million toward the new River Campus for the undergraduate men and added a surprise $6 million bonus, to be divided among the Eastman School of Music, the School of Medicine and Dentistry, and the College for Women—a dramatic reversal of his "not interested in education" verdict of twenty-six years before.[69]

As planning and construction got under way, other Eastman retainers besides architects Gordon & Kaelber showed up on the payroll. Landscape architect Alling Stephen De Forest drew up the first plan (from which the architects traced their forty-seven designs that were considered so alluring as to "draw blood from a turnip").[70] De Forest laid out the paths and fountains for the main quadrangle as an enlarged version of his 1902 plans for Eastman's formal gardens. A. W. Hopeman & Sons, who had accomplished the house-cutting-and-moving project of 1918 and the construction of the Eastman School and Theatre, became general contractors. Associated architects McKim, Mead & White—as usual in conflict with Eastman's ideas of simplicity, utility, and economy—lasted until 1927, when "Lawrence White seems to have got on the nerves of almost everybody around here by what they call his arrogant New York manners," Eastman wrote Babbott. "I like him in spite of his faults and in spite of the fact that he gets on my nerves occasionally also."[71]

McKim, Mead & White was replaced by Charles Adams Platt,[72] another nationally known exponent of the Georgian Revival. As the prodigal architects finally departed the scene, they left an important legacy in Philipp Merz, master of classical detail, who designed the university seal, decorated the Rush Rhees Library doors and staircases with wrought iron, and carved stone printer's marks and other symbolic decorative touches. Maquettes for two lifesize stone figures representing *Art* and *Industry*, destined to stand at the top of the twin grand staircases of Rush Rhees Library, evoked widespread protest because *Industry* was depicted holding a Kodak camera in her outstretched hand. Eastman was pleased by the gesture but unsure of which of the hundreds of models that had come off the assembly line since 1888 to feature. "Too crass," detractors declared, and after a faculty protest committee visited the president, a strange, boxy lamp of learning appeared on the finished statue.[73] Like Alfred Stieglitz, intellectuals and academics were wary of mass photography even though, in this case at least, it paid the educational bills.

During the years of construction (1927–30), Eastman's great interest was a Sunday check on its progress, chauffeur Harvey Padelford at the wheel. Perhaps reliving the building of 900 East Avenue, he was particularly fascinated by the moving of very large trees. One giant crashed to earth before his very eyes, and eventually became fireplace wood in the elegant new reading room of the Rush Rhees Library. Before architects' design could be translated into reality, contractors were required, if not to move mountains, to shave off the trees and greens of Oak Hill to receive the quad. "Drive me around town, Harvey," Eastman would say as the Packard or Lincoln or Cunningham rolled out of the driveway, "so the people will see I'm not dead yet." But then as the limousine passed Mount Hope he would ask, "Why are we going by the cemetery?"[74] Aware that in the building of the medical school and new undergraduate campus he was playing much more the role of conventional philanthropist than the one calling all the shots as in the case of the music school and theater, he was aware, too, that his role as Rochester's great benefactor and number one citizen was approaching its final curtain.

Music in Every Direction

"What you do in your working hours determines what you have. What you do in your play hours determines what you are." Eastman's famous dictum to Kodak Park workers in the 1920s became even more his own formula for living during that decade. He phrased it as a rhetorical question when discussing with a reporter his grand new music scheme and its connection to the gradual shortening of the workday: "What is going to be done with the leisure thus obtained? Do not imagine that I am a reformer—far from that. I am interested in music personally and I am led thereby, merely to want to share my pleasure with others." At a time when the five-day work week was only a working-man's dream, Eastman saw it coming. He felt precious leisure would be wasted unless new forms of recreation were provided.[1]

Those who shared in his pleasure could find the experience fatiguing. "GE is absolutely alcoholic about music," an exhausted Lillian Norton declared upon returning from a whirlwind visit to New York over the New Year of 1925. Twelve times in six days the trio of host plus "Parson and Parsonette," as Eastman called the rector of St. Paul's Church and his wife, had trotted off to the opera and theater as well as to the Morgan Library and Metropolitan and Frick museums. Twice they had trekked to the movies, and once they enjoyed a midnight supper at the Roosevelt Hotel. "The rest of the time we loafed," Eastman joked with George Dryden. The morning after the three returned to Rochester, a ready-to-go Eastman rang up the Norton household only to find Lillian breakfasting in bed. "I guess I tired out the young people—they are about forty," he bragged. Eastman reinforced Lillian's metaphor when he said: "I am not a musician. I come pretty close to being a musical moron because I am unable to whistle a tune, to carry a tune, or remember a tune. But I love to listen to music and in listening I've come to think of it as a necessary part of life. . . . There are no drawbacks to music: you can't have too much of it. There is no residual bad effect like overindulgence in other things."[2] Later his young music school director, Howard Hanson, would describe in more lofty tones Eastman's latest project, that of combining a collegiate institution for talented musicians, a community school dedicated to musical training from childhood on, and an orchestra supported by proceeds from the commercial booking of films.[3]

The goal of Eastman's "great music project," which would "afford this community all of the benefits of music in every direction," stemmed from his belief that "the trouble with this country is that it has too few listeners. There are probably enough performers already," he said shortly after the Eastman School opened and began adding to the ranks of performers. The schooling of listeners must start with schoolchildren, he vowed. In late 1918 the director of music in the public schools, who had plenty of teachers but few band and orchestra instruments, approached him. A previous study had indicated that a fund of $13,000 would provide about 250 instruments for primary and secondary school students. In response, in early 1919 Eastman provided $15,000 "for the purchase of such instruments," pianos being "outside the scope of my activities." The instruments would be owned by "the School of Music, which is about to be affiliated with the Rochester University." Eastman realized that "these bands and orchestras in the public schools are primarily to produce performers but they also are powerful influences in training and interesting listeners."[4]

But neither a school of music nor providing instruments for schoolchildren was enough for Eastman. Once the music idea took root, his energy and imagination were entirely focused on elaboration. The genius that had built a worldwide industry out of a revolutionary idea played with full force over the new field. Almost at once he visualized the project in its entirety. "The great project for training listeners is in the Eastman Theatre," he would say in 1923 in his own living room at the organizational meeting of the Subscribers Association to support a new Rochester Philharmonic Orchestra. The music Eastman had in mind all along was "orchestral music which, outside of opera, is the most expensive form of music that there is. The great orchestras of the country are only in the large cities," he noted.[5]

Eastman's reasoning for reducing costs by extending music's reach to theater audiences was based on the statistics that instead of playing to the usual 150,000 people per year (or 15,000 different individuals) a movie orchestra could play five hours a day to two million people a year. His theory was that "people who are not interested particularly in music, . . . will as they hear this music day after day come gradually to an appreciation of its beauty and the place it ought to occupy in their lives." This "theater" part of his "great project," both in terms of training listeners and raising money through movies to support a symphony orchestra, would never be understood by the conservatory-trained and -oriented first director of the Eastman School, nor by certain conductors who departed when their ideas differed from Eastman's.[6]

Two questions continue to intrigue. First, just how tone deaf was Eastman? He loved to foster that impression and, generally, everyone agreed with him. Once the Eastman School was opened he bragged about having flunked the Seashore tests used as part of the entrance examination. And when invited by Frank Seaman to join a "company of music sharks" in New York City, he declared he "should not dare to mix up with them. The very nice bunch that we have gathered here know all about my shortcomings and they do not waste their time trying to talk music with me."[7]

Second, at what point did Eastman fully commit himself to create the Theatre and School of Music? Was it 1918, when Eastman bought the Institute of Musical Art and presented it to the University of Rochester for use as a music school? Or earlier, in December 1916, when Charles Thoms, the real estate agent who had sold Eastman the Culver farm on which 900 East Avenue would rise, suggested a music hall on the very spot where the Eastman Theatre and School of Music would be built three years later? "What would you think of a project to build a Music Hall in Rochester?" inquired Thoms, the man Eastman had come down on so hard for not giving his quota to the Community Chest. "Our people are becoming very fond of music, due in large measure to the Dossenbach Orchestra, which you have sustained so generously. Rochester has some fine moving picture houses," Thoms argued, "but no adequate Auditorium in which to listen to a first class concert, either vocal or instrumental." Convention Hall and the Lyceum Theatre were inadequate. Even if the thought had not yet occurred to Eastman, which is unlikely, Thoms had put together an intriguing package for Eastman to mull over. "I do not know how much it would cost," Thoms concluded, "but I would like to subscribe for a box in the new Music Hall. One hundred subscribers would build the whole thing."[8] Or, one person could build the hall and the subscribers could support the orchestra, which is the way it would happen.

As early as April 1915 Claude Bragdon thought that Eastman "will surely build . . . a music hall." Also that same spring, organist and choral conductor George Barlow Penny, a founder in 1910 of the Rochester Conservatory of Music (which was not an accredited school but a merging of piano, voice, theory, and violin lessons), told his orchestration class that George Eastman was going to build a new school of music.[9] (Penny in 1915 consolidated his conservatory with the DKG Institute and joined its faculty as dean. He would continue on the faculty of the Eastman School.) Since Thoms, Bragdon, or

Penny were not intimates of Eastman, how they *knew* is hard to determine. Most probably it was just in the air, a rumor based on Eastman's intense interest in music for his own personal enjoyment combined with the extravagant largess of his civic-minded gifts to Rochester, which were already outpacing anything previously given to the city.

Perhaps he was thinking about it even earlier in the century, when he installed his giant theater organ and began holding regular music programs in his home, financially supported the summer program of music in the parks, or helped mop up the deficits incurred by local orchestral groups. In 1904 Rush Rhees had architects place a music school on the master plan for the university campus. All Rhees needed was the right donor, and it is possible he had Eastman in mind from the beginning. Perhaps Hermann Dossenbach, violinist and conductor, planted the seed in 1900, when he put together a group of experienced players as the small orchestra initially bearing his name. From the beginning the Dossenbach Orchestra was plagued by financial troubles and Eastman was one of a group of music lovers who picked up the annual deficit. In a manner reminiscent of aristocratic Europe, or an idea Eastman perhaps picked up from the Dickmans' soirees, Dossenbach began playing for Eastman at least as early as February 1902 in the Soule House, presumably as a soloist, as his fee for services was $20. After the move to the mansion in 1905, Eastman drew a "Quintette" from Dossenbach's Orchestra to play formal programs of chamber music Sunday and Wednesday evenings for the next fifteen years. (On evenings when quartet music was played, the Dossenbach Quintette obligingly became the Dossenbach Quartette.) By regularly employing these musicians Eastman was also further subsidizing the Rochester Orchestra. Over the years the Dossenbach groups were transported to Oak Lodge in North Carolina by their own railroad car and housed in a special cabin with practice and bunk rooms. Other times, when the patron was on vacation, he picked up the tab for the quintette to play for Alice Whitney, Mary Mulligan, the Walter Hubbells, or Almon and Delia Eastman who often stayed at 900 East Avenue when Cousin George was away, or even the Albrights in Buffalo, donors of the Albright Art Gallery there.

In 1911 Eastman, Emily Sibley Watson, her brother Hiram Watson Sibley, Rhees, Mary Mulligan, and six others formed a Musical Council for Rochester, the first act of which was to send Dossenbach to Berlin for a year of study in harmony and the violin. Dossenbach's Berlin stay was followed by visits to Dresden, Nürnberg, Rotenburg, Munich, Luzerne, Mainz, Bonn, Kohn, Brussells, The Hague, and London. Eastman and the Giffords once tracked Dossenbach down through the Berlin police station. Once contact was established, Dossenbach wrote enthusiastic letters to Eastman, chronicling "a year of uninterrupted practice, the most profitable of my life" and increasingly sharing Eastman's liking for chamber music by Haydn, Mozart, Schubert, and Beethoven.[10] For his part, Eastman kept Dossenbach informed of the quintette's progress in its leader's absence. When Dossenbach returned to Rochester, a committee of nine guarantors, with Eastman and Sibley the largest underwriters, reorganized Dossenbach's enterprise as sixty players, mostly professional musicians, under the rubric The Rochester Orchestra. Six concerts a season were scheduled at the Lyceum Theatre. The "few generous lovers of music" subscribed $15,000 for the season, Eastman's contribution to what he variously called "the Dossenbach Fund" or "the Dossenbach matter" being $2,000.[11] At the same time he was also bailing Rhees out of a musical "May Festival" that had lost large sums of money.

In these same years Eastman helped pick up the deficit for the Rochester Symphony Orchestra, founded about 1901 as a group of amateurs and students who performed free concerts in the spacious auditoriums of the East and West high schools. He subscribed to concerts by the Community Chorus, and concerts sponsored by the Tuesday Musicale, a group founded by cultivated ladies about 1890. The musicale sponsored the bringing to Rochester of symphony orchestras from other, usually larger, cities—an expensive proposition. From at least 1904 on, Eastman was an underwriter and often subscribed extra funds toward eliminating the deficit. He also hired the soloists the musicale brought to Rochester to perform at his own Wednesday or Sunday programs.[12]

Music had been part of the Rochester scene since at least 1820 through the traditions of the large German immigrant settlement. Jenny Lind and other visiting European artists gave recitals in the commodious Corinthian Hall that opened in 1849. Amateur orchestral ensembles and choral societies flourished and culminated in the first Rochester Philharmonic Orchestra, which existed from 1865 until the mid-1880s. Eastman's grand project, which appeared to many Rochesterians to be the culmination of a century's growing concern for music in the community, may have germinated during the 1890s when he first organized trips to the New York opera, and bought Aeolian pianos and organs with their canned music for the Soule House and Oak Lodge. Eastman did remark that his support of music prior to 1900 was given "on hearsay," because he had not "had time to give serious attention to music."[13] Many monied Rochesterians installed pipe organs in their homes in the 1880s and gave musicales, and those with cultivated musical tastes were becoming known to Eastman by the end of the century.

The Eastman School of Music had many conventional precedents in the music conservatories of nineteenth-century America, but the Eastman Theatre, a financial as well as artistic marriage of his two loves, music and film, was pure George Eastman. In that era silent movies were regularly accompanied by a theater organ and sometimes a movie orchestra, but only Eastman begot a scheme whereby showings of movies in a cavernous 3,500-seat auditorium were mandated to financially support a symphony orchestra regularly playing serious music. "If only it had worked," Howard Hanson sighed later. "Think of the symphony orchestras across the country which could have been thus supported." All of these influences serve to belie the bilious critic who wrote, upon the opening of the Eastman School of Music in 1922, that here was "the world's greatest experiment in attempting to exchange money for culture." Much more than money was involved. Despite his placing a music building on the 1904 master plan, Rhees admitted that the realization of such plans was "somewhat in the future." For years he had been resistant to suggestions of a music school without endowment or academic standards. A master at matching the buildings he wanted with the right donors, and knowing of Eastman's devotion to his mother, Rhees could easily have planted the seed that grew into a magnificent school memorializing Maria. In linking music to the memory of his mother, Eastman became uncharacteristically willing to "spend money like water," as Rhees would later describe the process.[14]

One element that entered the mix and brought matters to a head was the financial plight of Rochester's chief music school. The Institute of Musical Art was founded in 1913, in a house adjacent to the university campus, by Hermann Dossenbach and Alf Klingenberg, a Norwegian pianist who had trained in Germany. "DKG" was prefixed to the institute in 1914 when Oscar Gareissen, voice teacher and recital soloist, joined the original partners. Then in 1915 the institute consolidated further with the Rochester Conservatory of Music, whose director, George Barlow Penny, was among those agitating for a university-sponsored school of music in Rochester.[15] In 1917, with Klingenberg as director, the institute faced increasing financial difficulties with its provisional charter from the state's board of regents due to expire the next year. Taking matters into her own hands, the brash and direct Mrs. Klingenberg called upon Eastman, without appointment, managing to gain access to his office and inveigling a contribution from him. In April 1918, following a conference with Rhees, Eastman purchased the school and its equipment for $28,000, "in order," as Rhees phrased it, "that a new corporation may be organized to operate the Institute in the interest of musical education in Rochester, any profits accruing from the operation . . . to be turned back into the Institute for the improvement of its work." Also at that first private talk, Eastman and Rhees agreed only that the real estate title would either be vested in the university, which would place it at the disposal of the institute free of rental charges, or that the property would "come to the University if the new corporation shall go out of business or cease to fulfil the functions for which it is established." Current expenses would have to be undertaken elsewhere, "a condition I most cheerfully undertake to meet," said Rhees, "by asking for subscriptions to such an underwriting." July and August 1918 agreements, drawn up by Walter Hubbell, called for the school's trustees to resign and for Klingenberg to remain as director for five years at a salary of $4,000 a year.[16]

Eastman soon decided that the quaint Queen Anne house would never do as Rochester's music center. Adding a codicil to his will in July 1918, he advised his niece Ellen Dryden that "the proper disposition of the house and lot at 900 East Avenue . . . with fixtures and such furnishings as you do not want . . . would be to give it to the University of Rochester for a music school. . . . I shall rely upon you to carry out this plan." At what point he began to think that he "wanted to see the action during my lifetime," and that he would therefore undertake a "project to build a Music Hall in Rochester" is not clear. Indications are that between the purchase of the institute and 12 December 1918, when Rhees had the university's state charter amended to allow for establishing a professional music school, he thought and conversed, with Rhees and others, until a master plan gradually evolved. The codicil to that ever-changing will was to make sure the project went ahead in case he died suddenly before a new school could be built.[17]

On 14 February 1919 Eastman wrote to a vacationing Rhees at Ormond Beach that "things concerning the Music School have been moving quite rapidly." From Oak Lodge Eastman had lined up former architect, former mayor, inventor of the mail chute, bank president, and now realtor James G. Cutler to get options on some properties centrally located in the city, particularly for persons traveling by trolley. When he got home he had Gordon & Kaelber draw up plans to see "if the lot would accommodate everything we need." When he saw that it did, he gave Cutler "directions to take the property." Cutler and Hermann Dossenbach called at Kodak Office to say that at the urging of Rhees an underwriting committee headed by George Todd had been formed to "sell the seats for the 1919–1920 orchestra concerts and asked if the plan was agreeable to me. I told them I had some plans affecting the musical situation here that were not quite ready to disclose but might have a bearing or what should be done for the orchestra and that I would be able to talk about it in a few days."[18] Shortly afterward the *Democrat & Chronicle* announced publicly for the first time that George Eastman planned to build "a Concert Hall and School of Music . . . surpassed by no other in the world."

The February 1919 day that Eastman learned about the orchestra underwriting committee, over lunch at 343 State Street, he told Todd (and Rhees in a letter) that his plan was "to devote the music hall to motion pictures six days of the week, putting all of the profits into the music hall orchestra." Todd must surely have been amazed at this concept; in Florida, Rhees was startled to learn that the university was to have a movie theater. "The minor Medicis of Rochester," Howard Hanson was to state later, "were not particularly pleased by having Mr. Eastman come in, because they had been the leaders in the arts and in music and suddenly this man comes in with all of his money and plants a great music school in the middle of the city and plants a great symphony orchestra there and an opera company and an opera department. Well, who *was* he taking over culture in Rochester? What did he know about music? There was quite of bit of that kind of talk when I came [in 1924] although I don't think anyone turned down an invitation to his home."[19]

Eastman's plans went on apace. There could be two orchestras, he told George Todd, a "small" orchestra of about fifty-five to accompany the silent movies and a large symphony of about ninety for concerts, although, Eastman allowed, "the whole of my plan could be carried out without having a big orchestra at all." Soon Todd's group would become the Subscribers Association, dedicated to the support of the new Rochester Philharmonic Orchestra. In 1930, when the core Eastman Theatre Orchestra was renamed the Rochester Civic Orchestra, the supporters grew from six hundred to many thousands and became the Civic Music Association.[20]

Eastman must have expected Todd to opt for the full philharmonic orchestra and raise the necessary money, because Eastman had already hired, in July 1918, a versatile young British pianist and "Lieder singer," Arthur Alexander, to be his general music director and advisor. Born in New Zealand in 1891, Alexander had been sent to England at an early age where he garnered many prizes as a student, debuted in Vienna in 1912, and did a little composing, but made his greatest reputation as a pianoforte teacher.[21] Alexander's first act in Rochester was to bring in a new first violinist, Arthur Hartmann. He would shortly personify the ecstacies of electrifying music and agonies of financial and personal difficulties that Eastman would face in this new breed of European musician coming to conservative Rochester. The town would be alternately amazed, diverted, and scandalized by Hartmann and his ilk. Hartmann and Alexander, "the newcomers among the musicians," as Eastman called them in a letter to Ellen, would also represent a threat to Eastman's old violinist and conductor, Hermann Dossenbach. Eventually the Dossenbach Quintette would be eased out of their twice-weekly musicale schedule at Eastman House although they still played occasionally for Eastman or were sent by him to Kodak Park. The quintet was replaced by the new Kilbourn Quartet, a group of European musicians imported specifically for this purpose. The Kilbourn Quartet members would also hold the principal chairs in their respective sections of the philharmonic and teach at the new music school.

Apparently Klingenberg had recommended Alexander, and Eastman, of course, immediately had Frank Babbott check the man out. Babbott reported that "he is a remarkable musician and excellent teacher, who had three years in Paris . . . a better pianist than singer as his voice is a little 'pinched' on the upper notes . . . due in part, to cigarette smoking. He is a typical artist in temperament and has the artistic disregard of practical things." In reply, Eastman had his own assessment: "I find Alexander has a very unusual personality for a musician. He seems to be entirely devoid of the petty jealousy which possesses most of them and he is a most talented man. He can play the organ better than anybody I ever heard; he is an extremely fine pianist and everybody likes his singing. I think he is going to help buck up the musical situation here quite a bit."[22]

On the home front Eastman was doing his bit to buck up the music situation as well. He had finished enlarging his conservatory in September 1919 and had installed there a second organ. Alexander's $10,000 retainer (a hefty sum for a musician in those days) directed him to oversee the music at Eastman's house and help at the Institute of Musical Art, but Eastman had larger plans for the young musician. "It would be a much more interesting experiment," he wrote, "to have a new man like Alexander tackle the job than a man who had already made a reputation as a director." He worried, however, that Alexander, while "enamored with Rochester and crazy about leading an orchestra" would eventually be lured back to Paris. "If he connects up with us, he will spend both summers in England studying under Beecham."[23]

This meant, of course, that Dossenbach was out. The "one fundamental and unchangeable purpose" of the "great musical project which has been undertaken here in Rochester," as Eastman called it in the talk he delivered to the founders of the Subscribers Association in his own living room, "is to afford this community all of the benefits of music in every direction." His plan included "offering Mr. Dossenbach the leadership of the music hall orchestra, with the understanding that he could not in any event become the leader of the big orchestra." A few days after talking with Todd, Eastman "had an interview with Dossenbach and told him about the scheme. . . . In discussing the matter of his competence to fill the position of director of a big orchestra I was very frank. . . . The next night Mrs. Mulligan had a heart to heart talk with Mr. Dossenbach and was very much surprised to find that when he learned that the underwriting committee would go on with the old orchestra another year and in all probability until the movie orchestra could be organized he was perfectly satisfied."[24] In the end Dossenbach turned down the position of conductor of the movie orchestra. One can only guess that in his mind "perfectly willing to work in harmony" was not the same thing as "being under" Alexander.

No sooner had Eastman's music scheme been disclosed then another Rochester Medici announced plans for the David Hochstein Memorial Music School. Hochstein was Rochester's prodigy violinist whose education in Paris, Berlin, Vienna, and St. Petersburg Eastman had been subsidizing for years. He had also purchased three violins for Hochstein's use: first a Gagliano in 1914 (although it cost $1,500, it proved inadequate and was exchanged in favor of an $1,800 instrument), then a 1735 Carlo Landolphi, and, finally, a 1715 Stradivarius. Each belonged to Eastman until Hochstein was able to pay for it on the installment plan. Hochstein soon found concert life hard work compared to his carefree student days. Although he opened in Carnegie Hall upon his return to the United States in 1914 to rave reviews in the *New York Times*, he was not the sustained success in New York (where the competition included Jascha Heifitz, Mischa Elman, and Efrem Zimbalist) that he had been in Rochester and Buffalo, where his patrons showered him with kudos and funds. His letters to Eastman reveal increasing frustration and disillusionment. He divided his time between New York and Rochester, where he taught at the Institute of Musical Art. Perhaps out of frustration with his lagging career, Hochstein enlisted in the American Expeditionary Forces in 1917. He was listed as missing in action 15 October 1918, less than a month before the Armistice was signed, but it was the end of January 1919 before he was officially declared dead. By April Rochester musicians and Emily Sibley Watson had organized a memorial concert in Convention Hall and in June a masque, "The Gift of Music," played to five thousand people who crowded onto a school playground near the Hochstein home. Within months Mrs. Watson had purchased for a neighborhood music school the former Hochstein home across the Genesee River from Kodak Office, where newly arrived Irish, Polish, and Russian immigrants had settled in the city since the 1880s. The David Hochstein Music School Settlement opened on 2 January 1920 when 570 pupils applied and 472 were accepted. Francis E. Cunningham, of the carriage and car firm, was president of a twenty-member executive board and Harold Gleason, who by then was Eastman's private organist, was named director. Although Eastman was not a member of the Hochstein board he was able to fit what he described as "a settlement school in the Polish district of the city providing instruction for children of limited means" nicely into his music plans. Not only did it give his private organist employment; it would also give advanced students of the Eastman School practical teaching experience.[25]

In organizing a major new music conservatory, an adequate library is a major priority. Fortunately, a distinguished musical library was already in the possession of the university. It was augmented by works already at the DKG Institute, some orchestral music purchased from Dossenbach, and the works Eastman was able to locate in Europe through his never-fail agent, Thacher Clarke. In 1904 Elbert Newton, Rochester church organist, had discussed the need for a library of music compositions and publications with Hiram Watson Sibley, son of a founder and the first president of Western Union. The younger Sibley, a collector of various objects ranging from ivories to paintings to armor, was interested and commissioned Newton to begin hunting down standard works of music, which in the end came to about eight thousand volumes. The collection was housed for the next seventeen years in Sibley Hall, which the elder Sibley had built on the university's Prince Street Campus and which was open to the public. Spacious new quarters were prepared in 1921 in the new Eastman School to accommodate the library, which even then Eastman was able to describe as "the third or fourth largest musical library in the United States."[26]

Rhees outlined an avalanche of gifts descending upon the library once plans for the new school were revealed—so many gifts that the catalogers could not keep up and a moratorium had to be called until it could be determined what was needed. Arriving unsolicited on Eastman's doorstep were everything from a Schubert song book from Dr. Leon Lilienfeld, a Viennese chemist who had been puttering along for decades with a cellulose ether process for Kodak film and who also helped import Kilbourn Quartet musicians such as Joseph Press and Vladimir Resnikoff, to boxes of American mountain songs, to old librettos. Eastman decided that Thacher Clarke, his long-time patent expert for Europe, cultural mentor, old cycling companion, highly effective "head hunter," and on occasion, industrial spy, could also be his "musical expert for Europe" and negotiate for the purchase of libraries of orchestral scores. Clarke's own library at Harrow was legendary. "It will be the most economical plan," Clarke offered on 18 February 1920, "for you to let me buy the music which the new School will require, rather than to obtain it through importers. . . . The saving ought to amount to one half, or even more." Save the duty, too, a practical Eastman wrote, by shipping the music directly to the university rather than to Kodak. And so by mid-March Clarke was off to France, Switzerland, Italy, and Germany with quartet and chamber music lists drawn up by Alexander and Hartmann. But a strange law had just been passed in Germany "prohibiting the exportation of paper in any form," thus limiting all music published there. Clarke moved on to sources in Switzerland and was in Paris on Eastman's musical library mission when he suffered a heart attack and died on 23 September 1920. One of the great Kodak characters thus passed from the scene; no longer would he go up and down the Danube on a barge, scotch and soda in hand, conversing with the employees of the Kodak factory at Budapest in Magyar or one of the other dozen or so languages he spoke.

With Clarke gone, Eastman reassigned the music negotiations in Europe to a new team he assembled consisting of Dr. Oscar L. Harries, a Buffalo man who currently headed the Paris branch of Kodak; Frank Mattison and Charles Case of Kodak Limited; a music expert by the name of Notte; Harold Gleason, who was traveling in Europe at the time looking at organs to help him design them for the school and theater; and Donald B. Gilchrist, University of Rochester librarian. Clarke had been deep in negotiations with Jean Salis of Boston, who reputedly had a collection of five thousand pieces of printed music stored in Paris and Nice, which he was willing to sell for $6,000. Gilchrist went to Boston and got the price reduced to $5,500. Eastman had his Kodak representative in Washington rush Salis's passport through, and Harries was directed to meet Salis in Paris and pay him $3,000 "securing guarantee." A slippery Salis proceeded to lead Harries a merry chase: There was no guarantee except "the suggestion on Salis's part that we go to his apartment and look over his . . . furniture and pictures, so that we could see he was responsible." Salis insisted on dollars even though his contract with Clarke "stipulated he be paid in francs." Part of the collection was in Paris, part in Dax, part in Bordeaux, and Salis had borrowed large sums "pledging his music as security with his lender having the right to rent the music until the debt was paid." Upon further investigation Harries was "led to think that this music was never his own property but that he was simply selling it on commission." Harries finally decided that Salis's verbal statements, even when supported by a notarized affidavit, had no credence whatsoever. Yet because Notte had examined the music itself, verifying that "the purchase is well worth the money and all that he saw was in good condition," Eastman insisted on continuing to deal with Salis. Alice K. Whitney wrote to Rhees on 7 December 1920 when twenty-nine cases of music were delivered to Gilchrist that "the Salis transaction has come to a satisfactory conclusion, notwithstanding Dr. Harries' 'gloom.'" All through 1921 and 1922 Eastman had Mattison filling out the "sets of music purchased from Mr. Salis" in Berlin, Leipzig, Paris, and London. Then in April 1923 Mattison received word that "the School of Music now has all the music it desires." This would be temporary, as scores would always be needed for new generations of students and the Sibley Music Library would continue to expand.[27]

Eastman worried excessively about Hiram Watson Sibley's dissatisfaction with the plain finish of the paneling in the Sibley Library. But Sibley assured Eastman that no criticism was intended in his "comment that some modest decoration to the plain surfaces above the woodwork might at some time be applied" and that the "room is complete as it stands and eminently fitted to receive the library." In 1925 Sibley gave $50,000 toward the expansion of his library, earmarked for rare musical manuscripts. Barbara Duncan, who came from the Boston Public Library in 1921 to serve as librarian, was under orders from Sibley to "buy something we can talk about." Duncan sought out rare collections at library sales and auctions, including what is still the library's oldest item, the "Rochester Codex," a collection of treatises handwritten by German monks of the twelfth century. Sibley died the same year as Eastman; like his sister Emily, he left no endowment to support what he had started. Yet as a result of many efforts and sources, the Sibley Music Library is now the largest academic collection in the Americas.[28]

Separate from this deliberate combing of the world to assemble music for the Sibley Library was the mad scramble to get the contemporary popular scores needed for the movie orchestra. Here the practical Eastman emerged again. As he wrote Ray Ball, university treasurer: "Don't you think it would be a good plan to get some stamps 'The Property of the Eastman Theatre' and stamp all the music which we purchase? . . . I understand there is liable to be pilfering. . . . The stamps . . . should have a distinctive design so the mere shape would disclose the identity."[29] It amazed many people that a man who had such a renowned ability for grasping the larger essentials could handle details with equal facility—and could spare the time for them. After the theater was finished, Eastman hovered over it with relentless devotion. If he was not actually present, the possibility that he might arrive suddenly kept everyone on their toes. In a sense he is still there: Every mural, marble block, and chandelier is a reminder of his meticulous supervision.

In contrast to the 3,500-seat Eastman Theatre's lavish magnificence there was an exquisite, intimate, and delicate auditorium seating 500 that would be the setting for chamber music. Eastman called it Kilbourn Hall, in remembrance of his mother, and intended it to be the central feature of the school. Intimacy rather than grandeur would be stressed, the donor said, "so that the attention of the listener would not be distracted from the music by too assertive decoration." The color schemes for the two auditoriums were supervised by Ezra Winter, an artist of national reputation, who was also awarded the contract for the painted frieze and decorative scheme for ceiling. Thomas B. Wadelton, who had done Eastman's dining room in 1905, created the paneled ceiling under the direction of Larry White, who was for once allowed to soar. Winter was such a perfectionist that he mounted the scaffolding himself to affix the finishing touches. Then came the acid test as Eastman (the man who supposedly had a "tin" ear) and others came to the hall to check out the sound: "The Quartet made a trial of the acoustics . . . and some of the critics thought the room was a little too resonant and others thought it a little too dead. I heard them play this morning and concluded, with a number of others, that the acoustics appear to be perfect. No difference can be detected in any of the seats."[30] A small portrait of Maria Eastman, her son's favorite, painted from life by Robert MacCameron, was loaned by the Drydens and hung on the stage for the opening night of 4 March 1922.

Practical as well as aesthetic matters engaged Eastman's steel-trap mind. One goal was to have his music school "mark the highest development in America in musical equipment." Apparently none of Klingenberg's equipment was used; the organ from the old Institute of Musical Art, for example, was sold to a church in New Hampshire, and between November 1920 and July 1923 eighteen new organs were purchased, including thirteen practice organs, three teaching organs, and an organ for the theater and Kilbourn Hall. Costs ranged from $3,500 for a practice organ to $78,705 for the grand theater organ of more than 10,000 pipes and 140 stops built by the Austin Organ Company of Hartford, Connecticut.[31] Harold Gleason, Eastman's personal organist, engaged four organ consultants "who examined and gave written opinions of the specifications for the Theatre and Kilbourn Hall organs" for $25 each. Gleason traveled to inspect organs in Oberlin and the Wanamaker store in Philadelphia, visited organ manufacturers Skinner, Austin, Wurlitzer, and Moller, and attended the Northeast Conservatory class in Motion Picture Playing. Joseph Bonnet, the famous French organist engaged to teach at the school, was scheduled to dedicate the Skinner organ in Kilbourn Hall in mid-April 1922; when the Skinner company did not deliver on time, it heard from Eastman that "Your failure to have the organ ready before Mr. Bonnet sails for France is not only a disappointment to us but will cause a large financial loss and this is to notify you that I shall hold you responsible."[32]

The Austin Organ was reported to be the largest theater organ in the world at the time of construction. Eight divisions—Great, Swell, Choir, Solo, Orchestral, Echo, String, and Pedal—were all separate organs, each larger than the average church or theater organ. Weighing forty-five tons, its electric circuits used several thousand miles of wire; the largest pipe was thirty-two feet tall and weighed over four hundred pounds. "The console is mounted on an elevator and turnstile and can be moved from orchestra pit to stage as desired," the *Post-Express* reported. "This console [also] controls and plays a grand piano by means of a movable player placed over the piano keys." The theater organs, Eastman wrote proudly, "are two of the most important instruments built thus far representing the latest and most comprehensive thought of modern organ engineering and musical development. . . . Organ builders are constantly enlarging the capacity of their product for equivalence to orchestral effects." The Austin organ had to be amplified in 1926. It was situated backstage in an ideal position "for most of our work," Eastman told a consultant, "but when we want to compel people to stick cotton in their ears it is not quite loud enough."

A studio in the theater was equipped with a Wurlitzer orchestral organ with all modern instrumental equivalents and complete facilities for screening pictures. Eastman instructed Alexander to "get our friends among the producers to let us have spare copies of . . . *new* pictures of rather old releases."[33] Eastman pressed for the rising platform for organ and orchestra, an idea he copied from the Hippodrome in New York, because it eliminated the confusion of players filing in and taking their seats. He foresaw a new profession of theater organist emerging and publicized a course in "Organ Accompanying of Motion Pictures" taught by his theater organists who were, he noted, "past masters of the art." Organists had to be improvisers and quick change artists of the first order, continually scoring a new and comprehensive weekly program. When all organs were in and playing, Eastman was so pleased that he wrote the makers about their "great success. Just to commemorate the affair I am sending you a Kodak." With such an investment in the giant theater organ, plus another Wurlitzer organ in the projection room, and a class in theater organ playing in the offing, it is no wonder that Eastman chose to ignore the coming of "talkies."

Flags of many nations streamed above the marquee when the Eastman Theatre opened its doors for the glittering "Dress Performance" on the evening of

2 September 1922. Clayla Ward was there in her glory and finery to observe car after car gliding up to the entrance for that first 9 o'clock performance. Splendid dignitaries emerged and promenaded into the theater in full evening dress. A dozen limousines remained parked across Gibbs Street, chauffeurs chatting softly together and smoking until the carriage call indicated their charges had issued forth. George Eastman arrived with his guests, Rush and Harriet Rhees. Expressionless, he stood rigidly still for a moment, acknowledged the applauding crowd with a deep bow, and headed straight for his four reserved seats, front row right, 42 to 46 in the mezzanine (which he always paid for whether he occupied them or not).[34] The inconspicuous (to the rest of the audience) mezzanine could accommodate numerous private parties sandwiched as it was between the vast main floor with its rich if chilly grandeur and the equally capacious balcony. The mezzanine promenade quickly became Rochester's "Peacock Alley." As many people came to see the most palatial theater in America and the parade of fashionably dressed social leaders as came to see the movies or hear the music.[35] Eastman, the entrepreneur of music for the masses, wanted every seat in the house to be a good one. (Unlike Carnegie Hall, there were to be *no* boxes in his theater.) Since the auditorium was curved rather than a simple rectangle, the floor had to be concave so that seats on the same row would be at the same elevation. Consequently the theater had one of the first "dished floors" ever built.[36] Ironically, because the exclusive mezzanine was tucked under the balcony for the privacy of the elite, the well-heeled suffered the worst acoustics in the house.

Two days later, on Labor Day, the public streamed in for the official opening. "Performances De Luxe" of motion pictures accompanied by carefully selected orchestral or organ music were scheduled for 2:15, 7, and 9 P.M. Each "programme" opened with Arthur Alexander or his assistant Victor Wagner conducting an orchestra of fifty members decked out in the uniforms of a marching band. This was followed by "Eastman Theatre Current Events," a one-reel film produced by Fox Films that showed various aspects of the new building, and then by "Music Interpreted Through the Dance." In the latter, Swedish dancer Esther Gustafson interpreted "Russia," through Rachmaninoff's "G Minor Prelude," and "The South at Work," through Dvořák's "Humoresque in A Minor." Next came an "Eastman Theatre Magazine" of short subjects that included color footage of John Capstaff's Kodachrome process of 1914, projected "for the first time on any screen." The program that first week had Russian overtones, beginning with Tchaikovsky's *1812 Overture*. The feature film was Rex Ingram's production of *The Prisoner of Zenda*—"precisely as now shown at $1.50 prices at Astor Theatre, New York." A spine-tingling "Organ Exit" with Dezso d'Antalffy or John Hammond on the great Austin theater organ completed the show. A month later the theater hosted its first opera, a whole week of *Aida* by Verdi, produced by the San Carlo Opera Company. Eastman's "nice houseful of guests" and Rochester's large Italian community gave the company the greatest reception in its history—nearly full houses for eight performances. "The way the Italian people turned out was remarkable even for such a music loving nation," Eastman told the consul. The Boston and New York symphonies came in November along with the first solo recital by pianist Ignace Jan Paderewski. The famous names in the music world—Pavlova, John McCormack, Toscanini, Walter Damrosch, Isadora Duncan, Mischa Elman, John Charles Thomas, Nellie Melba, Madame Ernestine Schuman-Heink, Jascha Heifetz, Pablo Casals, Josef Hofmann, Paul Whiteman, Fritz Kreisler, Roland Hayes, the Metropolitan Opera Company, Marcel Dupre, the Russian Ballet, the Ukranian Chorus, the London String Quartet, the Cleveland Orchestra—soon made Rochester a regular stop. Eastman's music egalitarianism showed in the sale of tickets, which was on a first-come basis in order to avoid any "class distinctions." Admission for afternoon shows ranged from twenty cents for the Grand Balcony to fifty cents for the mezzanine; evening prices ranged from thirty-five cents to a dollar. One section of the mezzanine, however, was reserved for the six hundred Subscribers Association patrons, who contributed at least $150 a year.[37]

In its own time the Eastman Theatre was as remarkable as the Radio City Music Hall would be later. In the early 1920s there were few theaters in the country to compare with it. Four that did were the Rialto, the Rivoli, the Capital (seating 5,000), and the Roxy theatres in New York City—all the achievements of a great showman, Samuel L. Rothapfel. "Roxy," as the showman was universally known, was originally considered to run the Eastman Theatre. Jules Brulatour recommended Roxy for a short-term contract only, and Robert Lieber in Indianapolis warned that Roxy was "exceedingly extravagant in his conduct of a theatre venture." Negotiations did fail, probably because Roxy was such a strong personality and nobody was going to run this show except Eastman. And so Roxy didn't get the job and the earnest but eventually ineffective Charles Goulding was chosen. When he did not work out, William Fait Jr. came and went as did Eric Thacher Clarke, son of Eastman's old colleague.[38]

When Rush Rhees first learned of Eastman's plan to build a motion picture theater as part of the music school, the news "nearly gave me apoplexy." He recovered when he learned that Eastman planned to endow the complex for $2 million plus the $5 million that would eventually go for the buildings themselves, roughly $2.5 million for each. Ultimately he would spend about $17 million on the complex.[39] Rhees's initial shock when he realized that he, a university president and clergyman, would be running a movie house was a residual effect of the movie's initial reputation as a purveyor of frivolous and morally suspect entertainment for lowlifes. By 1919, however, movies were no longer "flickers"—they now featured Roman legions and mighty sea battles in many reels, and spiritually uplifting messages as well. Instead of a mechanical piano to accompany them, the services of a organ or orchestra were enlisted. Movies were now respectable and popular with all social classes. The auditoriums where they were shown underwent a similar epic transformation. Seeking to outdo the splendors of the rented opera houses, movie impresarios built palaces of marble and decorated them with all that was ornate in chandeliers and other fixtures. Eastman, for one, always thought movies were respectable—they used a great supply of film. The profits to Kodak since 1895 from the sale of ciné film through Jules Brulatour outweighed the profit from amateur still photography sales. And, as movies became mainstream entertainment, some were even beginning to call them "art."

At the Eastman Theatre, movies in total darkness were eliminated by a special lighting system developed by the Kodak Research Laboratories "which makes it possible to supply sufficient light in all parts of the theatre for patrons to find seats without halting or groping, see all the objects in the auditorium and read the printed programme. . . . This improvement removes the discomfort, inconvenience and moral hazard inescapable when audiences are assembled in darkened auditoriums and, it is hoped, will overcome existing prejudice of parents . . . against motion picture entertainment."[40] Some were intimidated by Eastman's enforced rules of decorum. In 1923, after Charles Goulding was fired, Eastman tried to hire Rothafel (who by then had dropped a "p" from his last name) as a "consulting director" but Roxy's New York employers forbade it. Roxy came once, then "delayed writing to you because I don't think you are going to like what I am going to say" about the movie theater, an orchestra for Rochester, and the opera:

> The people are not coming to your theatre as they should because they are afraid they are watched too much and while they are anxious to patronize, they are not as much at home in the Eastman Theatre as they are in the other theatres. The theatre itself this time appeared to me cold and forbidding. . . . I found that the spirit in the theatre itself [is] not a wholesome one and can attribute it mostly to the fact that the people therein are afraid of you. I feel that it is absolutely a waste of time, money and effort for you to try to create a symphony in Rochester . . . because Rochester is not ready for a symphony. Not even if you had the finest conductor in the world is it going to be a success. . . . Mr. Coates, if he is given enough latitude and money will give you the nucleus of a great orchestra, although he will not do it in the first, second or even the third year. . . . While I admire Mr. Rosing, I do not think the plan for Grand Opera is feasible for Rochester.[41]

Eastman did not hold Roxy's frank views against him. But Arthur Alexander, Eastman's music director, vigorously opposed Roxy coming even "to see one of our shows and make suggestions," declaring, "If you bring Roxy, I'm through." Eastman finished that conversation with "You're through."[42]

With the school and theater Eastman was starting a new career. Just as he had critiqued L. B. Jones' camera and film ads in the 1890s, he made notes commenting on theater advertising layouts, the size of lettering on screen announcements, or drawings for cartoons. He answered petty complaints from moviegoers. His daily inspections were so punctual that the nervous staff and students could set their watches by his arrival each morning on his way to work. He stayed close always to the theater/school exchequer. On the dot of 9 A.M. he appeared in the office of Arthur See, secretary-manager of the Eastman School, with the usual query, "What's the worst you know?" See had already positioned the daily financial report on the lower right-hand corner of the blotter on his desk. A polio victim who spent most of his painful life on crutches, See did not like Eastman, and Eastman was wary of See, especially after the latter moved on to become secretary of the Civic Music Association in 1930 and began manipulating his contracts with both the school and CMA in such a way that his salary was doubled. Eastman immediately spotted this and dropped See from the school's payroll. Yet See outlasted all the theater managers, to say nothing of Klingenberg and Alexander, both of whom Eastman fired. He was still secretary of the CMA when he died in his sleep in 1953.[43]

At 5 P.M., on his way home from work, Eastman stopped by the theater to examine the day's attendance receipts. Many afternoons he stopped first at Wahlgreen's Drug Store across East Main from the theater for a ten-cent malted, which came with a free cookie (two free cookies when Mr. Eastman was present).[44] Late at night Eastman would steal into the theater, alone or with guests, to check on late ticket sales or preview new movies. During the day Marion Folsom had been drawing up charts and doing statistical studies measuring the audience appeal of various films. Often at 11 P.M. on Sunday, after the last guests had left the musicale and while he was still too wound up to sleep, Harvey, the chauffeur, drove him to the theater so he could personally screen the latest arrivals until 1 or 2 A.M. When Rush Rhees received letters of complaint about Greta Garbo and John Gilbert's eroticism in Clarence Brown's 1927 silent *The Flesh and the Devil*, Eastman examined it and reported that "of course all of these so-called sex pictures are objectionable but I saw nothing unusually so, or that could be cut out except perhaps the unusually prolonged kissing." Eastman later told Rhees's secretary Carl Lauterbach, who handled these kinds of complaints, "If the theatre is compelled to cut out everything that could be put in this class it would have to close its doors."[45]

Through Klingenberg, Eastman negotiated for over a year with Jan

Sibelius to teach counterpoint and composition at the school, and in January 1921, press notices appeared that Sibelius had been engaged. Telegrams and editorials praised "the selection as an augury of the standard which will prevail in your admirable institution."[46] In August 1920 Klingenberg had gone to Stockholm, cabling back that Sibelius wanted $20,000 for the academic year. Eastman agreed and assumed that the matter was settled, but later Sibelius begged off, pleading ill health.[47] Anxious to recruit an internationally famous composer, Eastman and company considered Sergei Rachmaninoff. Finally Klingenberg arranged for Christian Sinding (1856–1941), talented pianist, composer, and personal friend, to come to Rochester, where he taught theory and composition for two years (1920–21), his only venture outside Norway. (Sinding is best remembered for one of music's great chestnuts, *Rustle of Spring*, which brought his name into many a genteel parlor in Europe and the Americas. His symphonies, sonatas, and concertos are overshadowed today, even in his native Norway, by those of his greater compatriot, Edvard Grieg.[48]) Upon arriving in Rochester, Sinding composed a work for organ dedicated to Eastman. "As Mr. Sinding does not speak English, he has tried to express his feelings in this piece of music 'Hymnus' for the organ," his wife Augusta Sinding wrote to Eastman, "composed to tell you how he appreciates all you have done for the music and all you are going to do for the music. He is trying to thank you in this way."[49]

Selim Palmgren (1878–1951), Finnish composer, pianist, and conductor, arrived from Helsinki in 1923 as a teacher of composition. His were mostly choral (in Swedish or Finnish) or orchestral works or small-scale piano pieces incorporating Finnish folk rhythms. Clearly, the gentle Klingenberg's Scandinavian contacts made an impact in forming the early faculty, and Palmgren occasionally played at Eastman House for the Sunday musicales. During those first two years of the Eastman School, the portals were open wide to many an international artiste. Pierre Augieras, French pianist, gave lessons at the school. Sandor Vas from Hungary and Frederick Lammond from Scotland taught piano. Joseph Bonnet from France, foremost organist of the time, was succeeded by his countryman Abel Descaux. Swiss-born Ernest Bloch taught theory before returning to Cleveland. Thomas H. Yorke Trotter brought a special rhythmic technique of teaching music to children from the Royal Academy of London. Members of the Kilbourn Quartet, all first chairs in the Rochester Philharmonic who also taught violin, were the Russian Samuel Belov, the Czech Vladimir Resnikoff, the Hungarian Arthur Hartmann, and the Paris-educated Gustave Tinlot. Joseph Press, the leading cellist of the time, spoke only German and had to be met at the boat by interpreters hastily assembled by Kodak executives in New York City. Gerald Maas and Paul A. Kefer both trained abroad. Briton Thomas Austin-Bell and Russian Nicolas Konraty taught voice—and unlike the majority of the above, both stayed for twenty years. Alexander himself was a New Zealander, the globe-trotting Albert Coates was Anglo-Russian by birth, and Eugene Goosens hailed from Great Britain. And then there were legacies from the DKG Institute of Musical Art—the Norwegian-born Klingenberg, and Americans George B. Penny, Lucy Call, Mildred Brownell Mehlenbacher, and Arthur See.

Eastman's "great vision" of "building musical capacity on a large scale from childhood" led to the school being established not only as a collegiate institution within a university, but also as a music school for children and adults from the Rochester community. From 1921 on there has been a Preparatory Department (later renamed Community Education) that offered not-for-credit, noncollegiate instruction to the community at large; there have been twenty thousand-plus lessons since 1921. But with all the great people and the community programing, something was lacking. The Eastman School *was* a part of the university. A liberal education along with a conservatory training and technical knowledge of music had been the goal in getting the university rechartered so it could have a school of music and this goal was not being achieved. Conservatory training was being provided to students who were mostly local—without dormitories, it was hard to attract students from any distance—and primarily women, just as the DKG Institute had done. Indeed, Eastman liked to josh, when asked to give to this or that college for women, that he was already supporting the education of women through the school of music. He did not, however, claim as he did with the school for dental hygienists or his father had with the Eastman Commercial College of 1842 that he had created a new profession for women.[50]

Eastman and Rhees sought more dynamic leadership at the head of the music school and decided not to renew Klingenberg's contract in 1923. They then went looking for "1. An American . . . or at least a man of English speech . . . who could make our school a factor in the development of American music without running into the danger of narrow provincialism; 2. A man whose education was general as well as musical; 3. A man with administrative experience in a school of music associated with a college of arts and science; 4. A man of wide general musical interest rather than a man prominent for virtuosity in one branch of music; . . . and 5. A man of high character as well as tact in dealing with other men, and power to lead both colleagues and students."[51] The designation of "a man" was important because when women applied for the position, they were told by Eastman that "I cannot say anything encouraging to you because it seems imperative that we have the post filled by a man."[52]

Albert Coates, Eastman's music director in 1924,[53] along with Walter Damrosch, conductor for the New York Symphony, met a young musician at the American Academy in Rome, the first to receive the coveted Prix de Rome for composition.[54] In 1923 Coates and Damrosch both invited the twenty-seven-year-old Howard Hanson from Wahoo, Nebraska, who had composed his first piece at age seven ("a short and sad work in three-quarter time") to conduct his new *Nordic Symphony* with the Rochester and New York orchestras respectively.[55] After the Rochester concert Hanson was invited to 900 East Avenue to meet Rhees and Eastman. Not really knowing what was up, the young musician found himself in an intense interview with the articulate sixty-three-year-old college president and the taciturn seventy-year-old industrialist. Hanson left, agreeing to write a multipage brief on his opinion of the place of a professional music school in a university. Returning to his beloved Rome, he soon found a cablegram on the doorstep of the American Academy offering him the directorship of the Eastman School of Music. But before that, according to Raymond Ball, then treasurer of the university and later president of the Lincoln Alliance Bank, Eastman did have one doubt about Hanson. Why did he wear that goatee? Did it hide a weak chin? Ball was delegated to snoop. At the American Academy in Rome, Ball approached and swore to secrecy another American musician, Randall Thompson, later professor at Harvard. Thompson had no opinion on the configuration of Hanson's chin, but certainly could attest that the conductor was in no way weak: "My god," said Thompson. "Howard is president of the student body. We call him 'Benito.'"[56]

And so on 15 September 1924 Howard Hanson—lanky, blond, six weeks shy of his twenty-eighth birthday, but supremely confident in his own abilities to do almost anything in the music line—arrived in Rochester. He brought along his invalid Swedish-immigrant parents whose sole support he was and with whom he would live until his marriage in 1946. It was the beginning of a remarkable association between a young man and a young school that would bring worldwide distinction to both. Hanson created the Eastman School in his own image. The students called him Uncle Howard behind his back; he knew all their backgrounds, called each by name, and heard every exam himself. He prided himself on being a teaching dean. He created the crackerjack student orchestra, the Eastman Philharmonia, which he took to Carnegie Hall yearly. Hanson introduced the Doctor of Musical Arts in creation or performance (previously only given for musicology).[57] Unlike his predecessor, Hanson fell into line with Eastman's pet idea of the movie theater supporting the philharmonic concerts. "Mr. Klingenberg was so antagonistic to the whole theatre enterprise that we were not able to get his cooperation but with Dr. Hanson it is entirely different."[58] Hanson understood Eastman: "He was essentially a simple man, but there were complexities, and severity was the armor of his shyness."[59]

Eastman attended the annual Festival of American Music concerts, which Hanson initiated, and met with the composers who brought new works to be performed at the Eastman Theatre, Kilbourn Hall, or Eastman House. Hanson was prepared to argue with Eastman that America must have writers as well as performers of music only to find that Eastman agreed easily. Eastman let the young composer go on for quite some time before saying, "You're right. It is self evident."[60] The school moved quickly toward professional status after the coming of Hanson. It more than doubled its original enrollment and two annexes were built. A studio building, five stories high and available in 1924, housed the new opera department and was used for operatic and orchestral rehearsals and ballet training. A "bridge of sighs" (similar to the one that linked Kodak Office and the Camera Works) crossed Swan Street from the annex to the stage entrance of the theater. "The school has been carefully weeded for unpromising talent," Hanson reported to Eastman. By the time of Eastman's death, half of the students came from outside New York State. And Eastman lived to see his school lead in several fields—composition, the development of music theory, and orchestral and operatic performance.

An opera buff since the 1890s and a member of the board of directors of the Metropolitan Opera Company in New York since November 1920, Eastman had been cogitating about how to bring opera to Rochester when, on a transatlantic liner, he met "a somewhat eccentric, ostentatiously mannerist Russian tenor named Vladimir Rosing," as Nicolas Slonimsky would describe him, and unlikely as it seems, the American Opera Company was born.[61] "American" meant that all operas were sung in English but as the department developed, most of the instructors were Russian expatriates, fleeing from the Revolution. Eastman favored opera in English because he considered it foolish to tell a long and complicated story that people couldn't understand.[62] From the start it was to be only an experimental department at the school, financed for two years only from its premiere performance of 20 November 1924, although Rosing had been on Eastman's payroll since the summer of 1923. Eastman saw an opera class at the school as a way of getting "good singing acts" for the theater, because, as he told Roxy, "we are too far away from the supply of professional talent to do it in the way you are doing it so successfully." His goal for the 1923–24 season was "to earn enough to finance the opera class. . . . With all of our mistakes we are going to get through the year with a whole skin, and a little to the good over."[63] When the opera program was announced, it met with great approval from the Julliard Foundation and the American Academy of Teachers of Singing, both of New York, as filling a void. Russians were very much in fashion just then in the art and music worlds and Rosing had received rave reviews in London from the likes of George Bernard Shaw and Ezra Pound and as a result had landed a contract for a Canadian tour. He sang his Russian songs in a highly dramatic manner—drawing in his cheeks when performing Mussorgsky's *Songs of Death*, scratching himself all over for *Song of the Flea,* or dropping his jaw to portray the village idiot.[64]

Rosing immediately began recruiting his improbable staff from among the hundreds of emigre Russian musicians then in London and Paris (many of whom spoke no English). George Todd, Jack Warner,[65] and Rosing had alerted Eastman about a new play in London, the director of which was twenty-three-year-old Rouben Mamoulian, born in the Caucasus Mountains of Georgia of Armenian parents, a graduate of Moscow University in criminal law who had spent his evenings at the Moscow Art Theatre studying acting, writing, and directing. Tall, dark, and bespectacled, Mamoulian had produced *Rigoletto*, *Faust*, *Tannhauser*, and Gilbert and Sullivan operettas in Moscow, and would go on, after he left Rochester, to direct the first stage production of *Porgy and Bess* in 1935 to say nothing of a number of film classics including *Dr. Jekyll and Mr. Hyde*, *Queen Christina*, and *Becky Sharp*, as well as many musicals. Mamoulian received a lengthy Eastman telegram recruiting him to help organize and direct the opera company and to teach "dramatic action." Mamoulian had just accepted a job at the Theatre des Champs-Elysees in Paris but decided to go with the unknown American millionaire's offer and asked to be let out of the Paris commitment.[66]

For the first year or so Mamoulian did not care for Eastman at all. During the three years he spent in Rochester, Mamoulian directed the American Opera Company in a dozen major productions, although he was not enamored of opera in English. When Eastman asked him to take charge of all the musical presentations in the theater, Mamoulian agreed, mainly because he wanted to cook up a half-hour story with dialogue, dancing, and singing—"I had that bee in my bonnet before I ever did *Porgy and Bess* or *Oklahoma* or *Carousel*." But when Eastman tried to tell Mamoulian how it should be done, the two got into a shouting match. Not since William Hall Walker bowed out of the Kodak Company had anyone told Eastman to his face how outrageous he was being over some small point. When the argument was spent, Eastman stalked out but within the hour a messenger was back with an autographed Luboshev photograph of Eastman: "With my best regards to Rouben Mamoulian." After that Mamoulian found Eastman fascinating. When Mamoulian reached what he considered "the end of my street" in Rochester, he told Eastman he was going to New York. "New York is tough," Eastman counseled, not unsympathetically since he gave Mamoulian two months to try it out with a guaranteed job if he returned. Mamoulian went—"Nobody wants me," he said—and briefly returned.[67]

On 31 October 1923 "George Eastman Kodak Rochester" received a telegram from Southampton, England: "SAILED HAPPY RETURNING ROCHESTER SLONIMSKY COACH WITH ME REGARDS GREETINGS ROSING." This meant that Rosing had found his American opera coach and accompanist in Nicolas Slonimsky, age thirty, whose working English vocabulary when he alighted at Rochester's New York Central Station consisted of "Yes," "Please," and "Thank you." But Slonimsky could still take conducting lessons from Rochester Philharmonic director Albert Coates who, having been born and raised in St. Petersburg by a Russian mother, spoke Russian fluently. Slonimsky was well known to Rosing, having toured France, Belgium, and Spain with him in 1921 and 1922 as his accompanist.

"The formula for an American Opera Company is obvious," says Slonimsky with a pinch of irony. "Get four Russians and assign them roles—Rosing is producer, Mamoulian stage director, Coates conductor, Slonimsky coach." And it worked. Eastman liked the boisterous Russians and forgave their antics, which in others would have been cause for reprobation. Eastman gave Joseph Press $6,000 to buy a new cello through Harold Gleason. Press picked up the cello for $4,000 and pocketed the change. After agonizing as to where his loyalties lay, Gleason told Eastman what had happened. "I'm glad you told me, Harold, but Press is Russian. These people have different standards than we Americans. He doesn't look on that as stealing. He sees it as a good business deal, a chance to pick up a little extra money."[68]

Rosing taught a class in "mental training" at the Eastman School that began with the recitation of the incantation, "Every day in every way we are getting better and better." He then instructed his class to flex the muscles of their brains. When Mamoulian quietly pointed out that there are no muscles in the brain, Rosing retorted, "Nonsense, if there were no muscles in the brain, we couldn't make a mental effort." Radio broadcasting was the latest miracle of the age; Eastman and Frank Gannett were arranging a hookup with the new station WHAM, which would broadcast concerts from Kilbourn Hall and the Eastman Theatre. (Eastman chose those thunderous call letters, WHAM, as he had once conceived "Kodak.") So Rosing included "mental radio," his term for telepathy and clairvoyance, in his course as a natural extension of wireless communication. Rosing's own memory needed lots of propping: When he sang lead roles in *Faust* and other operas, he planted scraps of paper with the words of the recitatives hidden in the scenery. This worked fine until an unsuspecting stage hand removed all the cue cards and Rosing had no recourse but to repeat, with assorted facial grimaces, the first line of an aria over and over and over again.[69]

At the Eastman School Slonimsky composed his first and last ballet entitled *The Prince Goes a-Hunting*. The scenario was by a young Paul Horgan, who later turned from music to become a novelist and historian, directed by the skeptical Mamoulian, and orchestrated by Vittorio Giannini. Selim Palmgren, the eminent Finnish composer and visiting professor, critiqued the ballet and found it highly derivative. Alas, Slonimsky agrees. The only copy of this early effort lies in state in the Sibley Music Library and Slonimsky hopes that it is never exhumed.[70] These incidents and more are delightfully captured in Paul Horgan's first novel, *The Fault of Angels*, a *roman à clef* about the early days of the Eastman School and Theatre, which won the Harper Prize in 1933.

The Eastman Theatre Ballet was created by the London-trained Enid

Knapp Botsford, a young Rochesterian then studying classical ballet in New York. In exchange for a place to teach, she would produce ballets, earning her keep through lessons. The ballet school started with six girls in February 1923; within a year enrollment had increased to two hundred. Operatic snatches and bits of ballet were used between movie reels at the Eastman Theatre.[71] Rush Rhees was a bit nervous, however, that the Baptist trustees of his university would not understand a dancing school. Indeed, Rhees and Eastman were meeting opposition to movies scheduled for Sunday, films with too much suggestive sex, and the Wednesday Philharmonic concerts that conflicted with the midweek services in many of Rochester's Protestant churches. To accommodate his many clergyman friends, including Clarence Barbour who became president of Brown University, and Clinton Wunder who went on to be affiliated with the Hollywood Bowl and Academy of Motion Picture Arts and Sciences, Eastman changed his own midweek musicales from Thursday night to Wednesday night so that the Philharmonic could play in the Eastman Theatre on Thursday night. And Rhees, an ordained Baptist minister, presided over the orderly secularization of the University of Rochester. He never would have gotten $51 million from Eastman if he had not.

While Rochester and the world watched these events with growing interest, backstage at the Eastman Theatre and School during the years 1925 and 1926 one of the most important artistic events in the history of America was quietly taking shape. It began with a 1911 performance by dance pioneer Ruth St. Denis, who along with her rival Isadora Duncan had broken with classical ballet. Martha Graham saw that performance and never forgot it. In 1916, at age twenty-two (old for an apprentice dancer), she joined the Denishawn Company, founded in 1914 by St. Denis and her husband, Ted Shawn. When, in 1925, after years of performing between animal acts with the Greenwich Village Follies, Graham was hired by Rouben Mamoulian to train dancers for routines between-movie acts at the Eastman Theatre, the only technique she knew was Denishawn. But soon Ted Shawn was demanding $500 for the use of the material. Martha refused, partly because of her innate penury and partly because she didn't have $500, and so had to create a wholly new technique for her Rochester students. (In later years Graham charged students $500 to use her material and technique when away from her supervision.)[72]

Up to that moment the Eastman dance students had as their teacher a restrained and proper but earthy Swedish nature dancer, Esther Gustafson, who thought that eyeliner was an instrument of the devil. In order to shock the students into a new attitude, Graham appeared in a clinging red silk kimono with a long slit up each leg and full makeup.

In April 1926 "Martha Graham and Dance Group" performed eighteen numbers in New York City, the iconoclastic "Dance Group" being a trio from the Eastman School—Evelyn Sabin, Thelma Biracree, and Betty MacDonald. A month later the same trio performed *Flute of Krishna*, choreographed—in those days they said "arranged"—by Graham, in the Eastman Theatre. A twelve-minute "Flute" was filmed in the Kodak studio of the Eastman School using the two-color Capstaff Kodachrome process.

Despite a studio of her own, all the students she could want, and a generous attitude on the part of both Howard Hanson and Eastman, when it was time to renew her contract, Graham got as far as signing "M," then put the pen back down on Hanson's desk.[73] Except for *Flute of Krishna*, she left few traces of her year and a half at the Eastman School. What Rochesterians did not understand, she records in her autobiography, was that dance was going to develop into an art, and not remain an entertainment in the spirit of Radio City Music Hall (founded a decade later) and that all her Rochester superiors wanted were "revues suitable for the Eastman Theatre." And so she returned to Manhattan to continue developing her revolutionary new dance language and stage aesthetic and to become, perhaps, the most important and influential American artist ever.[74]

VI

The Final Decade

Dear Mr. Eastman

"I suppose one secret of your wonderful success in life has been that you knew what you wanted to do and—shutting out the world—did it." Thus wrote Susan Brown, perceptively, on 6 March 1931 to her old beau and recently rediscovered friend, George Eastman. Susan went on to enumerate the conflicting emotions she, and most people, experience in trying to decide what to do next: "Pick the freesia . . . go to the bank to sign my Federal Income Tax return, answer letters that should be answered, or . . . write to you." She chose the latter as "the thing I most want to do," but after so many years of no communication, and perceiving that he was now a world figure, could not bring herself to write "Dear George." The salutation on Susan's letters reads "Dear George Eastman."[1] Susan was right in seeing Eastman's life as more focused than most—even when he had six or seven projects going, each moved deliberately from conception through execution and then, when his work was done, on to the next. The years following 1919 were no exception—the decade after he reached the age of sixty-five was as active and productive as any earlier period.

Late in the summer of 1919 he gave a gala banquet at the Genesee Valley Club to announce Rochester's new music and film center to city dignitaries, Kodak directors, university trustees and administrators, and above all, visiting motion picture figures. Some of them—Will Hays, Adolph Zukor, Carl Laemmle, D. W. Griffith, Jesse Lasky, Marcus Loew, Sydney Cohen, F. J. Godsol, Douglas Fairbanks, Winfield R. Sheehan, Joseph Schenck, Max Fleischer—entered his "Sunday letterbook" as Eastman correspondents of the 1920s. Then, just before leaving for a vacation in British Columbia, he circulated to Kodak people in Rochester an eloquent appeal for loyalty and calm in the atmosphere of panic following the Russian Revolution. Eastman admitted that living and working conditions were not yet ideal anywhere, "but they can only continue to improve with mutual confidence and co-operation." His workers responded, individually and by factory unit, pledging their loyalty and alertness.[2]

At Kodak the old order was passing. The deaths of Henry Strong and Thacher Clarke "cast a shadow over the whole organization." William Gifford retired as managing director of Kodak Limited in 1919 (he died in 1922 as did Jack Robertson, manager of the Camera Works. James Havens and James Haste were also gone before the end of the decade.)[3] Gifford was replaced by Frank Mattison. Because Eastman wanted an American point of view represented in the British management, Charles Case was sent to Kingsway as Mattison's administrative assistant. Simon Haus was sent back to supervise new construction at Harrow along with Walter Bent who, like Case, was deemed a "comer." Two chemists were dispatched from Rochester to Vienna to help Dr. Leon Lilienfeld produce practical cellulose ether. Jules Brulatour was sent to deal with the chaotic ciné film market on the Continent, where he was aided by Janson, now recovered from his wartime experiences in Berlin. William Stuber, master emulsion maker, was sent to Europe to share his new faster emulsion formulas and portrait plates with the Kodak branches.

The fall and winter of 1919–20 were the seasons of Eastman's emergence as a national figure. Although he turned down the invitation of ambassador James W. Gerard, president of the Society of the Genesee, to be guest of honor at the annual banquet in New York, and would continue to turn down that honor until 1931 when Thomas J. Watson, president of IBM, managed to convince him, his identity as MIT's mysterious "Mr. Smith" slipped out with the sale of some of the Kodak stock he had given the institution. In January 1920 the funeral for Richard Maclaurin, the MIT president who had so adroitly coaxed a new campus from Eastman only to die unexpectedly just before he was to announce the identity of the mysterious "Mr. Smith," was held in Boston's historic Old South Church; Eastman was at Oak Lodge and thus unable to be present as honorary pallbearer. When asked in June 1920, Eastman said he thought Pierre Samuel du Pont was too rich to be president of MIT. He also declined to intervene with a good word for Darragh de Lancey, who was breathlessly running for the office too. Eventually Samuel Stratton was chosen, followed by Karl Compton in 1930. However, MIT's George Eastman Research Laboratory for physics and chemistry was conceived and built during Eastman's lifetime, although he probably never saw the building.[4]

Eastman's refusal to make speeches—"It would embarrass me beyond words," he told the Society of the Genesee, an organization of men and women from Upstate New York who had achieved success—did not shield him from an enormous increase in accolades (notably honorary life membership in the National Association of the Motion Picture Industry), begging letters, proposals of marriage, and vivid "biographies" of the Kodak King. Eastman's life in the 1920s was summed up in the reply to yet another begging letter: "I am so full of various undertakings I could not possibly take on another." That attitude lasted until the next intriguing project came across his desk. The flood of begging letters having increased to monumental proportions, Alice Whitney was designated to interview the beggars and decide if their propositions fit Eastman's philosophy and goals. "Every time my name appears in connection with any new philanthropic stunt," Eastman noted, "I get a batch of letters trying to interest me in various things." In the 1920s a printed card was sent to those who obviously had no chance at an audience; this act alone outraged many of the beggars who became irate, abusive almost, about not getting a personal reply or audience. As usual, everyone thought that his or her case was unique. But as Alice Whitney Hutchison patiently explained in 1930: "If you could know how many letters similar to yours he is constantly receiving I am sure you would understand that he could not possibly dictate individual replies to them. . . . No one could meet the wishes of all who write to him for assistance and he feels that the only fair thing to do is to treat them all alike."

She informed the news media that "Mr. Eastman desires to avoid personal write-ups as much as possible," and that irritated the fourth estate. By the late 1920s, as his physical strength and energy began to ebb, Eastman had basically lost his sense of humor and detachment when looking at the proliferation of requests. No longer did he comment wryly, as he did to Babbott in 1919, about the woman who wrote offering to adopt six babies and bring them to Eastman House so they could raise them together. Instead, he began having his secretary sit in on all interviews where the caller might want money or some other commitment. By the end of the decade he was complaining that everyone who came calling, came with a hand out.

He said no to Episcopal Bishop William T. Manning: "I am unable to respond to the appeal for the Cathedral of St. John the Divine because I make it a rule not to contribute to religious enterprises, not because I am unsympathetic with them but because not being a religious man I prefer to spend my money in other directions." When Nicholas Murray Butler, president of Columbia University, cabled an involved request for him to join a conference of "industrialists, soldiers, peacemakers, and noted aviators" on disarmament, he cabled back: "I DO NOT FEEL THAT IN THE PRESENT CONDITION OF AFFAIRS I WANT TO PUT MYSELF ON RECORD AS A PACIFIST STOP IF THAT IS WHAT YOUR LONG TELEGRAM MEANS I SHALL HAVE TO DECLINE."[5] Butler often solicited Eastman on Columbia's behalf as well but without success. Other colleges and universities that tried and failed to get a foot in the door of Eastman House in the 1920s included Columbia, Georgia Tech, Swarthmore, Western Maryland, Pacific University, New York University, Auburn Technology, William and Mary, Princeton, University of Virginia, Washburn College, Kansas Wesleyan, Colby College, and Albion College. "I am afraid there is not much prospect of my making any more large gifts to universities," he told one and all. However, the University of Buffalo and Syracuse University were given token amounts of $5,000, "just as an evidence of my neighborly interest in your splendid enterprise,"[6] and Cornell received $100,000 in 1927 because Eastman was solicited by young Walter Todd, son of his friend and codirector of the Eastman Theatre, George Todd. Stevens Technology (which was the institution to which William Hall Walker left the bulk of his estate) received $50,000. Smith, Wellesley, Mount Holyoke, Bryn Mawr, Elmira, Bennington, and Barnard heard that "I have always drawn the line on women's colleges . . . simply because I am more interested in other branches of education."[7]

On the other hand, he built a dental center for Meharry Medical College, a black institution in Nashville, Tennessee. Meharry, founded in 1876, was still the "only college for the training of Negroes in medicine, dentistry, pharmacy, and nurse-training west of the Allegheny Mountains and south of the Mason and Dixon Line," Eastman was told. "A population of about eight million Negroes live in this vast area." In 1929 Eastman contributed $200,000 toward a building and equipment, providing the services of Harvey Burkhart, director of the Rochester Dental Dispensary, and Will Kaelber, architect.[8]

Eastman did contribute to Helen Keller, the Eugenics League, the Brookings Institute, the American Academy in Rome, and Margaret Sanger's group that was trying to legalize the distribution of birth control information. Helen Keller first appealed to Eastman as "a friend to humanity" in 1924, asking him to allow his now well-known name to be included on the National Committee of the American Foundation for the Blind. Keller was a friend of East Avenue neighbors Edmund and Carolyn Lyon, who had been influential in founding the Rochester School for the Deaf. Keller appealed to Eastman again in 1930 and received a "wonderful Valentine" for $10,000.[9]

Warring factions of the population control movement vied for Eastman's support. Early on he supported the Voluntary Parenthood League. But its unbusinesslike methods made him ripe for the aggressive, no-nonsense approach of Margaret Sanger, chairman of the New York-based Committee on Federal Legislation for Birth Control in the 1920s. Sanger arrived on his doorstep, lunched at 900 East Avenue, and went away with $10,000. In August 1929 Sanger reported that "there are now 25 clinics operating in the

United States. Many physicians are giving Birth Control information to their patients in accordance with the law of the state in which they practice." She was pressing for changes in federal statutes that made it "illegal to give (by mail) the address of a physician or a clinic to one making the request." Eastman became "a member of the Endorsing Committee of one thousand" prominent people. In 1930 Sanger was one of those who conveniently misinterpreted the increasingly feeble man's intentions (he said he would give $2,500 for each $25,000 raised toward her $100,000; she tried to get $2,500 as a start of each $25,000). Multiple incidents of this kind involving not just Sanger but Robert Brookings, Irving Fisher of the Eugenics League, and others who appear to have thought they could put one over on Eastman, soured him on the parade of beggars for good causes.[10]

It is not surprising that someone interested in euthanasia, or the good death, as set forth by the ancient Stoic philosophers, would also espouse eugenics, or the good birth, a concept originating in Plato's *Republic* and revived in the late nineteenth century in the wake of social Darwinism and a growing belief in the perfectibility of the human species. In 1923 Eastman became a charter member of the Eugenics Society of America, founded by Irving Fisher, then a professor at Barnard, and later Yale. By 1925 the society had 312 contributors, most of whom gave $10 a year—"a large sum for the ordinary scientific man who constitutes a large part of our list," Fisher wrote. Eastman subscribed $10,000 a year. The utopian goals of this new "science" included nothing less than the eventual elimination of "orphanages, tuberculosis, reformatories, jails, and institutions for the feeble-minded and insane" and "the building of schools and institutions of progress in their places." Eastman also toyed with backing physicians claiming to be on the trail of a cancer cure. He asked his own researcher, George Whipple, to investigate each appeal and since Whipple reported one after another to have no basis in fact or backing from the scientific community, Eastman never did contribute to a "cancer cure." Similarly, he became interested in 1925 in studies and experiments with gifted children in New York City, sending the material on to Rush Rhees to "look over and let me know what you think sometime." What appealed to Eastman was that it dovetailed with eugenics ("a civilization turning its attention from promoting stupidity . . . to promoting genius and leadership") and also with the Seashore tests then in use at the Eastman School of Music for testing musical aptitude. The leaders of the gifted child study, Mr. and Mrs. A. W. Wiggam, journeyed to Rochester, noting to Eastman "that there was not only no bric-a-brac about your house but was also none about you." In the end, Eastman appears to have decided not to support a project confined to a locality outside Rochester. Eventually he became disillusioned with eugenics too (Marion Gleason was present at the breakfast when he told Fisher he would not be renewing his pledge). By then eugenics had become a controversial movement that influenced the passage of sterilization laws in twenty-four states aimed at various "social misfits," and which would be forever discredited by Adolf Hitler's program for a "master race."[11]

But Marion Gleason felt the concept had a profound effect on Eastman personally, as his health began to fail and he felt more and more useless. It was then, Gleason said, that he decided that all that cash in the bank (about $25 million) was not doing anything but keeping a sick man going. It was, Gleason told interviewer Roger Butterfield in the 1950s, a perfectly logical next step for him to step aside so that his money could be put to work.

When the Institute of Government Research was organized in Washington in 1916, with Frank J. Goodnow (president of Johns Hopkins) and Robert S. Brookings as officers, Eastman began subscribing $1,000 a year and was appointed a director. By 1921 Brookings was chairman and also head of the Institute of Economics, a research organization of the Carnegie Corporation that "interpreted the economic data which form the basis of national and international policies." He also founded the Robert S. Brookings Graduate School of Economics and Government. In 1924 Eastman pledged $50,000 each year for seven years to the Brookings School and was elected a trustee. Twenty George Eastman Fellowships of $1,000 a year were established. In 1928 Julius Rosenwald, chief executive of Sears, Roebuck and Company, announced that he would give $1 million to the Brookings Institute (also called Institution) on the condition that Eastman also subscribe $1 million. Eastman was astounded at this development, informing the delegate from Brookings that "doubtless the condition made by Mr. Rosenwald . . . was made under a misapprehension, that as a matter of fact the major part of my wealth has already been distributed and the balance of it has been largely allocated to matters in which I was especially interested." But then Eastman agreed "to leave the matter open" so that the possibility that he would contribute could still be used as leverage with other funding sources.[12]

Franklin Delano Roosevelt, for whom Eastman had procured chemicals and binoculars during the war when he was Assistant Secretary of the Navy, appealed for a movie camera and, between the lines, for monetary support of his "Hydrotherapeutic Center at Warm Springs, Georgia." Eastman and FDR had met on several occasions in Washington, notably in 1917 when Roosevelt requested Eastman's counsel, presence, and aid on a war matter. In 1927 Roosevelt as vice president of the Fidelity and Deposit Company (he would be elected governor of New York in 1928 and president in November 1932) penned a note requesting a movie camera to record the poliomyelitis patients under treatment in the ninety-degree sulphur springs of the spa.

Warm Springs had been the property of George Foster Peabody (who also put the bite on Eastman frequently to contribute to his museum and various archeological expeditions), when it was noted that a young man afflicted with polio had spent three summers in the swimming pool there and graduated from helplessness and braces to a cane. FDR, who "had an attack of poliomyelitis in 1921, spent several weeks exercising and swimming in the pool during the fall of 1924 and spring of 1925" before deciding that he and others had improved enough for him to buy the property from Peabody and incorporate a foundation for the treatment of about twenty patients there in the winter of 1927. Even before that, Roosevelt wrote to Eastman in a letter marked "PERSONAL" that he foresaw "a great field of usefulness for Moving Pictures" in the treatment of polio. Roosevelt had in mind filming the patients' movements so that doctors could track their improvement. "And," the future president continued, "if the patients, themselves, can see just how they are walking, they can correct faults and understand what the Doctor is intending to have them do much more easily than by the most elaborate explanations. So far as I know," this letter concluded, "this is a new idea, but I think is a very practical improvement in the treatment of these cases."[13]

Eastman sent a Cine Kodak and told Roosevelt to visit the Kodak "place in Atlanta" and pick up a projector. "I am very much interested in the treatment of poliomyelitis," he wrote, without mentioning that his sister Katy had been similarly confined to a wheelchair for most of her short twenty years.[14] Roosevelt invited Eastman to Warm Springs, "for I am sure that you would be interested in the very remarkable work which the Foundation is conducting for the rehabilitation of cripples, the most of them victims of infantile paralysis."[15] The association continued and in 1930 Eastman invited Governor Roosevelt to be a houseguest at 900 East Avenue during his visit to Rochester's horse show. FDR accepted, but at the last minute cancelled his whole trip.

Eastman was preoccupied in the 1920s with putting his money to work for causes during his lifetime, and with disseminating his large holdings of Kodak stock so that his death would not throw it all on the market at once and thus depress the price and bring harm to the company. His plans in both respects were carefully considered and worked out. The formal dining room of Eastman House, which on Wednesday evenings was set for dinner for twenty with an orchid at each lady's place and pink and white carnations in abundance, was the ambience that Eastman as showman choose for his dramatic announcement of 8 December 1924. After observing that "men who wait to distribute their money until after they die are pie-faced mutts," he picked up a fountain pen and in the presence of ten men representing four educational institutions, signed away $30 million. Then he smiled and remarked quietly, "Gentlemen, now I feel better." Benefiting were the Massachusetts Institute of Technology, Hampton and Tuskegee institutes, and the University of Rochester—the preferred instruments of perpetuating a lifetime of largess begun with his generous (for its time and his salary) gift to Mechanics Institute in 1886.[16]

In May 1920 Kodak announced its first postwar increase in the price of film, both ciné and still. As Eastman explained to B. C. Forbes, business writer and editor, labor and material had increased at least 100 percent (silver, of which Kodak consumed 6 percent of U.S. production, was up 200 percent) and the users of ciné film, formerly the struggling Independents, now the movie moguls of Hollywood and Beverly Hills, could well afford a 20 percent increase in the price of raw film. In May 1920, too, the last team of draft horses left Kodak Park forever. Ever since the railway spur had been brought in, freight cars had been drawn along the in-park rails by teams of these equines. This method eliminated hazards of fire, smoke, and cinders, but was slow and subject to winter weather delays. Then someone figured out a locomotive could be charged with steam generated in the power house—and for the next thirty years the "canned steam" engines were the work horses, until diesels replaced them as they did on the main line.[17] That same month Eastman joined the board of directors of the Metropolitan Opera, wrote the foreword and an article, "Medical Miscreants" for the new company house organ, *Kodak Magazine*, and supervised the setting up of a new department of medical photography. In July he followed his preliminary scouting party to Kingsport, a small, planned community started by the Clinchfield Railroad in the Cumberland Mountains of Tennessee. For $1 million Kodak purchased a government war factory there built for the manufacture of wood alcohol. As a result of Eastman's visit, the company purchased three hundred acres adjoining the original thirty-five. The idea at this point was to build a gelatin factory and a saw mill for sawing Kodak's own lumber. Later, Eastman thought, it might be possible to develop a plant in Kingsport for the production of photographic chemicals. "Kingsport is the same latitude as Oak Lodge in a beautiful valley at 1800 ft elevation," Eastman observed, "one of the nicest towns I have ever seen, with only 10,000 inhabitants, only one of which is a foreigner."[18]

The government antitrust suit whose aim was the breaking up the Kodak "monopoly" had been dragging along for six years until 1921, when Eastman heard that a new man was handling the company's case in the Attorney General's office. In January Kodak cancelled its pending appeal to the Supreme Court and twenty years of uncertainty ended with the consent decree of 1 February. With Kodak's buying of other photographic companies effectively stopped by the antitrust decision, investing profits to develop the

Kingsport factory for the manufacturing of basic raw materials needed for film manufacture represented a legal way for Eastman to maintain control of the photographic materials business. Tennessee Eastman also insured the company independence from other firms that might raise prices, halt production because of labor problems, or leak formula secrets. A chain reaction was inadvertently set up: Acetone spun first for safety film to replace the volatile nitrocellulose film base, for example, would also enter the marketplace as an Eastman-made textile.

Perley Smith Wilcox, the mechanical engineer out of Cornell who had joined Kodak in 1897 to design and construct machinery for making film but was baptized by fire during his two-year supervision of Eastman's home generator and the ensuing battles with the Marine Engine Company, was put in charge of the Tennessee Eastman operation. Eventually Wilcox would rise to the honorary position of chairman of the board of the Eastman Kodak Company without ever serving as president or chief executive officer.[19]

The telegram arrived on 13 March 1920 from Frank Vanderlip:

> A DISTINGUISHED JAPANESE COMMITTEE IN WHICH BARON SHIB-USAWA BARON MEGATA PRINCE TOKUGAWA . . . ARE MOVING FIGURES IS INVITING SMALL GROUP OF AMERICANS TO MAKE AN UNOFFICIAL VISIT TO JAPAN AS THEIR GUESTS . . . VISIT . . . WILL . . . LAY FOUNDATION FOR PERMANENTLY FRIENDLY RELATIONS . . . ALL EXPENSES PAID . . . I PROFOUNDLY DESIRE YOU MAKING ONE OF THE PARTY

Eleven men accepted the invitation to go to Japan from 10 April to 30 May 1920 and while Eastman did not make friends easily, three of these eleven and their wives became close friends and at least four others entertained Eastman or made occasional trips to Eastman House. The three best friends were J. Lionberger Davis, bank president from St. Louis; Julian Street, journalist and novelist, Princeton; and Agnes and Seymour Cromwell. Agnes Whitney Cromwell was the first woman to serve on the board of education in New Jersey and Seymour was the vice president of the New York Stock Exchange. Following Seymour's sudden death in 1925 after being thrown from a horse (and after everyone thought he was out of danger), Agnes Cromwell and son Whitney came to Rochester for an extended visit. "The breaking up of such an ideal partnership is one of the most tragic things I have ever known," Eastman told Julian Street, and from then to the end of his life, Eastman saw a lot of Agnes Cromwell.[20]

Frank Vanderlip, banker; Lewis Clarke, president of the American Exchange Bank; Lyman Gage, former Secretary of the Treasury; Darwin Kingsley, president of the New York Life Insurance Company; and Jacob Gould

Schurman, former president of Cornell, were less intimate acquaintances on the Japan trip. That Vanderlip did not know Eastman before is evident by his telegram noting that "MRS EASTMAN IS INVISTED." In lieu of a wife—"The notice was too short," he joked[21]—Eastman ordered a new frock suit and silk hat as requested by the Japanese, and took along his doctor, Edward Mulligan.

Back in 1909 Eastman had declined to "act as a member of the Manufacturers' Committee to entertain the Japanese visitors." Ostensibly they were businessmen on a "goodwill" visit to Rochester but he suspected them of snooping. "For business reasons, we do not wish to have them inspect our factory," he wrote.[22] He did, however, agree to serve "on the General Committee for the entertainment of the Japanese Commissioners . . . with the understanding that it involves no arduous service." From that time on he read assiduously about Japan. In 1910 he told Murray Bartlett, then president of a university in Manila, that he was "reading a book that impressed me greatly, bearing on Japan and her relations with the United States. Probably you have seen it, *The Valor of Ignorance*. It is discouraging to think that all of your good work in the Philippines is merely preparing the way for the Japanese occupation. Now that they have assumed charge of Korea I suppose the Philippines will be their next objective."[23] His words would prove prophetic.

The Japan that Eastman would visit was a land largely unknown to Americans of the time. By the late nineteenth century, Japan had emerged from feudalism, replacing the *samurai* or warrior class with a modern army and navy and proclaiming its first constitution with a divine emperor as head of state in 1889; by the 1890s the country was beginning to adopt an aggressive foreign policy. Education was made compulsory and European and American experts were invited to teach Western methods to the Japanese. During a war over Korea, Japan defeated China in 1895, gaining Formosa and rights in southern Manchuria. When Russia asserted claims in Korea and Manchuria, the czar's sluggish nation was roundly defeated by Japan and in a treaty negotiated by Theodore Roosevelt in 1905, Russia gave up claims in Korea and gave Japan a railway and leases in Manchuria. During World War I, Japan seized the German-held city of Tsingtao in China and German-owned islands in the Pacific and extended its influence in China. The League of Nations then gave Japan a mandate over the Marshall, Caroline, and Mariana islands. The era of liberal Japanese leaders lasted until the prime minister was assassinated in 1930 and militarists gained ascendancy.

Fifteen liberal Japanese statesmen and businessmen who were intensely interested in bringing about a better understanding between Japan and the United States were the hosts during Eastman's 1920 visit to Japan. Eastman was a guest of Baron Mitsui, whom the *Kodak Magazine* called "a sort of Japanese Pierpont Morgan." Nearly all Japan's industry was controlled by eight family groups or industrial trusts, the most important of which were the Mitsui and Mitsubishi. Eastman stayed at "one of Mitsui's villas, built in European style and kept exclusively for the entertainment of distinguished foreign guests." He was given a ride through the palace gardens in the emperor's Rochester-made Cunningham car—the imperial chrysanthemum symbol having been woven into the upholstery in the Rochester factory.[24] Two banquets given by the photographic dealers honored him (with several more planned that he was not able to attend). As reporters noted, "What time he could snatch from the set-piece program arranged for the party, was spent in visiting dealers' shops and photographers' studios. Not all, of course, for in Tokio there are between six and seven hundred studios. This will give some idea of the extent to which professional photography is practiced in that country." As for the amateur trade, Eastman observed that "the Japanese are almost as addicted to the Kodak habit as ourselves." Charles Ames's "big books" bore that out, showing that in 1920 "the Japanese trade is twenty-five times what it was ten years ago [1910]. It could be written in five figures then—now it takes seven fairly sturdy ones." Ames's books showed, too, that the demand for amateur supplies had increased faster in Japan during the same period than in any other country in the world. "The Japanese want the best of Kodaks, the best lenses money can buy, and one order we saw called for 200 Graflex cameras," the *Kodak Magazine* marveled. During the war Seed and Stanley (i.e., Kodak) plates took over from European sources and in 1920 Eastman found the Japanese switching from glass plates to portrait film. Artura paper was used in almost every professional studio.[25]

The Japanese, Eastman decided, had the ability to assimilate the ideas of others "to the point of genius" and wondered if this was what "has made her the powerful nation she is today." The Japanese army was patterned after Germany's, her navy after England's, and her industrial development after that of the United States, he observed. Perhaps Eastman admired this trait because he, too, was an assimilator and innovator rather than originator and inventor as was, for example, Edison. Interviewed extensively after his return (with the interviews reproduced in Japanese for a Tokyo newspaper), Eastman criticized "the bad European style architecture" that was ruining Tokyo. "I believe a lot of the lack of sympathy with the Japanese in these days comes from their having ceased to be the underdog," he noted.[26] He made some other cogent remarks, which his traveling companion Julian Street, a professional writer, quoted in a book he wrote about Japan upon his return, sending the galleys to Eastman for comments: "It is discouraging to talk to the average American citizen or citizeness about the Japanese. They almost invariably ask "Do you think they are sincere" or some other wholly irrelevant question. Nine out of ten of them seem to think that anything will excuse our treating the Japanese in an insulting manner and that unless the latter can be shown to be entirely altruistic there is no reason why we should be their friend."[27] Eastman's strong views may have been triggered by a letter from Dundas Todd, a Kodak dealer in Victoria, British Columbia. Todd conceded that he had "admired the Japanese for . . . their conception of art, which is entirely free of the phallic base characteristic of the Occident" but "be that as it may, the Japanese are not liked as they are held to be as tricky as Satan himself. Their word is worthless." Eastman remained stubbornly apolitical and nonjudgmental about the Japanese in his interviews but not all of his companions followed his example. In interviews with the *New York Times*, Darwin Kingsley referred to Japanese troops on the Chinese and Manchurian railways, permanent barracks elsewhere in China, troops in Siberia, Manchuria, and Korea—and drew hostile letters in rebuttal from the Japanese. But Eastman was so complimentary that Baron Mitsui wrote that "you have carried away with you such clear understanding of this country which you are now so sympathetically interpreting to your people. . . . I simply marvel at your masterly grasp of the situation here in spite of the comparatively brief visit." J. Lionberger Davis, president of the Security National Bank Savings and Trust Company in St. Louis, recalled that "when it was proposed that the group should make a public statement of their opinion on American-Japanese relations, [Eastman's] conviction that a joint statement would be unwise could not be shaken by plausible persuasion."[28]

On the return trip from Japan, Eastman and Mulligan were assigned to a very small stateroom alongside the Davises. The ship's captain offered Eastman a larger cabin, but he refused, preferring to remain in the slim passageway they got to calling *Mulligan's Alley*. "And there, after dinner each evening," Davis wrote, "the four of us who lived in the 'alley' repaired for a glass of cordial which Mr. Eastman dispensed in glasses hung in the netting of a clothes rack above one of the bunks. I can see him yet in his little black cap looking like a chemist as he took down the glasses and filled them with liquid cheer."[29]

In November 1921 Viscount Shibusawa came to Rochester leading a group of seven Japanese, including a publisher and banker. Breakfasting at Eastman House, they moved on to enjoy oyster soup, broiled lamb chops, apple pie, cheese and apples, cigars and cigarettes at Kodak Park for lunch. The seven visitors autographed a specially printed souvenir menu (with a photograph of the park on the outside) for Eastman. Eastman contributed to the American Lectures at Doshisha University in Kyoto, a Japanese university with strong ties to a consortium of eleven American educational institutions, but he declined to be a lecturer himself.[30]

In September 1923 an earthquake and fire reduced 80 percent of Tokyo and Yokohama to ashes. Returning home from hunting in Alaska with the Nortons, Eastman found that the Rochester Community Chest, of which he was president, had contributed $25,000 to the relief fund. Although these voluntary contributions did much for Japanese-American goodwill, California laws denying citizenship to American-born children of "aliens ineligible to citizenship," upheld by the Supreme Court in 1924, negated any positive effect and caused new irritation. Eastman was an honorary member of the National Committee on American Japanese Relations working against the law by education. He did not, however, favor admitting Japanese as citizens in unlimited numbers.[31]

By the middle of the 1920s Eastman was deep into planning his last great adventures. The Africa trips would be his closing assertions of will, the final bursts of the vaunted Eastman energy, and the source of deep friendships.

Trust Your
Organization

◼ ▪ ▪ ────────────────────────────────────

"I think that this has been the happiest period of my entire life," Eastman told Osa Johnson in 1926 at the end of his first African safari. Soon after he retired as president of the Eastman Kodak Company in 1925, he packed his bags and went off to Africa for six months. "I want to let Stuber and Lovejoy get used to the saddle," he explained. His employees joked that he wanted to take two six-month vacations a year but they knew, too, how much he trusted the organization he had so carefully built. Big-game hunting was on Eastman's mind as early as 1891 when he told Frank Seaman that he hankered to stalk tigers. He didn't get to India but Africa *was* in his destiny, and the seeds of those safaris were planted in a jewelry store in Missouri. The owner, John Johnson, acquired the exclusive sales agency there for Kodak cameras and supplies. It was Johnson's son Martin, born in 1886, who took up photography, married Osa Leighty, traveled to Africa, and introduced Eastman to the continent.[1]

In 1907, two years before Theodore Roosevelt's big shoot, Eastman was inquiring of the great safari companies of Nairobi about "outfitting hunting parties in British East Africa" based on tales of elaborate safaris prepared for wealthy clients and described in the *London Express*. At least once, in 1910, Eastman toured North Africa by rail "and was actually snowed in on the railroad in the Atlas Mountains on the Biskra [Algeria]."[2] So he was intensely interested when Frank Seaman took a 3,500 mile trip across Africa north of the Sahara "with only the sun to steer by" during the winter of 1922. Eastman was pushing seventy and his friends and cousins warned him that equatorial Africa was a dark continent full of known and unknown dangers—which seemed to make him even more anxious to go there.[3]

By early 1923 the Johnsons, having run out of money, returned to the United States to release their film *Trailing African Wild Animals*, mostly miscellaneous footage of lions and rhinos but with some action shots of Osa chasing three elephants around Lake Paradise that amazed reviewers. Eastman tried to buy it for the Eastman Theatre but the price of $2,000 was too high. The film was finally sold to Rochester's Regent Theatre for $500 "but the Regent lost money on it at that. . . . Rochester movie goers are fed up on game pictures," Eastman told Seaman on 26 May 1923, "and won't attend a performance where they are the feature." Sometime between then and 14 July, Martin and Osa boarded the train for Rochester, intent on getting Eastman to become one of several backers who would put up $150,000 with an 8 percent return to allow Martin "to spend five years in the heart of the best game country in Africa, so far away from civilization that I will not be molested in the work, and there make an accurate, authentic study of the free, unmolested wild life as it still exists, a record that will live long after the animals are gone, and an invaluable contribution to the future generations."[4] According to Osa's account of seventeen years later, it was not hard to gain "admittance to the great executive's presence, but after a five minute audience with the slim, tired man, in which we presented everything just about as badly as possible, we found ourselves being politely escorted to the door." Eastman told them he lacked the time to look at pictures because his day was all tied up. Their experience was typical of that of the many others who sought Eastman money.[5]

The Johnsons did not give up. Through Kodak's motion picture department, Martin submitted the proposition in writing. Of the $150,000 he wanted, Martin had $60,000, mostly in lots of $5,000, and needed a big name. So he pulled out all the stops: "Now Mr. Eastman, . . . I know you . . . are helping to make this a better world. . . .[etc. etc.] If you object to a proposition so personal, I would make arrangements to do it as a strict [American] Museum [of Natural History] project." Mention of the museum, which was sponsoring and releasing Johnson's films, apparently made Eastman reconsider. He contacted Henry Fairchild Osborn, the director; Carl Akeley, sculptor of vanishing breeds; and Jimmy Clark, taxidermist. Akeley and Osborn gave Johnson high marks for his wild life cinematography and his refusal to sensationalize despite the "poor box office" for travelogues. Daniel E. Pomeroy, vice president of Bankers Trust in New York, patron of the American Museum of Natural History and later a donor along with Eastman of its African Hall, and president of the Martin Johnson African Expedition Corporation, brought the Johnsons to Eastman House and it was then that Eastman changed his mind. On 31 July Johnson thanked Eastman "for the confidence you have shown by concluding to subscribe [$10,000] in our African work. . . . We both hope to have the pleasure of seeing you in Africa. Should you come, we would meet you in Nairobi and take you into the finest game country in the world. We will promise that you will be healthier and feel ten years younger than when you arrived."[6]

In December 1923 the Johnsons left for *Four Years in Paradise*, the title of Osa's 1941 book. It was hardly a practical scheme. Five mule-drawn wagons, 4 oxcarts, 4 trucks, 6 overloaded cars, and 230 porters lugged 255 crates of supplies, including Martin's $50,000 camera equipment, across the desert as 100 African workers began construction of the village on a rise above the elephant trail. A grass-roofed home with kitchen, bath, fireplace, library, and furniture from wood and vines, shelves for the library, and curtains all fashioned by Osa formed the center of a complex that included a guest house, staff housing, tool shop, cow house, poultry yard, and one-acre vegetable garden planted with seeds from Kansas. Martin kept his sponsors informed of their progress with "diary letters": "twenty thousand feet of the prettiest, sharpest negatives . . . every inch full of interest . . . an elephant film that will live for ages . . . some fine rhino and a little buffalo; . . . lots of . . . native life, birds, butterflies . . . all important in making up my story of Africa.'"[7]

The Johnsons kept tempting Eastman to join them, and two years later, in 1926, he did achieve an African safari, seeing it as a last chance to hunt the largest, most exotic animals in the world. Preparations for these six months were the most elaborate of Eastman's long camping history even though Martin wrote that he need only pack as if he were going to London, that he could use the Johnsons' guns, and that his khakis would be stitched up in a day by Indians in Nairobi. But the Johnsons did not realize what an Eastman trip entailed. In the shipping department of Kodak Park more than two hundred small equipment boxes of uniform size were assembled and numbered for the native porters to carry on their heads. One key fit boxes that held guns and ammunition, one fit cases containing personal effects, and another fit the food cases. Eastman took "three cameras with lenses of different focal length and a full supply of film; also a couple of Kodaks for ordinary hand work. While I shall want to make a Cine Kodak record of my trip, I do not intend to let the work of making pictures interfere with the pleasures of the trip." He designed an air bed fitted with "side pontoons" and topped by a layer of sheepskin. "It will roll up closer than a mattress," he told Akeley and Pomeroy, whose sleeping gear he was also preparing. By November 1925 his "African outfit" consisting partially of saddles, tables, folding chairs, cots, beds, three Mannlicher guns, two Winchester guns, one hundred pounds of coffee, canned milk, pineapple, grapefruit, and apricots, and butter "to help make the cuisine" palatable, was all set to go "although we do not expect to leave until the middle of March" 1926. Ordered and waiting on the other side were "two Buicks, one touring and the other a truck, and two Chevrolets, one touring and the other a station wagon."[8]

In addition to the hunting party of Eastman, Akeley, and Pomeroy there was a work party from the American Museum of Natural History. "The Museum has a project to build an 'African Hall,'" Eastman wrote, "in which there will be installed forty habitat groups, of which our party has agreed to furnish six." Eastman, his personal physician Audley Durand Stewart (the retired Edward Mulligan's partner), and Pomeroy set sail on 13 March 1926, and this seventy-two-year-old was not to return from safari until seven months later. For his age the crisp and crusty traveler's health was good although he still suffered from the frequent colds and sore throats that had plagued him since the 1890s; Stewart was forever swabbing his throat or otherwise attempting to treat minor symptoms with little results. He had inexplicably lost a fair amount of weight and developed a mild case of diabetes that effectively curtailed the jams and jellies he loved. Yet the increased activity of the Africa trips would counteract the diabetes and he began to regain some of the lost weight.[9] In London, Eastman attended to Kodak and Eastman Dental Center business for six days. Then he went to Paris for a little over a week, where he met Charles Pathé, respected adversary of long standing. Together they pondered how best to bring order to Europe's raw film situation and the conversation laid the groundwork for the formation of Kodak-Pathé in 1928.[10] In April the trio left by ship for Africa.

Then Eastman traveled on to Mombasa and from there to Nairobi by train. The safari began in the Kedong valley, thirty-five miles south of Nairobi, where Eastman plunged into cooking for the group as well as his shooting assignment to "complete the buffalo group" for the African Hall. Mpishi, the Johnsons' Swahili cook, "stood and watched in awe as one after another there emerged delicious muffins, corn bread, beaten biscuits, graham gems, lemon tarts and huckleberry pie. Mr. Eastman also rigged up an ingenious device which consisted of a collapsible automobile canvas pail attached to a hose for a shower bath." A runner delivered the news to the Johnsons at Lake Paradise that their benefactor was on the way. Eastman found Paradise Lake, "our farthest north objective point and the one we have looked forward to with the greatest interest, . . . fully up to our expectations." Anticipating his arrival, the Johnsons had built a special log house with fireplace for his and Stewart's occupancy. "A steep roof thatched with straw on small poles [was] held in place by rawhide thongs. There are pegs on the walls upon which to hang our things and all around the top is a string of Osa's hunting trophies." The house was along the elephant trail so that Eastman could film on his new 16 mm Cine-Kodak camera the six-ton giants as they lumbered by on their way to the lake.[11]

The other houses were "made of wattles, plastered with mud and thatched with straw . . . on various levels following the undulations of the ridge and consist of a living and dining room with fireplace and dirt floor, a kitchen and sleeping house for the Johnsons, a guest house, a bath house, a workshop where the Delco electric generator is, the laboratory [Martin's darkroom for developing film] and a storehouse where the supplies are kept." Pomeroy occupied the guest house while Percival (Eastman's white hunter) and Pomeroy's white hunter lived in tents. Osa had made shelves for her library and curtains for her windows. One thing that entranced Eastman was Osa's gift for imposing orderly domesticity on the wilderness. It was a standing joke that if Martin left a tent standing for more than two days, Osa would have curtains on it. She collected stones for the various fireplaces, made furniture from wood and vines, and planted a one-acre vegetable garden. Workers built corrals for sixteen cows and a poultry yard for two hundred chickens. "The ground slopes from this string of houses away from the lake to the shamba or garden," Eastman wrote, "and below that is the native village of huts" of the men employed for the compound.[12]

From Paradise Lake Eastman dispatched handwritten memos to Alice Whitney to "have 12 or 15 lbs of fresh ground corn meal and graham flour put up separately in friction top tin cans," sterilized in the incubator at Kodak Park, to be sent to Martin Johnson along with Golden Bantam sweet corn seed for planting. He delighted in the fare, especially Osa's fresh milk, cream cottage cheese, and buttermilk, as well as the caviar, freshly baked bread, candied sweet potatoes, wild-buffalo oxtail soup and game or fowl roasted over an open fire, all served on a linen-spread table with candles and vintage wine in crystal goblets. Indeed, accounts of Osa's exploits fill his *Chronicles of an African Trip*. Martin is hardly mentioned.

Safari hunts took place both before and after Eastman's visit to Paradise Lake. Big-game hunting was once considered the height of manly pursuits for aristocrats, including American industrialists and presidents, and indeed Eastman had a noted naturalist along who did not disapprove of all of this banging away at beasts. Part of Carl Akeley's concept of conserving rare species was to take stuffed specimens back to the museum. The Johnsons did insist that no shooting take place in the lake area because the animals there felt safe and trusted the humans. Eastman stayed strictly within the conservation laws of the time: only five lions per safari, no females with cubs too young to survive on their own, no elephants with tusks under thirty inches. And he pondered the question of the purpose of all those trophies when he wrote from Africa on this first trip: "Whether anybody is justified in killing a lot of wild animals (mostly harmless) just for the pleasure of taking home so-called 'trophies' to show his friends and bragging (inferentially at least) of his prowess as a hunter is a matter . . . of viewpoint . . . that of the sportsman or that of the sentimentalist."[13] Fearlessness, some might say foolhardiness, in the face of danger was part of the credo of the African hunter. For Eastman the thrill of the kill on safari was augmented by the thrill of being in constant danger. It was enough to get his septuagenarian blood circulating. One time, Eastman wrote, "we ran across a rhino. As his horns were not good specimens I thought I would try making a Cine-Kodak of him." With the

Johnsons and Percival, the white hunter, watching in frozen fascination, Eastman started toward the animal, cranking his little camera as he went until he stood within twenty yards of the rhino. Suddenly the rhino lowered his head and charged. At that point, Osa recorded, Eastman "stood quietly . . . facing the animal and then, when snorting and ferocious, it was within perhaps fifteen feet of him, he simply sidestepped it, like a toreador and actually touched its side as it passed. . . . The rhino, growing momentarily more enraged, whirled to make a second charge, when Percival's gun brought him down."[14]

"The affair could not have been more perfect if it had been staged and was the opportunity of a lifetime," was Eastman's conclusion. The rhinoceros had been five paces from the cameraman when Percival finally shot him and two paces when he fell. But this imperfect rhino was not Eastman's goal. Plans to return to Africa were made as soon as it became apparent there would not be time on this trip to go after elephants. Months after Eastman had returned to Rochester, he was entertaining a distinguished group of surgeons with his African reels.[15] As he showed the rhino film, a buzz of consternation and vigorous scolding began which, because it was a silent film and spoke in a universal language, did not interfere with anyone's understanding of the episode. "Terrible," said one doctor. "You shouldn't have taken that risk." "The powder might have been wet," shouted another. "Bad business, George," cried a third. Why hadn't he moved sooner, the famous surgeons wondered. Why wasn't he more frightened? When the protests had subsided to a dim roar, Eastman said in a quiet voice, "Well, you've got to trust your organization."[16]

Late in November 1926, a cable from Africa brought the news that Carl Akeley had died in the midst of his work on material for his African Hall project. Because of the backing Eastman and other members of the safari had provided, the project did not die with Akeley but was carried through as a memorial to the skill and artistry of the man who had conceived it. Eastman contributed $100,000. Shortly after that Martin had a (photographic) flashlight accident in Africa in which he was badly burned. Then came news that Martin and Osa had taken sick while trying to climb Mount Kenya. The Johnsons were above the timber line at 14,000 feet when Martin contracted bronchitis and a high fever and Osa double pneumonia.[17]

The New York Times published and then syndicated Eastman and Johnson's photographs in their Sunday rotogravure section in December 1926. Indeed, so anxious was the Times to get the scoop, that they "sent a man to meet Mr. Eastman in Europe."[18] At first opposed to the project, Eastman later "changed my mind. . . . You may syndicate the African pictures if you will give credit in all cases to Martin Johnson for the photography." Eastman had to copyright the "800 or 900" photographs initially as he had no power to do so in Johnson's name. The Eastman Theatre showed excerpts from his and Johnson's movies. Eastman exhibited his and Osa's hunting trophies in the corridor of the music school. Thirty-two skulls were donated to the Rochester Municipal Museum, where they had the redeeming feature of serving to educate the public. "Visitors who have seen the exhibit have expressed surprise at the length of the horns of these strange African creatures," a newspaper noted. "Naturalists who have examined them say that the antlers of such animals as the Roberts gazelle, Grant's gazelle, the eland, kongone, topi, and impala, all represented in the collection, had their horns protected from breakage by the corrugations and ridged spirals that are found upon them."[19] Coats of topi animal skins were made for Alice Whitney (who became Mrs. Charles Hutchison in December 1927, about the time she received the coat) and Jane (Mrs. Audley) Stewart. "My carpenter is experimenting with the rhinoceros skin for my library table," Eastman wrote, "with every indication of success."[20] Stewart imported a live cheetah as a pet but at his wife's behest, kept it in the garage. "The cheetah is getting along finely," Eastman reported to Percival's little daughter, "although the weather is very cold."[21] Then one day the cheetah got loose and after a merry chase by the Rochester police ended up a resident of the Seneca Park Zoo.[22] As for Eastman, he arrived home just in time to see his cherished city manager plan finally succeed at the polls. "I am not certain which is safer," Will Hays wrote him, "a political boss or a rhinoceros hunter who shoots a rhinoceros with a camera at five paces."[23]

In May 1927 Osa asked the Almighty to protect Lake Paradise as a sanctuary forever as she and Martin made the long descent for the last time. Martin had shot and developed more than two hundred thousand feet of movie film. "You know he never thinks of anything but Photography," Osa confided to Eastman from her sick bed in March 1927. "He says you perfected everything worth while in Photography, and it was the biggest thing that ever happened to him to be with you in Africa. . . . You would think to hear him talk that you had come out here just to visit him. . . . I have never seen him so pleased as he was with the Eastman Theatre program when the pictures were billed as the Eastman-Martin Johnson African Hunt Pictures. . . . I am longing to see you and talk to you."[24]

The Johnsons returned to New York to work on the editing of their films, which would be released through regular motion picture channels to defray the expenses of the safari and return the money to the investors. By then Eastman had invested an additional $6,500. The film was viewed by Famous Players, First National, Pathé, Loew, Metro, Zukor, and various other movie companies and moguls. Movies were about to change from silents to talkies in the late 1920s, and fortunately the Johnsons had recorded, "hippo in sound, elephant in sound, and the pigmies in sound." *Simba*, a sympathetic portrait of a ferocious lion, released in 1928, was one result, extravagantly praised and eventually a box office success.[25] Eastman wrote Pomeroy that he had "not heard an unfavorable word said except that some thought the phonograph talk by Martin was unintelligible and added nothing to the picture. . . . [But] the children of some of my friends were, as they put it, 'crazy about it.'"[26] The Johnsons endured an arduous schedule of four personal appearance shows a day with *Simba* plus newspaper and radio interviews and club appearances. "Oh! how sick I am of this show business really I would just love to . . . go on some nice trout stream with you," Osa wrote Eastman. But offers of personal appearance contracts of upwards of $100,000 poured in.[27]

Nine months after the Johnsons' return to American shores, according to Osa's book, Eastman showed up at their office in the museum, reminded them they had promised he would get to shoot an elephant, and asked them to return to Africa with him. "In view of what you say about my going back to Africa," he wrote Martin on 18 April 1927, "I hate to tell you but I have chartered a steamboat leaving Khartoum 20 January 1928 for a trip up the White Nile; and I am trying to get Phil [Percival] to go with me. Audley is slated for the party and my friends the Nortons, who went with me two years ago into the Cassiar region." But Stewart had to decline on the grounds that he could not be away from his practice again that long. Albert David Kaiser, tutor of Eastman Dryden and the pediatrician who had accompanied Eastman on several of the western trips, would go as his doctor. George and Lillian Norton said no—he could not leave St. Paul's. "Why not?" Eastman asked petulantly. "I don't see why not if you really wish to go." Norton explained that St. Paul's was paying him a salary, that he enjoyed his work, and that the trip came at the busiest part of the year. "All that can be arranged," said Eastman. "If I thought it would be possible to dissuade him easily," Norton wrote in 1967, "I was mistaken. It was a month before he accepted the fact that I could not go."[28]

In the end, the Nortons did not go to Africa but they would meet Eastman in Paris on his way home, at a time carefully planned to coincide with the rector's vacation. From there they would tour Avignon, Vichy, and Nice in southern France, then the Riviera, motor on to Genoa, Florence, and Venice, and back through Switzerland. All expenses would be paid from the time the Nortons boarded the train in Rochester and a letter of credit issued—which they never used, to Eastman's everlasting annoyance—for $9,000 to cover incidentals or emergencies.

For his second trip to Africa Eastman would not go in by safari from British East Africa, the usual route, but lease a launch from Thomas Cook's at Cairo and follow the Nile toward its source. When rapids made further water travel impossible, the party switched to cars and trucks driven in from Nairobi. The Johnsons could film crocodiles and hippos along the Nile, then head down to the Serengeti Plain of Tanganyika to record the awesome spectacle of wildebeests in migration. From there they could go on to the Belgian Congo where they had ambitious plans to film the first all-talking motion picture made entirely in Africa and featuring a tribe of pygmies living in the Ituri Forest.[29] After keeping Eastman dangling for months, in September 1927 they agreed to go. "LOUD CHEERS FOR THE SUDAN TRIP," Eastman cabled happily. As he did with the Nortons, he issued a letter of credit for Kaiser and the Johnsons. Martin prepared a press release for the newspapers that were "already pestering for interviews . . . so that they are sure to get things straight." Johnson stated his own mission in conservationist terms so as to keep it distinct from Eastman's already well-publicized elephant hunt.

Shooting an elephant had become an obsession with Eastman, who looked at it as a last chance. "I am trying to pull off another trip to Africa this winter," he told an old camping companion before embarking, "and then I guess I will be about through."[30] (Eastman's compulsion to shoot an elephant has a nice symbolic link, albeit unnoticed at the time, to his defeat of the county Republican machine with his city manager plan.) Arrangements were made for Eastman's second African adventure, which would take him into Egypt and down the Nile from Khartoum, with a scant two weeks in a tiny area at the juncture of the Sudan, Uganda, and the Belgian Congo, where elephants and the increasingly rare white rhinoceros could still be hunted. (Eastman persistently claimed to the press to be more interested in filming the rare albino rhino than in bagging one.) But the first thing he did upon receiving his resume of the trip was to shoot off a telegram to Frank Mattison, who had done the organizing: "DISAPPOINTED ITINERARY ALLOW SUCH SHORT TIME ELEPHANT HUNT." From then on he referred to it as "a two weeks' dash into the interior after elephants." Next he openly admitted to wanting to bag a rare white rhino that even then was on the endangered list in many parts of Africa. Percival had about used up his influence in Uganda so Eastman wrote his friend Baron de Cartier in Brussels who had offered him special facilities in the Congo: "Do you think there is any chance of my being able to get permission to shoot one white rhino in the northeastern corner of the Congo? I understand they are on the protected list but that sometimes exceptions are made." Finally on 11 October 1927 permission was granted "to take a white rhino in Uganda" and plans to go into the Belgian Congo were cancelled.[31]

A just-issued General Electric refrigerator was shipped directly to Khartoum but his sudden attack of shingles right before the trip gave rise to great concern among Eastman intimates, who wrote Alice Whitney Hutchison of their shock at the change in his appearance, his frailty, and lack of "pep." The secretary acknowledged that he was "really ill. . . . I regretted that he had to start . . . before he had recovered [but] felt relieved to have him get away from continuous conferences from early morning until late at night. It was not surprising that his nerves went on a strike."[32] Cousins Delia, Carrie, and Mary worried again about his safety, but he reassured them that the Nile trip was "probably a safer but not so pleasant a trip as the one to British East Africa." A director of one of the conservation organizations that Eastman supported admonished him that "even very young men have died long before their time on account of that terrible African climate."[33] Babbott put in his two cents: "I was very much worried when you went the last time and yet you came back looking better than you had for years. Now, my dear fellow, is it not wise to let well enough alone? I do not like to think of you so far away." Even Thomas Baker sent out a warning from Australia about "the pitcher which goes too often to the well."

Eastman ignored them all and with Kaiser left Rochester on 12 December 1927 for New York where they and the Johnsons boarded the *Berengaria* for Cherbourg two days later. Lord Riddell and Secretary Garrett of the Royal Free Hospital met Eastman at his Paris hotel to receive £200,000 ($1 million) with which to let the contracts for the London dental clinic. The party spent the Christmas holidays in Nice with the family of Nels Bouveng of Kodak Limited. From Genoa they steamed to Alexandria, took the boat train to Cairo, and from the Shepheards Hotel ("not as luxurious as I imagined," said Eastman) in Cairo left for Khartoum by sleeper train.

By an act of will Eastman was now in Africa with his ten trunks of 1A Kodak cameras, Cine Kodak cameras, telescopes, cooking utensils, ammunition, camp bedding, medical supplies, shot guns, fishing equipment, and Martin Johnson's film, working his way south from Cairo. For the stretch between Khartoum and Rejaf where rapids made the Nile treacherous, Eastman had chartered a rather luxurious stern-wheel steamer, the *Dal*, from the Sudan government. "With its twenty-seven staterooms, the *Dal* was commodious indeed for our small party of four," Osa marveled. Eastman called it alternately "the little steamship" and "a little stern wheel motor boat." Besides the steamer itself, there was a double decker barge or scow, the lower deck being for donkeys and natives and the upper deck for equipment, and a steel dinghy. The host made sure that the chef, stewards, room boys, and crew were up to Eastman's exacting standards. He installed his new electric refrigerator, four cases of "good Scotch whiskey" and three cases of Pommery Extra Sec from England, ten dozen cans of Nestle's Pure Thick Cream, forty-eight cans of grapefruit without sugar, fresh Australian butter, and plenty of bottled water and food, including a supply of live chickens, goats, and sheep. The Post Bran Chocolate Company sent along a batch of bran chocolate; Campbell Church, Eastman's Oregon guide, sent some "alligator dressing" ("I never heard of such a thing," said Eastman), and a Kodak Park employee sent his "secret cure for snakebites." "Mr. Eastman . . . prepares his pastries and puddings on the boat as he would in camp," Kaiser wrote the Drydens.

The party sailed up past Luxor and the Valley of the Kings, which East-man found more impressive than the Pyramids, past Assuan and the second cataract. On up the White Nile, the *Dal* stopped where a Hollywood crew was filming. The professionals obliged by making a reel of the Eastman party. Paddlewheeling on through the land of the Berbers the travelers arrived at the Egyptian Sudan. The leisurely trip was broken frequently by shore trips to take footage of gazelle, elephants, crocodiles, and hippopotami. Huge Nile perch, some upwards of three hundred pounds, were fair game for fisherman Eastman. At the thatched-roof village of Kodok along the Nile photographer Johnson shot footage of the Kodak man strolling through Kodok.

Philip Percival met the group at Rejaf with a fleet of motor cars that drove to Uganda. There they left the cars and took on fifty porters and two skin-ners for a foot safari. Mindful of his seventy-three-year-old client's delicate health and dwindling energies, Dr. Kaiser contrived a sedan chair for East-man. With his debilities in mind, Eastman wrote a note one night and handed it to Kaiser: "In case of my death on this trip I want you to have my body cremated. If my death should take place on safari I also want you to cremate my body, digging a hole in the sand and placing the remains there for the ashes are not to be taken back to America." The quote is not exact, because the original would be lost, but Kaiser kept the sense of it in mind and eventually prevented Eastman's burial in Waterville and facilitated his ashes being placed at Kodak Park by his recollection of the note.

In Uganda Martin Johnson photographed white rhinos and native pyg-my life. On 2 February Eastman got his white rhino and shortly thereafter an elephant for the wall of his conservatory at 900 East Avenue. When the dead old elephant was turned over, it was seen that he had but one tusk. "That's all right," said Eastman, who was deep into his own false teeth, "we'll have a false one made for him." (Actually two wooden tusks were made, to lighten the hanging load, and the real ivory tusk mounted for display from the floor.)[34]

Eastman predicted the end of safaris. In 1927 he wrote: "In regard to the large hordes of wild animals in Tanganyika, . . . they tell me that they are likely to diminish very rapidly now that they can be reached so easily from Nairobi by . . . automobile, which can roam freely over the plains where they feed." In Cairo Eastman turned in the *Dal* and he and Kaiser joined fifty other Americans on a trip to the Valley of the Kings to visit the recently opened tomb of King Tutankhamen. They returned from Luxor to Cairo on the night train, a run of about 440 miles, scheduled from 6 P.M. to 8 A.M. Eastman, in an effort to save pennies, changed his reservations from first class to an old wooden sleeping car, which caught fire in the middle of that March night. He escaped the fire wearing one slipper and one shoe plus a pair of dress trousers over his bright green silk pajamas. The next day new clothes had to be purchased: "I never shopped so much in my life," an exhausted Eastman protested. Gone were the guns, the passports, and the letter about cremation. "Never mind," he said. "I don't need them. I've never felt so good as I do now."[35]

Again the big-game hunter was lionized. His second adventure was the cover story of *Time* magazine of 16 April 1928. (This was also the period when Henry Luce was trying unsuccessfully to get Eastman to back his new magazines *Time* and *Fortune*.)[36] "The scientific importance of George Eastman's second leisurely hunt," said *Time*, "lay chiefly in the cinema films. . . . Of lesser importance were the rare white rhinoceros and the more common water buck which he killed so that he might give them to the Natural History Museum at Rochester." The friendship between Osa and Eastman continued, as she took him by letter to the Ituri Forest with its trees a hundred feet high, its orchids and delightful song birds, its pygmy people, elephants, buffalo, okapi, monkey, and "the African grey parrot who whistles in the morning, a very cheeky bird." As usual, domesticity got top billing: "We have the cutest little dining room made out of sticks and leaves. . . . We had a hundred Pigmies building it. I do wish you were here to help me make pies."[37]

In late 1929 George Dryden and Eastman Dryden, his son, went on safari with the Johnsons. Eastman was in his element helping them prepare, packing up trunk after trunk of Eliza's suet pudding and Eliza's foaming sauce, "24-3 lb cans of biscuit mixture, 12 cans of corn muffin mixture which can be used for gems or corn bread but will have to have fresh eggs with it, 12 cans of graham gem mix," bran muffin mix, and mapleine (which Osa and GE thought as good as maple syrup and not so costly!). "I shall have a heart pain thinking that you are not with us to help us eat them," Osa wrote. "I shall miss you more than I can say especially when we serve lion chops to Mr. Dryden for dinner."[38]

When the Johnsons brought *Simba* to Rochester in March 1929 they stayed at Eastman House. The visit led to an exchange of pictures. "I, therefore, decided to have one of mine framed for you, and perhaps you would put it on your desk," said the note with Osa's picture. He did, and sent her four of his own pictures—one of himself before the oil painting Philip de Laszlo was doing for MIT, one of his redecorated conservatory, one of his garden, and the Luboshev "corporate" portrait of 1921 (his own favorite). The two of him the Johnsons had framed, the portrait for their New York apartment, and the other for their African walls. The Johnsons begged him to go to Africa with them one more time. Osa was insistent. "I think I shall take you back to Africa with me, and just take care of you. Don't you think I would make a good nurse? We would simply play, make pies, and muffins." But Eastman had already decided he would never see that wonderful place again: "I much regret that I am too old to go to Africa again," he told Dick Burkhart.[39]

Eastman's last Thanksgiving was spent at Oak Lodge with the Drydens, the Whipples, and his nurse. At Ellen's suggestion, because she thought they might "pep him up," he invited the Johnsons to join them. "I could send a car to either railroad. . . with love GE," he wrote them by shaky hand. Unfortunately the Johnsons could not come and sent Wenatchee apples in their stead.[40] Earlier in the spring of 1931, Eastman had appeared to other friends as weak and listless, lacking in animation. But on the beautiful sunny Sunday of 12 July 1931 a remarkable change was apparent. His houseguests for the occasion of his seventy-seventh birthday were the Drydens and the Johnsons. During the morning all the Kodak directors assembled next door at the home of Charles and Alice Whitney Hutchison and in a casual group walked across the stepping-stone path and vista between the two mansions to greet the chairman of the board, who was with his guests on the east terrace. Gay and carefree conversation followed. Eastman was smiling and animated, appearing to have taken on a new youth. Osa wanted to photograph him and did so, capturing a wonderful relaxed likeness of him standing by the wisteria, hat in hand. For a day, the enjoyment of life was restored.

The summation of Eastman's feelings about Africa came after the first trip. To Alice Whitney and other friends he had written, from the viewpoint of the period and his own mature philosophy that science and technology hold the answers to age-old problems:

> The adventure is now over, and this adventurer with his mind filled with memories of many new things he has seen and experienced . . . is turning his face eagerly homeward, to a place where there is an abundance of pure water, where the great majority of the inhabitants are not hopelessly and unspeakably filthy, where the mosquitoes are not allowed to spread disease, where the roads are smooth and the streets clean, where the four seasons follow each other in glorious sequence, where there is music, art and science, and boundless scope and unlimited opportunity for development of all that is admirable in man, and above all where he hopes to enjoy the priceless privilege of a few more years of contact with the friends whom he has gathered about him during the course of a long, interesting and eventful life.[41]

But to the Johnsons, as he was stepping on the train, he said with a wink: "Back to the world of fraud and front."[42]

Diminuendo

■ ■ ■ ────────────────────────────────────

From the vantage of 1930, Eastman could look back on a half century of organizing photography, music, health care, municipal government, a self-sufficient urban estate, life in Rochester, and education in general, and establishing these projects on whole new plateaus of efficiency. On the way to simplifying photography and making it accessible to the masses, he created giant film-manufacturing and photo-finishing industries, with subsidiary and less-encompassing camera works and eventually, thanks in part to the government antitrust suit, a whole new textile industry in Tennessee. Like other modern corporations, the Eastman Kodak Company was structured as a pyramid and thus, not unlike a primitive tribe. Eastman was the tribal chief, the board of directors and vice presidents were the tribal elders, and the workers the base of the pyramid. Eventually the time arrived to name a new chief.

The Kodak reorganization of 1921, hampered by the government suit aimed at splitting Kodak into separate companies, had created a tentative organizational structure with five vice presidents in charge of four principal functions—manufacturing, photographic quality, sales promotion, and legal matters. Titles and charts aside, Frank Lovejoy remained at the heart of the operation. For the next four years Eastman gradually withdrew from the active management, with Lovejoy assuming more and more of the responsibilities for a new generation of leadership. But there was the knotty problem of what to do with William Stuber, older than Lovejoy in both years of life and years of service. Stuber also commanded the second largest salary in the company, testimony to the importance of the emulsion expert. How best could Eastman recognize his central role? First, he created a whole new position—chairman of the board, which he himself assumed. Next, Stuber was named president, a largely honorary position that Henry Strong had occupied from 1880 to 1919, but one that entitled Stuber to pack his Kodak Park bags and move to the penthouse of 343 State Street.[1] There were grumblings as Stuber moved in. Lovejoy heard the decision from Eastman before it was announced and apparently swallowed whatever disappointment he felt. Stuber was abroad when the decision was reached and "was leaning on a taffrail photographing Gibraltar when a wireless operator brought him the news that he had been made president of the Eastman Kodak Company."[2]

"Who Runs Eastman?" asked a magazine article in 1932, shortly after the company's founder had died. "A group of seven senior executives who meet every Tuesday morning in a conference room adjoining the office of General Manager Frank W. Lovejoy," the article answered. "Two notable features of these cabinet meetings are (1) that it has been five years [1927] since Mr. Eastman even attended them, and (2) that their decisions are made by a majority vote. A richness of age and service is also distinctive. The four senior members[3] have not only a combined age of 255 years, but a combined Eastman experience of 143 years."

Eastman's share of ownership in the company decreased dramatically as a consequence of his 1924 gifts to Kodak employees and educational institutions. As he stepped down from the presidency and general managership of the company he assumed, like Strong had, an honorific position. Albert K. Chapman, whose office was adjacent to Eastman's, related in 1954: "Then there came the time when he was in his office less and less frequently. It came to be news when he was there. The word would go round—Mr. Eastman is in today. Somehow or other that made it a better day for all of us. Finally he came no more."[4]

Eastman began thinking about the post–GE Kodak early in the 1920s, as he ruminated to Andrew Pringle:

> We are getting old and have got to pass over the divide before many years. I am sixty-nine but do not as yet feel my age and am still going strong. When I go I hope I shall have things in shape so they will go on just the same. What I would like to do is just fade out of the picture and not go out with a bang. There is a lot of young blood in the Company and I am trying to organize it so people will say after I am gone that the old man was not the whole thing after all.[5]

A smooth transition was so important that once the new management team had been named, Eastman went off to Africa for six months. He wrote Helen

Carter, "The Kodak Company gets along so well without me that I am gradually lengthening my vacations." Still, he was not a man who retired easily. And so he now turned to "my one remaining hobby"—calendar reform.

"Mr. Eastman admired persons who combined idealism with practical usefulness," Marion Folsom told an interviewer in 1940. One such person was Moses B. Cotsworth, British statistician, who when introduced to Eastman in 1924 had already spent twenty-five years advocating the adoption of the thirteen-month calendar and had exhausted his financial resources. Cotsworth presented Eastman with a mass of papers and pamphlets describing the history and uses of the calendar along with how his plan would simplify it and allay confusion. Eastman perceived Cotsworth as working on calendar reform for the good of humanity, without expectation of personal benefits, but he added a caveat. "There may be kinks," he said, as he instructed Folsom to send a pamphlet and questionnaire to one hundred persons—bankers, businessmen, university professors, editors, superintendents of schools, and labor leaders—asking their reaction. A large proportion answered, probably, Folsom thought, "because of Mr. Eastman's personal letter." Of those, 90 percent thought the plan good; those who opposed cited the difficulty of change. "If the people we've written can't find any kinks, and we can't, it must be a good thing."[6]

In a staggering effort to get the whole world to change from the Gregorian calendar to the Cotsworthian, Eastman decided to take Cotsworth under his wing. He set up a budget and assigned Folsom, along with Eugene Chrystal and Oscar Solbert, public relations director and staff member respectively, to manage the finances and help with promotion. The new calendar would have thirteen equal months of twenty-eight days each. Tentatively the extra month was called "Sol" and the extra day in the year would be a holiday, "World Peace Day," falling between Christmas and New Year. Easter would be fixed and all holidays (except Christmas and Thanksgiving) would fall on a Monday. Only the last provision, of course, was ever widely adopted. Kodak adopted the new calendar in 1928 to maintain their own records of sales so that comparisons with earlier years could be made more accurately, and also to plan manufacturing operations and budgeting. (In the mid-1980s, even Kodak went back to the uneven Gregorian months.)[7]

The other new project of the late 1920s that caught Eastman's fancy was the Oxford professorship that Abraham Flexner talked him into establishing. Through Dr. Frank Aydelotte, secretary of the Association of American Rhodes Scholars and president of Swarthmore College, Eastman offered $200,000 (later raised to $300,000) for what would be called "The George Eastman Visiting Professorship" of Balliol College. The professor, Eastman wrote, "should be an eminent American" citizen and come from a different field of study and a different part of the country each year, receive a salary equivalent to an Oxford professor's, plus supplements to raise it to the prevalent American standard, and a free residence. Naturally Eastman took a special interest in the Oxford "Eastman House," insisting that the heating and bathroom facilities of the old house be fixed up so that the "temperature will not vary more than one degree no matter what the outside temperature may be." Recalling his English sojourns, he stipulated: "I want to make sure that the American professor has a place to live in where he will not have to wear a shawl over his back while he is eating his breakfast, or wait ten or fifteen minutes to get some hot water at the tap."[8]

Eastman met Thomas Edison again after many years and for the first time on a social level at a luncheon honoring the great inventor at New York's Ritz Hotel in 1924. Frank Tichenor of the Edison party introduced them. Tichenor drew himself up to Edison's best ear and shouted, "I'd like you to meet Mr. Eastman." Edison stiffened with surprise and looked puzzled. "George Eastman?" "Yes," replied Eastman, extending his hand. Edison beamed. "I've heard a lot about you," he said. "I bought a dynamo from you about 1885," shouted Eastman. "Was it any good?" Edison wondered. Eastman: "Pretty good machine. I've got it yet, and it still works." "That's fine," the inventor responded. "And say, your film is pretty good too."[9]

Eastman's attitude toward praise, honors, monuments, memorials, and the like extended to honors for others as well as himself. He accepted Henry Ford's invitation to come to a party at Dearborn, Michigan, for Edison in 1929 on the fiftieth anniversary of the invention of the incandescent light and asked Will Hays, the movie czar, to accompany him by sleeper train. Hays recalled that while Eastman was pleasant and cordial as the two walked about seeing everything, meeting people, listening to speeches, and more, he seemed to remain unmoved by all the praise that was being lavished not only on Edison but on himself for his role in photographic and motion picture achievements. Hays was enthusiastic about the whole affair and of course wondered about his companion's quiet reactions but Eastman remained his usual unexpressive self. (Later Eastman wrote MLG—May Love Gifford—that "although I got thoroughly tired out at the Ford Edison Celebration it was worth it. Really it was wonderful.") Finally as the train was pulling into Rochester and the two were about to separate with Hays going on to New York, Eastman said, "Yes, I guess it was all worthwhile. But you can't measure the value of such things. The doing of it was its own reward."[10]

Nearing Port Sudan on the Red Sea in 1926, Eastman wrote a letter that told of his dream of a new full-color process for amateur movies. Eastman described the process in detail, the steps by which it would be produced and marketed, the advertisements announcing it. He forecast booming sales and a drain, as in the early days, on inventories of film, cameras, and projectors. His vision was a year early. After a decade of talk and conjecture, a relatively simple process that used an attachment of filters to both the Cine-Kodak camera and projector to add color to the 16 mm film was ready to be marketed. Any reasonably careful photographer could now record his life and good times in living color. The major shortcoming of the process was a grid of fine lines, similar to early television. But the pictures were bright and colorful, the process was easy to use, and the boom to Kodak stock when this new technology was announced was considerable. Hollywood was then producing only black-and-white silent films; color and sound would be future developments for professionals and movie houses.

The announcement party was planned for August 1927 at Eastman House. Arrangements were in the hands of Colonel Oscar Solbert, Kodak's quintessential public relations man who knew everyone from the prince of Wales to General Pershing, and the latter's presence was earnestly desired. But the general was living in quiet retirement in Virginia and refused to make any personal appearances. Solbert had been on Pershing's staff during the Great War, and had witnessed the signing of the Armistice in a railroad car. So the colonel didn't just write or phone the general; he hopped a train to Black Jack's hideaway and the general did show up in Rochester.[11]

Edison appeared with his whole family after having one of his male secretaries phone ahead to Eastman's cook with a recipe for tapioca pudding, cooked slowly for two hours, and toast, very thin and baked a la Melba for one hour, to be prepared for all his meals since he ate nothing else. Horace S. Thomas, L. B. Jones's son-in-law, was one of the go-fers sent to the train station with four Lincolns and their drivers to meet all the trains and direct the guests, depending on their place in the pecking order, to 900 East Avenue, to the Genesee Valley Club, or to a hotel. Three sleepers from New York brought the Edisons to Rochester. The first arrived at 6 A.M. bearing the Wizard of Menlo Park himself. Horace Thomas shouted a greeting. "All right, young man," Edison shouted back, "we'll wait for Mrs. Edison and the others." Eventually Mrs. Edison, son Charles and his wife Caroline, and son Ted and his young bride arrived, and all the Edisons were off to Eastman House for a tapioca and Melba toast breakfast.[12]

Soon the gardens were filled with famous men being recorded in the morning by the new movie process so that they could watch themselves in living color in the afternoon. The showing on two screens with shades pulled to darken the living room was greeted with spontaneous applause. In between, the group was trotted off to Kodak Park for lunch. Adolph Ochs, publisher of the *New York Times*, came upon Eastman in the conservatory, changing his own Cine-Kodak film. "Would you like to see how to load one of these?" he asked with a combination of boyish offhandedness and a salesman's instinct for the kill.[13] When asked to comment on the new process by the local Rochester press, Ochs replied that "it is beyond my ability to express an opinion. We stand on the threshold of a new era. This development gives one the impression that nothing is impossible."[14]

Others attending were Professor Michael I. Pupin, physicist at Columbia University, who said he saw the first motion picture in Berlin in 1886; Dr. Edwin E. Slossen, editor of Science Service; Major General James G. Harboard, president of the Radio Corporation of America; Hiram Percy Maxim, inventor and president of the Amateur Cinema League, Dr. E. F. W. Alexanderson, one of the inventors of television; Sir James Irvine, chemist and vice chancellor of St. Andrew's University in Scotland; Owen D. Young, chairman of the board of the General Electric Company; Dr. G. K. Burgess, director of the United States Bureau of Standards; Frederick E. Ives, early color film experimenter; John J. Tigert, United States commissioner of education; Karl A. Bickel, president of United Press; Roy Howard, chairman of the board of Scripps-Howard newspapers; Kent Howard, general manager of Associated Press; H. E. Ives of the Bell Telephone laboratories; Frank David Boynton, superintendent of schools, Ithaca; David Lawrence, publisher of the *United States Daily*; Dr. Henry Fairchild Osborn, president of the American Museum of Natural History; and Dr. Leo H. Baekland, the inventor of Velox paper and the first "plastic," bakelite.

"What do you think of the new process?" reporter Henry Clune wrote on a slip of paper for the deaf Edison. "'Fine,' was the prompt reply of the famous inventor. . . . 'It is entirely simple.' Then with a gracious smile, he added, 'I worked at it myself many years ago, but I made a failure of it.' . . . Asked if he believed the process could be applied to television, Mr. Edison said he did not know."[15]

In February 1924 the Myricks of Oak Lodge sustained a double tragedy from the pneumonia that swept through the family. Edward Mulligan Myrick took sick and died—"a bright boy and with a good deal of promise," Eastman lamented. "Henry Myrick has lost one of his most promising children, a boy about sixteen, named Edward Mulligan [Myrick]. He died from pneumonia after an operation for appendicitis." Two or three other members of the family, including Mary, Henry's wife, were ill with pneumonia. Mary also died in that scourge of February 1924.[16]

The Oak Lodge story does not have a happy ending. Every week for almost thirty years, Henry Myrick sent Eastman his penciled list of farm workers, the number of hours each worked, and the amount each was owed by the boss. When Myrick made an arithmetical error, Eastman was sure to catch it: "There appears to be some error in our account."[17] But it never occured to him that Myrick might pad the hours of some of the workers and pocket the difference. "I have always paid everything that Henry put up to me without any questions," he explained to R. C. Dunn, his North Carolina attorney in 1931 when, as an old man who had lost his "pep" and zest for life, he asked George Dryden to look into the matter. "Apparently [Myrick] has got into very careless habits," he wrote, bending over backward to give Myrick the benefit of the doubt. "From what Dryden tells me I think it would be a good plan for you to call Henry up to your office and question him pretty closely. . . . I am trusting Henry with a good deal of money and responsibility and he is getting chronically in debt."[18]

For years Eastman had worried about Myrick's lack of money sense, his haphazard way of paying back the loans that Eastman extended from time to time, and his weakness for fancy cars that were beyond his means. In 1924 he admonished Myrick that "some of the Rochester friends tell me that you have been writing them begging letters. This is highly improper and I want you to let me know who put you up to it." Myrick continued to send his weekly list, but Eastman found himself writing "You still haven't answered my question how you came to send out the begging letters." The car remained a sore point, too, because "I was afraid you were getting into additional debt. It seems to me unwise for a man in your position to undertake such an expense. These salesmen play upon your pride and desire to own a conspicuous thing and do not care how much they involve you in difficulties. You are already heavily in debt and very much behind in your payments for your farm. If the notes were in the hands of a bank they would long ago have held you up."[19] Finally he agonized to Dunn: "After looking into affairs I wish you would advise me what is best to do—fire Henry and his gang or try to reform him. I might say that if he *has* got careless very likely part of the fault is mine for having put too much faith in his honesty. In my business I have accountants who look after such things but my private affairs are not so well organized."[20]

The hardest news Eastman had to bear in late 1931 was that Myrick had been cheating him for years, padding the payroll with field hands who were long gone, dead, or in school when reported to be working, or working one-third the hours Henry reported. Dryden uncovered the mess and along with Dunn, reported it to Eastman. Whether the few dollars saved by Eastman's reluctant firing and evicting of Henry was worth the mental anguish the old man experienced by feeling that his Oak Lodge "experiment" with black tenants had failed (coming on the heels of the "failure" of the Eastman Theatre plan), is hard to gauge. Eastman's last visit to Oak Lodge was Thanksgiving 1931; illness confined him to his room. "At the end of our stay I discharged Henry and hired a white man as superintendent under the supervision of my lawyer, Mr. Dunn," he wrote Nell Newhall. "I hope things will go better. . . . Henry has turned out to be a weak scoundrel and has taken money from the payroll, [etc. etc.]. No harm has been done except the loss of the money, which has been going on . . . for several years. It probably began while I was in Africa."[21]

The 1920s began with a high point in his relations with his only nephew, Royal Vilas Andrus, as Uncle George received "a telephone message . . . telling me he was [in Rochester] attending a convention of the Todd Protectograph salesmen."

> I invited him to come out to breakfast with me and he appeared this morning at half past seven, as dapper as you please. I asked him if he was still one of the foremost salesmen. He said: "No sir. I am the first. That is what you wanted, wasn't it?" I said, "Yes, of course." . . . He asked no advice, so I gave him none. Altogether he appeared very well but there is something very hard about his face which is not particularly reassuring. However, pride in his record may keep him going.[22]

Then came the big blowup when Royal discovered that the allowance Uncle George had been sending him monthly was the interest on a trust fund created from his grandmother's estate about which he had never been told. The usual string of sicknesses and begging letters began anew. In 1931 Eastman turned the whole Royal problem over to George Dryden, along with $5,000 to retire Royal's current $3,000 debt and pay for his health care.[23]

The importance to Eastman of the success of his grandiose music plans is evident in a 1923 letter to Andrew Pringle: "The Music School has given me more fun in my old age than anything I ever tackled. When you come to think of it, it is a joke that one who is totally devoid of all musical ability is trying to steer one of the biggest musical enterprises that has ever been proposed."[24] But with the advent of sound motion pictures, Eastman's music-cum-movies scheme for the Eastman Theatre edged toward a premature demise. Even more devastating was the block booking of motion pictures. Hollywood production studios were building their own theaters across the country and independent theaters like the Eastman could no longer manage to book any movie they wanted. Just to obtain some of the better films, Eastman and George Todd acquired a group of Rochester theaters.

Eastman's dislike of sound pictures meant that for once he was not leading the pack. "Talkies are fakery," he claimed. Edison had solved the problem of "a phonograph accompanying film" early on, but people did not like it. He was not alone in considering silent movies a breed apart, a whole different art form. Silent movie players became international stars who "spoke" to everyone regardless of language. Eastman eventually accepted the inevitable, agreeing with colleague Leon Gaumont that talkies were about to take over the world, but that still did not make him like this turn of events.[25]

As the Eastman Theatre began to fail financially, Eastman's desperate petty economies in his $17.5 million complex increased. He chastised Arthur See for sending out the bulletin with a two-cent (first-class) stamp. Was there a way, he wondered, short of plunging the theater into total darkness, of reducing the $2.88-per-hour cost of operating the chandelier? He had a white elephant on his hands and so was easy prey for the next episode. In the fall of 1928 he decided with extreme reluctance that "the Eastman Theatre has not made a financial go of it" and signed a ten-year lease with his friend Adolph Zukor of Paramount Publix to run the movie part. For the next three years the theater was a glitzy movie palace except for the Thursday night concerts. Publix immediately began redecorating with screaming banners and ice boxes in the lobby. Artists, architects, and the general public, who by this time had grown to love "their theatre," petitioned Eastman angrily. "I hope the talk of redecorating is only gossip," Lawrence Grant White wrote, "and that you will use your influence to keep the decorations as they are at present."[26]

"My dear Lawrence White," a resigned Eastman replied. "Our contract with the Publix people prevents their making any permanent changes without consent. . . . In order to 'pep up' the interior they have hung a red curtain in the proscenium arch that would break your heart. It nearly did that to mine and I am not so sensitive as you are. They talk about covering the murals with hangings to regulate the sound of the talkies. If they decide to do this we will try to mitigate the horror of their color scheme."[27] Eastman even offered to pay one-half of the expenses if Publix changed those offensive red curtains, "a glaring atrocity, . . . for something that would pass the approval of McKim, Mead & White." Two years into its ten-year lease, Paramount threw up its hands and returned the theater to the university as a luxurious but almost empty landmark. Zukor and Paramount failed, not because Eastman banished them but because Rochester would not accept their innovations. The town had taken a very special pride in its new theater and people were affronted to have it cheapened. These factors plus the advent of the Depression made the Eastman Theatre a grand failure in its donor's opinion and, according to friends, his most bitter disappointment.[28]

Eastman's interest in musical enterprises began to wane as he concentrated most of his dwindling energies on demonstration projects of dental health for children. He remained an interested listener and spectator of music projects but never again a sponsor. On Christmas Day 1930 a program of choral and organ music was broadcast nationwide from the conservatory at Eastman House, which he heard from the Dryden home in Evanston to which he had fled to escape the broadcasters. His own version fudged: "I did intend to invite the Drydens down to Rochester for Christmas," he told

"Dearest Nell" Newhall, "but finding that I wasn't up to it I accepted their invitation to go to Chicago." When a youthful William S. Paley, president of the Columbia Broadcasting System, ecstatic about the quality of the show, asked whether it could be arranged to continue broadcasting from the conservatory on Monday afternoons, Eastman replied diffidently, "I would not be opposed to it but would not be interested enough to bear any of the expense connected with it." Ten days before he died he summoned Arthur See to Eastman House. He could barely walk across the room, See recalled in 1950, but there was as much fervor as ever in his voice when he said: "See, I'll never endow the orchestra. If the people want it, let them support it" through the Civic Music Association.[29] He did, however, lavishly endow the music school and during the Depression Howard Hanson was able to contribute $100,000 a year from that endowment for the support of the Rochester Philharmonic Orchestra.

By the 1920s Eastman's long friendship with Mary Mulligan had passed through several stages as Mary herself articulated in the letters that often followed a spirited spat about the Eastman Theatre. Mary was forever groping to understand her reticent friend and draw some response from him. In the beginning of the century she had organized not only his musical evenings but almost his entire social life for him. She wrote and produced elaborate little dramas for Eastman House in which the guests arrived costumed as one of his paintings (Clayla Ward loved to come as Rembrandt's dissipated young man, Katharine Whipple as Joshua Reynolds's glamorous *Mrs Provis of Bath*).[30] Gradually Eastman took charge of his own music and planned his own fun. Then younger couples such as the Nortons and the Whipples replaced the Mulligans as vacation companions, and he went away without so much as a goodbye to Mary or an itinerary for her so that she had to call Miss Whitney to learn his address.[31] These humiliations plus the fact that he no longer hung on her every word in musical matters led Mary to experience a profound sense of loss. She "felt more unhappy than you will ever know . . . that you no longer asked nor desired my advice and that I passed long ago into a class of friends of whom you have many instead of remaining in a rather exclusive position in your regard." Mary recoiled at the proliferation of amateur local talent in the Eastman Theatre: "It has been one of my chief wishes that anything with which your name was associated would be of the finest texture and so I winced at the cheap stunts put in the Eastman Theatre which I could regard elsewhere with indifference. I insist on keeping you on a pedestal. Please don't get off!" She was particularly irritated with Eastman's coolness and secrecy regarding his plans for the theater and was astounded to learn that even without consulting her, he was in pursuit of professionals to raise the caliber of the performances: "You did not put me in possession of the facts—I had not the faintest notion that you were planning to call in an expert of Mr Coates's calibre. He is indeed a 'big gun' and will reach the target."[32]

Lest he think her petulant, she assured him that "my affection for you will continue through the years and until my death—it is independent of your feeling for me—You can hurt my feelings but you cannot destroy my friendship. . . . Life is too sad too short and too enigmatic to let go of our friends." Eastman found their disputes exhilarating, and while he could not express himself as articulately as she could in words, friends observed his body English. One saw him leap over the shrubbery in front of the Mulligan porch after a summer evening there—instead of sedately exiting by the preordained steps—before sprinting the short block home along East Avenue to Eastman House. Thus the merry-go-round controversies did not really lessen the friendship. Mary and George had an disagreement once about the relative importance of ordinary human beings versus artists. "Suppose there was a shipwreck and you had to choose between saving me or Fritz Kreisler," Mary goaded. "You would have to take Kreisler." "No," said George, quietly. "You're more important to me, Mary."[33]

And despite the changing nature of the friendship during the 1920s, Mary *was* important to him. So much so that he may not have been prepared for the profound sense of loss he felt when life did indeed become "too sad too short and too enigmatic." Mary of the "indefatigable energy" that would "tire the average man out, dancing all evening with no one to keep up with her," had, since her 1921 bout with influenza, a weakness in her lungs. In July 1927 Eastman suddenly cancelled a vacation and hurried to New York to meet the *Homeric* after cabling: "MY DEAR ED I AM SIMPLY HEART BROKEN AT THE TERRIBLE NEWS." Mary, with husband and daughter Molly, had been touring France and upon arriving in London seemed "very ill" with what her physician husband initially thought was malaria but shortly decided was pneumonia. Within three days, despite the best medical care of time and place, she was dead. Reeling, Eastman described "her going" as "an almost unbelievable tragedy." A little more than a year later Edward Mulligan died, too, of complications of diabetes. "Both of the Mulligans are gone now," said their friend Eastman and he never did rally from that dual loss.[34]

Two years later Eastman lost another close friend with the death of Lillian Norton. "My acquaintance with the Nortons is a great joy to me," he wrote in 1927. "They are good sports, among other things." He looked forward to their vacations together and the weeks in New York on theater sprees, which he liked to describe as "wild dissipation." He even started attending services at St. Paul's again; Sunday mornings he would watch from an upstairs room until spotting Lillian walking the short block from rectory to church, catch up to her for the last few paces, and ask with a grin if he could join her. He would then invite them to join him for Sunday noon dinner.[35]

In the fall of 1927 Lillian had a mastectomy and appeared to recover rapidly. Eastman took the Nortons to Oak Lodge and Lillian "came home looking as well as I have ever seen her." But by late 1928 she was "not well," her husband's euphemism for the spread of the cancer. Her activities were greatly curtailed and Eastman declined a Metropolitan Opera spree with Otto Kahn to host a birthday dinner for Lillian. Most nights Eastman walked the half-block to the rectory at 6 P.M. just as George Norton was getting home. Lillian did not improve and by late fall of 1928 her terminal condition was obvious. Unknown to her husband, Eastman kept in touch with the doctors. In March 1929 doctors informed Norton that time was brief for Lillian and soon Norton was summoned to Eastman House. Lillian's three doctors heard Eastman announce that he was taking charge, getting Lillian away from the surroundings in which she had been sick for so long, and providing her with some good fresh North Carolina air.[36]

"I'm in your hands," Norton said finally, with some relief. Two days later, Lillian, George, and son Johnny, along with a trained nurse Eastman had hired, boarded the *Grassmere* for Oak Lodge. Lillian was happy and comfortable for two weeks. But on 25 March it was apparent that she had entered the terminal stage. Eastman talked with her for half an hour and then said goodbye, leaving her with her family. "Goodbye GE," she said, as if she was taking leave of a social call. "I've had a wonderful time. Thank you for everything." The next morning she died and Eastman again took charge, sending Norton and Johnny out for a horseback ride while he drove the thirteen miles to Enfield for an undertaker and to wire ahead to Rochester. Back in Rochester Eastman said goodbye once again. Appearing at the rectory door at 6 P.M. with an orchid, he asked the maid if he might open the casket and pin it to Lillian's dress. He left for New York immediately after the funeral (as he had left for Boston immediately after his mother's funeral) and wrote Norton from there, saying in part, "When I get back I hope I shall see something of you. Don't drift away."[37]

In a letter to John Hemenway, childhood companion, Eastman noted that he had "reached the advanced age of sixty-six." Although he said in 1907 when his mother died after several years as an invalid that he had no desire to live on in that condition, it was another decade before thoughts on death and dying turn up regularly in his letters. "The condition of [Cousin] Henry [Eastman] and [his wife] Frankie too certainly is sad," he wrote Almon in 1916. "What a blessing it would be if we could all drop dead when we get to a point where we have to give up."[38] And when, a year later, Henry died, Eastman wrote Henry's son Albert: "It is sad to contemplate the passing of such good men as Cousin Henry. Even when the body is worn out and the mind weakened it seems hard to let them go." And further to Almon: "The time always comes when it is better to go than stay and I suppose we must face the thing philosophically." (Eastman apparently did face Almon's death in 1924 at age eighty-three philosophically because he had been ill for a long time with no hope of recovery. After Almon's death, Eastman stepped up his letters and visits to Delia in Waterville, because she was now alone and had been so dependent on her husband.)

He began talking in an abstract way about the "right to die," his dislike of monuments, and his advocacy of cremation: "I am thoroughly out of sympathy with any proposition which looks to the preservation of human corpses. I am an advocate of cremation and think that the very last thing that should be done would be to cumber the soil with a lot of concrete boxes containing festering human matter."[39] Since the carbuncle of 1888 that "nearly snuffed out my life," he had not been really sick. In 1917 he bragged to have climbed Mount Whitney "about 2,500 ft. from where we left our horses. This took about four hours. I was particularly well pleased that old age does not yet prevent my climbing as high as 14,500 ft. Also that I could go into the mountain streams every morning for a cold bath."[40] Well into his sixties his unlined face gave him such a youthful appearance that strangers to Kodak asked to see his father, assuming he was too young to be the head of such an enterprise. But by 1927 his vigor was declining. "An hour or two a day is all that I spend at the office and I take a nap of about an hour in the middle of the day when I go home to lunch, something I have never done before. So far I have not discovered that there is anything special the matter with me but I am having some investigations made at the Medical School." He had tests done at the Mayo Clinic as well. "I am suffering much from colds," he wrote friends. "I take a 'shotgun' vaccine every week. My physician is skeptical." The man who used to sit through two opera performances a day now worried that "I could not sit through an opera at all." The man who wrote two hundred thousand letters now said, "It worries me exceedingly to have to write anything and I am getting too old to make the effort. . . . This weakness is hanging on from my cold. I had myself examined by the experts at the Medical School but they could not find anything the matter with me except old age." On 2 June 1927 Audley Stewart consulted with William McCann of the university's medical center regarding a respiratory infection that tired Eastman unduly and disturbed his sleep. Records show that his prostate gland was enlarged (but not cancerous) and that he had moderate senile arteriosclerosis. Contrary to persistent rumor of later years, cancer was not found, his gastrointestinal series was negative, and the Wasserman test of 1927 was negative—which squelches the rumor that he suffered from syphilis. In October 1928 his medical records list an umbilical hernia, edema, and congestive heart failure. During 1929 the edema increased, his heart was

flabby, and he complained of insomnia as well as nausea from digitalis tox-
icity. Arthritis of spine and hips was getting worse. Probably most emo-
tionally painful for such a fastidious man, he experienced urinary inconti-
nence day and night. Walter Alvares of the Mayo Clinic was called in and his
prognosis was guarded but bleak. Eastman took the news quietly. He could
look for no improvement.[41]

Periodically he perked up. "My health is excellent," he snorted in 1928.
Yet later that year he admitted that "nowadays I am only spending about two
or three hours at business. . . . I go home to luncheon and take a nap immediately after." The opening of his new penthouse office in 1931 brought
another revival of spirits, but when he received a letter from his old bank
colleague, Tom Chester, age eighty-six, "ten years more than I am," he
noted:

> I see you are in about the same condition I am; you have to have your
> letters written by a nurse. For six months I have been in the hands of a
> nurse. She does not do much except hand me different kinds of pills, or
> drinks, some of which are very good . . . orange juice with lemon, . . .
> or extract of liver which is not only dirty looking but dirty tasting.
> However, I am able to get around the house and strong enough to read
> murder mysteries. My average per day is just under two. I have not been
> down to business.[42]

He resigned as president of the Rochester Community Chest and from many
other boards. "I am getting to a time in life where I am withdrawing from all
activities of this kind . . . finding it necessary to cut out all such functions."
Just before going to Africa for second time he came down with a painful
attack of the shingles. He rallied and went to Africa, but photos taken of him
on that second trip show a rapidly aging and not very happy Eastman.

In December 1929 he cancelled a trip to New York where he planned to
spend Christmas with Ellen Maria Dryden Moller and her family, which then
included two small children. "It was just as well I staid home," he told Agnes
Cromwell, "because I had a little attack Christmas." Earlier that fall he had
been at Oak Lodge "and staid in the house pretty much all the time which is
quite unusual for me. . . . I do not feel sick but just good for nothing. The
joke of it all is that it does not seem to worry me much to remain at home. I
spend most of my waking hours alternately lying on the sofa and reading
murder stories. I am in the midst of one that has already disposed of three
crooks and it is not finished yet."[43]

By March 1930 he was still confined to the house, getting out for a ride
occasionally and to the office about once a week. William Stuber, president of
the Eastman Kodak Company, sent him a special "emulsion" for his health:
"Take 15 drops of Tincture of Iodine in a glass of water twice a day, for 10

days. After this repeat the dose once a week for four weeks and then once a month indefinitely. Before retiring take a drink of Scotch or Rye whiskey in a large glass of hot water. . . . I have used this for the past four years and have found it very beneficial."[44]

Eastman's final major trip to the Pacific coast in 1930 was an attempt to move the clock back to "accumulate the pep I have lost," as he told Charles Edison. He had been confined to the house for three months, going out for an automobile ride "only when I feel like it which is not necessarily every day because I am very comfortable in the house. Sitting by the fire, dozing on the sofa, and reading murder stories is not so bad as you may think," he told Nell Newhall, but then decided that a geographical cure and one last hunt for the Kodiak and grizzly bears that had so far eluded him might do what the doctors could not. At Easter the Dryden family was with him at Oak Lodge as he enjoyed vicariously tales of the three-month African safari George and Eastman Dryden had just spent with the Johnsons.[45]

"To ascertain whether a change would buck me up," he explained to Helen Carter, "I undertook a trip which I enjoyed very much although it did not buck me up any too much." But he gave it his all. He dismissed Minnie Mason, the nurse who had accompanied him to Oak Lodge, chartered Campbell Church's *Westward*, invited Campbell Jr., the owner's son who on an earlier trip had been a crew member, along with his young wife to come along as guests, lined up Audley Stewart, and left Rochester for Prince Rupert north of Vancouver on 18 May 1930.[46]

Friends were worrying about him. George Dryden wrote a letter to Charlie Hutchison marked "Please destroy." (Alice Whitney Hutchison filed it.) "I was with Mr Eastman on his [private railroad] car when he passed through Chicago," Dryden wrote. "To me he appeared to be very weak and seems to have lost his usual pep."[47] Alice kept everyone at bay by explaining that he would be gone six weeks for his health and no mail would be forwarded. "The bears in June have just come out of their winter haunts and are mostly near the shore looking for salmon," Eastman wrote. He got his bear, but in a somewhat farcical way for a man who had faced a rhino's charge. "The grizzly was seen from the yacht . . . while I was reading in the cabin with no expectation of hunting any more that day." Since Eastman had trouble walking, Church suggested they slip off the yacht and stalk by canoe. Even his own gun was gone; Stewart had borrowed it to go off hunting *on foot* and it was a mortification to Eastman that he was not able to do the same. So he grabbed the gun at hand that had telescopic sights ("my eyes are getting too old to use an open sight") and started out. "He did the paddling and when we got to within eighty to ninety yards of the bear on shore I let him have it. There was plenty of light and it was an easy shot. It was too late to skin him so punctured him and left him where he was until the next morning."[48]

On 25 June the *Westward* was back in Vancouver and Eastman felt well enough to make one last swing around the west by private railroad car. The itinerary went from Seattle to Portland, then to Yosemite and on to San Francisco where they stayed five days. In Los Angeles the morning was spent with Kodak people and the afternoon at the Fox studios, traveling about California in the limousine belonging to Jules Brulatour, who had shifted his working headquarters from New York to California, following the movie industry. He was pleased with Kodak's "outfit at Hollywood . . . tasteful and not too extravagant, considering the surroundings. The only thing I criticized was the lighting in the auditorium and I frankly gave some suggestions." The lion in winter told Brulatour that "I think it is our duty to set an example in lighting." He flew over the city in the Goodyear blimp—"My first ride in a lighter than air machine."[49] Then on to Pasadena to see the Huntington Library and art collection, which included some superb Gainsborough and Reynolds paintings, including the *Blue Boy* he had once hung in Eastman House and sent back.[50]

In Pasadena he called on Susan Brown, whom he had long ago dispatched to Europe with a bunch of violets when they were both quite young, who had written him love letters when he was a youth, and who had rekindled the friendship with a letter in 1927. At that reunion he invited her to visit Eastman House. Next to San Diego and the Grand Canyon, where he celebrated his seventy-sixth birthday by going to the kitchen and watching the chef prepare his cake. Once home he noted in green pencil that he weighed 142 pounds. "I covered the whole coast from Juneau down to Agua Caliente in Mexico where the gambling hell is," he told "Dearest Nell. . . . It is uncertain when, if ever, I shall get out to the Northwest again. I am afraid my hunting days are over."[51]

Susan Brown did indeed make a "memorable visit to you" at Eastman House in September 1930; for a few days fifty intervening years were minimized. Eastman pulled out an impressive array of photographic scrapbooks replete with his "chronicles of many adventures" as the two sat on the leather sofa before the fire in the sitting room. His boyhood friend soaked up the ambience of flowers and music "rolling out of those great organs," admitting later that "not a day has passed that thoughts of you have not been in my mind, as you are ever enshrined in my heart." Once back in Pasadena, Susan in her seventies was acutely aware that roles were now reversed. Her promising musical career had never taken off, while the anonymous bank clerk's name had become a household modifier to the famous Kodak trademark. She continued to begin her letters, "Dear George Eastman," even while confessing to a "love that never dies." Although "you have received no letter in visible form," Susan wrote, "many many are lying at Love's dead-letter office, unclaimed by you."[52]

When Eastman sent her the cleaned-up, dried-up Ackerman biography, she put off reading it, fearing that it would further distance them by "taking

you from me—emphasizing your greatness and, by contrast, my insignifi-
cance!" In reply, Eastman ignored Brown's references to love and friendship
but immediately picked up on Chiang, Susan's little sick dog, which reminded him of his first dog, the one the Erie Canal boatman stole, and he
continued to live out their relationship through sanitized correspondence.
"I cried all night," he remembered. "I never had another dog," he wrote,
conveniently forgetting all the hunting dogs, to say nothing of Herro, his
guard dog of the 1920s who bit people. "It's a shame you never had another
dog," Brown finally replied, tongue in cheek, "and worse still that you never
helped people Rochester with your *own* children."[53]

In September 1931 Thomas A. Edison died. "He did more than any other
man has done to make this world an easier, pleasanter, better world to live
in," said Eastman through his PR department. "His death closes a career that
set the tempo for an unparalleled era of invention. For the most part, his
accomplishments will be measured from the standpoint of pure science.
But . . . along with his wizardry in matters electrical went a human kindliness that endeared him to the whole world. Our relations began early—in
1882 I think it was—when we purchased a small electric lighting plant from
Edison for the rooms where our chemical work was done. But the most
interesting incident was in 1889, when Edison was working to perfect his
Kinetoscope, a nickel-in-the-slot machine, where, after dropping the nickel,
one peered through a peep-hole and saw a few feet of motion pictures—the
forerunner of the present screen pictures. He had been unable to get a
suitable material for his negatives and prints, when one day he heard about
the transparent Kodak film. He sent for a few feet, and after a trial said,
'We've got it boys. Now work like H____l.'"[54]

While Eastman could remember his association with Edison with pleasure
and accept his passing after a long and fruitful life, he was less sanguine
about the last illness (perhaps Alzheimer's) of his longtime friend and attorney, Walter Hubbell. Confined to his bed for over two years, Hubbell died in
January 1932. Eastman saw it as "a gruesome death . . . one of the finest
minds I have ever known reduced to a doddering idiot," and he was profoundly affected.[55]

Fausta Menignari, Italian sculptor, came to live at Eastman House for a
month or so in 1930 while she worked on a bust for the Rome and Paris
dental clinics. The bust—a form of art that Eastman hated—portrayed Eastman as haughty and an imperial, hooknosed, and tight-lipped Old Roman.
The bust, which the clinics thought magnificent and the Harrow museum
asked to acquire, was reproduced on the cover of the commemorative program of the February 1931 Society of the Genesee tribute to Eastman. After
a decade of saying No, No, No, he capitulated to Thomas Watson, another

Upstate New York business genius, entrepreneur, and IBM founder, whom Eastman greatly admired, and literally dragged himself to New York for the ordeal of the public tribute. He shut himself up in a hotel room and refused to see anyone but old friends—Frank Babbott, Hattie Strong—until he was escorted into a cavernous coliseum of 1,200 noisy well-wishers. He then dragged George Dryden to sit next to him at the head table because, as he told Dryden, "I don't have to talk to you."[56]

"I just can't imagine you sitting really at ease in that throne-like chair," chortled Susan Brown. "I believe Dr. Rhees right when he calls you incorrigibly modest, and half say 'Thank Heaven that he is'—but such being the case can imagine how you must have mentally squirmed as he told you to your face what Rochester thinks of you." Susan further wrote about her enchantment with the 1857 ambrotype of Eastman, age three, reproduced in the Ackerman book, "before that beautiful mouth had thinned into a line" and suggested that his string quartet play Cesar Franck's quintet in E Minor "in memory of me." She closed her last letter to him with the last word:

"Good by, elusive friend."[57]

"My Work Is Done"

■ ■·━━━━━━━━━━━━━━━━━━━━━━━━━━━━━━━

"I just want to fade away, not go out with a bang," George Eastman said when he retired.[1] It was not to be. The final act of his life was a dramatic one and, like everything else in it, carefully planned and executed.

Death was no stranger to him. His father died after a chronic, deteriorating illness of at least a year. He had watched his mother's slow, debilitating death; she spent the last two years in a wheelchair. When she was gone, he "cried all day. I couldn't help myself." And then he told friends: "I don't want to live that long." One sister was in a wheelchair all her short life and died at twenty, the other died at forty, leaving two young children.

Close business associates Charles Abbott, Frank Noble, and George Dickman succumbed unexpectedly and painfully in the prime of life. Josephine Dickman, Mary Mulligan, Louise Gifford, and Lillian Norton all died before their time. Walter Hubbell, George Todd, and James Havens suffered protracted illnesses while their faculties deteriorated. These cases greatly distressed Eastman. "God keep me from being like them," he said. "Doesn't it seem strange that the clearest minds I have ever known should be taken this way?" he asked rhetorically. "That is the sad thing about illness."[2]

In 1912 he had the macabre experience of reading his own obituary and was not at all affected. Among those listed as having gone down with the *Titanic* was a Mr. Eastman. A San Francisco newspaper wrote that George Eastman, founder of Kodak, had perished, and the report spread. While not subscribing to a belief in any afterlife, he was never morose about his final demise. Indeed, once when Eastman was greeting guests he overheard a man ask Charlie Hutchison, then Kodak's chief emulsion maker, what would happen to the mansion if anything happened to Eastman. Hutchison's reply was: "Oh, I imagine he'll leave it as a home for retired emulsion makers." Eastman was so convulsed with laughter that the reception line was temporarily thrown out of gear.[3]

He thought about death when he was still in good health, expressing strong feelings about graveyards cluttering up the landscape and the advantages of cremation. He had always controlled the circumstances of his life; as his health began to fail, particularly control over bodily functions, he discovered the one area beyond his power of direction. Nothing in his life prepared him to face the indignities of old age. The dread of living with a darkened mind, of not being able to deal with people, issues, or the disposal of property with his wits intact—these were the fears that gathered in Eastman's mind as old friends, one after another, said farewell to earth and he began to retire to the loneliness of old age.

His philosophy of life was one of work and service and when the work was done, rest. More and more the correspondence of his last decade foretold his last words. When considering one philanthropy or another, he would end with: "I am convinced my work in that area is done." Or he would say, "Others can carry on. My real work is done." Once, in 1928, he wrote: "Most of my stuff is finished. I am getting pretty well down to the dregs now and it is not feasible for me to take on anything new. I am just cleaning up."[4] Or he would write: "I am trying to pull off another trip to Africa this winter and then I guess I will be about through."[5]

His friends and acquaintances, beginning with Helen Strong, were always after George Eastman to adopt a religious attitude toward life. The humanistic philosophy remained even though some of his best friends were clergymen with whom he enjoyed debating the ethics of suicide. "What can a man do about getting old?" he would ask George Norton. "It's the one thing you can't beat. It gets you in the end."

"What do you think of suicide?" he would further bait Norton, a man whose friendship he cemented when in his seventies. "Take for example a man with an incurable disease who has discharged all his obligations and has no one dependent on him. What is there ethically against his committing suicide?" Norton would patiently explain that every man has some influence in the world and that we owe it to others not to let them down but to live as long as we can. "By God," Eastman exploded, "I don't owe any man a damned thing."[6]

He tried the same sentiments out on his doctors. No one seemed to notice the uncharacteristic self-pity creeping in, or the cry of a lonely man: "When a man is alone and hasn't anybody interested in him, there's no reason for getting old. If he has a family, it different of course." He quizzed Audley Stewart, his regular physician, about the efficacy of strychnine, dropping the subject when he learned it caused convulsions. Another time he said abruptly, "Audley, you're always listening to my heart. Just where is it?" Dr. Stewart gave a professional thump or two.

"Outline it for me."[7]

Late in 1930 Eastman's physical deterioration was diagnosed by specialists from the Mayo Clinic and Strong Memorial Hospital as hardening of the cells in the lower spinal cord. Stewart called it atherosclerosis of the spinal cord. This affected the nerves leading to his legs and made him unsteady on his feet. (Physicians in the 1990s speculate that today's CAT scan might reveal that he suffered from spinal stenosis, a condition that makes walking difficult and painful.)[8] The condition was beginning to affect the nerves leading to the vital organs.

The once vigorous man accustomed to bounding up stairs two at a time now shuffled along in great pain, inexplicably weepy and depressed, dragging one foot behind. Stephen Cornell, head of Canadian Kodak, found Eastman leaning against a wall as he made his way from his office to the elevator and Cornell's eyes filled with tears. Aware that employees were observing his physical failings, Eastman more and more stayed away from the office and had Alice Whitney Hutchison walk across the grand vista between their two homes to take dictation. George Whipple said years later: "The only period of Mr. Eastman's life that really bothered him was the last few months, when he was deteriorating pretty rapidly and losing control of his sphincters." Eastman again asked for a prognosis and Audley Stewart replied that the condition was progressive and irreversible. Eastman knew he was headed for invalid status—confined to chair or bed, waited on constantly by nurses.[9]

When Martin and Osa Johnson arrived to celebrate his seventy-seventh birthday, Eastman called H. R. Patterson, Frank Crouch's son-in-law and a Camera Works employee. "I want you to show the Johnsons all through the new tower," he told Patterson. "I'm not sure I'd better go with you. Can you act as guide?" Then he tried to tag along anyway but failed at the bottom of the circular stairway leading to the observation platform. Clinging to the railing, he motioned the others ahead. Then from the platform, Patterson heard him calling for help so he returned and assisted the boss up the stairs to the top. Once on the platform he just stood there for a while looking out, then pointed out the landmarks of his life: the house on Jones Avenue where he lived when he started the business, the Ambrose Street house where he lived when the Kodak camera and transparent film were first marketed, the Soule House at 1050 East Avenue, then 900 East Avenue, the Eastman School of Music, Kodak Park, and the Hawk-Eye factory hard by the lower falls of the Genesee River. His whole life lay before him in a panorama: the physical evidence of his trials and successes. The new Kodak tower in which he stood was George Eastman's last building project. He would never set foot in it again.[10]

Methodically he said goodbye to old favorites in a wobbly hand.

DEAREST NELL,

I got back from the Drydens, having had a very quiet, agreeable time. My routine was after a late breakfast to sit on the porch and doze all day until late in the afternoon, when George and his chauffeur would take us out to ride in the cool of the evening. Any spare time I used reading murder stories. . . . After a grapefruit I went to bed at half past ten.

I took the nurse with me . . . and she did not have a very strenuous time; just seeing that the different kinds of pills were handed to me at the right time and not too many of them. I was willing to take them in almost any amount unless I was safeguarded. . . .

Sister [Ellen Maria Dryden Moller] has developed a real flair for building and furnishing and has a most admirable outfit. She keeps the kids in one compartment, where they can be washed up and taken out and paraded without annoying the guests.

I have settled down to a realization that my work is done; and also a realization that I have built up an organization that can operate the very complicated work of the company with at least as good results as have ever been attained before.

The thing that annoys me most is that I cannot write letters as fluently as I would like to. . . . I like to get letters from you, as many as you can find time to write, if you will only let me make an occasional postcard take the place of a good long letter. . . .

With lots of love
Uncle George[11]

Retiring to the sun belt never crossed his mind. Ever the confirmed Rochesterian, he wrote Minna Edison in February 1932 that "I would rather spend my winters in Rochester than so far south. We have had some beautiful winter days . . . very little snow but a falling almost every day or two so that the ground has been white and clean, which makes a very pleasant outlook."

The Wednesday dinners grew fewer, then ceased. The Sunday musicales dwindled from 150 guests to only a handful; finally the musicians played to an empty house, with the owner confined to his room. The pile of murder mysteries grew as Eastman feverishly read and reread them, tossing them uncharacteristiclly on the floor as he finished another volume. (Stewart later speculated that he read at least one detective story a day looking for the perfect death potion.) Many of the books came from Scrantom's, the shop where as a boy he had scooped up armsful of Oliver Optic stories. Now it was Harvey Padelford's turn to scoop up the latest thrillers for him. Mysteries and cowboy stories had pulled him through the crisis of 1882 when he woke up in a cold sweat fearful that the spoiled plates would destroy his business; perhaps he felt they might prop up his waning vigor now that he could no longer embark on adventures himself. When Eastman read he usually sat for hours at a time on a leather setee, placed between two long couches in front of the fireplace in his sitting room, always dressed in a business suit and shoes, not slippers. No one had to read to him although Minnie Mason, his nurse, or Molly Cherbuliez, his housekeeper, tuned the radio for him all day and late into the evening. They selected musical programs; he listened and read at the same time unless it was the Rochester Philharmonic or something special. Then he would lay aside the book. After 11 P.M. Miss Mason let him tune for himself. He joked with her a bit. Once when he had trouble getting up from the couch, she said, "Let me at him; I'll get him up!" Audley Stewart commented, "The powerful Katrinka!" and henceforth Eastman called her that. In going through doors he would wait for her to precede and then say "Scat, Powerful Katrinka," pretending to shoo her through. The dread of being dependent and unable to manage his own affairs loomed larger and larger. And the hard truth is that he was unnecessarily isolated from friends and visitors by overzealous hired help soliticious for his health.[12]

"There isn't much to live for," he told George Norton. "All that most people come here for is to have me sign on the dotted line." When he witnessed Eastman practically begging his guests not to leave, Norton agonized, remembering the crisp independence of earlier years.

During Thanksgiving of 1931 at Oak Lodge with the Whipples and the Drydens a curious choking sound in the middle of the night brought the guests rushing to his bedside. It was only a nightmare. Later, George Whipple said: "It would have been so fitting if he could have died there, in the place he dearly loved, the one place where he could relax."[13] Upon returning to Rochester he fell in his bath and had to call for Young and Nathaniel to carry him back to bed. He spent most of his time in the large bedroom suite in the southwest corner, so carefully shielded that he began to think all his friends had deserted him. The public had no notion that he was ill. The Drydens knew he was sickly but not that he was despondent: he wrote them about going to Oak Lodge in the spring.

"Instead of Young to attend him," Katharine Whipple said, "he was surrounded by grim old grey-haired nurses. . . . That dragon of a housekeeper grew more and more vitriolic and impossible as his friends were not allowed to see him . . . lonely and seemingly forsaken, with all the money in the world."

"I wish you would come over and have lunch with me," he told Katharine when he finally got to a phone.[14]

"I wish you would stop in regularly so I can have something to look forward to," he told Norton.

On the fourth of March he returned the key to the garage of the Eastman School of Music with the note, "I shall not be needing this any more." On the eighth he wrote to May Gifford that he was so "discouraged about getting my writing hand in shape so you could read it" that he was resorting to the typewriter. "I wish you would write to me and let me know how you are but do not expect me to write you. . . . I am sitting up every day and usually go out for a ride but am not any stronger." He wrote that he was "laying my plans to go down to Oak Lodge about the 12th of April," indicating that at that moment, at least, no irreversible decision had been reached (unless, of course, he was deliberately trying to divert suspicion). He wrote Ellen that he was "ordering a private car for . . . the 12th of April. Let me know if that will suit you and George. Who would you like to have go down with us?" He wrote R. C. Dunn, his Enfield lawyer, that he would "wait until I get down to the Lodge about the middle of April before deciding about matters." Vivrette, the white supervisor, was not working out any better than Henry. Indeed after Eastman's death, Alice Whitney Hutchison declined to pay Vivrette for four cows he had purchased because "the amount is so in excess of the estimate quoted Mr. Eastman February 10."

The mess at Oak Lodge and the thought of trying to cope with it in April may have forced his hand. On 9 March he wrote some letters of introduction to Lord Riddell and Reginald Garratt for Rush Rhees, then leaving for Europe. On 11 March he wrote his goodbyes to Agnes Cromwell:

> I have thought of you many times but have not been in shape to write anything cheerful.
>
> For several months I have not been out to business except on special occasions for a few hours. While I have not been ill in bed at any time I have not had energy enough to do anything worthwhile.
>
> It is not likely that I shall get down to New York in the near future so there is no prospect of seeing you much as I would like to. I wish very much that I might see you and have a talk with you.[15]

On 12 March he told publishers Houghton-Mifflin, who asked if they should send him 350 copies of Ackerman's *George Eastman*, that he had "all the copies of my biography that I shall want."

Unfinished business, relating to some $8 million in cash and $14 million in high-grade bonds and stock still in his possession, haunted him.[16] By the terms of his will Ellen would get $200,000 outright, plus Oak Lodge, and her children would receive $100,000 each. These were the largest personal bequests, followed by a long list of smaller amounts for the household staff. The pearl stick pin, purchased at Tiffany's in London in 1898, was to go to Frank Lovejoy, the only employee mentioned. (The will, however, was drawn up in 1925 and the stick pin was lost in the African train fire.)

On Wednesday 9 March, Kodak attorney Milton K. Robinson was summoned to draw up new codicils. Robinson was surprised; he had never done any of Eastman's personal work. Alice always typed the will and codicils with amounts left blank. Witnesses never saw anything but the last page.

Excluding the personal bequests, Eastman had decided to leave everything to the University of Rochester, eliminating MIT and Cornell from an earlier version of the will. "I've done other things for them," he told Robinson.[17] His house was to go to the university as well, designated as the official presidential residence, with a $2 million endowment for upkeep.

The will was very long and took several days to revise, but Eastman was patient and even seemed more cheerful. He made sure the dental dispensary contracts were worded with such precision that they could not be changed after his death: "Suppose something were to happen to me. Would there be any hitch? Are these contracts clear as to how the money should be paid in Europe and set up so that Burkhart can act?"

He insisted on looking over each contract Alice brought, almost as a delaying tactic. Robinson read them out loud one clause at a time as Eastman slowly paced the room. Then he looked each one over again and finally said, "Yes, I guess that's right."

"There was an extra caution and shrewdness about him that week," Robinson would recall. "He was not in bed. One foot dragged—but his mind was clear and without my asking he told me why he was making the changes." But Robinson also saw "an old man chained to a nurse and a housekeeper, who were keeping people away. Why? He's never been a recluse," Robinson thought, "but a leader of his social set and the envy of thousands of people."[18]

Wednesday it snowed and snowed; a school bus full of children was stuck for a time in a drift. When the driver went for help, the older children cared for the younger ones and a jolly time was had until rescuers appeared. Thursday, Eastman wanted to see the drift where the incident occurred and invited the Whipples to accompany him. "The trained nurse went along, sitting with the chauffeur and turning around to interrupt in a maddening manner," Katharine Whipple remembered. "He talked very little, and seemed rather limp. Once or twice he said, 'You don't know how grateful I am to you for coming with me this afternoon.'" Then subtly, with just a "turn left here" or "right there" he began guiding the tour. In a roundabout way the car passed Kodak Park, glided into town by Kodak Office, took off along the Genesee toward the medical school, by the hospital and river campus and back into town to glimpse the music school and theater, the women's campus, and the dental dispensary.

"I knew afterwards he was seeing it for the last time and saying goodbye. I am glad I didn't know it then."[19]

On Friday Harvey Burkhart stopped by before leaving for Europe on the business of establishing dental clinics in Paris, Stockholm, and Brussels. He walked to the window in Eastman's bedroom and looked down on a sea of icy-covered branches glistening in the sun. He commented on its beauty. Eastman agreed. When Burkhart started for the door, Eastman raised his hand to object. "Don't go yet. Stay a little longer," he pleaded.[20]

Saturday Eastman called Robinson back with more changes to the will, which would be signed Monday. Eastman specified his witnesses—Frank Crouch, Marion Folsom, Albert K. Chapman. "What about Jean Hargrave?" he asked. Eastman was concerned that Hargrave was going to feel left out, but wondered, "Could an attorney also be a witness?" New York law required two witnesses; Eastman always had at least three. George Dryden was in town that day and enjoyed a champagne lunch with Eastman. Sunday at noon the Whipples called for an appointment to return. "We spoke to the butler who spoke to the housekeeper who spoke to the nurse." They were allotted fifteen minutes.

When Katharine went to kiss Eastman goodbye, she noticed how feeble he appeared in his dressing gown. He had difficulty in rising and she had to brace herself to steady him. At the door she couldn't bring herself to turn around "to make the usual silly remark and blow him a kiss." Outside, her husband said, "He looked at you as if he never expected to see you again."

Sunday evening Eastman sat silently before the embers of a dying fire with Harold Gleason: "We sat together . . . without a word being said, although I had a strange feeling that he wanted to tell me something. Finally, as the nurse appeared, he said, 'Goodbye Harold.' He waited a moment and in almost a whisper continued, 'Don't let anything happen to the School.'"[21]

Monday, 14 March 1932, young Elizabeth Vaughn arrived as usual to provide the breakfast music. "Don't play this morning," Eastman said. "Come and talk to me instead." Elizabeth's teacher from Leipzig was visiting. "Yes, bring him to see the organ," Eastman said, "but I can't meet him." During their visit the nurse went by the door, clearing her throat each time. Elizabeth stood up to go and he took both her hands in his. "Tell your teacher how much I enjoyed your playing," he said, slowly kissing both of her hands and cheeks.[22]

Alice Hutchison came in to take dictation and recorded one letter—to Thomas Jean Hargrave, attorney and Kodak vice president:

MY DEAR HARGRAVE:—

In naming Robinson as attorney to handle my will I don't want you to think that this action is prompted by any lack of confidence in or regard for you but merely because I want to do something for him personally in return for many personal services that he has rendered me.

As you know I have the highest regard for you and in fact it was largely my idea that you occupy your present position in the Kodak Company.

I am also very glad to include you personally as one of the attorneys in the matter of my will.[23]

Alice did not type the letter until several days later and so it was never signed.

At 11:15 the Kodak contingent arrived. "We had a nice, normal visit," Chapman recalled. Eastman insisted on placing their chairs for them in his room and even joked with Frank Crouch. The fountain pen balked as he began to sign the will and Crouch suggested that he could afford to buy a new one.[24]

"You shouldn't kick about this pen, Crouch. You gave it to me."

Eastman signed, and the witnesses after him. As they left Alice came in to get the will and he reminded her of his practice of giving anyone who witnessed his signature a $10 gold piece. As she started toward the door, he called to her, "Oh, Miss Whitney, get them $20 gold pieces." When Mrs. Hutchison reached the bottom of the stairs she wondered if she had heard right and returned to the bedroom. On the way she met the nurse and the two walked toward the door. The nurse opened it without knocking. Eastman was standing with his back to them. He wheeled around and seemed angry.

"Did you say $20 gold pieces?" the secretary wondered.

"That's right." He laughed with relief. The women closed the door.

He put a Lucky Strike in a small black and gold folding holder, smoked it, and snuffed it out. He placed the cigarette in an ash tray, and carefully refolded the holder. He capped his pen, removed his glasses and skull cap, lay down on the bed, folding a wet towel over his chest to prevent powder burns, pointed the muzzle of a Luger automatic to the spot Stewart had outlined, and pulled the trigger. It was 12:50 P.M.

Alice heard the crack from the stairs and rushed back. On the night table was a piece of yellow-lined paper with the words in balky ink:

> To my friends
> My work is done—
> Why wait?
> GE[25]

Next to the note was his mother's sewing basket. Inside, two of her gloves were rolled up into tight little balls.[26] Later found, hidden in the bookcase, was a second Luger. Eastman covered the alternative to the last.[27]

Audley Stewart and George Norton were called but when they came Nathaniel Myrick could not speak in greeting. Leroy Snyder of the *Times-Union* was summoned to handle publicity but when his own reporters arrived he turned them away without explanation. The stock market was shaky enough from the suicide of the match king Ivan Krueger, aged fifty, another prominent capitalist. Snyder pocketed the Eastman note. In the corridor of the Eastman School a janitor saw the light that illuminated Eastman's portrait for years flicker and go out. When he went for a replacement, he heard of the death.

The Drydens were called and an Evanston operator listened in. She made two calls—to the newspapers and the stock exchange. The news was out. Kodak stock shuddered and slumped six points but within a few days recovered: The company was sound.

Elizabeth Vaughn had gone downtown shopping and saw the black headlines of the first *Times-Union* "EXTRA" starring at her: "GEORGE EASTMAN IS DEAD; END COMES AT HOME HERE." Suicide was not confirmed by the Rochester press until 2 P.M., when a suspicious Hearst reporter said to one of the fifteen uniformed policemen and plainclothesmen enveloping Eastman House: "People say that someone shot Mr. Eastman." "Hell no," the detective snapped back. "He shot himelf."

At the Eastman Kodak Company the elevator boys knew even before the witnesses returned. "Such rumors are common," A. K. Chapman scoffed in disbelief when told. "We just saw him. He was fine."[28]

Tough and taciturn George Whipple wept openly.

The next day, the Ides of March, Lewis Bunnell Jones of the Eastman Kodak Company issued an obituary that began with a personal note: "My anxiety is that he should not be misunderstood: George Eastman played the game to the last. By his own hand he lived his life, and by his own hand he ended it."[29] A simple if massive wreath was affixed to the door of Eastman House. Solomon Young and Nathaniel Myrick, having served Eastman twenty-nine and twenty-one years respectively, stood at attention at the house entrances beginning at 9:30 A.M. when the first "of the almost unending human line filed its way . . . past the casket and out into the yard . . . the procession ending only with arrival of the hour set for the funeral."

A little-known vaudeville performer sent a five-foot high bower of roses with the note, "Thank you for all that you have done for the colored race."

"The tribute which George Eastman, in his modesty, disapproved of in life, was paid to him in death by people of all classes," Frank Gannett's *Times-Union* said.

The funeral took place at 3:30 P.M. on Thursday, 17 March at St. Paul's, an unusual event in itself since at that time death by suicide usually meant no burial from an Episcopal church. Lilies from Eastman's own greenhouses, such as banked the altar in memory of Maria Eastman every Easter since 1908, now filled the sanctuary. George Norton officiated, assisted by Murray Bartlett, president of Hobart and William Smith Colleges, and Bishop Ferris. Rush Rhees read the lesson. The absence of a eulogy of "fulsome praise" in the Episcopal service was "especially fitting," Norton noted, "in view of Mr. Eastman's aversion to pomp and show. . . . His achievement and generosity to mankind are his eulogy."[30]

Admittance to the church was by invitation only, and every seat in the church and parish halls was filled. Active pallbearers were George Whipple, Audley Stewart, Charles Hutchison, Albert Kaiser, Albert K. Chapman, and Martin Johnson. Harvey Burkhart was en route to Europe; Frank L. Babbott in Brooklyn was too ill to attend, and Howard Hanson was inexplicably omitted from the pallbearers.[31] A section was reserved for out-of-town visitors: Osa Johnson, actress Hope Hampton and her husband Jules N. Brulatour, Lord Riddell, Carl Ackerman (now dean of the Pulitzer School of Journalism at Columbia University), president Karl Compton leading the MIT contingent, Charles and Caroline Edison, Theodore Edison, Frank Mattison and the rest of the overseas Kodak complement, among others. World figures from Mussolini to Ghandi sent condolences. Amplifiers on the façade of St. Paul's relayed the service to crowds outside and radio station WHAM carried it nationwide. East Avenue was cordoned off in a scene not duplicated before or since.[32] Silent crowds lined each side of the rain-soaked avenue.

The Massachusetts Institute of Technology and University of Rochester cancelled classes for the afternoon. Besides Kodak, the Red Cross, the Eastman School of Music, the Rochester Dental Dispensary, the Lincoln-Alliance Bank and branches, and the law offices of Hubbell, Taylor, Goodwin, Nixon & Hargrave were closed. At 3:30 P.M. the lights in all Rochester movie houses dimmed for one minute. At the same moment the long-silent bell in A. J. Warner's city hall, which had tolled the end of the Civil War and for Frederick Douglass and Susan B. Anthony's funerals, was struck seventy-seven times, "one blow for each full year of the great industrialist's life."[33]

Inside the church Harold Gleason and the Kilbourn Quartet played Eastman's favorites—movements from the quartets of Haydn and Mozart, Howard Hanson's *Vermeland*, and the *Benedictus* of Max Reger, plus a choral prelude by Bach Eastman would not have requested. For the finale, Gleason had saved his most pointed selection. Back in 1921 at a dinner in honor of Dame Nellie Melba, Gleason had played *Marche Romaine*, a vigorous piece arranged from a Gounod opera but also known as the *Marche Pontificale*, originally composed in 1869 for the Vatican Council that declared Papal Infallibility. Eastman liked it and increasingly asked to hear it. At first he called it simply "the march," then "my march," and by 1929, "my funeral march." The last time Gleason played it for Eastman was during the summer of 1930.

> He was sitting at his breakfast table as if in deep thought. Suddenly he called out in a firm voice, "Harold, please play my funeral march." When I finished he fairly shouted, "We'll give 'em hell when they carry me out the front door.[34]

"'The march' was not the kind of music one would expect to hear at a funeral," Gleason thought as he sat at the organ on 17 March 1932, "but he had never failed me, and I would not fail him. At the conclusion of the service, as the casket was being carried from the church, I began the triumphal 'Marche Romaine' with full organ. The effect was thrilling, and I cannot think of a more appropriate benediction for my friend, George Eastman."[35]

Epilogue:
The Homecoming

■ ▪ ▪ ─────────────────────────────────

"A photograph is a secret about a secret," said photographer Diane Arbus, shortly before she took her own life at age forty-eight. "The more it tells you, the less you know." The same could be said for the act of suicide.

Eastman's suicide was a hard, wrenching experience for his friends. He thought that because he had no immediate family, had taken care of all his obligations, and had his affairs in order that he would not be missed. Optimism and enthusiasm for life were characteristics of the man. His infirmities from an incurable degenerative disease destroyed that enthusiasm and even, apparently, an abstract interest in what was coming next at a fascinating moment in world affairs. He decided that now he was one of those cluttering up the world. Eastman's attitude toward suicide was Roman, not Judaeo-Christian. According to Seneca, one of Eastman's most favored philosophers, the wise man lives as long as he ought, not as long as he can. But his friends were not Roman Stoics.

Audley Stewart, who had lost his father at age seven and had come to think of Eastman as a father, was devastated. "It was a bleak day," he told interviewers many years later. "I never found anything to criticize, or saw him do anything that was not right, except his last act."

Hiram Marks met Rush Rhees at the train station after the latter cut short his European trip. Tears rolled down the cheeks of the university president.

"These are the saddest days I have ever known," Alice Whitney Hutchison wrote.[1] It was 11 April 1932, and she was closing Eastman's office forever.

One of her last duties was the annual order for thousands of Holland bulbs: "This is not a company order. Please send to 900 East Avenue." Replying to a telegram from Robert Moton, principal of Tuskegee, she started to write in the present tense and switched midsentence: "At no time has Mr. Eastman's mentality been affected and he was gaining strength and going out to ride every day, as well as giving daily attention to his correspondence. His sudden passing was a very great shock."

Reaction ran the gamut from shock to grief but there was very little reaction to the suicide itself. The national newspapers were laudatory about Eastman's career and worldwide influence and their editorial eulogies were reverential, "regardless of the nature of the sunset."

Eastman had not provided in his will for Emma Cope Bassatt, his cousin in Los Angeles whom he had been supporting in small ways for years and who was slowly dying of cancer. (In their last exchanges of a lifetime of correspondence, Eastman wrote of his great sympathy for Emma's condition and his thankfulness that he was not suffering from anything so terrible as her disease.) Nor had he provided for the Cope twins at Cornell and Rennsalear Polytechnic Institute. But Alice quickly fixed it with the executors that a trust fund was established and deposited at the University of Rochester and breezily wrote Walter Cope, Emma's brother and the twins' father that "arrangements are being made to pay for Mrs Bassatt's care in Los Angeles from a special fund established by Mr. Eastman so that it will not be necessary for her to go through the ordeal of being moved across the country. . . . From the same fund it will be possible to carry on the expense of the education of your two sons, Donald and Wilfred, which was undertaken by Mr. Eastman."[2] With the Cope transactions, Alice's work of more than forty years as Eastman's only private secretary was done as well. She lived on in retirement and precarious health until April 1937 in the house the Hutchisons had built across the vista from Eastman House. Her husband Charles would reach his centennial year, retiring from Kodak in 1952 and dying in 1974. His bequest of more than $25 million to the University of Rochester made him the third largest donor in the university's history after George Eastman and Joseph C. Wilson, founder of the Xerox Corporation.[3] In 1954 Hutchison anonymously presented the university with a circular monument to George Eastman to be located at the center of the Eastman Quadrangle of the River Campus.

The George Eastman Memorial Monument, with its framework of marble and living trees, was built at Kodak Park in 1934, unveiled in silence by Ellen Dryden on 15 September before one thousand people, and dedicated by

Rush Rhees on behalf of the board of directors of the Eastman Kodak Company. Beneath a massive central stone pillar his ashes are interred in a bronze urn within a steel box. On one side of the stone the carved figure of a woman raises the flame of aspiration and on the opposite side, a crouching male figure represents the science of photography. The monument to the man who did not believe in monuments is simple to the point of starkness with the only inscription, "George Eastman, 1854–1932," on the edge of the disc on which the pillar stands. The monument is in a startling yet significant place: just inside the principal entranceway to Kodak Park, surrounded by that bustling industrial complex—a place where work not rest is the principal activity, the workplace that George Eastman built.

ABBREVIATIONS AND NOTES ON SECONDARY SOURCES

■ ■ ■ ──────────────────────────────────────

Abbreviations

The following abbreviations are used in the notes and photo captions to designate individuals or colletions of primary source materials:

GE: George Eastman

MKE: Maria (pronounced Mah-rye-ah) Kilbourn Eastman

GWE: George Washington Eastman

HAS: Henry Alvah Strong

GEC: George Eastman correspondence. These are letters by Eastman or occasionally members of his staff that have been preserved in forty-one outgoing letter press books, dating 1879–1932, each either one thousand pages or (into the 1920s) five hundred pages in length. These letter books were at the Business Information Center of the Eastman Kodak Company, Rochester, N.Y., when the author did her research but are now at the George Eastman House, International Museum of Photography and Film. Letters dating 1881–84 are missing; only transcribed summaries exist.

INC-GEC: Incoming George Eastman correspondence, filed chronologically in boxes, 1890–32. These, too, were at the Eastman Kodak Company and are now at the George Eastman House.

GEH: George Eastman House, International Museum of Photography and Film, Rochester, N.Y.

HAS: Henry Alvah Strong correspondence, Strong to Eastman, 1884–98. Now at George Eastman House.

EKC: Eastman Kodak Company. As far as the author knows, this material,

SN-EKC: mainly pertaining to Kodak business and employees, is still in the company archives.

SN-EKC: Stenographer's notes for the missing correspondence, 1881–84, Eastman Kodak Company.

UR: Signifies that the collection is in the Department of Rare Books and Special Collections, Rush Rhees Library, University of Rochester. Five collections of materials relating to George Eastman are located here.

     1. RGE-UR: Recollections of George Eastman at the University of Rochester are 137 interviews recorded in 1939 and 1940 for a proposed biography by Andre Maurois. They were conducted under the direction of Frank Lovejoy, president of the Eastman Kodak Company, and Oscar Solbert of Kodak's Public Relations Department.

     2. GEC-UR: George Eastman correspondence at the University of Rochester. The collection consists of over seven hundred letters written between 1864 and 11 March 1932. More that half are personal ones to his mother and niece. Some correspondence belonging to George Washington and Maria Kilbourn Eastman is also here, as well as a journal kept by Maria Eastman.

     3. BUTT-UR: The Eastman Butterfield Collection at the University of Rochester consists of a set of notes, interviews, and printed information gathered in the 1950s by Roger Butterfield as resource material for a proposed biography of Eastman. The collection also contains printed material distributed by Eastman Kodak to its stockholders, notes and clippings about the development of photography in general, and specific information about the Eastman Kodak Company. The collection was the gift of Roger Butterfield to the university in September 1971.

     4. More than four thousand photographs.

     5. ERM: Eastman research materials: newspapers clippings, Whipple scrapbooks relating to Eastman, and certain other scrapbooks and oral histories.

BRAG-UR: Collection of correspondence, architectural plans and drawings, scrapbooks, printed material, and memorabelia relating to Claude Bragdon at the University of Rochester.

MIT: Institute Archives and Special Collections, Massachusetts Institute of Technology Libraries, Cambridge, Mass.

Notes on Secondary Sources

Key secondary works must begin with the only full-length authorized biography: *George Eastman* by Carl W. Ackerman (Boston and New York: Houghton Mifflin, 1930). Commissioned as "a history of the company as I am connected to it" and edited by the subject, it is weak on Eastman's personal side. Long out of print, it may be found in older libraries. The best brief biography is "The Prodigious Life of George Eastman," by Roger Butterfield, *Life* magazine (26 April 1954). The best contemporary interview is Terry Ramsaye's "Little Journeys to the Homes of Famous Film Magnates: George Eastman," *Photoplay* (July 1927):46–47, 109–15. (Ramsaye, Eastman noted, "slings an airy, sketchy and friendly pen.")

Newspaper and magazine coverage began in 1880 with Eastman's advent into dry-plate photography and increased when he introduced the roll holder and paper-backed film in 1884. A lengthy discussion of the Kodak camera, probably written by Eastman himself, was titled "Instantaneous Photography," *Scientific American* (15 September 1888):159, 164.

Eastman's scathing letter corrected the *New York Sun*'s draft of "George Eastman, the Man behind the Kodak." But that article, finally published 3 November 1912, p. 5, was the first authorized newspaper biography. Earlier, he had written, or at least approved, the entry about himself appearing in Guy S. Rix, *Eastman Family of America* (Concord, N.H.: Press of I. C. Evans, 1901), 801–6. Other Kilbourn and Eastman genealogy sources include *Genealogy of the Harvey Eastman (1777–1829) Branch of the Eastman Family* (privately printed, 1917), commissioned by George Eastman, researched and written by Charles R. Eastman and others (EKC); *History of the Kilbourn Family* (privately printed, 1917), commissioned by Eastman (EKC); *Ballard Genealogy* (unpublished ms., n.d.), available at the University of Rochester Library.

Herbert L. Baldwin's "Life Story of George Eastman the Kodak King" was published in seven installments by the *Boston Post* ("a somewhat sensational paper of large circulation," Eastman wrote), beginning 1 February 1920. "Philanthropy under a Bushel" appeared 21 March 1920 in the *New York Times*. Samuel McCoy, "Eastman Embarks on a New Adventure: Gives Away His Wealth and Seeks Broader Life in Watching Benefits of Philanthropy, appeared in the *New York Times Magazine*, 28 December 1924. Shorter articles from the *Times* and *Rochester Democrat & Chronicle* (the latter is unindexed) are too numerous to list.

Newspaper and magazine coverage was extensive at the time of Eastman's death. The *New York Times* covered it on the front page and editorial page, with articles on inside pages and in subsequent editions. Exhaustive coverage was given in all five Rochester papers. Lewis B. Jones's lengthy obituary, *Rochester Democrat & Chronicle*, 15 March 1932, 2, 4, was published by Kodak as a pamphlet and distributed gratis for years. Eastman's controversial will was published in many papers in 5 April 1932 editions. The Massachusetts Institute of Technology covered his death at length in publications, as it had earlier written about him as the once-anonymous benefactor who built a whole new campus for the school.

Oscar Solbert's "George Eastman, Amateur," *Image* (November 1953):49–56—reprinted as a pamphlet—and Beaumont Newhall's "The Photographic Inventions of George Eastman," *Journal of Photographic Science* (March–April 1955):33–40, deal with Eastman as pioneer in photography for the masses.

Summary information appears in *Who Was Who in America, 1897–1942*, in encyclopedia articles, and in *Eastman Kodak Company: A Brief History*, published for Kodak's centennial, 1980. Longer sketches are in the *Dictionary of American Biography* (New York: Scribner's, 1944), 21:274–76; and *The National Cyclopedia of American Biography* (New York: James T. White, 1937), 26:32–33.

The *University of Rochester Library Bulletin* 26, no. 3 (Spring 1971) is devoted to reminiscences by Roger Butterfield, Marion Folsom, Howard Hanson, Marion Gleason, Harold Gleason, Enid Knapp Botsford, Arthur May, and George W. Goddard. Other *Library Bulletin* articles include "'Key' to the Eastman Scrapbook," by Katharine Whipple ([Fall 1965]:4–18); and "My Friend George Eastman," by George E. Norton ([Fall 1967]:3–13). The University of Rochester printed Roger Butterfield's "George Eastman's Vision of University" and reminiscences by Ernest Pavior and Howard Hanson in its *Rochester Review* (September 1954):10–13, 26–30.

Three volumes of Blake McKelvey's four-volume history of Rochester trace Eastman's influence on the city, as do the magazine *Rochester History* (1939 to date) and the Rochester Historical Society's *Publication Fund Series* (1922–48, 24 vols). The most complete account is in McKelvey's *Rochester, the Quest for Quality, 1890–1925* (Cambridge: Harvard University Press, 1956).

Celebrating the centennial of Eastman's birth, *Rochester Commerce* (July 1954) featured articles by Frank E. Gannett, Ernest Pavior, Thomas F. Robertson, Lee McCanne, Dr. Albert Kaiser, Arthur Kelly, Dr. Audley Stewart, and Blake McKelvey. The Rochester Historical Society's *Genesee Country Scrapbook* for 1954 included the first publication of some Eastman letters written during his boyhood and on his first trip abroad plus reminiscences by the Rev. George Norton, John R. Slater, Frank Gannett, Caroline Werner Gannett, and Francis S. Macomber.

Fictional accounts of Eastman appear in Paul Horgan's *Fault of Angels* (New York: Harper and Brothers, 1933) and Henry Clune's *By His Own Hand* (New York, Macmillan, 1952). More factual accounts are found in Horgan's "How Dr. Faustus Came to Rochester," *Harpers* (April 1936):506–15; and Clune's *Main Street Beat* (New York: Norton, 1947). A personal view is found in Claude Bragdon's autobiography *More Lives Than One* (New York: Knopf, 1938), 76–81.

Many of the above sources were recorded by Karl Sanford Kabelac in his "George Eastman: A Bibliographical Essay of Selected References," *University of Rochester Library Bulletin* 27, no. 1 (Winter 1971–72):33–38. Further references were recorded by Elizabeth Brayer, "George Eastman," *Read More about It: An Encyclopedia of Information Sources on Historical Figures and Events* (Ann Arbor: The Pierian Press, 1989), 3:180–82.

Eastman suppressed many attempts to record his life, notably one commissioned by Kodak in 1923 and written by Isaac Marcossen, and others proposed by Julian Street, J. J. Kennedy, Arthur Gleason, and Samuel Crowther. And so, when asked to recommend such an account, he would reply curtly, "I have no biography." In 1928, however, his secretary, Alice K. Whitney directed correspondents to articles in *Leslie's Weekly* (8 February 1917); *System* magazine (31 January 1917):78; Samuel Crowther, *System* magazine 38 (October 1920):607; *Outlook* 139 (7 January 1925):24; *American* magazine 91 (February 1921):36; *Literary Digest* 83 (27 December 1924):36; and B. C. Forbes, *Men Who Are Making America*, 1917. Other contemporary articles include Peter F. O'Shea, "He Made This an Age of Pictures: A Snapshot of George Eastman at 72," *Everybody's* June 1926 54, no. 6 18–25, 174, 176, 178; B. C. Forbes, "How Big Business Men Grew Rich," *Hearst's for March* (1920):72–73. *Pathfinder Magazine* 8 (October 1927) contains an article about Eastman's fabrication of the word "Kodak."

Reese V. Jenkins, *Images and Enterprise: Technology and the American Photographic Industry, 1839–1925* (Baltimore and London: Johns Hopkins University Press, 1975), is an excellent history of the photographic industry and technology that naturally concentrates on its leader, George Eastman. Of all secondary sources, only Jenkins, Butterfield, and Ackerman are based on the rich primary source of Eastman's extensive correspondence.

Beaumont Newhall, *A History of Photography* (New York: The Museum of Modern Art, 1964), is a classic text of the art history of photography but of minimal importance as an Eastman bibliographical reference. Brian Coe, curator of the Kodak Museum, London, wrote *The Birth of Photography: The Story of the Formative Years, 1800–1900* (London: Ash & Grant, 1976), with two chapters of references to Eastman not found elsewhere.

Robert Taft, *Photography and the American Scene* (New York: Macmillan, 1938), functions as advocate for the underdog in the *Goodwin/Ansco v. Eastman Kodak* patent suit re the invention of film. Taft's errors of facts and dates suggest that Kodak denied him access to basic Eastman facts and correspondence in the 1930s; hence this flawed account in an otherwise classic history. (He writes, for example, that Eastman went to Europe in 1879 to learn the dry-plate process, even though Eastman was commercially producing plates already, and does not know that Eastman and Walker were experimenting with flexible film for at least two years before Goodwin's first application.)

Fritz Wenzel, *Memoirs of a Photochemist* (Philadelphia: American Museum of Photography, 1960), presents interesting sidelights on the photographic industry, particularly concerning Kodak's leading American competitor, the Ansco company. So do William and Estelle Marder in *Anthony: the MAN, the COMPANY, the CAMERAS* (Pine Ridge Publishing Company, 1982).

Douglas Collins, *The Story of Kodak* (New York: Harry N. Abrams, 1990), is a seamless narrative of how the company changed the course of photography and social history with a stream of inventions and discoveries, beginning with Eastman. T. H. James, *A Biography-Autobiography of Charles Edward Kenneth Mees* (Rochester: Photographic Research Laboratories, Eastman Kodak Company, n.d. but ca. 1991), was written by a longtime Mees associate. "George Eastman said, 'Kodak,'" by Richard Condiff appeared in *Smithsonian* 19, no. 3 (June 1988). *George Eastman*, by Oscar N. Solbert (Rochester: The George Eastman House of Photography, 1953), is a booklet by the then director of Eastman House. "You Press the Button, We Do the Rest," by Bernard Weisberger appeared in *American Heritage* 23, no. 6 (October 1972). "Journey into the Imagination: The Kodak Story" (Rochester: Eastman Kodak Company, 1988) is an accurate outline of Eastman's career.

Other sources dealing with Eastman's photographic processes and apparatus include Jim and Joan McKeown, *Collectors' Guide to Kodak Cameras* (Grantsburg, Wis.: Centennial Photo Services, 1981); Rudolph Kingslake, *The Rochester Camera and Lens Companies* (Rochester: The Photographic Historical Society, 1974); Eaton S. Lothrop Jr., *A Century of Cameras from the Collection of the International Museum of Photography at George Eastman House* (Dobbs Ferry, N.Y.: Morgan & Morgan, 1973); Frank Brownell Mehlenbacher, "Frank A. Brownell: Mr. Eastman's Camera Maker," *Image: Journal of Photography and Motion Pictures of the International Museum of Photography at George*

Eastman House 26, no. 2 (June 1983); Donald C. Ryon, "Development of the No. 1 Kodak Camera" (Rochester: The Photographic Historical Society Symposium, 1970); and Jane Baum McCarthy, "The Two-Color Kodachrome Collection at the George Eastman House," *Image* magazine (Rochester: George Eastman House, 1987), 1–12. This issue of *Image* contains an extensive bibliography of the subject. Kodak Trade Circulars, *Kodak Magazine*, and various Kodak directors' reports, annual reports, and summaries of board minutes were also consulted by the author.

Sources that tie Eastman to Rochester include Jesse L. Rosenberger, *Rochester: The Making of a University* (Rochester: University of Rochester, 1927); Arthur May, *A History of the University of Rochester, 1850–1962* (Rochester: University of Rochester, 1977): John Slater, *Rhees of Rochester* (New York: Harper and Bros., 1946), 156–177 and *passim*; George Corner, *George Hoyt Whipple and His Friends: The Life-Story of a Nobel Prize Pathologist* (Philadelphia: J. B. Lippincott, 1963); Dexter Perkins, Charles Riker, George H. Whipple, and others, *The University of Rochester: The First Hundred Years, 1850–1950* (Rochester, 1950); Grace N. Kraut, *An Unfinished Symphony: The Story of David Hochstein* (Rochester, 1980); Elizabeth Brayer, *MAGnum Opus: The Story of the Memorial Art Gallery* (Rochester: Memorial Art Gallery of the University of Rochester, 1988); Elizabeth Brayer, *Our Spirit Shows: Rochester Sesquicentennial, 1834–1984* (Rochester: Rochester Sesquicentennial, Inc., 1984); and Andrew D. Wolfe, *Views of Old Rochester and the Genesee Country from Indian Days to 1918* (Rochester: Marine Midland Trust Company, 1970). Various *Reports of the [University of Rochester] President and Treasurer*, 1904–1932 and beyond add more information.

Sources dealing with Eastman's interest in medicine and health include Edward C. Atwater, "A Modest But Good Institution . . . and Besides There Is Mr. Eastman," *To Each His Farthest Star: University of Rochester Medical Center, 1925–1975* (Rochester: UR Medical Center, 1975), 3–36; George H. Whipple, *Planning and Construction Period of the School and Hospitals, 1921–1925: School of Medicine and Dentistry, Strong Memorial Hospital, Rochester Municipal Hospital* (Rochester: University of Rochester, 1957); Virginia Jeffrey Smith, *A Century of Service: Rochester General Hospital, 1847–1947* (Rochester, 1947).

Aspects of Eastman's vision to build musical capacity on a large scale from childhood are found in *American Architect* (23 February 1923); Margaret Bond, "Howard Hanson Remembered," *Rochester Review* (Spring 1981):1–8.; Margaret Bond, "Mr. Eastman's Theatre," *Rochester Review* (Summer 1980):16–19; Howard Hanson, "Music Was a Spiritual Necessity," *University of Rochester Bulletin* (Spring 1971):88; Nicolas Slonimsky, *Perfect Pitch: A Life Story* (Oxford: Oxford University Press, 1988), 81–85; Stewart B. Sabin, "A Retrospect of Music in Rochester," *Centennial History of Rochester, New York* (Rochester: The Rochester Historical Society Publication Fund Series, 1932), 2:69; Agnes de Mille, *Martha: The Life and Work of Martha Graham* (New York: Random House, 1956, 1991); Martha Graham, *Blood Memory* (New York: Doubleday, 1991), 108; and Vincent A. Lenti, "The Preparatory Department: Historical Origins of the Eastman School of Music and Its Commitment to the Education of the Rochester Community" (Rochester, 1978).

Sources that show the Eastman influence elsewhere include Francis E. Wylie, *M.I.T. in Perspective* (Boston: Little, Brown, 1975), 46, 54, 57, 87; and Henry Greenleaf Pearson, *Richard Cockburn Maclaurin* (New York: Macmillan, 1937). Osa Johnson,

I Married Adventure: The Lives and Adventures of Martin and Osa Johnson, and *Four Years in Paradise* (Philadelphia: J. B. Lippincott 1940, 1941), are sassy and humanizing accounts of Eastman's two safaris. Each Johnson book has a chapter about Eastman. George Whipple, *George Eastman: Picture Story of an Out-of-doors Man* (privately printed, n.d., ca. 1930s), illustrates many of Eastman's other camping trips during the 1920s.

Various publications of the Eastman dental clinics in Rochester, London, Paris, Stockholm, and Rome, too numerous to list and in the language of each country, show still other aspects of Eastman's life. The Ackerman biography has been excerpted and printed in Japanese, and various illustrated pamphlets in that language have been produced for more than seventy years. Pierre Clement, *Kodak-Pathé: Histoire et Evolution* (Paris, 1987) and Jean-Claude Gautrand, *Publicites Kodak, 1910–1939* (Paris: Contrejour, 1983), contain biographical information. The latter text is also in English.

Elizabeth Brayer, "Mr. Eastman Builds a House," *The Brighton Pittsford Post*, 19 April 1979 to 3 April 1980, comprises forty-three newspaper articles. A scrapbook of these articles is in the Department of Rare Books and Special Collections, University of Rochester Library. Other articles by the same author appeared as "The Great Removal Project" (Parts I and II), *Rochester Review* (Fall 1980, Winter 1981); and "The Eastman Touch: George Eastman and the University of Rochester" (Summer 1980). Also, "GE: A Biographical Essay," *Eastman House* (Rochester: privately printed for friends, guests, and patrons, January 1990), 15–27; and "The Eastman House Gardens: Simplicity and Tranquility" (Rochester: privately printed for friends, guests, and patrons, June 1990), 1–17. The first booklet contains a restoration report by William Seale; the second, a historical commentary, "The Restoration of the Historic Landscape at George Eastman House," by Gerald and M. Christine Klim Doell. Essays by Brayer ("George Eastman, Collector") and Donald Rosenthal ("Barbizon Paintings in the George Eastman Collection") appeared in the exhibition catalog, *The George Eastman Collection* (Rochester: Memorial Art Gallery of the University of Rochester, 1979).

Young adult works about the subject include Brian Coe, *George Eastman and the Early Photographers* (London: Priority Press: 1973)—the best of the lot and an excellent introduction for adults too. Other children's works include Joanne Landers Henry, *George Eastman, Young Photographer* (Indianapolis: Bobbs-Merrill, 1959), which is largely fictionalized; and Barbara Mitchell, *Click: A Story about George Eastman* (Minneapolis: Carolrhoda Books, 1986), which contains errors in facts and dates. Burnham Holmes, *George Eastman*, Pioneers in Change series (New York: Silver Burdett Press, 1992), is apparently based on Ackerman and accurate. Kazuhiko Fukuda's *Eastman, Kindai Shashin no Chichi* (Tokyo: Iwasaki, 1958) is written in Japanese.

Works by Eastman himself are *Chronicles of an African Trip* (Rochester: privately printed, 1926), his first journey to East Africa as recorded in letters to his secretary; and (edited by) Kenneth M. Cameron, *Chronicles of a Second African Trip* (Rochester: The Friends of the University of Rochester Libraries, 1987), his second trip, also recorded in letters to Alice Whitney Hutchison.

Public documents consulted include the twenty-eight patents granted to George

Eastman personally from 1879 to 1923. Judicial decisions, available in most law school libraries, include "Opinion," *United States v. Eastman Kodak Co.* et al. August 24, 1915. U.S. Circuit Court, Western District of New York, v. 226, *Federal Reporter*, p. 65; *U.S. v. EKCo., Abridged Transcript of Record* (10 vols., 4,200 pp.) and *Supplemental Brief and Argument for Defendants* (80 pp.); *Goodwin Film & Camera Company v. Eastman Kodak Company*, 213 *Federal Reporter* 231 (1914); "Goodwin File Wrapper and Contents," U.S. Patent Office, in *Goodwin v. EKCo.*, 3575–3830; Blair testimony, *U.S. v. EKCo., Abridged Transcript of Record* (10 vols., 4,200 pp.) and *Supplemental Brief and Argument for Defendants* (80 pp.), 1914; "Testimony on Behalf of the Defendants," record on Appeal, *United States v. Eastman Kodak Co. and Others*, 1913–14.

Unpublished sources, found in private collections, include Beaumont Newhall's notes for a pictorial biography of Eastman, made in the 1950s, and Robert Johanson's notes for a biography, n.d., F. W. T. Krohn, *Early Kodak Days* (unpublished, 1932), is available at the University of Rochester Library, Department of Rare Books and Special Collections. Typescripts, "Outline History of European Kodak Companies," and M. D. Gauntlett, "An Outline History of Kodak Limited, 1885–1975," are at the Eastman Kodak Company. Wyatt Brummitt, head of public relations at Kodak during the 1960s, wrote *George Eastman of Kodak*, a 332-page typescript of forty chapters, all but the early ones devoted to a year of Eastman's life. Undocumented, it nevertheless remains an invaluable resource found in a few private collections.

NOTES

Prologue: The Housewarming

1. Paul Horgan, *Fault of Angels* (New York: Harper and Brothers, 1933), 41. In this *roman à clef* about the Eastman School of Music, Horgan writes that Mr. Ganson (George Eastman) "looked like a gentle reproduction of Julius Caesar." Interview with Dr. C. E. K. Mees, director of Kodak Research Laboratories, who also compared Eastman to Caesar, 9 January 1940 (RGE-UR).

2. Walter Hubbell to GE, 8 September 1912 (INC-GEC).

3. Interviews with Henry Willis, 13 February 1940, and W. S. Bent, 26 February 1940 (RGE-UR).

4. *American Amateur Photographer*, ca. 1900 (INC-GEC).

5. Frank Lusk Babbott to GE, 1906 (INC-GEC).

6. Interviews with Pagie Macomber, 17 November 1950 (EKC), and Marie Cherbuliez, 24 January 1940 (RGE-UR).

7. Interview with Hattie Strong, 28 February 1940 (RGE-UR).

8. Interviews with Henry Thayer, 4 January 1940, and J. L. Gorham, 2 January 1940 (RGE-UR).

9. GE to J. T. Clarke, Harrow, England, 30 September 1905 (GEC).

10. Letter from William Vaughn to author, 1985.

Chapter 1: Eastmans and Kilbourns

1. GE to Samuel Fry, R. W. Thomas, Harvey Reynolds, Wratten & Wainwright (London), and Romain Talbot (Berlin), 23 July 1879 (GEC).

2. Kilbourn and Eastman genealogy sources include *Genealogy of the Harvey Eastman (1777–1829) Branch of the Eastman Family* (privately printed, 1917), commissioned by George Eastman, researched and written by Charles R. Eastman and others (EKC); Guy S. Rix, *Eastman Family of America* (Concord, N.H.: Press of I. C. Evans, 1901), 801–6; *History of the Kilbourn Family* (privately printed, 1917), commissioned by GE (EKC); *Ballard Genealogy* (unpublished ms., n.d.) (UR); many letters from cousins, etc. (INC-GEC) (GEC); and interviews by author with Eastman family members in Waterville in 1989 and Mariana, Florida, in 1988.

3. Stella Eastman Ford, Huntington, W.Va., to GE, 14 December 1924 (INC-GEC).

4. Maria K. Eastman to Emily Kilbourn Cope, 3 October 1842, 10 October 1843 (INC-GEC).

5. Exactly why George Eastman was not baptized as an infant is unclear. Tommy Cope wrote of attending the Baptist church in Waterville with Aunt Maria and Uncle George so it appears that as long as the father lived, his denomination, one that practices adult baptism, was espoused by the family.

6. MKE to Emily Kilbourn Cope, 1830s (INC-GEC).

7. George Harvey Genzmer, "Harvey Gridley Eastman," *Dictionary of American Biography* (New York: Charles Scribner's Sons, 1958), 602.

8. Almon R. Eastman to GE, 6 December 1901 (INC-GEC).

9. MKE to Emily Kilbourn Cope, 1840s letters (GEC-UR) and (INC-GEC-GEH). Maria's toothaches are noted in these letters.

10. Blake McKelvey, Rochester city historian for many years, was probably the first to call Rochester America's first boomtown.

11. MKE to Emily Kilbourn Cope, 23 July 1845 (INC-GEC).

12. A photostat of this page from the Eastman family bible is at the UR library.

13. The tradition that Eastman was born in the Stafford Avenue house, which was moved to the gardens of the George Eastman House, International Museum of Photography and Film, Rochester, N.Y., in 1954 and to the Genesee Country Museum, Mumford, N.Y., in 1979, has been challenged. Dorothy Eastman (third cousin twice removed to George) of Waterville said in 1989 that as Maria Eastman's 1854 confinement approached, she and her daughters moved to the Eastman family homestead several miles from Waterville in the township of Marshall and moved back to the house on Stafford Avenue when her son was several months old. We know, too, that George Washington Eastman was commuting between Waterville and Rochester in 1854.

14. Eastman's obituary in the *Waterville Times* of 15 March 1932.

15. MKE to Emily Kilbourn Cope, 23 July 1845 (GEC).

16. Roger Butterfield made these notes in the 1950s from the *Waterville Journal* and *Waterville Times* (BUTT-UR).

17. Henry Clune, 13 April 1930, *Rochester Democrat & Chronicle*, quoted from A. J. Warner's daybook, then owned by J. Foster Warner but now lost: "On Jan. 25, 1850 and several days thereafter, Andrew J. Warner was engaged on plans for the home of George Washington Eastman, father of George Eastman."

18. Thomas Kilbourne (sic) Cope to Edward and Emily Cope, 2 August 1852 (GEC-UR).

19. GWE to Thomas K. Cope, 17 August 1852 (INC-GEC). This reference is the only evidence that an older son was born. It is possible the date is wrong, and the letter written in 1854 after GE was born (in which case he apparently did have a middle name). Or GWE could be referring to a nursery worker (unlikely). There are still unmarked stones in the original Eastman burial ground but no such grave was moved ca. 1900 when GWE's and Katy's were moved to the Waterville cemetery.

20. *Rochester Daily Union*, 12 July 1854, quoted by Robert Johansen, unpublished ms. (EKC).

21. Herbert L. Baldwin, *Boston Post*, 3 February 1920.

22. Letter, George Edward Norton to Marion Gleason, 15 April 1939 (RGE-UR),

quoted in George Norton, "My Friend George Eastman," *University of Rochester Library Bulletin* 23, no. 1 (Fall 1967).

23. *New York Leader*, 6 October 1855 (BUTT-UR).

24. H. Paul Draheim, "When Hops Were King," Waterville sesquicentennial booklet, 44–46; *Waterville Times*, 15 September 1855 (BUTT-UR).

25. *Waterville Times*, 7 May 1858 (BUTT-UR). GWE lists "Dahlias, Verbenas, Phlox, Petunias, Fuchsias, Heleotropes (sic), Geraneums (sic), Salvias, German Stocks, Chrysantheums (sic), Monthly Roses . . . in Pots." Fuchsia and Heliotrope were Maria Eastman's favorite flowers. Interview with Katharine Whipple (RGE-UR).

26. GWE to Thomas K. Cope, 17 August 1852 (INC-GEC): "I have bot a farm located here in the village just opposite my house containing 10 acres for which I pay three thousand dollars. I intend to set it all out to fruit. Principally pears." The *Waterville Times* stated that thirty thousand of the forty thousand trees were pear trees (BUTT-UR).

27. Ibid. Thomas K. Cope to father and mother at North Guilford, Chenango Company, 2 August 1852. The Rev. Cope was a circuit rider during this period. Thomas K. Cope to Emily K. Cope, 26 July, 9 August 1852 (INC-GEC).

28. The *Waterville Times* ran this announcement: "Sudden Death. George Washington Eastman of Rochester and formerly of this place, died . . . on Sunday last [27 April 1862], after an illness of only four days. His remains were brought to his brother Horace on Tuesday and interred in the Eastman burying ground on the following day." The death was not as "sudden" as the Waterville paper was led to believe. The *Rochester Union and Advertiser*, with reporters on the scene, stated the case with more detail: "The announcement of the death of George W. Eastman will not surprise anyone who has known him intimately for a year past. He has been in a condition that rendered him liable to die at almost any moment for months. He was attacked with a brain disorder on Friday and expired on Sunday morning."

29. Henry Clune interviewed GE on several occasions in the 1920s as a reporter for the *Rochester Democrat & Chronicle*. Clune incorporated this scene in his novel, *By His Own Hand*, based on Eastman's life, by having the protagonist say: "My father was always in debt. He couldn't manage himself. Debt was his natural condition. . . . As a boy I'd lay awake nights and hear my mother and father talking about them. It seemed to me there was a monster on the doorstep and his name was debts. I swore I'd never repeat my father's errors," 45.

30. GE to H. H. Eastman, 19 November 1865 (GEC).

31. Interviews with Darwin Smith's daughter, Mrs. C. Storrs Barrows, 19 January 1940, and Jacob Bernstein, 16 and 23 February, 6 March 1940 (RGE-UR).

32. Eastman's early ledgers, 1868–74 (EKC). Maria didn't like the idea that his job included cleaning the cuspidors but then added to Louisa Knorr, her nurse: "George wasn't any better than other boys, not too good to do honest work." Interview with Louisa Knorr, 13 February 1940 (RGE-UR).

33. Entry in second ledger, 1868–74, 1 August 1870 (Katie's ride) (EKC). *Thrift Advocate*, Rochester Savings Bank, May 1923.

34. Ibid. Interview with Tom Brown, 6 February 1940 (RGE-UR). Interview with Marie Cherbuliez.

35. GE to Uncle Horace Eastman, 1864 (GEH). Among Eastman's effects after his

death was a well-thumbed small black leather *Book of Common Prayer* dated "July 12 1874" (probably a present from his mother for his twentieth birthday) and a *Hymnal of The Protestant Episcopal Church,* signed "Rochester New York Geo Eastman pew 99 Trinity Church" (BUTT-UR).

36. Alvah Strong, *The Autobiography of Alvah Strong (1809−1885)* [written in 1880, privately printed, n.d., probably in the 1910s or 1920s], 100−105 (STRONG-UR).

Chapter 2: An Amateur There

1. Santo Domingo was renamed the Dominican Republic after the first break with Spain in 1844. However, Eastman, like many others, continued to use the older name. The Spanish did resume rule briefly (1861−63), but U.S. intervention forced them out.

2. *System* magazine (30 October 1920):607: Carl W. Ackerman, *George Eastman* (Boston and New York: Houghton Mifflin, 1930), 23−24. Robert Johanson (unpublished ms., 1951), ch. IV-1 (EKC). Francis Macomber, *Reminiscences* (unpublished ms., 20 April 1944), 14 (EKC). The men at the bank who worked with Eastman tell another story of Eastman's entry into photography: It began with the bank's janitor, a bachelor who lived in the basement and devoted his spare time to photography. He would set up his tripod and camera to photograph the iron fountain of "little Black Sambo" in the bank's courtyard. Eastman's interest in the janitor's pastime was greater than that of the other young men and when the janitor heard the clerk was going to Santo Domingo, he suggested, "Take my camera along." As far as we know, Eastman did not buy a camera until November 1877. Of course, the janitor and the photographer's assistant on the Powell Survey may have been the same person. Major John Wesley Powell had explored the Grand Canyon for the government in 1871. So heartbreakingly difficult was the task of getting pictures that Powell's two professional cameramen quit. John K. Hillers, an oarsman who had picked up some photographic knowledge from them, carried on and later gained fame for his work. Hillers would become a loyal Eastman customer.

Also, Charles Forbes's daughter believed her father had sparked Eastman's interest and wrote to Eastman in the 1920s about their early relationship. He did not contradict her story (INC-GEC).

Forty years later, GE chartered a yacht and while cruising the coat of Haiti with friends, suddenly found Samana Bay on his chart and decided it was time to finally see it.

3. Johanson ms., III-1, 4 (EKC). Johanson, a Kodak employee, had access to the trustees' minutes of the period and interviewed Thomas H. Husband, who came to Rochester in the late 1860s, landed a job at the bank, and boarded with the Eastmans. Eastman filled the clerkship left by the death of W. A. Hubbard. Among those competing was Samuel Durand, brother of Eastman's close friend Mary Durand Mulligan. Ten votes were cast, with Eastman getting five. Finally, on the third ballot, he received six.

4. The purchases of the pictures are recorded in Eastman's second early account book. The first began 1 March 1868 when he was still thirteen and ends 18 March 1874, when he was nineteen. There are spaces ruled off in this book for the ensuing

months of 1874, April through December, and headed in pencil with names of months, but no entries. Book 2 begins with April 1876, when Eastman was almost twenty-two, with expenses relating to the moving into the Jones Street house. Less than a year later he plunges with great energy into his hobby—photography.

5. Eastman's early account books are at UR and GEH.

6. Interviews with Gertrude S. Achilles, 9 February 1940, and E. D. Leary, 22 January 1940 (RGE-UR). Leary was a neighbor, schoolmate, and beau of Gertrude.

7. Letters from Susan Brown to GE, 1927–30 (INC-GEC), and interviews with Gertrude S. Achilles and E. D. Leary, 1940 (RGE-UR). Letters from GE to his mother in the 1894 refer to calling on "Miss B."

8. GE to the Rev. W. W. Walsh, Petosky, Mich., 6 August 1891 (GEC). Other quotes are from the first interview Eastman authorized, in *System* magazine (October 1920).

9. Louise Hart Orwin to GE, 15 November 1924 (INC-GEC): "Upon inquiry we [the seminary girls] were told that the blonde young man . . . was George Eastman."

10. Letter to Roger Butterfield from Forbes's daughter, 1955 (BUTT-UR). Interviews by Jean Ennis in 1950 with friends and relatives of George Monroe. An advertisement for the Rochester Savings Bank in the *New York Times*, 9 November 1955, features the old fountain in the bank courtyard that Eastman "loved to photograph."

11. The wet-plate negative of Eastman's first photograph was found in an old trunk in the home of George B. Dryden, Evanston, Ill., in 1955, shortly after the death of Eastman's niece, Ellen Andrus Dryden. It was given by Dryden to Oscar Solbert, director of the George Eastman House of Photography. See articles in *Genesee Country Scrapbook* (Rochester: Rochester Historical Society, 1955), vol. 6, and *Image* (Rochester: George Eastman House, 1955).

12. Interview with George B. Selden (son), 1940 (RGE-UR).

13. *System* (October 1920).

14. David Gibson, retired head of the Patent Museum at Eastman Kodak Company, has noted that Eastman's subscription to the *British Journal of Photography* began with the issue containing Bennett's formula.

15. GE to M. Carey Lea, Shoemakerstown, Pa., 6 February 1879 (GEC).

16. *Philadelphia Photographer* (January 1880).

17. GE to F. Dundas Todd, 12 August 1920 (Scoville camera) (GEC). Ackerman identifies the negative as "One of G. Eastman's first gelatine negatives winter 1879–80." Beaumont Newhall, director of Eastman House, identified the house as the residence of Charles P. Ham, president of the Ham Steam Gauge & Lantern Company, for the *Rochester Times-Union*, 1954.

18. GE (London) to MKE, 1 June 1879 (UR). The original of this letter is on long-term loan to the Royal Photographic Society.

19. Brian Coe, *The Birth of Photography* (London: Ash & Grant, 1976), 38.

20. GE to MKE, 6 June 1879 (GEC-UR).

21. GE to Mawson & Swan, 13 October 1879 (GEC).

22. GE to Hazeltine & Lake, 1 February 1880 (GEC): "Your favor Jan 23 enclosing certificate of Patent Office of the filing of the Final Specifications of my patent is received."

23. GE to Messrs. Hazeltine, Lake & Company, copy to S. Fry & Company,

16 October 1879 (GEC): "Mr Selden my soliciter here thinks the provisional specifications [for the U.K. patent] too broad, at least for the American patent. In getting the papers ready for my patent he found [two similar] American patents [of 1866 and 1874]. . . . In view of this we confined our claims to the applying of a gelatinous sensitive compound to the *underside* of a glass plate by means of the apparatus described."

24. GE to J. B. Church, 27 April 1887 (GEC).

25. GE to W. B. Bolton, 11 September 1879; GE to C. F. Richardson, Wakefield, Mass., 15 February 80; GE to Harris H. Hayden, 11 September 1891; GE to S. Fry, 8 December 1879, 23 February 1880, 1 April 1880; GE to Hazeltine & Lake, 8 December 1879, 2 May 1880 (GEC).

26. GE to MKE, 8 October 1878 (GEC-UR).

27. GE to Mawson & Swan, 13 October 1879 (GEC).

28. GE to MKE, 8 and 13 October 1879 (GEC-UR).

29. GE to S. Fry, 2 July 1880 (GEC).

30. GE bought the hardware to make a hammock on his birthday 12 July 1877, probably with a cash gift from his mother or other well-wisher (LEDGER-UR).

31. Florence Glaser's name is spelled Glasser in some company and court records.

32. Information gleaned from the first letter book, 1879–90 (GEC).

33. GE to H & L, 4 July 1880 (GEC).

34. GE letters of 23 July 1880 to Samuel Fry, R. W. Thomas, Harvey Reynolds, and Wratten & Wainwright (GEC).

35. Testimony in court by Florence S. Glaser, 17 January 1895. Hattie Brumen was the mother of *Rochester Democrat & Chronicle* reporter Henry Clune, who occasionally described in his column, "Seen and Heard," how his mother had coated plates by hand for George Eastman.

36. GE to the Eastman Photographic Materials Company Ltd. (EPMCo), London, 23 April 1896 (GEC-GEH).

37. GE to Romain Talbot, 5 August 1880 (GEC-GEH).

38. Information on the Anthonys summarized from William and Estelle Marder, *Anthony, the Man, the Company, the Cameras* (Amesbury, Mass.: Pine Ridge Publishing Company, 1982); and Reese V. Jenkins, *Images and Enterprises* (Baltimore and London: Johns Hopkins University Press, 1974).

39. Early letter book and later correspondence over many years between Eastman and George Monroe (GEC) (INC-GEC). Coe, *Birth of Photography*.

40. GE to E. & H. T. Anthony, 18 August 1880 (GEC-GEH).

41. GE to F. Dundas Todd, British Columbia, 12 August 1920 (GEC).

42. Jenkins, *Images and Enterprises*, 69–74, 78–80, 221–30.

43. Johanson ms. V-1, p. 4 (EKC).

44. Gertrude Strong Achilles to GE, 20 March 1921 (INC-GEC).

45. Interview with Benham Cline, photographer (BUTT-UR).

46. *Rochester Daily Union & Advertiser*, 1 January 1881, 1.

47. GE to Hattie Strong when the latter sent him a miniature of Henry, ca. 1913 (GEC-UR).

48. GE to MKE, 21 May 1882 (GEC-UR).

49. GE to Singer & Company, 17 March and 6 May 1881 (GEC).

50. Obituary for Almon R. Eastman, *Waterville Times*, 1924 (INC-GEC).

51. GE to A. R. Eastman, 4 November 1902 (GEC).

52. GE to MKE, 21 May 1882 (GEC-UR).

Chapter 3: Scoop the World

1. Interview by Kodak Public Relations with Tom Husband in 1940, quoted in Johanson ms. V-1, p. 4 (EKC). Harry Brewster, later the bank president and a U.S. congressman, would eventually invest heavily in the Eastman Kodak Company and make Eastman a trustee of the bank.

2. Carl W. Ackerman, *George Eastman* (Boston and New York: Houghton Mifflin, 1930), 42–43. The notebook that Ackerman describes as "worn . . . stained with chemicals, soiled by constant fingering, and now brown with age" is apparently no longer extant.

3. The new plant was listed at 211 State Street in the 1882 city directory, and at 341 State in the 1884 directory, a result of a number change. Physically, however, the building stood on the site of the present Kodak Office, now numbered 343 State Street.

4. C. E. Kenneth Mees, *Photography* (London: G. Bell and Sons, 1936), 67; Robert Taft, *Photography and the American Scene* (New York: Macmillan, 1938), 382–83. Although many modern gelatin experts discount the "mustard" story as a tale not worth perpetuating, because it cannot be proven or refuted, it was published in 1936 by one of Eastman's own experts—Dr. C. E. Kenneth Mees, director of the Research Laboratories. Mees's associate, Dr. Samuel Sheppard, discovered that a minute trace of sulphur was the sensitizing agent in gelatin (made from the clippings from the skins of calves). Mustard oil is rich in sulphur. "Presumably the calves obtain the oil from the plants they eat, so the amount present depends upon the pasturage that they have had," Mees wrote. Too much sulphur, Sheppard also discovered, could have the opposite effect, of desensitizing the emulsion. Taft also wrote in 1938 that the trouble was that the gelatin lacked the sulphur-bearing compound necessary for sensitivity.

5. Lewis B. Jones, *Biography of George Eastman* (Rochester: Eastman Kodak Company, 1932), 3–4. This booklet is a public relations department reprint of the 15 March 1932 *Rochester Democrat & Chronicle* obituary. Lew Jones would have heard the plate story from Eastman.

6. Wyatt Brummitt, *George Eastman of Kodak* (unpublished ms., ca. 1960), 14 (EKC).

7. *Philadelphia Photographer* 20 (1883): 61, 191. Walker and Forbes originally took on William Reid and the firm became Walker, Reid and Forbes. Then Forbes left to form his own company (which survived until 1904), being replaced by James Ingles, "late of Montreal"; and the firm became Walker, Reid and Ingles. The Rochester Optical Company was formed by William Reid and W. F. Carleton.

8. GE to A. Henderson, Montreal, 21 April 1887 (GEC); Rudolph Kingslake, *The Rochester Camera and Lens Companies* (Rochester: The Photographic Historical Society, 1974), 6; Reese V. Jenkins, *Images and Enterprise* (Baltimore and London: Johns Hopkins University Press, 1975), 351; *Philadelphia Photographer* 20 (1883); letters from Wm. Reid to GE in 1905, 1919, and 1921 (INC-GEC). In 1919 GE wrote W. H.

Reid, Steuben Sanitorium, Hornell: "I do not see how you can call yourself the originator of amateur photography. You followed Walker and even he never made any claim to that effect. I began my work before he did his. I was filling up my factory when he first became interested but I do not claim . . . to be the *originator* of amateur photography. There were two amateurs here in Rochester before I knew anything about the art."

9. F. W. T. Krohn, *Early Kodak Days*, unpublished ms. 1932 (RGE-UR); William Hall Walker's letters to GE (INC-GEC) over two decades bear out Krohn's assessment of his volatile, rapidly changing moods. While Walker may not be a tragic figure, he is certainly a pathetic one.

10. GE affidavit of 1892 in Goodwin case, *Complainant's Record* v. 5, 24, U.S. District Court of Western N.Y. Quoted in Taft, *Photography and the American Scene*, 384. Sources are numerous, including GE to M. B. Philipp, 18 October 1889 (GEC).

11. *Rochester Union*, 13 December 1884. The meanings of the words "film" and "amateur" have changed. In 1884 film was any flexible and therefore rollable material. Professional photographers made portraits in studios for money, whereas amateurs took to the field to capture views for their own use. Lightweight equipment such as film was obviously a great advance for these outdoor photographers. Under Eastman's influence, "amateur" would come to mean "untutored."

12. GE to Vernon Welch, Kensington, S.W., London, 16 March 1885 (GEC).

13. That Eastman was so far ahead of Ford in mass production methods was noted by Roger Butterfield in his article "The Prodigious Life of George Eastman," *Life* magazine (26 April 1954).

14. GE to B. C. Forbes, 20 February 1917 (GEC).

15. Emerson Peet to GE, 8 May 1883 (INC-GEC).

16. GE to Curtis Guild, 3 October 1884 (GEC); Ackerman, *George Eastman*, 49. The family fortunes made by the right decisions around the magical year of 1884 are legendary. Edmund Frost Woodbury, Strong's partner in the whip business, at first said no, but soon changed his mind. All the Kodak stock he bought was passed on to his only child John, dividends always reinvested, and followed suit by John's only child Margaret, an intrepid doll collector who was fond of telling people that "George Eastman used to live in my backyard" (as her grandfather's tenant—but in a comfortable cottage one lot removed from the yard, and not in a tent, as her statement might imply). By the 1970s E. F. Woodbury's investment was worth $80 million, which was used to build and endow the Margaret Woodbury Strong Museum in Rochester. Brackett Clark, paint store owner and barrel stave manufacturer, seemed to sense, as his neighbor and whip maker Henry Strong had, that the barrel and buggy stage of American industry was over. He opted for the future with an investment of $9,000, and his son George chipped in another $1,000. After Eastman's death, George Clark was the largest individual Kodak stockholder on the planet, and, needless to say, an incredibly wealthy man. Edwin O. Sage, a shoe manufacturer and fellow church member with the Strongs, bought one hundred shares. John Kent, Rochester portrait photographer, who photographed such local luminaries as Susan B. Anthony and whose assistant "old Sam Wardlow used to cuss you [Eastman] out for dropping a 'pepper box' lens then sticking your foot out and saving it," grew to value those days when the young Eastman hung out in his shop: He bought one hundred shares and

suddenly found himself vice president of the corporation. Henry Achilles, a book-keeper in the Monroe County Savings Bank who had recently married Gertrude Strong, bought thirty-five shares, while Dr. Ruben Adams took a flyer for twenty—he later named his California ranch "The Diamond Twenty" for the rich rewards he reaped. Tom Husband, Eastman's bank colleague, invested $1,000, and when he retired his Kodak stock was worth more than the total of his lifetime salary.

17. GE to G. W. Andrus, 14 October 1884 (GEC).

18. MKE to Emily K. Cope, 31 March 1888 (INC-GEC).

19. GE to W. H. Walker, 31 May 1885 (GEC): "The negatives print twice as quick as when cold oiled, or about as quick as the average glass negative."

20. GE to G. W. Andrus, 16 September 1884 (GEC).

21. GE to W. H. Walker, 30 April 1887 (SN-EKC).

22. GE to HAS, 8 February 1893 (GEC); GE to Charles Abbott, 1901 (GEC).

23. *Goodwin Film & Camera Company v. Eastman Kodak Company*, 207 *Federal Reporter* 351 (1913), v. 1, 353.

24. Ibid.

25. Solar enlargers were large, bulky, and expensive and had to be readjusted every time the sun moved or went under a cloud. The concentrated heat could set the internal woodwork of the enlarger on fire or break the glass negative during prolonged exposure.

26. GE to Scovill Manufacturing Company, 25 June 1885 (GEC).

27. GE to S. C. Beach, New York City, 16 May 1885 (CEC).

28. GE to William H. Walker, 7 November 1886 (GEC).

29. GE to Edward L. Wilson, editor, *Philadelphia Photographer*, 20 December 1886 (BUTT-UR); GE to David Cooper, 8 March 1886 (SN-EKC).

30. GE to Gus D. Milburn, San Francisco, 27 March 1886 (GEC). GE to Pinkerton Detective Agency, 19 September 1887 (GEC). Testimonial from Pickering, 29 April 1886: "Delighted with roll holder. Shall use it exclusively for all my landscape work. Shall teach its management to all my students" (EKC). GE to Henry Lomb, 30 April 1887 (GEC). Six years later, the Mechanics Institute would combine with Rochester's older center for learning and be officially renamed the Rochester Athenaeum and Mechanics Institute. In the 1940s it would again be renamed the Rochester Institute of Technology.

31. GE to W. Irving Adams, Scovill, 7 January 1887 (GEC): "Mr. Cooper left us on the 1st of January. We understand he is endeavoring to work up a bromide paper company in the interest of Anthony. Any information that you can give us on the subject will be very gratefully received."

32. GE to David Cooper, New York City, 2 August 1885, 22 March 1886 (GEC).

33. GE to David Cooper, Hartford, 2 April 1886 (GEC).

34. GE to Seth C. Jones, 9 April 1886, 2 June 1886 (GEC). GE to his dealers, 3 May 1887 (EKC); see also Jenkins, *Images and Enterprise*, 71, 85, 104, 106, 166.

35. GE to Washington Irving Adams, 7 January 1887. GE to W. H. Walker, 15 February and 30 April 1887; GE to J. B. Church, 27 April 1887 (GEC).

36. *Rochester Democrat & Chronicle*, 10 February 1888.

37. HAS to GE, February 1888 (INC-GEC).

38. Interview with Dr. Hans Thacher Clarke, 1953 (EKC).

39. Ibid.

40. Jenkins, *Images and Enterprise*, 135–40.

41. GE to Blair Camera Company, Boston, 21 and 25 February 1887 (GEC).

42. GE to Dr. Robert Aberdeen, Syracuse, 15 April 1887 (GEC).

43. GE to W. J. Stillman, 22 and 26 October 1887; GE to W. I. Adams, 23 November 1887 (GEC).

44. GE to W. J. Stillman, 26 October 1887 (GEC).

45. Complainant's Record, v. 5, Exhibits, United States District Court, Western District of New York *Goodwin Film & Camera Company* v. *Eastman Kodak Company* (1913–14), 4. Eastman's first mention of Goodwin is in a letter to Church & Church, 25 January 1892 (GEC). In 1887 he was unaware, apparently, of Goodwin's filing.

Chapter 4: " . . . We Do the Rest"

1. GE to Scovill Manufacturing Company, 25 June 1885; GE to W. J. Stillman, 6 July 1888 (SN-EKC).

2. GE to George H. Cook, New York, 20 May 1886; GE to F. J. Soldan, Peoria, 9 April 1886 (SN-EKC). Perhaps the European model contained a plate holder because of the failure of the roll-film system or paper film to achieve the popularity Eastman had hoped or because film was not as available in Europe.

3. The George Eastman House, International Museum of Photography and Film, has only a reproduction of Eastman's Detective camera. The story of the Eastman Detective camera is contained in twenty-two GE letters dating from 5 April 1886 to 12 March 1888 (SN-EKC).

4. GE to W. J. Stillman, 22 October 1887 (GEC).

5. GE testimony in the U.S. Patent Office before the examiner of interferences, *George A. Waters v. George Eastman, Interference, Photographic Shutters*, No. 13,825, 9 May 1992, 6. Fred F. Church represented Eastman, George H. Selden represented Waters. In addition, the camera carried a "patented May 5, 1885" notice on it, alluding to two Eastman–Walker roll-holder patents. Even after the camera had been on the market for some time, Eastman continued to purchase patents—a roll-holder patent from T. Taylor in November 1889, for example—to maintain this protection. Interestingly, however, the name of the Eastman Dry Plate and Film Company was nowhere in evidence anywhere on the camera.

6. In earlier cameras, after the shutter had been released, the lens had to be capped while the shutter was cocked again to avoid exposing the film or plate.

7. GE to C. W. Hunt, 15 September 1888 (GEC).

8. Interview by author with Nicholas Graver, photographer, historian, and collector.

9. GE to C. W. Hunt, 15 September 1888 (GEC).

10. *Pathfinder*, (8 October 1927).

11. Eastman's further etymology of the word "Kodak" was contained in an interview: "I devised the name myself. A trade mark should be short, vigorous, incapable of being mis-spelled to an extent that will destroy its identity, and—in order to satisfy trade mark laws—it must mean nothing. If the name has no dictionary definition, it must be associated only with your product and you will cease to be known as produc-

ing a 'kind of anything.' The letter 'K' had been a favorite with me—it seemed a strong, incisive sort of letter. Therefore, the word I wanted had to start with 'K.' Then it became a question of trying out a great number of combinations of letters that made words starting and ending with 'K.' . . . Instead of merely making cameras and camera supplies, we make Kodaks and Kodak supplies. It became the distinctive word for our products."

12. GE to W. J. Stillman, 6 August 1888 (GEC).

13. Johnston's most famous shot was the last photograph of President William McKinley before he was assassinated on 6 September 1901. When Eastman learned she had taken it with a Kodak No. 4 Bull's-Eye Special, he included it in Kodak advertising. Johnston was later admired for her photographs of Hampton Institute and Tuskegee Institute, colleges heavily endowed by Eastman. Douglas Collins, *The Story of Kodak* (New York: Harry N. Abrams, 1990), 110.

14. Cornelia J. Hagan to GE, 4 November, 1 and 7 December 1887, 3 January, 18 April, 8 May, 13 June 1888, 1 October 1889 (INC-GEC).

15. *Waters v. Eastman*, 13.

16. Nora F. (Mrs. Charles) Rasmussen (wife of the photographer who made the remark) to GE, 19 September 1923 (INC-GEC). GE to Nora Rasmussen, 29 October 1923 (GEC).

17. GE to MKE, 15 July 1888 (GEC-UR).

18. Ellen's photo is captioned "Unknown photographer. George B. Dryden Collection. International Museum of Photography at George Eastman House."

19. GE to S. T. Blessing, New Orleans, 23 July 1888 (GEC).

20. Jim and Joan McKeown, *Collectors Guide to Kodak Cameras* (Grantsburg, Wis.: Centennial Photo Service, 1981), 8–9.

21. GE to W. H. Walmsley, 6 and 18 June, 6 July 1888 (GEC).

22. The twenty-one letters from GE to Kilbourne Tompkins were written between 19 March and 15 June 1888 (GEC).

23. Carl W. Ackerman, *George Eastman* (Boston and New York: Houghton Mifflin, 1930), 76–79.

24. There is disagreement as to the length of these tables. "Twelve glass coating tables 80 ft. long" is from F. W. T. Krohn, "*Early Kodak Days*" (unpublished, 1932) (RGE-UR). In 1925 Eastman wrote that the first coating tables were one hundred feet long (GEC).

25. GE to J. B. Church, 3 March 1889 (SN-EKC).

26. Ackerman, *George Eastman*, 83.

27. *Homeopathic News* 3 (1891).

28. Beaumont Newhall, *The History of Photography* (New York: The Museum of Modern Art, 1964), 118. Cleveland used his Kodak all day long while on a fishing trip with Joe Jefferson.

29. Ed Hickey to GE, 1890 (INC-GEC).

Chapter 5: England and America

1. GE to W. H. Walker, 5 May 1889 (GEC).

2. Walker to Eastman correspondence 1886–92 (EKC); F. Walter T. Krohn, *Early*

Kodak Days (unpublished typescript, 1932) (RGE-UR); GE to W. H. Walker, 9 February 1892 (GEC): "big feet."

3. George Dickman obituary, 1898 (EKC); W. H. Walker to GE, 12 April 1891; Dickman to Eastman correspondence 1892–98 (INC-GEC).

4. GE to MKE, 30 March 1890 (GEC-UR).

5. GE to W. H. Walker, September 1890 (GEC).

6. GE to Henry A. Strong, 21 October 1889 (GEC).

7. GE to H. A. Strong, 26 October 1889 (GEC).

8. Organization of English company and reorganization of American company from EKC files. *Outline History of European Companies, Kodak Limited* (unpublished typescripts, n.d.) (EKC).

9. GE to W. H. Walker, November 1890 (GEC).

10. W. H. Walker to GE, 11 November 1890 (INC-GEC).

11. W. H. Walker to GE, 11 November 1890 (INC-GEC); GE to W. H. Walker, November 1890 (GEC).

12. *Social Notes*, 29 December 1892 (EKC); W. H. Walker to GE, 20 April and 2 May 1892 (INC-GEC); GE to George Dickman, 18 March 1893 (GEC). GE to HAS, 22 February 1893 (GEC). Walker planned to continue some personal film experiments on the side. The Celluloid Company was producing continuous film without joint marks on a wheel for Blair; Walker thought he could do the same on a cloth or paper support. Eastman thought otherwise. He gave Walker friendly but firm advice: "I will state what I think to be the defects of your plan, not with a view to discouraging your experiments but to enable you to avoid them. . . . You could not use the support over and over again, the mat surface is not equal to sandblasting and will not hold the emulsion, therefore . . . inferior to Celluloid . . . , film not free from wrinkles and buckles, and no gelatin backing."

13. GE to HAS, 16 February 1893 (GEC); HAS to GE, 7 February 1893 (Strong box INC-GEC).

14. GE to George Dickman, 18 March 1893 (GEC).

15. GE to George Dickman, 19 January 1893 (GEC).

16. HAS to GE, 7 February; GE to HAS; London, 16 and 22 February 1893 (GEC); GE to William H. Walker, 15 March 1893 (GEC). Walker did receive patents for a wheel method of casting film in 1893, six years before that method was adopted at Kodak Park.

17. GE to MKE, 11 August 1892 (GEC-UR); GE to G. W. de Bedts, 18 October 1892 (GEC); G. Dickman to GE, 16 March 1894 (INC-GEC); GE to HAS, 2 May 1894 (GEC).

18. GE to George Dickman, 7 March 1893 (GEC).

19. George Dickman to GE, 5 October 1898 (INC-GEC).

20. GE to George Dickman, 16 September 1893 (GEC).

21. GE to HAS, Tacoma, 15 and 17 June 1890 (GEC). Walter Hubbell testified before the Common Council of Rochester in 1892 about the pollution caused by the Court Street film factory and this was undoubtedly one reason Eastman looked for a factory site outside city limits. At the State Street factory, company offices and the emulsion room were on the ground floor. Three emulsions were made: *Permanent* for a slow and contrasty bromide paper, *Peerless* for film, and *Special* for mixing with

either emulsion to vary the quality (such as to produce Extra Rapid Bromide paper). Transparent film and glass plates were coated at the Court Street factory. The dope was set and seasoned under movable wooden covers with counterweights, which were lowered several times over the twelve coating tables to form tunnels.

22. GE to Miss Tompkins, 9 September 1891 (GEC).

23. GE to Harris Hayden, August 1891 (GEC).

24. Krohn, *Early Kodak Days* (RGE-UR).

25. GE to William H. Walker, March 1891 (GEC).

26. Frank Brownell Mehlenbacher, "Frank A. Brownell: Mr. Eastman's Camera Maker," *Image: Journal of Photography and Motion Pictures of the International Museum of Photography at George Eastman House* 26, no. 2 (June 1983): 1–9. Interviews with Frank Dugan, 17 November 1950, Mrs. Mary Dugan, 24 November 1950, Mrs. Frank E. Mehlenbacher and Raymond F. Brownell, 30 November 1950 (EKC). The "someone" who nixed the "Collapsing Kodak" was L. B. Jones.

27. Reese V. Jenkins, *Images and Enterprise* (Baltimore and London: Johns Hopkins University Press, 1974), 142.

28. GE to J. B. B. Wellington, 16 April 1892 (GEC). Carl W. Ackerman, *George Eastman* (Boston and New York: Houghton Mifflin, 1930), 68.

29. Ibid.

30. GE to HAS, 19 August 1891 (GEC).

31. Interviews by Jean Ennis and other Kodak interviewers with Thomas J. Craig, 25 July 1950, 29 January 1951 (EKC).

32. GE wrote to Mrs. Sage in longhand and either never mailed the letter or made a handwritten copy (INC-GEC).

33. Interview by Jean Ennis with Minnie Hoefler Cline, ca. 1950 (EKC). Minnie's impressions are echoed in Eastman's letter to a dealer, "Friend Partridge," in 1889: "Nobody in our factory knows what we are going to make except the foreman and the chemist. The rest think we are going to make glass plates on a large scale and by a new process. Address correspondence to me *personally*."

34. Ibid.

35. Interview with Charles F. Hutchison, Kodak Park, 17 October 1950 (EKC).

36. GE to Henry and Homer Reichenbach, Gus Milburn, and Carl Passavant, 1 January 1892; GE to Moritz B. Philipp, 2 January 1892 (GEC).

37. GE to George Dickman, 27 March 1893 (GEC). This long letter, which addresses Dickman for the first time as "Managing Director" and urges him to build a Solio plant, shows that GE was suspicious of both Wellington and Krohn.

38. GE to William H. Walker, 18 February 1892 (GEC).

39. *The Hartford Courant*, 1934, clipping in employee files (EKC).

40. Darragh de Lancey, September 1897 (Box 8, INC-GEC); Walter Krohn, *Early Kodak Days*; Interviews with Minnie Hoefler Cline, de Lancey (EKC), and Charles Hutchison, 1940 (RGE-UR).

41. Jenkins, *Images and Enterprise,* 146; GE to Cellulod Zapon Company, 1892 (GEC).

42. Jenkins, *Images and Enterprise,* 93–95, 167–68, 192–95; Rudolf Kingslake, *The Rochester Camera and Lens Companies* (Rochester: The Photographic Historical Society, 1974); Eaton S. Lothrop Jr., "The Camera Industry of Rochester, N.Y." (Rochester:

The Photographic Historical Society booklet, 1974). In 1995 the name of the building was Hawkeye Plant.

43. GE to Cornelia Hagan, 27 January 1892; GE to W. H. Walker, 26 November 1891 (GEC).

44. Krohn, *Early Kodak Days*, GE to George Dickman, 31 July 1893 (GEC).

45. GE to the Eastman Photographic Materials Company, Limited, 19 December 1892 (GEC); *Democrat and Chronicle*, 14 February 1893 (INC-GEC).

46. GE to H. A. Strong, 8 and 14 February 1893 (GEC).

Chapter 6: Prayers and Paper Wars

1. GE to W. H. Walker, 2 February 1892 (GEC); W. H. Walker to GE, 24 February 1892 (INC-GEC).

2. GE to George Monroe, 6 December 1893 and 21 March 1912 (GEC). Monroe never did drop the subject of his firing. In 1912, twenty years after the episode, Eastman wrote: "I cannot agree with you at all when you speak of de Lancey's revenge, or when you refer to his advancement at your expense. His judgment of you at the time may have been right, or may not, but it was absolutely honest. All he was interested in was to have the emulsion department run successfully. As to Butler I can say nothing except that while he did get temporary advancement he soon demonstrated his own incompetency and was dropped. Now as to your loyalty, my recollection is that at the time I doubted it but the main reason for letting you go was the feeling that you were not big enough to handle the job. Your own indiscretions probably induced me to act more abruptly than I otherwise would. As time has gone by the feeling that you were not loyal has worn away and I now am ready to debit you only with indiscretion. Of course at that time everyone was on edge as to disloyalty on account of the actions of the Reichenbach crowd and this should have, I think, caused you to have been unusually careful in not laying yourself open to any suspicion. In view of what I have done for you [many loans and gifts over the years] you must realize that I bear you no ill will whatever."

3. GE to the *Chicago Tribune*, 7 November 1892 (GEC); *Denver Republican*, 11 December 1892 (INC-GEC).

4. Plates were in use through the 1930s, according to Nicholas Graver, historian and collector. The Kodak Research Laboratories of 1995 still does some precision work on plates because they are so flat and smooth and capable of small runs of special emulsions.

5. GE to William Stuber, 18 December 1893 and 4 January 1894 (GEC). According to David Gibson, former head of the Kodak Patent Museum, there is no evidence other than Eastman's word that such a "transparency plate department" existed at this time but the six sizes offered to photographers in 1886 had increased to twelve sizes by 1896, so someone made this part of the business grow. Most probably it was William Stuber.

6. Interview with William G. Stuber (EKC).

7. Ibid.

8. GE to William H. Walker, 5 March 1892 (GEC).

9. Wyatt Brummitt, *George Eastman of Kodak* (unpublished ms., ca. 1960).

10. GE to W. G. Stuber, 25 September 1894 (GEC).

11. William G. Stuber to Howard Senier, 11 December 1894; Eastman Kodak Company to Howard Senier, 7 and 11 December 1894; GE to George Dickman, 7 November 1894 (GEC).

12. GE to Walter Krohn, 26 June 1894; GE to Church & Church, 11 April 1892 (GEC).

13. George Dickman to GE, 15 March 1894 (INC-GEC).

14. GE to HAS, 8 August 1893 (GEC).

15. Eastman–Blair correspondence in GEC and INC-GEC. Summary of minutes of Eastman Company and Eastman Kodak Company at EKC.

16. GE to Moritz B. Philipp, 31 October 1894 (GEC).

17. GE to M. B. Philipp and E. P. M. Co. Ltd., 28 May 1895 (GEC). In 1892 Eastman tried to get an injunction against Turner's Boston Camera Company for infringing the Eastman–Walker roll-holder patent, a strategy he had used so effectively against Blair in removing the Kamaret camera from the market. But the Turner injunction was denied in July 1894.

18. GE to Henry A. Strong, 13 December 1894 (GEC).

19. Walter Krohn, *Early Kodak Days* (unpublished ms.: 1932), 22. (RGE-UR).

20. POP was pronounced by the three initials—P.O.P.—not as "POP," a nickname for a father. The collodion formula was introduced in England in 1864 and brought to this country by Carl Christensen of Denmark. It captured the imagination of a group of businessmen who founded the American Aristotype Company, naming their company for the European trademark.

21. GE to Joseph Thacher Clarke 3 February 1896 (GEC); Brummitt ms.

22. GE to George Dickman, 2 September 1893 (GEC); Walter Krohn, *Early Kodak Days* (ms., 1932), 19–20 (RGE-UR); [Stuber's contract] (GEC).

23. GE to S. H. Mora, 17 January 1894; GE to George Dickman, 17 August 1893 and 12 February 1894 (GEC).

24. GE to George Dickman, 22 December 1894 (GEC).

25. GE to Eastman Photographic Materials Company, Limited, 19 and 21 December 1892 (GEC). Eastman is using "Aristotype" in a generic sense, meaning printing-out paper. Several firms—American Aristotype, New York Aristotype, New Jersey Aristotype—used the term in their company names.

26. GE to Henry A. Strong, 13 November 1894 (GEC).

27. GE to Henry A. Strong, 17 October 1894 (GEC); GE to Eastman Photographic Materials Company, Limited, 19 and 21 December 1892 (GEC); GE to H. Lieber, 19 November 1894 (GEC). Reese Jenkins, *Images and Enterprise*, 94.

28. GE to William H. Walker, 3 December 1894 GEC).

29. GE to C. A. Stacy, 26 February 1894 (GEC).

30. GE to Carbutt, 3 March 1894 (GEC).

31. GE to HAS, 1893 (GEC); Carl Ackerman, *George Eastman* (Boston and New York: Houghton Mifflin, 1930), 103.

32. GE to George Dickman, 19 December 1894; Alice K. Whitney to GE, Cedar Rapids, 14 and 17 December 1894 (GEC).

33. GE to Charles S. Abbott, November 1892, 26 August 1893 (GEC); Ackerman, *George Eastman*, 103–104.

34. GE to George Dickman, November 1894 (GEC).

35. GE to Henry A. Strong, 21 November 1894 (GEC); GE to M. Phelps, 31 January 1895 (GEC).

36. GE to George W. de Bedts, 15 February 1893 (GEC); GE to M. B. Phelps, 14 February 1893 (GEC); GE to HAS, 9 February 1893 (GEC).

37. Lest the reader think that Eastman didn't really mean to win all these suits but was just using them to keep his competitors in court constantly, David Gibson notes: "Having read the trial transcript [for the suit against the Buffalo Argentic Paper Company] and all the work that went into it, even building machines based on earlier patents and a copy of the Allen & Rowell machine, and pursuing the suit for about two years, I have no doubt that GE really meant to win this suit."

38. GE to the Eastman Photographic Materials Company Limited, 5 December 1892 (GEC).

39. GE to Henry A. Strong, 8 December 1894 and 8 July 1895 (GEC).

Chapter 7: Photos by the Mile

1. Carl W. Ackerman, *George Eastman* (Boston and New York: Houghton Mifflin, 1930), 66. Ackerman does not identify the source of this report.

2. GE to Paul Garrett, Weldon, S.C., 3 December 1903; Eastman Kodak Correspondence School manual, 1903.

3. GE to Homer Croy, Forest Hills, Long Island, N.Y., 20 March 1917 (GEC).

4. Edison Phonograph Works to Eastman Dry Plate Company, 30 May 1889 (EKC); Ackerman, *George Eastman*, 64, 209.

5. W. K. L. Dickson to the Eastman Company, 2 September 1889 (EKC). Dickson asked for the film for his "astronomical arrangement" to disguise the fact that he was working on motion pictures. GE to Reichenbach, 23 July 1891 (GEC).

6. GE to Henry Reichenbach 8 December 1891 (GEC). Even before the wheel method of manufacturing film was perfected, discussions were held at Kodak Park about doubling and even tripling the length of the two hundred-foot glass tables and extending the buildings so that longer sections of film could be produced and the cutting and pasting routine reduced. Eastman vetoed the idea.

7. GE to William H. Walker, 22 February 1896 (GEC).

8. GE to Thomas Baker, Melbourne, 20 June 1918 (GEC): "It looks as if glass plates are doomed [for x rays]. . . . The Government has taken all we could make."

9. Wyatt Brummitt, *George Eastman of Kodak* (Eastman Kodak Company, ca. 1960, unpublished ms.), 72–73 (EKC).

10. GE statement on the occasion of Edison's death, 15 September 1931 (GEC).

11. GE to Darwin P. Kingsley, 15 March 1923 (GEC).

12. GE tribute, 15 September 1931 (GEC).

13. HAS to GE, 12 and 15 October 1896 (GEC); HAS to T. Edison, 31 August and 17 September 1896 (GEC); HAS to Mutoscope, 24 August and 14 September 1896 (GEC).

14. GE to George Dickman, 13 and 24 February 1896 (GEC).

15. George Dickman to Hedley Smith, 22, 24, 27, and 30 June 1896 (GEC).

16. Ackerman, *George Eastman*, 127.

17. GE to George Dickman, 16 February 1897 (GEC).

18. GE testimony, *United States v. Eastman Kodak Co.* et al., 24 August 1915, U.S. Circuit Court, Western District of New York, *Abridged Transcript of Record* (10 vols., 4,200 pp.) and *Supplemental Brief and Argument for Defendants* (80 pp.).

19. GE to Hedley Smith, 3 May 1907 (GEC); Ackerman, *George Eastman*, 209–10. Eastman and Edison did not meet again until 1924 at a New York luncheon in Edison's honor, given by the motion picture industry. At that second meeting, both men had forgotten about the 1907 conversations.

20. Ackerman, *George Eastman*, 222.

21. GE to M. B. Philipp, 2 December 1907 (GEC); Ackerman, *George Eastman*, 213.

22. Ackerman, *George Eastman*, 219.

23. Ibid., 224.

24. GE to William Gifford, GE to Thomas Baker, 1909 (GEC)

25. GE to J. Thacher Clarke, 1910 (GEC); Ackerman, *George Eastman*, 225.

26. Details about Jules Brulatour from interview by author with General Edward Peck Curtis, 1980.

Chapter 8: The Gay Nineties

1. GE to City [Rochester], July 1887 (GEC).

2. A. S. Barnes to MKE, 24 April 1887 (INC-GEC): "Dear Madam . . . The diminished sale of the Book for the past two years makes my offer a desirable one for you."

3. GE to A. M. Koeth, 30 September 1886 (GEC): "I decided not to purchase your lot. My principal reasons are that the lot has not sufficient frontage on the avenue in proportion to its depth and width at the rear end and that for a residence the situation is not so good as the land next in the direction of the city." GE to J. M. Kirk, 9 September 1886 (GEC), is an inquiry concerning land on the Charlotte road for a factory. The Court Street factory was originally Walkers dry plate factory; Strong bought it from him in 1884. In 1994 it was demolished to make room for Bausch and Lomb corporate headquarters garage.

4. GE to Charles Crandall, 25 September 1894 (GEC).

5. GE to MKE, 25 May 1890 (GEC-UR).

6. GE to George W. Andrus, 16 and 20 August 1891 (GEC).

7. George W. Andrus to MKE, 14 August 1886 (INC-GEC).

8. Interview with Francis S. Macomber, 17 December 1950 (EKC).

9. Lizzie Colman to GE; Harris Hayden to GE (INC-GEC); GE to MKE, November 1887 (GEC-UR).

10. Incoming correspondence, Box 1 (INC-GEC).

11. GE to MKE, 10 April 1890 (GEC-UR).

12. GE to MKE, 30 March 1890 (GEC-UR).

13. GE to MKE, 30 April 1890 (GEC-UR).

14. GE to MKE, 10 April 1890 (GEC-UR).

15. Ibid.

16. Ibid.

17. GE to MKE, 18 April 1890 (GEC-UR).

18. Ibid. He was home by 4 May 1890. GE to G. W. Andrus, 15 July 1890 (GEC-UR).

19. The original note to Dr. Lee is at the University of Rochester Library (RGE-UR).

20. F. T. Walter Krohn, *Early Kodak Days* (unpublished ms., 1932) (RGE-UR).

21. Cornelia B. Atwood, Hamilton, N.Y., to GE, 14 December 1924 (INC-GEC).

22. William H. Walker to GE, 1890 (INC-GEC).

23. Paul Fussell, "The Fate of Chivalry and the Assault upon Mother," Thank God for the Atom Bomb and Other Essays (New York: Summit Books, 1988), 221–48.

24. GE to MKE, 14 February 1891 (GEC-UR).

25. Paul Fussell, "The Fate of Chivalry and the Assault upon Mother," 221–48.

26. GE to W. H. Walker, 14 June 1890 (GEC).

27. Interview with Albert W. Jacobs, 3 April 1940 (RGE-UR).

28. GE to James Cunningham, 21 December 1891, January and February 1893, August 1893; GE to Central Park Riding Academy, 21 November 1893 (GEC); Rufus K. Dryer (for Cunningham) to GE, 30 January, 5 February, 31 March 1892 (INC-GEC).

29. Krohn, *Early Kodak Days*, 9.

30. GE to director of General World's Columbian Exposition in Chicago, 29 July 1891 (GEC).

31. The Kodak camera models available in 1893, according to David Gibson, Kodak Patent Museum, were the Nos. 1, 2, 3, and 4 Kodak camera; Nos. 3 and 4 Junior Kodak, both film and plate models; 4, 5, and 6 Folding Kodak; ABC Ordinary; ABC Daylight; and also glass-plate models of the C Ordinary and the Nos. 4 and 5 Folding Kodak cameras.

32. GE to HAS, Tacoma, 16 May 1893 (GEC); Handout on "World Fairs in Which Kodak Has Participated" (EKC).

33. GE to the Eastman Photographic Materials Company, June, 1893 (GEC).

34. GE to HAS, 16 May 1893; GE to William H. Walker, 22 May 1893 (GEC).

35. GE to HAS, 3 September 1891 (GEC).

36. Adolph Stuber, son of William G. and a vice president of the Eastman Kodak Company for many years, identified Stuber, L. B. Jones, C. E. K. Mees, F. J. Lovejoy, and M. B. Folsom as the five lieutenants.

37. GE to George W. De Bedts, 15 February 1893 (GEC).

38. Background material on L. B. Jones in writeup of August 1965 in the (historical) employee files (EKC).

Chapter 9: Prince Henry and the Earl of East Avenue

All quotes in this chapter from HAS to GE are from letters kept in one box (INC-GEC).

1. Interview with Thomas Craig, 1950 (EKC); HAS to S. N. Turner, 9 October 1895 (EKC).

2. HAS to GE, 1888 (INC-GEC). See Carl W. Ackerman, George Eastman (Boston and New York: Houghton Mifflin, 1930), 74–75.

3. GE to HAS, 24 May 1889 (GEC).

4. GE to HAS, 29 March 1894 (GEC).

5. GE to HAS, 17 July 1894 (GEC).

6. GE to HAS, 29 October 1894 (GEC).

7. GE to HAS, 29 October 1894; GE to A. N. Fitch, 30 December 1895 (GEC).

8. HAS to GE, box of letters from Strong to Eastman, various dates, 1880s and 1890s (INC-GEC). HAS to GE, 1 April 1897 (GEC): "APRIL FOOL!"

9. GE to HAS, 30 November, 3 and 19 December 1894 (GEC).

10. GE to HAS, 26 February 1894; GE to The Plenty Horticultural and Skylight Works, 9 May 1894; GE to Josephus Plenty, 16 May 1894; GE to MKE, 3 October 1895 (GEC).

11. GE to Harris H. Hayden, 29 September 1894 (GEC).

12. Marguerite Hubbell, [Soule House] (Landmark Society of Western New York: unpublished ms., n.d.).

13. GE to Almon R. Eastman, 30 October 1894 (GEC).

14. GE to HAS, November 1894; GE to A. R. Eastman, 28 and 30 September 1894, 16 September 1895 (GEC).

15. GE to J. B. Tiffany, 28 February and 4 April 1898; GE to Hayden Furniture Company, 18 November 1898 (GEC).

16. GE to George Dickman, 23 and 28 January 1896; GE to Frank Seaman (who found Toku), 17 August 1899 (GEC).

17. GE to HAS, January 1895 (GEC).

18. Interview with Murray Bartlett, 26 March 1940 (RGE-UR).

19. GE to George Dickman, 6 May 1895 (GEC).

20. Ed Hickey to GE, 30 July 1896 (INC-GEC).

21. Interview by author with Dr. James Sibley Watson Jr., ca. 1980.

22. GE to George Dickman (dish), 18 March 1896 (GEC); Cornelia Hagen to GE, June 1895 and Lily Fenn to GE, 2 March 1896 (Box 6 INC-GEC).

Chapter 10: A Salute for the Czar

1. Interview with Carl Fisher, 4 January 1940 (RGE-UR).

2. GE to Edmond Seymour, 2 January 1894 (GEC).

3. GE to George W. Andrus, 19 March 1893; GE to A. H. Overman, 23 July 1895 (GEC).

4. GE to William H. Walker, 25 February 1895 (GEC).

5. GE to MKE, 9 July 1892 and July 1896 from Russia (GEC-UR).

6. GE to MKE, September, October 1891 (GEC-UR).

7. Ibid.

8. GE to MKE, 9, 15, 17, 23, 30 July, 5 August 1892 (GEC-UR).

9. Ibid.

10. Ibid.

11. GE to MKE, 11 August 1892 (GEC-UR).

12. Ibid.; interviews with Mildred Brownell Mehlenbacher, Frank Dugan, Mary Dugan, and Raymond Brownell, 1950 (EKC).

13. George Dickman to GE, 29 September 1896 (INC-GEC).

14. George Dickman to GE, 10 October 1896 (INC-GEC); GE to George Dickman, January 1897 (GEC).

15. This painting has since been returned to Eastman House, where it is prominently displayed over the fireplace in the living room.

16. Claude Bragdon, *More Lives Than One* (New York: Alfred A. Knopf, 1938), 80; interview with George B. Selden, 2 February 1940 (RGE-UR); GE to MKE, 25 September 1895 (GEC-UR).

17. GE to MKE, 9 and 13 July 1896 (nightshirts); 17 and 24 July, and n.d. 1896 (Russia) (GEC-UR).

18. Ibid.

19. GE to MKE, 30 and 31 July, 3 and 5 August 1896 (GEC-UR).

20. GE to MKE, 6 September 1896 (GEC-UR); Murray Bartlett interview, 26 March 1940 (RGE-UR).

21. GE to MKE, 15 September 1896 (GEC-UR).

22. GE to MKE, 27 September 1896; 27 October 1894 (GEC-UR); GE to G. Dickman, 9 November 1896 (GEC).

23. GE to HAS, March 1899 (GEC); Carl Ackerman, *George Eastman* (Boston and New York: Houghton Mifflin, 1930), 152.

24. Interviews with Charles F. Hutchison, 8 January 1940 (RGE-UR); 17 October 1950 by Jean Ennis, 25 December 1974 by James M. Albright (EKC).

25. GE to HAS, 11 April 1895 (GEC-GEH).

26. Ibid.

27. GE to HAS, 19 and 27 March, 19 November 1895 (GEC). The messages went in a special Kodak code (not in Morse code, available to all) in which a word stood for another word and the messages made no sense as received—except to the managing director in London, who had the same Kodak code book.

28. Wyatt Brummitt, *George Eastman of Kodak* (Eastman Kodak Company, ca. 1960, unpublished ms.), 81–82 (EKC).

29. GE to the Eastman Photographic Materials Company, 23 April 1896 (GEC). In less than two years (1888–90), the original Kodak camera had been augmented by Nos. 1, 2, 3, and 4 Kodak cameras, Nos. 3 and 4 Kodak Junior, and Nos. 4 and 5 Folding Kodak cameras. Then in 1891 came the A, B, and C Daylight and A, B, and C Ordinary Kodak cameras plus a special glass-plate camera. These were followed by the Nos. 4 and 5 glass-plate Folding Kodak and Nos. 3 and 4 Junior glass-plate Kodak cameras of 1892. Even in the depression year of 1893, the No. 6 Folding Kodak, a monster camera, was introduced. The customer could thus shoot almost any conceivable size negative. As the economy improved the number of different models increased even more. In 1894 the Kodet, Folding Kodet, and Folding Kodet Junior models were introduced, followed by the Bullet and the Bulls-Eye (which Eastman purchased from Samuel Turner) cameras of 1895. Because "the cheap camera trade is growing," Eastman introduced the Flexo Kodak film camera, selling for $5, and the Eureka camera, a "cheap [$3.20] dry plate outfit" with "cheap cartridge rollholder" optional, as he told Dickman, all "to get the ground covered ahead of our competitors." Nevertheless, he assured the public that the Eureka camera was "an instrument

that can be depended upon" with "no uncertain or untried devices for cheapening cost and no clumsy attempts at making it a magazine camera."

30. GE to George Dickman, 29 July 1897 (GEC).

31. GE to the Eastman Photographic Materials Company, 23 April 1896 (GEC).

32. GE to HAS, 22 July 1899, GE to Brownell, 1898; HAS to GE, 10 January 1898, 6 March, 26 May 1900 (GEC).

33. GE to Albert Jay, 1898 (GEC).

34. GE to George Dickman, 29 July 1897 (GEC).

35. GE to E. O. Sage, 23 August 1897 (GEC).

36. GE to HAS, 1 July 1899 (GEC); *F. W. Lovejoy: The story of a practical idealist*, (Rochester: Eastman Kodak Company, 1947). 18; *Boys Grown Tall: A story of American Initiative* (Rochester: Democrat and Chronicle, 1946), 89–90.

37. Ibid.; GE to Francis A. Walker, 19 June 1896 (GEC); GE to Harriet Gallup, 25 January 1896 (GEC). It was the rug Eastman purchased in Paris for the de Lanceys that gave rise to the rumor, passed from rug merchants in Paris to rug merchants in Rochester, that Eastman was engaged. The rug, in this rumor, was for his betrothed.

38. HAS to GE, 15 November 1897 (GEC). GE to J. W. Millington, 1897 (GEC).

39. GE to MKE, 18 July 1897 (GEC-UR); GE to A. H. Overman, 5 February, 24 July, 23 August 1897; GE to E. O. Sage, 16 August 1897; GE to George Dickman, 10 May 1898 (GEC).

Chapter 11: GE versus Albion's City

1. "Preference shares" (U.S. "preferred stock") is stock assured by a corporation's charter of dividends before any are paid on the "ordinary shares"(U.S. "common") and usually also having preference in distribution of assets. The dividends of preference shares was specified whereas dividends on ordinary shares depended on how well the company was doing. Myron Peck's tirades fill the INC-GEC boxes from 1890–3. Eastman's lengthy replies are in GEC, 1890–93.

2. GE to George Dickman, 3 February 1897 (GEC).

3. GE to MKE, 6 March and 15 April 1897 (GEC-UR).

4. GE to MKE, 2 October 1897 (GEC-UR).

5. GE to MKE, 29 October 1897 (GEC-UR).

6. HAS to GE, 18 October 1897 (GEC) Walter S. Hubbell to GE, 24 March 1898 (INC-GEC).

7. HAS to GE, 18 October, 8 November 1897 (GEC); GE to MKE, 31 October 1897 (GEC-UR).

8. GE to MKE, 14 and 18 September 1897 (GEC-UR).

9. GE to MKE, 15 April 1897 (GEC-UR).

10. GE to MKE 4, 9, 17 November 1897 (GEC-UR).

11. GE to MKE, 16 October 1897 (GEC-UR). Eastman was confused. He meant not the queen of England, but Princess Alexandra of Wales.

12. GE to MKE, 16, 22, 27, 31 October, 4 and 9 November 1897 (GEC-UR).

13. GE to MKE, 24 and 27 November, 1, 4, 11 December 1897 (GEC-UR). Whitney accompanied Eastman on all his trips to London during 1897.

14. GE to MKE, 19 January 1898 (GEC-UR).

15. GE to MKE 15, 19, 23, 28 January, 2, 5, 11, 16 February 1898 (GEC-UR); Carl W. Ackerman, *George Eastman* (Boston and New York: Houghton Mifflin, 1930), 138.

16. GE to MKE, 9 November 1898 (GEC-UR); Ackerman, *George Eastman,* 134.

17. GE to MKE, 11 February 1898 (GEC-UR).

18. Ackerman, *George Eastman,* 136–37.

19. GE to George Dickman, April 1898; GE to William H. Walker, 3 May 1898 (GEC). The *Maine* was blown up 15 February 1898; Congress voted $50 million for defense on 9 March; the armistice was signed 12 August, and the peace treaty in December 1898.

20. GE to MKE, 1898 (GEC-UR); recapitalization of 1898 documents (EKC).

21. Ackerman, *George Eastman,* 142.

22. GE to MKE and HAS, 11 and 12 November 1898 (GEC-UR).

23. GE to MKE, 15 November 1898 (GEC-UR).

24. GE to MKE, 23 December 1898 (GEC-UR).

25. Printed card signed by F. M. Crouch, cashier, 15 February 1899 (EKC).

26. Interview with Louisa Knorr, 13 February 1940 (RGE-UR).

27. GE to Andrew Pringle, 1899 (GEC).

28. GE to Charles S. Abbott, 23 December 1899 (GEC). Andrew Pringle to GE, 7 April and 4 May 1899 (INC-GEC).

29. Interviews with Murray Bartlett and Raymond Ball, 1940 (RGE-UR); MKE to GE, 14 November 1898 (GEC-UR); GE to F. Colson, 1923 (GEC). Instead, thanks in part to a hundred years of Kodak business, the Alliance became the Lincoln Alliance, then the Lincoln Rochester, and finally the Chase Lincoln bank.

30. GE to HAS in Honolulu, 13 March 1899 (GEC). Interviews with Charles F. Hutchison, 1940 (RGE-UR); 1950 (EKC).

31. It also recalls Eastman's childhood habit of frequenting bookstores just to read the font of all knowledge, the encyclopedia: "I had an argument about Gothic architecture and quoted Clarke's opinion that buttressing and not pointed arches was the important factor. But I can't find printed proof, not even in the Encyclopædia Brittanica."

There is no evidence that Eastman and Babbott ever saw each other after pre-school days although some of Babbott's family remained in Waterville and they kept up with each other's careers. Then as 1896 approached and Eastman was preparing to send out advance models of his pet, the Folding Pocket Kodak camera, he impulsively added Frank's name to the list and received a reply that was to erase thirty years of separation. "Dear George," Babbott wrote. "It was my great pleasure to receive your new year greeting and . . . the beautiful camera. I shall indeed be glad to begin my work in this new line [with] . . . a fine group of my three children and wife whom I hope you will soon meet. In many ways your gift takes me back to my Waterville life when you and I found much in our ambitions that was common to us both. I hope we may renew that friendship, for there are no new friends that are quite the same as the old ones." The friendship was renewed and stayed constant for thirty-six years. Frank L. Babbott to GE, January 1896 (INC-GEC).

32. This is one version of how Eastman met the Mulligans. Another that has come

down in the Mulligan family is that both Eastman and Edward Mulligan were suitors for the hand of the vivacious Mary Durand, daughter of a railroad president. Since the Mulligans were married in 1892, it seems unlikely that Eastman would have been traveling then in the same social set as the prominent Durand family.

33. GE to HAS, 20 March 1899 (GEC).

34. GE to Harris H. Hayden, 6 April 1899 (GEC); GE to HAS, 5 April 1899 (GEC).

35. GE to HAS, 1 July 1899; GE to Moritz B. Philipp, 24 March 1899; GE to George Davison, 27 March 1899 (GEC). Eastman prepared for the increased capacity to produce film by instructing Brownell to design a $1 camera to further hook the public on snapping pictures.

36. GE to Darragh de Lancey, 25 and 27 March 1899 (GEC): "It never occurred to me that Stuber and Lovejoy were not working together. . . . I do not see that their interests clash. Stuber is interested in emulsion, Lovejoy in dope. . . . It makes little difference whether Lovejoy had to ask Stuber to do the emulsion part or Stuber had to ask Lovejoy to do the dope part. . . . These are little matters. I think I fully appreciate the work that both men are doing and I do not think they are likely to gain or lose by such matters as these."

37. GE to Frank Lovejoy, June 1900 (GEC).

38. GE to HAS, 14 April 1899 (GEC); GE to J. Foster Warner, 1898 (GEC); GE to George Davison, July 1899 (GEC); GE to HAS, 26 July 1899 (GEC) It was in this basement vault that George Eastman's correspondence, both personal and business, incoming and outgoing, was housed until April 1990, when it was moved to the George Eastman House. His letters to his mother were sent to his home and remained there until they were moved to the Department of Rare Books and Special Collections, Rush Rhees Library, the University of Rochester, in the 1960s.

39. GE to M. J. Calihan, 10 August 1898 (GEC).

40. GE to George Davison and E. W. Peet, 6 June 1900; GE to M. B. Phelps, 5 June 1900 (GEC).

41. GE to MIT, 5 June 1899 (GEC); GE to Darragh de Lancey, 9 December 1898 (GEC).

42. GE to A. H. Overman, December 1899 (GEC).

43. Sources for material on Mechanics Institute in GEC: GE to L. P. Ross, 13 and 20 February 1900; GE to Messrs. Thayer and Co., New York City, 4 August 1900; GE to Walter S. Hubbell, 20 February 1900; GE to J. Foster Warner, 25 April 1900; GE to E. O. Sage, 15 August 1900. Dedicatory brochure at Rochester Historical Society.

Chapter 12: The Power of Combination

1. "Opinion," *United States v. Eastman Kodak Co.* et al., 24 August 1915, U.S. Circuit Court, Western District of New York, v. 226, *Federal Reporter*. *United States* v. *Eastman Kodak Company* (*U.S.* v. *EKCo.*), U.S. Circuit Court, Western District of New York, 24 August 1915, no. A-51; appeal to U.S. Supreme Court, petition: 8 March 1916; withdrawn: February 1921, *Abridged Transcript of Record*, 10 vols. (4,200 pp.), available in Appellate Case File No. 25,293, Legislative, Judicial and Diplomatic Records Division, National Archives, Washington, D.C.   and *Supplemental Brief and Argument*

for Defendants c. 80 pp.)—available at the Rochester Public Library, Rochester, N.Y., and 226 *Federal Reporter* 62 (1915).

2. GE to Moritz B. Philipp, 12 August 1898 (GEC).

3. $42,955.22 for building, machinery, and real estate that had cost $91,640 plus assets of $25,000.

4. GE to Moritz B. Philipp, 12 August 1898 (GEC).

5. Ibid., Henry Verden to GE, 10 August 1899 (INC-GEC); GE to Henry Verden, 21 August 1899 (GEC).

6. Combined, Eastman invested $126,588 in the four companies, expecting them to do a business of about $250,000 a year.

7. GE to HAS, 3 February 1898 (GEC); GE to W. H. Walker, 7 June 1894 (GEC).

8. HAS to GE, London, 10 February 1898 (GEC).

9. Ibid.

10. GE to HAS, 14 April 1899 (GEC); Blair testimony, *U.S. v. EKCo., Abridged Transcript of Record* (10 vols., 4,200 pp.) and *Supplemental Brief and Argument for Defendants* (80 pp.), 1914.

11. Interview with Charles Ames, 4 January 1940 (RGE-UR) (BUTT-UR).

12. GE to John Palmer, December 1899; 27 September and 11 October 1901; (GEC).

13. GE to Moritz Philipp, 12 September 1898 (GEC); "Goodwin File Wrapper and Contents," U.S. Patent Office, in *Goodwin v. EKCo.*, 3575–3830.

14. Unidentified document in INC-GEC, 1893, presumably written by Goodwin interests as the allegation is not true.

15. Copy of Kodak Trade Circular, September 1901 (BUTT-UR).

16. GE to George Davison, 11 August 1902 (GEC).

17. GE to George Davison, 6 March 1898 (GEC). The *Democrat & Chronicle*, 5 August 1898.

18. GE to Moritz B. Phillipp, 25 June and 14 August 1901 (GEC).

19. Ibid.

20. Ibid., The essence of Eastman's version was later confirmed by Frederick A. Anthony in his testimony, *Goodwin v. EKCo.*, 1296.

21. *Kodak Trade Circular*, January 1902 (BUTT-UR); Reese V. Jenkins, *Images and Enterprises* (Baltimore and London: Johns Hopkins University Press, 1975), 251; *Kodak Trade Circular*, January 1902 (BUTT-UR).

22. GE to Moritz B. Philipp, 9 December 1904 (GEC).

23. GE to Moritz B. Philipp, 6, 17, and 28 May, 12 June 1902 (GEC). Jenkins, *Images and Enterprises*, 253.

24. Ibid., 205–6.

25. *Record on Appeal*, 476–82. According to a July 1957 interview with Netta Ranlet by C. M. Podolin (EKC), Bonbright took the Defender stock off his friend's hands with great reluctance and only as a favor. In 1945 the Du Pont Company purchased Defender.

26. GE to George Davison, 23 October 1900 (GEC).

27. GE to F. Dundas Todd, Victoria, B.C., 12 August 1920 (GEC).

28. HAS to GE, 1900 (INC-GEC).

29. GE to MKE, 1898 (GEC-UR); GE to Rudolf Sulzberger, Dresden, 17 April 1902 (GEC).

30. GE to Kodak Limited directors, 30 March 1899 (GEC).

31. GE to HAS, 13 March 1899 (GEC).

32. GE to Kodak Limited directors, 30 March 1899 (GEC).

33. GE to GEPACO, 12 June 1899 (GEC).

34. GE to C.S. Abbott, 11 July 1899 (GEC).

35. Jenkins, *Images and Enterprises*, 192–93; Fritz Wentzel, *Memoirs of a Photochemist* (Philadelphia: American Museum of Photography, 1960), 79. Velox was based on a formula for an unwashed chlorobromide emulsion, published in Europe in 1881 by J. M. Eder and G. Pizzighelli. This versatile formula was five hundred times as fast as albumen but still slow enough to be handled and developed in subdued "gaslight" and capable of being exposed when brought in close proximity with the same artificial light.

36. Story related by Baekeland to Professor Ralph H. McKee, Columbia University, who related it to C. B. F. Young, Douglasville, Ga., who sent it to *Smithsonian*, October 1985.

37. GE to Kodak Limited, 20 July 1899 (GEC); GE to Alfred T. Jay, 5 September 1899 (GEC).

38. GE to Kodak Limited, 12 June 1899 (GEC).

39. GE to Charles S. Abbott, 13 July 1899; GE to Simon Haus, 7 June 1900 (GEC).

40. GE to Harris H. Hayden, 9 August 1899 (GEC) Jenkins, *Images and Enterprises*, 206. Eastman's Permanent Bromide remained in the catalogs from 1886 until 1917. Velox is still made as a single-weight glossy paper for contact prints, "designed to fit the requirements of the amateur photographer's negatives," a recent catalog states. Regardless of how hard Kodak Park and Jamestown tried, they could not turn out a platinum paper that satisfied the rigorous demands of the minuscule market of art photographers.

41. GE to George Davison, 15 March 1902 (GEC).

42. GE to HAS, 26 July 1899 (GEC)., GE to George Davison, 26 July 1901; GE to G. Cramer, Messrs. Stanley Bros., L. F. Hammer, 31 July 1901 (GEC).

43. Charles S. Abbott to GE, 23 July 1902 (INC-GEC).

44. GE to Charles S. Abbott, 10 November 1902 (GEC).

45. GE to George Davison, 16 November 1899 (GEC). Rudolf Kingslake, *The Rochester Camera and Lens Companies* (Rochester: The Photographic Historical Society, 1974), 35.

46. GE to George Davison, 18 September 1902 (GEC). Carl W. Ackerman, *George Eastman* (Boston and New York: Houghton Mifflin, 1930), 182.

47. "Brownies," the preface to all Cox books read, "like fairies and goblins, are imaginary little sprites who are supposed to delight in harmless pranks and helpful deeds. They work and sport while weary households sleep, and never allow themselves to be seen by mortal eyes." Cox believed that because children are prone to mischief, Brownies could vicariously do things children might wish to do: slide down a bannister or climb a tree and then bend it down over Niagara Falls, only to have it spring back and pitch them into the rushing water. Cox's Brownies had a penchant

for good deeds—fixing a sick widow's spinning wheel, fetching the village parson's wood—and their sports included the fads of the period: tobogganing, baseball, tennis, bicycling—but not photography. Eastman Kodak saw to that.

48. GE to George Dickman, 16 April 1896 (GEC); also GE to Edmond Seymour, 2 January 1894: "Photography is not a fad anymore than bicycling. It is used as a means for getting useful results and has increased steadily from the very discovery of Daguerre."

49. Wyatt Brummitt, *George Eastman at Kodak* (Rochester: Eastman Kodak Company unpublished ms., ca. 1960), 94–95. Hoping to better the dollar Brownie, Samuel N. Turner, former competitor and proprietor of the American Camera Company, designer of the Bulls-Eye camera and the daylight-loading cartridge, whom Eastman had recently bought out, suddenly resurfaced. Turner, who was put on a $100-a-month retainer by Eastman to turn over his ideas to the company, proposed a "Winkie" camera to sell for fifty cents. Although Eastman was initially extremely interested, asking Turner for a model, he also warned that to sell it at that price, the camera would have to be produced for a mere quarter. That, apparently, proved to be the unsurmountable barrier. No Winkies were ever marketed. However, the idea of a disposable camera never really died, and in the 1980s came to fruition.

50. Kodak advertisements (EKC); Roger Butterfield, "The Prodigious Life of George Eastman," *Life* magazine (26 April 1954): 154.

51. *People v. Gillette*, 3, 161, quoted by William Safire, *New York Times* magazine, March 1981.

52. Employee files on L. B. Jones (EKC).

53. Frank Brownell Mehlenbacher, "Frank A. Brownell: Mr. Eastman's Camera Maker," *Image: Journal of Photography and Motion Pictures of the International Museum of Photography at George Eastman House* 26, no. 2 (June 1983): 9. Brownell stayed until 1906, when he resigned to go into business for himself.

54. Ackerman, *George Eastman*, 183–86; Brummitt ms., 111–13.

55. GE to HAS, 1 July 1899 (GEC); HAS to GE, 27 September 1899 (GEC). GE to M. B. Phi and C. S. Abbott, 8 July 1901 (GEC).

56. GE to George Davison, 28 June 1900, 13 and 26 December 1900 (GEC); GE to F. Lovejoy, 21 July 1900 (GEC); GE to President, International Association of Machinists, 4 March 1901 (GEC). Ackerman, *George Eastman*, 157–64.

57. Interview with Harry M. Fenn, Kodak employee (1892–1936) and brother of Albert O. Fenn, 15 April 1939 (RGE-UR). After Eastman became intensely interested in calendar reform in the 1920s, the rumor got started that the two large chimneys erected at Kodak Park were 365 feet high, representing the number of days in the year, and 366 feet high, representing leap year.

58. GE to Arthur W. McCurdy, 7 August 1903 (GEC); Brummitt ms. 128–29.

59. GE to Thomas Baker, 22 June 1910 (GEC).

60. GE to Moritz B. Philipp, 15 June 1907, GE to F. Mattison, 23 January 1911 (GEC).

61. GE to M. A. Seed, 15 July 1903 (GEC): "Cover all celluloid scrap and shavings with solvent. . . . It will ignite if put in a warm place, [or from] the sun's rays through a bubble in the window."

62. GE to HAS, 19 February 1914 (GEC). In the Autographic cameras, a carbon

tissue between the paper and the film removed the light protection wherever the stylus pressed and when a negative was developed, name and date were preserved for posterity.

63. GE to George Davison, 16 July and 11 October 1900; GE to Andrew Pringle, 5 November and 31 December 1900 (GEC).

64. GE to George Davison, December 1907 (GEC).

65. Interview with Ronald Davison, 1954 (UR-BUTT).

66. GE to Messrs. William B. Dana Co., J. A. Terrens-Johnson, secretary, stock exchange, London, 5 September 1902 (GEC); GE to Henry Verden, 5 October 1901 (GEC); GE to Meedy's Manual, New York City, 15 March 1902 (GEC). Authorized capital was $10 million in 6 percent cumulative preferred shares and $25 million in common.

67. *Directors' Report*, Eastman Kodak Company, January 1902. GE to Henry Verden, 5 October 1901 (GEC); GE to Henry Huiskamp, Seed Dry Plate Company, 18 July 1901 (GEC): GE to Meedy's Manual, New York City, 15 March 1902 (GEC); Circular to Kodak Shareholders, 20 June 1902 (EKC).

68. GE to George Davison, 6 March 1899 (GEC).

69. GE to George Davison, 15 August 1899 (GEC).

70. Ibid.

Chapter 13: Crazy about Color

1. GE to Joseph Thacher Clarke, 3 June 1904 (GEC).

2. Notes to the author from Thomas Howard James, associate of C. E. Kenneth Mees, made after reading a draft of this chapter. Also Carl Ackerman, *George Eastman* (Boston and New York: Houghton Mifflin, 1930), 229–32.

3. GE to Moritz B. Philipp, 26 April 1904 (GEC).

4. GE to Frank W. Lovejoy, 3 May 1904 (GEC).

5. GE to George Davison, 26 May 1904 (GEC).

6. GE to George Davison, 28 April, 25 and 26 May 1904 (GEC).

7. GE to Joseph Thacher Clarke, 5 May 1910; GE to Moritz B. Philipp, 10 May 1910 (GEC). The color processes appeared in the *Photographischen Industrie*, no. 6 (1909).

8. GE to Moritz B. Philipp, 9 January 1908; GE to Joseph Thacher Clarke, 9 June 1905; GE to Simon V. Haus, 23 June 1905 (GEC).

9. GE to Darragh de Lancey, 20 June 1906; GE to HAS, 6 February 1908 (GEC).

10. GE to Frederick Monsen, 10 November 1909; GE to Darragh de Lancey, April 1910 (GEC).

11. GE to Joseph Thacher Clarke, 5 May 1910; GE to James Haste, 20 May 1910, GE to Thomas Baker, 29 August 1910 (GEC).

12. Clarke himself was an accomplished musician. Considering the later resolution of the intricacies of Kodak's color processes by two musicians, or the fact that Louis Condax, who perfected the dye transfer process, was an amateur violinist and expert violin maker, some conclusions might be drawn.

13. GE to Darragh de Lancey, April 1910 (GEC).

14. GE to Joseph Thacher Clarke, 29 April 1910; GE to Baker, 7 June 1909, GE to

Joseph Thacher Clarke, 29 April 1910, GE to Messrs. Church and Rich, 11 May 1910; GE to Joseph Thacher Clarke, 2 June 1910; GE to Darragh de Lancey, 20 November 1910 (GEC). De Lancey had left Kodak in 1900, although he continued to correspond with Eastman for the rest of the latter's life.

15. GE to Joseph Thacher Clarke, 4 January 1910 (GEC). AGFA, now written Agfa, stands for Achtung für Gesellchaft Aniline.

16. Almost marketed by Pathé in 1914, a modified Berthon process would be acquired by Kodak in 1925 and marketed in 1928 as the "Kodacolor" motion picture process.

17. GE to Moritz B. Philipp, 7 October 1910 (GEC).

18. GE to Joseph Thacher Clarke, 16 May 1910 (GEC).

19. GE to Joseph Thacher Clarke, 27 May 1910, GE to Spath, 29 May 1913 (GEC).

20. GE to Joseph Thacher Clarke, 12 June 1911 (GEC).

21. Wratten & Wainwright had an earlier contact with Kodak when George Dickman sent Frederick P. Wratten, the second son of S. H. Wratten (who shared the directorship with Mees), to Kodak Park in the 1890s to work on the sluggish dry-plate emulsion. Young Fred Wratten died prematurely at the age of twenty-five in 1899.

22. Wyatt Brummitt, *George Eastman of Kodak* (Rochester: Eastman Kodak Company, ca. 1960, unpublished ms.), 208. There is no evidence from the correspondence that Eastman visited Bayer at this time. But although he claimed in November 1911 that he was not visiting Germany on this trip in February he reported to Strong he had been to Paris, Turin, Milan, Venice, Munich, Nuremberg, Jena, Berlin, and Nancy. A stop in Elberfeld to see Duisberg was possible if unlikely since Bayer had recently instituted suits against Kodak's NI film infringing theirs in both France and the United States.

23. Ackerman, *George Eastman*, 241.

24. GE to L. Gaumont, Paris, 26 February 1912 (GEC); GE to HAS, 16 February 1912 (GEC); Ackerman, *George Eastman*, 240.

25. GE to L. Gaumont, 21 January 1914; GE to Joseph Thacher Clarke, 21 January 1914; GE to Moritz B. Philipp, 22 January 1914 (GEC).

26. GE to George L. Herdle, director, Memorial Art Gallery; GE to L. Gaumont, 1914 (GEC).

27. Haste, Mees, Capstaff, Stuber, Hutchison, Noble, Lansing, DiNunzio, Hopkins, Wills, Cline, L. B. Jones, Spensler, Barnes, Robertson, Folmer, Ruttan, Wilcox, Ames.

28. G. Hammer Croughton was the critic.

29. GE to Ellen Andrus Dryden, 10 November 1914 (GEC).

30. (Historic) employee files (EKC).

31. Joseph Wechsberg, "Whistling in the Darkroom," *The New Yorker* (10 February 1956): 61ff.

32. Ibid. In his "dream letter" to Lovejoy, Eastman referred to the Keller-Dorian lenticular process. Berthon was the first to disclose the use of lenticular film for color reproduction, but A. Keller-Dorian made substantial improvements that brought the process closer to a practical one. The two inventors formed the *Societe Keller-Dorian-Berthon*, but by 1925 Berthon had severed his connection and the three-color process

became known as simply Keller-Dorian. Source: Author's interview with T. H. James, ca. 1991.

33. Interview by author with Earl Kage of the Kodak Research Laboratories. Charles Edward Kenneth Mees, *From Dry Plates to Ektachrome Film: A Story of Photographic Research* (New York: Ziff-Davis, 1961), 211.

34. Ibid. The terms were an immediate payment of $30,000 shared and an annual salary of $7,500 each, with all future patents to belong to the company.

35. (Historic) employee files (EKC).

Chapter 14: The Garden of Eden

1. MKE to GE, letters from January 1898 to January 1899, Box 1, folder 11 (GEC-UR).

2. GE to W. J. Stillman, 23 June 1900; GE to Effie Stillman, February 1901 (GEC). Effie was the daughter of W. J. Stillman, one-time Scovill employee and editor of the *Photographic Times* whom Eastman had urged in 1887 to develop a simple film camera. When Stillman showed no interest, Eastman went on to develop for himself "a little roll holder breast camera" that he called the Kodak. Later Eastman would buy paintings by Effie that he didn't want just because W. I. Lincoln Adams—formerly of Adams & Scovill—told him that she was destitute.

3. GE to Robert MacCameron, May 1902; GE to Ellen Andrus Dryden, 14 April 1927 (GEC). Interview by author with Marguerette MacCameron, the artist's daughter, ca. 1980. The MacCameron portrait was given to Ellen Andrus Dryden and returned to Rochester briefly to hang as the centerpiece of the stage of Kilbourn Hall for the opening of that auditorium of the Eastman School of Music in March 1922. In 1927 Eastman decided to have portraits painted by Philip de Laszlo from two ca. 1850 daguerreotypes of his parents that he borrowed from cousin Emma Cope Bassett of Pasadena. After writing all his cousins to see if they remembered the color of Maria's eyes and hair, he had Ellen take the MacCameron portrait to a glass eye maker "to match up the color" as "the most accurate way of getting what we want."

4. Interview by Oscar Solbert with Dr. Murray Bartlett, 26 March 1940 (RGE-UR). Material on Bartlett confirmed by interview by author with his daughter, Blanchard Bartlett Walker, December 1990. Roger Butterfield, "Reminiscences of George Eastman: An Introduction," *University of Rochester Library Bulletin* 26, no. 3 (Spring 1971):54.

5. GE to A. H. Overman, 17 March 1899 (GEC).

6. GE to A. H. Overman, 19 October 1900, 7 May and 27 August 1901 (GEC).

7. John Carlova, "The Stanleys and Their Steamer," *American Heritage* (February 1959):40–45, 84–87.

8. GE to Messrs. Stanley Bros., 20 and 25 March 1902 (GEC).

9. GE to Charles S. Abbott, 12 May 1903 (GEC-UR).

10. GE to Charles S. Abbott, 20 August 1901 (GEC).

11. 1911 letterhead (INC-GEC).

12. GE to the American Association of Automobiling of Rochester, 1901 (GEC).

13. GE to Charles S. Abbott, 11 March 1903, 15 April 1904 (GEC).

14. Frank Seaman to GE, 24 June 1914 (INC-GEC).

15. GE to A. H. Overman, 29 June 1898 (GEC).

16. Interview with Miss Louisa J. Knorr, 13 February 1940 (RGE-UR).

17. GE to E. W. Peet, 16 May 1899 (GEC). George Eastman Dryden stated in a 1989 interview that he had always understood that Nell's tuition and expenses were paid by Uncle George.

18. Personal correspondence, GE to MKE and Ellen Andrus, and MKE and Ellen to GE, Box 1, folders 12, 13, 14, George Eastman Papers, 1899–1901 (GEC-UR). Interview by Beaumont Newhall with George B. Dryden, 1950s (BUTT-UR).

19. Ibid.

20. Ibid. Ellen Andrus to GE, 7 May 1901 (INC-GEC); GE to MKE, May 1901 (GEC-UR); GE to Ellen Andrus Dryden, 14 May 1912 (GEC).

21. GE to MKE, 1901 (GEC-UR); GE to Royal V. Andrus, 2 February and 13 June 1905, 22 and 29 March 1906 (GEC); Royal V. Andrus to GE, 15 October 1900 (INC-GEC).

22. GE to Royal V. Andrus, 28 October 1907, 21 and 25 June 1909 (GEC); GE to Edward Eastman, 22 June and 22 September 1909 (GEC).

23. GE to Royal V. Andrus, 26 June 1907 (GEC); Royal V. Andrus to GE, 1907–11 (INC-GEC); GE to Albert N. Eastman, Chicago, 7 September 1910 (GEC).

24. GE to Royal Vilas Andrus, 2 February 1905, 25 June 1909, 12 August 1909; GE to George Dryden, 10 April 1911 (GEC).

25. Marion Gleason, "The George Eastman I Knew," *University of Rochester Bulletin* (Spring 1971): 98–99.

26. GE to Hedley M. Smith, 21 March 1905 (GEC).

27. Telephone interview with Schuyler Townson, ca. 1980. The Soule House would pass through various incarnations; it was a boarding house that became the scene of a murder, and the administrative office building of the Asbury United First Methodist Church.

28. Butterfield, "Reminiscences," 54. Interview with Murray Bartlett, 1940 (RGE-UR).

Chapter 15: The House That George Built

Material in this chapter formed the basis of a series of forty-three articles by Elizabeth Brayer published in the *Brighton-Pittsford Post* between April 1979 and April 1980 under the general rubric "Mr. Eastman Builds a House."

1. According to Blake McKelvey, Kimball's mansion on Troup Street in Rochester's Third Ward could be seen from Maria's boarding house; this claim is, however, unlikely because the Kimball house was not built until after the Eastmans left the Third Ward. Yet everyone knew of the landmark house and Hattie Strong stated that one of Eastman's goals from childhood was to provide his mother with a coachman and carriage so she could go "calling" as Mrs. Kimball did.

2. GE to John Foster Warner, GE to Charles J. Hoffman, September 1903 (GEC). Also George Eastman House Construction Papers, 1902–6 (GEHCP-UR).

3. GE to Messrs. C. Keur & Sons, Hillegom, Holland, January 1902; GE to Frank Seaman, July 1902 (GEC).

4. GE to Charles S. Abbott, 28 June 1902; GE to J. Foster Warner, 3 July 1902; GE to Alling S. DeForest, 3 July 1902 (GEC); Charles Thoms to GE, 14 June 1902 (INC-GEC); Jean Czerkas, "Alling Stephen DeForest, Landscape Architect, 1875–1957," *Rochester History* 51, no. 2 (Spring 1989):5, 20.

5. GE to J. Foster Warner, 3 July 1902, 13 April 1903; George Eastman House Construction Papers, 1902–6 (GEHCP-UR). Samuel Howe, "The Residence of Mr. George Eastman, Rochester, N.Y.," *Town & Country* (8 August 1914):18.

6. GE to Frank Lusk Babbott, 2 October, 4, 12, 29 November, 24 December 1902 (GEC).

7. Lawrence Grant White, *Sketches and Designs by Stanford White* (New York: The Architectural Book Publishing Company, 1920); Claude Bragdon, *More Lives Than One* (New York: Alfred A. Knopf, 1938).

8. Edgerton R. Williams, [*commemorative booklet for the opening of*] The Third Monroe County Courthouse (Rochester: Monroe County, 1896); GE to Frank Lusk Babbott, 8 December 1902 (GEC).

9. GE to W. R. Mead, 29 December 1902 (GEC). That a thousand dollars was a lot for an architectural critique in 1902 is the opinion of Paul Malo, architect, architectural historian, and author of *Landmarks of Rochester and Western New York*, as expressed in a letter to the author ca. 1980.

10. William Seale, consultant to the Eastman House restoration of the 1980s, wrote of the "airy, light splashed staircase which seems to fly in space" in his *Historic Furnishings Plan: George Eastman House Rochester* [unpublished, 1988]. Warner–Mead correspondence is at the New-York Historical Society.

11. GE to HAS, 8 January 1902 (GEC).

12. GE to F. L. Babbott, 13 December 1904 (GEC).

13. Charles A. Coolidge to GE, 11 June 1920 (INC-GEC).

14. Frank Seaman to GE, 10 February 1911 (INC-GEC).

15. Limpert visited Eastman House on 28 March 1957 with this information.

16. Interview with Ben Cline, 10 January 1940 (RGE-UR).

17. GE to John Foster Warner, 2 January 1903; GE to W. R. Mead, 11 April 1903 (GEC).

18. Elizabeth Brayer, "Who Was the Architect and Where Are the Plans?" *Brighton-Pittsford Post*, 14 June 1979. The New-York Historical Society, repository of the records of the McKim, Mead & White office, has a thick file of three-way correspondence among Eastman, Warner, and Mead.

19. GE to G. D. Arnold, Buffalo, 13 August 1902; GE to E. W. Robertson, 17 April 1903 (GEC). Alfred Simon was the photographer.

20. GE to Sayre Fisher, 15 June 1903; GE to J. F Warner, 15 June and 3 August 1903; GE to William R. Mead, 11 April 1903 (GEC).

21. GE to Charles S. Abbott, 17 August 1903 (GEC).

22. GE to Frank Haddleton, 19 November and 20 December 1903, 26 January 1904; GE to J. Foster Warner, 19 November 1903 (GEC). Also (GEHCP-UR).

23. GE sent his Paris manager, Hedley M. Smith, to the Ritz Hotel in April 1903 to check out where the room clocks had been made as he wanted them for his house.

24. GE to A. H. Davenport, 30 June 1908 (GEC). Babbott had been particularly anxious that Eastman have some of John "LaFarge's stained-glass work," and when that did not work out, Bacon designed these based on modes of transportation. Eastman always thought them "somewhat out of drawing." What became of them is not known. The roundels now in the windows are 1990 simulations.

25. Interview by Jean Ennis with Minnie Cline, 1 February 1951 (EKC).

26. GE to Frank L. Babbott, 2 June 1905; GE to Francis H. Bacon, 19 December 1904, 2 June 1905 (GEC).

27. Correspondence between Thacher Clarke and GE, 1910 to 1919 (when Eastman finally enlarged the conservatory) includes much mention of the proportions and how they might be improved (GEC).

28. Interview with Julian Street, who accompanied GE to Japan in 1920, 25 March 1940 (RGE-UR).

29. GE to J. F. Warner, 31 December 1903; GE to Hiram W. Sibley, 24 March 1904 (GEC). Whether Winter completed the paintings and whether they were ever installed is not clear. They have not been in the elevator since at least the 1950s.

30. GE to J. Foster Warner, 18 July 1904 (GEC).

31. Blake McKelvey, *East Avenue's Turbulent History* (Rochester: Rochester Public Library and Society for the Preservation of Landmarks in Western New York, 1966), 24–25.

32. Letters between J. Foster Warner and William R. Mead (N-YHS).

33. GE to Frank L. Babbott, 16 and 19 November 1903; GE to R. de Quelin, Hayden Company, 1 March 1904; GE to Francis H. Bacon, A. H. Davenport, and W. R. Mead, 21 March 1904; GE to C. F. King, 24 March 1904 (GEC). Also (GEHCP-UR).

34. George Eastman House Construction Papers (GEHCP-UR). The pickled oak is a gray finish more associated with the 1950s than 1905. Restorers in 1988 found that it was the original, however, and Eastman himself describes the dining room walls as gray oak.

35. Today several of Bacon's watercolor designs hang in the Davenport Memorial Foundation (A. H. Davenport's former house in Malden, Mass.), attesting to his skill as designer and colorist.

36. GE to Francis Henry Bacon and McKim, Mead & White, 1904; GE to Eugene Glaenzer, 14 January 1905 (GEC).

37. All of these facts can be gleaned from the George Eastman House Papers at the University of Rochester.

38. Interview by author with Edward Ribson, ca. 1980. Ribson's father was an architect in Warner's office, where the theory of the creosoted rounds as the reason for no more Eastman commissions was propounded.

39. GE to William R. Mead, 24 February 1906 (GEC). The Eastman Fund at Amherst College is still supporting artistic projects relating to the Mead Art Museum at Amherst.

40. George Eastman House Construction Papers, 1902–6 (GEHCP-UR).

41. GE to Charles S. Abbott, 27 February 1904 (GEC).

42. The Rochester Orphan Asylum is now the Hillside Children's Center. The Eastman Cottage sustained fire damage in the 1950s and was rebuilt as the audi-

torium and social center of the Hillside Children's Center. It now bears almost no resemblance to the shingle-style cottage of 1906.

43. GE to Ellen A. Dryden, 28 March, 11 and 13 April, 25 and 29 July 1905 (GEC). In the end, the Drydens did not build in 1905 but rented a house. In 1919 they would purchase a lot in Evanston and build a near-replica of Eastman House.

44. GE to Kay-Scheere Company, 29 and 31 July 1906 (GEC). Interview with Louisa Knorr, 13 February 1940 (RGE-UR). Interview with Charles D. Carruth (BUTT-UR).

45. Letter from Victoria R. Powers to Oscar N. Solbert, 12 February 1940 (RGE-UR).

46. A. H. Harrison to GE, January 1906 (INC-GEC).

47. GE to Francis H. Bacon, 7 August 1905 (GEC).

48. GE to G. A. Audsley, New York City, 20 December 1902 (GEC).

49. George Eastman House Construction Papers (GEHCP-UR) and George E. Fisher's diary, courtesy of Frank B. Mehlenbacher.

50. Archer Gibson to GE, 22 October 1917 (INC-GEC).

51. GE to Heins, 1919 (GEC).

52. GE to George E. Fisher, 14 June 10 (GEC).

53. Interview with Hermann Dossenbach, 22 March 1940 (UR-RGE). Dossenbach Quintette members were Hermann Dossenbach, conductor and first violinist; J. B. Paddon, second violinist; George Henrickus, violist; Biedrich Vaska, cellist; and Theodore Dossenbach, violinist.

54. Harold Gleason, "Please Play My Funeral March," *University of Rochester Library Bulletin* 26, no. 3 (Spring 1971): 112.

55. Interview with Mrs. Harold Kimball (daughter of Charles F. Pond of the Rochester Savings Bank and a frequent Oak Lodge visitor), 12 February 1940 (RGE-UR).

56. Interview by Roger Butterfield with Albert Eastwood, January 1954 (UR-BUTT).

57. Henry H. Eastman to GE, 12 June 1907 (GEC-INC). Henry Tompkins, George Tompkins, Russell Kilbourn, Emma Cope Bassett, Elizabeth Kilbourn, Martin E. Luce, Jennie Hall, Mary Kilbourn Miller, Mary Eastman Southwick, Carrie Eastman Benedict, Henry A. Eastman, Emeline Eastman Webster, and Almon Eastman. The last five listed were the children of Joseph Porter Eastman of Kingsville, Ohio, and George Eastman's closest relatives of his own generation.

58. GE to George B. Dryden, 16 June 1907 (GEC).

59. GE to HAS, July 1907 (GEC). GE was away 6 to 19 July 1907.

60. GE to Ellen A. Dryden, 29 July 1907; GE to Royal Vilas Andrus, July 1907 (GEC). Maria K. Eastman Will (BUTT-UR).

61. GE to dealers, 26 June 1907 (GEC).

Chapter 16: From Oak Lodge to Tuskegee

1. John Slater, *Rhees of Rochester* (New York and London: Harper and Brothers, 1946), 167.

2. GE to W. A. Spivey, 17 November 1925 (GEC).

3. Henry Myrick to GE, 7 February 1911 (INC-GEC). In 1911 Henry Myrick got a raise but had to gently remind Eastman of such: "Now Mr Eastman you sent me a check for $25 instead of $30. You told me you were going to give me $30 [a week] this year. Your obedient Henry Myrick."

4. GE to HAS, 27 February 1909 (GEC).

5. Letter to author from Stuart Wood, 25 November 1986. Oak Lodge was left by bequest to Ellen Dryden. During World War II the U.S. government insisted that all the pine trees be cut and used in the war effort. In the 1950s, when the Drydens no longer owned the property, the lodge burned to the ground. Another house was built on its foundations by A. K. Hines.

6. Letter to Oscar Solbert from Anna D. Hubbell, 28 February 1940 (RGE-UR).

7. William Gifford to GE, 1910 (INC-GEC); GE to W. S. Gifford, 31 August 1910 (GEC).

8. Letter to Oscar Solbert from Anna D. Hubbell, 28 February 1940 (RGE-UR).

9. Ibid.

10. GE to Frank Seaman, 1903 (GEC). The school at Bricks, North Carolina, was under the auspices of the American Missionary Association in New York City.

11. Charles S. Abbott to GE, 14 March 1903 (INC-GEC): "From what I can learn I believe there is more than *one* reason why you are through with the slow [steamship] line—They blacklist people who deal themselves four sevens and hand out a flush & four sixes at the same time—You cannot expect to work an S. S. line more than once in two or three years like this."

12. Letter to Oscar Solbert from Anna D. Hubbell, 28 February 1940 (RGE-UR). Eastman would have processed snapshot film only; ciné film had to be sent to the factory.

13. Francis Macomber, *Reminiscences* (Rochester: unpublished typescript, 1944), 7 (author's collection).

14. Letter to Oscar Solbert from Anna D. Hubbell, 28 February 1940 (RGE-UR); letter to Oscar Solbert, from Hattie Strong, 28 February 1940 (EKC).

15. Kodak interview with Francis Macomber, 17 November 1950 (EKC). "Reminiscences," paper Francis S. Macomber read to Kent Club, 20 April 1944 (author's collection).

16. GE to Paul Garrett, 1 March 1904, 22 February 1912 (GEC).

17. GE to Murray Bartlett, Philippines, 17 May 1911 (GEH).

18. GE to Charles S. Abbott, 28 May 1903 (GEC).

19. GE to N. H. Shepherd, Rocky Mount, N.C., 5 November 1915 (GEC).

20. GE to the Rev. Murray Bartlett, 17 May 1915 (GEC).

21. Interview by author with James Henry Myrick Jr., 1980. Myrick Jr. moved to Rochester about 1932 and worked at Kodak Park until his retirement. At first he lived with his brother Nathaniel, who continued as butler at Eastman House while it was the residence of the University of Rochester presidents, 1932–47.

22. GE to Henry Myrick, 7 December 1911 (GEC).

23. GE to A. E. Akers, 12 May 1919; GE to Almon R. Eastman, 21 May 1919 (GEC); Julius Rosenwald to GE, 20 January 1922 (INC-GEC). Rosenwald contributed approximately $4 million to 1,198 schools for black children. The twenty-four "Rosenwald" schools in Halifax County were two-room buildings; the Eastman school had five rooms.

24. Ibid.

25. GE to Frankie Myrick, 8 May 23 (GEC).

26. GE to A. E. Akers, 1 June 1923 (GEC).

27. GE to A. E. Akers, 8 May, 14 June 1923 (GEC).

28. Du Bois (1868–1963), educated at Fisk and the University of Berlin and the first African American to be awarded a Ph.D from Harvard, taught history and economics at Atlanta University (1897–1910). As an ardent advocate of complete racial equality, Du Bois openly discounted Washington's views of African Americans as a subservient minority in a white society. He served as the director of publication for the NAACP (1910–32) but broke with the organization for ten years. A visit to the Soviet Union convinced him that the advancement of blacks could best be achieved through communism. Awarded the Lenin Peace Prize in 1959, he joined the Communist Party in 1961 and became a citizen of Ghana that year too.

29. Robert Moton to GE, 17 May 1923 (INC-GEC).

30. Rev. James E. Rose to GE, 10 December 1924 (INC-GEC).

31. GE to Rev. James E. Rose, 15 November 1924 (GEC).

32. GE to F. N. Doubleday, Page & Co. 30 November 1901 (GEC).

33. GE to HAS, 5 March 1909 (GEC).

34. Booker T. Washington to GE, May 1915 (INC-GEC); GE to Booker T. Washington, 8 November 1915 (GEC).

35. GE to the Hon. Seth Low, Bedford Hills, N.Y., 22 November 1915 (GEC); R. R. Moton to GE, 25 November 1916 (INC-GEC).

36. Rush Rhees to GE, 1921 (INC-GEC)

37. John J. Mullowney to GE, 8 October 1929 (INC-GEC).

38. GE to J. Small, 1924 (GEC).

39. GE to George Davison, 14 May, 10 June, 23 July 1907 (GEC).

40. Statement by GE, quoted in what appears to be a press release pertaining to the Tuskegee–Hampton campaign, n.d., but filed in 1924 (INC-GEC).

Chapter 17: Dalliance

1. GE to Fred Freeland Walker, Boston, 22 May 1911 (GEC): "I have a Jersey Heifer which I desire to ship to Petersham."

2. GE to Mrs. George Dickman, 7 June 1911 (GEC).

3. GE to MKE, 29 August 1895 (GEC-UR).

4. GE to John P. Leach, Littleton, N.C., 31 May 1906 (GEC).

5. Interview with Nathaniel Myrick by Jean Ennis, 28 November 1950 (EKC).

6. GE to Farmers Loan & Trust Company, New York City, 15 August 1912 (GEC).

7. Unidentified clipping in Tenquall Scrapbook, no. 1, p. 45 (Rochester Public Library). In 1895 Eastman described Sunnyside, the Dickman home in Hampstead, England as "an old curiosity shop."

8. Interview by author with Delight Haines, Petersham Historical Society, 3 September 1992.

9. GE to Josephine H. Dickman, 3 July 1914 (GEC).

10. GE to Josephine H. Dickman, 12 November 1913 (GEC).

11. GE to director, United States Geological Survey, Washington, D.C., 5 August 1907 (GEC).

12. GE to Josephine H. Dickman, 4 April 1914 (GEC). Harriet Dana was a neighbor of the Dickmans in England; her husband died three months after George Dickman died.

13. GE to W. H. Walker, New York City, 4 January 1910, 3 March 1915; GE to J. H. Dickman, 27 April 1910 (GEC).

14. Interviews with Frank Macomber, 1940, 1950s (RGE-UR) (EKC).

15. GE to Mrs. Alice Conkling, 22 June 1911 (GEC).

16. Interview by Jean Ennis with Marie Cherbuliez, 26 May 1950 (EKC).

17. GE to Ellen A. Dryden, 6 December 1916 (GEC).

18. GE to Ellen A. Dryden, 14 December 1916 (GEC).

19. Birney Parsons to GE, 16 and 28 March 1917; GE to Birney Parsons, 17 and 22 March, 19 April 1917; GE to Charles Caryl Coleman, 11 February 1924 (GEC).

20. Louise Gifford to GE, 22 December 1915 (INC-GEC).

21. Louise Gifford to GE, 15 and 22 December 1915; 3 February 1916 (INC-GEC).

22. Louise Gifford to GE, 3 February 1916; J. H. Dickman to GE, 15 May 1916; May L. Gifford to GE, 23 May 1916 (INC-GEC).

23. GE to Edward Bausch, 23 July 1920 (GEC).

24. Marion Gleason, "The George Eastman I Knew," *University of Rochester Library Bulletin* 26, no. 3 (Spring 1971): 97.

25. Interviews with Harold Gleason, 1940, 1955, 1972 (UR).

26. Ibid. Harold Gleason, "Please Play My Funeral March," *University of Rochester Library Bulletin* 26, no. 3 (Spring 1971): 112.

27. Ibid. GE to Arthur Alexander, 3 October 1919 (GEC).

28. Gleason, "Please Play My Funeral March," 120.

29. Interviews with Clayla Ward, 1940 (RGE-UR), 1950 (EKC). Primary material in the Frank Hawley Ward Papers, Department of Rare Books and Special Collections, Rush Rhees Library (UR).

30. Marion Gleason, "The George Eastman I Knew," *University of Rochester Library Bulletin* 26, no. 3 (Spring 1971): 95–103.

Chapter 18: Frozen Music: GE and His Architects

1. Marion Folsom, "A Great Man," *University of Rochester Library Bulletin* 26, no. 3, (Spring, 1971) 63.

2. GE to EPMCo., December 1892 (GEC); "Rochester's Crystal Palace" (pamphlet), December 1892 (INC-GEH). The bridge resembled the Bridge of Sighs in Florence, Italy, over which condemned prisons walked to their execution. Whether Frank Brownell, whom Eastman continually hounded in an effort to increase the production of cameras, ever sighed on his daily march to the boss's office, is not known.

3. GE to McKim, Mead & White, 28 February, 24 April, 26 December 1906; 17 January 1907; GE to Paul Garrett (Norfolk, Va.), 12 June 1906; GE to HAS, 7 June 1906 (GEC). The Kodak Office on West 23d Street was featured in the international edition of *The American Architect and Building News* of 4 May 1907.

4. Nicholas Pevsner, *Studies in Art, Architecture and Design Victorian and After* (Princeton: Princeton University Press, 1968), 179–80.

5. GE to Edwin Gordon, 16 May 1910, 15 June 1923; GE to Walter Hubbell, 9 March 1910; GE to Wm. S. Gifford, 11 April, 23 May, 20 October, 4, 5, 19, 22 December 1910, 27 February, 6, 11 April, 13, 30 October 1911; GE to Thomas Baker, July 1911; interview with Charles E. Case, 8 January 1940 (RGE-UR).

6. GE to Charles Crandall, J. Foster Warner, Claude Bragdon, Gordon & Madden, and Hutchison & Cutler, 14 July 1911 (GEC).

7. GE to William R. Mead, 20 September 1912; GE to McKim Mead & White, 24 December 1912; GE to HAS, 27 March, 15 October 1913 (GEC).

8. GE to Edwin S. Gordon, 24 June 1927 (GEC).

9. GE to Edwin S. Gordon, 31 October 1929 (GEC).

10. Interview with Paul Favour, 3 January 1940 (RGE-UR).

11. Nahum Ellan Luboshez (1869–1925), born in Russia, came to America as a child, worked in photographic studios especially as a retoucher, went back to Europe, joined Kodak as a special demonstrator, and improved x-ray photography to such a point that he was given the Progress Medal of the Royal Photographic Society. The corporate portrait-photograph of Eastman by Luboshez, by which the world knows him best, is dated "London, June 29, 1921."

12. Interview with Ben Cline, 10 January 1940 (RGE-UR).

13. Claude Bragdon, *More Lives Than One* (New York: Alfred A. Knopf, 1938). Edwin S. Gordon, "Autobiography of the Life of Edwin S. Gordon" (unpublished ms.)

14. GE to Edwin S. Gordon, 21 January 1908 (GEC).

15. The renaming of City Hospital as Rochester General was to dispel the notion that it was a municipal institution. Instead, City Hospital was organized by the Rochester Female Charitable Society in 1845, expanding greatly under an entirely female board of managers two decades later as three thousand Civil War disabled came straggling home.

16. Rush Rhees to GE (INC-GEC). Interview by author with Dr. James Sibley Watson Jr., 1980. John Gade was attached to the Belgian consulate at the time the Eastman Dental Clinic in Brussels was dedicated and represented the U.S. government at that ceremony.

17. Edwin S. Gordon to GE, 21 May 1915 (INC-GEC).

18. Interview with Leroy E. Snyder, 22 January 1940 (RGE-UR).

19. Ibid. Edward Harris to McKim, Mead & White, 1924 (N-YHS).

20. GE to Charles Crandall, 1902 (GEC).

21. Bragdon, *More Lives Than One*, 77.

22. Claude Bragdon, "The Rochester Passenger Station," *The American Architect* 100, no. 1982 (17 December 1913): 237–38.

23. James G. Cutler to GE, 14 March 1906 (INC-GEC).

24. Carl Schmidt, *My Life as an Architect*, privately published, n.d. Schmidt, an architect in the office of Gordon & Kaelber, wrote that Bragdon did the elevations.

25. Claude Bragdon to Eugenie Bragdon, 18 April 1916 (Bragdon collection-UR).

26. Claude Bragdon to Eugenie Bragdon, 29 June 1915 (Bragdon collection-

UR). The YMCA building of 1914 was virtually built by Eastman too, since he contributed $250,000 of the $750,000 budget. Because he asked that his name not be mentioned, Bragdon may not have known this.

27. Bragdon, *More Lives Than One*, 77–78.

28. Claude Bragdon to Eugenie Bragdon, n.d. (BRAG-UR).

29. Claude Bragdon to Eugenie Bragdon, 2 June 1915 (BRAG-UR); Claude Bragdon to GE, 11 June 1917 (INC-GEC).

30. Claude Bragdon to Eugenie Bragdon, 2 June, 15 and 16 October 1915 (BRAG-UR).

31. Bragdon, *More Lives Than One*, 78. The answer was typical of GE's turndowns during this wartime period: "NO THINK MONEY CAN BETTER BE SPENT BUYING AMBULANCES" he had just wired the Russian Liberty Fund.

32. Bragdon, *More Lives Than One*, 76.

33. Directly west of the Ross property was the Robinson house, designed by J. Foster Warner in 1892 for W. Gorsline. After Eastman House became a museum, the Robinson house was acquired and demolished and the area blacktopped for a parking lot.

34. Claude to Eugenie Bragdon, Genesee Valley Club stationery, n.d., ca. 1916 (BRAG-UR).

35. The similarity of the Bragdon garden to Hestercome was first noted by Katherine Rahn, landscape architect, Buffalo, N.Y., who was in charge of the 1984 restoration of that garden. Bragdon's letter to Eugenie confirms that attribution.

36. Bragdon, *More Lives Than One*, 77.

37. Mary Hallock Greenewalt to GE, 17 December 1921 (INC-GEC); GE to Mary Hallock Greenewalt, December 1921 (GEC).

38. Bragdon, *More Lives Than One*, 79.

39. GE to Ellen Dryden, April 1917 (GEC).

40. Paul Malo, architect, "George Eastman and his Architects" (unpublished paper, The Landmark Society of Western New York, ca. 1970).

41. Claude Bragdon to Fritz Trautman, 25 April 1918 (BRAG-UR).

42. Interview by author with Walter Strakosh, Genesee Valley Club historian, 1990. Eastman was president of the club (1921–22) when the club moved from its original building (which Bragdon was too young to have designed) to an 1832 rambling historic home. On 11 February 1921 Gordon & Kaelber were engaged to plan an addition. Eastman could well have recommended his favorite firm and the building committee acquiesced just because of his general standing in the community. But the club had to borrow money from local banks for this addition. A gift of $50,000 plus the proceeds from the sale of the old clubhouse would seem to have made borrowing unnecessary.

43. Burt L. Fenner to Gordon & Kaelber, 1 July 1919; Burt L. Fenner to William Mead, 25 July 1919 (N-YHS).

44. McKim, Mead & White to GE, 1 October 1919 (N-YHS).

45. Interview by author with Gertrude Herdle Moore, director of Memorial Art Gallery (1922–62), ca. 1980.

46. Burt L. Fenner to William R. Mead, 22 August 1919 (N-YHS); Burt L. Fenner

to William Mitchell Kendall, 7 August 1919 (N-YHS); Burt L. Fenner to William R. Mead, 12 July 1919 (N-YHS).

47. GE to McKim, Mead & White, 7 August 1919 (N-YHS).

48. Burt L. Fenner to William R. Mead, 12 July, 22 August 1919 (N-YHS).

49. Edwin S. Gordon, to GE, 29 March 1920 (INC-GEC).

50. GE to Frank Lusk Babbott, 21 November 1918 (GEC).

51. GE to A. W. Hopeman, 3 November 1921; GE to Frank L. Babbott, September 1921 (GEC). In 1972 these wallpaper scenics, blackened with age and beyond repair, were replaced by an identical set—the last available from the original woodblocks. The major change of the 1972 renovation was to remove the ten thousand pipes of the defunct organ for a modern air-conditioning system.

52. Margaret Bond, "Mr. Eastman's Theatre," *Rochester Review* (Summer 1980): 16–19.

53. Lawrence Grant White to Robert Burnside Potter, 1 March 1922 (N-YHS).

54. Lawrence Grant White to GE, 1921 (INC-GEC).

55. William G. Kaelber to Lawrence G. White, 2 February 1920 (N-YHS).

56. In 1925 White would use Zenitherm again for a Fountain Court addition for the Memorial Art Gallery of the University of Rochester.

57. Lawrence Grant White to William G. Kaelber, 8 December 1921 (N-YHS).

58. Interview by author with Rochester Philharmonic director and conductor, David Zinman, ca. 1978. Zinman said the Eastman Theatre acoustics were "pretty good, better than many halls" and blamed its dual function for the problems. In newspaper interviews, Mark Elder, Zinman's sucessor, urged the philharmonic management to build a new hall with better acoustics.

59. Eastman was a life member of the board of managers of the Memorial Art Gallery of the University of Rochester from its founding in 1912 until his death in 1932. But because the gallery was given by Emily Sibley Watson in memory of her son, James G. Averell, and because there was a tacit division of cultural labors—the Watsons did art, Eastman did music—he did not involve himself heavily in the gallery as far as collections or exhibitions were concerned. He did, however, bequeath his art collection of some sixty paintings and prints to the university and hence to the gallery.

60. Interview with Clarence Livingston, 5 March 1940 (UR-RGE).

61. Ibid.

Chapter 19: The Platinum-Mounted Farm

1. Interviews with Harvey Padelford, 1 February 1940 (RGE-UR) 15 July 1950 (EKC) (BUTT-UR).

2. John White Johnston to GE, 31 May 1929 (INC-GEC).

3. Interviews with Harvey Padelford, 1 February 1940 (RGE-UR), 15 July 1950 (EKC) (BUTT-UR).

4. Interview with Gustave Tinlot, 25 January 1940 (RGE-UR).

5. Nicolas Slonimsky, *Perfect Pitch* (Oxford and New York: Oxford University Press, 1988), 84.

6. Interviews with Howard Hanson, 15 April 1939, 17 January 1940, 1950s (by Roger Butterfield), 23 June 1972 by Adrienne McLennon (UR).

7. George Dryden told Beaumont Newhall that George Washington Eastman had a weakness for alcohol (BUTT-UR).

8. Interviews with Marie Cherbuliez and Eugene Goosens (EKC) (UR).

9. GE to J. J. Kennedy, 27 December 1921 (GEC); GE to William H. Anderson, The Anti-Saloon League, 12 December 1923 (GEC).

10. GE to Julius Rolshoven, 3 and 8 October, 12 December 1904; 21, 23, 28 February, 17 May 1905; 31 August, 26 November 1906 (GEC); Julius Rolshoven to GE, 4 October, 4 November, 13 December 1904, 8 January, 26 February 1905 (INC-GEC).

11. Eastman purchased the old master paintings through M. Knoedler and the contemporary works through William Macbeth, both New York dealers.

12. GE to Delia Eastman, 2 June 1925 (GEC-GEH).

13. Jean Czerkas, "Alling Stephen DeForest, Landscape Architect, 1875–1957," *Rochester History* 51, no. 2 (Spring 1989): 5, 20.

14. Samuel Howe, "The Residence of Mr. George Eastman at Rochester, New York," *Town & Country* (8 August 1914): 18-19, 34. Article reprinted in *American Country Houses of To-Day*, 322–25.

15. Excerpt from Eastman's will: "I hereby give, devise and bequeath to the University of Rochester the land and buildings constituting my homestead. . . . It is my desire that the university use this property as a dwelling place for its president . . . [and] that such property should be kept as near as possible in the same state as at the time of my decease. . . . If after the ten years the trustees of the University of Rochester conclude that the use of the property indicated is inadvisable, then I have no objection to their making such other disposition of it . . . as they may think best for the interests of the university" (EKC).

16. GE to Arthur Colgate, 20 September 1902 (GEC).

17. Ibid.; Arthur Colgate to GE, 29 August 1902 (INC-GEC).

18. GE to Alling S. De Forest, 13 July 1905 (GEC).

19. William S. Riley, Commissioner of Parks, to GE, 17 January 1924 (INC-GEC).

20. Most maids of the period wore gray in the morning and white in the afternoon.

21. Interview with Elizabeth Peoples, 1971 (EKC).

22. Ibid.

23. Ibid.

24. Terry Ramsaye, "Little Journeys to the Homes of Famous Film Magnates," *Photoplay* (July 1927).

25. James R. Quirk to GE, 8 December 1921 (INC-GEC).

26. GE to Frank L. Babbott, 28 June 1927 (GEC).

27. Ramsaye, "Little Journeys."

28. GE to Terry Ramsaye, 20 June 1927; GE to Frank L. Babbott, 28 June 1927 (GEC).

Chapter 20: Mr. Smith Goes to College

Secondary sources for this chapter are Arthur May's published *A History of the University of Rochester, 1850–1962* (Rochester: printed by Princeton University Press, 1977) and particularly the unabridged, annotated typescript of same at the UR Library; Jesse Leonard Rosenberger, *Rochester, The Making of a University* (Rochester: printed by the University of Chicago Press, 1927); John Slater, *Rhees of Rochester* (New York and London: Harper and Brothers, 1946); Henry Greenleaf Pearson, *Richard Cockburn Maclaurin* (New York: Macmillan, 1937); Francis E. Wylie, *MIT in Perspective* (Boston, 1976); and Carl W. Ackerman, *George Eastman* (Boston and New York: Houghton Mifflin, 1930). Also consulted were issues of *The Tech*, MIT student newspaper; various archival materials, displays, and memorabilia at the MIT archive; and annual reports of the University of Rochester president. Portions of this material was published as "The Great Removal Project, " I and II, by Betsy (Elizabeth) Brayer in *Rochester Review* (Fall 1980, Winter 1980–81). The MIT story is contained in letters and telegrams from GE to Richard Maclaurin, 2, 6, 7, 8 March, 3 and 9 April, 22 May, 7, 14, 21 June, 14 and 17 December 1912; 13 and 14 January, 2, 5, 9 June 1913; 13 and 19 February, 14 December 1914; 14 June, 29 October 1915; 2, 3, 19 June, 25 August 1916; GE to Benjamin Strong Jr. or Seward Prosser (Bankers Trust Company, New York City), 14 June 1912; 9 June 1913; 14 January, 25 November 1914; 14 June, 23 October 1915; 30 August, 15 December 1916; 19 January 1917; 18 June 1919; GE to Coleman du Pont, 23 January 1920; GE to Frank Babbott, 14 June 1915 (GEC); and Richard Maclaurin to GE, 29 February, 6, 7, n.d. March, 18 June, 1 July, 12 December 1912; 10 January, 10 February, 12 and 23 May, 4 and 13 June 1913; 15 and 16 February, 29 June 1914; 4, 8, 11 April, 19 May, 19, 20, 24, 25 June, 19 October 1915; 1 and 9 March, 23 and 27 May, 6 and 15 June, 27 August, 11 and 22 October, 22 November, 2, 4, 11, 15 December 1916; Richard Maclaurin to Francis R. Hart (Old Colony Trust Company), 22 January 1914; Coleman du Pont to Richard Maclaurin, 2 April 1912; Benjamin Strong to GE, 17 June 1912; 15 January 1914 (INC-GEC). Correspondence between GE and MIT continued through 1929 but is not covered in this chapter.

1. The two women were Helen Barrett Montgomery, who went on to become the first woman member of the Rochester Board of Education, and Mrs. George Hollister, who is quoted. Later, Mrs Hollister said of Eastman: "He could change his mind grandly" (EKC interviews).

2. GE to the Hon. Timothy I. Woodruff, New York City, 2 May 1912 (GEC): "Dr. Hill . . . is rather cold and unsympathetic, and not much of a 'mixer.'"

3. The university's color was dandelion yellow. Later it became blue and yellow, yellow alone having been ascertained to represent cowardice.

4. Harriet S. Rhees, "Rochester at the Turn of the Century," *Rochester Historical Society Publication Series* 20 (1942): 69–86. Ernest A. Paviour, UR'10 and UR trustee, gives a somewhat different account of the conversations between Rhees and Eastman. Since she was there, I have used Mrs. Rhees's account.

5. University of Rochester Report of the President, 1906 (UR).

6. Rush Rhees to GE, 7 March, 3 April 1904 (INC-GEC); GE to Rush Rhees, 13 December 1906 (GEC).

7. GE to Frank L. Babbott, 27 June 1908 (GEH).

8. Report of the President, 1909 (UR).

9. University of Rochester Report of the President, 1912, UR (a public document).

10. Issues of *The Cloister Window* (the women students' weekly publication), *The Campus* (men's weekly) (UR); Betsy Brayer, "The Great Removal Project," part I, *Rochester Review* (Fall 1980): 1–7.

11. John R. Slater, *Rhees of Rochester* (New York and London: Harper and Brothers, 1946), 166.

12. GE to Professor Thomas Drown, 3 November 1891 (GEC).

13. After Welles Bosworth learned Eastman's identity in 1920, he began to badger, flatter, and cajole the Kodak man, showering him with blueprints or gifts (which Eastman sent back) with the hopes of getting another Eastman commission. On 25 October 1921 Bosworth wrote: "Whether or not anything should turn my way in connection with the Rochester University, I am deeply interested to further our acquaintence [sic]. You forget how many years I was working with you in the background of my thought. I wonder . . . when I might come up and take dinner with you in Rochester?" On 10 May 1922 Eastman returned a light fixture with the note: "It would be a sin to keep it if I could not use it. Please do not attempt to replace it with anything else. I rather dislike the idea of presents and I have you in constant remembrance through the use of the nice little memorandum diary which you sent me" (GEC) (INC-GEC).

14. GE to Frank Lusk Babbott, 15 June 1915 (GEC).

15. Interviews with George A. Carnahan, 28 February 1940 (RGE-UR); C. E. Kenneth Mees, 9 January 1940 (RGE-UR), 1950s (BUTT-UR); and Jeremiah G. Hickey (brother of Bishop Hickey), 31 January 1940 (RGE-UR) and 1950s (BUTT-UR).

16. GE to Lewis L. Clarke, New York City, 31 December 1928 (GEC).

17. GE to William L. Chenery, *New York Times*, 30 January 1920 (GEC).

18. Press release announcing gifts of $30 million to the University of Rochester, MIT, Hampton and Tuskegee Institutes, 8 December 1924 (INC-GEC)

19. Mrs. Kuno Franks, Cambridge, Mass., to GE, 2 August 1915 (INC-GEC).

20. GE to Helen Arnold, 28 December 1905 (GEC).

21. GE to Helen D. Arnold, 28 December 1905, 27 December 1912 (GEC).

22. Blake McKelvey, *Rochester: The Quest for Quality* (Cambridge, Mass.: Harvard University Press, 1956), 140.

23. GE to Norris L. Gage, Ashtabula, Ohio, 15 September 1911 (GEC).

Chapter 21: "Pull" Is a Verb

1. The name of the widow and her son—who eventually achieved great success in the business world—is withheld. Nevertheless, the story appears to be true rather than apocryphal. The slogan "Pull is a verb" is also attributed to GE by Jeremiah G. Hickey, president of Hickey-Freeman Company and brother of Bishop Thomas F. G. Hickey, McQuaid's successor and close neighbor of Kodak Office. J. G. Hickey's friendship with Eastman began when the latter named him as one of ten trustees of the Bureau of Municipal Research. Interview, 31 January 1940 (RGE-UR). There are many Eastman letters chiding employees who lack "push."

2. GE to John Mumford, Harper and Brothers. New York City (not for publication), 7 April 1908 (GEC).

3. *New York Herald Tribune*, 15 March 1932.

4. Carl Ackerman, *George Eastman* (Boston: Houghton Mifflin, 1930), 193.

5. "A man who has fun with his wealth" by Arthur Gleason (INC-GEC).

6. GE to Henry Strong, 26 February 1912; GE to William S. Gifford, 25 February 1912 (GEC). In the mid-1990s Eastman Kodak and IBM remain the major non-unionized corporations. Thomas J. Watson of IBM (1874–1956) was also a native of Upstate New York and a friend of Eastman. He was employed by the National Cash Register Company, which had influenced Eastman in 1898 to start a suggestion system for employees. In 1914 he joined the Computing-Tabulating-Recording Company as its president. In 1924 he changed the name of the firm to International Business Machines Corporation, turning it into a multimillion-dollar business that employed sixty thousand in two hundred offices by the time of his death, held 1,500 patents, and manufactured six thousand models of business machinery. Corporate research and development led to the automatic digital computer in 1944.

7. GE to James Haste, 14 June 1911 (GEC).

8. GE to William H. Walker, 29 March 1912 (GEC).

9. Address by Dr. Albert K. Chapman, 8 July 1954, Chamber of Commerce luncheon marking centennial of George Eastman's birth.

10. GE to Frank Babbott, 13 March 1912 (GEC).

11. GE to HAS, 6 March 1912 (GEC).

12. GE to HAS, 26 February 1912 (GEC).

13. GE to HAS, 20 March 1912 (GEC).

14. GE to Charles S. Whitman, 13 April 1917 (GEC).

15. GE to Rush Rhees, 23 October 1921 (GEC).

16. GE to HAS, 20 March 1912 (GEC).

17. GE to the board of directors, Eastman Kodak Company, of New Jersey, 2 April 1919 (EKC).

18. GE, *System* magazine interview, 1927, 751.

19. GE to HAS, 12 March 1919 (GEC).

20. GE to Eliot G. Mears, Harvard, 6 April 1914; Marion B. Folsom, "A Great Man," *University of Rochester Library Bulletin*, 26, no. 3, 57–80.

21. Ibid. Joseph Alsop, "He Sparked a Revolution," *Saturday Evening Post* (5 December 1955): 19, 132–36.

22. GE to Eliot G. Mears, Harvard, 8 June 1914; GE to Frank Mattison et al., 3 July 1914; GE to Marion B. Folson, 17 June, 3 July 1914; GE to F. M. Crouch, 1 October 1914 (GEC).

23. Folsom, "A Great Man," 58.

24. Ibid., 59. "Marion Bayard Folsom: Biographical Information," 31 July 1958 and undated; interview with Marion B. Folsom, 22 February 1940; employee files (EKC).

25. Alsop, "He Sparked," 132.

26. Folsom, "A Great Man," 59.

27. Folsom, "A Great Man," 61.

28. GE memo, March 1920 (EKC).

29. Interview with Marion B. Folsom, 22 February 1940 (EKC).

30. GE to HAS, 1914; GE to the Rev. Paddock, 4 June 1921 (GEC).

31. GE to H. W. Forster, Independence Bureau, 7 January 1919 (GEC).

32. "Consumers choose Kodak No. 1 in U.S. for quality": headline, referring to the independently conducted Total Reserch Corp. EquiTrend study, *Rochester Democrat & Chronicle,* 16 March 1995, 1.

33. Meadowbrook and Koda-Vista prospectuses (author's collection).

34. Alsop, "He Sparked," 134.

35. Eastman Kodak Company memo, 1929 (EKC).

36. Interview with Marion Folsom, 22 February 1940 (RGE-UR).

Chapter 22: My Hometown

This chapter, more than any other, relies on the secondary source Blake McKelvey, *Rochester: The Quest for Quality, 1890–1925* (Cambridge: Harvard University Press, 1956).

1. Arthur Gleason, "A man who has fun with his wealth" (INC-GEC).

2. *Upstate Magazine, Rochester Democrat & Chronicle,* 8 February 1987, 15.

3. Roger Butterfield, "Reminiscences of George Eastman: An Introduction," *The University of Rochester Library Bulletin* 26, no. 3 (Spring 1971): 53.

4. GE to C. M. Thoms, 20 May 1921 (GEC).

5. GE to John D. Rockefeller, 12 June 1920 (GEC).

6. GE to Joseph T. Alling, 31 December 1912; GE to Almon R. Eastman, 19 June 1920 (GEC).

7. GE to Lewis P. Ross, 17 August 1906 (GEC); Lewis P. Ross to GE, 20 August 1902, 5 February 1906 (INC-GEC). Eastman also gave $50,000 in 1913 to Stevens Institute of Technology in Hoboken, N.J.

8. Carlton Gibson to GE, 14 March, 19 June, 19 September 1915; Rush Rhees to GE, 11 and 22 March 1915; A. W. Lindsay to GE, 1 March 1915; minutes of the executive committee of Mechanics Institute, 28 June 1916 (INC-GEC); GE to Carlton Gibson, 7 June 1912, 5 March 1915, 4 November 1921; GE to Rush Rhees, 16 May 1910 (GEC).

9. Jasper H. Wright to GE, 22 August 1917 (INC-GEC).

10. Letter from Kendall Castle to many interested parties, 1924 (INC-GEC). The committee that studied "whether or not a practical plan could be made whereby Mechanics Institute would be organized as a School of the University of Rochester" included Joseph Alling, Raymond Ball (for the university), Edward Bramley, Kendall B. Castle (for the university), George Eastman, James Gleason, Edward Halbleib (for Mechanics Institute), Carl Lomb, Herman Russell (for the institute), Roland Woodward, Harry Wareheim (for the Community Chest), and George Todd (INC-GEC).

11. The Rochester Orphan Asylum was originally the Rochester Female Asylum for the Relief of Orphans, renamed the Hillside Home for Children in 1921 and, from 1938, the Hillside Children's Center.

12. GE to Mrs. William Sage, 18 August 1902 (GEC).

13. GE to Cyrus Paine, president, Rochester Orphan Asylum, 2 June 1919 (GEC).

14. GE to William Bausch, 20 July 1901 (GEC); Elizabeth Farrar to GE, 28 March 1905 (INC-GEC); C. C. Laney, Board of Park Commissioners, to GE, 5 October 1905

(INC-GEC); GE to C. C. Laney, 13 October 1905 ; GE to the Right Rev. B. J. McQuaid, 11 April 1905 (GEC).

15. GE to Hiram H. Edgerton, 5 December 1908, 31 May, 15 June 1911; GE to Mrs. Gurney T. Curtis, 24 February 1912 (GEC).

16. GE to W. S. Hubell, 19 February, 17 July 1906, 23 January 1908; GE to Dr. H. S. Durand, 24 April 1906, 25 January 1907, 1 February 1908; GE to William S. Riley, 23 May 1912 (GEC).

17. Henry S. Durand to GE, 28 August 1922; H. S. Durand to Mayor Clarence D. VanZandt, 13 July 1922 (INC-GEC).

18. Ibid. GE to Edward Ziegler, New York, 24 December 1926 (GEC).

19. Henry S. Durand to GE, 4 December 1923; list of trees planted at Durand–Eastman Park, 2 April 1915 (INC-GEC).

20. GE to Henry S. Durand, Los Angeles, 12 December 1923 (GEC).

21. Interview with Harvey Padelford, 15 July 1950 (EKC); *National Magazine* to GE, 26 November 1917 (INC-GEC).

22. GE's speech on opening of Chamber of Commerce, 1917 (INC-GEC). Lord Northcliffe came to Rochester in 1917, GE to J. Thacher Clarke, 1917 (GEC); the airplane ride was 1918' GE to Frank L. Babbott, 24 July 1918 (GEC).

23. Edwin S. Gordon to Burt Fenner, McKim, Mead & White, 27 September, 3 October 1924; Burt Fenner to Edwin S. Gordon, 29 September 1924 (N-YIIS). Built as the Kimball Tobacco factory in the 1880s from plans by architect-turned-mayor James G. Cutler, the building was owned by the Cluett-Peabody shirt company at the time of Eastman's purchase.

24. Harland Bartholomew to GE, 3 and 29 January, 18 December 1930 (INC-GEC); GE to Harland Bartholomew (GEC).

25. GE to Dr. Clarence A. Barbour, New York City, 4 January 1913 (GEC). Barbour had been minister of the Lake Avenue Baptist Church, was then employed by the national YMCA, and would return to Rochester as the president of the Rochester Theological Seminary.

26. GE to Hattie Strong, 4 June 1913 (GEC).

27. Abby A. Rockefeller to GE, 6 October 1927 (INC-GEC).

28. Anna D. Hubbell to GE, 29 December 1917 (INC-GEC).

29. Alexander M. Lindsay to GE, 14 May 1918 (INC-GEC). When Eastman organized the War Chest and Community Chest he brought together for the first time for a single appeal Protestant, Catholic, and Jewish charities.

30. Blake McKelvey, *Rochester, The Quest for Quality, 1890–1925* (Cambridge: Harvard University Press, 1956), 165–66.

31. GE to Max Lowenthal, 4 December 1913 (GEC).

32. GE to E. R. L. Gould, 14 March 1911 (GEC).

33. GE to F. L. Babbott, 18 May 1911 (GEC).

34. GE to George B. Dryden, 26 September 1911; GE to H. C. Sievers, 2 October 11 (GEC).

35. GE to W. E. Riley, 19 December 1911; John J. Burnet to GE, 18 December 1911 (INC-GEC); GE to E. R. L. Gould, 19 February 1912 (GEC).

36. GE to E. R. L. Gould, 12 March 1912 (GEC).

37. GE to W. E. Riley, 19 December 1911 (GEC).

38. Edwin A. Rumball to GE, 11 April, 22 June 1912 (INC-GEC); GE to E. R. Gould, 26, 29, 30 March 1912; GE to Rev. Edwin Alfred Rumball, 1 April 1912 (GEC).

39. GE to Henry A. Smith, 21 November 1925 (GEC).

40. McKelvey, *Rochester, The Quest for Quality,* 73–85.

41. Paul Horgan, *The Fault of Angels* (New York and London: Harper and Brothers, 1933), 41.

42. Frederick A. Cleveland to GE, 20 November 1914 (INC-GEC).

43. F. A. Cleveland to GE, 19 February 1915 (INC-GEC).

44. Dr. Rush Rhees, president of the University of Rochester; George W. Todd, president of the Chamber of Commerce; Walter S. Hubbell, attorney; James Sibley Watson, capitalist; James Goold Cutler, ex-mayor, architect, Cutler Mail Chute Company; Edward Bausch, Bausch and Lomb; Abram J. Katz; president, Stein-Block Company (men's clothing manufacturers), Henry W. Morgan, president, Morgan Machine Company; Andrew J. Townson, Sibley, Lindsay & Curr Company; and Jeremiah G. Hickey, president, Hickey-Freeman Company. McKelvey, *Rochester, The Quest for Quality,* 316.

45. Interview with LeRoy E. Snyder, 22 January 1940 (RGE-UR).

46. Charles Mulford Robinson to GE, 13 March 1915 (INC-GEC).

47. W. S. Hubbell to GE, 21 April 1915 (INC-GEC).

48. GE to Frank L. Babbott, 3 December 1927 (GEC).

49. Leroy Snyder to E. W. Villeneuve, Commissioner, City Hall, Montreal, Quebec, 24 February 1917 (INC-GEC).

50. GE to M. Bartlett, 24 December 1915 (GEC).

51. GE to Hon. George Aldridge, 21 April 1917 (GEC).

52. GE to George Aldridge, 20 September 1918 (GEC).

53. LeRoy E. Snyder to GE, 8 October 1918 (INC-GEC).

54. J. G. Schurman to GE, 8 January 17 (INC-GEC).

55. Interview with Leroy Snyder, 22 January 1940 (RGE-UR).

56. GE to Leroy Snyder, 4 October 1918 (GEC).

57. GE to James W. Routh, 21 February 1920 (GEC).

58. GE to James W. Routh, 2 March 1921 (GEC).

59. GE to James W. Routh, 27 July 1921 (GEC).

60. GE to George B. Dryden; GE to Will Hays, 23 September 1927 (GEC).

61. Interview with W. Earl Weller, 15 February 1940 (RGE-UR).

62. GE to A. R. Hatton, 5 January 22 (GEC).

63. GE to A. R. Hatton, 9 April 1922 (GEC).

64. Isaac Adler, "The City Manager Movement," *Rochester Historical Society Publication Fund Series XVIII,* 300.

65. Interview with Eastman, 8 December 1924, quoted in Ibid.; John R. Slater, *Rhees of Rochester* (N.Y., 1946) 172; and Blake McKelvey, *Rochester: The Quest for Quality,* 323. Interview with Isaac Adler (BUTT-UR).

66. GE to O. J. Price, 31 March 1927 (GEC).

67. GE to Daniel E. Pomeroy, 9 October 1929 (GEC).

68. GE to Harry J. Bareham, 8 October 1929 (GEC).

69. GE to Frank Gannett, 22 September 1927 (GEC).

70. Earl Weller to GE, 27 June 1925 (INC-GEC).

71. Interview with W. Earl Weller, 15 February 1940 (RGE-UR).

Chapter 23: Manifest Destiny

1. GE to HAS, 20 December 1894 (GEC).

2. GE to William S. Gifford, 30 October 1911; GE to Moritz B. Philipp, 10 February 1913; GE to HAS, 3 February 1914 (GEC).

3. GE to J. J. Kennedy, 18 July 1913, 2 March 1914 (GEC).

4. GE to A. Siloman, Vereinigte Fabriken Photographischer Papiere, Dresden, 15 October 1913; GE to Moritz B. Philipp, 3 April 1913 (GEC).

5. GE to William Gifford, 18 August 1913 (GEC).

6. *Goodwin Film & Camera Company v. Eastman Kodak Company*, 213 *Federal Reporter* 231 (1914).

7. GE to Thomas Baker, 1 April 1914 (GEC).

8. GE to HAS, 30 March 1914 (GEC).

9. Ibid. GE to HAS, 24 February, GE to Frank L. Babbott, 12 February, GE to Benjamin Strong Jr., 27 March 1914 (GEC).

10. Including the Celluloid Company, the Raw Film & Supply Company, Jules Brulatour (for Lumière), the Eclectic Film Company, Pathé Freres, and Pathé Exchange, Inc.

11. Fritz Wentzel, *Memoirs of a Photochemist* (Philadelphia: American Museum of Photography, 1960), 100.

12. *Rochester Union & Advertiser* and *Rochester Herald*, 27 March 1914; *Wall Street Journal*, 22 April 1914.

13. GE to HAS, 30 March 1914 (GEC).

14. GE to Andrew Pringle, 30 March 1914 (GEC).

15. Clipping from Chicago Tribune, 1904 (BUTT-UR).

16. Clippings from Hearst papers, *Boston American* and *New York American*, 8 August 1907 (BUTT-UR).

17. GE testified in court with words like these on 9 November 1914.

18. GE to HAS, 10 May 1912 (GEC).

19. GE to William S. Gifford, 2 April 1914 (GEC).

20. GE to Rush Rhees, May 1914 (GEC); Carl W. Ackerman, *George Eastman* (Boston and New York: Houghton Mifflin, 1930), 280.

21. In the 1980s the Bayer Company, having long since gone out of the film business and being perhaps best known for its aspirin, was acquired by the Eastman Kodak Company. In the 1990s it was sold.

22. "Opinion," *United States v. Eastman Kodak Co.* et al., 24 August 1915, U.S. Circuit Court, Western District of New York, v. 226, *Federal Reporter*, 65.

23. *U.S. v. EKCo.*, *Abridged Transcript of Record*, (10 vols., 4,200 pp.) and *Supplemental Brief and Argument for Defendants* (80 pp.).

24. "Opinion," *U.S. v. EKCo*, 70.

25. GE to L. Goffard, 16 April 1907 (GEC).

26. "Opinion," *U.S. v. EKCo.*, 79.

27. Ibid., 80.

28. Ibid., 76.

29. GE testimony, *U.S. v. EKCo.*

30. GE testimony, U.S. v. *EKCo.*

31. Ibid.

32. James S. Havens, counsel of the company, to Dudley Field Malone, January 1917 (GEC).

33. Alice K. Whitney to GE, 25 August 1915 (GEC).

34. GE to Allan C. Ross, associate editor, *Democrat & Chronicle*, 6 November 1916 (GEC).

35. Ackerman, *George Eastman*, 284.

36. GE to J. J. Kennedy, 5 September 1917 (GEC).

37. Ibid.

38. GE to E. A. Whittier, 18 June 1917 (GEC).

39. GE to HAS, 14 December 1917 (GEC).

40. GE to editor of the *Sunday Sun*, 4 September 1912 (GEC).

41. GE to Samuel Crowther, 25 October 1916 (INC-GEC).

42. *Financial World*, 23 October 1974.

43. GE to Murray Bartlett, 24 December 1915 (GEC).

44. GE to Daniel E. Pomeroy, 21 December 1920 (GEC).

45. "A Stieglitz Talk at a New York Art Center," ca. 1924 taken down by Rebecca Strand, Center for Creative Photography, The University of Arizona, N. 1 March 1976, 7.

46. *Kodak Magazine* 1, no. 10 (March 1921): 1–4.

47. Ibid.

48. GE to William S. Gifford, Ormond Beach, 14 February 1921 (GEC). Supporting this claim were the figures that in 1920 portrait and commercial films yielded $1,850,000 as against plates of $1,900,000.

49. GE to Ernest Willard, 24 February 1921; GE to Frank L. Babbott, 31 January 1921 (GEC).

50. Roger Butterfield, "The Prodigious Life of George Eastman," *Life* magazine, (April 1954).

Chapter 24: Over There

Ackerman and Brummitt have good secondary accounts of Kodak activities during World War I.

1. Writer Elizabeth Hardwick coined the phrase "All writing is profoundly unmarried."

2. Interview by Georgia Gosnell with Mrs. Harvey Padelford, wife of Eastman's chauffeur, 1989.

3. Marion Gleason was interviewed about Eastman many times. On 15 May 1939 she wrote a six-page letter to Andres Maurois, then contemplating a biography of

GE. She spoke to Roger Butterfield in the 1950s, on radio in 1976, on tape to John Kuyper of the GEH in 1986, and on television in 1980. All these sources were consulted.

4. Interview by author with Anne Mulligan, ca. 1990.

5. Interviews with Gertrude Strong Achilles, 9 February 1940, and E. D. Leary, 22 January 1940; Susan Brown to GE, 2 December 1927, 27 August, 9 September, 22 December 1930 (INC-GEC).

6. Interview by Jean Ennis with Nathaniel Myrick, 28 November 1950 (EKC).

7. GE to Mrs. Charles Newhall, December 1913 (GEC).

8. William S. Gifford to GE, 13 May 1911, 18 March 1913 (INC-GEC). GE to Carey Williams Jr., Ringwood, S.C., 23 February 1912 (GEC).

9. GE to Katherine Gifford, April 1912; also letters to caterers and Tiffany's (GEC).

10. GE to Frank L. Babbott, 12 December 1913 (GEC).

11. Letter from Victoria Powers to Oscar Solbert, 12 February 1940 (RGE-UR). Henry Clune describes Eastman's New Year's ball (although he was not in attendance) in *The Rochester I Know* (New York: Doubleday & Company, 1972) 253–59.

12. GE to W. A. Taprell, 27 August 1914 (GEC).

13. Alice K. Whitney to F. L. Babbott, 8 August 1914, GE to F. L. Babbott, 25 August 1914, GE to Thomas Baker, 28 August 1914, GE to W. S. Gifford, 31 August 1914, GE to E. H. Janson, 25 August 1914 (GEC); the prince of Wales to GE 15 August 1914 (INC-GEC).

14. GE to Thomas Baker, 2 June 1915; GE to HAS, 9 March 1915 (GEC).

15. GE to William H. Walker, 10 June 1917 (GEC).

16. Harriet Dana Walker to GE, 19 May 1918 (INC-GEC).

17. GE to Alice K. Whitney, July 1916; GE to the Rev. Murray Bartlett, 14 September 1916 (GEC).

18. GE to Mary Mulligan, 13 July 1917; GE to W. N. Duane, New York City, 9 November 1917; GE to Alexander M. Lindsay, 16 October 1915 (GEC); GE to Ellen Dryden, 12 December 1917 (GEC-UR); interview by author with Jocelyn Carp, who was employed by the Friendly Home in the 1980s.

19. Carl Akerman, *George Eastman* (Boston and New York: Houghton Mifflin, 1930), 292–93.

20. GE to William S. Gifford, 15 December (GEC): Henry Ford quote; GE to Janson, 23 December 1916 (GEC).

21. Interviews with Isaac Adler, 23 April 1940, and Mortimer Adler, 16 May 1940 (RGE-UR).

22. GE to Franklin Delano Roosevelt, 11 December 1917; Franklin Delano Roosevelt to GE, 28 March 1918 (GEC).

23. GE to Alexander Lindsay, 11 March 1918 (GEC).

24. GE to Alexander Lindsay, 8 February 1918 (GEC).

25. Interview with Hans Clarke, 8 April 1953 (EKC).

26. GE to Jules E. Brulatour, 1 October 1917 (GEC).

27. GE to Henry Myrick, April 1917; GE to HAS, 1 June 1917 (GEC).

28. GE to Henry P. Davison, 8 March 1918 (GEC).

29. The ten key Rochesterians were Albert Eastwood, Foulkes, Edward Miner, George Todd, Woodward, Ernest Willard, James G. Cutler, Mortimer Adler, Dr. William Taylor, and Bishop Thomas F. Hickey.

30. GE to Joseph T. Alling, 28 March 1918 (Alling was heading the YMCA activities at Camp Dix in New Jersey for the duration of the war) (GEC): "The only one who opposed the idea was Mr. Lansdale [of the YMCA] but his argument did not impress anyone. . . . It was voted to have a third meeting and decide the matter definitely. . . . The same men were present and in addition Mr. Gerard Dahl, Vice President of the Chase National Bank, New York, who has charge of the forthcoming Red Cross drive for the Atlantic Division. He made mainly the same argument that Lansdale did and although he made a most favorable impression he did not convince anybody and the vote was unanimously against him."

31. GE to Albert B Eastwood, 8 November 1918 (GEC).

32. In 1917 Eastman subscribed $2.5 million in bonds of the $31 million raised in Rochester for the $5 billion War Loan, of which $3 billion was loaned to the Allies.

33. GE to HAS, 21 March 1918 (GEC).

34. GE to Luther B. Wishard, LLD, New York City, 9 May 1918 (GEC).

35. GE to Joseph Alling, 28 March 1918 (GEC).

36. GE to Cyrus F. Paine and nineteen other Rochesterians, 15 May 1918 (GEC).

37. GE to C. E. Scott, American Red Cross, Washington, D.C., 23 March 1918 (GEC).

38. GE to Almon R. Eastman, 4 June 1918 (GEC).

39. In 1921 Eastman wrote to Charles Thoms, the real estate man who sold him the Culver farm in 1905, and encouraged him in 1916 to build "a grand music hall" for Rochester. "I am in receipt of your . . . check for $500 for the Community Chest. . . . If all the rich men of this town subscribed in the same proportion to their means we would not have any charities here worth while. . . . You are reputed to have made yourself a millionaire and yet you want to contribute an amount which measures up only to what is given by dozens of salaried men. . . . Your proposition that because you lost some money last year justifies you in penalizing the charities is wholly untenable. . . . You have not visibly altered your way of living."

40. GE to Albert B. Eastwood, 8 and 12 November 1918 (GEC).

41. GE to William Gifford, 3 and 18 January 1919 (GEC); Wyatt Brummitt, *George Eastman of Kodak*, 270.

42. GE to Ellen Dryden, January 1919 (GEC).

43. GE to Almon R. Eastman, 15 October 1918 (GEC).

Chapter 25: Kodak Man to Be World's Doctor and Dentist

Secondary sources for this chapter are: *To Each His Farthest Star, University of Rochester Medical Center 1925–1975* (collected essays); Harvey J. Burkhart, "Centennial History of Dentistry in Rochester," *The Rochester Historical Society Publication Fund Series* 13 (1934):281–320; George Corner, *George Hoyt Whipple and His Friends;* Abraham Flexner, *Autobiography;* Arthur May's published *A History of the University of Rochester, 1850–1962* (Rochester: University of Rochester, 1977) and particularly the unabridged, annotated typescript of same at the UR library; John Slater, *Rhees of Roches-*

ter (New York and London: Harper and Brothers, 1946). As always, the primary sources were the incoming and outgoing George Eastman correspondence, now housed at the George Eastman House. Portions of this material was published as "The Great Removal Project," I and II, by Betsy (Elizabeth) Brayer, *Rochester Review* (Fall 1980, Winter 1980–81).

1. GE to Abraham Flexner, 13 June 1929; GE to William H. Walker, 30 July 1915 (GEC): "My favorite headline is 'Kodak Man to be Rochester's Dentist.'"

2. Interview with George Carnahan, 28 February 1940 (RGE-UR).

3. Interview with Albert D. Kaiser, 19 January 1940 (RGE-UR).

4. GE to Teddy Marceau, 20 December 1909; GE to Colonel Theodore C. Marceau, 20 December 1909 (GEC).

5. GE to Dora Winsor, 9 March 1917 (GEC).

6. GE to Robert Lieber, 6 October 1922 (GEC).

7. "Sonny" story from Georgia Gosnell; chauffeur story quoted by Marion Gleason in *University of Rochester Library Bulletin* (Spring 1971). Halloween story told author by Allen Macomber, who was one of the boys who went trick-or-treating to Eastman House.

8. Interviews with Marion Gleason and Charles Turpin, 12 February, 15 May 1940 (RGE-UR).

9. GE to Cousin Mary Eastman Southwick, 12 May 1923 (GEC); GE to Ellen A. Dryden, 4 January 1921 (GEC); Interview by author with George Eastman Dryden, February 1989; Eastman Dryden to GE, 1920 (INC-GEC).

10. GE to Cyrus H. K. Curtis, Philadelphia, 18 June 1923; also GE to R. J. Caldwell, New York City, 21 December 1917; GE to Ernest Sturride, London, 14 April 1927 (GEC).

11. MKE to Emily Kilbourn Cope, 1840s and 1850s (GEC); interview with Netta (Mrs. Robert) Ranlet, 1940 (RGE-UR).

12. Burkhart's son Richard, a dentist in New York City, then made new dentures for Eastman every few years.

13. Interview with Harvey J. Burkhart, 19 January 1940 (RGE-UR).

14. Early Rochester dentists made the record books in other ways too. The first gold crown used in capping a broken-down tooth was made by Dr. John B. Beers. And the first repeating rifle was the invention of an itinerant Rochester dentist, Edward Maynard, in 1851. The first practical rapid fire gun was invented by Josephus Requa, dentist, in 1863. The first attempt to organize a dental protective association against attacks by those holding patents on appliances and methods was in Rochester.

15. Carl Ackerman, *George Eastman* (Boston and New York: Houghton Mifflin, 1930), 386.

16. Ibid.

17. The author found this scrapbook and renderings in the attic of the architects' offices in 1978. The Rochester Dental Dispensary became the Eastman Dental Dispensary in 1947, when a new director succeeded Harvey Burkhart, who died in 1946, and the Eastman Dental Center in 1965, reflecting perhaps the falling out of favor of the word "dispensary."

18. Harvey Burkhart, "Centennial History of Dentistry in Rochester," *Rochester Historical Society Publication Series* (Rochester: Rochester Historical Society, 1934), 307. GE to Hon. Simon Adler, Thaddeus Sweet (Speaker of the Assembly), Albany, 3 and 24 March 1916; GE to Charles S. Whitman, governor, 30 March 1916 (GEC).

19. Burkhart, "Centennial History of Dentistry."

20. GE to New York State Dental Society, 1915 (GEC).

21. GE to Robert C. Shumway, 30 August 1915 (GEC).

22. In 1918 these rates were modified to family income not exceeding $15 a week for a two-child family, $20 for three children, and $24 for four.

23. GE to William Bausch, 22 July 1920; GE to the trustees of the Rochester Dental Dispensary, 25 June 1920 (GEC); Burkhart, "Centennial History of Dentistry."

24. Ackerman, *George Eastman*, 391.

25. GE to Ernest Willard, Florida, January 1921 (GEC). Archival publicity material in the library of the Eastman Dental Center, Rochester, N.Y.

26. George Eastman, "Medical Miscreants," *Kodak Magazine* (June 1921): 4–5; GE to KODAK PARIS (telegram), 15 April 1921 (GEC).

27. Wm. F. Von Dohlen to GE, 12 November 1920 (INC-GEC). GE to Rush Rhees, 27 July, 9 August 1920; GE to Dr. Edward W. Mulligan, Loon Lake, 4 August 1920; GE to Helen Carte, Honolulu, 11 October 1920 (GEC).

28. GE to Dr. Winford H. Smith, Johns Hopkins Hospital, 28 December 1920 (GEC).

29. GE to Ernest Willard, January 1921 (GEC).

30. GE to Abraham Flexner, 13 June 1929 (GEC).

31. GE to Lord Riddell, 26 June 1929 (GEC).

32. Josephine Dickman was especially prone to bad toothaches and cancelled numerous social occasions because of them.

33. Ackerman, *George Eastman*, 477–80.

34. GE to Cesare Sconfietti, 4 June 1929 (GEC).

35. F. F. Robison to GE, October 1929 (INC-GEC); GE to F. F. Robison, Grafton W. Va. 28 October 1929 (GEC).

36. Abraham Flexner, "Carnegie Bulletin Number Four" (1910); Edward C. Atwater "A Modest but Good Institution," *To each his farthest star* (Rochester: University of Rochester Medical Center, 1975), 8–9.

37. Abraham Flexner, *I Remember: An Autobiography* (New York: Simon and Schuster, 1940), 180.

38. Ibid. Burkhart, "Centennial History of Dentistry", 307–9.

39. Abraham Flexner, *I Remember: An Autobiography*, 180–81.

40. GE to Hiram Watson Sibley, 24 November 1908 (GEC).

41. Betsy Brayer, "Health Care in an Ongoing Society," *Our Spirit Shows: Rochester Sesquicentennial, 1834–1984* (Rochester: Rochester Sesquicentennial Inc., 1984), 64–73.

42. GE to Gov. Nathan Miller, 8 January 1922 (GEC).

43. GE to George Goler (GEC); Quote from *Democrat & Chronicle* article about GE's plans for health care in Rochester, ca. 7 November 1921 (INC-GEC); GE to William R. P. Emerson, 1920 (GEC); ten letters from Emerson to Eastman, 1920–21 (INC-GEC). Hillside Home later became the Hillside Children's Center, reflecting

the change in attitude toward these words. "Asylum" originally was meant to imply a haven from a heartless world. But the connotation of a place where crazy people went led to its being discarded. "Home" then underwent a similar transformation. One wonders what will follow the now neutral, antiseptic, and rather heartless "center" in the future.

44. Flexner, *I Remember: An Autobiography*, 183; GE to Frank L. Babbott, 15 March 1920 (GEC).

45. GE to Frank L. Babbott, 22 March and 14 June 1920 (GEC).

46. GE to John D. Rockefeller Sr., 12 May 1920 (GEC). Eastman continued: "In this case it is not only the money contribution that this community appreciates, but the cooperation of your organization, without the skilled services of which the mere money would be impotent to obtain success."

47. GE to Harvey J. Burkhart, 8 April 1921 (GEC).

48. According to Walter Hubbell to GE, 24 June 1920 (GEC), Hattie Strong received the income from one-fourth of Henry's residuary estate to revert to his children upon Hattie's death (INC-GEC).

49. Helen Strong Carter to GE, 22 March 1920 (INC-GEC). GE to Helen Strong Carter and Gertrude Strong Achilles, 2 March 1920 (GEC)

50. GE to Gertrude Strong Achilles, March 1920 (GEC): "I can appreciate your feeling that you do not want to tie yourself up in any way where you could possibly be cramped for money and it would be far from my desire to put you in any such position."

51. GE to Gertrude Strong Achilles, 10 March 1921 (GEC).

52. Ibid., 31 March and 4 October 1920; GE to Rush Rhees, 12 August 1920 (GEC).

53. Correspondence files of the Hooper Foundation, 1914–22, were made available to and quoted by George W. Corner, *George Hoyt Whipple and His Friends: The Life-Story of a Nobel Prize Pathologist* (Philadelphia: J. B. Lippincott, 1963), 113–14.

54. GE to Frank L. Babbott, 11 August 1921 (GEC). George W. Corner, *George Hoyt Whipple*, 115.

55. Ibid.

56. GE to Rush Rhees, 7 July 1923 (GEC).

57. George H. Whipple, *Planning and Construction Period of the School and Hospitals, 1921–1925: School of Medicine and Dentistry, Strong Memorial Hospital, Rochester Municipal Hospital* (Rochester: University of Rochester, 1957)

58. Corner, *George Hoyt Whipple*, 138–55. Whipple's narrowing in on young American men for his staff may also be an indication of his own narrow conception of for whom the field of medicine should be open. There is evidence that anti-Semitism was rampant at the medical school in early days. See Arthur Kornberg, *For the Love of Enzymes, The Odyssey of a Biochemist* (Cambridge: Harvard University Press, 1989). Kornberg writes of his student days: "My first shock at Rochester was hearing anti-Semitic remarks. . . . The worst was being denied academic awards and research opportunities because I was Jewish. I particularly coveted the pathology fellowship. . . . The fellows were chosen by George H. Whipple—Nobel laureate, chairman of the department, dean of the school, and God of the Rochester medical universe." Despite being first in his class, Kornberg was not offered any fellowship.

59. Arthur May, *A History of the University of Rochester* (Princeton: Princeton University Press, 1977), 188.

60. Flexner, *I Remember: An Autobiography,* 184.

61. Betsy Brayer, "The Great Removal Project," I, *Rochester Review*, Fall 1980.

62. Ibid. *Rochester Alumni Review,* June–July 1930.

63. Ibid.

64. Ibid.

65. Betsy Brayer, "The Great Removal Project," I and II, *Rochester Review* (Fall 1980, Winter 1980–81).

66. Ibid.

67. Ibid. May, *A History,* 217.

68. Ibid. GE to Rush Rhees, 13 July 1923 (GEC); GE to Ellen Dryden, 8 December 1924 (GEC).

69. John Rothwell Slater, *Rhees of Rochester* (New York and London: Harper and Brothers, 1946), 171.

70. May, *A History,* 216.

71. GE to Frank L. Babbott, 24 May 1927 (GEC).

72. Charles Platt (1861–1933) was primarily a country-house designer—perhaps the best of the post-1900 period; his houses borrowed from the Georgian period, the Italian Renaissance, and the French eighteenth century without being heavily in debt to any one period. His gardens—he was a landscape architect, too—had a delicate charm.

73. GE to Rush Rhees (GEC). Interview by author with Gertrude Herdle Moore, 1980. The faculty protest committee was spearheaded by Dexter Perkins, history professor, and Gertrude Herdle (Moore), director of the university's Memorial Art Gallery.

74. Interview with Harvey Padelford, 1 February 1940 (RGE-UR).

Chapter 26: Music in Every Direction

1. Kodak Park speech, 20 October 1928 (EKC); "Philanthropy under a Bushel", *New York Times*, 21 March 1920.

2. GE, December 1920 (GEC); "Philanthropy under a Bushel".

3. Howard Hanson, "Music Was a Spiritual Necessity," *University of Rochester Library Bulletin* (Spring 1971):88.

4. GE to C. H. Miller, director of music, Department of Public Instruction, 13 January 1919 (GEC).

5. Agenda for organizing the Subscriber's Association, 1923 (INC-GEC).

6. Ibid.

7. GE to Frank Seaman, 10 January 1922 (GEC).

8. C. E. Thoms to GE, 19 December 1916 (INC-GEC).

9. Jean Ingelow, original graduate of the DKG Institute (class of 1915), recalled a picnic in the spring of 1915 when "Professor George R. Penny told the students about a new school of music that George Eastman was going to build and he said for us all to be thinking of it." Vincent A. Lenti interviewed Ingelow in May 1978 and made her notes available to me.

10. Hermann Dossenbach to GE, 3 February, 28 March, 12 June 1912 (INC-GEC).

11. Walter Sage Hubbell to GE, 23 July, 8 August 1912 (INC-GEC).

12. GE to Mrs. J. H. Boucher, 9 December 1904; GE to Frank S. Upton, 5 March 1923; GE to W. E. Walters, 19 May, 2 June 1922 (GEC); Rochester Tuesday Musicale to GE, 21 March 1922 (INC-GEC).

13. Stewart B. Sabin, "A Retrospect of Music in Rochester," *Centennial History of Rochester, New York*, v. 2, *The Rochester Historical Society Publication Fund Series*, 1932, v. 11, 69.

14. Interviews with Howard Hanson, 15 May 1939, 17 January 1940 (RGE-UR); also filmed interview with Adrianne McLennon, 1972. John R. Slater, *Rhees of Rochester* (New York: Harper, 1946), 57. The billious critic wrote for *Time* magazine.

15. Vincent A. Lenti, *The Preparatory Department; Historical Origins of the Eastman School of Music and Its Commitment to the Education of the Rochester Community* (Rochester: typescript ms., 1978), 1.

16. Rush Rhees to GE, 5 April 1918 (INC-GEC). Walter S. Hubbell to GE, 12, 16 19, 23 July, 1 August 1918 (INC GEC).

17. GE to Ellen A. Dryden, 30 July 1918 (GEC).

18. GE to Rush Rhees, 14 February 1919 (GEC).

19. Howard Hanson, filmed interview with Adrienne McLennon, 23 June 1972 (UR).

20. GE to George Todd, February 1919 (GEC). At present the organization is called Rochester Philharmonic Orchestra, Inc.

21. *Grove's Dictionary of Music and Musicians*, 5th ed., ed. Eric Blom (New York: St. Martin's Press; London: Macmillan, 1954), A: 104.

22. Frank L. Babbott to GE, 22 October 18 (INC-GEC); GE to Frank L. Babbott, 9 November 1918 (GEC).

23. GE to Rush Rhees, 14 February 1919 (GEC).

24. Ibid.

25. GE to David Hochstein and violin makers, 1912–17 (GEC); David Hochstein to GE. 22 letters, 1912–7; Rush Rhees to GE, 26 and 29 March and 30 April 1923; The David Hochstein Music School Settlement statement, 1 July 1922 (INC-GEC); Grace N. Kraut, *An Unfinished Symphony: The Story of David Hochstein* (Rochester, 1980), 71–75; *The Rochester Historical Society Publication Fund Series* (Rochester, 1922–38), 3, 11, 33–34, 47; 74. Quote from GE to Howard W. Cutter, 18 February 1920 (GEC).

26. Rush Rhees to GE, 1 July 1920 (INC-GEC).

27. GE to Rush Rhees, 30 October, 12 November and 7 December 1920, 5 February 1923 (GEC).

28. GE to Hiram Watson Sibley, 24 March 1922 (GEC); Hiram W. Sibley to GE, 29 March 1922 (INC-GEC). Only the Library of Congress, the New York Public Library, and the Moscow University Library have larger collections of musical manuscripts, with the Bodleian at Oxford probably having the most treasures. In 1937 a separate structure was built on Swan Street to house the collection—the first music library in the United States to have its own building. In 1989 a new block-long, $18 million building called Eastman Place opened with the library occupying the second,

third, and fourth floors (the last from *Notes* 20, no. 5 [August 1989], publication of the Eastman School of Music, University of Rochester).

29. GE to Ray Ball, 1923 (GEC).

30. GE to Prof. James M. White, University of Illinois, 3 March 1922 (GEC).

31. Skinner organ for Kilbourn Hall, $55,000 (November 1920) with about 90 stops and designed by Harold Gleason; grand theater organ from Austin, $78,705 (December 1920); nine seven-stop practice organs M. P. Moller, Hagerstown, $14,000 (December 1920); one M. P. Moller, Hagerstown fifteen-stop studio organ, $7,750 (December 1920); fifteen-stop Steere studio organ, $8,416 (January 1921); Wurlitzer, $10,250 (March 1922); three organs M. P. Moller Inc., $10,500 (July 1923), Marr & Colton, Warsaw $3,800 (July 1923). Ernest M. Skinner, Boston, suggested that practice and teaching organs be put into the attic instead of studios themselves, thereby giving room for more practice organs and making the studios more attractive. Eastman told Rob Jessup (11 February 1921) in Salt Lake City that he understood Austin people built the organ for the Mormon Tabernacle.

32. GE to Skinner Organ Company, Boston, 30 March 1922 (GEC).

33. GE to Arthur Alexander, 3 October 1922 (GEC).

34. Interview with Mrs. Hawley (Clayla) Ward, 12 January 1940 (RGE-UR).

35. Henry Clune, *five Oclock* 1, no. 4 (13 May 1924) (GE's picture on cover). During the intermission of *La Boheme* at Eastman Theatre by Metropolitan Opera, Clune noted that Eastman was "in earnest conversation with Mrs. Harold Gleason, content to pass up the rest of the promenaders and rest his eyes on the blue and silver vision that was Mrs. Harold. Meanwhile Harold, the organ wizard, forbore to stray far away."

"The official promenade was scheduled for the interval between Acts 2 and 3, but so like an intimate family was the distinguished audience that many chatted across the aisles between scenes or introduced their large parties of guests to neighbors."

36. Interview by author with Carl F. W. Kaelber Jr., architect, 1977.

37. *Programme for the Opening of the Eastman Theatre*, 4 September 1921. GE to Julian Street, 23 October 1922 (GEC); GE to G. Sconfietti, 23 October 1923 (GEC). The list of visiting artists during the early years of the Eastman Theatre was compiled by the author from George Eastman's incoming correspondence.

38. Robert Lieber to GE, 11 June 1919; Jules Brulatour to GE, 14 July 1919 (INC-GEC).

39. The eventual expenditure by Eastman of $17,567,000 on school and theatre is quoted from Vincent A. Lenti, *The Preparatory Department*, 6; However, in GE to L. F. Loree on 28 February 1924 (GEC) is this quote:"The School and Theatre are in one building and the approximate cost was something like five million dollars. It was difficult to keep the costs separate but it has been estimated that they were pretty evenly divided between the two departments. The building was built during a strike of the building trades and the total cost was far above what the normal would be."

40. Since this is quoted from the program for the theater's opening, it is likely that it was written by Eastman himself.

41. Samuel Rothafel to GE, 24 July 1923 (INC-GEC).

42. Interview with Harold Gleason, ca. 1954 (BUTT-IN-UR).

43. Interview by Jean Ennis with Arthur See, 1953 (EKC).

44. Interview by author with Byron Johnson, former Preparatory Department student, ca. 1980.

45. GE to Carl Lauterbach, 14 February 1927 (GEC).

46. Otto H. Kahn to GE, 26 January 1921 (INC-GEC).

47. In November 1920 Rush Rhees wrote Sibelius: "All of us connected with The University of Rochester and its School of Music are greatly delighted by the report which Mr. Alf Klingenberg gives of his visit with you at Helsingfors this last summer and your agreement to spend a year at our Eastman School of Music" (INC-GEC). In February 1921 Eastman wrote Otto Kahn: "We were very fortunate in getting hold of Sibelius. The fact that he is a friend of our Director, Mr. Klingenberg, was the deciding influence" (GEC).

48. Paul Turok, "Norwegian Surprises, From Opera to Symphony," *New York Times*, 12 February 1989, H-29. Sinding may be due for a reevaluation. Turok wrote upon the release of a new recording of Sinding's Der Heilige Berg, written in 1914, that "the last thing one would have expected from Sinding is a first-rate opera," calling Sinding's "opera sounds . . . lightened, aerated Wagner"—which may be why his music appealed to Eastman.

49. Augusta Sinding to GE, undated letter, ca. December 1920 (INC-GEC).

50. Eastman's typical response to appeals from women's colleges is contained in a letter to Mrs. William Ely of 26 December 1919 (GEC), asking him to contribute to the Smith College campaign: "I have always drawn the line on women's colleges, not because I have any lack of appreciation for the good they are doing in the education of the world but simply because I am more interested in other branches of education and do not care to spread my efforts too much."

51. This compilation of traits that Rhees and Eastman were looking for comes from several sources, including a letter, Rhees to GE, 16 October 1929 (GEC), in which Rhees reports what he told Ackerman for that biography. Also Hanson's several interviews and recollections 1939, 1940, 1950, 1954, and the articles he wrote for the *University of Rochester Library Bulletin* in Spring 1971.

52. GE to Nellie C. Cornish, Seattle, 12 July 1923 (GEC).

53. Coates shared the directorship this year with Eugene Goosens.

54. The Prix de Rome was previously only open to painters, sculptors, and classical scholars.

55. *Baker's Biographical Dictionary of Musicians*, 5th ed., revised by Nicolas Slonimsky (New York/London: G. Schirmer, 1971), 655. Margaret Bond, "Howard Hanson Remembered," *Rochester Review* (Spring 1981) :1–8. Interviews with Howard Hanson: 15 May 1939, 17 January 1940 (RGE-UR); 1950s interview by Jean Ennis (EKC) (BUTT-UR); filmed interview by Adrienne McLennon, 23 June 1972 (UR).

56. Interview with Raymond Ball, 12 May 1939 (RGE-UR); McLennon interview with Hanson.

57. Bond, "Howard Hanson Remembered," 3.

58. GE to Eric T. Clarke, 31 January 1927 (GEC).

59. Ennis interview with Hanson, ca. 1950.

60. Interview with Howard Hanson, 15 January 1939 (RGE-UR).

61. In June 1989 Nicolas Slonimsky told the author that it was Eastman who met

Rosing. Slonimsky made the same assertion in a *New Yorker* article. Other accounts say George Todd met Rosing on the steamer.

62. GE to Vladimir Rosing, 3 November 1926 (GEC). Although Eastman favored opera in English, he complained mightily to Rosing in this letter about the poor diction of the performers.

63. GE to S. L. Rothafel, Capitol Theatre, New York City, 25 July 1923 (GEC).

64. Nicolas Slonimsky, *Perfect Pitch: A Life Story* (Oxford and New York: Oxford University Press, 1988), 81–85.

65. Andrew Jackson (Jack) Warner II was the son of J. Foster Warner, architect of Eastman House.

66. Interviews with Mamoulian (EKC) (UR). Mamoulian did go back to Paris and his old employer—thirty-two years later, in 1955, he took a special production of *Oklahoma* to the Theatre des Champse-Elysees.

67. Ibid.

68. Interview by author with Nicolas Slominsky, May 1989; Interview with Harold Gleason 1940 (RGE-UR).

69. Ibid.; Slominsky, *Perfect Pitch*, 81–91.

70. 1989 interview by author with Slominsky.

71. Enid Knapp Botsford, "A Vison Shared," *University of Rochester Library Bulletin* (Spring 1971): 127.

72. Agnes de Mille, *Martha: The Life and Work of Martha Graham* (New York: Random House, 1956, 1991), 79–80.

73. Martha Graham, *Blood Memory* (New York: Doubleday, 1991), 108. Evelyn Sabin, one of Martha's dancers, married Leopold Mannes, one of the inventors of Kodachrome film mentioned in chapter 13.

74. Ibid., 79; de Mille, *Martha*, 417.

Chapter 27: Dear Mr. Eastman

1. Susan Brown to GE, 6 March 1931 (INC-GEC).

2. GE to Kodak employees, 15 July 1919 (INC-GEC). The letter read in part: "Conditions within the city are such that I feel, as I go away, that I should leave with you a warning against the dangers that menace you and your homes and the institution to which a great bulk of you are so loyal. . . . [Some] citizens have refused to admit that there was a lurking danger . . . fostered by professional agitators and nourished by the gullible and ignorant. . . . Don't let us make that mistake here in Rochester . . . [with] propaganda that, if followed to its full conclusion, can bring us only to the pitiable condition of prostrate, starving Russia. . . . It is by no means wholly the affairs of the company . . . that I have in mind in putting this matter before you. Your comfort and prosperity and the growth and prosperity of the company are inter-dependent. The management and the employees have always gotten along wonderfully well. There is probably no concern of equal size in the country that has had less friction. . . . We of the management, are anxious not merely that you take pride in your work and in the excellence of the goods that the company produces, but that there shall be opportunity for every one of you. We want you to have comfortable homes and healthy surroundings. We want your children to

have good schools and want them to be enveloped in an atmosphere that will make of them good citizens. . . . None of these things are attainable where anarchy reigns . . . where . . . our property, our lives, our women and children, even our jobs, are at the mercy of the mob leaders who fatten on the very fanaticism that they fan into flame. Fortunately, there has been little of this spirit of destruction within our organization. We have been builders, not destroyers. We have seen working conditions improve. . . . Men and women, its up to you. It's in your hands to strangle it, pull its fangs, kill it. And I have faith that you will."

Employees of each department wrote to the effect that they "fully appreciate the dangers set forth and desire to assure Mr. Eastman of our loyal support not only as members of the Kodak Organization but as true American citizens."

3. Gifford's widow, May, remained a close friend and correspondent of GE, visiting Oak Lodge and Eastman House often. She was one of the last people he wrote to in March 1932.

4. Rubbing the nose of the bronze bas-relief plaque of Eastman in the lobby before taking an exam has been the good-luck ritual of many generations of MIT students. Consequently the nose is much shinier that the rest of the bas-relief.

5. GE to W. T. Manning, 15 May 1930 (GEC); GE to Nicholas Murray Butler, 1 October 1931; N. M. Butler to GE, 29 September 1931 (INC-GEC).

6. GE to Walter Cook, University of Buffalo, and Charles Flint, Syracuse University, ca. 1920, 1927 (GEC).

7. GE to Mrs. William Ely (on behalf of Smith College), 26 December 1919 (GEC).

8. GE to William G. Kaelber, 29 July 1929 (GEC). GE to John Mullowney, 23 September and 3 October 1929 (GEC)

9. Helen Keller to GE, 12 December 1924, 10 and 15 February 1930 (INC-GEC); GE to Helen Keller, 13 February 1930 (GEC): "Of course I have known about you and your work for many years and have looked upon it with much sympathy and appreciation. It just happens that my philanthropic work has taken other channels and it is now too late to open up any new ones. However, I do not want to say no to your appeal, so I am sending you herewith a check for $10,000 for your undertaking."

10. Margaret Sanger to GE, 28 August, 23 September, 6, 16, and 20 November 1929, 4 and 12 April 1930 (INC-GEC). GE to Margaret Sanger 15 November 1929 (GEC).

11. GE to Irving Fisher, 23 January 1923 (GEC); Irving Fisher to GE, 11 January 1923, 9 January 1925 (INC-GEC).

12. GE to Robert Brookings, 7 December 1927 (GEC).

13. Franklin Delano Roosevelt to GE, 18 August 1927 (INC-GEC).

14. Eastman seemed to suffer a selective amnesia when it concerned his childhood. Interestingly, so did his great nephew about his childhood when this writer interviewed George Eastman Dryden, age eighty-seven, in 1989 concerning what he remembered about Uncle George, Eastman House, Rochester, etc. Katharine Whipple noted too that GE never mentioned his sisters although this is not entirely accurate. He mentioned Katy to relatives like Cousin Delia who would have known her. There are no known photographs of sister Katy or Ellen, although Royal Andrus, ca. 1900, mentions having found one of his mother.

15. FDR to GE, 10 September 1927; n.d., Box 107, October 1928–January 1929; 30 August 1930 (INC-GEC).

16. GE to Fellow Employees of the Kodak Company, 8 December 1924 (GEC).

17. Wyatt Brummitt, *George Eastman of Kodak* (Rochester: unpublished type-script., ca. 1960), 271.

18. GE to George B. Dryden, 19 July 1920 (GEC).

19. Perley S. Wilcox testimony, *U.S. v. EKCo*, 446–47. Letters in the George Eastman House Construction Papers, 1902–6 (GEHCP-UR).

20. A law was passed in 1921 allowing women to serve on the New Jersey Board of Education. GE to Julian Street, 19 January 26 (GEC).

21. GE to Almon R. Eastman, 19 March 1920 (GEC).

22. GE to J. Warren Cutler, 27 September 1909 (GEC).

23. GE to Murray Bartlett, 2 July 1910 (GEC).

24. Letter from Peter Cunningham to the author, 3 December 1988. "I remember as a young boy seeing a limousine being built for the emperor at the factory with the chrysanthemum symbol woven into the upholstery."

25. Articles quoting GE in *Democrat and Chronicle and Herald*, June 1920.

26. GE to Robert Mathes, 1 July 1920 (GEC).

27. GE to Julian Street, 9 October 1920 (GEC).

28. Letter from J. Lionberger Davis to Frank Lovejoy, 23 April 1940 (RGE-UR).

29. Ibid.

30. GE to Dr. Jacob G. Shurman, 11 April 1921 (GEC). Many incoming letters, of 1921 pertain to Doshisha University (INC-GEC).

31. GE to Almon R. Eastman, 9 June 1920 (GEC); GE to Viscount E. Shibusawa, 29 October 1923 (GEC).

Chapter 28: Trust Your Organization

Sources for this chapter include Osa Johnson, *I Married Adventure* (Philadephia: J. B. Lippincott, 1940) and *Four Years in Paradise* (Philadelphia: J. B. Lippincott, 1941).

1. Osa Johnson, *I Married Adventure*, 306; GE to Frank Babbott, 1920 ("employees joked") (GEC).

2. GE to David G. Longworth, Nairobi, 7 December 1907; GE to Frank L. Babbott, 8 March 1910; GE to Frank Seaman, 9 April 1910 (GEC).

3. Frank Seaman to GE, 27 April 1922 (INC-GEC); GE to Frank Seaman, 9 May 1922, 26 May 1923 (GEC). The cousins who wrote in worried tones were Delia Conger Eastman, Carrie Eastman Benedict, and Mary Eastman Southwick.

4. GE to Frank Seaman, 26 May 1923; GE to Carl Laemmle, Universal Pictures, 6 June 1923 (GEC).

5. Osa Johnson, *I Married Adventure* (Philadelphia/New York/London/Toronto: J. B. Lipincott, 1940), 266–70.

6. Ibid.; Martin Johnson to GE, 14 and 31 July, 1 August 1923; Carl Akeley to GE, 26 July 1923; Sydney Colgate to GE, 12 November, 11 December 1923; GE to Daniel E. Pomeroy, 20 and 24 December 1923; Martin Johnson, *What I am trying to do: Why now is the Time to Get a Permanent Motion Picture of Untouched Africa. Some of My*

Plans for Photographing Natives and Wild Animals, and How I am Going About it" (galley proofs, ca. 1923) (INC-GEC); GE to Martin Johnson, 30 July, 2 August, 19 November 1923; GE to Sydney Colgate, 8 December 1923; GE to D. E. Pomeroy, 21 and 27 December 1923; GE to W. H. Eaton, Doubleday, Page & Company, 30 June 1923; GE to Auburn Electrical Supply Company, 14 July 1923 (GEC).

7. Martin Johnson (Lake Paradise) to GE, 4 December 1924, 23 April, 1 June, 22 September, 19 and 31 December 1925 (INC-GEC).

8. GE to Martin Johnson, Nairobi, 20 and 27 November 1925; GE to Carl Akeley, 20, 25, 27 November 1925; GE to Daniel Pomeroy, 27 November, 1 December 1926, 9 January 1926; GE to Kodak Park, 3 December 1925; GE to Professor Walter C. O'Kane, 2 December 1925, 1 January 1926; GE to Metropolitan Camp Goods Company, 25 November 1925; GE to The Cannister Company, 19 December 1925 (GEC).

9. Albert David Kaiser, "The George Eastman I knew" (unpublished monograph: prepared for the Philosopher's Club, ca. 1956); interviews with Dr. Albert D. Kaiser, 19 January 1940, 1950s (RGE-UR) (BUTT-UR).

10. Wyatt Brummitt, *George Eastman of Kodak* (unpublished ms., ca. 1960), 302 (EKC). While in Paris on this trip Eastman apparently became excited over the possibilities of fluorescent tube lighting and according to G. Signoret in *Theses et Travaux* tried to get the inventor of the fluorescent tube, Professor J. C. Risler, to go to Rochester as a member of the Research Laboratories staff. Supposedly Eastman, having seen the dancer, Lois Fuller, perform her celebrated "ballets fluorescents" at the Opera, prevailed upon her to convey his invitation, baited with a first-class one-way passage of the *S. S. Olympic*, to Risler, who refused to be seduced away from Paris.

11. Osa Johnson, *I Married Adventure*, 294–97; GE to Alice K. Whitney, 20 June 1926 (GEC). Letters from Eastman to Whitney formed a kind of diary and the secretary began sending them around to special friends such as Rush Rhees (who asked if it was all right for his wife to read them too). Later illustrated with photographs by Eastman and Martin Johnson, the letters were privately published in July 1927 as a book of 5,595 copies, *Chronicles of an African Trip*, and sent to Eastman's friends and Kodak employees worldwide.

12. Eastman, *Chronicles of an African Trip* (privately printed for the author, 1927), 37.

13. Ibid., 86–87.

14. Osa Johnson, *I Married Adventure*, 298–99.

15. The Committee on Medical Motion Picture Films of the American College of Surgeons had just been formed by Will Hays, former postmaster general and now president of the Motion Picture Producers & Distributors of America. Hays believed "that to have the motion picture and use it only for entertainment is just as sensible as to have the English language and use it only for novels," and had persuaded an international convocation of surgeons to consider "the value of films of unusual surgery that could be shown to more students than could crowd into the balcony of an operating theater." In November 1926 Hays contacted Eastman for film and financial support. Eastman's interest was immediate, including the pledging of about $300,000 of the $500,000 deemed necessary to promote surgical films. He then invited the committee to come to Rochester for one of his famous house parties, which consisted of wide-ranging discussion of the subject at hand, a tour of Kodak Park, the music school and theater, the university, and the dental dispensary (all

described to prospective guests as "some of the interesting things we are doing here"), and ending with dinner cum musical and motion picture entertainment at his home.

16. Will H. Hays, *"Re: George Eastman"* 10 March 1942, a five-page typewritten reminiscence (EKC).

17. GE to Martin Johnson, 16 December 1926; GE to C. F. Church, 16 December 1926; GE to General Charles F. Stokes, 3 December 1926; Martin Johnson to GE, 12 December 1926; Alice L Seixas (Pomeroy's secretary) to GE, 9 December 1926 (INC-GEC).

18. C. M. Graves, Sunday Picture Section, *New York Times*, to L. B. Jones, EKC., 15 October 26; L. B. Jones to C. M. Graves, 18 October 1926 (INC-GEC).

19. The trophies were exhibited in October 1927. GE wrote to Clark, his taxidermist, on 27 January 1927: "Although you have the complete skins of the lions I suppose you understand that the heads only are to be mounted; one with an open mouth. I do not care to have any rugs. . . . Can you make any suggestions as to what can be done with the lion skins?"

20. GE to Leslie J. Tarlton, Safariland Ltd. Nairobi, 24 January 1927 (GEC).

21. GE to Joyce Percival, 27 January 1927 (GEC).

22. Interview by the author with Dr. James Stewart (son of Dr. Audley Stewart), 7 February 1990.

23. Will Hays to GE, 22 September 1927 (INC-GEC).

24. Osa Johnson to GE, 19 March 1927 (INC-GEC).

25. Osa to GE, 31 January 1929 from Miami (INC-GEC)."Simba has been going over great," Osa exulted.

26. GE to Daniel E. Pomeroy, 10 September 1928 (GEC).

27. Osa Johnson to GE, 27 February 1929 (GEC).

28. GE to Martin Johnson, 18 April 1927; GE to Hiram W. Sibley, 1927 (GEC); George E. Norton, "My Friend George Eastman," *University of Rochester Library Bulletin* 23, no. 1 (Fall 1967): 7.

29. Dick Houston, "Martin and Osa Johnson, Game to the End," *Smithsonian Magazine* 17, no. 8 (November 1986): 144–55.

30. GE to North Duane, 6 September 1927 (GEC).

31. GE to Hon. Robert Silvercruys, charge d'affaires of Belgium, Washington, D.C., 15 July 1927 (GEC); Daniel E. Pomeroy to GE, 11 October 1927 (INC-GEC).

32. A. K. W. Hutchison to George B. Dryden, 10 January 1928 (GEC).

33. Elizabeth North Muller, National Life Conservation Society, Division of Wild Life Protection, to GE, 2 December 1927 (INC-GEC).

34. A. K. W. Hutchison to Robert J. Jessup, Glandale, Calif., 6 February 1928 (GEC).

35. Kaiser interviews and unpublished paper on GE cited earlier. Eastman wrote letters to Alice Whitney Hutchison during this trip as he had on the first safari but chose not to publish them. They were published in 1987 by the Friends of the University of Rochester Libraries as *Chronicles of a Second African Trip*, illustrated with photographs of that trip by Martin Johnson and George Eastman.

36. GE to Henry R. Luce, 28 February 1930 (GEC): "My dear Mr. Luce: Thank you for the copy of Fortune. In answer to your inquiry, I think it is a very striking and

creditable publication. It is so fine that I dislike to criticize it but since you ask me for my frank opinion, I think it is too bulky."

37. Osa Johnson to GE, n.d., received July 1928 (INC-GEC).

38. Osa Johnson to GE, n.d., 1929 (INC-GEC). Interview by author with George Eastman Dryden, February 1989.

39. Martin Johnson to GE, 12 December 1926; Osa to GE, from Pittsburgh, Pa., 27 February 1929 (INC-GEC); GE to Dick Burkhart, 16 July 1929 (GEC).

40. GE to Osa, 4 and November 1931 (GEC).

41. GE to A. K. Whitney, 12 September 1926, reprinted in *Chronicles of an African Trip*, 86–87.

42. Osa Johnson, *I Married Adventure*, 303.

Chapter 29: Diminuendo

1. Interview by author with Dr. Albert K. Chapman, 1980; Wyatt Brummitt, *George Eastman of Kodak* (unpublished typescript, ca. 1960) (EKC); Reese Jenkins, *Images and Enterprise, Technology and the American Photographic Industry, 1839 to 1925* (Baltimore and London: Johns Hopkins University Press, 1975), 328. In 1907 Stuber's title became "Sensitive Goods Expert . . . under the immediate direction of George Eastman, Treasurer of said Kodak Co." The terms of his contract stated that "Stuber not to engage in or be interested in, directly or indirectly, any other photographic business that the EKCo. during the term of his life." (This yellow dog clause was negated by the antitrust decision of 1921.) Stuber said in 1940 that Eastman's most outstanding characteristics were loyalty to and encouragement of employees and recalled that about 1896 he had been so discouraged by the batches of bad emulsions he was getting that he tendered his resignation. "How many batches are you making a day?" Eastman wondered. "Two, and occasionally I get one good one," Stuber replied. "Well," said Eastman, declining to accept the resignation, "Why don't you make four batches a day and then maybe we'll get more good ones." In 1907, unbeknownst to Stuber, George Davison and Simon Haus complained bitterly about Stuber to Eastman, who wrote the English contingent: "You need not pay any attention to what is said about or by Mr. Stuber. . . . Although Mr. Stuber has been indiscreet in his talk [threatened to leave the company] this can be said of him, that up to the present time he has never endeavored to evade his obligation to the company. . . . There are so many things required in order to make a success at this day in the photographic manufacturing business that the company is not greatly alarmed at what any man can do. [This is far from the way Eastman felt when Reichenbach left.] All of our big competitors today can make good emulsion; some of them can make mighty good film; lots of them good plates and paper; some of them have been in business longer than the Kodak Co. and people have left the Kodak Co. to go into business, but with very few successes." GE to George Davison, 13 May 1907 (GEC).

In 1914 Stuber was again unhappy with his contract, still the most lucrative in the company after Eastman's, to which Eastman responded, "I had forgotten the exact terms of our contract but on looking it up it seems to me that you have misinterpreted it. I wish you would look it over carefully and then come up and talk it over. You have certainly made a splendid record with the company and can hardly blame us if we want to continue your services for another five years." GE to W. G. Stuber, Kodak Park, 20 May 1914 (GEC). Actually, Stuber was bored by the monotony of his job; "It is my desire to alleviate the monotony of your work as much as possible," Eastman agreed. Stuber was then given a trip to Australia, ostensibly to help Baker with his emulsion. In 1918 Stuber assumed charge of emulsions for photographic papers in addition to films and plates, and in 1919 he became vice president in charge of photographic quality.

2. Rose R. Stuber, *William G. Stuber* (Rochester: privately printed, 1951), 26.

3. Lewis B. Jones, age sixty-six (1892); William G. Stuber, sixty-eight (1894); Frank W. Lovejoy, sixty-one (1897); Rudolph Speth, treasurer (1902); Dr. Charles Edward Kenneth Mees, fifty (1912); plus the youngsters Thomas Jean Hargrave, head of the legal department and a partner in Hubbell, Taylor, Goodwin, Nixon & Hargrave; and Albert F. Sulzer (MIT, 1901), Kodak Park manager.

4. Dr. Albert K. Chapman, "Address," Chamber of Commerce Luncheon, Rochester, 8 July 1954.

5. GE to Andrew Pringle, 23 July 1923 (GEC).

6. Interview with Marion B. Folsom, 22 February 1940 (RGE-UR).

7. Carl W. Ackerman, *George Eastman* (Boston and New York: Houghton Mifflin, 1930), has a lengthy acount of Eastman's calendar project, on pp. 469–74. Eastman Kodak Company has a voluminous archive too. Interview with Marion Folsom, 22 February 1940 (RGE-UR).

8. GE to Frank Aydelotte, 11 June 1929 (GEC) The fifty or so Eastman professors since 1930 have included four Nobel Prize winners. Felix Frankfurter in law, Linus Pauling in chemistry, Lionel Trilling in English, and George Washington Corner, first chairman of the University of Rochester's Department of Anatomy, were among those who resided for a year or two at Eastman House, Oxford.

9. Ackerman, *George Eastman*. Both Eastman and Edison had apparently forgotten their 1907 meeting in Orange, N.J., to discuss the Motion Picture Patents Company.

10. Will H. Hays to Frank Lovejoy, 10 March 1942 (EKC and RGE-UR).

11. Letter from Horace S. Thomas, Nokomis, Fla., to Mrs. Thomas Gosnell, 29 June 1989 (author's collection).

12. Ibid.

13. Interview with Franklin P. Ellis, Kodak Public Relations Dept., who was standing nearby, 29 December 1939.

14. Henry W. Clune, *Democrat & Chronicle*, 31 July 1928, 1.

15. Ibid. Television as well as color photography was not only in the air but expected on the market momentarily. Hindsight shows that neither color photography for amateurs nor television would be commercially viable and thus available to the mass market for some years—color film with the Kodachrome of 1935 and television not until almost 1950. Yet the Drydens worried about their Kodak stock in 1928. Ellen's portfolio was quite lopsided, George wrote Uncle George, and if television was now going to make film photography obsolete, wouldn't it be better if she diversified? Predictions of the demise of film photography continue in the 1990s.

16. GE to Delia Conger Eastman, 14 and 17 February 1924 (GEC).

17. GE to Henry Myrick, 30 January 1914 (GEC).

18. GE to R. C. Dunn, 11 March 1931, GE to George B. Dryden, 4 September 1931 (GEC).

19. GE to Henry Myrick, 21 December 1922, 10 March 1924, 17 December 1930, 22 January, 4 June 1931 (GEC).

20. GE to R. C. Dunn, 3 January, 8 May, 18 August, 16 December 1931, 8 January 1932 (GEC).

21. GE to Nell Newhall, 14 January 1932 (GEC).

22. GE to George B. Dryden, August 1921 (GEC).

23. GE to Royal Vilas Andrus, 29 May 1931; GE to George B. Dryden, 4 September 1931 (GEC).

24. GE to Andrew Pringle, 23 July 1923 (GEC).

25. GE to Leon Gaumont, 2 June 1919 (GEC); GE to Darragh de Lancey, 2 July 1920 (GEC).

26. Lawrence Grant White to GE, 3 June 1929 (INC-GEC); GE to Arthur See, 28 September 1930; GE to Rush Rhees, 27 August 1930; GE to Clarence Livingston, 20 January 1931 (GEC).

27. GE to Lawrence Grant White, 12 June 1929 (GEC).

28. GE to Madelon and Albert Coates, 14 February 1929; GE to Eugene Goosens, 13 February, 23 March 1929; GE to Ray Ball, 4 June 1929; GE to Adolph Zukor, 9 September 1931; interview with Clayla Ward, who felt the disappointment over the Eastman Theatre contributed to Eastman's final discouragement, 12 January 1940 (RGE-UR).

29. GE to William S. Paley, 3 January 1931 (GEC); interview with Arthur See, 13 October 1950 (EKC).

30. Interview notes by Roger Butterfield with Albert and Eleanor Eastwood, 1950s (BUTT-UR).

31. Mary Mulligan to GE, 15 September 1923 (INC-GEC).

32. Mary Mulligan to GE, n.d., ca. 1923 (INC-GEC); GE to Mrs. Edward Mulligan, 31 May 1923 (GEC).

33. Interview with C. E. K. Mees (EKC).

34. Interview with Albert Eastwood (EKC).

35. GE to J. Lionberger Davis, February 1927 (GEC).

36. GE to George B. Dryden, 30 November 1927 (GEC).

37. Interviews with George E. Norton, 13 February 1940 (RGE-UR) and 1954 (BUTT-UR).

38. GE to Almon Eastman, 30 October 1916 (GEC).

39. GE to Daniel Burmaster, 6 May 1918 (GEC).

40. GE to Frank Lusk Babbott, 8 September 1917 (GEC). The carbuncle of 1888 was close to the carotid artery. Eastman stayed home from work for five weeks and Minnie Hoefler and other Kodak "girls" decided that he would be distressed if they "didn't pay him a visit," so all tramped over to Ambrose Street in a body. Eastman seemed pleased with the impromptu visit. Later, when Eastman's power and wealth effectively separated him from the rest of society, Minnie Hoefler Cline marveled at her early audacity.

41. According to two lectures by Dr. James Bartlett, psychiatrist, it is impossible to tell from this distance in time whether Eastman's depressive characteristics were

reactive or endogenous, whether he suffered from a classic major depressive illness or whether his depression was reactive to symptoms. Bartlett's lecture was entitled "The Death of George Eastman" and given 25 October 1988 as part of a University of Rochester series and again, with more medical details, to the Rochester Medical Society on 7 March 1990.

42. GE to Tom Chester, Santa Barbara, 23 June 1931 (GEC).

43. GE to Agnes Cromwell, 27 March 1930 (GEC).

44. William G. Stuber to GE, 24 January 1930 (INC-GEC). How Stuber got the scotch or rye during Prohibition is not explained.

45. Interview by author with George Eastman Dryden, 1989.

46. GE to Helen Strong Carter, 27 July 1930; GE to Lord Riddell, 16 July 1930 (GEC).

47. George B. Dryden to Charles Hutchison, 13 June 1930 (INC-GEC).

48. GE to Charles Edison and Daniel Pomeroy, 17 July 1930 (GEC); GE to Helen Carter, 31 July 1930 (GEC).

49. GE to A. B. Cleaves, Goodyear Tire & Rubber Company, Louisiana, 19 July 1930 (GEC).

50. Interview by Bill Beeney with Nathanial Myrick, *Democrat & Chronicle*, 1953.

51. GE to Evangeline Newhall, 22 July 1930 (GEC).

52. Susan Brown to GE, 9 and 27 September 1930, 6 March 1931 (INC-GEC).

53. GE to Susan Brown, 28 February 1931 (GEC); Susan Brown to GE, 28 September 1930; 1931 (INC-GEC).

54. Press release signed George Eastman, 15 September 1931 (INC-GEC).

55. GE to H. C. Reiner, St. Louis, 16 January 1932 (GEC).

56. GE to Harvey Burkhart, 27 October 1930; GE to Thomas J. Watson, 5 October 1930, 3 February 1931; GE to F. L. Babbott, 15 and 20 January, 11 February 1931; GE to Osa Johnson, 15 January 1931; GE to Fausta Menignari, 6 June 1931 (GEC); interview by Beaumont Newhall with George B. Dryden, 1954 (BUTT-UR).

57. Susan Brown to GE, 6 March 1931 (INC-GEC).

Chapter 30: "My Work Is Done"

Portions of this chapter appeared as an article entitled "The Day George Eastman Died" in the Wolfe Newspapers in April 1980. The article has been reprinted several times.

1. GE to Andrew Pringle, 23 July 1923 (GEC).

2. Interview with Milton K. Robinson, 8 February 1940 (RGE-UR).

3. Interview with Charles Hutchison, ca. 1950 (EKC).

4. GE to Prof. R. V. D. Magoffin, Archeological Institute of America, 19 November 1928 (GEC).

5. GE to North Duane, 6 September 1927 (GEC).

6. George Norton, "My friend George Eastman," *University of Rochester Library Bulletin* 23, no. 1 (Fall 1967): 3–14.

7. Interviews with Audley Durand Stewart, 18 January 1940 (RGE-UR), 1954 by Beaumont Newhall (BUTT-UR), and ca. 1956 by Roger Butterfield (BUTT-UR).

Stewart listened to Eastman's heart on all his visits, stopping by once a week unless Eastman was under the weather, then it was every day. He came mornings after breakfast and saw him in the sitting room. They had discussed several poisons such as strychnine, cyanide, and arsenic.

8. Interview by author with Dr. James Bartlett, psychiatrist and head of Strong Memorial Hospital in the 1980s. Bartlett had access to Eastman's medical records.

9. Interview with S. B. Cornell, 10 April 1940 (RGE-UR).

10. Interview with H. R. Patterson, ca. 1955 (BUTT-UR).

11. GE to Evangeline (Nell) Abbott Newhall, 26 August 1931 (GEC).

12. Interview with Miss Minnie Mason, 6 March 1940 (RGE-UR).

13. Interview with George Whipple, 20 August 1969 (ERM-UR): "He had a horror of losing control of his intestinal track or any other part of his organism. The last visit we had at Oak Lodge he was beginning to lose control of his sphincters. . . . Some people who didn't know said he had cancer but I had enough association with him so that I realize that the thing that he couldn't endure was the loss of control of his sphincters so that he'd occasionally urinate when he didn't want to and pass feces when he didn't want to. Of course, that's a very unpleasant business especially for a person who wanted to be immaculate in every conceivable way. When I saw this developing at the last visit at Oak Lodge I was hoping that something would happen like a stroke and kill him because I knew how unhappy he was. So, when he took the matter into his own hands, it was no surprise to me, and I hadn't the slightest feeling that he did wrong."

14. Interviews with Katharine Whipple, 15 January 1940 (RGE-UR) and ca. 1955 (BUTT-UR); letter from Katharine Whipple to André Maurois, 15 May 1939 (RGE-UR); Katharine Whipple, "Key to the Eastman Scrapbooks" (ERM-UR).

15. GE to Agnes Cromwell, 11 March 1931 (GEC).

16. Eastman's estate totaled $25,561,641.60, including the mansion and grounds. Of that the University of Rochester received $19 million, the Rochester Dental Dispensary $1 million, everything else less. His peak fortune has been estimated at about $125 million; when he died it was one-fifth of that. Had he not been a philanthropist but simply hoarded and invested his money, it has been estimated that would have been worth $300 million at his death.

The principal gifts made during his lifetime since 1900, not including his annual contributions to the Community Chest of $250,000 each year, were:

University of Rochester
$35,500,000
Massachusetts Institute of Technology
19,500,000
Kodak stock distributed to employees
6,000,000
Tuskegee Institute
2,362,000
Hampton Institute
2,000,000

Chamber of Commerce Building
1,350,000
London Dental Clinic
1,300,000

17. In 1927 Eastman made a gift of $150,000 to Cornell through Walter Todd, son of his friend and Eastman Theatre colleague, George L. Todd. But because coroner David Atwater wrote on the death certificate that Eastman was temporarily insane when he committed suicide, Cornell took the case to court. A. K. Chapman and Marion Folsom testified that he wasn't and the case was dismissed. Atwater said he always wrote that for suicides, so that in case the person was of the Roman Catholic faith, he could be buried in Holy Sepulchre Cemetery.

18. Interviews with Milton K. Robinson, 8 February 1940 (RGE-UR), by Roger Butterfield, ca. 16 March 1954 (BUTT-UR); "Milton K. Robinson on Eastman," 16 April 1951 (EKC).

19. Interviews with Katharine Whipple, 1940, 1954; "Key To the Eastman Scrapbooks," by Mrs. George Hoyt (Katharine) Whipple, *University of Rochester Library Bulletin* (Fall 1965): 18.

20. Interviews with Dr. Harvey J. Burkhart, 19 January 1940 (RGE-UR) and ca. 1954 (BUTT-UR).

21. Harold Gleason, "Please Play My Funeral March," *University of Rochester Library Bulletin* 26, no. 3 (Spring 1971): 122.

22. Interview by author with William Vaughn, 1985.

23. GE to Thomas Jean Hargrave, 14 March 1932 (GEC).

24. Interviews by author with Albert K. Chapman, ca. 1980–82.

25. The present location of Eastman's suicide note is not known to the author. It has, however, been reproduced several times and copy prints of it are located at the George Eastman House, at the Eastman Kodak Company, and in the author's collection.

26. Interview by Jean Ennis with Molly Cherbuliez, who remembered the sewing basket, 1950s (EKC).

27. Eastman kept the gun he used in a small locked drawer in a desk in his bedroom where Young was not supposed to look. But Molly Cherbuliez knew it was there. Stewart said if he had known about the gun beforehand, "it would have disappeared." Stewart was the only one who suspected suicide, particularly after the "strychnine" and "where is my heart" episodes. The other gun was found behind books after death by the Drydens. This information is from a Stewart interview with Roger Butterfield in the 1950s.

28. Interviews by author with Albert K. Chapman, 1980–82.

29. Journalist Henry Clune would write a *roman à clef* novel about George Eastman. Henry W. Clune, *By His Own Hand* (New York: Macmillan, 1952).

30. *Rochester Times-Union*, 17 March 1932, 8.

31. That Hanson was generally thought to be "full of pride and ego" was heard by the author in interviews with Dr. Albert K. Chapman and others. Frank Babbott died the next year, 1933, of complications from kidney disease.

32. The Rochester funeral of Frederick Douglass in 1895 was described in con-

temporary accounts as second in size to Abraham Lincoln's. There were marching bands in the Douglass procession, however.

33. *Rochester Times-Union*, 17 March 1932, 8.

34. Harold Gleason, "Please Play My Funeral March," 122–24.

35. Ibid. Following the service, the cortege wended its way to Mount Hope Cemetery Chapel and Crematorium, where George Norton led the commitment services and the body was later cremated. Policeman Milton Wahl, charged with making sure all went well during the cremation, stole a piece of the casket that has since been given to Eastman House by his great-granddaughter. Eastman Dryden, representing the family, would later carry the ashes to Kodak Park where they were interred and a massive stone memorial built. (Originally Eastman was to be buried in Waterville next to his parents and sister Emma Kate, but Albert Kaiser's recollection of Eastman's Africa letter—which had burned in the train fire—specifying cremation and local interment, led Kodak officials to press for the change.)

Epilogue: The Homecoming

1. Alice K. Whitney Hutchison to Tony Babb, Kodak's man in Los Angeles, 11 April 1932 (GEC): "I wish you and Gretchen would come and cheer us up."

2. Alice K. Whitney Hutchison to Walter Cope, 21 April 1932 (GEC).

3. The Kodak company could have fathered xerography as well as photography. But through Dr. C. E. Kenneth Mees, who was essentially a chemical man, Kodak consistently turned down Chester Carlson's dry photographic process, basically a physics operation. Other objections came from top management: Thomas Jean Hargrave, president, saw all kinds of antitrust problems looming if Kodak undertook the new process. Eventually Carlson sold it to the tiny Haloid (photographic paper) Company, then headed by Joseph Wilson, who took the ball and ran with it, renaming the process xerography and his rising company Xerox.

INDEX

Library of Congress Cataloging-in-Publication Data

Brayer, Elizabeth.
George Eastman : a biography / Elizabeth Brayer.
p.   cm.
ISBN 0-8018-5263-3 (alk. paper)
1. Eastman, George, 1854–1932.   I. Title.
TR140.E3B73   1996
338.7'61681418'092—dc20
[B]
                                                       95-9513